Lecture Notes in Computer Science 14719

Founding Editors

Gerhard Goos
Juris Hartmanis

The series Lecture Notes in Computer Science (LNCS), including its subseries Lecture Notes in Artificial Intelligence (LNAI) and Lecture Notes in Bioinformatics (LNBI), has established itself as a medium for the publication of new developments in computer science and information technology research, teaching, and education.

LNCS enjoys close cooperation with the computer science R & D community, the series counts many renowned academics among its volume editors and paper authors, and collaborates with prestigious societies. Its mission is to serve this international community by providing an invaluable service, mainly focused on the publication of conference and workshop proceedings and postproceedings. LNCS commenced publication in 1973.

Norbert A. Streitz · Shin'ichi Konomi
Editors

Distributed, Ambient and Pervasive Interactions

12th International Conference, DAPI 2024
Held as Part of the 26th HCI International Conference, HCII 2024
Washington, DC, USA, June 29 – July 4, 2024
Proceedings, Part II

 Springer

Editors
Norbert A. Streitz ⓘD
Smart Future Initiative
Frankfurt am Main, Germany

Shin'ichi Konomi
Kyushu University
Fukuoka, Japan

ISSN 0302-9743   ISSN 1611-3349 (electronic)
Lecture Notes in Computer Science
ISBN 978-3-031-60011-1   ISBN 978-3-031-60012-8 (eBook)
https://doi.org/10.1007/978-3-031-60012-8

This Springer imprint is published by the registered company Springer Nature Switzerland AG
The registered company address is: Gewerbestrasse 11, 6330 Cham, Switzerland

If disposing of this product, please recycle the paper.

Foreword

This year we celebrate 40 years since the establishment of the HCI International (HCII) Conference, which has been a hub for presenting groundbreaking research and novel ideas and collaboration for people from all over the world.

The HCII conference was founded in 1984 by Prof. Gavriel Salvendy (Purdue University, USA, Tsinghua University, P.R. China, and University of Central Florida, USA) and the first event of the series, "1st USA-Japan Conference on Human-Computer Interaction", was held in Honolulu, Hawaii, USA, 18–20 August. Since then, HCI International is held jointly with several Thematic Areas and Affiliated Conferences, with each one under the auspices of a distinguished international Program Board and under one management and one registration. Twenty-six HCI International Conferences have been organized so far (every two years until 2013, and annually thereafter).

Over the years, this conference has served as a platform for scholars, researchers, industry experts and students to exchange ideas, connect, and address challenges in the ever-evolving HCI field. Throughout these 40 years, the conference has evolved itself, adapting to new technologies and emerging trends, while staying committed to its core mission of advancing knowledge and driving change.

As we celebrate this milestone anniversary, we reflect on the contributions of its founding members and appreciate the commitment of its current and past Affiliated Conference Program Board Chairs and members. We are also thankful to all past conference attendees who have shaped this community into what it is today.

The 26th International Conference on Human-Computer Interaction, HCI International 2024 (HCII 2024), was held as a 'hybrid' event at the Washington Hilton Hotel, Washington, DC, USA, during 29 June – 4 July 2024. It incorporated the 21 thematic areas and affiliated conferences listed below.

A total of 5108 individuals from academia, research institutes, industry, and government agencies from 85 countries submitted contributions, and 1271 papers and 309 posters were included in the volumes of the proceedings that were published just before the start of the conference, these are listed below. The contributions thoroughly cover the entire field of human-computer interaction, addressing major advances in knowledge and effective use of computers in a variety of application areas. These papers provide academics, researchers, engineers, scientists, practitioners and students with state-of-the-art information on the most recent advances in HCI.

The HCI International (HCII) conference also offers the option of presenting 'Late Breaking Work', and this applies both for papers and posters, with corresponding volumes of proceedings that will be published after the conference. Full papers will be included in the 'HCII 2024 - Late Breaking Papers' volumes of the proceedings to be published in the Springer LNCS series, while 'Poster Extended Abstracts' will be included as short research papers in the 'HCII 2024 - Late Breaking Posters' volumes to be published in the Springer CCIS series.

I would like to thank the Program Board Chairs and the members of the Program Boards of all thematic areas and affiliated conferences for their contribution towards the high scientific quality and overall success of the HCI International 2024 conference. Their manifold support in terms of paper reviewing (single-blind review process, with a minimum of two reviews per submission), session organization and their willingness to act as goodwill ambassadors for the conference is most highly appreciated.

This conference would not have been possible without the continuous and unwavering support and advice of Gavriel Salvendy, founder, General Chair Emeritus, and Scientific Advisor. For his outstanding efforts, I would like to express my sincere appreciation to Abbas Moallem, Communications Chair and Editor of HCI International News.

July 2024   Constantine Stephanidis

HCI International 2024 Thematic Areas and Affiliated Conferences

- HCI: Human-Computer Interaction Thematic Area
- HIMI: Human Interface and the Management of Information Thematic Area
- EPCE: 21st International Conference on Engineering Psychology and Cognitive Ergonomics
- AC: 18th International Conference on Augmented Cognition
- UAHCI: 18th International Conference on Universal Access in Human-Computer Interaction
- CCD: 16th International Conference on Cross-Cultural Design
- SCSM: 16th International Conference on Social Computing and Social Media
- VAMR: 16th International Conference on Virtual, Augmented and Mixed Reality
- DHM: 15th International Conference on Digital Human Modeling & Applications in Health, Safety, Ergonomics & Risk Management
- DUXU: 13th International Conference on Design, User Experience and Usability
- C&C: 12th International Conference on Culture and Computing
- DAPI: 12th International Conference on Distributed, Ambient and Pervasive Interactions
- HCIBGO: 11th International Conference on HCI in Business, Government and Organizations
- LCT: 11th International Conference on Learning and Collaboration Technologies
- ITAP: 10th International Conference on Human Aspects of IT for the Aged Population
- AIS: 6th International Conference on Adaptive Instructional Systems
- HCI-CPT: 6th International Conference on HCI for Cybersecurity, Privacy and Trust
- HCI-Games: 6th International Conference on HCI in Games
- MobiTAS: 6th International Conference on HCI in Mobility, Transport and Automotive Systems
- AI-HCI: 5th International Conference on Artificial Intelligence in HCI
- MOBILE: 5th International Conference on Human-Centered Design, Operation and Evaluation of Mobile Communications

List of Conference Proceedings Volumes Appearing Before the Conference

1. LNCS 14684, Human-Computer Interaction: Part I, edited by Masaaki Kurosu and Ayako Hashizume
2. LNCS 14685, Human-Computer Interaction: Part II, edited by Masaaki Kurosu and Ayako Hashizumc
3. LNCS 14686, Human-Computer Interaction: Part III, edited by Masaaki Kurosu and Ayako Hashizume
4. LNCS 14687, Human-Computer Interaction: Part IV, edited by Masaaki Kurosu and Ayako Hashizume
5. LNCS 14688, Human-Computer Interaction: Part V, edited by Masaaki Kurosu and Ayako Hashizume
6. LNCS 14689, Human Interface and the Management of Information: Part I, edited by Hirohiko Mori and Yumi Asahi
7. LNCS 14690, Human Interface and the Management of Information: Part II, edited by Hirohiko Mori and Yumi Asahi
8. LNCS 14691, Human Interface and the Management of Information: Part III, edited by Hirohiko Mori and Yumi Asahi
9. LNAI 14692, Engineering Psychology and Cognitive Ergonomics: Part I, edited by Don Harris and Wen-Chin Li
10. LNAI 14693, Engineering Psychology and Cognitive Ergonomics: Part II, edited by Don Harris and Wen-Chin Li
11. LNAI 14694, Augmented Cognition, Part I, edited by Dylan D. Schmorrow and Cali M. Fidopiastis
12. LNAI 14695, Augmented Cognition, Part II, edited by Dylan D. Schmorrow and Cali M. Fidopiastis
13. LNCS 14696, Universal Access in Human-Computer Interaction: Part I, edited by Margherita Antona and Constantine Stephanidis
14. LNCS 14697, Universal Access in Human-Computer Interaction: Part II, edited by Margherita Antona and Constantine Stephanidis
15. LNCS 14698, Universal Access in Human-Computer Interaction: Part III, edited by Margherita Antona and Constantine Stephanidis
16. LNCS 14699, Cross-Cultural Design: Part I, edited by Pei-Luen Patrick Rau
17. LNCS 14700, Cross-Cultural Design: Part II, edited by Pei-Luen Patrick Rau
18. LNCS 14701, Cross-Cultural Design: Part III, edited by Pei-Luen Patrick Rau
19. LNCS 14702, Cross-Cultural Design: Part IV, edited by Pei-Luen Patrick Rau
20. LNCS 14703, Social Computing and Social Media: Part I, edited by Adela Coman and Simona Vasilache
21. LNCS 14704, Social Computing and Social Media: Part II, edited by Adela Coman and Simona Vasilache
22. LNCS 14705, Social Computing and Social Media: Part III, edited by Adela Coman and Simona Vasilache

47. LNCS 14730, HCI in Games: Part I, edited by Xiaowen Fang
48. LNCS 14731, HCI in Games: Part II, edited by Xiaowen Fang
49. LNCS 14732, HCI in Mobility, Transport and Automotive Systems: Part I, edited by Heidi Krömker
50. LNCS 14733, HCI in Mobility, Transport and Automotive Systems: Part II, edited by Heidi Krömker
51. LNAI 14734, Artificial Intelligence in HCI: Part I, edited by Helmut Degen and Stavroula Ntoa
52. LNAI 14735, Artificial Intelligence in HCI: Part II, edited by Helmut Degen and Stavroula Ntoa
53. LNAI 14736, Artificial Intelligence in HCI: Part III, edited by Helmut Degen and Stavroula Ntoa
54. LNCS 14737, Design, Operation and Evaluation of Mobile Communications: Part I, edited by June Wei and George Margetis
55. LNCS 14738, Design, Operation and Evaluation of Mobile Communications: Part II, edited by June Wei and George Margetis
56. CCIS 2114, HCI International 2024 Posters - Part I, edited by Constantine Stephanidis, Margherita Antona, Stavroula Ntoa and Gavriel Salvendy
57. CCIS 2115, HCI International 2024 Posters - Part II, edited by Constantine Stephanidis, Margherita Antona, Stavroula Ntoa and Gavriel Salvendy
58. CCIS 2116, HCI International 2024 Posters - Part III, edited by Constantine Stephanidis, Margherita Antona, Stavroula Ntoa and Gavriel Salvendy
59. CCIS 2117, HCI International 2024 Posters - Part IV, edited by Constantine Stephanidis, Margherita Antona, Stavroula Ntoa and Gavriel Salvendy
60. CCIS 2118, HCI International 2024 Posters - Part V, edited by Constantine Stephanidis, Margherita Antona, Stavroula Ntoa and Gavriel Salvendy
61. CCIS 2119, HCI International 2024 Posters - Part VI, edited by Constantine Stephanidis, Margherita Antona, Stavroula Ntoa and Gavriel Salvendy
62. CCIS 2120, HCI International 2024 Posters - Part VII, edited by Constantine Stephanidis, Margherita Antona, Stavroula Ntoa and Gavriel Salvendy

https://2024.hci.international/proceedings

Preface

The 12th International Conference on Distributed, Ambient and Pervasive Interactions (DAPI 2024), an affiliated conference of the HCI International Conference, provided a forum for interaction and exchanges among researchers, academics, and practitioners in the field of HCI for DAPI environments.

The DAPI conference addressed approaches and objectives of information, interaction, and user experience design for DAPI Environments as well as their enabling technologies, methods, and platforms, and relevant application areas. The DAPI 2024 conference covered topics addressing basic research questions and technology issues in the areas of new modalities, immersive environments, smart devices, etc. On the other hand, there was an increase in more applied papers that cover comprehensive platforms and smart ecosystems addressing the challenges of cyber-physical systems, human-machine networks, public spaces, smart cities, and nature preservation. The application areas also include education, learning, culture, art, music, and interactive installations.

Two volumes of the HCII 2024 proceedings are dedicated to this year's edition of the DAPI Conference. The first focuses on topics related to Designing, Developing and Evaluating Intelligent Environments, and Smart Cities, Smart Industries and Smart Tourism. The second focuses on topics related to Intelligent Environments for Health and Wellbeing, Smart Ecosystems for Learning and Culture, and Multimodal Interaction in Intelligent Environments.

The papers in these volumes were accepted for publication after a minimum of two single-blind reviews from the members of the DAPI Program Board or, in some cases, from members of the Program Boards of other affiliated conferences. We would like to thank all of them for their invaluable contribution, support, and efforts.

July 2024

Norbert A. Streitz
Shin'ichi Konomi

12th International Conference on Distributed, Ambient and Pervasive Interactions (DAPI 2024)

Program Board Chairs: **Norbert A. Streitz**, *Smart Future Initiative, Germany,* and **Shin'ichi Konomi**, *Kyushu University, Japan*

- Pedro Antunes, *University of Lisbon, Portugal*
- Kelvin Joseph Bwalya, *Sohar University, Oman*
- Katrien De Moor, *Norwegian University of Science and Technology (NTNU), Norway*
- Morten Fjeld, *Chalmers University of Technology, Sweden*
- Nuno Guimaraes, *Instituto Universitário de Lisboa - ISCTE, Portugal*
- Kyungsik Han, *Hanyang University, Korea*
- Jun Hu, *Eindhoven University of Technology, Netherlands*
- Eiman Kanjo, *Nottingham Trent University, UK*
- Nicos Komninos, *Aristotle University of Thessaloniki, Greece*
- H. Patricia McKenna, *AmbientEase/UrbanitiesLab Initiative, Canada*
- Tatsuo Nakajima, *Waseda University, Japan*
- Guochao Peng, *Sun Yat-Sen University, P.R. China*
- Elaine M. Raybourn, *Sandia National Laboratories, USA*
- Carsten Röcker, *TH OWL, Germany*
- Tomoyo Sasao, *The University of Tokyo, Japan*
- Reiner Wichert, *Darmstadt University of Applied Sciences, Germany*
- Chui Yin Wong, *Intel Corporation, Malaysia*
- Woontack Woo, *KAIST, Korea*
- Mika Yasuoka-Jensen, *Roskilde University, Denmark*
- Takuro Yonezawa, *Nagoya University, Japan*
- Yuchong Zhang, *KTH Stockholm, Sweden*

The full list with the Program Board Chairs and the members of the Program Boards of all thematic areas and affiliated conferences of HCII 2024 is available online at:

http://www.hci.international/board-members-2024.php

HCI International 2025 Conference

The 27th International Conference on Human-Computer Interaction, HCI International 2025, will be held jointly with the affiliated conferences at the Swedish Exhibition & Congress Centre and Gothia Towers Hotel, Gothenburg, Sweden, June 22–27, 2025. It will cover a broad spectrum of themes related to Human-Computer Interaction, including theoretical issues, methods, tools, processes, and case studies in HCI design, as well as novel interaction techniques, interfaces, and applications. The proceedings will be published by Springer. More information will become available on the conference website: https://2025.hci.international/.

General Chair
Prof. Constantine Stephanidis
University of Crete and ICS-FORTH
Heraklion, Crete, Greece
Email: general_chair@2025.hci.international

https://2025.hci.international/

Contents – Part II

Smart Ecosystems for Learning and Culture

Contents – Part I

Smart Cities, Smart Industries and Smart Tourism

Intelligent Environments for Health and Wellbeing

Enhancing Human-Healing Environment Interaction Framework: Based on Two Applications

Jinghao Hei[1] and Jing Liang[1,2](✉)

[1] College of Design and Innovation, Tongji University, Shanghai, China
{heijinghao,12046}@tongji.edu.cn
[2] J Design LAB, Shanghai, China

Abstract. This study explores the evolving relationship between humans and healing environments, propelled by advances in spatial intelligent perception technology. From smart healthcare to home care, the medical field has witnessed substantial growth in intelligent environments. The paper envisions three future focus of human interaction on healing environments according to literature review. Then 5 user experience elements suitable for healing environment were identified: user research, functional analysis, narrative structure, experience design, and specific design, and 4 design processes were identified: observation, framework, elements, and solution. The paper proposed a design framework to articulate the interplay between user experience and design elements in the healing space. In the two design cases, we applied intelligent simulated natural light lighting systems with narrative methods, enhancing the interaction between users and the environment. Questionnaire assessments were designed and provided to verify the validity of the design framework.

Keywords: Healing Environment · Design · narrative design · interaction

1 Introduction

Humans respond cognitively and emotionally to the built environment, which embodies the interaction between people and the environment [14]. The interaction between humans and the environment takes place in our daily lives on a daily basis. With the ongoing advancement of spatial intelligent perception technologies, the interaction between humans and the environment increasingly requires intelligent feedback. From intelligent healthcare to in-home care, the medical industry has a robust tradition in the intelligent setting as a result of the necessity to monitor the user's physical well-being and the more stringent demands in all areas. In the coming years, the domain of human-computer interaction (HCI) will have to prioritise its attention towards the therapeutic setting.

At present, intelligent environmental feedback and interaction research is emerging in an endless stream, and robots and environmental devices with high cognitive and recognition ability have received a lot of attention [9, 17]. How does the environment assess and categorise individuals' requirements, and what sort of internal reasoning is employed to acquire knowledge and provide input, in order to establish an intelligent system on an environmental scale? This might potentially be one of the future paths of human-computer interaction [29].

Health is a state of complete physical, mental and social well-being. In recent years there has been increasing interest in the role of technology and the built environment as part of the holistic treatment of patients. The therapeutic setting is a fusion of architectural and environmental design elements that are conducive to patient well-being [12]. This has led to the emergence of the concept of healing environment, which refers to the constructed environment that is perceived as a mechanism for healing in the therapeutic journey. This encompasses both the physical and emotional aspects, such as lighting, colour, music and spatial expansiveness [15, 25].

The field of environmental interaction technology has been continuously advancing, and healing environment systems are discovering novel methods to provide feedback as the level of user demand for a healthy environment transitions from physical health to mental health to social health. The aim of this study is to present a design framework that delineates the correlation between user and design concepts, objects, and emotions within the healing environment.

2   Literature Review on Healing Environment Design

In this section, we describe the existing literature in the field of healing environment design, which suggests analogies around evidence-based medicine for design elements in healing environments, and offers possible potential for how healing environments intersect with HCI technologies. We found three main interactive factors in the design of healing environment, namely concept design, object design and emotional design.

2.1   Concept Design in Healing Environments

The field of architectural design has been progressing with the development of human productivity, but the concept of architectural design has always been closely related to the natural environment, especially in a highly specialized functional built space such as the healing environment.

Natural and Healing Environment.   Natural scenes play a particularly important role in productive human life [18]. Ulrich proposed that the main mechanism by which natural light affects healing activities is its effect on human attention and physiology [23]. On the other hand, although people perceive color differently, the natural variation of solar color temperature over time has evolved over a long history as a fundamental element of human regulation of biological rhythms [16]. From the perspective of environmental psychology, Ulrich proposing the Stress reduction theory, which suggests that human beings produce a 'restorative response' through exposure to a specific natural environment. Stress reduction theory suggests that people will develop a "restorative response" through exposure to a natural environment, i.e. by introducing natural elements to stimulate positive emotions [22]. Because the design of the healing environment is often limited by pain and clinical practice, so it only makes sense to introduce natural, dynamic elements as lightly as possible into the healing environment.

Simulated Natural Lighting and Healing Environment. Naturalistic lighting is a form of dynamic lighting that artificially simulates the same trends as daylight, based on the cycles of solar insolation in the natural environment. The US WELL Building Standard proposes to create light environments that are most conducive to visual, physiological, and psychological well-being. 2007 saw the launch of AmbiScene by Philips, which is programmed to dynamically change the light environment in real-time and since then the development of natural lighting has entered a new phase. Cajochen tested the effect of LED lighting simulating the morning daylight spectrum on human circadian rhythms, suggesting that dynamic lighting simulating the daylight spectrum has a positive effect on subjects' minds and bodies [5]. Full-spectrum lighting was first proposed by John Ott in the middle of the last century to give artificial light sources similar characteristics to natural light and is primarily used to describe electric light sources that are similar to the natural light spectrum [19]. Simulating natural light system has the characteristics of low cost, easy intelligence and easy installation, which is very useful for deepening the concept of naturalization of healing environment.

2.2 Object Design in Healing Environments

During the development of design, the relation between design and creation technology has always been exact and close, and the evolution of new technology has constantly given birth to new creation objects and methods. The four-order design proposed by Richard Buchanan (2001) divides design objects into four areas: symbols using text and graphics as media; objects; interaction; system and environment [2]. Medicine objects that exist objectively in the environment is divided into two parts according to whether the environment design can intervene. Among them, medical monitoring equipment and medical operating equipment each have strict and necessary medical clinical norms for management or product optimization, so in the perspective of design thinking to examine the healing environment, we designers should pay attention to the "objects" that can be designed outside the medical equipment.

Narrative Objects that Combine Medical Functions. The concept of narrative, which is highly regarded in both health and design, is fundamental to healing environment design. Narrative medicine theory effectively combines medical knowledge with principles of storytelling, facilitating interdisciplinary [6]. However, the design object of the physical healing environment has been undervalued with narrative medicine theory. The possibility exists for improved healthcare delivery through improved communication and cooperation between designers, medical practitioners, and patients if narrative medicine theory is included in physical environment design.

Prudent Choices of Materials, Forms and Colors. Florence Nightingale suggested that patients would recover more quickly from illness when cared for in an environment with ventilation, cleanliness, and basic hygiene [18]. Building on this idea, Wilson proposed the "pro-biotic hypothesis," which suggests that people prefer non-artificial environments that have life or life-like forms [27]. Integrating these principles into design can contribute to the overall well-being of individuals undergoing medical treatment or recovery.

2.3 Emotional Design in Healing Environments

To explore how environmental design can emotionally support users of the medical environment, designers need to consider emotional design from a systematic perspective. With the advancement of design thinking, we now need to work towards investigating more profound emotional requirements and utilizing these various emotional needs to improve user experiences during the interaction process of designing items and users. In addition to the move towards more emotional industrial items, the built environment places a strong priority on emotional design [30].

Bidirectional Environmental and Social Expression of Emotional Feedback. Burge has described the relationship between the symptoms of sick building syndrome (SBS) and the indoor environment of buildings [4, 26]. The emotional design of the healing setting should not only consider the patients' good emotional adjustment, but also the emotional adjustments of the patients' family members, the medical staff, and other social factors. Some others noted that the provision of privacy, encouraging family interactions, and facilitating comfort through a sense of belonging and interaction to nature were among the key themes [14, 24, 28].

Combined Influence of Multiple Senses. Highly emotional design present a more intimate and efficient image in people's lives. Patients' not only physical but psychological treatment became increasingly prevalent healing environment design indicators [21]. Physiological adjustment and emotional intervention can effectively regulate patients' circadian rhythm and produce positive psychological intervention [13]. Rosa et al. (2021) focused on the psychological causes of forest therapy, suggesting that natural irritate of varying brightness is one of the main factors in producing physical and psychological effects in forest therapy [20]. These acknowledge the potential for innovation via the enhancement of the integration of several senses.

3   Methods

In this chapter, the questionnaires were designed based on user preferences and evaluation index. The reasons and specific details for formulating the indicators of the table are explained below.

3.1   Questionnaire of User Preferences in Healing Environments

Gola et al. (2016) distinguished the main elements in the built environment of palliative care from endogenous and exogenous aspects [11]. So before building the design framework, we developed a user research questionnaire (see Table 1.) to consider the environmental design of the treatment scenario, including six categories of design preferences. It is distributed electronically to patients, peers, healthcare professionals and designers to investigate the needs of different users for treatment scenarios. The 6 design preferences correspond to the three dimensions of lighting design, objects design, and emotional triggers summarized in the literature review.

Table 1. Index of user preferences in healing environments (Source: the authors).

Indicators		Index	
X1	Occupation	Medical worker; patient; Accompanying family; Designers; other	
X2	Gender	Male; female	
X3	Age group	Under 18 years old; 18–25; 26–30; 31–40; 41–50; 51 to 60; Over 60	
A1	Spatial illumination	Score range (0–100) (With extreme brightness diagram)	
A2	Simulated natural dynamic illumination (N/Y)		
A3	Color combination	CP1	Natural color
		CP2	COLOR-Warm
		CP3	COLOR-Cold
		CP4	Colorless phase
		CP5	High saturation color
A4	Material combination	MP1	Flexible material (Cloth, sponge…)
		MP2	Hard materials (Plastic, wood, rubber…)
		MP3	Material of moderate hardness (Marble, steel, glass…)
A5	Smell	(N/Y)	Score range as Very disagree (1)- Very agree (5)
A6	Sound	(N/Y)	Score range as Very disagree (1)- Very agree (5)

Lighting design includes two factors: spatial illumination and simulated natural dynamic illumination, which aims to understand the user's expectation of the key daily illumination of the healing scene.

Object design includes color and material. To understand the color matching in the ward that the user wants most. Also to investigate users' preferences for touch and look of tactile materials in healing scenes and guide the selection of materials for contacts. These two groups are more abstract, so we provide sample materials in the form of settlements to help users understand, such named as CP1 & MP1.

Although the above four design elements have included the conventional environmental design content, in order to increase the possibility of emotional discussion, we added A5 and A6 as additional preference options, hoping to find more new possibilities for people to interact with the healing environment by expanding the scope of investigation.

3.2 Questionnaire of Healing Environment Design Evaluation

Based on the Good Milieu Index proposed by Friis [8] and the environmental emotion index proposed by Chen et al. [7], We successfully concluded the formulation of a comprehensive user study questionnaire, comprising 3 primary indicators (see Table 2.).

Table 2. Questionnaire of User's feedback in healing scenarios (Source: the authors).

Indicators		Index			
B1	Design concept recognition	Very disagree (1); Disagree (2); Unsure (3); Agree (4); Very agree (5)			
B2	Healing functional satisfaction	Very disagree (1); Disagree (2); Unsure (3); Agree (4); Very agree (5)			
B3	Space atmosphere satisfaction	Multiple options available (up to 4)			
		P1	Involved	N1	Alone
		P2	Warm	N2	Passionless
		P3	Peace	N3	Noisy
		P4	Interesting	N4	Boring
		P5	Bright	N5	Dark
		P6	Free	N6	Constrained
		P7	Clear	N7	Disordered

The questionnaire was distributed electronically to patients, healthcare professionals, and designers to assess user perceptions and evaluations of this healing environment application using naturalistic lighting.

4 Results of User Preference Factors in Healing Environment Design

A total of 98 questionnaires were returned, and after checking the valid questionnaires and screening the questions, 2 questionnaires with problems and distorted answers were removed, and the final number of valid questionnaires was determined to be 96. The basic information of the sample is shown in the table below (see Table 3.).

According to the results of the questionnaire survey (see Table 3.), more than half of the users are more concerned with space lighting (A1) and space color (A2) when it comes to prioritizing their needs. The majority of users preferred the illumination of the healing environment to be brighter than the normal working environment, with nature-like colors and landscapes, and the use of soft materials (e.g. fabric) and moderate materials (e.g. wood) to create a healing environment, and the use of simulated nature sounds to relieve patients' anxiety. Therefore, the design focus of the lighting design for healing scenes is how to combine the color and sound elements of nature with dynamically changing soft lighting to create a complete user experience.

Table 3. Demography of research respondent (Source: the authors).

Classification	Number of respondents	Sample proportion (%)
Male	32	33.3
Female	64	66.7
Under 18 years old	13	13.5
18–25 years old	26	27.1
26–30 years old	22	22.9
31–40 years old	28	29.2
41–50 years old	6	6.3
51–60 years old	1	1.0
Medical care personnel	31	32.3
Patients	13	13.5
Attendants	25	26.0
Designer	27	28.1

Based on Pearson method, this paper conducts correlation analysis of user preference design factors in rehabilitation environment to analyze the two problems (see Table 4). First, do a user's occupation, gender, and age affect design preferences for healing environments? Secondly, do different environmental design preferences attract or repel each other?

Table 4. Correlation analysis of user preference design factors (Source: the authors)

	X1	X2	X3	A1	A2	A3	A4	A5	A6
A1	0.284**	−0.026	0.007	1.000**	−0.019	−0.085	−0.029	−0.119	−0.036
A2	0.050	−0.043	−0.178	−0.019	1.000**	−0.011	−0.028	0.025	0.060
A3	−0.108	0.075	0.068	−0.085	−0.011	1.000**	−0.166	−0.143	−0.109
A4	0.208*	0.089	−0.265**	−0.029	−0.028	−0.166	1.000**	−0.216*	0.006
A5	0.131	0.055	0.284**	−0.119	0.025	−0.143	−0.216*	1.000**	−0.001
A6	0.101	−0.046	0.095	−0.036	0.060	−0.109	0.006	−0.001	1.000**

$* p < 0.05 ** p < 0.01$

The results show that:

1. There is no correlation between X2 and design preferences. The effect of gender on the design preference of healing environment is not obvious;
2. The correlation coefficient values between X3 and A4, A5 are significant. Specifically, there is a significant negative correlation between X3 and A4, and a significant positive correlation between X3 and A5. There is a significant negative correlation between A4 and A5. The influence of age on design preferences for healing environments is

evident, especially with regard to materials and smells. The older the age, the more likely to obtain less spatial satisfaction from spatial materials, and more likely to improve satisfaction from the treatment of environmental odors;
3. There was no correlation between A1, A2, A3, A6 and the other five design factors. Healing environment design preferences do not have the characteristics of clusters.

5 Design Applications

Based on the developed experience design framework, this paper experimented with real projects in the PICU of Shanghai Children's Medical Centre and Sino-Danish Child-Friendly Space of Suzhou High-speed Railway New Community respectively to concretize the design process in the design framework in practice.

5.1 Design Framework Construction

Design thinking is a way of linking and designing four orders of design to turn 'spacing' into 'environment' [3]. Design thinking is increasingly used in a variety of real-world contexts to improve people's comfort with a product or service by focusing on the user experience so that the user feels respected in the process.

However, little research has been conducted on how design thinking practices fit in with established design approaches in the healing environment. This study provides insights into possible approaches for practitioners in the field of healing environment by digging deeper into the interdisciplinary capabilities of design thinking.

Sara Beckman developed a new framework of the innovation process in 2007 [1], in which participants are asked to exercise four competencies by constructing connections between the concrete and abstract worlds, alternating between analysis and synthesis to generate new designs, and requiring participants to engage in concrete experience and abstract conceptualization, reflective observation and active experimentation (Fig. 1).

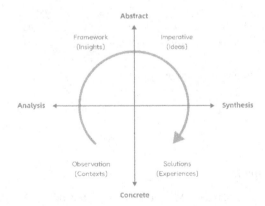

Fig. 1. The Innovation Process framework proposed by Sara Beckman (2007)

However, the framework only provides a universal framework for the innovation process, and its application in various fields still requires the user to be adept at integrating the framework with specific design purposes. Therefore, this paper will integrate the elements of experience design based on this framework to provide a reference experience for the design of healing environments.

Jesse James Garrett proposes that user experience refers to "how a product relates to and functions in the outside world" [10]. For example, how people "touch" and "use" the " corresponding products, and proposes five dimensions of user experience, namely strategy, scope, structure, framework, and performance, based on which he proposes a complete set of user experience elements. Therefore, to better serve the users of the healing environment, we combine the experience design theory with the design process to develop a design framework for the healing environment.

Due to the special nature of the healing environment design, combined with the five elemental levels of experience design proposed by Jesse James, the five elements of user experience suitable for the healing scene were first identified: user research, function analysis, narrative structure, experience design, and specific design (see Fig. 2), and four design processes of observation, framework, essentials, and solutions were identified. The design framework is much more focused on the relationship between user and environment, and more easy-to-operate (see Fig. 3).

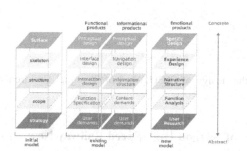

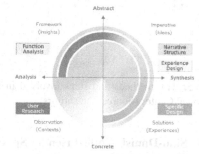

Fig. 2. Design experience element framework (Source: the authors).

Fig. 3. Simulated natural light lighting experience design process framework (Source: the authors).

5.2 PICU of Shanghai Children's Medical Centre

Using the design framework developed in this paper, a total of 10 specific processes were carried out (see Fig. 4 and 5.) to meet the objective of relieving stress and providing a positive psychological effect on the children receiving palliative care. Based on user research, the main theme of the space was healing, warmth, and sunshine for the children and parents receiving palliative care. The focus of the design, in this case, is on "how to relieve children's medical anxiety", and the overall environment is used to create the spatial imagery of the traveling bus. The interior of the ward is designed to simulate daylight with portholes for the children, allowing them to swim in the sea as if they were in a submarine. The wall-hung windows have a soft natural light system that changes dynamically over time to regulate the child's physiological rhythms and reduce the impact of the stress of being away from home on the child's life and rest.

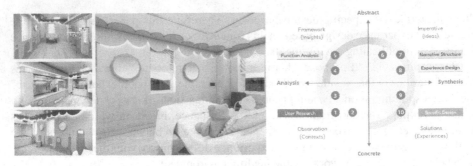

Fig. 4. Application of experiential design process framework of simulated natural light lighting in PICU Ward of Shanghai Children's Medical Center (Source: the authors).

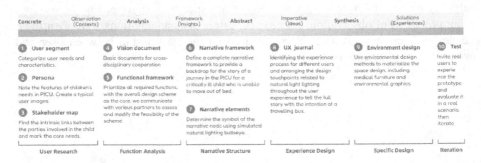

Fig. 5. The methods and steps involved in the design of PICU Ward of Shanghai Children's Medical Center (Source: the authors).

5.3 Sino-Danish Child-Friendly Space of Suzhou High-Speed Railway New Community

Using the experience design framework developed in this paper, a total of 10 specific processes (see Fig. 6 and 7.) were carried out to rehabilitate and promote social inclusion for vulnerable groups of children such as orphans and children with disabilities. In this case, the design focuses on the question of "how to encourage children to learn and socialize" by creating a fairytale-like combination of spaces through the overall environment, using "forest therapy" to create a dynamic landscape in the environment with naturalistic lighting design to relieve children's stress and negative emotions [20].

5.4 Design Evaluation

The results of the questionnaire show that almost all respondents approved of the narrative concept of the project and expressed satisfaction with the atmosphere of the ward. Among the descriptions of the space, brightness (P5) was the most noticed and recognized indicator, followed by interesting (P4) and warm (P2), which shows that the design of the proposed natural light lighting, guided through the Experience Design Process framework, has had a positive effect in the healing space (Table 5).

Fig. 6. Application of experiential design process framework of simulated natural light lighting in Sino-Danish Child-Friendly Community in Suzhou (Source: the authors).

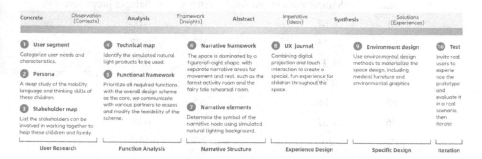

Fig. 7. The methods and steps involved in the design of Sino-Danish Child-Friendly Community in Suzhou (Source: the authors).

6 Discussion

The study has several limitations. Firstly, the assessment of feasibility as a framework is not comprehensive. Secondly, the empirical instances only include a single type of user. Lastly, additional investigation is required to evaluate the quality of the study and the influence of the constructed environment on patient outcomes.

Secondly, for modern people, who often live and work in a way that is not synchronized with nature, then how to compensate for the need for nature is also a topic that needs to be discussed.

However, this study did not discuss the classification of occupations completely and systematically, and the questionnaire was only collected as basic information in the design. Surprisingly, occupation is correlated with spatial illumination preference and spatial material preference, there is a positive correlation between X1 and A1, A4, which may be a topic worthy of further classified research in the field of environmental design.

Table 5. Evaluation feedback results (Source: the authors).

Indicators	Results			
	index		Sample proportion (%)	
B1	<3 (Very disagree; Disagree)		0.00	
	3 (Unsure)		5.21	
	>3 (Agree; Very agree)		94.79	
B2	<3 (Very disagree; Disagree)		2.08	
	3 (Unsure)		11.46	
	>3 (Agree; Very agree)		86.46	
B3	Positive attitude		86.46	
	index	Sample proportion(%)	index	Sample proportion(%)
	P1	26.67	N1	0.00
	P2	44.15	N2	6.77
	P3	31.27	N3	6.77
	P4	60.70	N4	0.00
	P5	81.86	N5	0.00
	P6	19.32	N6	0.00
	P7	9.20	N7	13.54

7   Conclusion

As spatial intelligent perception technology continues to advance, there is an increasing demand for more intelligent feedback in the interaction between humans and the environment. Smart healthcare to home care exemplifies the medical field's extensive practical application of intelligent environments, driven by the necessity to monitor users' physical functions and meet stringent requirements in various aspects. Looking ahead, the field of human-computer interaction (HCI) must place a greater emphasis on healing environments.

As for concept design, we should focus on adjusting the circadian rhythm of the patient and relieving anxiety. The most significant features of the light environment during the day, i.e. changes in light intensity and light color correspond to two parameters, illuminance, and color temperature, and a full spectrum of LED lighting that simulates natural light has a positive effect on human health. For object design, with emotional design as the core, in addition to medical devices, we need to pay attention to color and material, and combine object design with medical narrative, and combine narrative medicine methods to help create environmental concepts.

The main goal of this study is to look at more possible connections between the healing environment and its users in the future, building on the study of the link between people and their surroundings. Through literature review, the author analyzed the user preference factors that will promoted the design of healing environment, and obtained the correlation conclusion that the design factors affected the user satisfaction through the questionnaire. By combining design elements and traditional design process and innovating, an innovative design framework is added to describe the connection between users and healing environment and two case applications are finished. Through the analysis of user feedback, it is proved that the design of healing environment based on the relationship between users and environment can significantly improve user experience.

Acknowledgments. This study was funded by the International Knowledge Centre for Engineering Sciences and Technology (IKCEST) under the Auspices of UNESCO, Beijing 100088, China.

Disclosure of Interests. The authors have no competing interests.

References

1. Beckman, S.L., Barry, M.: Innovation as a learning process: embedding design thinking. Calif. Manage. Rev. **50**(1), 25–56 (2007)
2. Buchanan, R.: Design research and the new learning. Des. Issues **17**(4), 3–23 (2001)
3. Buchanan, R.: Introduction: design and organizational change. Des. Issues **24**(1), 2–9 (2008)
4. Burge, P.: Sick building syndrome. Occup. Environ. Med. **61**(2), 185–190 (2004)
5. Cajochen, C., et al.: Effect of daylight LED on visual comfort, melatonin, mood, waking performance and sleep. Lighting Res. Technol. **51**(7), 1044–1062 (2019)
6. Charon, R.: Narrative medicine: Honoring the stories of illness (First issued as an Oxford University Press paperback). Oxford University Press, United Kingdom (2008)
7. Chen, G., Wang, C., Liu, F., Wang, F., Li, S., Huang, M.: Estimate of public environment-emotional index based on micro-blog data. In: 2016 IEEE International Conference on Internet of Things (iThings) and IEEE Green Computing and Communications (GreenCom) and IEEE Cyber, Physical and Social Computing (CPSCom) and IEEE Smart Data (SmartData), pp. 854–858. IEEE (2016)
8. Friis, S.: Characteristics of a good ward atmosphere. Acta Psychiatr. Scand. **74**(5), 469–473 (1986)
9. Gan, Y., et al.: Integrating aesthetic and emotional preferences in social robot design: an affective design approach with Kansei engineering and deep convolutional generative adversarial network. Int. J. Ind. Ergon. **83**, 103–128 (2021)
10. Garrett, J.: Customer loyalty and the elements of user experience. Des. Manag. Rev. **17**(1), 35–39 (2006)
11. Gola, M., Francalanza, P., Galloni, G., Pagella, B., Capolongo, S.: Architectures for paediatric palliative care: How to improve quality of life and environmental well-being. Annali dell'Istituto Superiore di Sanità **52**(1), 48–55 (2016)
12. Gross, R.: Healing environment in psychiatric hospital design. Gen. Hosp. Psychiatry **20**(2), 108–114 (1998)
13. Hao, L., Cao, Y., Cui, Z., Zeng, K., Shao, R.: Research trends and application prospects on light and health. China Illum. Eng. J. **28**(6), 1–15, 23 (2017)
14. Higuera-Trujillo, J.L., Llinares, C., Macagno, E.: The cognitive-emotional design and study of architectural space: a scoping review of Neuroarchitecture and its precursor approaches. Sensors **21**(6), 2193 (2021)
15. Huisman, E.R.C.M., Morales, E., Van Hoof, J., Kort, H.S.M.: Healing environment: a review of the impact of physical environmental factors on users. Build. Environ. **58**, 70–80 (2012)

16. Li, Y., Liu, L.: An empirical study on the influence of color learning on color perception. Art Des. Res. **4**, 63–69 (2021)
17. Musick, G., Hauptman, A.I., Flathmann, C., McNeese, N.J., Knijnenburg, B.P.: Recommendations with benefits: exploring explanations in information sharing recommender systems for temporary teams. Int. J. Hum. Comput. Interact. 1–17 (2023)
18. Nightingale, F.: Notes on nursing: What it is, and what it is not. Lippincott Williams & Wilkins, United Kingdom (1992)
19. Ott, J.N.: Health and Light. Pocket Books, New York (1983)
20. Rosa, C.D., Larson, L.R., Collado, S., Profice, C.C.: Forest therapy can prevent and treat depression: Evidence from meta-analyses. Urban For. Urban Greening **57**, 126943 (2021)
21. Schweitzer, M., Gilpin, L., Frampton, S.: Healing spaces: elements of environmental design that make an impact on health. J. Altern. Complement. Med. **10**(supplement 1), S-71-S-83 (2004)
22. Ulrich, R.S.: Visual landscapes and psychological well-being. Landsc. Res. **4**(1), 17–23 (1979)
23. Ulrich, R.S., et al.: ICU patient family stress recovery during breaks in a hospital garden and indoor environments. HERD: Health Environ. Res. Des. J. **13**(2), 83–102 (2020)
24. Van De Glind, I., De Roode, S., Goossensen, A.: Do patients in hospitals benefit from single rooms? A literature review. Health Policy **84**(2–3), 153–161 (2007)
25. Van den Berg, A.E.: Health impacts of healing environments; a review of evidence for benefits of nature, daylight, fresh air, and quiet in healthcare settings. UMCG (2005)
26. Wang, M., Li, L., Hou, C., Guo, X., Fu, H.: Building and health: mapping the knowledge development of sick building syndrome. Buildings **12**(3), 287 (2022)
27. Wilson, E.O.: Biophilia. Harvard University Press, Cambridge (1986)
28. Wong, K., McLaughlan, R., Collins, A., Philip, J.: Designing the physical environment for inpatient palliative care: a narrative review. BMJ Support. Palliat. Care **13**(1), 45–51 (2023)
29. Yang, X., Wang, R., Tang, C., Luo, L., Mo, X.: Emotional design for smart product-service system: a case study on smart beds. J. Clean. Prod. **298**, 126823 (2021)
30. Zhao, M., Chen, J.-T.: Emotional interactive design of industrial products. In: 2021 2nd International Conference on Intelligent Design (ICID), pp. 10–13 (2021)

Design Proposal for a Chatbot with Mental Support Functionalities Based on Artificial Intelligence

Leonel Hernandez Collante[1]([✉]), Aji Prasetya Wibawa[2], Hugo Hernandez Palma[3],
Mario Orozco Bohorquez[4], Jonny Rafael Plazas Acevedo[5],
and Angelica Jimenez Coronado[6]

[1] Faculty of Engineering, Institución Universitaria de Barranquilla IUB, Barranquilla, Colombia
lhernandezc@unibarranquilla.edu.co
[2] Faculty of Engineering, Universitas Negeri Malang, Malang, Indonesia
aji.prasetya.ft@um.ac.id
[3] Department of Industrial Engineering, Corporación Universitaria Latinoamericana CUL,
Barranquilla, Colombia
hhernandez@ul.edu.co
[4] Department of Computer Science and Electronics, Universidad de La Costa CUC,
Barranquilla, Colombia
morozco5@cuc.edu.co
[5] Escuela de Ciencias Básicas, Tecnología e Ingeniería, ECBTI, Universidad Nacional Abierta y
a Distancia, Barranquilla, Colombia
jonny.plazas@unad.edu.co
[6] Department of Business Transformation, Business Administration Program, Corporación
Unificada Nacional de Educación Superior CUN, Barranquilla, Colombia
angelica_jimenezco@cun.edu.co

Abstract. Mental health, an essential component of overall well-being, faces persistent challenges globally. Despite its crucial importance, adequate care remains elusive due to various barriers. Among these, the lack of access to mental health services, the associated social stigma, and the lack of trained professionals stand out. These barriers create significant gaps in providing quality services, leaving many needing more support. Artificial intelligence (AI) emerges as a powerful tool to address these challenges in the current era, characterized by increasing interconnectedness and technological advancements. Chatbots, powered by AI, represent an innovation that offers virtual care in an accessible and personalized way. Available 24/7, these chatbots can adapt to users' needs, marking a promising global solution to improve mental health care. This research project focuses on developing a virtual assistance prototype based on artificial intelligence, specifically a chatbot. The main objective is to provide effective and personalized support, overcoming accessibility limitations and guaranteeing user privacy. The integration of artificial intelligence seeks to create a tool that not only offers a high-quality treatment experience but also dynamically adapts to the individual needs of each user. The research will cover various crucial aspects, from technological considerations to ethical aspects, social acceptance, and evaluation of treatment effectiveness. The integration of artificial intelligence is perceived as a significant contribution to the

N. A. Streitz and S. Konomi (Eds.): HCII 2024, LNCS 14719, pp. 17–31, 2024.
https://doi.org/10.1007/978-3-031-60012-8_2

health sector, establishing an interdisciplinary effort that fuses computer science, psychology, ethics, and technology to address critical issues in the field of mental health.

Keywords: Artificial intelligence (AI) · mental well-being · care · health systems · mental health

1   Introduction

Mental health is an essential part of a person's overall well-being. However, adequate care remains a global challenge despite its importance due to many barriers, including lack of access to care, associated stigma, and shortage of professionals. These barriers create gaps in the provision of quality service.

In an increasingly connected and technological world, artificial intelligence (AI) has become a powerful tool capable of eliminating some of these barriers. AI encompasses various techniques and algorithms that allow machines to learn, reason, plan, and make decisions. These capabilities are achieved through big data processing, pattern identification, algorithm optimization, and simulation of cognitive processes [1]. Furthermore, AI has become an interdisciplinary field combining computer science, statistics, mathematics, neuroscience, and psychology knowledge to develop increasingly attractive systems. Its applicability is diverse, from computer vision that allows machines to recognize objects in images to natural language processing that facilitates communication between humans and computer systems. These transformative capabilities of AI are being explored in various industries; however, [2] notes that AI relies on the simulation of human cognitive processes, such as learning and problem-solving, to achieve behavioral intelligence in machines. This similarity to human thinking has led to the development of machine learning algorithms and data processing techniques that allow machines to gain knowledge from past experiences, adapt to new situations, and make informed decisions. For [2], to achieve intelligent behavior in machines. This similarity to human thinking has led to the development of machine learning algorithms and data processing techniques that allow machines to gain knowledge from past experiences, adapt to new situations, and make informed decisions.

With chatbot developments that offer the opportunity to provide virtual care in an accessible and personalized way. These chatbots are available 24/7 and can adapt to individual user needs, providing a promising solution to improve healthcare worldwide. The study developed by [3] describes developing and implementing an AI-powered chatbot to navigate mental health resources during and after the COVID-19 pandemic. Techniques include creating flowcharts to guide chatbot development, entity extraction, and using open-source artificial intelligence algorithms to improve conversational functionality. The results show that the chatbot can effectively identify and recommend appropriate mental health resources to users.

The present research project focuses on developing a proposal, based on the literature review of the topic, of a virtual assistance prototype (chatbot) based on artificial intelligence to provide effective and personalized support. The chatbot is designed to address accessibility limitations and user privacy.

By integrating artificial intelligence, we aim to create a tool to provide a quality treatment experience while adapting to the user's needs. The research will address several key aspects, including technology, ethics, social acceptance, and effectiveness of treatment. The integration of artificial intelligence aims to contribute to health care significantly. The program is an interdisciplinary effort that combines computer science, psychology, ethics, and technology to address critical health problems (Fig. 1).

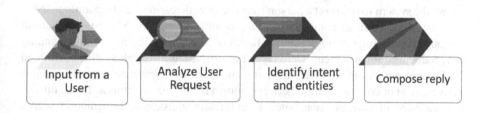

Fig. 1. Chatbot Function

In this project, the SCRUM methodology was used, which proposes an incremental development of the system requirements throughout the network, identifying clear and concise activities in its iterations to implement a technological infrastructure prototype in a network simulator that serves as a strategy to improve the processes of a solution that provides care to users who require this type of service. The rest of the paper is organized as follows: the general concepts of chatbot and AI are exposed, presenting the appropriate literature review. Subsequently, the methodology used for the development of the study is exposed. Then, the project's expected results are presented and culminated with the general conclusions and future work.

2 Conceptual Framework and Literature Review

2.1 Conceptual Framework

- Chatbot: Many institutions have implemented chatbots or conversational agents to communicate with their target audiences. According to [4], they are instant messaging channels designed so that users or clients can create conversational threads with companies and ask questions that are answered quickly. These responses are based on all the information stored in the databases that feed the chatbot. But to reach these systems, a path of technological development had to be followed.
- Artificial Intelligence: AI can be defined as "the ability of a system to interpret external data, learn from it, and use it flexibly to achieve a specific objective." [5] can also be defined as "the science of achieving machines do the things that would require intelligence if they were done by people" [6]. That is, Artificial Intelligence is the science that takes advantage of the capacity of computers to store incalculable amounts of data and then, through robotic systems, can use all that data to provide answers as a human being would do with all that knowledge.

- Expert Systems in Specialized Areas: According to [7], an Expert System is a set of programs capable of solving problems in a specific area of knowledge or knowledge that ordinarily require human intelligence. These systems simulate the learning, memorization, reasoning, communication, and action processes of a human expert in a particular science, allowing them to be used as an automated consultant.
- Natural Processing Language (NPL): For a chatbot or an expert system to work, the first thing that must be done is for the machine to be able to process natural language. This natural language processing (NPL), also called linguistic computing, allows the system to interpret a person's language with learning and reasoning. "NLP was designed for human-computer translation with empirical data languages. Natural language processing develops computational techniques for learning, understanding and producing human content" Cerdas [8]. For [9], NPL is a discipline within Artificial Intelligence and computational linguistics that aims to investigate natural language as an element of communication between human beings and machines. Its usefulness is manifested in various areas, such as automatic translation, information search systems, and intelligent interfaces, such as chatbots, which allow users to interact with a machine.

2.2 Literature Review

The scope of the application of AI in an area as important as health care and control is being explored, and its limits are yet to be established. However, the most relevant contribution of the studies reviewed is that Artificial Intelligence, when used in health care, will significantly improve patients' quality of life and allow faster and more effective care. In the future, AI will be an indispensable tool in the diagnosis and treatment of many diseases, as stipulated in the studies developed by [10–13]. In this same sense, [14] mentions that the introduction of chatbots significantly impacts society. With the creation of virtual assistants, chatbots have become a popular entity in conversational services. [15] for their part, chatbots as a new information, communication, and transaction channel allow companies to reach their target audience through messaging applications such as Facebook, WhatsApp, or WeChat. Compared to traditional chats, humans do not handle chatbots; the software leads through conversations. The latest chatbot developments in customer services and sales are notable.

In the existing literature, works like the prototype proposed by the project have been found. In which the importance of the implementation of AI-based chatbots for the treatment of patient's mental health is highlighted. The first corresponds to a comparative analysis developed by [16]. [17] their research mentions that chatbots have evolved rapidly in numerous fields in recent years, including marketing, support systems, education, healthcare, cultural heritage, and entertainment. In this article, we first presented a historical overview of the evolution of the international community's interest in chatbots. The motivations driving the use of chatbots were then discussed, and the usefulness of chatbots in various areas was clarified.

A more technical view is presented by [18], which describes the design options, architecture, and algorithms used in chatbots.

According to Koulori et al. [19], a health chatbot is necessary for several reasons. Firstly, it is hoped that chatbots can help improve awareness and understanding of mental health among young adults, who may be unwilling or unable to recognize mental health symptoms and may lack awareness about the support available and where they can find information. Secondly, chatbots can be a helpful tool for concerned families and friends by helping them identify symptoms or understand a young adult's mental illness. Third, it is hoped that chatbots can provide more accessible and more convenient access to mental health care, which may be especially important for people living in rural or remote areas. Fourth, chatbots are expected to be valuable for people who prefer privacy and confidentiality when seeking mental health help. Fifth, chatbots are expected to be useful for people with difficulty communicating verbally, such as people with autism spectrum disorders. Sixth, chatbots are expected to be a helpful tool for people with difficulty accessing mental health care due to financial or insurance barriers. Seventh, chatbots are expected to be valuable for people needing immediate support outside traditional mental health care hours.

According to [20], the accessibility and effectiveness of mental health services. Health chatbots are expected to be able to provide personalized and adaptive interventions that fit the individual needs of patients, which can improve the quality of care and reduce costs associated with healthcare. Additionally, health chatbots are expected to be able to collect data continuously and in real-time, allowing researchers and healthcare professionals to monitor and evaluate patient progress more effectively in the future.

In addition, developing a chatbot prototype for mental health support is essential from the environmental area because it can contribute to reducing the ecological impact of mental health care. In a study by [21], mental health chatbots could optimize the use of physical resources in medical facilities, as they would not require physical consulting space or related inputs, thus reducing the ecological footprint associated with the care infrastructure of traditional medical.

In addition, [22] explains that as technology advances, the development of health chatbots is becoming a necessity in the economic area. In the future, health chatbots are expected to be an essential tool to improve efficiency and reduce costs in the healthcare sector. Chatbots can help reduce the workload of healthcare professionals, which in turn can reduce healthcare costs.

3 Methodology

3.1 Research Methodology and Design

The methodology for developing a chatbot dedicated to mental and emotional support is based on a review of the scientific case study related to the psychological needs of users and best practices in the field of chatbots for mental health. A quantitative research approach will be used to know the approximate number of people who require immediate attention in mental health. It should be noted that this approach is appropriate for collecting numerical and statistical data, which will allow identifying the population that requires such health care faster and in a more timely manner [23]. This review will provide a solid foundation for understanding specific chatbot requirements. Once clear objectives have been established, such as improving the accessibility and personalization of emotional assistance, the agile Scrum methodology will be adopted to develop the project [24]. This choice is justified by its ability to offer flexibility and encourage continuous collaboration between an interdisciplinary team. Figure 2 shows the stages of the project.

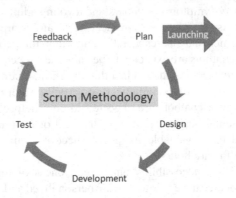

Fig. 2. Scrum Methodology

This project is based on already proven technological knowledge. Therefore, it is a non-experimental project. The non-experimental type of research is characterized by not intervening or manipulating the variables or the application of controlled treatments in a specific environment and only focuses on the observation and collection of existing data, allowing the analysis of phenomena as they occur in their natural context without trying to intervene.

Research design is transversal. This type of design consists of a study methodology that focuses on observing phenomena at a given time, thus allowing data to be collected using different tools (surveys, questionnaires, or measurements). The cross-sectional design is characterized by analyzing the variables of interest at a single point in time.

The research proposal will adjust to the Descriptive model since it will seek to describe the needs of the population that suffers from mental health problems and does not find timely care. Likewise, how technological tools can effectively help these people will be investigated. This type of research will be chosen since it will allow us to understand the variables of the project better. Figure 3 shows the activities to be developed in each phase of the study:

Team training will be critical, ensuring the presence of technical experts in artificial intelligence and software development, as well as mental health professionals. Constant collaboration with stakeholders, demos at the end of each sprint, and regular interviews will allow continuous feedback that will inform the iterative development of the chatbot.

Iterative development will be carried out in two-week sprint cycles, where the chatbot's functionalities will be built, tested, and improved continuously. User testing at the end of each sprint will ensure the effectiveness and usability of the chatbot, allowing adjustments to the design and functions based on user responses.

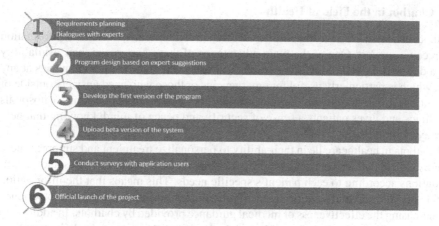

Fig. 3. Activities of each phase

Regarding the feeding of artificial intelligence, APIs will be integrated to allow access to relevant and updated data sources. These APIs will provide contextual information and real-time updates to enrich the chatbot's responses and keep you informed about the latest developments in the field of mental health. Figure 4 shows the general architecture of a chatbot:

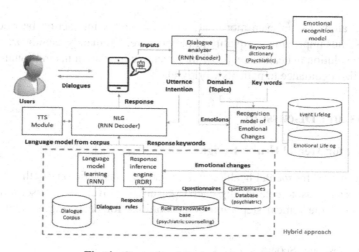

Fig. 4. General architecture of a chatbot

Implementing strong privacy measures, advanced security protocols, and compliance with specific health regulations will be crucial to ensuring the confidentiality of user information. In collaboration with ethics experts, ethical evaluation will be an ongoing activity.

3.2 Chatbot in the Field of Health

Chatbots in healthcare have transformed the way individuals access medical information and receive support. One of the main advantages of these systems is their availability 24 h a day, seven days a week. This means that users can make medical inquiries at any time, which is particularly useful for emergencies or those who need answers outside of conventional office hours. This constant availability relieves busy phone lines in hospitals and clinics and gives patients a sense of security and peace of mind, knowing that help is always within reach.

Chatbots in healthcare lie in their ability to personalize treatment and support. These systems collect data on user interactions, allowing them to tailor responses and recommendations according to each patient's specific needs. This means that the information provided is relevant and specific to each individual, improving the patient experience and increasing the effectiveness of medical guidance provided by chatbots. In addition to providing medical information, healthcare chatbots also play a crucial role in providing emotional support to patients. In particular, chatbots designed for mental health offer a safe space for people to express their feelings and concerns. These systems can provide relaxation techniques and tips for managing stress and sometimes refer users to mental health professionals if necessary.

Not only does this help reduce anxiety and stress in patients, but it can also be a vital tool for those facing mental health issues. As technology advances, even more improvements are expected in health chatbots. Deep learning algorithms and pre-trained language models make these systems more sophisticated in understanding and generating human language.

This will allow for an even more natural and complex interaction between users and chatbots, thus improving the quality of patient care. Ultimately, healthcare chatbots represent a revolution in healthcare, providing accurate information, emotional support, and personalized guidance to patients worldwide.

4   Results and Discussion

4.1   Chatbot for Mental Health Design

Designing a chatbot for mental health requires careful consideration of ethical and privacy concerns and a user-centered approach to ensure effectiveness and user satisfaction [25]. Here are some critical steps and considerations for designing a mental health chatbot:

- Define Purpose and Scope:

    - Clearly define the chatbot's purpose (e.g., providing emotional support, coping strategies, psychoeducation).
    - Determine the scope of the chatbot, including the types of mental health issues it can address.

- User-Centered Design:

  - Conduct user research to understand the target audience's needs, preferences, and concerns [26].
  - Design a user-friendly interface that is easy to navigate, ensuring accessibility for users with different needs.

- Empathy and Compassion:

  - Implement a conversational style that conveys empathy and understanding.
  - Use supportive and non-judgmental language to create a safe space for users.

- Privacy and Security:

  - Prioritize user privacy and confidentiality. Communicate how user data will be handled and stored.
  - Implement security measures to protect sensitive information.

- Risk Assessment and Crisis Response:

  - Develop a robust risk assessment protocol to identify users at risk of self-harm or harm to others.
  - Provide crisis response information and, when necessary, seamlessly connect users to emergency services.

- Personalization:

  - Allow users to customize their experience based on their preferences and needs.
  - Implement machine learning algorithms to adapt the chatbot's responses based on user interactions over time.

- Evidence-Based Content:

  - Ensure that the chatbot's information and advice are evidence-based and align with established mental health guidelines.

- Feedback and Iteration:

  - Collect user feedback regularly to identify areas for improvement.
  - Iteratively update the chatbot based on user input and evolving mental health knowledge.

- Integration with Professionals:

  - Consider integrating the chatbot with mental health professionals when more personalized or intensive support is needed.

- 24/7 Availability:

  - Aim for 24/7 availability to provide support whenever users may need it. Include disclaimers about the limitations of automated support.

- Educational Resources:

  - Provide educational resources on mental health topics to empower users and enhance their understanding.

- Ethical Considerations:

  - Be transparent about the chatbot's automated nature and limitations.
  - Avoid making diagnostic claims and encourage users to seek professional help [27].

The design process should involve collaboration with mental health professionals, psychologists, and users to ensure that the chatbot is a valuable and ethical tool for mental health support. The design is in the initial phase of this project, and a series of expected results have been defined. This phase is essential to ensure that the chatbot meets the needs of the people it is intended to serve.

Once we have developed a set of requirements, we can analyze the survey results. This analysis will help us better understand the needs of people with psychological health conditions and ensure that the chatbot meets those needs. Table 1 shows the expected results:

Table 1. Expected Results of the Project

Expected Results	Description
Integration with Health Professionals	Expectation: Collaborate with medical staff for comprehensive care
	Implementation: Facilitate communication between the chatbot and health professionals, allowing coordinated supervision and monitoring
Universal Access	Expectation: Provide global access to emotional support services 24/7
	Implementation: Integration into digital health platforms and collaboration with medical institutions for broad distribution
Effective Personalization	Expectation: Adapt to individual user needs
	Implementation: Use of machine learning algorithms to understand and adjust chatbot interaction based on specific responses and needs

(*continued*)

Table 1. (*continued*)

Expected Results	Description
Education and Awareness	Expectation: Reduce the stigma associated with mental health
	Implementation: Include educational features within the app to encourage social understanding and acceptance of mental health challenges
Social Impact Measurement	Expectation: Contribute positively to the well-being of society
	Implementation: Conduct social impact studies to evaluate how the application positively affects mental health at a community and global level

4.2 Chatbot Implementation

The implementation of a mental health chatbot can offer numerous benefits, both for users and healthcare providers. Figure 5 shows some key advantages.

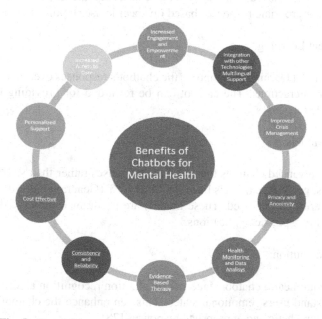

Fig. 5. Key Advantages of a Mental Health Chatbot Implementation

Implementing a mental health care chatbot involves combining technical aspects with ethical considerations. Creating a chatbot for mental health consists of the use of various artificial intelligence (AI) techniques and algorithms, among which can be mentioned:

- Natural Language Processing (NLP):

    - Algorithms: NLP algorithms are fundamental for processing and understanding human language. Techniques like tokenization, part-of-speech tagging, named entity recognition, and sentiment analysis are employed.
    - Libraries/Frameworks: Popular NLP frameworks include spaCy, NLTK (Natural Language Toolkit), and Hugging Face's Transformers.

- Machine Learning (ML) Algorithms:

    - Intent Recognition: ML algorithms often recognize user intents and map them to appropriate responses. This is crucial for understanding the purpose behind user inputs.
    - Classification Models: Supervised learning models, such as support vector machines (SVMs) or deep learning models like recurrent neural networks (RNNs) or transformers, can classify user input into predefined categories.

- Decision Trees and Rule-Based Systems:

    - Decision trees and rule-based systems can guide the conversation flow and determine appropriate responses based on specific user inputs or situations.

- Reinforcement Learning:

    - Reinforcement learning can improve the chatbot's responses over time by learning from user interactions. The chatbot can be rewarded for providing helpful and appropriate responses.

- Generative Models:

    - For more advanced chatbots that generate responses rather than selecting predefined ones, generative models like OpenAI's GPT (Generative Pre-trained Transformer) series can be used. These models are pre-trained on large datasets and fine-tuned for specific applications.

- Emotion Recognition:

    - Some mental health chatbots incorporate emotion recognition algorithms to better understand users' emotional states. This can enhance the chatbot's ability to provide empathetic and appropriate responses [28].

- Deep Learning for Personalization:

    - Deep learning techniques can be applied to personalize the chatbot's responses based on user interactions, adapting to individual preferences and needs.

- Data Analytics and User Profiling:

  - Data analytics and profiling algorithms may analyze user interactions, preferences, and patterns. This information can be leveraged to improve the chatbot's performance and offer personalized support.

- Ethical AI Considerations:

  - Implementing algorithms that ensure ethical considerations, such as prioritizing user privacy, avoiding bias, and maintaining transparency about the chatbot's limitations.

It's important to note that the choice of algorithms depends on the specific goals and requirements of the mental health chatbot. Additionally, collaboration with mental health professionals and adherence to ethical guidelines are crucial aspects of the development process to ensure the chatbot is safe, effective, and beneficial for users.

5 Conclusions and Future Works

The research is in a crucial planning and design phase, where the foundations are being established for developing an innovative and effective tool in the mental health field. The meticulous selection of natural language processing algorithms and predictive models and priority attention to user privacy and security reflects this project's commitment to technical and ethical excellence. The user interface, designed to be friendly and intuitive, ensures the user experience is accessible to a diverse audience.

Consideration of early feedback through usability testing demonstrates an orientation toward adaptability and continuous improvement. Furthermore, the possibility of integrating emerging technologies, such as emotion detection, suggests a futuristic vision to enrich the chatbot's ability to understand and address users' emotional needs further.

In conclusion, this project aims to develop a mental support chatbot based on artificial intelligence and establish standards of excellence in privacy, accessibility, and adaptability. The combination of technically and ethically sound approaches and the vision to incorporate emerging technologies significantly supports the aspiration to improve mental health care through innovation and artificial intelligence. Continued progress in this direction promises to contribute positively to the mental health field and end users' well-being.

References

1. Russell, S.J., Norvig, P.: Inteligencia Articial un Enfoque Moderno, Segunda. Pearson Education, Madrid (2004)
2. Cobo Cano, M., Lloret Iglesias, L.: Inteligencia Artificial y Medicina. Madrid (2023)
3. Noble, J., et al.: Developing, implementing, and evaluating an artificial intelligence-guided mental health resource navigation chatbot for health care workers and their families during and following the COVID-19 pandemic: protocol for a cross-sectional study. JMIR Res. Protoc. **11**(7) (2022). https://doi.org/10.2196/33717

4. Zarabia, O.: Implementación de un CHATBOT con Botframework: Caso de Estudio, Servicios a Clientes del Área de Fianzas de Seguros Equinoccial. Escuela Politécnica Nacional (2018)
5. Kaplan, A., Haenlein, M.: Siri, Siri, in my hand: who's the fairest in the land? On the interpretations, illustrations, and implications of artificial intelligence. Bus. Horiz. **62**(1), 15–25 (2019). https://doi.org/10.1016/j.bushor.2018.08.004
6. Jackson, P.C.: Introduction to Artificial Intelligence, 3rd edn (2019)
7. Badaro, S., Ibañez, L.J., Agüero, M.: SISTEMAS EXPERTOS: Fundamentos, Metodologías y Aplicaciones. Cienc. Tecn. **1**(13), 349–364 (2013). https://doi.org/10.18682/cyt.v1i13.122
8. Cerdas, D.: Historia de la Inteligencia artificial relacionada con los Chatbots. https://planet achatbot.com/historia-inteligencia-artificial-relacionada-con-chatbots/
9. Jurafsky, D., Martin, J.H.: Speech and Language Processing (2024)
10. Sulaiman, S., Mansor, M., Abdul Wahid, R., Nor Azhar, N.A.A.: Anxiety assistance mobile apps chatbot using cognitive behavioural therapy. Int. J. Artif. Intell. **9**(1), 17–23 (2022). https://doi.org/10.36079/lamintang.ijai-0901.349
11. Viduani, A., et al.: Assessing mood with the identifying depression early in adolescence chatbot (IDEABot): development and implementation study. JMIR Hum. Factors (2023). https://doi.org/10.2196/44388
12. Neto Jai Hyun Choi, S., Fontes de Azevedo Costa, A.L., Simone Lopes Moreira, R., Saito Regatieri, C.V., Rogério dos Santos, V.: Development of a chatbot to identify depression through a questionnaire. J. Psychiatry Psychiatr. Disord. **06**(01), 25–35 (2022). https://doi.org/10.26502/jppd.2572-519x0151
13. Troya-Capa, C., Mocha-Brito, L., Cabrera-Sarango, M.: Revisiónsistemática de literatura: Inteligencia Artificial aplicada a la predicción de pensamientos suicidas. In: Proceedings del Congreso Estudiantil de Inteligencia Artificial Aplicada a la Ingeniería y Tecnología, pp. 1–8 (2020). https://ieeexplore.ieee.org
14. Gupta, A.: Introduction to AI chatbots. Int. J. Eng. Res. Technol. **9**(07), 255–258 (2020). https://doi.org/10.17577/ijertv9is070143
15. UmstZein, D., Hundertmark, S.: Chatbots: an interactive technology for personalized communication and transaction. IADIS Int. J. www/Internet **15**(1), 96–109 (2018)
16. Martínez-García, D.N., Dalgo-Flores, V.M., Herrera-López, J.L., Analuisa-Jiménez, E.I., Velasco-Acurio, E.F.: Avances de la inteligencia artificial en salud. Dominio de las Ciencias **5**(3), 603 (2019). https://doi.org/10.23857/dc.v5i3.955
17. Adamopoulou, E., Moussiades, L.: An overview of chatbot technology. In: Maglogiannis, I., Iliadis, L., Pimenidis, E. (eds.) AIAI 2020. IAICT, vol. 584, pp. 373–383. Springer, Cham (2020). https://doi.org/10.1007/978-3-030-49186-4_31
18. Huang, X.: Chatbot: Design, Architecture, and Applications (2021)
19. Koulouri, T., Macredie, R., Olakitan, D.: Chatbots to support young adults' mental health: an exploratory study of acceptability. ACM Trans. Interact. Intell. Syst. **12**, 1–39 (2022). https://doi.org/10.1145/3485874
20. Boucher, E.M., et al.: Artificially intelligent chatbots in digital mental health interventions: a review. Expert Rev. Med. Devices. **18**(sup1), 37–49 (2021). https://doi.org/10.1080/17434440.2021.2013200
21. Omarov, B., Narynov, S., Zhumanov, Z.: Artificial intelligence-enabled chatbots in mental health: a systematic review. Comput. Mater. Continua **74**(3), 5105–5122 (2023). https://doi.org/10.32604/cmc.2023.034655
22. Høiland, C.G., Følstad, A., Karahasanovic, A.: Hi, can I help? Exploring how to design a mental health chatbot for youths. Hum. Technol. **16**(2), 139–169 (2020). https://doi.org/10.17011/ht/urn.202008245640
23. Perez Castaños, S., Garcia Santamaria, S.: Cómoinvestigar en Didáctica de las Ciencias Sociales? Fundamentos metodológicos, técnicas e instrumentos de investigación, no. May (2023)

24. Schwaber, K., Sutherland, J.: 2020-Scrum-Guide-Spanish-Latin-South-American (2020). https://scrumguides.org/docs/scrumguide/v2020/2020-Scrum-Guide-Spanish-Latin-South-American.pdf

25. Crosas Batista, M., Mora Ayala, E.: La era de los asistentes conversacionales: Guía para diseñar, implementar y entrenar un chatbot (2022)

26. Neebal: Mobile App Development: A Roadmap to Success, Avoiding the Common Pitfalls. https://www.neebal.com/blog/mobile-app-development-a-roadmap-to-success-avoiding-the-common-pitfalls

27. García-lópez, A., Girón-luque, F.: La integración de la inteligencia artificial en la atención médica: desafíos éticos y de implementación. Universitas Medica **64**(3), 1–18 (2023). https://doi.org/10.11144/Javeriana.umed64-3.inte

28. Carmona, M.C., Laura, A., Carvajal, F.E.: Experienciaemocional de adultos al usar un chatbot operado con inteligencia artificial Nicolás Rodríguez Valero. Universidad de Antioquia (2023). www.udea.edu.co

Embracing Virtual Reality: Understanding Factors Influencing Older Adults' Acceptance

Qian Li[1] , Qian Liu[1(✉)] , Qingyang Tang[2] , and Qingwei Liu[2]

[1] School of Journalism and Communication, Beijing Normal University, Beijing, People's Republic of China
qianliu@bnu.edu.cn
[2] School of Journalism, Fudan University, Shanghai, People's Republic of China

Abstract. The growing concern over the aging population has heightened the focus on elderly mental health and well-being, positioning Virtual Reality (VR) technology as a potential remedy; this underscores the importance of understanding older adults' perspectives and attitudes towards VR. In this study, 29 participants over 60 years old from Beijing were recruited and their attitudes towards, as well as willingness to use, VR were analyzed through semi-structured interviews based on the Unified Theory of Acceptance and Use of Technology (UTAUT2). The study found that factors such as performance expectancy (PE), hedonic motivation (HM), physiological sensations (PS), and patriotic feeling (PF) were widely mentioned among the elderly group, while factors such as effort expectancy (EE), facilitating conditions (FC), and social influence (SI) were relatively less mentioned. The study provides new insights into the understated role of EE in older adults' VR technology acceptance, the significant impact of socio-cultural factors, and the critical need to address the digital divide and specific challenges the elderly face with VR technology. Practically, it identifies essential factors influencing VR acceptance among the elderly, offering guidelines for user-friendly, culturally adaptive, and inclusive design.

Keywords: Virtual Reality · Elderly · Acceptance of Technology · UTAUT2

1 Introduction

The rapid aging of the global population has increasingly brought the quality of life and well-being of the elderly into the spotlight of societal concern. According to the World Health Organization (WHO), by 2050, there will be 2 billion people aged 65 and older globally, with a significant proportion, up to 80%, in low- and middle-income countries [1], intensifying the challenges societies face in accommodating an aging population. In this context, leveraging emerging technologies such as Virtual Reality (VR), which offers immersive and interactive experiences, is considered crucial for enhancing the quality of life in the elderly [2, 3].

VR is a computer-simulated environment that allows interaction within an artificial three-dimensional space, where users are immersed through specific interactive devices

N. A. Streitz and S. Konomi (Eds.): HCII 2024, LNCS 14719, pp. 32–54, 2024.
https://doi.org/10.1007/978-3-031-60012-8_3

such as goggles, headsets, gloves, or bodysuits [4]. VR is widely believed to have a growing presence among the elderly, encompassing medical rehabilitation [5], social interaction [6, 7], cognitive therapy [3, 8], and leisure activities [9, 10]. These applications not only effectively improve the quality of life and health of older adults, but also introduce them to refreshing and engaging entertainment and social experiences.

While older adults could greatly benefit from technology use, barriers such as fear of technology and skill deficiencies may inhibit their engagement [11]. What's worse, the current VR market primarily caters to younger consumers, frequently overlooking the unique needs and perspectives of older adults. In contrast to younger users, elders typically have a less favorable experience when engaging with VR [12]. Hence, comprehensive research should be undertaken to investigate how VR technology is perceived and adopted by older adults, along with the factors that influence its acceptance. This study, through in-depth interviews with the elderly, investigates the key factors influencing their acceptance of VR. It aims to better understand their interaction with new media technology and offer insights for VR product design, which in turn helps to improve the quality of life of older adults.

2 Literature Review

2.1 Older Adults and VR Technology

The term 'older adults' is conventionally defined as individuals aged 60 and above [13]. In this age group, individuals frequently encounter challenges: physiologically, marked by slowed metabolism, weakened immunity, and reduced physical functions [3]; cognitively, characterized by an increased risk of disorders such as Alzheimer's disease [14]. Social isolation, stemming from changes in economic and social resources, the passing of family members, and shifts in family structure and mobility, is also an undeniable challenge [15]. Not only do these factors limit older people's social opportunities, they also exert a significant negative impact on their physical and mental health.

In recent years, the increasing utilization of VR among the elderly population signifies both its growing prevalence and its potential to effectively address the challenges faced by older adults. This is supported by a scoping gray literature review of 39 documents, which identified VR as one of the eight emerging technologies that could fulfill the diverse care and support needs of the elderly [2]. As an intervention, VR has demonstrated significant efficacy in enhancing the physical health of the elderly. It not only aids in physical exercise, boosting their fitness levels [3], but also enhances balance [16], and spatial navigation abilities [17], thereby reducing the risk of falls. Additionally, VR is utilized in facilitating post-stroke motor rehabilitation in the elderly [18]. In terms of cognitive improvement, VR has also shown significant effects. For example, Gamito et al. found that VR environments were more effective in improving cognition, executive function, attention, and visual memory among the elderly, compared to traditional cognitive intervention methods [19]. Similarly, Appel et al. observed that immersive VR experiences contribute to enhanced cognitive function in older adults, a key factor in preventing cognitive decline [8]. VR, extending beyond its tangible benefits in the physical and cognitive realms, emerges as a valuable tool in revolutionizing the social and emotional conditions of the elderly. By facilitating a novel socialization paradigm,

VR mitigates feelings of isolation among this demographic, enabling them to surpass physical barriers and immerse themselves in activities otherwise constrained to real-life settings, such as virtual rock climbing [7]. Brimelow et al. further demonstrated that VR was beneficial to older adults with severe cognitive impairment in alleviating apathy and increasing activity levels [20].

However, despite the numerous benefits offered by VR technology, its widespread adoption and acceptance among the elderly remain challenging. This demographic typically exhibits lower acceptance of emerging technologies, which may be attributed to factors like cognitive abilities, technological proficiency, health status, and attitudes towards new technologies [21]. Research indicates that willingness to use technology tends to decline with age [22]. Furthermore, a survey conducted by Qualtrics revealed that among 1,148 American seniors, VR had the lowest acceptance rate at only 15%, compared to other emerging technologies such as internet-connected cameras, smart home appliances, smart homes with built-in personal digital assistants, assistive robots, autonomous vehicle [23]. However, this does not imply a lack of recognition for VR among the elderly. In fact, research has found that seniors consider VR technology to be useful, easy to use, and enjoyable, indicating a positive attitude towards this new technology [24]. Intriguingly, as noted by Kuo, Chen, and Hsu, even with a positive disposition towards technology, the elderly still face difficulties in adopting and using it due to various reasons [25].

The above reveals a fundamental consensus: while VR technology has the potential for positive effects within the elderly population, its adoption seems to face more and more complex obstacles compared to other emerging technologies. Therefore, a thorough investigation into the factors influencing the acceptance of VR technology by the elderly is crucial for promoting its widespread use within this demographic.

2.2 UTAUT2

To understand how older adults accept and use VR technology, researchers typically employ various models. For example, Jeng et al. used sports commitment model and theory of planned behavior (TRA) [26] to investigate the continuous intention of older adults in VR leisure activities, and found that subjective norms and perceived behavioral control are two significant predictors [27]. Manis and Choi proposed the virtual reality hardware acceptance model (VR-HAM) to validate the negative correlation between older adults' age and their perceived ease of use for technology [28]. Sancho-Esper et al. utilized the technology acceptance model (TAM) [29] to study older adults' attitudes and intention to use VR in tourism, and found that perceived usefulness (PU) and perceived ease of use (PEOU) were effective in influencing older adults' intention to use VR [30]. Syed-Abdul et al. used TAM to study the acceptance and use of VR among older adults and found that PU, PEOU, curiosity and enjoyment (CE), subjective norms (SN), and user experience (UE) were significant predictors [24]. TAM is one of the most commonly used models for studying technology acceptance among older adults [3], however, researchers argue that it does not sufficiently consider physiological and socio-psychological characteristics of older adults, as well as cultural and social contexts of use [10, 31].

The Unified Theory of Acceptance and Use of Technology (UTAUT), compared to models such as TAM, offers a more holistic evaluation of older adults' technology adoption, encompassing a broad range of factors such as socio-psychological status, attitudes, motivations, and the influence of external elements like familial support. UTAUT, proposed by Venkatesh et al. in 2003, is a comprehensive model widely used to explain the intent to adopt and use new technologies, showcasing its robustness by accounting for 70% of the variance in users' adoption and utilization intentions [32]. Venkatesh et al. integrated the independent variables of eight models, including theory of reasoned action (TRA), technology acceptance model (TAM), model of PC utilization (MPCU), theory of planned behavior (TPB), innovation diffusion theory (IDT), social cognitive theory (SCT), combined TAM and TPB (C-TAM-TPB), and motivation maneuver model, into four core constructs: performance expectancy (PE), effort expectancy (EE), social influence (SI), and facilitating conditions (FC). PE refers to the extent to which individuals perceive that using the system can aid their work; EE refers to the extent to which individuals are expected to exert effort in using the system; SI measures the extent to which use of the system is impacted by peer groups; and FC assesses individual perceptions of organizational support in terms of technology and equipment availability for system use. The researcher also pointed out the moderating variables that have a significant effect on the core variables, namely gender, age, voluntariness, and experience. In 2012, Venkatesh et al. enhanced the UTAUT model with UTAUT 2, which accentuated the consumer context by adding three new predictors—hedonic motivation (HM), price value (PV), and habit (H)—to the original four core variables, thus broadening its applicability [33].

Some researchers have used the UTAUT and its extended models to study elderly people's acceptance of technology. Asghar et al. employed the UTAUT model in a survey exploring seniors' perceptions of a remote assistance system designed for locating items in the kitchen, finding that the elderly considered the system usable and easy to use [34]. Chen and Chan developed a new model based on UTAUT and discovered through a survey of 1,012 elderly people in Hong Kong that personal attributes (like age, gender, education, gerontechnology self-efficacy, anxiety, as well as health and ability characteristics) and FC were more predictive of technology use than traditional attitudinal factors like PE and PEOU [21]. In VR, Money et al. analyzed elderly individuals' think-aloud, post-task, and follow-up interview transcripts using the UTAUT framework, revealing high usability of VR games and the influence of PE, EE, and SI on their acceptance and use [35]. Focusing on older adults' acceptance of social VR technology and the factors influencing it, Shao and Lee found that older adults had a significant preference for social VR, especially for entertainment (32.4%) and medical therapy (31.3%) functions, demonstrating that SI, PEnjoy (also known as HM in UTUAT2), and PE were important indicators [7].

Existing studies largely employ the UTAUT model to probe into VR acceptance among the elderly, yet the application of UTAUT2 remains unexplored. UTAUT2, tailored for consumer contexts as opposed to UTAUT's organizational focus, aligns better with analyzing older adults' VR engagement. Notably, UTAUT2's newly added HM is crucial in older adults' entertainment-focused VR adoption, underscoring enjoyment alongside usability and utility [36, 37]. This study, therefore, utilizes UTAUT2 to delve into elderly consumers' attitudes and acceptance of VR, leading to the research question: What are the key factors within the UTAUT2 framework that influence the older adults' acceptance of VR technology?

3 Methodology

To delve into factors influencing the elderly's acceptance of VR, semi-structured in-depth interviews and thematic analysis were employed. The chapter will sequentially detail the data collection and analysis methods, procedure, and materials used.

3.1 Data Collection

Semi-structured interviews were employed for data collection, primarily because VR, as an emerging media technology, might be unfamiliar to many participants, and interviews facilitate concept clarification. Additionally, in-depth interviews are proven effective for older adults, who tend to prefer dialogue-based communication [7, 16, 36, 38–42]. Furthermore, considering possible vision challenges or literacy differences in the elderly, interviews are also utilized in quantitative surveys to ensure clarity and understanding [21, 43].

3.2 Analysis

In this study, thematic analysis was utilized to analyze interview data, an approach particularly effective for interpreting findings [44]. The researchers first classified data within the UTAUT2 model's theoretical framework [45], then inductively developed sub-themes from the condensed data, elucidating various aspects of VR acceptance among the elderly. Nvivo software facilitated independent coding by two coders, with cross-validation ensuring coding reliability. A high Cohen's Kappa score of 0.87 indicated strong agreement in theme identification and categorization.

3.3 Coding and Themes

UTAUT2 is frequently employed as a foundational framework in qualitative research, aiding in question formulation, data coding, and analysis. Rempel and Mellinger leveraged UTAUT for coding qualitative data like interview outcomes using the Naturalistic Work-Practice Method, finding factors like expected productivity increase and EE critical in encouraging literature management tool usage [46]. Hyche crafted a qualitative instrumental collective case study design based on UTAUT, formulating questions from its structural and theoretical bases to analyze semi-structured interviews, particularly for rural users' videoconferencing system acceptance [47]. Gaviola applied UTAUT as a conceptual structure to investigate postgraduate students' mobile learning experiences and analyze the data [48].

This study, grounded in the UTAUT2, tailors its factors to the specific context of VR usage by older adults. Key variables are defined as follows:

- Performance expectancy (PE): seniors' beliefs in VR technology's potential to enhance their productivity, entertainment experiences, or daily life quality.
- Effort expectancy (EE): perceptions of the energy and effort needed to learn and use VR, focusing on device usability and interface intuitiveness.
- Social influence (SI): the perceived impact of social groups on seniors' decisions to use VR technology.
- Facilitating conditions (FC): the external elements perceived as supportive of VR usage, such as technical assistance and resource availability.
- Hedonic motivation (HM): the pleasure and satisfaction seniors derive from using VR.
- Price value (PV): seniors' cost-benefit evaluation of VR technology, considering both purchase and usage costs against perceived value.
- Habits (H): older adults' general media usage habits.
- Experience (E): the seniors' prior experience specifically with VR technology.
- Physiological feelings (PF): seniors' physical and physiological responses when using VR, a new factor added to address issues like cybersickness.

Issues such as cybersickness and the weight of VR equipment, not commonly addressed in traditional 2D technologies, present unique challenges. Research indicates a negative correlation between the vertigo experienced from cybersickness and the perceived usability of VR [49]. Poor health conditions also impede the use of VR for enhanced experiences [7]. Thus, the elderly's feelings towards VR devices were significantly associated with comfort and potential physical discomfort. Understanding these factors provides a more comprehensive insight into older adults' acceptance of VR, particularly considering their heightened sensitivity to physical comfort.

- Others: the category that is not directly aligned with the specified variables.

3.4 Procedures

This study, conducted in a community at a Beijing neighborhood, targeted right-handed individuals over 60 without heart disease. Participants, after giving informed consent, were equipped for the experiment and viewed an 8-min video. Post-viewing, one-on-one semi-structured interviews delved into their subjective experiences, VR perceptions and expectations, willingness to re-watch or recommend, and prior media use. Each participant received a 50 RMB reward. Notably, two individuals couldn't complete the experience due to severe cybersickness. The study, ethically reviewed and approved, gathered 29 interview recordings, each about 30 min long.

3.5 Device and Stimuli

In this study, the VR device used was the Pico G2 4K glasses. This device is an all-in-one VR headset, which is particularly suitable for the elderly population with its lightweight body and easy-to-use interface. The Pico G2 4K provides a wide 101° field of view and a high refresh rate of 90 Hz, which ensures the viewer's experience. Participants watched *VR China*, an 8-min film produced by National Geographic China, which presents a narrative of human-nature harmony in China, featuring diverse landscapes, cultural heritage, and modern achievements across various regions. This film offers a VR experience ideal for elderly viewers, featuring calming, familiar visuals that require minimal interaction with VR controllers.

4 Results

4.1 Performance Expectancy

All 29 elderly participants discussed the performance expectancy (PE), with the direct source of their PE being the experience of watching movies using VR devices, primarily centered on immersive experiences, variety in viewing experiences, and convenience.

Twenty-five elderly participants focused their assessment of VR on the strength of immersion and realism. VR, by breaking the limits of time and space and enhancing realism through immersive techniques, gave them a sense of being physically present. The "immersive experience" was highlighted as a significant feature of VR devices, as perceived by most of the elderly participants.

> *"Compared to watching on TV, the VR experience provides a more intense three-dimensional feel and a broader view, offering a different experience from the TV screen. Additionally, it allows interaction with the virtual environment, enabling me to observe various scenes at will, as if being there in person."*

> *"Especially the part about the large bamboo raft, it felt very beautiful, like I was actually sitting on the raft. The section about the Summer Palace, particularly the Long Corridor, also made me feel deeply immersed. The Forbidden City, too, these places provided me with a strong sense of immersion."*

Not only did the participants perceive VR as superior to traditional film and television, but seven elderly individuals also believed that VR offers broader, more diverse viewpoints, richer details, and unique perspectives, enabling observation of scenes that are typically difficult to notice in real life. Due to VR's beautification and three-dimensional effects on landscapes, a significant number of them thought that the scenery in VR films was even more beautiful than in reality, suggesting that VR viewing is an ideal way to appreciate scenery.

> *"The real-life viewing experience can't compare with VR, as VR offers a much more thorough picture, with a wider field of view and broader perspective."*

> *"I think that for certain scenes that are hard to see with the naked eye, VR allows us to observe them closely, making the viewing experience more enjoyable, even surpassing our own vision."*

Additionally, ten elderly participants found VR to be highly convenient. They appreciated that VR allows seniors with physical limitations or age restrictions to comfortably experience world-famous landmarks and natural sceneries from home, thereby enhancing their quality of life.

"Currently, especially among the elderly, there is a significant demand for VR. Their physical condition might not be suited for traveling outdoors, but their mood and cognitive state remain positive. Due to age restrictions, some travel groups do not accept them, making VR devices sufficient for these seniors. They can use them anytime to fulfill their needs for travel and sightseeing."

However, two elderlies questioned the value of VR. They believed that for certain activities and contents, such as news broadcasts and sports events, the immersive experience provided by VR was not necessary and might not be the best choice.

"I don't need to feel immersed. Keeping a certain viewing distance allows me to better enjoy and understand the news or the enjoy the sports program."

4.2 Effort Expectancy

Effort expectancy (EE) in this study mainly includes time and learning costs. Surprisingly, only a few elderly participants (N = 6) mentioned EE, generally finding the device user-friendly. This ease of use might be due to the device's straightforward operation, mainly involving turning it on and starting playback. Additionally, a researcher assisted with VR device operation, possibly reducing the seniors' direct experience of learning difficulty.

"It's pretty simple, not that complicated, and I think it's okay."

However, some older adults also expressed concerns about difficulties in learning and memorizing the operation of the VR device.

"If I have this device at home, I would need to set it up myself. If I forget how it works, then I wouldn't know how to make it work again."

"My memory isn't good. I can't operate the VR, and I can't remember it at all."

4.3 Social Influence

The social influence (SI) aspect mainly refers to the impact of external social environment, friends, and family on elderly individuals' use of VR.

Eight seniors mentioned that their decision to use VR was influenced by family and societal factors. In Chinese families, it's common for elderly people to live with children or grandchildren, often playing a crucial role in caring for younger generations or assisting with household tasks. Personal interests and leisure activities, like watching VR, are sometimes secondary to family responsibilities or education needs.

"If my child wants (a VR device), I'll buy it for them."

"You see, although the device looks nice, it's not really useful for my kids (grandchildren). So, I don't think I would buy it myself."

"This indeed poses a new challenge in family education, there's a certain contradiction. The devices are usable, and the price is reasonable, within an acceptable range. But I'm reluctant to accept it, you know? Sometimes, I really wish to hide it

so the children won't find it. Yes, this is my inner conflict, you can surely understand this feeling. Actually, the device itself is quite good."

In addition, there was also one participant whose attitude towards the use of new technologies such as VR was also influenced by macro-social changes in the country.

"Think about it, my hometown is changing, not only Henan, but the whole of China is undergoing changes for the better. Isn't it? Our older adults should also all keep up with the times and follow this pace of progress."

4.4 Facilitating Conditions

The interviews revealed that although fewer elderly people (N = 7) directly mentioned facilitating conditions (FC), their discussions reflected considerations of external support and resources needed for VR use. FC includes the accessibility of devices, ease of obtaining help and support, and adaptability of the technological environment.

One key aspect participants focused on was the internal guidance features of the devices, indicating a need for clear, understandable instructions to help them start using VR and access its content.

"The reason I don't accept (VR) is that there is no start (cue) (after) putting it on."

In addition, the widespread availability and accessibility of VR devices are key factors influencing the elderly's acceptance and use of VR. The unfamiliarity of elderly individuals with VR technology and a lack of awareness about its prevalence can lead to reservations about using it. Their comments underscore the need for broader promotion and education about VR to increase its adoption among the elderly.

"This device is not as ubiquitous as television, nor is it as readily available online as news."

"There's a need to enhance the promotion of VR technology to make more people aware and understand it. Many of us haven't heard of VR; honestly, it's my first time too. If everyone is familiar with VR, knows what it's about, the acceptance level might be very different, right?"

Besides, some elderly participants called for the need for additional assistive devices or functions to adapt VR to their viewing habits, relating to technological adaptability. They suggested VR features and designs catering specifically to the visual and operational needs of older users.

"I personally think if VR could be further improved, especially to cater to older users, like incorporating features to slow down video playback, it would be better."

Lastly, while not directly related to VR, the elderly stated the extra support they might need when using smart technologies. This reflects the need for more assistance and resources in adapting to new technologies like VR, which could include easy-to-understand instructions, practical help from family or friends, or even professional training. This need for additional support highlights the challenges older users face in adapting to technology, and points to the need for society and technology providers to consider and implement more comprehensive support measures for this group to better utilize new technologies.

"Like internet-connected smart TV box, after someone taught me how to use it a few times, I managed to operate it successfully by myself once or twice."

4.5 Hedonic Motivation

Hedonic motivation (HM) mainly reflects the pleasure or enjoyment derived from using VR devices. Most seniors (N = 20) indicated VR's role in improving mood, bringing positive emotional experiences. This effect arises from the immersive and entertaining experiences VR offers, providing an escape and emotional uplift.

"(After watching the VR film), my mood immediately improved. It felt like entering another world, sweeping away my worries with its beautiful scenery."

Additionally, participants believed that the cognitive stimulation and novel experiences of VR also brought them joy and a sense of satisfaction, especially when they explored new content or learned new knowledge.

"This is the first time I've ever (watched a VR video), the feeling's quite new ... I feel quite thrilled and excited."

Some individuals also cited that VR not only provided sensory comfort and new experiences but also assisted them in emotionally revisiting past memories or exploring places they cannot physically reach, thereby strengthening their emotional connections to these memories or locations and enhancing their sense of happiness.

"I was really happy watching the video. I have visited many of those places, and watching the video felt like revisiting them. Being from Harbin, seeing Heilongjiang, Liaoning, and Jilin in the video felt particularly close to my heart. I've been to Hangzhou and Shanghai, and only Hainan is left to visit. Watching these videos gave me a very familiar feeling, like recalling past stories. The video is so realistic; it looks just like the real thing."

Finally, a few respondents also brought up the social interaction aspect within VR, which proved to be of significant value to the elderly. Through this form of interaction, they could experience a sense of social participation, not only alleviating feelings of loneliness but also greatly enhancing their emotional well-being.

"[VR is] useful for improving mood, for example, if my daughter can't come to visit me in time in the future, interacting with this device should help a little bit."

4.6 Price Value

The concept of price value (PV) for the elderly in evaluating VR devices encompasses a comprehensive assessment of the relationship between the device's cost and its perceived value. This includes sensitivity to costs and evaluation of benefits from the investment. Among the 29 elderly participants, 20 expressed that PV directly influences their decision to purchase and use VR devices. Generally, they expect the price to match their valuation of the device, staying within a reasonable range.

The elderly primarily focused on the price of VR, preferring lower-cost options for what they consider a "crowd-pleaser." If the price is too high, they may opt for more economical entertainment methods like watching TV, despite potentially lower clarity compared to VR. Their purchasing decisions were influenced by their financial situation, leaning towards mid-to-low priced devices, with acceptable price ranges varying significantly, from tens to thousands of RMB.

"If you ask me whether I'd like to buy it, my answer is definitely yes, as long as the price is right. The device looks good and can help me relax, and I'd like to have one. But the price has to be taken into consideration because, after all, it's not a necessity."

"If the price is too high, I'd rather just watch TV. While the picture quality of TV may not be as good as VR, it's good enough for my viewing needs."

Furthermore, some respondents also expressed that when considering a purchase, they placed importance not only on the price but also on the equipment's value. This encompassed whether the device suited their needs and whether it provided content of good enough quality. Their comprehensive evaluation of price and value led them to adopt a more accommodating stance towards the cost when making a decision, believing that as long as the value matched the price, the investment was worthwhile.

"It depends on how well it works in the future. If the device is a perfect fit for me and the video content provided is comprehensive and complete, then I might consider purchasing one. Yes, I think it's worth investing some money to get such an experience."

4.7 Habit

Habits (H) refers to the elderly's previous media usage preferences. In interviews, many elderlies (N = 22) discussed their habits with old and new media and technologies, and how these habits affect their acceptance of VR. They often compared VR to familiar media (e.g., phones, TVs, newspapers) to assess its acceptability.

Some, already accustomed to smart devices and open to emerging technologies, showed active interest in trying VR. Their exploratory nature and willingness to embrace new things makes it easier for them to accept VR.

"I like to try something relatively new... I think it should be good to accept it (VR)."

Conversely, some elderly individuals, due to their long-standing reliance on traditional media like television and radio, might have a conservative attitude towards adopting new technologies such as VR. They might feel that existing media sufficiently meet their needs and considered learning and adapting to new technologies as unnecessary or challenging.

"Nowadays, watching TV is very convenient, especially for news. So, for me, there's no need to buy a VR device."

"I find watching TV more casual, while using VR requires wearing the device and sitting still. When watching TV, I can multitask or just listen to the audio if I need to do something else, keeping me connected. But with VR, it feels like I'm cut off from my surroundings, completely disconnected once it's on."

Lastly, interviewees claimed that traditional media like TV and movies offered a relatively passive viewing experience in a stable and predictable media environment, whereas VR provided an active, immersive experience, which could make them uncomfortable or uninterested in VR's novel visual experiences and content types.

"I think the effect is so-so. Wearing VR glasses feels too close, not as comfortable as watching TV or a phone because you can adjust the distance from your eyes with a phone. The VR glasses are too close, a bit uncomfortable to use."

"TV watching is relatively calm, not 3D, but more stable, comfortable. In contrast, VR effect is more varied and intense."

4.8 VR Experience

Out of 29 elderly participants, the vast majority (N = 21) had no prior experience with VR. Generally, past tech experience significantly impacts their acceptance, learning pace, and efficiency in using VR. Experienced users may grasp VR operations quicker and explore its various features and content more willingly.

Among the three seniors with VR experience, although their experiences varied, all showed a positive attitude towards VR technology. One owned a VR device received from his company, while the other two had brief experiences (mostly like occasional glimpses while their grandchildren were using VR). All three showed a strong interest in using VR and a willingness to recommend it to family and friends, with the VR owner being particularly more enthusiastic in endorsing it than the others.

"I experienced VR before, it was distributed by my company. Everyone got one, completely free. ... Honestly, I would be willing to buy (a VR device)."

Additionally, five elderly participants had experienced VR-related technologies like 3D movies and dome screens. These individuals, after their experiences, were generally positive, finding VR to be better and more convenient than 3D or dome experiences, and willing to recommend it to others.

"I had a similar experience at the Reform and Opening-Up exhibition, but that didn't require glasses, it was a screen surrounding on all sides. It showed scenes since the Reform and Opening-Up, very impressive, felt like being there. ...This VR experience is better (than the previous ones), and I plan to recommend it to my partner and daughter."

4.9 Physiological Feelings

Physiological feelings (PF) are about older people's own physiological conditions and physiological experiences during VR use. Given the general physical state of the elderly, adapting VR experiences to their physiological traits is vital. These sensations aren't just determined by actual conditions but also by the elderly's subjective assessments. Often, psychological rejection is a bigger barrier than physical aversion [50].

Cybersickness is a common discomfort among the elderly using VR, with symptoms like motion sickness. It can manifest as overall discomfort, fatigue, headache, eye strain, stomach awareness, nausea, dizziness, vertigo, hiccups, sweating, and blurred vision when exposed to VR environments [51]. Although a few elderly users (N = 4) didn't report any discomfort, 15 experienced mild dizziness or eye discomfort, and 10 felt no discomfort. This phenomenon usually occurs in the initial stages or when the VR content moves rapidly, but many adapt over time.

> "Although I occasionally feel a bit dizzy when using VR, it usually subsides naturally after a short while."

The elderly participants in the study shared their physiological experiences when using VR for movie watching, highlighting several concerns. They mentioned potential hazards to their eyes, such as visual fatigue and dryness, as reasons for their reluctance to use VR. Additionally, maintaining a specific posture for extended periods led to neck and back tension and pain. For those with hearing issues, loud audio in VR could cause ringing or discomfort. They also expressed apprehension about intense visual and auditory stimuli in VR environments, fearing it could trigger blood pressure or heart issues. Overall, these experiences suggest a need for careful consideration of physical limitations and comfort when designing VR experiences for the elderly.

> "At my age, I don't think it's good to use VR often. Given my health issues, like high blood pressure and poor hearing, I think using it for a long time might not be suitable. I'd enjoy it for maybe half an hour or forty minutes, but no longer. A lighter device might be more appropriate for our age group."

> "I don't really like and don't really go for VR. It is still a bit difficult for me to accept it. I feel a bit scared when using VR. We older people now prefer to live a more peaceful and quieter life and are less thrill-seeking."

4.10 Patriotic Sentiment

In the interviews, 21 older adults showed strong patriotic sentiment after watching the VR film. Patriotic sentiment (PS) refers to an individual's deep affection and pride for their country, often including an identification with and respect for the nation's history, culture, achievements, and values. This response was likely due to the VR content's vivid presentation of China's natural landscapes and urban scenes, using immersive VR technology to showcase the country's beauty and development. The high-tech approach enhanced the viewing experience's realism and impact, and stirred deep feelings about the nation's achievements in the elderly. They saw the vastness of China's landscapes, the prosperity of its cities, and the richness of its culture through the VR film, which made them feel very proud and honored. Additionally, contrasting past and present changes, the elderly were moved by the rapid development and progress of the country, sparking stronger patriotic sentiments. Many expressed that VR technology allowed them to experience the country's beauty from a new perspective, instilling hope and confidence in the nation's future.

"(I) feel extremely excited and thrilled, witnessing the continuous rollout of new products and advanced technologies in our country. It makes me feel the ongoing development and progress."

"After watching the film, I feel immensely proud. The rate of China's development is astonishing, far beyond what I had imagined. Our generation's experiences are completely different from the younger ones. We have lived through a journey from poverty to gradual prosperity. Looking back now, these changes are indeed monumental."

5 Discussion

5.1 Summary of Findings

This study explored older adults' acceptance and use of VR technology using semi-structured in-depth interviews based on the UTAUT2 model. The results showed that most older adults were open to embracing VR, consistent with previous research [52]. After experiencing VR, older adults most frequently mentioned the variables of performance expectancy (PE), hedonic motivation (HM), physiological feelings (PF), patriotic sentiment (PS), habit (H), VR experience, and price value (PV), garnering attention from over 70% of the participants. In contrast, facilitating conditions (FC), social influence (SI), and effort expectancy (EE) were mentioned at relatively low rates. While these interview results cannot provide quantitative data to support the relationship between these factors and VR use and acceptance, they offer valuable insights into our understanding of older adults' attitudes toward VR.

Frequently Mentioned Factors. First, the importance of effort expectancy (EE) in this study deviates from previous research. While PE was most mentioned by the elderly, EE was least referred. Slightly different from the TAM model [29] or the UTAUT, UTAUT2 models [32, 33], which all emphasize the important influence of PE and EE on technology use. Previous studies also confirmed their importance for elderly VR use [5, 10, 30, 42, 53, 54], and it is even pointed out that EE (usability/usefulness in the original article) is a key factor for VR acceptance among the elderly [3]. The low mention of EE in this study might be due to unstable effects, as Syed-Abdul et al. (2019) observed that ease of use typically predicts usage intention less than usefulness [24]. Additionally, Ma and Liu's meta-analysis, based on 26 empirical studies, showed that the significance of the relationship between EE and acceptance failed a security test [55], and other studies showed no direct link between EE and VR usage intention [7, 56, 57]. Secondly, the nature of the task could be a factor. The elderly watched VR films with researchers' help, involving simple operations without complex interaction or independent use, possibly reducing their focus on the difficulty of operating the device. Another study, where elderly participants completed VR experiences with assistance, found that all elderly subjects considered VR to be very easy to use [30]. Lee et al. suggested that when technology or tasks were easy, perceived ease of use might have less or no impact on acceptance [58].

Secondly, hedonic motivation (HM) also emerged frequently. This indicates that the elderly consider not only the practicality and usability of VR but also place significant importance on the emotion and experiences it brings, highlighting its role in providing pleasure and emotional fulfillment. Researchers have found that the entertainment and fun aspects of VR significantly influence its acceptance and use among the elderly [5, 10, 36, 37, 40, 42, 54]. Specifically, Kim and Hall claim that consumers' perceived enjoyment significantly affects their flow state, and this flow state substantially influences their subjective well-being and continued usage of VR [9].The older adults interviewed perceived that using VR satisfied their desire for novel experiences, and might also help them to alleviate loneliness and elevate their mood. Moreover, VR enables them to emotionally revisit memories or explore unreachable places, thereby strengthening their emotional connection with these memories or locations. As older adults watch VR films and recall their pleasant pasts, it creates an effect akin to nostalgia therapy. Nostalgia therapy, effective and recognized globally, is particularly beneficial for the elderly, enhancing their sense of worth, confidence, happiness, and adaptability [59], illustrating VR's extensive therapeutic potential beyond entertainment to emotional and psychological wellness.

Then, in our study, we observed that elderly participants displayed strong patriotic sentiment (PS) after watching VR films, a finding not mentioned in previous research. Beyond VR's ability to evoke strong emotions [60], it is more likely that such emotions are shaped by a combination of cultural factors and historical experiences. China, as a collectivist society, emphasizes the close connection and mutual dependence between the individual and collective entities, including family, society, and the nation, within its cultural context [61]. Studies indicate a significant correlation between collectivism and patriotism [62]. Particularly for the older adults in this study, who were generally born between 1940 and 1960 and experienced crucial historical periods in China, such as the founding of New China, and the Reform and Opening-Up. This generation possesses a more intense collective mindset than any generations that followed [63]. This generational perspective amplifies their patriotic emotions when engaging with VR content portraying China's evolution and natural beauty. Such emotions underscore their deep national ties and pride in the country's advancements. It's crucial to recognize, however, that this patriotic sentiment might manifest differently across various cultural contexts. Elderly acceptance of VR is shaped by cultural and societal backgrounds [64, 65], with cultural norms and histories influencing VR content perception and emotional response [66]. Future research could delve into the influence of these patriotic sentiments on elderly VR acceptance across cultures, examining their impact on usage and experience.

Next, among the physiological feelings (PF), cybersickness had less of an impact on older adults. Throughout the VR experience, all older adults successfully completed it, except for two participants who withdrew due to severe cybersickness. While some individuals did experience mild cybersickness, these symptoms were typically temporary and could be alleviated. This contrasts with some research suggesting age was associated with cybersickness [67], and that increasing age might lead to an increased risk of cyber-sickness [68, 69]. However, a meta-analysis of variables associated with cybersickness rejected the connection between age and cybersickness [70]. What's more, occurrence of cybersickness in older adults using VR wasn't high [13, 43], and was even less reported than in younger adults [71, 72]. This may be because motion sickness susceptibility decreases with age [73, 74]. In addition, almost all of the older adults in this study reported stronger immersion, and it was found that stronger immersion was associated with weaker cybersickness [70]. In conclusion, and there was no significant association between cybersickness and willingness to use VR in older adults [10]. In summary, most previous studies have primarily focused on cybersickness as a physiological response, potentially overlooking other aspects. It should be noted that a study showed there was no significant association between cybersickness and willingness to use VR in older adults [10]. Therefore, it may be necessary to examine other physiological factors that influence older adults' acceptance of VR. Although researchers have concluded that older adults, even those with mild cognitive impairment, could safely use VR [14], there are still some risks associated with VR use in older adults. The elderly, being more sus-ceptible to falls, may encounter physical discomfort when using VR, such as the burden of a heavy helmet or sensory overstimulation from sounds and images [38], necessitating further research.

Other variables frequently mentioned by older adults after experiencing VR were habit (H), VR experience, and price value (PV). This aligns with the findings of previous studies [53, 75] and reaffirms the significance of these factors in older adults' acceptance and usage of VR.

Less Frequently Mentioned Factors. Although older persons were less likely to bring up facilitating conditions (FC) and social influence (SI), these aspects warrant discussion.

FC reflects users' perception of the resources and support needed for using a particu-lar technology [32]. Huang found that FC significantly predicted older adults' acceptance of technologies [56]. Xu et al. indicated that FC might not directly affect usage intention but improved it indirectly via usability [10]. This underscores FC's importance for the elderly, as they may require more external assistance to overcome challenges in using VR. Seifert and Schlomann pointed out that, in comparison to younger individuals, the elderly faced disparities in skills and access, creating a digital divide that might impede their adoption and effective use of VR [69]. In the context of older adults using VR, the accessibility of the equipment is a clear concern. However, the need for additional sup-port and assistance can often be overlooked. Older adults may require more external help and resources to navigate the challenges associated with VR usage. It's noteworthy that the less frequent mention of FC by older adults in interviews doesn't necessarily imply a lack of need; rather, it could indicate an unawareness of these needs. It was discovered that older adults, particularly those with diminished cognitive abilities, struggled more to recognize the resources needed and to anticipate the challenges they might encounter with VR [14]. This highlights the importance of considering the provision of neces-sary support and resources when designing VR experiences for older adults. Timely and effective assistance can provide a sense of psychological security for older adults engaging with technology [76]. This support can be effective training [77], or assistance from family, friends, or the community [27].

Prior research has found that social influence (SI) can sometimes significantly predict VR usage intentions [7, 53], while other times it cannot [75]. It's apparent that the social and cultural environments of the subjects in these studies differ. Similarly, a cross-cultural study by El-Masri and Tarhini found that in Qatar, SI could significantly predict VR acceptance, but this was not the case in the United States [78]. According to Hofstede and Hofstede (1991), Chinese society is considered a typical collectivist society. In such a cultural context, emphasis is placed on the tight connections and interdependence between individuals and collectives (such as family, community, and nation) [61]. This means that an individual's behavior and decisions are often influenced by social relationships and collective interests. This was confirmed in our interviews; the decision of the elderly to accept and use VR largely depends on surrounding factors, such as family, friends, and society. If they believed that using VR might have adverse effects on the younger generation (such as addiction or eye damage) or impact family relationships, they were very firm in their decision not to use it.

5.2 Contributions

This study employed the UTAUT2 model to analyze qualitative interview data regarding the use of VR by the elderly, representing a significant endeavor. The theoretical and practical contributions are as follows.

Theoretical Contributions. From a theoretical standpoint, this paper first introduces new insights into EE within the UTAUT2 model. The study finds that when elderly individuals use VR technology, EE (i.e., ease of use VR) is not frequently mentioned. This may be due to several factors: the excessive ease of use and fun aspect of VR might lead the elderly to overlook the difficulty of using the technology; a lack of independent VR experience could prevent them from accurately describing the difficulty of use; and the presence of external support might also reduce the focus on effort expectancy. Considering the insignificant role of EE in this study, combined with its significant impact in most related research, it's reasonable to speculate that EE might play a mediating role in the elderly population, rather than being a key factor directly affecting their technology acceptance. This hypothesis has been tested in the general population [57], and future research could more comprehensively explore the relationship between EE and PE among the elderly.

Secondly, this study highlights the importance of socio-cultural factors in research on the elderly's acceptance of VR. Especially within the Chinese elderly population, we observed a notable "patriotic sentiment" and a tendency for family needs to outweigh personal needs, reflecting characteristics of collectivist culture. This finding underscores the necessity of cross-cultural studies. Future research can delve deeper into how cultural factors influence technology acceptance and usage by comparing the attitudes of the elderly from different cultural backgrounds, as well as exploring the specific needs of elderly populations in various cultural contexts.

Lastly, the study suggests focusing on the difficulties and discomforts experienced by the elderly when using VR, as well as assisting them in bridging the digital divide to share the benefits of virtual reality. As an emerging technology, VR's acceptance and user experience have garnered widespread attention. However, research on the specific challenges and needed assistance for the elderly using VR remains relatively scarce. Furthermore, while VR-induced cybersickness is a significant issue, there's insufficient focus on other physiological discomforts caused by the unique psychological and physiological needs of the elderly population, with correspondingly fewer design and improvement measures.

Practical Contributions. This study has identified key factors influencing the elderly's acceptance of VR technology and offers several guidelines for the application and improvement of VR among the elderly, specifically:

- Simplified operation: ensuring an intuitive and user-friendly interface with reduced complexity will make it easier for the elderly to get started.
- Feedback and support systems: considering incorporating assistive features such as voice subtitles and prompts during the design phase. Additionally, provide immediate technical assistance and guidance during the VR usage process, addressing potential challenges and issues faced by the elderly. For instance, assistance can be offered through online help centers, telephone support, or live chat.
- Enhanced social support and outreach: strengthening the promotion and education of VR technology to help the elderly understand and accept it, while providing essential social support and assistance, such as involvement of family members and technical training.
- Device lightness and comfort: taking into account the elderly's need for lightweight and comfortable devices, designing lighter and more portable equipment will enhance usability.
- Marketing strategies: when promoting and designing VR for the elderly, emphasize the specific benefits and value brought by VR, not just its ease of use, such as improving quality of life, enhancing family relationships, and aiding physical exercise.
- Developing elderly-friendly VR content: creating VR content tailored to the needs of the elderly, like serene-paced scenic documentaries. Minimize visual and auditory stimuli, for example, by adjusting color saturation and contrast, reducing fast-moving or flashing images, and modifying volume and sound frequency to suit the hearing range of the elderly.
- Cultural adaptability: considering the impact of cultural background on technology acceptance, the design should cater to the specific needs and expectations of elderly users from different cultural contexts. This involves integrating cultural sensitivity and relevance into VR experiences to resonate more deeply with the elderly.
- Emotional connection and entertainment value: developing VR content that can evoke emotional responses and provide entertainment value for the elderly, such as nostalgia therapy and immersive travel experiences. Also, consider creating VR content with social features, like enhanced virtual character interactions, to increase the elderly's social participation and immersion.
- Safety and health considerations: special attention should be given to the safety and health of the elderly in the design process, such as reducing the risk of cybersickness and considering physical stability while using VR.

5.3 Limitations

However, this study has certain limitations. Firstly, as it relied on semi-structured interviews, the results were more qualitative, lacking quantitative data support to establish correlations or causal relationships. Secondly, the limited sample size, along with the subjects being mainly from a specific residential area in Beijing, might not accurately represent the attitudes and perceptions of the broader elderly population across China. Finally, as a short-term study, it lacks the ability to longitudinally track changes in the elderly's use of VR. Future research should increase the sample size and employ more quantitative methods for data support. It can also expand the geographical and socio-economic background of the study subjects to better represent the elderly population. Moreover, conducting long-term studies to track and analyze the continuous changes and long-term impacts of VR usage among the elderly is recommended.

Acknowledgments. This study was supported by Fundamental Research Funds for the Central Universities (No. 2021NTSS52) and the Beijing Social Science Fund (grant No. 19XCC015).

Disclosure of Interests. The authors have no competing interests to declare that are relevant to the content of this article.

References

1. World Health Organization: Ageing and health (2022). https://www.who.int/news-room/fact-sheets/detail/ageing-and-health
2. Abdi, S., Witte, L.D., Hawley, M.: Exploring the potential of emerging technologies to meet the care and support needs of older people: a Delphi survey. Geriatrics **6**(1), 19 (2021)
3. Tuena, C., et al.: Usability issues of clinical and research applications of virtual reality in older people: a systematic review. Front. Hum. Neurosci. **14**, 93 (2020)
4. Tham, J., Duin, A.H., Gee, L., Ernst, N., Abdelqader, B., McGrath, M.: Understanding virtual reality: presence, embodiment, and professional practice. IEEE Trans. Prof. Commun. **61**(2), 178–195 (2018)
5. Mascret, N., Delbes, L., Voron, A., Temprado, J.-J., Montagne, G.: Acceptance of a virtual reality headset designed for fall prevention in older adults: questionnaire study. J. Med. Internet Res. **22**(12), e20691 (2020)
6. Kalantari, S., et al.: Using immersive virtual reality to enhance social interaction among older adults: a cross-site investigation. Innov. Aging **7**(4), igad031 (2023)
7. Shao, D., Lee, I.-J.: Acceptance and influencing factors of social virtual reality in the urban elderly. Sustainability **12**(22), 9345 (2020)
8. Appel, L., et al.: Older adults with cognitive and/or physical impairments can benefit from immersive virtual reality experiences: a feasibility study. Front. Med. **6**, 329 (2020)
9. Kim, M.J., Hall, C.M.: A hedonic motivation model in virtual reality tourism: comparing visitors and non-visitors. Int. J. Inf. Manag. **46**, 236–249 (2019)
10. Xu, W., Liang, H.-N., Yu, K., Wen, S., Baghaei, N., Tu, H.: Acceptance of virtual reality exergames among Chinese older adults. Int. J. Hum.-Comput. Interact. **39**(5), 1134–1148 (2023)
11. Huygelier, H., Schraepen, B., van Ee, R., Vanden Abeele, V., Gillebert, C.R.: Acceptance of immersive head-mounted virtual reality in older adults. Sci. Rep. **9**(1), 1–12 (2019)

12. Liu, Q., Wang, Y., Tang, Q., Liu, Z.: Do you feel the same as I do? Differences in virtual reality technology experience and acceptance between elderly adults and college students. Front. Psychol. **11**, 573673 (2020)

13. Singh, R., Upadhyay, A.: Mental health of elderly people. J. Psychosoc. Res. **9**(1), 61–70 (2014)

14. Arlati, S., et al.: Acceptance and usability of immersive virtual reality in older adults with objective and subjective cognitive decline. J. Alzheimer's Dis. **80**(3), 1025–1038 (2021)

15. Courtin, E., Knapp, M.: Social isolation, loneliness and health in old age: a scoping review. Health Soc. Care Community **25**(3), 799–812 (2017)

16. Kiselev, J., Haesner, M., Gövercin, M., Steinhagen-Thiessen, E.: Implementation of a home-based interactive training system for fall prevention: requirements and challenges. J. Gerontol. Nurs. **41**(1), 14–19 (2015)

17. Merriman, N.A., Roudaia, E., Romagnoli, M., Orvieto, I., Newell, F.N.: Acceptability of a custom-designed game, CityQuest, aimed at improving balance confidence and spatial cognition in fall-prone and healthy older adults. Behav. Inf. Technol. **37**(6), 538–557 (2018)

18. Aramaki, A.L., Sampaio, R.F., Reis, A.C.S., Cavalcanti, A., Dutra, F.C.M.S.E.: Virtual reality in the rehabilitation of patients with stroke: an integrative review. Arq. Neuropsiquiatr. **77**(4), 268–278 (2019)

19. Gamito, P., Oliveira, J., Alves, C., Santos, N., Coelho, C., Brito, R.: Virtual reality-based cognitive stimulation to improve cognitive functioning in community elderly: a controlled study. Cyberpsychol. Behav. Soc. Netw. **23**(3), 150–156 (2020)

20. Brimelow, R.E., Dawe, B., Dissanayaka, N.: Preliminary research: virtual reality in residential aged care to reduce apathy and improve mood. Cyberpsychol. Behav. Soc. Netw. **23**(3), 165–170 (2020)

21. Chen, K., Chan, A.H.S.: Gerontechnology acceptance by elderly Hong Kong Chinese: a senior technology acceptance model (STAM). Ergonomics **57**(5), 635–652 (2014)

22. Perrin, M.A.: Tech adoption climbs among older adults. Pew research center: Internet, Science & Tech., 17 May 2017. https://www.pewresearch.org/internet/2017/05/17/tech-adoption-climbs-among-older-adults/

23. Kadylak, T., Cotten, S.R.: United States older adults' willingness to use emerging technologies. Inf. Commun. Soc. **23**(5), 736–750 (2020)

24. Syed-Abdul, S., et al.: Virtual reality among the elderly: a usefulness and acceptance study from Taiwan. BMC Geriatr. **19**(1), 1–10 (2019)

25. Kuo, H.-M., Chen, C.-W., Hsu, C.-H.: A study of a B2C supporting interface design system for the elderly. Hum. Fact. Ergon. Manuf. **22**(6), 528–540 (2012)

26. Ajzen, I., Fishbein, M.: A Bayesian analysis of attribution processes. Psychol. Bull. **82**(2), 261–277 (1975)

27. Jeng, M.Y., Yeh, T.M., Pai, F.Y.: The continuous intention of older adult in virtual reality leisure activities: combining sports commitment model and theory of planned behavior. Appl. Sci. (Switzerland) **10**(21), 1–14 (2020)

28. Manis, K.T., Choi, D.: The virtual reality hardware acceptance model (VR-HAM): extending and individuating the technology acceptance model (TAM) for virtual reality hardware. J. Bus. Res. **100**, 503–513 (2019)

29. Davis, F.D.: Perceived usefulness, perceived ease of use, and user acceptance of information technology. MIS Q. **13**(3), 319 (1989)

30. Sancho-Esper, F., Ostrovskaya, L., Rodriguez-Sanchez, C., Campayo-Sanchez, F.: Virtual reality in retirement communities: technology acceptance and tourist destination recommendation. J. Vacat. Mark. **29**(2), 275–290 (2023)

31. Chen, K., Chan, A.H.S.: A review of technology acceptance by older adults. Gerontechnology **10**(1), 1–12 (2011)

32. Venkatesh, V., Morris, M.G., Davis, G.B., Davis, M.G.: User acceptance of information technology: toward a unified view. MIS Q. **27**(3), 425–478 (2003)
33. Venkatesh, V., Thong, J.Y.L., Xu, X.: Consumer acceptance and use of information technology: extending the unified theory of acceptance and use of technology. MIS Q. **36**(1), 157 (2012)
34. Asghar, Z., Yamamoto, G., Taketomi, T., Sandor, C., Kato, H., Pulli, P.: Remote assistance for elderly to find hidden objects in a kitchen. In: Giokas, K., Bokor, L., Hopfgartner, F. (eds.) EHealth 360°. LNICSSITE, vol. 181, pp. 3–8. Springer, Cham (2017). https://doi.org/10.1007/978-3-319-49655-9_1
35. Money, A.G., Atwal, A., Boyce, E., Gaber, S., Windeatt, S., Alexandrou, K.: Falls sensei: a serious 3D exploration game to enable the detection of extrinsic home fall hazards for older adults. BMC Med. Inform. Decis. Mak. **19**(1), 85 (2019)
36. Lin, C.S., Jeng, M.Y., Yeh, T.M.: The elderly perceived meanings and values of virtual reality leisure activities: a means-end chain approach. Int. J. Environ. Res. Publ. Health **15**(4), 663 (2018)
37. Yeh, T., Pai, F., Jeng, M.: The factors affecting older adults' intention toward ongoing participation in virtual reality leisure activities. Int. J. Environ. Res. Publ. Health **16**(3), 333 (2019)
38. Coldham, G., Cook, D.M.: VR usability from elderly cohorts: preparatory challenges in overcoming technology rejection. In: 2017 National Information Technology Conference. NITC 2017, pp. 131–135, September 2017
39. Farrow, S., Reid, D.: Stroke survivors' perceptions of a leisure-based virtual reality program. Technol. Disabil. **16**(2), 69–81 (2004)
40. Korsgaard, D., Bjøner, T., Nilsson, N.C.: Where would you like to eat? A formative evaluation of mixed-reality solitary meals in virtual environments for older adults with mobility impairments who live alone. Food Res. Int. **117**(February), 30–39 (2019)
41. Renaud, K., van Biljon, J.: Predicting technology acceptance and adoption by the elderly. In: Proceedings of the 2008 Annual Research Conference of the South African Institute of Computer Scientists and Information Technologists on IT Research in Developing Countries Riding the Wave of Technology - SAICSIT '08, pp. 210–219, October 2008
42. Roberts, A.R., De Schutter, B., Franks, K., Radina, M.E.: Older adults' experiences with audiovisual virtual reality: perceived usefulness and other factors influencing technology acceptance. Clin. Gerontol. **42**(1), 27–33 (2019)
43. Huygelier, H., Schraepen, B., Van Ee, R., Vanden Abeele, V., Gillebert, C.R.: Acceptance of immersive head-mounted virtual reality in older adults. Sci. Rep. **9**(1), 4519 (2019)
44. Alhojailan, M.I.: Thematic analysis: a critical review of its process and evaluation. In: WEI International European Academic Conference Proceedings, Zagreb, Croatia, October 2012
45. Crabtree, B.F., Miller, W.F.: A template approach to text analysis: developing and using codebooks. In: Crabtree, B.F., Miller, W.L. (eds.) Doing Qualitative Research, pp. 93–109. Sage Publications Inc., Thousand Oaks (1992)
46. Rempel, H.G., Mellinger, M.: Bibliographic management tool adoption and use: a qualitative research study using the UTAUT model. Ref. User Serv. Q. **54**(4), 43–53 (2015)
47. Hyche, H.L.: exploring and understanding rural educator perceptions of a video conferencing technology system through the UTAUT lens. Doctoral dissertation, Keiser University. ProQuest dissertations and Theses Global (2018)
48. Gaviola, K.W.: Understanding student experiences using smartphones as learning tools. Doctoral dissertation, Walden University (2020). https://scholarworks.waldenu.edu/cgi/viewcontent.cgi?article=11394&context=dissertations
49. Voinescu, A., Morgan, P.L., Alford, C., Caleb-Solly, P.: The utility of psychological measures in evaluating perceived usability of automated vehicle interfaces – a study with older adults. Transport. Res. F: Traffic Psychol. Behav. **72**, 244–263 (2020)

50. Zhou, Y.: The rising of digital vulnerable group: the influential factors of Wechat adoption and use among senior citizens. Journal. Commun. **7**, 66–86 (2018)
51. Kennedy, R.S., Lane, N.E., Berbaum, K.S., Lilienthal, M.G.: Cybersickness questionnaire: an enhanced method for quantifying cybersickness. Int. J. Aviat. Psychol. **3**(3), 203–220 (1993)
52. Haesner, M., Wolf, S., Steinert, A., Steinhagen-Thiessen, E.: Touch interaction with Google Glass – is it suitable for older adults? Int. J. Hum. Comput. Stud. **110**, 12–20 (2018)
53. Barsasella, D., et al.: Acceptability of virtual reality among older people: ordinal logistic regression study from Taiwan. In: Proceedings of the 2019 6th International Conference on Bioinformatics Research and Applications, pp. 145–151, December 2019
54. Ren, Z., Zhou, G.: Analysis of driving factors in the intention to use the virtual nursing home for the elderly: a modified UTAUT model in the Chinese context. Healthcare **11**(16), 2329 (2023)
55. Ma, Q., Liu, L.: The technology acceptance model: a meta-analysis of empirical findings. J. Organ. End User Comput. (JOEUC) **16**(1), 59–72 (2004)
56. Huang, F.-H.: Adapting UTAUT2 to assess user acceptance of an e-scooter virtual reality service. Virtual Reality **24**(4), 635–643 (2020). https://doi.org/10.1007/s10055-019-00424-7
57. Sagnier, C., Loup-Escande, E., Lourdeaux, D., Thouvenin, I., Valléry, G.: User acceptance of virtual reality: an extended technology acceptance model. Int. J. Hum.-Comput. Interact. **36**(11), 993–1007 (2020)
58. Lee, M.K.O., Cheung, C.M.K., Chen, Z.: Acceptance of internet-based learning medium: the role of extrinsic and intrinsic motivation. Inf. Manag. **42**(8), 1095–1104 (2005)
59. Cully, J.A., LaVoie, D., Gfeller, J.D.: Reminiscence, personality, and psychological functioning in older adults. Gerontologist **41**(1), 89–95 (2001)
60. Tian, F., Wang, X., Cheng, W., Lee, M., Jin, Y.: A comparative study on the temporal effects of 2d and VR emotional arousal. Sensors **22**(21), 8491 (2022)
61. Hofstede, G., Hofstede, G.J.: Cultures and Organizations: Software of the Mind. McGraw-Hill, New York (1991)
62. Schmitz, S.: Patriotism and collectivism: a within culture analysis. Unpublished bachelor thesis, University of Illinois (1992). https://www.ideals.illinois.edu/items/96406
63. Ma, J., Hu, Z., Gocłowska, M.A.: Cultural orientation in China: differences across five generations of employees. Soc. Behav. Personal. Int. J. **44**(4), 529–540 (2016)
64. Mondellini, M., et al.: User experience during an immersive virtual reality-based cognitive task: a comparison between Estonian and Italian older adults with MCI. Sensors **22**(21), 8249 (2022)
65. Quan-Haase, A., Williams, C., Kicevski, M., Elueze, I., Wellman, B.: Dividing the grey divide: deconstructing myths about older adults' online activities, skills, and attitudes. Am. Behav. Sci. **62**(9), 1207–1228 (2018)
66. Li, Q., Liu, Q., Chen, Y.: Prospective teachers' acceptance of virtual reality technology: a mixed study in rural China. Educ. Inf. Technol. **28**(3), 3217–3248 (2023)
67. Ramaseri Chandra, A.N., El Jamiy, F., Reza, H.: A systematic survey on cybersickness in virtual environments. Computers **11**(4), 51 (2022)
68. Arns, L.L., Cerney, M.M.: The relationship between age and incidence of cybersickness among immersive environment users. In: IEEE Proceedings of Virtual Reality, pp. 267–268. IEEE, March 2005
69. Seifert, A., Schlomann, A.: The use of virtual and augmented reality by older adults: potentials and challenges. Front. Virtual Reality **2**, 639718 (2021)
70. Howard, M.C., Van Zandt, E.C.: A meta-analysis of the virtual reality problem: unequal effects of virtual reality sickness across individual differences. Virtual Reality **25**(4), 1221–1246 (2021)

71. Dilanchian, A.T., Andringa, R., Boot, W.R.: A pilot study exploring age differences in presence, workload, and cybersickness in the experience of immersive virtual reality environments. Front. Virtual Reality **2**, 736793 (2021)
72. Drazich, B.F., et al.: In too deep? A systematic literature review of fully-immersive virtual reality and cybersickness among older adults. J. Am. Geriatr. Soc. **71**(12), 3906–3915 (2023)
73. Paillard, A.C., et al.: Motion sickness susceptibility in healthy subjects and vestibular patients: effects of gender, age and trait-anxiety. J. Vestib. Res. **23**(4–5), 203–209 (2013)
74. Saredakis, D., Szpak, A., Birckhead, B., Keage, H.A.D., Rizzo, A., Loetscher, T.: Factors associated with virtual reality sickness in head-mounted displays: a systematic review and meta-analysis. Front. Hum. Neurosci. **14**, 96 (2020)
75. Yein, N., Pal, S.: Analysis of the user acceptance of exergaming (fall- preventive measure) – tailored for Indian elderly using unified theory of acceptance and use of technology (UTAUT2) model. Entertain. Comput. **38**, 100419 (2021)
76. Saracchini, R., Catalina, C., Bordoni, L.: A mobile augmented reality assistive technology for the elderly. Comunicar **23**(45), 65–73 (2015)
77. Tsai, H.Y.S., Rikard, R.V., Cotten, S.R., Shillair, R.: Senior technology exploration, learning, and acceptance (STELA) model: from exploration to use–a longitudinal randomized controlled trial. Educ. Gerontol. **45**(12), 728–743 (2019)
78. El-Masri, M., Tarhini, A.: Factors affecting the adoption of e-learning systems in Qatar and USA: extending the unified theory of acceptance and use of technology 2 (UTAUT2). Educ. Technol. Res. Dev. **65**(3), 743–763 (2017)

Learning to Effectively Identify Reliable Content in Health Social Platforms with Large Language Models

Caihua Liu[1] , Hui Zhou[1], Lishen Su[1], Yaosheng Huang[1], Guochao Peng[2],
Dayou Wu[3], and Shufeng Kong[2(✉)]

[1] School of Artificial Intelligence, Guangxi Colleges and Universities Key Laboratory of AI
Algorithm Engineering, Guilin University of Electronic Technology, Jinji Road, Guilin 541004,
Guangxi, China
[2] Sun Yat-Sen University, Xingang Xi Road, Guangzhou 510275, Guangdong, China
kongshf@mail.sysu.edu.cn
[3] International Institute for Advanced Data Management Study, Hong Kong, China

Abstract. With the widespread accessibility of the Internet, individuals can effortlessly access health-related information from online social platforms. However,
the veracity of such health-related content is often questionable, posing a significant challenge in ensuring the content quality and reliability. The exponential
growth in daily data generation necessitates the integration of artificial intelligence
to assess the reliability of content shared on these platforms. In this paper, we
focus on Large Language Models (LLMs) due to their outstanding performance.
We introduce Health-BERT, a novel model built upon the BERT architecture. We
fine-tuned Health-BERT using a carefully curated dataset from a prominent health
information forum. Our experiments demonstrate the remarkable capabilities of
our model, achieving an impressive accuracy rate of 94% even with relatively limited training data. This highlights the exceptional knowledge transfer capabilities
of LLMs when applied to health-related content. Our model will be open-sourced,
with the hope that this initiative will improve the identification of content reliability
in health contexts.

Keywords: Large Language Models · Knowledge Transfer · Health-related
Content · Reliability Assessment

1 Introduction

The widespread accessibility of the Internet has fundamentally transformed the way individuals access health-related information. Through online social platforms, the Internet
has effectively democratised knowledge, empowering people to seek answers to their
health concerns, explore medical treatments, and engage in discussions about well-being
[1]. In this digital age, the ease of access to a vast repository of health-related information
is undeniably beneficial. However, this wealth of information also presents a significant
and pressing challenge: the quality and reliability of online health-related content. The

N. A. Streitz and S. Konomi (Eds.): HCII 2024, LNCS 14719, pp. 55–67, 2024.
https://doi.org/10.1007/978-3-031-60012-8_4

reliability of health-related content available on the Internet spans a wide spectrum, ranging from content grounded in evidence-based research and medical expertise to speculative and potentially harmful information. This variability in content reliability is a source of legitimate concern for individuals who turn to social platforms for health information. The consequences of relying on unreliable health-related content can be dire, potentially leading to misdiagnosis, misguided treatment choices, and even health risks [2].

Amidst this landscape of information abundance and variability, artificial intelligence (AI) emerges as a promising solution to address the challenge of assessing the reliability of health-related content from social platforms. Previous research efforts have primarily focused on establishing criteria for evaluating the content reliability for health social platforms [3] and promoting health and media literacy among internet users [4]. While these efforts are valuable, they often place the onus of content evaluation on individuals, requiring them to critically assess the reliability of content they encounter. However, there has been limited attention dedicated to developing automated methods that can efficiently and effectively determine the reliability of health-related content. This paper centers its focus on the pivotal role of Large Language Models (LLMs) in meeting this challenge. LLMs have gained widespread recognition and acclaim for their exceptional performance in natural language understanding tasks [5–7], making them well-suited for the complex task of assessing the reliability of health-related content.

Leveraging the capabilities of LLMs, we introduce Health-BERT, a novel model built upon the foundational BERT (Bidirectional Encoder Representations from Transformers) architecture. The choice of BERT as the basis for our model is grounded in its remarkable ability to grasp context, semantics, and language intricacies effectively. BERT, a transformer-based architecture, has been pre-trained on massive amounts of text data, allowing it to capture nuanced patterns and relationships within language [8, 9]. To equip Health-BERT with the knowledge and contextual awareness necessary to make informed judgments about the reliability of health-related content, we undertake the task of curating a training dataset. This dataset is sourced from a prominent health information forum, encompassing a wide spectrum of health-related discussions on cardiovascular diseases. The dataset ensures that Health-BERT is exposed to health-related content, allowing it to learn and adapt to health contexts.

Subsequently, we embark on the crucial step of fine-tuning Health-BERT on this curated dataset. Fine-tuning is an iterative process involving rigorous training and validation, designed to enable the model to accurately distinguish between reliable and unreliable health-related content. By fine-tuning Health-BERT on the dataset, we ensure that the model can generalise its learning health-related topics and contexts. The experimental results of our study are both remarkable and encouraging. Health-BERT achieves an impressive accuracy rate of 94% when assessing the reliability of health-related content. Notably, this high level of accuracy is achieved even when the model is trained on a relatively limited dataset. These results underscore the exceptional knowledge transfer capabilities of LLMs, particularly when applied to the health domain.

The contributions of this paper can be summarised into three key aspects:

- Introduction of an LLM-based model, Health-BERT, designed to assess the reliability of content shared on health social platforms. Health-BERT represents a significant step towards automating content reliability assessment in the health domain, relieving individuals of the burden of manual evaluation.
- Development of a real-world health social platform discussion dataset, meticulously curated to support the training and validation of Health-BERT. This dataset captures the diversity and complexity of health-related discussions found online, making it a valuable resource for future research in this domain.
- Experimentation that showcases the effectiveness of our model in accurately assessing the reliability of health-related content. Our results provide compelling evidence of the potential of LLMs in addressing the challenge of reliable health information dissemination in the digital age.

The subsequent sections of this paper are organised as follows: Sect. 2 reviews related studies and provides a technical background on transfer learning. Sect. 3 outlines the research methods employed in this study, while Sect. 4 presents the evaluation results of the classification model for content reliability assessment based on the dataset. Sect. 5 delves into the implications and limitations of our research, and finally, Sect. 6 concludes this study.

2 Related Studies

To better understand the research background of this study, this section depicts related studies concerning content reliability and classification, along with the technical underpinnings of LLMs that embrace transfer learning employed in this study.

2.1 Reliability

As mentioned, previous research has paid much attention to establishing the criteria for assessing the content reliability on social media [3]. For example, Keshavarz identified objectivity, currency, accuracy and usability as the components used to evaluate the reliability of the content shared on social media [3]. In this study, reliability pertains to the trustworthiness of health information shared on the social platforms, contingent upon the accuracy of health-related content (namely, text) that is the scope of the study. In light of this, we can have a better chance to label the reliability of the content acquired from health social platforms. On the other hand, researchers posited that alongside the development of relevant criteria, improving individuals' health and media literacy plays an important role in evaluating the reliability of content [4]. While these studies have made diverse contributions to advance the research field, there has been a paucity of concerted efforts aimed at the development of an automated method to assist individuals in discerning the reliability of content. The present study thus attempts to take advantages of AI techniques to solve this problem.

2.2 Content Classification

Content classification, also called content categorisation, is a fundamental task in natural language processing (NLP). It aims at assigning labels or tags to various text units (in the present study we focus on textual content), like sentences, queries, paragraphs, or documents and finds many applications in fields such as question answering, spam detection, sentiment analysis and news categorisation [10]. Text data can derive from various sources, making content classification a versatile tool for organising and extracting valuable information from textual content. Content classification can be performed through either manual annotation or automatic labeling methods [11]. Due to that the expanding volume of text data emerge in industrial applications, automated content classification (e.g., based on AI techniques such as machine learning models and deep learning models) is increasingly utilised in practice. Among hundreds of the models, deep learning based pre-trained language models or LLMs (e.g., BERT, ERNIE, GPT) have drawn lots of attention to a technique called transfer learning in NLP [12]. Compared to traditional machine learning, transfer learning removes the necessity of creating task-specific language models. In this context, the knowledge acquired during the training of a model for a specific task or domain can be reused to address downstream tasks or domains [9], better assisting in content classification. In this study, the content shared on health social platforms can be categorised into two distinct groups: reliable content, denoted by the label "1" and unreliable content, denoted by "0". This essentially frames the issue as a text classification challenge. Leveraging an LLM, we can minimise the data collection effort from health social platforms to a manageable scale, followed by the labeling of this data. Subsequently, this LLM can be fine-tuned and tailored to suit our specific task. Accordingly, we select transfer learning technique in the present study to ascertain the reliability of content by performing a content classification task.

2.3 Transfer Learning

Transfer learning refers to a model's ability to leverage knowledge gained from one domain or task and proficiently apply it to another [9]. In the realm of NLP, LLMs have demonstrated impressive transfer learning capabilities, particularly in domains or tasks that exhibit similarities [13, 14]. LLMs have been successfully applied in diverse content classification tasks, e.g., topic classification and sentiment analysis [15] and can be improved and fine-tuned based on the following base models as shown in Table 1.

As shown in Table 1, the majority of LLMs leverage a bidirectional language model. Especially, BERT utilises a bidirectional Transformer encoder to combine both left and right context for predicting masked words, thereby enhancing the semantic representation capacity of word vectors and showing significant advantages in natural language understanding [22]. For the Chinese language, BERT series have demonstrated superior performance in various Chinese NLP tasks [23]. In this study, we select textual content posted on Chinese health social platforms as the study sample (since this research is supported and funded to investigate the reliability of health-related content posted on social media in the Chinese context). Accordingly, we use Bert-base-Chinese model improved based on BERT architecture and designed specifically for Chinese language as the foundation to fine-tune a model that assists in assessing the content reliability.

Table 1. A summary of base models related to LLMs in content classification.

Base model	Description	Training objectives			
		Bidirectional	Left-to-right	Right-to-left	Sequence-to-sequence
BERT	undergoes training through the masked language modeling task, where certain tokens within a text sequence are randomly concealed, and subsequently, these masked tokens are independently restored by taking into account the encoding vectors acquired from a bidirectional Transformer [16]	x			
ELMo	depends on the entire input sentence, utilising vectors generated by a deep bidirectional language model trained with a coupled language model objective on extensive text data [17]	x			
ERNIE	incorporates entity representations from the knowledge module into the lower layers of the semantic module and amalgamates contextual information and factual knowledge, enabling it to make predictions for both individual tokens and entities [18]	x			

(*continued*)

Table 1. (*continued*)

Base model	Description	Training objectives			
		Bidirectional	Left-to-right	Right-to-left	Sequence-to-sequence
GPT	predicts a text sequence word by word, from left to right, with each word prediction relying on the preceding predictions [19]		x		
UniLM	undergoes pre-training by engaging in three distinct language modeling tasks: unidirectional, bidirectional, and sequence-to-sequence prediction, and is accomplished by employing a shared Transformer network and deploying specialised self-attention masks to govern the context upon which the prediction relies [20]	x	x	x	x
XLNet	employs a pre-training technique that incorporates a permutation operation, enabling context to encompass tokens from both left and right, and also introduces a dual-stream self-attention mechanism to facilitate position-aware word prediction [21]		x		

3   Research Methods

This section describes the research methods used to develop the Health-BERT. Firstly, we talk about how we gathered textual data from Chinese health social platforms and screened the data for our experiment based on the developed criteria. Secondly, we outline the labeling procedure to assess the reliability of the screened data. Lastly, we present the experimental process and pertinent parameters.

3.1   Data Collection and Screening

In this study, we focus on the textual data shared on DXY Forum[1]. DXY Forum provides health information, discussions about diseases, and sharing of medical knowledge. It is one of Chinese largest professional social platforms in the medical field, with a wide user base of medical professionals, including doctors, medical students, and individuals interested in healthcare. DXY Forum serves as a platform for communication and learning, where individuals can find health-related topics and discussions. This forum generates approximately 1.5 to 2 TB of data every day. Furthermore, here we concentrate on the topic related to cardiovascular disease discussed on the forum for two reasons. First, the cardiovascular disease is one of the most prevalent topics discussed on the forum and in practice, and this forum community has a better chance to provide valuable data used for experiments in this study. Second, we have connections with experts who have professional knowledge in the cardiovascular disease and can help us label the screened data.

By using a web crawler tool, we gathered the original data (n = 1056 posts) from the cardiovascular disease forum community posted in April 2023. Due to the presence of empty posts, advertisements, and other format data (e.g., pictures and videos) in data collection that did not meet the requirements of this study, we developed a set of criteria to filter the data. See Table 2.

Table 2. Data screening criteria developed in this study.

ID	Exclusion criterion
C1	empty posts
C2	repetitive posts
C3	posts for advertising
C4	posts that ordinary users do not have the authority to view
C5	posts that contain pictures or videos
C6	posts that contain the content from other web links, guiding users to visit the links

---

[1] DXY Forum is available using the following link: https://www.dxy.cn/bbs/newweb/pc/home.

Based on the data screening criteria, we further removed 421 posts and then cut the textual content from the rest posts into 1180 independent complete sentences for data labelling. Since BERT can be applied to a small dataset, the filtered data was suitable for our study to explore the feasibility of utilising tranter learning technique in assessing the content reliability.

3.2 Data Labelling

To label the filtered data, we recruited experts with over ten years of experience in treating cardiovascular diseases. Each expert individually labeled the data, and they were required to label reliable content as "1" and unreliable content as "0". Any inconsistencies in labeling results were resolved through discussions to reach a consensus. After the data labeling process, out of 1180 sentences in our dataset, 1035 were labeled as "1" (reliable), accounting for 87.71% of the total, while 145 were labeled as "0" (unreliable), making up 12.29%. In light of this, we had the final dataset to conduct the experiment.

3.3 Experiment

For training the model, the length requirements for input text data need to be standardised, but the lengths of each sentence in the dataset varied. Hence, the input length of these texts needs to be unified. If the input data length is set to be too long, it may waste computational resources, and meaningless data padding can also affect the model's accuracy. If it is set too short, it may result in the discarding of a significant amount of potentially important information. By plotting the lengths of the labeled data as a clustered bar, as shown in Fig. 1, it shows that the majority of the content texts have lengths below 120 characters. Thus, the maximum text input length was set to 120 to preserve as much meaningful information as possible. In this study, the dataset was divided into training, validation, and test sets in a proportion of 80%, 10%, and 10%, respectively.

Our model was implemented with the Pytorch deep learning framework and the whole model was trained using the Adam optimiser [24] with a batch size of 32, a learning rate of 0.0002, and a weight decay ratio of 0.01 in an end-to-end fashion. We trained our model with the CrossEntropyLoss function for 10 epochs, and all experiments were carried out on a machine with a 4.2 GHz quad-core Intel i7 CPU, 16 GB RAM, and an Nvidia RTX 3090 24 GB GPU card.

In this study, we employed widely-used evaluation metrics, including accuracy, precision, recall, and f1-score [25], to assess the performance of the model to identify the content reliability. These four metrics are presented in Table 3.

4 Experiment Results

Our experiment results for the test set based on BERT as a baseline are presented in Table 4. The overall accuracy of content classification exceeded 85%, demonstrating that the model can be utilised to assess the content reliability.

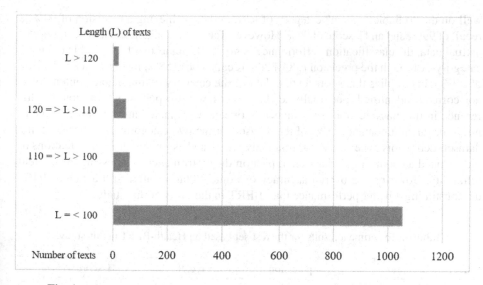

Fig. 1. Distribution of the lengths of the content texts in the dataset in this study.

Table 3. Evaluation metrics used to assess the performance of the model in this study.

Evaluation metric	Description	Formula
accuracy	how much correctly the model or classifier classifies the data	$\frac{TP+TN}{TP+TN+FP+FN}$
precision	how many positive identified classes were correct	$\frac{TP}{TP+FP}$
recall	how many actual positives were identified correctly	$\frac{TP}{TP+FN}$
f1-score	a balanced measure of precision and recall	$\frac{2\times precision\times recall}{precision+recall}$

TP: True Positive (a positive class is correctly predicted by the model or classifier)
TN: True Negative (the model or classifier correctly predicts a negative class)
FP: False Positive (the model or classifier incorrectly predicts a positive class)
FN: False Negative (the model or classifier incorrectly predicts a negative class)

Table 4. Experiment results for the test set based on BERT in this study.

Label	precision	recall	f1-score
0 (unreliable content)	0.73	0.56	0.63
1 (reliable content)	0.89	0.94	0.92
accuracy			0.86

After fine-tuning the model's hyperparameters, the results of the test set were improved. See Table 5. The table shows that in the test set, the model performed quite well on the "reliable content" category of textual data, achieving a precision of 94%, a recall of 99%, and an f1-score of 97%. However, for the "unreliable content" category of textual data, the classification performance is not as strong as that for "reliable content" category. Although the precision is 88%, the recall is only 58%, resulting in an f1-score of 70%. This implies that some textual data in the category of "unreliable content" was not correctly identified, potentially leading to a few false positives. The notable difference in the classification performance between "unreliable" and "reliable" content might be due to unbalanced size of the dataset for the two categories. Furthermore, the dataset used in this experiment was relatively small, and as a result, misclassifications of individual data points might have an impact on the performance of assessing the content reliability. However, the overall accuracy of content classification still achieved 94%, demonstrating a better performance than BERT in the tasks of this study.

Table 5. Experiment results for the test set based on Health-BERT in this study.

Label	precision	recall	f1-score
0 (unreliable content)	0.88	0.58	0.70
1 (reliable content)	0.94	0.99	0.97
accuracy			0.94

5 Discussion

This study took advantages of BERT architecture that embraces transfer learning capabilities in content classification, to assess the reliability of content shared on a Chinese health social platform. By collecting and filtering the data from the social platform, we had 1180 independent complete sentences in the dataset. Thereafter, two experts helped us to label this data for later experiment. The experiment results showed that the fine-tuned Health-BERT embraced better accuracy than the results from BERT in the context of the present study that can help assess the content reliability, addressing the challenge concerned in this study.

5.1 Implications

The present work has both academic and practical contributions. First, on the academic front, we illustrate how the application of LLMs embracing transfer learning capabilities can lead to the creation of an automated approach for assessing content reliability, offering our research methods as a valuable resource for developing tools and systems in this regard.

Second, in practical terms, we fine-tuned a content classification model (Health-BERT) based on BERT architecture that assists individuals in gauging the reliability of content. This model holds the great potential for monitoring and issuing early warnings concerning unreliable content distributed across health social platforms.

5.2 Limitations and Future Work

While this study has made contributions, it still has limitations. First, our dataset for training in the experiment was limited to only one specific topic (i.e., cardiovascular disease), and the collected text data was relatively small in size. Future studies are recommended to collect or utilise a broader range of health-related topics and a larger dataset to evaluate the model's performance. Second, this study only employed one type of LLMs (i.e., BERT) to explore the feasibility of assessing the content reliability. Our future work will involve comparing the experimental results among multiple LLMs. Last, in the present study, we did not develop specific criteria for data labeling and relied solely on the expertise, knowledge, and experience of the recruited experts in the field of cardiovascular diseases to label the collected and screened data. The criteria for data labeling need to be further improved in future research.

6 Conclusion

This study leveraged the advantages of BERT, which harnesses transfer learning capabilities for content classification, and fined-tuned Health-BERT to evaluate the reliability of content shared on a Chinese health social platform. After collecting and filtering data from the social platform, we obtained a dataset for labeling. The experimental results based on the labeled data demonstrated that LLMs can effectively determine the content reliability and our fined-tuned Health-BERT showed a better performance in the tasks than BERT. The implications of the study for both academics and practice are outlined in Sect. 5.1. We also propose future directions to overcome the limitations of the present study by covering a broad range of health-related topics and a larger size of datasets, comparing experiment results between different LLMs, and improving the criteria for data labeling.

Acknowledgement. This research was supported and funded by the Humanities and Social Sciences Youth Foundation, Ministry of Education of the People's Republic of China (Grant No. 21YJC870009). We would like to express our gratitude to Ms. Jiayu Chen for her valuable help in our data collection from the social platform.

References

1. Ukoha, C., Stranieri, A.: On the value of social media in health care. J. Technol. Behav. Sci. **6**, 419–426 (2021)
2. Borges do Nascimento, I.J., et al.: Infodemics and health misinformation: a systematic review of reviews. Bull. World Health Org. **100**(9), 544–561 (2022)
3. Keshavarz, H.: Evaluating credibility of social media information: current challenges, research directions and practical criteria. Inf. Discov. Deliv. **49**(4), 269–279 (2021)
4. Wang, Y., McKee, M., Torbica, A., Stuckler, D.: Systematic literature review on the spread of health-related misinformation on social media. Soc. Sci. Med. **240**, 112552 (2019)
5. Thirunavukarasu, A.J., Ting, D.S.J., Elangovan, K., Gutierrez, L., Tan, T.F., Ting, D.S.W.: Large language models in medicine. Nat. Med. **29**(8), 1930–1940 (2023)

6. Wu, Y., et al.: Autoformalization with large language models. Adv. Neural. Inf. Process. Syst. **35**, 32353–32368 (2022)
7. Min, B., et al.: Recent advances in natural language processing via large pre-trained language models: a survey. ACM Comput. Surv. **56**(2), 1–40 (2023)
8. Iqbal, F., Javed, A.R., Jhaveri, R.H., Almadhor, A., Farooq, U.: Transfer learning-based forensic analysis and classification of e-mail content. ACM Trans. Asian Low-Resourc. Lang. Inf. Process. (2023)
9. Qasim, R., Bangyal, W.H., Alqarni, M.A., Ali Almazroi, A.: A fine-tuned BERT-based transfer learning approach for text classification. J. Healthc. Eng. **2022**, 3498123 (2022)
10. Minaee, S., Kalchbrenner, N., Cambria, E., Nikzad, N., Chenaghlu, M., Gao, J.: Deep learning–based text classification: a comprehensive review. ACM Comput. Surv. **54**(3), 1–40 (2021)
11. Li, Q., et al.: A survey on text classification: from traditional to deep learning. ACM Trans. Intell. Syst. Technol. **13**(2), 1–41 (2022)
12. Taneja, K., Vashishtha, J.: Comparison of transfer learning and traditional machine learning approach for text classification. In: Proceedings of the 9th International Conference on Computing for Sustainable Global Development, pp. 195–200. IEEE, New Delhi, India (2022)
13. Lee, E., Lee, C., Ahn, S.: Comparative study of multiclass text classification in research proposals using pretrained language models. Appl. Sci. **12**(9), 4522 (2022)
14. Al-Twairesh, N.: The evolution of language models applied to emotion analysis of Arabic tweets. Information **12**(2), 84 (2021)
15. Ni, S., Kao, H.-Y.: KPT++: refined knowledgeable prompt tuning for few-shot text classification. Knowl.-Based Syst. **274**, 110647 (2023)
16. Devlin, J., Chang, M.-W., Lee, K., Toutanova, K.: BERT: pre-training of deep bidirectional transformers for language understanding. In: Proceedings of the 2019 Conference of the North American Chapter of the Association for Computational Linguistics: Human Language Technologies, pp. 4171–4186. Association for Computational Linguistics, Minneapolis, Minnesota (2019)
17. Peters, M.E., et al.: Deep contextualized word representations. In: Proceedings of the 2018 Conference of the North American Chapter of the Association for Computational Linguistics: Human Language Technologies, pp. 2227–2237. Association for Computational Linguistics, New Orleans, Louisiana (2018)
18. Zhang, Z., Han, X., Liu, Z., Jiang, X., Sun, M., Liu, Q.: ERNIE: enhanced language representation with informative entities. In: Proceedings of the 57th Annual Meeting of the Association for Computational Linguistics, pp. 1441–1451. Association for Computational Linguistics, Florence, Italy (2019)
19. Radford, A., Narasimhan, K., Salimans, T., Sutskever, I.: Improving language understanding by generative pre-training. https://www.mikecaptain.com/resources/pdf/GPT-1.pdf. Accessed 21 Aug 2023
20. Dong, L., et al.: Unified language model pre-training for natural language understanding and generation. In: Proceedings of the 33rd Conference on Neural Information Processing Systems, vol. 32, pp. 13063–13075. Neural Information Processing Systems Foundation, Inc, Vancouver, Canada (2019)
21. Yang, Z., Dai, Z., Yang, Y., Carbonell, J., Salakhutdinov, R.R., Le, Q.V.: Xlnet: generalized autoregressive pretraining for language understanding. In: Proceedings of the 33rd Conference on Neural Information Processing Systems, vol. 32, pp. 5753–5763. Neural Information Processing Systems Foundation, Inc, Vancouver, Canada (2019)
22. Chang, Y., Kong, L., Jia, K., Meng, Q.: Chinese named entity recognition method based on BERT. In: Proceedings of the 1st IEEE International Conference on Data Science and Computer Application, pp. 294–299. IEEE, Dalian, China (2021)

23. Lyu, P., Rao, G., Zhang, L., Cong, Q.: BiLGAT: bidirectional lattice graph attention network for Chinese short text classification. Appl. Intell. **53**(19), 22405–22414 (2023)
24. Kingma, D.P., Ba, J.: Adam: a method for stochastic optimization. In: Poster of the 3rd International Conference for Learning Representations. ICLR, San Diego, USA (2015)
25. Hassan, S.U., Ahamed, J., Ahmad, K.: Analytics of machine learning-based algorithms for text classification. Sustain. Oper. Comput. **3**, 238–248 (2022)

Wearable and Pervasive Architecture for Digital Companions in Chronic Disease Care

Guillermo Monroy Rodríguez[1], Sonia Mendoza[1],
Luis Martín Sánchez-Adame[2(✉)], Ivan Giovanni Valdespin-Garcia[1],
and Dominique Decouchant[3]

[1] Computer Science Department, CINVESTAV-IPN, Av. Instituto Politécnico Nacional 2508, San Pedro Zacatenco, Gustavo A. Madero, 07360 Mexico City, Mexico
`{guillermo.monroy,sonia.mendoza,ivan.valdespin}@cinvestav.mx`
[2] Design and Building Division, FES-Acatlán, UNAM, Av. Jardines de San Mateo s/n, Sta. Cruz Acatlán, Naucalpan de Juárez, 53150, State of Mexico, Mexico
`lmsanchez@sigchi.org`
[3] Department of Information Technologies, UAM-Cuajimalpa, Av. Vasco de Quiroga 4871, Santa Fe, Delegación Cuajimalpa, 05300 Mexico City, Mexico
`decouchant@cua.uam.mx`

Abstract. Nowadays, advancements in sensor technologies, microcontrollers, and radiofrequency systems have facilitated the development of systems capable of measuring various physical parameters in diverse environments. This progression underscores the necessity for seamless integration of these systems to accomplish diverse objectives. Digital companions, epitomizing this trend, are computer-assisted systems designed to synergize with human users. They are a nexus between rigorous process efficiency, voluminous data management, and human interactions. In response to the imperative for integrating these technological and scientific innovations, a compelling proposition has emerged to develop a digital companion architecture tailored to assist patients with chronic conditions such as diabetes. This proposed architecture comprises various services, including speech recognition and biometric monitoring control. These elements are integral to the system's ability to deliver tailored and effective responses to the user, aiming to enhance the quality of life for individuals suffering from this chronic disease. Preliminary evaluations of a prototype grounded in our architecture demonstrate a positive anticipated user experience.

Keywords: Digital Companions · Software Architectures · Diabetes · User Experience · Pervasive Computing · Wearable Technology

1 Introduction

Chronic diseases represent a significant global public health challenge. The World Health Organization (WHO) reported that conditions such as diabetes,

N. A. Streitz and S. Konomi (Eds.): HCII 2024, LNCS 14719, pp. 68–85, 2024.
https://doi.org/10.1007/978-3-031-60012-8_5

cardiovascular disease, and cancer account for an estimated 70% of all global mortalities [3]. The repercussions of these diseases extend beyond health implications, exerting considerable economic and societal burdens. Given the escalating prevalence of these conditions, there is an imperative need for innovative interventions that empower patients to manage their health effectively and subsequently enhance their quality of life. Digital companions are emerging at the forefront of these interventions-advanced computer-assisted systems adept at adapting to individual users, bridging the gap between rigorous data-driven processes and user-centric interactions [1].

Recent advances in wearable technology and pervasive infrastructure, including sensors, microcontrollers, and radiofrequency systems, underpin the feasibility of intelligent digital companions. These innovations enable comprehensive environmental monitoring and biometric analysis, providing real-time feedback and enhancing daily activities through ubiquitous computing [15]. Digital companions, evolving with cutting-edge natural language processing and machine learning techniques, offer personalized and adaptable interactions, moving beyond traditional constrained input modalities. This integration aims to improve decision-making, embodying the zenith of user-friendly, intelligent technology [9].

A meticulous examination of pertinent literature, including works by Anastasiadou et al. [5], Ahmed et al. [4], Sonntag [19], Rincón et al. [18], and Ghandeharioun et al. [11], reveals a predominant trend: many existing systems exhibit a reactive nature, often lacking predictive capabilities. This limitation curtails their potential to deliver tailored recommendations proactively. Furthermore, a significant proportion of these systems do not harness the capabilities of wearable devices, which could offer invaluable contextual insights to enhance user interactions. Hence, there is a significant opportunity to design an architecture that synergistically combines various Internet of Things (IoT) devices and wearables. This integration aims to enhance the capabilities of digital companions, particularly for individuals with chronic conditions like diabetes. Such an approach is promising for improving self-management and overall well-being, tailoring technological solutions to the specific needs of these patients.

Our proposal delineates a comprehensive architectural blueprint for digital companions, encapsulating the features mentioned earlier and ensuring adaptive, personalized user interactions. By seamlessly integrating ubiquitous infrastructure with wearable technology, the proposed architecture is poised to ameliorate the management of people with diabetes. Patients stand to benefit from real-time insights into their biometric health metrics, empowering them to make informed health decisions. The architecture comprises eight web services following the microservices paradigm, prioritizing fault tolerance and modular extensibility. Fundamental software design principles, such as high cohesion and low coupling, are meticulously incorporated and complemented by established design patterns, ensuring adaptability to future technological shifts. Additionally, the strategic integration of sensors, capable of monitoring a spectrum of biological parameters, infuses digital companions with a wealth of user-centric data. This data-driven approach continually enables digital companions to adapt to individual user profiles, fostering enhanced self-care and health management.

This paper is organized as follows. After presenting related work in Sect. 2, we explain in Sect. 3 the proposed architecture for digital companions and their components. Next, we present a running example for medical follow-ups in Sect. 4. Then, in Sect. 5, we describe and discuss the results of anticipated user experience tests conducted with individuals suffering from diabetes, who performed a set of tasks derived from our architecture. Finally, in Sect. 6, we provide a conclusion of the achieved work and some ideas for future research.

2   Related Work

In recent years, there has been a surge in the development of digital companions that aim to provide assistance in various aspects of daily life, including healthcare. This section discusses some of the existing digital companions that have been proposed and their limitations.

2.1   Digital Companions

The Educational Virtual Assistant (EVA) system [5] is a conversational digital companion designed to educate patients on proper chronic disease management. EVA uses machine learning algorithms to understand natural language and provide personalized recommendations to patients. However, EVA is reactive, cannot predict a patient's deterioration or behavior, and does not incorporate wearable devices.

Ahmed et al. [4] propose a conversational digital companion that utilizes a cognitive test to diagnose dementia in elderly patients. The system cannot predict a patient's deterioration or infer the patient's mental health status without explicitly soliciting information from the patient. The absence of wearable devices also limits the system's potential to become proactive.

Kognit [19] utilizes smart glasses and wearables to assist patients with cognitive impairment in reinforcing or recovering their memory during daily activities. The system is proactively centered around the patient, although there are no reports on the extent to which the proposed objectives have been achieved.

The Conversational Virtual Agent [2] resides within a smartphone application and is designed to assist patients with intractable cardiac fibrillation and a high risk of stroke. The system focuses on integrating GSR sensors to detect heart rhythm, although its interaction is not continuous. However, the system is neither proactive nor predictive.

EmmIR [18] is a social robot that provides cognitive support to the elderly for their activities of daily living. The system is equipped to display emotions to generate an empathetic response, but it lacks predictive capabilities and is not user-centered.

EMMA [11] is a virtual personal assistant that runs on a smartphone and uses psychological assessments to track the user's energy, positivity, and well-being. It determines whether intervention is required due to the user's risk of depression. EMMA is designed for all patients, particularly for those susceptible to depression. Nevertheless, the absence of wearables limits the acquisition of additional data to contextualize the user's situation.

Although these digital companions have shown potential, they have limitations. Most systems are reactive and do not incorporate predictive techniques, limiting their ability to become proactive and provide more personalized recommendations. Additionally, most systems do not use wearable devices, which could provide valuable contextual information to enhance the user experience. Therefore, there is room for improvement and innovation in developing digital companions for healthcare applications.

2.2 Reviews and Architectures

In their review, Ganesan et al. [10] explore the application of ambient assistive living (AAL) technology for elderly individuals with physical and cognitive impairments, emphasizing its potential to enhance daily living and social participation. The paper categorizes AAL technologies into tools for physical impairments, where technologies like force-resistive sensors are used to monitor activities like eating and sleeping positions, and wearable sensors on wrists and necklaces to track daily activities. For cognitive impairments, wearable and non-wearable sensors monitor daily life activities. PIR sensors are used for depressive patients, demonstrating how AAL technologies can support elderly populations through digital pillboxes and GPS reminders. The review also covers smart home technologies that implement various sensors for monitoring and assisting with both physical and cognitive impairments, contributing to the well-being and independence of the elderly. Additionally, the paper acknowledges the need for more extensive research on AAL technologies aimed at social participation and reducing caregiver burden.

Patro et al. [16] present an ambient assisted living predictive model for cardiovascular disease using supervised learning. The research highlights the significant role of IoT in healthcare, focusing on real-time patient monitoring and data analysis. To predict cardiovascular disease, the proposed system architecture integrates machine learning techniques, including multiple linear regression, LASSO regression, ridge regression, and decision tree classifiers. The study emphasizes the importance of data preprocessing, feature extraction, and machine learning training in developing an effective predictive model. The model's performance is evaluated based on precision, accuracy, and sensitivity, demonstrating the potential of IoT and machine learning in enhancing healthcare services and predictive diagnostics.

Qureshi et al. [17] conduct a detailed literature review on deep learning-based ambient assisted living for self-management of cardiovascular conditions. It explores the integration of wearable technologies, ambient assisted living, clinician management systems, and deep learning methods for cardiovascular diagnosis. The study emphasizes the role of these technologies in early disease detection, improved patient self-management, and enhanced clinician intervention. It also discusses the benefits of leveraging deep learning for analyzing complex biomedical data, highlighting its significance in improving healthcare services and predictive diagnostics for cardiovascular diseases.

While the studies by Ganesan et al. [10], Patro et al. [16], and Qureshi et al. [17] provide valuable insights into ambient assisted living and Artificial Intelligence (AI) techniques for cardiovascular diseases and elderly care, our work distinctly focuses on diabetes care across all age groups. Our architecture leverages existing AI tools to create personalized digital companions, integrating commonly used systems for tailored solutions. Unlike the specific applications for elderly care or cardiovascular diseases, our approach prioritizes adaptable and user-centric solutions, avoiding unnecessary complexities and aligning more closely with the diverse needs of diabetic individuals. This distinction underscores the originality and relevance of our proposal in the evolving landscape of digital health solutions.

3   Architecture for Digital Companions

This section outlines the architecture of our digital companions designed for healthcare applications. This includes a detailed description of both functional and non-functional requirements and the architectural components.

3.1   Functional Requirements

We have identified three recurring problems that patients have due to their health conditions:

1. **Appointment management**: It is challenging to manage appointments for clinical analysis and medical check-ups, either by the patient, the patient's family, or the person who supports them.
2. **Medical monitoring**: Usually, the patient does not record their actions, much less their relationship with any associated biomedical parameter.
3. **Adherence to medication intake**: It is difficult for patients to follow up on their medication intake, especially when there are more than three and at different times.

Actors: This proposal introduces four key actors: 1) the patient, 2) the patient assistant, 3) the physician, and 4) the digital companion. Each actor plays a distinct role, which a person or a system may fulfill.

The *patient* actor serves as the primary user of the digital companion and can request information through a range of interfaces, including voice commands, mobile apps, smart speakers, and other subsystems like smart bands.

The *patient assistant* actor, who may be a family member or a home health care professional, can access the same information if the patient cannot do so.

The *physician* actor can take many forms, including the treating physician, physician's assistant, or an automated system within a clinic or doctor's office. This actor can receive alerts and reports generated by the digital companion and interact with it through a mobile app or data exchange format to integrate with their hospital's systems. The physician may also ask the digital companion to pose questions to the patient, record their answers, and forward the information for further evaluation.

The *digital companion* actor serves as an intelligent entity capable of processing information from various channels and communicating with the other actors through both text and voice. This system enables seamless communication and information exchange between patients, their assistants, and physicians.

Use Cases: The proposed digital companion has various use cases, which include medical appointment management, medical follow-up, and support for medication adherence (see Fig. 1).

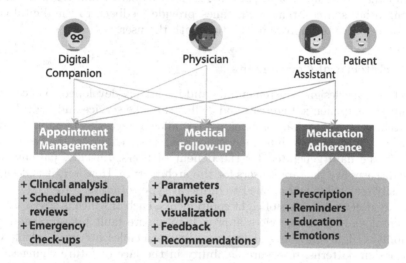

Fig. 1. Actors and use cases of the digital companion

The *medical appointment management* use case consists of managing clinical analysis, scheduled medical reviews, and emergency check-ups.

In the *medical follow-up* use case, the digital companion will send parameters to the physician for analysis and visualization, and the physician's feedback or suggestions will be provided directly by the physician or through the digital companion. It will also make recommendations in educational mode for patient support in medication adherence.

The *support for medication adherence* use case includes prescription input using a proposed format for information exchange, scheduling reminders for medication intake, informing patients about the correct way of intake or administration of medication, providing educational recommendations on the effects of medication or contraindications, and recording emotional feedback from the patient to report to the physician for analysis using machine learning to identify potential issues.

3.2   Non-functional Requirements

The design of the digital companion takes into account the following transversal characteristics:

1. **Adaptability**: The system must have a learning process available at all times to ensure that its behavior adapts precisely to the patient. Knowledge may eventually be discovered using data collected from the user's interactions with the digital companion.
2. **Embodiment**: The digital companion must have a personalization of character that resembles human behavior. This will help patients to feel a certain empathetic emotion and encourage adherence to the use of the digital companion to improve health habits and maintain monitoring of measurable parameters from wearables, embedded video cameras, and audio listening, among other sources, that at all times provide feedback to the digital companion in order to improve interaction with the user.

3.3   Architectural Components

The architecture design is incrementally and iteratively developed to encompass all required components. Figures 2 and 3 illustrate the service and logical views of the architecture of digital companions that allow integration of online services and devices, in addition to interconnecting ubiquitous computing infrastructure to exploit the data generated for the benefit of users. Initially, patients with chronic diseases are the target users for the architecture. However, it is designed to be easily extensible and applied to different types of users.

The architecture consists of eight components, each of which is a web service, and it employs the microservices approach to ensure fault tolerance and easy extensibility. High cohesion and low coupling principles are used, along with proven design patterns, to ensure flexibility in the face of future changes. The services that make up the architecture are:

1. **Speech Recognition**: It receives audio signals and identifies key phrases or commands from the sentences emitted to perform user-requested actions. Its duties include recognizing patient commands and translating and managing them as messages to be sent to the Broker Messaging service, which routes them to the appropriate service to orchestrate the system.
2. **Semantic Web Search**: It can receive queries and provide answers from the Knowledge Base designed for the digital companion. If the Knowledge Base cannot provide an answer, a search will be conducted online to obtain relevant information to update the Knowledge Base. The service is also responsible for inserting discovered patterns from the Behavioral Intelligence Service into the Knowledge Base and for inserting knowledge obtained from web searches.
3. **Biometric Monitoring**: It incorporates middleware to integrate various devices in the patient's environment. The service collects and structures biometric and behavioral patterns for further analysis by the Behavioral Intelligence Service, which generates knowledge for future use. The Biometric

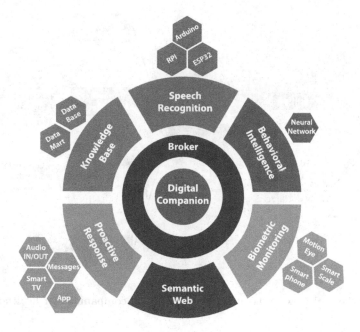

Fig. 2. Service view of the architecture of digital companions for healthcare

Monitoring service includes a smart band, a domotic system, a computer vision system, and a smart scale.

4. **Digital Companion Core**: It is responsible for gathering and coordinating data, information, and knowledge to create a feedback model to adapt the digital companion to the patient. Additionally, it establishes communication with appointment management systems, consolidates medical follow-up, and employs business logic to establish strategies for adherence to the patient's medication according to their profile.

5. **Behavioral Intelligence**: It analyzes data collected by the Biometric Monitoring and Digital Companion Core services using machine learning methods. It can accelerate the training of machine learning models, particularly Clustering and Classification models, using Edge AI devices. The service transmits the analysis results to the Semantic Web and Digital Companion Core services via the Broker Messaging service.

6. **Proactive Response**: It interacts with the patient to respond to requests and suggestions or provide information proactively to support the patient in improving their behavioral habits and health status.

7. **Broker Messaging**: It routes events through request queues that facilitate exchange between the various micro-services. The Broker Messaging service uses the Broker architectural pattern [6], which decouples software in a distributed manner, allowing system components to interact through remote calls or requests. This pattern includes a Broker component responsible for coordinating communication, dispatching other components,

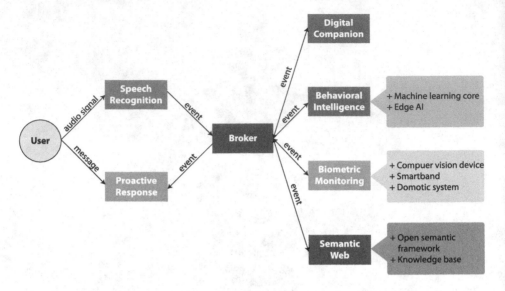

Fig. 3. Logical view of the architecture of digital companions for healthcare

redirecting requests, and transmitting the results of such requests or generated exceptions. In this way, this service manages the messages coming from
all the components, incorporating decoupling and asynchronous responses in
the architecture.

8. **Knowledge Base**: The architecture's knowledge base is structured to encompass the attributes of various entities, their interrelationships, and the mechanisms governing their transformation from one state to another. This repository is instrumental in enabling the digital companion to offer educational
recommendations tailored to the patient's needs. The knowledge base is
designed to succinctly encapsulate essential information, including tracking
ID, biometric and emotional states, the patient's specific situation or problem,
corresponding solutions or recommendations, and subsequent feedback for
enhancement of the knowledge base. The process of knowledge management
is vital in the collection, preservation, and accessibility of information generated within the patient's environment. Furthermore, validating the knowledge
base is critical in ensuring its reliability and utility. This validation is achieved
by employing the digital companion to transmit question-answer pairs to
medical experts for review. The knowledge base is continuously refined and
updated through this process, coupled with the application of machine learning classification methods. Such rigorous knowledge management ensures the
repository's accuracy and relevance, thus maintaining its value in healthcare.

4 Running Example: Medical Follow-Up

To show the viability of our proposed architecture of digital companions for healthcare, in this section, we detail a use case for medical follow-up, which consists of the following actions: 1) transmission of parameters to the physician; 2) analysis and visualization of the parameters obtained; 3) the physician's feedback or suggestions will be provided directly by themselves or through the digital companion; and 4) recommendations by the digital companion (educational mode). These actions involve several services of the architecture, so we focus on detailing the responsibilities of the associated services:

The *Biometric Monitoring* service has to obtain biological parameters from a smartphone, a smart band, a smart scale, and sensors linked to a microcontroller. This data is sent to the *Digital Companion Core* service to be persisted and associated with the patient profile. This service is also responsible for keeping the patient profile and filling out the extended clinical record, which must contain the minimum information required by NOM-024-SSA3-2012 and NOM-004-SSA3-2012 (Mexican Standards on Electronic Health Record Information Systems and Health Information Exchange) as well as the NOM-008-SSA3-2017 Standard, which deals with the comprehensive treatment of overweight and obesity.

The patient record will also have the treating physician, who will be able to respond to the notifications made by the digital companion and then communicate them to the patient and store them in their record. The records in the file will be analyzed by scheduled *Digital Companion Core* service tasks to generate information and knowledge that will be sent (anonymized) to the *Semantic Web Search* service to be persisted in the *Knowledge Base*. At the express request of the patient, the digital companion is also able to search first in the record, then in the *Knowledge Base* (managed by the *Semantic Web Search* service) if it has information on the matter or will refer the corresponding doubt of the patient to the treating physician. Similarly, the clinical analysis results will be stored in the file, preferably parsed to obtain the result information generally in PDF format or, if necessary, to access the laboratories' API to make a link that allows retrieving the results in the layout of the corresponding company. The latter requires programming the information exchange formats for each institution or company.

The *Behavioral Intelligence* service will also receive from the *Digital Companion Core* service information packages, not the entire clinical record, so that information exploration tasks can be executed or store the information in a Data Mart to be processed and obtain knowledge or concrete information that will allow the treating physician or a scientific research group to make decisions. This service will also feed the *Knowledge Base* (managed by *Semantic Web Search* service) that will have, among other information, the knowledge related to specific topics concerning the patient's health based on the analysis of their record. The information in this service is not specific to the patient record but is the product of knowledge discovery.

The communication between these services of the digital companion will always be done through the *Broker Messaging* service thanks to a messaging system and queuing of requests. This guarantees aspects such as fault tolerance in communication and asynchronous attention, among others.

5   Anticipated User Experience Analysis

In this section, we describe and discuss the results of anticipated user experience tests conducted with individuals suffering from diabetes, who performed a set of tasks derived from our architecture.

5.1   Tests

The Wizard of Oz (WoZ) technique, named after the eponymous novel, is a seminal method in interactive system design, particularly useful in the early stages of development. It involves a human operator clandestinely controlling a system while users interact with it as if it were fully autonomous [8]. This technique is invaluable for scenarios like ours, where understanding user interaction in real-world contexts is crucial. It facilitates data collection for AI training, allows observation of how users articulate requests and their expectations for responses, and helps identify potential interaction scenarios for future development [7].

The tests were conducted in a controlled environment where participants interacted with the "digital companion", believing it was fully autonomous. We asked users to speak into a microphone, receiving the companion's responses through speakers. Unbeknownst to the participants, these responses were crafted by a human using a text-to-speech generator. This setup enabled us to observe and record authentic user interactions, reactions, and feedback in real time.

The tasks derived from the proposed use cases were evaluated by a cohort of 20 individuals with diabetes. This group of participants comprised the authors' colleagues, friends, and relatives, representing an opportunity sample. The demographic distribution included 11 women and nine men, aged 38 to 81 years, with an average age of 55.15 years.

Before initiating the testing sessions, we gave participants an overview of the digital companion's intended purpose and the general idea behind its assistance for diabetic patients. We outlined the three tasks they were expected to perform: scheduling medical appointments, entering health data, and seeking dietary advice. However, to ensure authenticity in their interactions and gain genuine insights, we deliberately refrained from offering detailed instructions on accomplishing these tasks. This approach was adopted to observe the natural manner in which users would interact with the system, including how they formulated their requests and queries. It allowed us to capture a range of spontaneous user behaviors and verbal expressions, which are critical in shaping a user-centric and intuitive digital companion.

During the tests, participants were tasked with activities designed to mirror typical use cases for diabetic patients, not to assess the system's functionality but to gain insights for developing the actual digital companion in the future. For instance, in booking a doctor's appointment, we observed the participants' language patterns and how they specified appointment details like type, date, and time. This helped us understand the necessity for the system to request any missing information and to interpret vague phrases like "in the morning" or "in the afternoon".

In tasks involving health data entry, such as blood glucose and blood pressure readings, we focused on how participants communicated these measurements. The tendency to omit explicit units highlighted the importance of context-awareness in the system design.

Finally, when seeking dietary advice, we paid close attention to the type of language and detail the users preferred. They were usually straightforward and expected the same tone from the digital companion.

Following the interaction sessions, participants were asked to complete the AttrakDiff questionnaire. This gave us quantitative data on their perception of aesthetics, functionality, and overall user experience. Combining qualitative insights from the WoZ technique and quantitative data from the AttrakDiff questionnaire offered a comprehensive understanding of the interactions' strengths and areas for improvement.

We employed the AttrakDiff tool, a widely recognized questionnaire in user experience and usability research, especially in designing user interfaces and digital products. The AttrakDiff questionnaire comprises 28 word pairs, with responses measured on a Likert scale ranging from 1 to 7. This scale assesses the user's perception of the system's aesthetics, identity, originality, and practical utility. The questionnaire aims to gauge the user's initial attraction to the product and their satisfaction after use. Within this framework, 'attraction' is defined as a user's overall positive impression of the product, while 'satisfaction' pertains to how effectively the product meets the user's expectations [12].

5.2   Results

Figure 4 presents an overview of the evaluation using a "portfolio" plot. The vertical axis quantifies Hedonic Quality (HQ), whereas the horizontal axis measures Pragmatic Quality (PQ). Based on the interplay of these dimensions, the product's positioning spans various categories such as too self-oriented, self-oriented, desired, neutral, task-oriented, superfluous, or too task-oriented, as delineated in Hassenzahl's framework [13].

Two distinct shapes are identifiable in the plot. The product is represented by a blue square centrally located within a translucent blue rectangle, known as the 'confidence rectangle.' This rectangle illustrates the consensus in user evaluations of the product. A larger confidence rectangle indicates a broader range of user opinions about the product's categorization, whereas a smaller rectangle suggests a higher agreement among users. This plot feature enables an assessment of the variability in user perceptions of the product [13].

Notably, the confidence rectangle, in this instance, exhibits little dispersion, indicating a high degree of uniformity in user ratings. The product's placement at the intersection of the desired and task-oriented categories underscores its balanced orientation toward user satisfaction and task efficiency. Such positioning, far from being detrimental, conveys a positive user experience with a slight emphasis on task-specific utility.

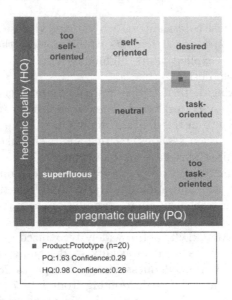

Fig. 4. Portfolio

Figure 5 displays the mean values for the AttrakDiff evaluation, which bifurcates Hedonic Quality into two facets: stimulation and identity. Consequently, AttrakDiff encompasses four dimensions: 1) *Pragmatic Quality (PQ)*, assessing the product's usability and effectiveness; 2) *Hedonic Quality-Identity (HQ-I)*, evaluating how the product resonates with the user's identity; 3) *Hedonic Quality-Stimulation (HQ-S)*, gauging the product's capacity to provide pleasure or satisfaction; and 4) *Attractiveness (ATT)*, reflecting the overall quality perception of the product [13].

Both Figs. 5 and 6 utilize a scale ranging from −3 to 3. Here, negative values suggest user aversion or displeasure towards the product, zero indicates neutrality and positive values imply attractiveness. The plot reveals that all dimensions score positively, affirming the product's acceptable quality. A detailed analysis shows PQ scoring at its highest, indicating superior usability and effectiveness. HQ-I achieves satisfactory levels, signifying reasonable user identification with the product. However, HQ-S scores the lowest among the dimensions, suggesting moderate satisfaction. The ATT dimension, denoting overall quality perception, achieves the highest score, indicating favorable overall product quality.

Figure 6 elucidates the mean values of semantic differentials. Extreme values in this context indicate aspects of the product that are either critically

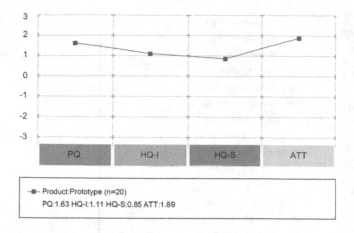

Fig. 5. Average values of participants

acclaimed or need improvement. Notably, the semantic differentials *isolating* and *undemanding* exhibit unfavorable values, ranging between 0 and −2, suggesting perceptions of the product as somewhat isolating and lacking complexity. While this may be perceived negatively, it also underscores the product's ease of use.

Conversely, positive values between 0 and 1 are observed in semantic differentials such as human, predictable, premium, bold, novel, and inviting. Most differentials, including straightforward, structured, manageable, stylish, and others, fall between 1 and 2, indicating a favorable user perception. The highest acclaim, with values between 2 and 3, is seen in simple, practical, professional, pleasant, likable, and motivating attributes.

Overall, the predominance of positive semantic differentials attests to the product's considerable acceptance. However, for optimal user satisfaction, the focus should initially be on improving aspects with negative ratings, followed by enhancing those rated between 0 and 1.

5.3   Discussion

Our application of the WoZ technique in the testing phase offered significant insights into user interactions and expectations, which are pivotal for developing our digital companion for diabetic patients. The nuances observed in how participants articulated their requests, and the type of information they omitted during tasks underscored the need for a context-aware system capable of handling incomplete data and interpreting natural language. For instance, the frequent omission of explicit units in health data entry tasks highlights the system's requirement to infer such details accurately. This exercise was invaluable in designing a system that comprehends and anticipates user needs.

Another critical observation was the users' preference for retrieving health data. Questions regarding the length of the audio response and handling multiple readings throughout the day were central to understanding user preferences for

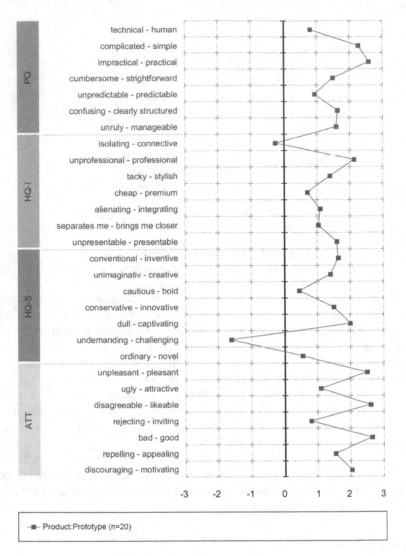

Fig. 6. Pairs of semantic differentials

data retrieval and interaction. This aspect is crucial in ensuring that the digital companion provides information in a manner that is both accessible and user-friendly. Our findings suggest that users prefer concise and direct responses, indicating a need for a system to deliver information efficiently without overwhelming the user.

The dietary advice task revealed that users generally found complex medical jargon confusing and preferred simpler, more straightforward advice. This indicates a significant opportunity for the digital companion to bridge the gap between medical information and user comprehension. The system can enhance user understanding and adherence to medical guidelines by delivering advice in layman's terms.

Additionally, this testing phase served as an exercise in Anticipated User Experience [14]. It allowed us to gauge user expectations and preconceptions about digital health assistants, shaped by their experiences with mainstream assistants like Alexa and Siri. This understanding is crucial in aligning our system with user expectations, especially considering the specialized nature of health-related assistance compared to general-purpose digital assistants.

A notable observation during the tests was the delay between user requests and the system's responses. Despite the human operator's ability to understand user requests better than any current AI system, the response time was noticeably slower than what would be expected from a fully automated system. This discrepancy highlights the importance of response speed in user satisfaction and the overall effectiveness of a digital companion. As we progress towards developing an autonomous system, optimizing response time will be a crucial area of focus to match, or even surpass, user expectations set by their experiences with existing digital assistants. The insights gained from our WoZ tests are instrumental in shaping the development of a digital companion that is not only technically proficient but also aligns closely with user preferences and expectations. These findings will guide us in creating a system that is user-centric, intuitive, and effective in aiding diabetic patients in their daily healthcare management.

6   Conclusions and Future Work

Digital companions have been developed to tackle the challenge of intelligent user interaction, simulating the ability to adapt to user requests or expressions. In order to understand the user and provide the impression of intelligence, it has been necessary to limit the universe of possibilities to avoid misinterpreting user commands. While conversational systems have proven helpful in achieving self-care goals, most digital companions rely on inputs restricted to multiple-choice formats. However, recent advancements in natural language processing have enabled digital companions to better identify ideas or commands expressed by users. By incorporating machine learning techniques into natural language processing, models have been trained to compress sentences and exhibit behavior closer to that of humans. As digital companions become more similar to humans, user confidence increases as they feel understood [9]. A major objective of digital companions is to assist users in decision-making, which is why they increasingly employ avatars or personalities that display emotions or communicate with users non-verbally in visual ways.

From the state of the art, it is clear that a great opportunity exists to propose an architecture that connects various devices to enhance the capabilities of digital companions, as the majority do not utilize Internet of Things devices and wearables. Furthermore, the incorporation of Ubiquitous Computing principles in terms of proactivity and availability at all times and in all places is a potential area for improvement. Partial integration of digital companions with smart displays, smartphones, smart bands, audio equipment, and other devices can leverage the devices currently available on the market. Lightweight processing could also be implemented on some devices to simplify computation on a server or in the cloud, taking care of security issues properly.

Additionally, the use of sensors to monitor biological parameters such as oximeters, glucometers, manometers, galvanic response sensors, cameras, and others is an aspect that can be capitalized upon in the proposed architecture. Such sensors provide digital companions with valuable information about users' health and activities, enabling them to learn and adapt to individual patients and facilitate their self-care.

As a future work, our intention is to achieve an agnostic integration of a speech recognizer. In addition, this component will be changed easily thanks to the use of design patters such as strategy or dependency injection.

References

1. AI: My name is Companion - Digital Companion. https://new.siemens.com/global/en/company/stories/research-technologies/artificial-intelligence/artificial-intelligence-digital-companion.html
2. Bickmore, T.W., et al.: Managing chronic conditions with a smartphone-based conversational virtual agent. In: Proceedings of the 18th International Conference on Intelligent Virtual Agents, pp. 119–124 (2018). https://dl.acm.org/doi/abs/10.1145/3267851.3267908
3. Non communicable diseases (2022). https://www.who.int/news-room/fact-sheets/detail/noncommunicable-diseases
4. Ahmed, S., Qaosar, M., Rizka, W., Sholikah, Y.,: Morimoto: early dementia detection through conversations to virtual personal assistant (2018)
5. Anastasiadou, M., Alexiadis, A., Polychronidou, E., Votis, K., Tzovaras, D.: A prototype educational virtual assistant for diabetes management. In: 2020 IEEE 20th International Conference on Bioinformatics and Bioengineering (BIBE), pp. 999–1004. IEEE (2020)
6. Buschmann, F., Meunier, R., Rohnert, H., Sommerlad, P., Stal, M.: Pattern-Oriented Software Architecture - Volume 1: A System of Patterns, Wiley Publishing (1996)
7. Choi, D.S., Park, J., Loeser, M., Seo, K.: Improving counseling effectiveness with virtual counselors through nonverbal compassion involving eye contact, facial mimicry, and head-nodding. Sci. Rep. 14(1), 506 (2024). https://doi.org/10.1038/s41598-023-51115-y
8. Dahlbäck, N., Jönsson, A., Ahrenberg, L.: Wizard of Oz studies: why and how. In: Proceedings of the 1st International Conference on Intelligent User Interfaces, pp. 193-200. IUI '93, Association for Computing Machinery, Orlando, Florida, USA (1993). https://doi.org/10.1145/169891.169968
9. Darcy, A., Daniels, J., Salinger, D., Wicks, P., Robinson, A., et al.: Evidence of human-level bonds established with a digital conversational agent: cross-sectional, retrospective observational study. JMIR Formative Res. 5(5), e27868 (2021)
10. Ganesan, B., Gowda, T., Al-Jumaily, A., Fong, K., Meena, S., Tong, R.K.Y.: Ambient assisted living technologies for older adults with cognitive and physical impairments: a review. Eur. Rev. Med. Pharmacol. Sci. 23, 10470–10481 (2019).https://doi.org/10.26355/eurrev_201912_19686

11. Ghandeharioun, A., McDuff, D., Czerwinski, M., Rowan, K.: EMMA: An emotionally intelligent personal assistant for improving wellbeing (2018). arXiv preprint arXiv:1812.11423

12. Hassenzahl, M.: The effect of perceived hedonic quality on product appealingness. Int. J. Hum. Comput. Interact. **13**(4), 481–499 (2001). https://doi.org/10.1207/S15327590IJHC1304_07

13. Hassenzahl, M., Burmester, M., Koller, F.: AttrakDiff: Ein Fragebogen zur Messung wahrgenommener hedonischer und pragmatischer Qualität, pp. 187–196. Vieweg+Teubner Verlag, Wiesbaden (2003). https://doi.org/10.1007/978-3-322-80058-9_19

14. Law, E.L.C., Roto, V., Hassenzahl, M., Vermeeren, A.P., Kort, J.: Understanding, scoping and defining user experience: a survey approach. In: Proceedings of the SIGCHI Conference on Human Factors in Computing Systems, pp. 719-728. CHI '09, Assoc. Comput. Mach., Boston, MA, USA (2009). https://doi.org/10.1145/1518701.1518813

15. Liao, Y., Thompson, C., Peterson, S., Mandrola, J., Beg, M.S.: The future of wearable technologies and remote monitoring in health care. Am. Soc. Clin. Oncol. Educ. Book **39**, 115–121 (2019). https://doi.org/10.1200/EDBK_238919

16. Patro, S., Padhy, D.N., Chiranjevi, D.: Ambient assisted living predictive model for cardiovascular disease prediction using supervised learning. Evol. Intell. **14**, 1–29 (2021). https://doi.org/10.1007/s12065-020-00484-8

17. Qureshi, M., Qureshi, K., Jeon, G., Piccialli, F.: Deep learning-based ambient assisted living for self-management of cardiovascular conditions. Neural Comput. Appl. **34**, 10449–10467 (2022). https://doi.org/10.1007/s00521-020-05678-w

18. Rincon, J.A., Costa, A., Novais, P., Julian, V., Carrascosa, C.: A new emotional robot assistant that facilitates human interaction and persuasion. Knowl. Inf. Syst. **60**(1), 363–383 (2019)

19. Sonntag, D.: Kognit: intelligent cognitive enhancement technology by cognitive models and mixed reality for dementia patients, p. 6

Framework of Occupant-Centric Measuring System for Personalized Micro-environment via Online Modeling

Mohammad Saleh Nikoopayan Tak[1] and Yanxiao Feng[2]([✉])

[1] Hillier College of Architecture and Design, New Jersey Institute of Technology, Newark 07102, USA
[2] School of Applied Engineering and Technology, New Jersey Institute of Technology, Newark 07102, USA
yf43@njit.edu

Abstract. Indoor environmental comfort has become increasingly important, necessitating occupant-centric systems that provide personalized comfort. This trend is particularly notable in light of the increasing frequency of extreme weather events associated with global climate change. This paper proposes a novel framework integrating real-time occupant feedback, multi-sensor data fusion, online modeling, and intelligent sensor technologies to dynamically tailor indoor micro-environments. The framework collects diverse data on built environment and personal health using environmental sensors and wearable devices. It employs online machine learning algorithms to analyze the database and automatically adjust environmental conditions in real-time to match occupants' preferences. In implementing this framework, advanced encryption are utilized to enable swift, localized data processing while preserving privacy. Multi-sensor fusion techniques are leveraged to integrate heterogeneous sensor data into an accurate assessment of occupant comfort. The user interface facilitates occupant feedback to continuously refine the system's reinforcement learning model. By personalizing comfort in a responsive, privacy-aware manner, this framework is expected to enhance occupant well-being and satisfaction, potentially enabling significant energy savings by avoiding overcooling and overheating. The framework represents an innovative application of smart and computing technologies, including deep learning and data fusion, to advance beyond static environmental setpoints. In anticipation of testing, it shows promise in revolutionizing occupant-centric comfort, fostering the creation of more adaptive and resilient indoor spaces.

Keywords: Real-time modeling · Multi-sensor fusion · Adaptive adjustment

1 Introduction

The study of enhanced indoor environmental comfort has become increasingly critical in recent years, reflecting a broader recognition of its impact on human well-being and productivity, as well as its significance in building resilience amidst global climate change. This shift towards occupant-centric control systems emphasizes a personalized approach to comfort, necessitating a departure from traditional methods that rely on static setpoints and overlook the individual's dynamic experience of comfort.

The advent of smart sensing technologies and wearable devices represents a significant advancement, providing an abundance of personalized indoor comfort profiles that encompass both the built environment and personal health indicators. However, the industry faces persistent challenges in effectively harnessing this data to provide coherent, real-time insights that cater to the occupants' unique preferences. Critical issues include maintaining data consistency, protecting data privacy, and developing advanced data fusion techniques capable of adapting in real-time to individual needs.

Recognizing the strategic importance of responsive and sustainable living spaces, this research aims to address these challenges by proposing a novel framework that integrates smart sensing technologies, real-time occupant feedback, and cutting-edge machine learning algorithms. By employing intelligent sensing technologies and online modeling, the framework seeks to dynamically customizes indoor micro-environments to elevate comfort and well-being. This approach not only enhances the immediate experience of occupants but also cultivate a synergistic relationship between individuals and their living spaces, with a special emphasis on supporting vulnerable populations particularly affected by environmental stressors.

The proposed solution presents a paradigm shift in indoor environmental monitoring, positioning itself as a significant contribution to the field. It aims to bridge the gap between data availability and actionable comfort optimization, ultimately enhancing the synergy between humans and their built environments through advanced technology and innovative modeling techniques. The following sections will articulate the development of this responsive system, elucidating how it addresses existing gaps and establishes a new standard for indoor environmental control.

2 Related Work

The concept of adaptive thermal comfort has gained significant interest over the years as researchers recognize the limitations of conventional static comfort models based on heat balance theory (Yao et al., 2009). Static models, relying on fixed temperature setpoints, fail to account for temporal and individual variations in thermal perception (Huang et al., 2013). In contrast, adaptive models incorporate key factors such as outdoor climate, past thermal history, and occupant preferences to offer a more nuanced understanding of comfort (Kim et al., 2018).

Several studies have explored data-driven adaptive comfort models using machine learning techniques. Ghahramani et al. (2015) proposed an online learning system using reinforcement learning to automatically adjust HVAC setpoints based on user feedback. While a significant step forward, their system did not fully leverage the richness of data available from environmental sensors and wearable devices. Park and Nagy (2018) developed neural network models for predicting personalized thermal sensation using wearable sensors, improving upon conventional offline regression models.

A key challenge in harnessing the full potential of sensing data is the development of robust data fusion techniques. As Li et al. (2017) discussed, combining data from heterogeneous sensors is non-trivial due to differences in sampling rates, measurement uncertainties, and synchronization issues. To address this, Dai et al. (2017) proposed a wearable multi-sensor fusion scheme using a hidden Markov model to integrate temperature, humidity, and heart rate data for personalized thermal comfort estimation. Liu et al. (2019) combined infrared imagery, CO2 sensors, and humidity data to estimate personalized comfort. However, research gaps remain in the fusion of the breadth of data needed for holistic comfort monitoring.

Privacy preservation is another critical consideration in adaptive comfort systems that rely on personal data. Lin et al. (2016) applied differential privacy techniques to smart meter data in buildings, enabling analytics while preserving individual privacy. Access control mechanisms, such as attribute-based encryption, restrict data access to only authorized users, facilitating the secure sharing of sensitive comfort-related data (Liang et al., 2015). Integrating such solutions can facilitate the wider adoption of personalized comfort systems. Federated transfer learning allows the training of a model across multiple organizations without sharing raw data (Liu et al., 2019). Despite these advanced techniques, effectively integrating them into holistic comfort frameworks remains an open challenge.

Overall, while significant research has explored adaptive thermal comfort and data-driven HVAC control, opportunities exist to develop a holistic framework addressing key gaps related to multi-sensor fusion, online learning, and privacy preservation. This research aims to fulfill this potential and advance the state-of-the-art. It introduces an adaptive framework designed to address these limitations by leveraging advanced computing-enabled architecture, integrating multivariate data sources, and employing privacy-preserving online machine learning algorithms. The proposed approach is expected to significantly advance occupant-centric and responsive indoor comfort.

3   Framework Design

In the realm of indoor environmental comfort, the proposed framework represents a significant departure from the conventional, static systems by introducing an occupant-centric model that leverages real-time data analytics and personalized environmental control. The proposed framework transcends conventional measurement systems by incorporating several layers of innovation, particularly in adaptive control, privacy preservation, and data integration (See Table 1). These advancements not only enhance the occupant experience but also contribute to the field of human-computer interaction (HCI) by offering fine-tuned control and increased transparency in system operations. This section outlines the structure of the proposed system and the envisioned applications that underscore its potential impact, especially in sensitive environments such as assisted living facilities.

Table 1. Key features of the proposed framework.

Feature	Traditional Approach	Proposed Framework
Modeling Approach	Static, based on fixed setpoints	Adaptive, based on real-time data and user feedback
Control System	Rule-based using temperature thresholds	Online learning model continuously optimized based on updated database
Data Sources	Measurements from individual wired sensors	Multi-sensor data fusion from environmental sensors and wearables devices
Responsiveness	Low, relying on fixed schedules	High, real-time adaptation possible
Personalization	Minimal, generalized group comfort zones	High, customized to individual via physiological feedback
Privacy Management	Limited considerations for data privacy	Encryption and federated learning for privacy preservation

3.1 System Architecture and Integration

As illustrated in Fig. 1, this framework signifies an evolution from the 'traditional measurement' process, which relies on offline modeling to set comfort temperatures based on general data, to an 'occupant-centric measurement' system. This system prioritizes the individual's experience by integrating a multitude of sensors that collect both environmental and personal data. It marks a shift to 'online modeling,' where the comfort zone is no longer static but rather a 'neutral comfort zone' that can be fine-tuned in real-time in response to active occupant feedback.

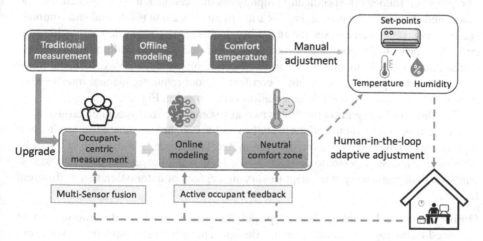

Fig. 1. Upgraded occupant-centric measurement and adjustment system.

The core of the proposed framework is smart wearable devices to measure an array of individual physiological metrics, including skin temperature, metabolic rate, and heart rate, along with portable environmental sensors to collect data on environmental factors such as air temperature, relative humidity, airflow, illuminance, acoustics, and indoor air quality. Physiological signals from wearables will be encrypted at the device before transmission for analysis. Through the sophisticated fusion of these diverse datasets, the system customizes the micro-environment at an individual level, taking into account factors factors such as age and seasonality.

The wearable device is supported by a platform—a smartphone APP that enables users to access data analytics insights and update their environmental preferences. This platform offers personalized feedback to individual data profile for continuously model training and optimization. Feedback from occupants is not merely passive data; it is an essential input that continuously informs the online learning model. This model evolves with each interaction, refining its suggestions and automatic adjustments to ensure they align more closely with the individual's preferences and well-being. Consequently, the mobile platform can actively send recommendations to the user, thereby promoting a human-in-the-loop adjustment system to enhance both comfort and energy efficiency.

The connection of wearable sensors and environmental has been tested for building system integration through a wireless mesh network protocol that allows data integration for IoT sensor networks. To synchronize sensing data from multiple data sources at the same time stamps, utilizing the processing platform with a web server to store, transfer and process data, is being increasingly explored (Feng and Wang, 2023). The processed outputs will feed into the online learning model to estimate and identify the neutral comfort zone. Such a platform has great potential for seamless integration with HVAC, lighting, and other building management systems to enact personalized comfort adjustments.

3.2 Implementation of the Proposed Framework

The proposed framework specifically emphasizes the feedback loop integrated into the model and showcases the practical application of this system in residential and commercial buildings such as an assisted living facility. In this setting, the system can either suggest adjustments to the occupant or staff or, if integrated with the building management system, automatically modify environmental conditions such as HVAC settings, lighting, and window positions to optimize comfort without requiring manual intervention. A control framework for the implementation is described in Fig. 2.

The described integration facilitates two key scenarios: staff-mediated adjustments where the system sends notifications to staff to take action, and automated environmental adjustments. In the latter situation, the system interfaces directly with building controls, offering a seamless response to occupants' needs. This dual capability ensures the system's versatility, allowing it to adapt to varying degrees of automation across different facilities.

Online Machine Learning. The proposed framework stands at the intersection of advanced technology and human-centric design. The adaptive control framework represents the next generation of environmental comfort systems. It moves beyond static,

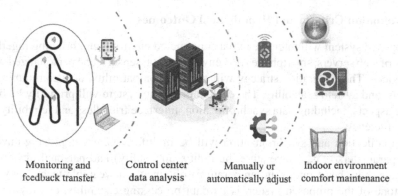

| Monitoring and | Control center | Manually or | Indoor environment |
| feedback transfer | data analysis | automatically adjust | comfort maintenance |

Fig. 2. Assisted living facility scenario.

one-size-fits-all settings, utilizing a combination of real-time data and occupant feedback to create a living environment that adjusts to the changing conditions and preferences.

The proposed online framework evaluates the state of the indoor environment in real-time, including the occupant's current comfort level, and takes actions that maximize a predefined function with continuously updated database. This function is tailored to prioritize occupant comfort, as well as energy efficiency, thereby aligning with the goals of sustainable and occupant-centric design. The efficacy of the prediction model in such scenarios is supported by research by Wei et al. (Automation Conference, 2017), which highlights the potential of deep reinforcement learning in reducing energy consumption while maintaining comfort.

Explainable Artificial Intelligence (XAI). Transparency in AI-driven systems is a growing field of interest, particularly in scenarios where the user's trust and understanding of the system's decisions are crucial. The proposed framework incorporates XAI principles to demystify the AI's decision-making process. By leveraging techniques such as feature visualization and saliency mapping, which have been discussed in detail by Samek et al.'s (IEEE, 2017), the system provides users with understandable explanations for the AI's actions.

The system's XAI component tackles a significant challenge in HCI: the frequently opaque nature of AI algorithms. By implementing guidelines from Gunning's work (Defense Advanced Research Projects Agency (DARPA), 2017), we ensure that users are not alienated by the complexity of AI. Instead, they are provided with an interface that offers clear, concise explanations for the AI's adjustments to the indoor environment. This not only enhances user satisfaction but also encourages more meaningful interaction with the system, potentially leading to more accurate feedback and further refinement of the AI model.

By integrating online machine learning and XAI, the framework respects the dynamic nature of human comfort, prioritizes energy efficiency, and values the trust and engagement of the occupants, embodying the true spirit of human-centered design in smart building systems.

3.3 Evaluation Criteria and Hypothetical Outcomes

The proposed system will integrate into a constructed environment, bringing together a network of web servers, smartphone APP, environmental sensors, and personalized wearable devices. The integration strategy will address compatibility, data communication protocols, and system scalability. The evaluation of the system will primarily be based on three aspects, including data synchronization, interface friendless and reliability, and energy efficiency.

Data collection and synchronization will be multifarious, encompassing environmental parameters (e.g., temperature, humidity, air quality) and personal physiological signals (e.g., heart rate, skin temperature) obtained via wearable technology. The cornerstone of the proposed system is its data processing capability, employing data fusion techniques for immediate data storage and preprocessing. Simultaneously, the time-stamped data should be obtained and integrated for online modeling.

The user interface will be meticulously crafted, following the principles of user-centered design, to ensure not only intuitiveness and ease of interaction but also the utmost reliability. This reliability will be ingrained in every aspect of the interface, fostering user confidence in the system's consistent performance. Additionally, the interface will facilitate seamless occupant feedback, empowering users to confidently personalize their environmental settings. Recognized as a critical touchpoint, the interface will play a pivotal role in enhancing occupant engagement.

A comparative analysis of energy consumption before and after the system implementation will provide insights into its efficiency. It is hypothesized that the system's ability to tailor environmental conditions to individual needs will lead to significant energy savings, reducing unnecessary heating, cooling, or lighting adjustments.

4 Discussion

The proposed system is expected to significantly enhance indoor comfort levels, and this personalization is anticipated to lead to increased occupant satisfaction and well-being. In the long term, the system could contribute to improved occupant health and productivity, as personalized comfort has been linked to these factors in existing literature. For example, Frontczak et al. (2012) found that occupants reported improved health, satisfaction, and productivity when they had control over their indoor environment. Similarly, Kim and de Dear (2012) demonstrated long-term reductions in sickness in occupants of buildings with enhanced comfort systems. The proposed system dynamically aligns HVAC and lighting to occupant presence and preferences, reducing unnecessary energy use while enhancing indoor comfort.

The framework's flexibility suggests it could be adapted for various building types and environments, thereby broadening its applicability and impact. The system's potential to cater to the specific needs of vulnerable populations, such as the elderly or those with health conditions, highlights its societal value. Its capacity for personalization and privacy preservation positions it as a valuable contribution to future smart building solutions.

While innovative, the proposed framework has certain limitations that must be acknowledged. Primarily, its effectiveness is yet to be validated in real-world environments. This testing phase is crucial for understanding practical challenges and the system's adaptability to diverse settings. Furthermore, the framework faces notable challenges due to its reliance on sensor accuracy and the complexity of integration with various building management systems. Ensuring the privacy and security of sensitive data, despite the advanced techniques employed, remains an area requiring vigilant attention and continuous improvement.

In contemplating the future development of this system, a broader perspective is necessary-one that not only addresses the current limitations but also enhance the system's capabilities. An intriguing and crucial avenue for future research is exploring the integration of indoor comfort systems with external climate prediction models. This integration forms the basis of what can be termed the occupant-centric building resilience framework. This expanded framework goes beyond optimizing indoor comfort in the present; it envisions enhancing building resilience in response to climate change. Integrating real-time external climatic data enables the system to proactively adjust to environmental changes, ensuring the sustained comfort and well-being of occupants even under fluctuating external conditions. The holistic approach surpasses traditional paradigms of indoor comfort systems that often operate independently of external environmental factors. The novelty of this approach lies in its proactive nature-anticipating and responding to external weather patterns, rather than merely reacting to internal environmental changes.

5 Conclusion

This paper has introduced a comprehensive framework for occupant-centric measurement and adjustment within indoor environments, designed to enhance comfort through personalized micro-environment control. The proposed framework represents a significant shift from conventional static models, advocating for a system that dynamically adjusts to individual preferences using real-time data and feedback. The novelty of the framework lies in its integration of multi-sensor data fusion, online modeling, and intelligent sensor technologies. It is designed to handle and respond to a diverse range of inputs from both the built environment and the occupants themselves, providing a level of personalization not previously achieved in existing systems. Theoretically, this approach has been suggested to enhance the immediate occupant experience and foster a harmonious relationship between individuals and their living spaces.

This research makes dual contributions. Firstly, it tackles the challenges of data consistency and privacy in smart environments by implementing advanced computing. Secondly, it introduces a system capable of real-time adaptability, thereby enhancing the responsiveness of indoor comfort control measures. The paper has additionally outlined an occupant-centric building resilience framework as a direction for future work, proposing the integration of indoor comfort models with climate prediction to proactively adapt to external environmental changes. This future work aims to extend the application scope of the framework and contribute to building resilience in the face of climate variability.

In conclusion, while the proposed framework is yet to be validated in situ, it provides a blueprint for the future of intelligent building systems, where comfort, energy efficiency, and user privacy are at the core of design and operation. The expected results of this research are anticipated to lead to the development of more adaptive and resilient living spaces.

Disclosure of Interests. The authors have no competing interests to declare that are relevant to the content of this article.

References

Dai, C., Zhang, H., Arens, E., Lian, Z.: Machine learning approaches to predict thermal demands using skin temperatures: steady-state conditions. Build. Environ. **114**, 1–10 (2017)

Feng, Y., Wang, J.: Alert-based wearable sensing system for individualized thermal preference prediction. Build. Environ. **232** (2023)

Frontczak, M., Schiavon, S., Goins, J., Arens, E., Zhang, H., Wargocki, P.: Quantitative relationships between occupant satisfaction and satisfaction aspects of indoor environmental quality and building design. Indoor Air **22**(2), 119–131 (2012)

Ghahramani, A., Tang, C., Becerik-Gerber, B.: An online learning approach for quantifying personalized thermal comfort via adaptive stochastic modeling. Build. Environ. **92**, 86–96 (2015)

Gunning, D.: Explainable artificial intelligence (XAI). Defense Adv. Res. Projects Agency (DARPA) Web **2**(2) (2017)

Huang, L., Ouyang, Q., Zhu, Y., Jiang, L.: A study about the demand for air movement in warm environment. Build. Environ. **61**, 27–33 (2013)

Kim, J., De Dear, R.: Nonlinear relationships between individual IEQ factors and overall workspace satisfaction. Build. Environ. **49**, 33–40 (2012)

Kim, J., Zhou, Y., Schiavon, S., Raftery, P., Brager, G.: Personal comfort models: predicting individuals' thermal preference using occupant heating and cooling behavior and machine learning. Build. Environ. **129**, 96–106 (2018)

Li, D., Menassa, C.C., Kamat, V.R.: Personalized human comfort in indoor building environments under diverse conditioning modes. Build. Environ. **126**, 304–317 (2017)

Liang, K., Susilo, W., Liu, J.K.: Privacy-preserving ciphertext multi-sharing control for big data storage. IEEE Trans. Inf. Forensics Secur. **10**(8), 1578–1589 (2015)

Lin, C., Song, Z., Song, H., Zhou, Y., Wang, Y., Wu, G.: Differential privacy preserving in big data analytics for connected health. J. Med. Syst. **40**, 1–9 (2016)

Liu, S., Schiavon, S., Das, H.P., Jin, M., Spanos, C.J.: Personal thermal comfort models with wearable sensors. Build. Environ. **162** (2019)

Park, J.Y., Nagy, Z.: Comprehensive analysis of the relationship between thermal comfort and building control research - a data-driven literature review. Renew. Sustain. Energy Rev. **82**, 2664–2679 (2018)

Ploennigs, J., Hensel, B., Dibowski, H., Kabitzsch, K.: BASont - a modular, adaptive building automation system ontology. In: IECON 2012–38th Annual Conference on IEEE Industrial Electronics Society (2012)

Samek, W., Wiegand, T., Müller, K.R.: Explainable artificial intelligence: understanding, visualizing and interpreting deep learning models. arXiv preprint arXiv:1708.08296 (2017)

Wei, T., Wang, Y., Zhu, Q.: Deep reinforcement learning for building HVAC control. In: Proceedings of the 54th Annual Design Automation Conference (2017)

Yao, R., Li, B., Liu, J.: A theoretical adaptive model of thermal comfort–Adaptive Predicted Mean Vote (aPMV). Build. Environ. **44**(10), 2089–2096 (2009)

Yang, Q., Liu, Y., Chen, T., Tong, Y.: Federated machine learning: concept and applications. ACM Trans. Intell. Syst. Technol. (TIST) **10**(2), 1–19 (2019)

VIT.IN: Visualizing Collective Stress with a Dynamic Painting

Danique Stappers and Jun Hu[(✉)]

Department of Industrial Design, Eindhoven University of Technology, Eindhoven,
Netherlands
j.hu@tue.nl

Abstract. Office workers face high working pressure, which could result
in chronic stress. These conditions affect their vitality and can lead to
health problems and burnout. VIT.IN is a dynamic painting that represents the collective stress level of employees. Based on the intensity and
duration of stress, the dynamic painting will partially morph towards
a more stressed or relaxed visualization. In an experiment with several
fictive scenarios, behavioral influences were explored related to changes
in collective stress. Social connections between colleagues, and general
organizational and social values seemed important behavioral influences.
Next to this, ethical boundaries were identified for real-life application.
Further investigation of these behavioral influences can unveil new triggers, aimed at encouraging healthier behavior amongst the working community.

Keywords: Data visualization · Collective stress · Behavior change ·
Digital art

1 Introduction

In 2019, 1.3 million Dutch employees faced burnout symptoms due to too high
working pressure. This raised the absenteeism costs to approximately 3.1 billion
euros, which makes the situation problematic for employers as well [21]. Even
though stress is a useful factor in completing tasks efficiently, a high workload
often requires high performance, leading to increased stress levels. Especially
when stress levels are increased for a longer amount of time, chronic stress can
be developed. This leads to serious health problems, such as headaches, insom-
nia, concentration issues, muscle tension, and eventually burnout when not taken
seriously [7]. Therefore, chronic stress prevention is essential for a healthy working community.

The European Union acknowledges the seriousness of work-related stress,
demonstrated in the European Framework for Psychological Risk Management
(PRIMA-EF) [22]. PRIMA-EF contains guidelines for EU companies defined by
the Institute of Work, Health and Organizations in 2008. International recognition of work-related stress has created a well-studied research domain. Lansisalmi

et al. (2000) emphasized the importance of investigating collective stress within organizations since it gives a holistic view [6]. However, most current studies are focused on individual stress. Within design research, investigating collective stress allows for managing and reflecting upon stress by shared data visualizations [23, 24, 26]. Nevertheless, behavioral influences in this direction, have not been investigated sufficiently.

Thus, within this study we have tapped into behavioral influences of collective stress within the field of design research. Office workers were targeted since they often face stress due to high workloads and working pressure, e.g. because of deadlines and time restrictions [8]. The research artefact is a digital collective stress visualization, to elicit behavioral insights in a hypothetical setting. First, we have designed an initial visualization through a co-creation session. Based on the received critique on a design demonstration day, we have derived two new visualizations. By comparing these visuals in a small user study, we have chosen the most empathic and artistic visual, which became the research artefact: VIT.IN (Vitality Insight) (Fig. 4). The following question will be answered through VIT. IN: "How does a dynamic painting, that represents data about collective stress, influence behavior amongst office workers in different fictive scenarios?"

We have used a combination of hypothetical choice experiments with elicitation interviews to answer the research question, while evaluating personality traits and VIT.IN's aesthetic quality quantitatively. With this study, we aimed to contribute to the field of design research by gaining insight into the value of collective stress visualizations among office workers. Investigating this newer domain of collective stress can unveil new triggers for a healthier behavior change. These triggers could be applied in future investigations to create a healthier working community.

2 Related Work

2.1 Visualizing Vitality

The vitality of office workers is a common topic within design research. Elvitigala et al. (2021) designed StressShoe [3], a sensor for measuring work-related stress amongst office workers, which could be attached to their shoes. When stress levels changed, there was a contextual change (desktop background), a message to manage stress (take a break, stretch), or interruptions (change in music). The measured stress was visualized in an app, which was perceived as most helpful for gaining insight into personal stressors. Ren et al. (2021) investigated the value of coping with and reflecting upon stress by mockup app Steadi [15]. Steadi allows for scheduling tasks, recommendation of breaks, and planning optimizations. In a small explorative study, it was found that Steadi helped with decreasing high stress levels amongst intensive tasks. However, a field study was not conducted. Sharmin et al. (2015) found that personal data visualizations allow for the development of individual interventions by stress experts [18].

Stimulight, a physical data visualization, was developed by Brombacher et al. (2019) to investigate the stimulation of physical activity amongst office workers, whilst tested with students [2]. It facilitated feedback for individual employees and the collective of them. They found by a thematic analysis, that individual data should be accessible since it could otherwise lack meaning for the user. A thematic analysis was also used to investigate the stress levels of aid workers [28], and in another study about break-taking and accompanied social behaviors of office workers [11]. Xue et al. (2017) developed ClockViz [25], a physical data visualization of collective stress amongst office workers. ClockViz was perceived as a valuable information tool. Additionally, Xue et al. (2019) created Affective-Wall [27], an interactive wall that visualizes both individual stress levels and those of the collective. AffectiveWall was deployed in group meetings and helped participants to interpret their stress levels in a better way. Both ClockViz and AffectiveWall demonstrated abstract and creative data visualizations compared to other studies. However, behavioral influences by collective data visualizations were not studied in these two studies.

2.2   Organizational Culture

According to Peters and Weggeman (2013), most European companies use a combination of the Rhineland Model (West-European capitalism) and Anglo-American capitalism [13]. The Rhineland Model has a social-economic focus where political democracy is applied, in order to preserve job security, public education and public healthcare. The Rhineland model has increased in popularity since the economic crisis of 2008, because it is the most economically stable model. This model is in contrast with the Anglo-American Capitalism, which has a purely economic focus on making money; this is not guarded by the government. Another socio-economic model is the Government capitalism, which is meant to provide income for the government, without political democracy [14]. The applied capitalism is reflected within the organizational culture. It determines the values and the ambiance of the work environment, also considering stress management and personal health of employees.

2.3   Behavior Change

Behavioral change theories are often about changing and maintaining a healthier behavior. Examples are the Integrated Behavioral Model (IBM) [10] theory and the Transtheoretical Model (TTM) [5]. IBM emphasizes that the intention a person has to perform a specific behavior is mainly dependent on their attitude, perceived norms, and personal agency. The attitude is influenced by their feelings (experiential attitude) and beliefs (instrumental attitude) associated with performing a behavior. The perceived norm is related to social factors: whether other people expect an individual will perform a certain behavior (injunctive norm), and the tendency of others to perform the behavior themselves (descriptive norm). Personal agency consists of the perceived control one feels related to the specific behavior, as well as to what extent they believe they are competent to perform the behavior (self-efficacy). When using IBM, elicitation interviews are used to determine behavioral influences such as triggers, constraints, and social aspects [10].

TTM defines stages accompanied with behavior change [5]. In this theory, the processes from pre-contemplation (no intention to change behavior) to contemplation (intention to change behavior sometimes) to preparation (preparing oneself to change behavior) are of relevance. These processes can be influenced by several factors, including consciousness-raising, self-re-evaluation, and environmental re-evaluation. These stages are followed by action and maintenance, to successfully change and sustain the desired behavior.

When evaluating behavioral aspects and stress, more meaningful insights could be gained by including the Big Five Personality traits [12]. These traits can reflect how certain people experience stress, cope with stress and how they will behave in general. They were mentioned within the Five Factor Model (FFM) which distinguishs the following traits: 'Neuroticism', 'Extraversion', 'Openness', 'Agreeableness', and 'Conscientiousness' [9]. Seibt et al. (2005) demonstrated the importance of investigating the relation between personalities and stress amongst office workers and teachers [17]. Additionally, Grant and Langan-Fox (2006) have found that combining the traits is valuable when investigating a stress-related topic, although this is fairly more complex [4].

In summary, prevention of chronic stress is essential to protect the working community. Awareness is raised, but behavioral triggers have remained unexplored in current design research about collective stress. Visualizing collective stress allows for a holistic view of organizational stress, which is most valuable when individuals can retrieve personal data from the visual [2,25,27]. Behavioral influences could be investigated by combining the open-ended characteristic of elicitation interviews [10]. Furthermore, it is important to evaluate personalities amongst the Big Five Personality traits within this context [17].

3   Design

3.1   Design Process

Visualizing Ambiances. The value of data visualizations has been demonstrated in previous studies about individual and collective stress. Especially the visualizations aiming at collective stress, characterized abstractness and creativity instead of graphs and specific numerical data. We agreed upon the development of an abstract visual based on grounds for novelty. Furthermore, a data visualization hidden in an artwork seemed less ethically concerning, because it does not reveal specific health conditions. This manner of visualizing seemed less serious and therefore a better dialogue enabler, from a first-person perspective [19]. We have executed a co-creation session with 4 participants to investigate individual differences and similarities about the ambiance of colors, shapes, artworks and data visualizations.

Beforehand, we explained the study and the participants signed consent forms regarding ethical considerations. All elements were handed to the participants as visualization cards, each participant was facilitated with the same set of cards. First, the participants had to sort these elements from relaxed to stressed in about 10 min. This was followed by a group discussion, in which participants could indicate whether some visuals triggered an ambiance instead of only visualizing it. The participants had a similar opinion about using softer colors for expressing a relaxed ambiance, whereas stronger and brighter colors indicated stress. When stronger colors were combined with softer colors, stress was visualized, but not triggered. One participant envisioned animated effects based on colors and size of the elements within the visual. Bigger, brighter and multi-colored elements would transform and move around quicker than smaller, darker and single-colored elements. The slower movement would indicate relaxedness whilst the quick movement could trigger stress. Some participants argued organic shapes to indicate relaxedness because of their 'soft edges'. Other students argued static shapes to be relaxed, because they are 'clear and easy to grasp'. After this first round of sorting the cards, participants were engaged to create their own visualizations for a stressed and relaxed ambiance. Overall results demonstrated 'connectedness' for relaxedness, whereas disconnection was demonstrated for stress (Fig. 1).

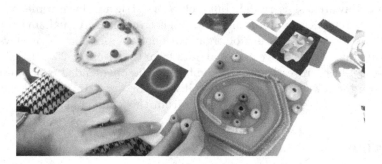

Fig. 1. Co-created artwork with on the left a whole (relaxed ambiance) and on the right this gets disconnected and the beats float out of the center (stressed ambiance).

From a theoretical perspective, Aronoff et al. (1988) found in an intercultural study that sharp edges and diagonals were more likely to represent hazards [1]. This third-person perspective enriches the empirical findings. Therefore, we have decided to express relaxedness with organic shapes and stress with increased straight lines and sharper angles. Furthermore, we have conducted knowledge about color combinations to express an ambiance, without triggering it. Additionally, animated effects should have minimized speed to prevent triggering stress. Consequently, we have gained the insight that relaxedness could be seen as a 'whole' in which individuals are connected. In contrast, an increased stress level would disturb this whole by disconnecting from the center.

A Morphing Artwork. Based on the takeaways from the co-creation session, we have created a dynamic artwork. We envisioned this artwork to be a dynamic painting, which could be attached to a wall in the office where most employees could see it. The artwork expresses a whole with pastel colors and organic shapes when the collective stress level is low (Fig. 2). When the collective stress level increases, the artwork will morph slowly and express stress by disconnection, the addition of bright and strong colors and sharper shapes. The visualized faces do not represent specific employees, but they represent the average collective stress level. The artwork itself was inspired by line art, which is abstract and often expresses humans. This way, we have used a style that generally represents faces, but also allows for empathizing when the deeper layer of collective stress is known. From a first-person perspective, it gives a feeling of safety that only people involved within the organization understand the deeper layer; whilst it will look like a general artwork for external people.

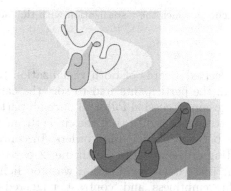

Fig. 2. First concept: when the collective stress level increases, the artwork will morph slowly and express stress by bright and strong colors and sharper shapes.

This morphing artwork was shown and explained to design students, coaches and professors for a public exhibition. Visitors often misinterpreted the faces as specific persons whilst they represented an average value. Feedback included that this neglection of individual data could cause demotivation to understand or act upon the visual.

Novelty. The feedback from the exhibition inspired us to create a new visual, with improved individual involvement. The facial elements of the previous visual were based on a first-person perspective, that human characteristics could assist in empathizing with the design. However, this was not evaluated. Therefore, two different themes of visualizations were created. One theme was based on traditional data visualizations, using a circle as the basis (Fig. 3. The other theme had an artistic focus, inspired by the previous visual with faces (Fig. 11.3). Both visuals were evaluated in a user study with 5 participants at the same time.

4 out of 5 participants, who participated in the previous study as well, were familiar with the collective stress topic. All participants were master students from Industrial Design, Eindhoven University of Technology.

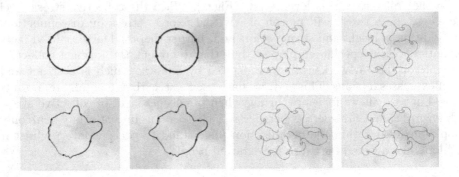

Fig. 3. Sorting experiment, in which the visualization with the faces was chosen as the final design

The participants received 4 cards of both visualization themes in a random order. In about 10 min, the participants had to sort the cards from relaxed to stressed per theme. A group discussion followed once all participants had sorted the cards. While all participants argued that the circle theme was easier to grasp, there were differences between participants' orders. In contrast, there were no differences in the sorting order of the facial theme. 2 participants argued that the background of the first circle visualization was too light combined with a thick circle border, this 'emptiness' and 'contrast' triggered stress. The other 3 participants understood their opinion, but experienced multiple colors as more stressful. All participants argued that the background of the first visualization of the facial theme is most relaxed, because of its warm, convenient and comfortable ambiance; without much contrast. One participant held the opinion that the doodle lines of the circles were more stressful than the peaks. Other participants argued that the increased amount of peaks caused asymmetry, thus interpreting more peaks as stressful. After discussing the sorting experiment, we requested the participants to explain differences in interpretation per theme. All participants found the facial theme most personal and emphatic, one participant mentioned: 'It allows me to translate data to a person right away and therefore makes me more conscious of how my colleagues are doing, otherwise I would probably neglect it'. However, personalization was concerning according two participants, one of them stated: 'I would prefer the circles, because these are less personal. Otherwise I am afraid that I get identified and that others will gossip about my stress levels.' The circle theme was most positively evaluated, on grounds of simplicity, colorfulness and craftmanship. The facial theme was evaluated best on diversity, meaning it was original and inventive. Based on this mixed-method experiment, we decided to continue with the facial theme. This theme allowed for conducting knowledge through a novel data visualization, since we value originality within design research. Furthermore, we believed that the evaluation of this theme would be more interesting. Namely, when we evaluated it with fictional stress-related data, we were enabled to explore behavioral triggers and ethical concerns; without violating ethical regulations.

3.2 VIT.IN

The resulting research artefact VIT.IN (Vitality Insights), aimed at the representation of collective stress. We have created VIT.IN to study the (negative) impact of increased stress levels, it was not a tool for finding the optimal stress level or showcasing the positive effects of stress. Another important note regarding VIT.IN is that this artefact was developed to investigate behavioral triggers related to collective stress visualizations, in a hypothetical setting. It has been evaluated amongst different fictional situations, without using real data or measuring equipment.

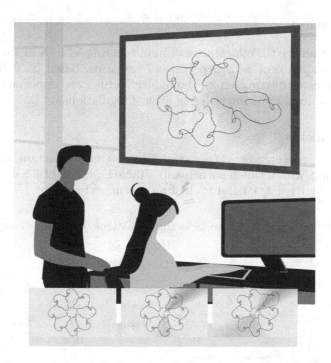

Fig. 4. VIT.IN scenarios. On the left, scenario 1: no stress measured. In the middle, scenario 2: some office workers experience an increased stress level. On the right, scenario 3: one colleague disconnects from the whole, due to an endured increased stress level, other colleagues experience an increased stress level.

We thought of combining individual data to create a whole since integrating individual data could create a more meaningful design [2]. We believed in the value of having a whole, while this principle was evident in the preliminary user studies. Each face within VIT.IN represents an employee, employees are only aware of which face is a representation of themselves, they have no information about their colleagues' data. The background colors demonstrated the amount of stress, whereas the soft pink represented the most relaxed ambiance; as a result of the sorting experiment (Fig. 4). Inspired by both preliminary user studies, a color changed to a stronger color when the stress level increased (Fig. 4). This color change occurred in the background of the face representing an employee who experienced an increased stress level. Next to the height of stress levels, the duration of an increased stress level is important to consider whether someone is suffering from chronic stress [7]. Therefore, the faces floated away from the center once someone experienced stress for a longer amount of time (Fig. 4). This disconnection resulted from both preliminary studies in which disconnection was perceived as a heavier effect than a color change. Therefore, disconnection was applied for serious health situations, whilst a color change represented a less hazardous health situation.

4   Evaluation

We tried to minimize the ethical risks of implementing VIT.IN in a real context, by doing an experiment with hypothetical scenarios, based on fictional data. This allowed us to discover ethical boundaries which are important for future studies on this topic, without violating ethical regulations.

4.1   Participants

Office workers were recruited via personal networks and Instagram. We have executed this study with 6 Dutch participants (Table 1). P2 and P6 had a managing function, whilst P1, P3, P4 and P5 had an executive function.

Table 1. Participants (P3 works at three locations of the same company)

Details Participant	Gender	Age	Job	Amount of hours per week	Direct Colleagues
1	Male	25	Executive	Full time	2
2	Male	51	Manager	Full time	7
3	Female	52	Executive	28	1, 4 and 2*
4	Female	55	Executive	16-20	4
5	Female	49	Executive	24	4
6	Female	51	Manager	Full time	2-5

This study was approved by the ethical committee of Eindhoven University of Technology, and we have used informed consent forms to clarify ethical regulations to the participants. Participation in this study was voluntary and without any compensation.

4.2   Material

We have made use of the following material to execute this study.

- Notebook or desktop for displaying VIT.IN.
- Adobe XD: an animation program of Adobe in which we have created VIT.IN. VIT.IN is displayed via this program to the participant.
- Printed or digital images of 3 different scenarios of the sketched version of VIT.IN (created in Adobe Fresco, Fig. 4).
- Informed consent form for ethical regulations.
- Notebook, writing down findings.
- Procedure: study protocol and questions for the semi-structured interview.
- Survey Big Five Personality traits by IDRLabs [20].
- In case of online user-study: Microsoft Teams.

4.3   Procedure

The user study was conducted in an environment in which participants felt most comfortable. The study with P1 was conducted online, and the other studies were conducted in a physical home setting. The study started with explaining the procedure and related ethical regulations, which were accepted by all participants via a signed informed consent form.

First, demographic and contextual information of the participants was collected. Such as personal information and whether the participant had experiences with work-related stress, and if it is a topic that could be discussed openly within their organization. Furthermore, the participant had to describe the amount of direct colleagues; in one room, most closely located; and the kind of connections with these colleagues. Then the research artefact VIT.IN was explained by 3 different scenarios of the sketched prototype (Fig. 14). We consciously chose to vary between the example and the actual prototype, to activate the participant to interpret the situations themselves, instead of repeating the example. The participants were informed that this study focused on investigating their behavior, related to VIT.IN, whilst this study was not about measuring and collecting real stress data. After the introduction was clear to the participant, the first scenario of VIT.IN was opened in our notebook, on full screen. We have indicated which avatar within VIT.IN represented the participant, whilst they received no information about which avatars represented their colleagues. Furthermore, the participants were informed that the location of their and their colleagues' avatars would change per day for ethical reasons. The situation was sketched to the participant, in which VIT.IN was attached to a wall where most employees could see it. We have emphasized imagining the scenarios in real-life, and answering as honestly as possible. Per scenario the following questions were asked, there were 7 scenarios in total (Fig. 5).

- How would you feel when this scenario occurs at your office?
- Does this depend on the situation, day or time?
- Would you do something with regard to this visual?

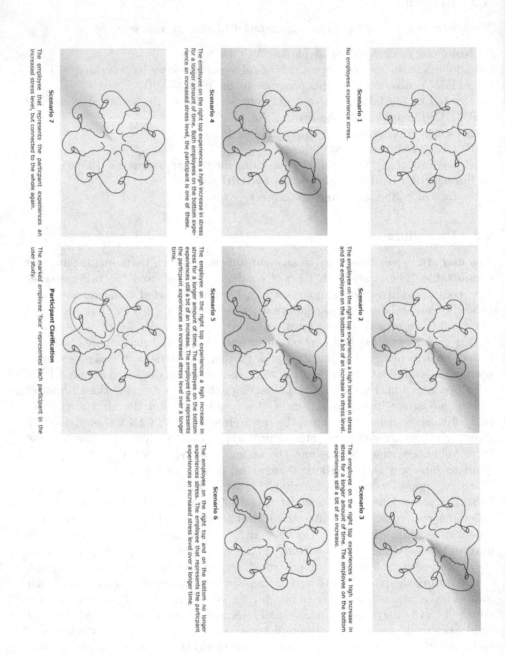

Scenario 1

No employees experience stress.

Scenario 2

The employee on the right top experiences a high increase in stress and the employee on the bottom experiences still a bit of an increase.

Scenario 3

The employee on the right top experiences a high increase in stress for a longer amount of time. The employee on the bottom experiences still a bit of an increase.

Scenario 4

The employee on the right top experiences a high increase in stress for a longer amount of time. Both employees on the bottom experience an increased stress level, the participant is one of these.

Scenario 5

The employee on the right top experiences a high increase in stress for a longer amount of time. The employee on the bottom experiences still a bit of an increase. The employee that represents the participant experiences an increased stress level over a longer time.

Scenario 6

The employee on the right top and on the bottom no longer experiences stress. The employee that represents the participant experiences an increased stress level over a longer time.

Scenario 7

The employee that represents the participant experiences an increased stress level, but connected to the whole again.

Participant Clarification

The marked employee 'face' represented each participant in the user study.

Fig. 5. The seven scenarios which were used for evaluation

– In case of a visual in which the participant experiences stress themselves:
  • If a colleague asks how you're doing, would you answer this honestly?
  • If a colleague asks to take a break would you accept this?
  • If a colleague asks if they can take some work from you, would you accept this?

The amount of questions was not limited to the above, since a semi-structured interview was conducted, based on elicitation interviews [10]. Participants had to explain their answers to the above-stated questions. Furthermore, participants had to elaborate upon their actions, if there were certain conditions under which they performed the mentioned action or not. In situations regarding social interactions, participants had to explain whether the connection between themselves and their colleagues influenced their behavior.

The hypothetical scenario experiment was followed by a short survey about the Big Five Personality traits via Microsoft Forms, with the addition of Dutch translations [20]).

4.4 Data Analysis

All collected information from the semi-structured interviews were carefully documented per participant. We have conducted a thematic analysis as an initial step, to create oversight in the qualitative interview data. We have created codes per kind of action that participants took hypothetically. Behavioral influences were coded as well (Table 2). We perceived an aspect as a behavioral influence when a change in the aspect correlated with a change in the participant's behavior. The codes were revised and combined into themes. We have linked the themes and corresponding codes per scenario, per participant. Eventually, we used these themes to compare how participants acted in a situation and whether this depended on certain social or contextual factors (behavioral influences). Participants will be discussed by 'P' followed by their number. The overall results were eventually analyzed by an expert with a dual background in both psychology and technology.

4.5 Results

Organizational Culture and Expectations. All participants indicated that they work in an organization in which topics like well-being and experiences with stress could be discussed openly. P2, P4, P5 and P6 mentioned this open environment several times in multiple scenarios. This open environment was according to these participants a ground for expecting colleagues to be honest about their feelings and have trust in their colleagues, 'they should know that we help each other in hard situations' (P2). Furthermore, P2 and P5 expected all other colleagues to help them, when they experienced stress. P5 indicated the following: 'I always take care of how others are feeling, so I expect them to take care of me in return. If they do not notice it, I will react snippy to them till they show interest in me.'. P1 and P4 had no expectations of receiving

Table 2. Actions participants would perform in a certain fictive scenario and based on a certain type of colleague. The kind of colleagues that the participants have are indicated behind the participant number with the same letter categories.

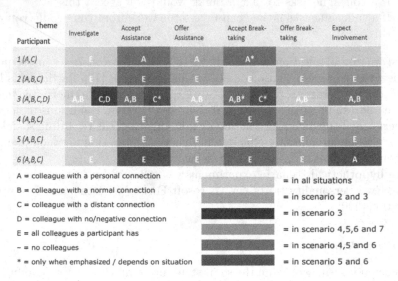

help in return, but would appreciate this. P6 expected colleagues with a close personal connection to help her in return, help from others was appreciated but not expected. P3 was the only participant who had colleagues with whom she had no connection. She indicated helping colleagues with a personal or normal connection, and also with a distant connection when this person was experiencing a serious stress level. She expected this help in return from the colleagues with a personal and normal connection, it was appreciated when a colleague with a distant connection showed interest. She did not appreciate help or show interest from colleagues with no connection, 'I have nothing to do with these colleagues, so I would prefer them to mind their own business. Furthermore, I would just say that everything is fine if they ask how I am doing, they do not need to know more.' (P3).

Investigate. All participants indicated that once there was a change within the visual displayed by VIT.IN, that they would try to investigate which colleague experienced the most stress from colleagues in categories A and B. P3 was the only participant who had experiences with colleagues with whom she had no connection (category D). Only in a situation which a colleague experienced serious stress for a longer time, such as in scenario 3, P3 would check upon colleagues within categories C and D. All participants except P3 would check up on colleagues within category C, but had no experience with colleagues of category D. Furthermore, P2, P3, P4, P5 and P6 indicated that they immediately had a colleague in mind, corresponding with an avatar facing the most stress, when scenario 2 and 3 were displayed. In a situation where VIT.IN did not represent the colleague that they first thought of, they would still try to find out who it would be; except for P3.

Involvement. The theme 'Involvement' was sub-divided within 'Assistance' and 'Break-taking'. We have used the code assistance for improving task division, either taking tasks from a colleague, dividing the tasks in a better way or prioritizing tasks. Furthermore, the code break-taking is about taking a short break from a work-related task such as, a short walk to the coffee machinery, take a walk outside or have a personal conversation in another room or location. In general, assistance was more frequently accepted and offered than break-taking.

Assistance. P4 and P5 both accepted assistance from all colleagues in scenarios 4,5,6 and 7 and offered it to all colleagues in scenarios 2 and 3. P2 differed from P4 and P5 by accepting assistance in scenarios 4,5 and 6, P6 only accepted assistance in scenarios 5 and 6, P6: 'I will not give any of my work to others when I am experiencing stress, even if they emphasize it I will not listen to them.' P1 accepted assistance in scenarios 4, 5 and 6 from a colleague with a personal connection (category A). P1 also offered assistance to a colleague within category A in scenarios 2 and 3. P3 accepted assistance from colleagues within categories A and B in scenarios 4,5 and 6 whilst she would only accept assistance sometimes from a colleague of category C in scenarios 5 and 6. P3 offered assistance to colleagues within categories A and B.

Break-Taking. P1 would accept a break only from colleagues within category A, when this offer is emphasized. Additionally, P1 would not offer a colleague to take a break when they feel stressed. In contrast, P5 would offer a stressed colleague to take a break, whereas she would not accept this offers herself in any situation, from any colleague. P4 and P6 would both offer all colleagues in scenarios 2 and 3 a break, whereas they would also accept this offer from all colleagues in scenarios 4, 5 and 6. P2 would offer any colleague in scenarios 2 and 3 to take a break, whilst he would accept this offer from any colleague in any scenario, P2: 'I would always accept an offer when colleagues ask me to have a coffee or a walk, also when the visual would not show that I am stressed. I prefer that people share their concerns with me, because they have noticed something and I think there is always an opportunity to learn from that.' P3 would offer colleagues in category A and B to take a break in scenarios 2 and 3. P3 would accept this offer from colleagues in category A and sometimes B in scenarios 4, 5 and 6, and sometimes from category C in scenarios 5 and 6.

Managing Personal Stress. P1, P2, P4, P5 and P6 would focus on themselves when they experience stress, P6: 'I will focus more on myself in this situation, I think that is also the best for the person who is experiencing stress since I will not be able to give good assistance.' P3 would still focus on helping others, when colleagues with a personal connection are feeling stressed. For P4 and P5 it would make a difference if they were the only ones from their colleagues who experienced stress. P4 indicated that it would raise personal doubts, 'I would think that there is something in my personal situation not going well, I would relate this to myself.' P5 indicated that it would feel different in a way of an unfair workload 'I would be frustrated if I am the only one experiencing this high workload and the rest would not help me.' P2 would report the disbalance in workload to other colleagues directly, but would not feel frustrated about this disbalance.

Personality Traits. The personality traits showed differences per participant (Fig. 6). P1 and P5 scored relatively high on 'Neuroticism', with a score of 50%. P3, P5 and P6 scored above 50% on openness, whilst P1, P2 and P4 scored below 38%. All participants scored above 75% on Conscientiousness and above 88% on Agreeableness. P2 till P5 scored 88% or higher on extraversion.

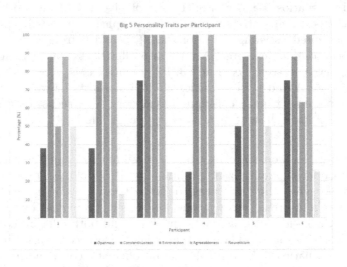

Fig. 6. Personality traits of the participants

Expert Evaluation. According to the expert evaluation, there was little correlation between personality traits and the behavior of participants per scenario. P1 and P5 both had a relatively higher score of the trait Neuroticism than other participants (Fig. 6). Furthermore, P1 would only accept an additional break when this is strongly emphasized by a colleague with a close personal connection, whilst P5 would never accept an additional break. Additionally, both participants indicated that they would work harder when they experienced stress, instead of taking more rest. Since neuroticism is related to stress management, this personality trait could result in this specific behavior, according to the expert.

5   Discussion

5.1   Challenge and Approach

We have evaluated VIT.IN in different fictive situations, to gain insight in behavioral influences by data visualizations about collective stress. We believe that this creates initial insights for chronic stress prevention amongst office workers.

We have found that the visualized data affected the (fictive) performed behavior of the participant. For some participants, the connection with other colleagues was an important aspect that influenced their behavior (P1, P3, P6). The presence of a personal connection could mean that someone would easily accept assistance or be involved with a colleague's well-being. In contrast, VIT.IN would not function as a dialogue enabler for colleagues who have no connection, since they would not engage in sharing health circumstances (P3). In this situation, the collective data visualization caused discomfort (P3). Furthermore, the values that organizations hold seemed important behavioral influences. Participants who emphasized that they work in an environment where personal well-being is valued, were more open to assisting all other colleagues and accepting this in return from all other colleagues (P2, P4, P5, P6). Lastly, the participants argued that their behavior was based on the visualized data, but it is not determined whether they would act differently without VIT.IN or if their fictive behavior corresponds with their behavior in real life.

5.2   Behavioral Influences

It is more common for a company that holds a Rhineland Model to look after employees' health [13,14]. All participants described their company as an open environment where personal health and stress could be discussed, which is in line with the Rhineland Model. However, we noted differences between the participants who only discussed this open environment when asked (P1 and P3) and participants who started about this topic themselves (P2, P4, P5 and P6). Namely, P2, P4, P5 and P6 were more involved with the collective of all colleagues instead of focusing on colleagues with most personal connections. Specifically, for P2 and P5 this functioned as a give-and-take situation, they offered help to all colleagues, but they expected their help in return. Other participants expected help from only colleagues with a closer connection, or from no colleagues, but it was appreciated. The only exception to this situation of social involvement is P3, who would not appreciate the involvement of colleagues with whom she has no connection. P3 was the only participant who had experiences with colleagues with whom she had no connection. This resulted in in-depth insights related to ethical and privacy regulations. From one side VIT. IN could assist a manager in these situations, to create a better ambiance between colleagues within an organization. From the other side, using a tool to improve collective well-being would be a paradox when it eventually leads to personal discomfort, isolation and embarrassment (P3). It is hard to determine whether this situation applies to the majority of employees who have no connection with their colleagues, but we have found that this situation is present for at least one employee. Therefore, when designing for the collective, there should be paid attention to individual effects concerning visualizing stress-related data.

5.3 Social Exchange

These kinds of give-and-take relationships were framed in a social exchange model [16]. Social give-and-take is about putting effort into a relationship while expecting this effort from the other in return. Disbalance in equal give-and-take relationships stimulates motivation to restore the balance. Furthermore, Schaufeli (2006) [16] has found that a disbalance in an inequal relationship in a working environment could lead to frustration and stress by a lack of behavioral rewards; which could eventually result in burnout. The correspondence between our findings and the theory of the social exchange model reflects the importance of applying collective stress visualizations, to keep each other in balance. Additionally, this is in line with the perceived norm someone holds concerning their behavior, the injunctive and descriptive norm [10]. The injunctive norm could trigger extra motivation to perform the behavior of being more involved with each other's well-being because it is expected, whilst the descriptive norm would stimulate performing this behavior because the person in question notices others' performing who perform this behavior. People's social behavior is determined by their personality traits, and these traits could also demonstrate insight in how stress is managed [4,12]. We have found that the relatively higher scores of P1 and P5 in neuroticism and their behavior of rejecting or rarely accepting additional breaks could create a logical connection. Analyzing this psychological data with an expert, gave us the insight that the mentioned connection could direct at not effective coping strategies with stress. However, the sample size and the amount of data are too small to conclude general findings from this information. Furthermore, there were no other valuable links found between personality traits and the fictive performed behavior, which was confirmed by the expert. More valuable results could probably be generated when the sample size is bigger, and when all participants work in the same organization, to limit the effect of differences in environmental factors.

5.4 Limitations

The limitations of our study include that the research artefact, VIT.IN, was partly inspired on user-studies with students. Since students are not the target group, this could be a possible declaration from the results of the visual quality of VIT.IN. Furthermore, we would like to emphasize that the findings of this study could be used as initial points for future work, but should not be generalized. Namely, our study was not executed with a representative group of the working community. Additionally, the behavioral influences were evaluated in different fictive scenarios and could vary from behavior in a real setting. Lastly, we did not conduct knowledge about the need or essence of a research artefact such as VIT.IN since we did not execute a separate control experiment to evaluate behavior without a collective data visualization.

5.5 Contribution and Future Work

We have investigated collective stress by a data visualization based on preliminary studies of Brombacher et al. (2019) [2], Xue et al. (2017) [25], Xue et al. (2019) [27]. Our findings are in line with theirs by demonstrating the value of collective stress, we have found that social and organizational values create an environment in which employees look after each other. Additionally, our study has built up on this by exploring these behavioral influences, that play a role in performing or not performing a specific behavior. More generally, these influences should be considered when designing interventions for a collective of employees, while they have an essential impact on the performance of a behavior. Furthermore, implementing collective stress visualizations in the context could raise ethical concerns. We have found that it could also cause discomfort and embarrassment when it involved colleagues who had no connection with each other. Therefore, it is an important note for the future studies, to carefully minimize the risk of participation in in-context studies. Furthermore, we would recommend to investigate collective stress with a control experiment, to evaluate a situation with a collective data visualization and a situation without. This can firstly demonstrate which behavior was actually performed by participants instead of thinking they would do so, and it can show whether there is a difference in behavior when the data visualization is present. Lastly, a more holistic view could be created when the sample size forms a good representation of the working community or at least a department of one company, which was not the case within this study.

6 Conclusion

Chronic stress is a problematic phenomenon within the Dutch working community, which eventually leads to burnout if not taken seriously. Awareness is raised, but behavioral influences should be discovered before current behavior can be changed to a healthier behavior. While investigating collective stress, we have focused on the whole of employees instead of focusing on individuals. This way, collective stress allowed us to include social and organizational factors, which play an important role within organizations and stress management. An experiment with several fictive scenarios was executed by a collective data visualization, VIT.IN. The found behavioral influences were mostly related to social connections between colleagues or expectations about the desired behavior of both organizations and colleagues. We have specifically contributed to the field of collective stress by investigating behavioral influences. We have identified initial influences that play a role in determining one's behavior. These influences need to be known before behavior change can be reached. Furthermore, we have found important ethical boundaries that should be respected. Namely, a collective data visualization could cause discomfort or shame among employees who have colleagues they have no connection with.

Therefore, we encourage future work on collective stress based on our found behavioral influences. Furthermore, we aim to discover other behavioral triggers in real-life settings, while considering the ethical boundaries found in this study. This way, our study could function as an initial point toward a healthier working community through chronic stress prevention.

References

1. Aronoff, J., Barclay, A.M., Stevenson, L.A.: The recognition of threatening facial stimuli. J. Pers. Soc. Psychol. **54**(4), 647 (1988)
2. Brombacher, H., Arts, D., Megens, C., Vos, S.: Stimulight: exploring social interaction to reduce physical inactivity among office workers. In: Extended Abstracts of the 2019 CHI Conference on Human Factors in Computing Systems, pp. 1–6 (2019)
3. Elvitigala, D.S., Scholl, P.M., Suriyaarachchi, H., Dissanayake, V., Nanayakkara, S.: StressShoe: a DIY toolkit for just-in-time personalised stress interventions for office workers performing sedentary tasks. In: Proceedings of the 23rd International Conference on Mobile Human-Computer Interaction, pp. 1–14 (2021)
4. Grant, S., Langan-Fox, J.: Occupational stress, coping and strain: the combined/interactive effect of the big five traits. Personality Individ. Differ. **41**(4), 719–732 (2006)
5. Jo, P.: The transtheoretical model and stages of change. Health behavior and health education: Theory, Research, and Practice, pp. 97–121 (2008)
6. Lansisalmi, H., Peiro, J.M., Kivimaki, M., IV.: Collective stress and coping in the context of organizational culture. Eur. J. Work Organ. Psy. **9**(4), 527–559 (2000)
7. Maslach, C., Leiter, M.P.: Burnout. In: Stress: Concepts, cognition, emotion, and behavior, pp. 351–357. Elsevier (2016)
8. Maulik, P.K.: Workplace stress: a neglected aspect of mental health wellbeing. Indian J. Med. Res. **146**(4), 441 (2017)
9. McCrae, R.R., Costa Jr, P.T.: More reasons to adopt the five-factor model (1989)
10. Montaño, D., Kaspryzk, D.: Theory of reasoned action, theory of planned behavior, and the integrated behavior model. In: Glanz, K., Rimer, B.K., Viswanath, K. (eds.) Health Behavior and Health Education: Theory, Research, and Practice, pp. 67–92 (2008)
11. Oliver, M., Rodham, K., Taylor, J., McIver, C.: Understanding the psychological and social influences on office workers taking breaks; a thematic analysis. Psychol. Health **36**(3), 351–366 (2021)
12. Petasis, A., Economides, O.: The big five personality traits, occupational stress, and job satisfaction. Eur. J. Bus. Manag. Res. **5**(4) (2020)
13. Peters, J., Weggeman, M.: Het Rijnland praktijkboekje: hoe maak je een Rijnlandse organisatie? Business Contact (2013)
14. Peters, J., Weggeman, M.: The rhineland way: reintroducing a European style of organisation. Business Contact (2013)
15. Ren, X., A. Sherif, S., Thijs, B., Lu, Y.: Steadi: proactively preventing burnouts among office workers through app-based workflow management services. In: 2021 13th International Conference on Bioinformatics and Biomedical Technology, pp. 196–202 (2021)

16. Schaufeli*, W.B.: The balance of give and take: toward a social exchange model of burnout. Revue internationale de psychologie sociale **19**(1), 75–119 (2006)

17. Seibt, R., Lützkendorf, L., Thinschmidt, M.: Risk factors and resources of work ability in teachers and office workers. In: International Congress Series, vol. 1280, pp. 310–315. Elsevier (2005)

18. Sharmin, M., et al.: Visualization of time-series sensor data to inform the design of just-in-time adaptive stress interventions. In: Proceedings of the 2015 ACM International Joint Conference on Pervasive and Ubiquitous Computing, pp. 505–516 (2015)

19. Smeenk, W., Tomico, O., van Turnhout, K.: A systematic analysis of mixed perspectives in empathic design: not one perspective encompasses all. Int. J. Des. **10**(2), 31–48 (2016)

20. Smith, R.: The big five traits and subtraits (2018). https://www.idrlabs.com/articles/2019/03/the-big-five-traits-and-subtraits/. Accessed 01 Feb 2024

21. TNO: Verzuimkosten door werkstress lopen op tot 3,1 miljard (2020). https://www.monitorarbeid.tno.nl/nl-nl/news/verzuimkosten-door-werkstress-lopen-op-tot-31-milja. Accessed 01 Feb 2024

22. World Health Organization and others: PRIMA-EF: guidance on the European framework for psychosocial risk management: a resource for employer and worker representatives (2008)

23. Xue, M.: Affectiveviz: Designing collective stress related visualization. Phd thesis, Department of Industrial Design, Eindhoven University of Technology (2021)

24. Xue, M., et al.: Co-constructing stories based on users lived experiences to investigate visualization design for collective stress management, pp. 652–663. DIS '23, Association for Computing Machinery, New York, NY, USA (2023). https://doi.org/10.1145/3563657.3596118

25. Xue, M., Liang, R.H., Hu, J., Feijs, L.: Clockviz: designing public visualization for coping with collective stress in teamwork. In: Proceedings of the Conference on Design and Semantics of Form and Movement-Sense and Sensitivity, DeSForM 2017. IntechOpen (2017)

26. Xue, M., Liang, R.H., Hu, J., Yu, B., Feijs, L.: Understanding how group workers reflect on organizational stress with a shared, anonymous heart rate variability data visualization. In: CHI Conference on Human Factors in Computing Systems Extended Abstracts, p. Article 27. Association for Computing Machinery, New Orleans, LA, USA (2022).https://doi.org/10.1145/3491101.3503576

27. Xue, M., Liang, R.H., Yu, B., Funk, M., Hu, J., Feijs, L.: AffectiveWall: designing collective stress-related physiological data visualization for reflection. IEEE Access **7**, 131289–131303 (2019)

28. Young, T.K., Pakenham, K.I., Norwood, M.F.: Thematic analysis of aid workers' stressors and coping strategies: work, psychological, lifestyle and social dimensions. J. Int. Humanitarian Action **3**(1), 1–16 (2018)

Design and Practice of Traditional Chinese Massage Experience Based on Augmented Reality

Chunxi Tian[1], Wenjun Hou[1,2,3(✉)], Yuze Gao[1], Bole Wu[1], and Sen Lin[1]

[1] School of Digital Media and Design Arts, Beijing University of Posts and Telecommunications, No.10 Xitucheng Road, Beijing 100876, China
hwj1505@bupt.edu.cn
[2] Beijing Key Laboratory of Network System and Network Culture, No.10 Xitucheng Road, Beijing 100876, China
[3] Key Laboratory of Interactive Technology and Experience System, Ministry of Culture and Tourism, No.10 Xitucheng Road, Beijing 100876, China

Abstract. This article explores the application of augmented reality technology in the field of traditional Chinese massage (TCM), aiming to provide users with an immersive and personalized massage experience at home. Through qualitative and quantitative research methods, this study identifies users' preferences and pain points and proposes a series of innovative AR massage design solutions, including AR massage route guidance, personalized experience, and disease diagnosis. This study also analyzes the potential of AR technology in medical education and practice. The application of AR technology provides new possibilities for TCM, enabling users to enjoy a more realistic, comfortable, and personalized massage experience at home. Meanwhile, AR technology can also provide users with more accurate disease diagnosis and health management, help users understand their own physical condition, and prevent the occurrence and development of diseases through massage health care. In addition, we compared the influence of video guidance, static guidance, and dynamic guidance in the AR massage learning environment through experiments and emphasized the excellent performance of dynamic guidance in massage gesture restoration and the sensitivity of virtual and real combinations. The results of this study provide new ideas and methods for the learning and practice of TCM, and also provide useful references for the practical application of AR technology in the medical field.

Keywords: Augmented Reality · Traditional Chinese Massage · Health care education · Dynamic Guidance

1 Introduction

1.1 AR: Transforming Healthcare Learning and Practice with Massage

Augmented Reality (AR) is one of the outstanding immersive experiences of the 21st century, narrowing the distance between scenarios and experiences. Kipper

N. A. Streitz and S. Konomi (Eds.): HCII 2024, LNCS 14719, pp. 116–135, 2024.
https://doi.org/10.1007/978-3-031-60012-8_8

and Rampolla [1] define Augmented Reality (AR) as the fusion of the real world and digital information. AR technology has triggered a profound transformation in multiple fields, including industries such as health and medicine, education and learning, tourism, design, and manufacturing. The rapid development of these fields has driven the widespread application and growth of AR technology in an unprecedented way [2,3]. Among them, embedding virtual learning and practical experience into the real physical environment is a major attempt provided by AR in the healthcare field. Although AR lacks a theoretical framework in the real healthcare field and is in its early stages, it has great potential in promoting healthcare learning and practice [4]. For example, AR has been used for interdisciplinary education and training purposes in formal and informal environments [5–7], and has been proven to have a lot of functional support in learning and practical scenarios [8–10].

1.2   AR-Enhanced Traditional Chinese Massage

Through literature research, we found that medical training and simulation, practical tools for healthcare, real-time feedback, and patient communication are more commonly used in the field of medical learning and practice, but massage is rarely used. However, massage is an effective method for relieving physical and mental stress and promoting functional regulation in healthcare practice. Therefore, we conducted pre-research interviews on traditional Chinese massage (TCM) and found that most users lack confidence in their own health status, and most users are interested in TCM but do not have a basic understanding of its concept.

At the same time, we also note that traditional learning materials often fail to attract people's attention to the learning process of physical health, which makes it relatively difficult to transfer knowledge of physical health [11]. In the current digital age, AR seems to be an ideal Application Area for providing dynamic guidance and massage learning practices, which can well combine spatial perception and natural interaction.

On the other hand, we observe that there is a lack of relevant teaching practice and interactive experience in the field of AR massage, which leads to users' difficulty in forming a real and interesting experience in the process of learning and preliminary practice of TCM, thus limiting users' active learning and practice of physical health.

Therefore, to better combine the practice of traditional Chinese massage with an AR immersive experience so that everyone can immerse themselves in learning and experiencing massage in a personal environment, we have designed a traditional Chinese massage experience design based on augmented reality. Based on TCM, this article aims to expand the TCM scene, advocate the continuity of TCM, and enrich the extension of personalized experience and diagnosis of TCM diseases through observation, listening, questioning, and palpation. By creating a massage experience under augmented reality, we enable individual users to self-diagnose and treat their diseases in a home environment; AI intelligently provides TCM plans, immerses themselves in massage experience or learning massage, shares massage data, etc. We created this AR experience to provide a reference framework that combines TCM learning with AR, provides continuous cross-time and space massage therapy and personalized experience for the home environment, reduces the learning cost and difficulty of TCM, and creates a multi-sensory experience of real-life and virtual environments.

2   Related Works

2.1   AR Traditional Chinese Massage Research

The use of VAMR technology to guide medical education has been a long-term research topic at home and abroad. VAMR enables learners to immerse themselves in clinical experiences in controllable contexts [11]. The application of AR in medical education is especially reflected in the ability to register imaging results and organ 3D models into real environments, providing more visual and interactive effects [12]. AR has good practical significance in promoting medical education and practice. Compared with traditional teaching methods, it is more intuitive and effective and can effectively avoid unexpected errors caused by lack of prior experience [11]. Chen M. designed and developed the application AnatoView, proving that the visual-spatial cognition required for medical understanding provided by AR can provide an efficient learning supplement for non-medical professionals [13]. Jose Gutierrez-Maldonado effectively improved the therapeutic effect of Anorexia nervosa (AN) by using VR-based body exposure therapy {a virtual reality-based body exposure therapy}. The experiential learning practice environment provided by AR applications can help medical learning and practice and promote learning rehabilitation. These necessary practical abilities are difficult to obtain from books, teaching courses, or two-dimensional multimedia (such as video) [15].

The teaching and practice of TCM should have strong skills, operability, practicality [15], and personalized experience [16]. Therefore, it is necessary to combine the learning of TCM with practice, and it is necessary to cooperate with new technologies and equipment to achieve more efficient future development and subjective initiative of practice. Shen Mingqiu and others proposed the use of simulated patients in massage teaching, effectively combining massage theory, technique training, and clinical application to cultivate students' ability to apply massage techniques [17]. Ding Yuxin and others proposed the massage training method of simulating clinical diagnosis and treatment, which greatly improved students' interest in massage techniques and participation in clinical practice and effectively improved the enthusiasm and learning efficiency of massage learners [15]. In the past, most of the research on TCM teaching tended to explore the practical level, effectively changing the phenomenon of simple book learning DE and effectively reinforcing learners' general clinical capabilities. However, the learning of TCM is more systematic, the learning cycle is longer, and the difficulty of getting started is greater, so it is difficult for ordinary people to get started with TCM only through books.

Combining TCM teaching with practical experience, improving learning efficiency, and further enhancing the massage experience of service recipients is still a challenging task. With the continuous development of various smart devices, such as smartphones and VAMR technology, there have been many explorations for the combination of TCM and smart devices. Taking Taiwan's Mei-Ting Su and others as examples [18], they used mobile-end AR technology to conduct research on the combination of intelligent devices for traditional Chinese massage. Their application not only recorded the acupoint pressing situation to provide users with medical information but also designed acupoint knowledge games to provide users with a more effective experience and acupoint knowledge education. Kuang Rongxin achieved intelligent calibration of back acupoints through algorithms, providing support for the subsequent design of traditional Chinese massage based on smart devices [19]. However, there are some shortcomings in the previous cases of combining TCM with smart devices. Based on smartphone devices, TCM massage is difficult to provide an immersive experience; the treatment course, as an important theory of massage, is difficult to effectively integrate into TCM combined with smart devices. The lack of this concept directly affects the therapeutic effect of traditional Chinese massage [20] In addition, current research based on smart devices has not effectively combined the theoretical content of TCM with practice. Although users can locate acupoints through smart devices and understand the targeted massage of acupoints, there is no concrete and effective explanation for common techniques such as pressing, pointing, pushing, and grabbing in TCM. This may make it difficult for users to understand and experience the characteristics of different techniques. Therefore, how to better integrate the theoretical concepts of TCM with the spatial perception and natural interaction of augmented reality (AR) experience to create a seamless learning environment is still an urgent research field that needs to be filled.

2.2 Practice Strategy

In order to solve these problems, this study aims to innovatively integrate TCM theory with practical operation, combined with AR technology, to provide richer and more intuitive learning and practical experience. By designing immersive smart device applications, we will focus on the integration of treatment theory to improve the efficacy of TCM. In addition, we will focus on concretizing the characteristics of TCM techniques so that users can effectively understand and experience different techniques in the massage process. Through this innovative combination, we expect to provide users with a more comprehensive and in-depth learning experience of TCM and promote the improvement of overall health concepts.

In our design, considering the limitations of mobile end devices AR, we turned to virtual reality Head-Mounted Display (HMD) technology to better achieve our design goals. HMD technology provides users with a more realistic experience in a computer-created virtual environment, with more natural interaction patterns and superior information layout. This technology can bring users a more immersive feeling [21]. However, in the process of creating personalized and specialized massage practices, we must carefully design how to cleverly integrate the learning methods of TCM into HMD technology in order to present the theme accurately and realistically. As previous studies have pointed out, the experience in AR is subjective, while the training process of therapeutic massage is highly variable [16]. In this context, we designed and preliminarily implemented an AR practice and experience framework based on TCM concepts, allowing users to personalize massage experiences at home. Our goal is to further explore and evaluate the feasibility and effectiveness of this attempt in learning and practicing massage concepts, providing a conceptual framework for subsequent design.

3   Application of Traditional Chinese Massage in Sub-health Management

Sub-health state refers to a state between health and disease, also known as the third state. Since it can be transformed into health or disease, it is often referred to as the "gray state," "pre-disease state," or "sub-clinical stage." Stage ". This includes no clinical symptoms or symptoms that feel mild, but there is an underlying pathological state [22]. According to a set of data published by the World Health Organization, the number of people in sub-health in China accounts for 70% of the total population, which means that more than 900 million people are in sub-health state. Shoulder, neck, and lumbar spine pain plague many office workers. There is no clear qualitative diagnosis of the disease and no abnormality in laboratory tests for such symptoms. Therefore, it is difficult for Western medicine to use specific methods or drugs for targeted Western medicine treatment. Therefore, more and more people Therefore, more and more people tend to seek traditional Chinese medicine (traditional Chinese medicine) treatment. Traditional Chinese medicine believes that a sub-health state is similar to" weakness. " Su Wen (220-211 BC, Han Dynasty) said:" If the soul is gone, the body is weak " [23]. As early as in "Nine Notes on the Year of Extension" (1636-1912 AD, Qing Dynasty), it is recorded that massage of the abdomen can supplement the body's abdominal massage can supplement the body's deficiencies, excrete waste from the body, and may also increase lifespan. Syndrome differentiation and treatment (the basic principle of Chinese medicine for understanding and treating diseases) means that the doctor records the patient's medical history, symptoms, and other clinical data. Diagnosis and diagnosis of diseases through the four methods of Chinese medicine (looking, smelling, asking, cutting) are used to analyze and determine treatment plans [24,25]. It closely follows the main pathogenesis of the disease, thus improving the clinical efficacy. Chinese medicine massage stimulates acupoints on the surface of the body through different techniques and conducts them to the relevant meridians and internal organs so as to achieve the therapeutic purpose [26]. The occurrence of physical sub-health is related to the dysfunction of the bladder meridian and viscera, and the bladder meridian is closely related to the viscera [27,28]. Pang Jie and other studies have found that massage therapy has a satisfactory clinical effect on the treatment of physical pain in sub-healthy people. They believe that massage can stimulate the human meridians to a certain extent through a variety of techniques, thereby reflexively stimulating the body's local and systemic responses [29]. Therefore, massage can dredge the meridians and promote qi and blood circulation, thereby relieving and eliminating pain. Therefore, massage therapy positively affects human sub-health pain [30]. Traditional Chinese medicine massage gives sub-healthy people another possibility, adjusting the overall balance of the body through non-invasive natural therapies to prevent diseases rather than just targeting specific symptoms or diseases, which gives it unique advantages in modern health management. In addition, traditional Chinese medicine massage provides personalized diagnoses according to the individual's physique and condition and treats them step by step according to the course of treatment, which can better prevent diseases in a targeted manner. "AR traditional Chinese massage" aims to incorporate traditional Chinese massage into people's daily health management. Through reasonable massage guidelines, personalized diagnosis and treatment, and course management, it can improve the cervical and lumbar spine and other diseases caused by sub-health.

4   Methods

Past studies have indicated the highly variable nature of the therapeutic massage training process, coupled with the subjective nature of the augmented reality (AR) experience for individuals. Concurrently, there is a discernible rationality and commonality in the interface design specifications of AR and the experiential processes associated with Traditional Chinese Medicine (TCM) massage. Consequently, our research approach involves a combination of qualitative and quantitative methods. Through in-depth interviews, we aim to gain a profound understanding of user perspectives, swiftly acquire pertinent information and dynamics, and augment sample size through questionnaire administration. This multifaceted methodology aims to identify commonalities and establish quantitative standards for design. By doing so, we mitigate the inherent subjectivity in interviews and reduce sample selection bias to a certain extent, thereby providing valuable guidance for subsequent phases of quantitative research and questionnaire design.

4.1   Interview Research

Participants were selectively engaged in preliminary interviews to validate their alignment with the specified target demographic for this study, comprising users aged 18 to 55. Their diverse experiences were categorized into four distinct groups: individuals with AR exposure but lacking massage experience; those with both AR and massage experiences; individuals devoid of AR exposure but unfamiliar with massage; and participants lacking AR exposure but possessing massage experience. Furthermore, participants were stratified into two subgroups based on their level of massage experience: novices and moderate users.

In addition to the aforementioned groups, an individual with extensive AR experience and a professional in Traditional Chinese Medicine (TCM) was enlisted for interviews, both of whom subsequently disclosed limited AR exposure and were excluded from further classification. The surveyed cohort consisted of six participants, all falling within the age range of 24 to 35.

Interview Preparation. We finalized the preparation and user recruitment process by October 19, 2023, utilizing a combination of semi-structured and situational interviews. User interviews were conducted on October 20 and 21, with the analysis of interview results commencing on October 22. Our research focused on the following interview outline.

- Introduction to Massage Experience: Delve into participants' past massage experiences, including aspects such as frequency, location, and overall satisfaction. Massage Expectations and Ideals: Gain insights into their expectations for an ideal massage, considering any distinctive needs or preferences they may have. Pain Point Discussion: Explore potential pain points users might encounter during the massage experience, covering aspects such as appointment challenges, service quality, etc.
- User Behavior Focus. Daily Massage Behavior: Examine users' routine massage practices, encompassing considerations such as the selection of massage time and duration. Behavioral Emphasis: Delve into the specific aspects that users prioritize during the massage process, potentially including factors like comfort levels and the proficiency of the massage technician.
- AR Massage Cognition and Interest. AR Technology Awareness: Evaluate the user's comprehension of AR technology, including whether they have prior experience with AR applications. AR Massage Interest: Investigate the user's level of interest in AR-enhanced massage, gauging their willingness to experiment with it and exploring their expectations regarding the transformative potential of AR in the realm of massage.
- Future Vision of AR Massage. AR Cognitive Landscape: Evaluate the user's cognitive proficiency in AR technology, discerning any positive or negative perspectives they may hold. Anticipated AR Massage Experience: Elicit the user's envisaged future of AR-enhanced massage, exploring their expectations regarding how AR could potentially address existing challenges or introduce novel experiential dimensions.

Interview Conclusion. After conducting in-depth user interviews, we have acquired valuable insights into the nuances of the massage experience, levels of AR technology awareness, and user expectations. The following outlines key questions posed during the interviews and highlights the anticipated benefits and expectations associated with the integration of AR technology with massage:

- Personalized Massage Experience: Users anticipate that AR technology will deliver personalized massage plans tailored to individual physical conditions and preferences.

- Real-time Feedback: Users expect AR to provide instantaneous feedback on the massage's effectiveness, aiding in a better understanding of the overall impact of the massage.
- Immersive Experience: Users express a desire for AR-enhanced massages to provide a heightened, immersive experience, enabling them to enjoy professional massage services within their homes.
- item Pain Points: Several users have encountered pain points, including issues related to inconsistent service quality and massage intensity falling short of expectations.

5   Questionnaire Survey

5.1   Questionnaire Design and Collection

In this study, a questionnaire was designed in combination with the findings of the above interview study and filled out on the online platform to deepen the target users through the questionnaire to understand the users' real thoughts, psychological state, the degree of understanding of Chinese massage and the psychological expectations of the AR experience. In the end, 243 valid questionnaires were obtained, of which men and women basically accounted for half each; among them, 35.72% were aged between 18 and 25, 23.15% were aged between 26 and 30, 18.73% were aged between 31 and 40, and 22.4% were aged over 41.

5.2   Questionnaire Data Analysis

Through Data Analysis, it was found that the people interested in AR traditional Chinese massage are mainly concentrated in the middle-aged and middle-aged groups, with fixed jobs or studies, sub-health with a large proportion (74.5% of self-evaluated people believe that they are in sub-health or lower health levels), 78.2% of people often feel back pain, waist pain, and neck pain, but there is no good treatment method. Data Analysis found that most people believe that regular massage helps maintain physical and mental health. They go for massage 1–2 times a year on average and do not pay much attention to the massage techniques. The professionalism of the massage, the creation of the massage environment, and the price are the main issues they consider. 54.5% of people who go for massages basically focus on shoulder and waist massages, and 35.1% choose full-body massages. They do not resist AR massage but doubt its effectiveness. If there is AR massage, they think it will be cheaper and more convenient, and the scenario is not limited; real-time physiological detection and periodic data feedback make them feel that the massage is more targeted. 27.19% of people In addition, the survey results also showed that the main motivation for customer engagement in massage is to relieve physical discomfort (65.77%); the rest believe that massage can relieve stress and relax (Fig. 1).

Question : The most appealing feature of the combination of AR and massage may be? [multiple choice]

options	sub-total	Proportion	
massage guide	190		78.4%
convenience	158		64.9%
Symptomatic treatment	129		53.3%
Interactive experience	94		38.7%
cheap	72		29.5%

Fig. 1. AR and massage combination characteristics

5.3   Findings

Based on interview findings, we formulated targeted questions related to users' concerns, expectations, and pain points, offering valuable insights for subsequent questionnaire surveys. User expectations for massage center around personalized experiences, appointment problem resolution, real-time feedback, and an immersive encounter. Regarding the integration of AR with massage, personalized experiences, real-time feedback, and appointment problem resolution are common user focal points.

A subsequent questionnaire survey deepened our understanding of the Target User group. Analysis of the data revealed that middle-aged and young individuals, constituting a significant portion of the sub-health state, are particularly interested in AR traditional Chinese massage. Users primarily seek massage to alleviate physical discomfort, displaying a general skepticism towards AR massage. However, users anticipate AR massage to bring convenience, real-time physiological detection, and periodic data feedback, believing these aspects enhance the relevance and efficacy of massage. Simultaneously, users' recognition of AR massage fostering parent-child relationships has garnered attention.

6   Experiment

The experiment aims to systematically explore the potential impact of different augmented reality (AR) operation guidance methods on massage learning efficiency. In particular, we will focus on comparing the effects of video guidance, static guidance, and dynamic guidance in learning massage techniques in order to deeply understand the unique impact of each guidance method on learners' learning outcomes. Through this study, we pursue the following objectives: to evaluate the differences in learning effects of different AR operation guidance methods in massage learning, aiming to identify the most effective guidance methods for learners to quickly master massage skills. To deeply analyze the changing trends of learning efficiency under different guidance methods in order to fully understand the advantages and limitations of each guidance method. Finally, to provide empirical research support for the design of AR operation guidance massage skills and to provide targeted guidance for technical improvement and educational design in related fields.

6.1 Participants and Devices

(1) Participants. In order to ensure the scientificity and effectiveness of the experiment, we will recruit experimental participants with the following characteristics and use specific equipment for the experiment: Recruitment criteria for experimental participants: We are recruiting adult participants with a strong interest in the field of massage learning, especially users with the following characteristics:

1. Massage experience: Participants need to have a beginner's level of basic massage skills, but no experience as a professional masseur is required.
2. Health status: Participants should have good physical health to ensure that they can complete the massage learning tasks in the experiment.
3. Normal vision: Since the experiment involves visual guidance, participants should have normal vision to ensure a clear perception of the AR-guided interface.

A total of 8 customers engaged in this experiment. The users were 4 males and 4 females, aged between 22 and 26, with an average age of 23.85 years (SD = 1.55). All participants had visual acuity or corrected visual acuity above 5.0 and no color blindness or color weakness. Among them, 3 participants had never used AR devices, and the remaining participants had a basic knowledge of AR devices. The experimental environment is built in Unity 3D. AR devices are used to intervene, and the guidance method is applied to the front of the helmet so that participants can see different guidance methods in AR and enhance perceptual learning. Other experimental equipment includes a set of camera equipment with recording and video functions. The experimenters are one recorder/host and one operator.

(2) Equipment. The experiment will be conducted on equipment with the following technical configurations: AR Devices (Quest Pro): The experiment will use AR-enabled head-mounted display devices, such as AR glasses, to provide participants with an immersive learning environment. By recruiting participants who meet the above conditions and providing corresponding AR devices, we will be able to obtain high-quality data in the experiment to more comprehensively understand the impact of different AR operation guidance methods on massage learning efficiency. In addition, filling out the subjective scoring questionnaire will provide learners with subjective feelings and experiences for the study, thereby providing a more comprehensive interpretation of the experimental results. This helps to make the experiment scientific and the results reliable.

6.2 Experimental Procedure

The experiment consists of a practice phase and a testing phase. During the experiment, participants were asked to wear AR devices for operation. During the practice phase, participants were first taught how to recognize guidance information. During the experimental phase of the subjects, each participant was asked to complete four types of massage gestures under four types of guidance information: 1. Press method: Use the palm root, thumb root, or elbow tip to focus on the surgical site and press vertically downward. 2. Finger kneading method: Use the fingertips to focus on acupoints for circular kneading, which is used for various parts of the body. 3. Finger-pushing method: Use the fingers to focus on the surgical site and push in a straight line in one direction, which is used for tendons. 4. Thumb partial pushing method: Place the radial sides of both thumbs on the forehead and push from the midline of the forehead to both sides. The order of the four gestures in each type of guidance information test is random.

Experimental Phase

1. Participants put on AR devices.
2. Under different types of guidance information, including pressing, finger rubbing, finger pushing, and thumb pushing, experiments were conducted with four massage gestures.
3. In each test type, the gesture prototype guidance video was displayed in the left window for 5 s, then disappeared, and the participants restored the same massage gesture based on the prompts in the right gesture area.
4. In each type of guidance information test, the order of the four gestures is random.
5. The average duration of the experiment was 30 min.
6. At the same time, the recorder recorded the experiment through audio and video equipment.

Experimental analysis was conducted using the four main massage gestures in traditional Chinese massage as examples. The experimental design was divided into four guidance methods: video guidance, static guidance, and dynamic guidance. 1. Press method: Use the palm root, thumb root, or elbow tip to focus on the surgical site and press vertically downward. 2. Finger kneading method: Use the fingertips to focus on acupoints for circular kneading, which is used for various parts of the body. 3. Finger-pushing method: Use the fingertips to focus on the surgical site and push in a single direction in a straight line, which is used for tendons. 4. Thumb partial pushing method: Place the radial sides of both thumbs on the forehead and push from the midline of the forehead to both sides. After the experiment, participants will fill out a questionnaire based on cognitive load, which refers to questionnaires designed by Hart [31] and Hwang [32]. The questionnaire will self-evaluate the participants' massage learning efficiency and score them on a five-point scale (5 represents the highest preference, 1 represents the lowest preference) (Table 1).

Table 1. Questionnaire

ID	Question
Perceived Usefulness	
Q1	It enables me to complete experimental tasks faster
Q2	It can improve my experimental efficiency
Q3	Overall, this is very useful to me
Perceived Ease of Use	
Q4	It takes a short time to understand the information conveyed
Q5	It is clear and easy to understand
Q6	It's easy to use this method for AR massage
Satisfaction	
Q7	I will recommend this method to others in the future
Q8	I feel satisfied using this method to complete experimental tasks
Q9	The method creates a pleasant interactive experience for me
Cognitive Load	
Q10	I have invested a lot of energy
Q11	I have put in a lot of psychological effort
Q12	It's easy to use this method for AR massage
Q13	I put in a lot of mental labor
Q14	Overall, the method to complete tasks is difficult for me

6.3   Results

Eye Movement Data. In this experiment, the evaluation indicators of eye movement data, such as heat map and annotation duration, were moved to the AR device through Quest Pro, realizing the function of obtaining eye movement data in real-time during the process of learning to use AR while operating, reducing the input of other devices and the limitations of AR devices, making the experimental data more intuitive to obtain feedback.

Questionnaire. Referring to Scholar Chen Chen's "Research on the Impact of Interaction Patterns on Learning Experience in Immersive Virtual Experimental Environments," we used seven indicators, including perceived usefulness, perceived ease of use, willingness to continue using, satisfaction, comfort, presence, self-awareness, and cognitive load, as indicators to evaluate personal massage learning efficiency, which can reflect users' learning situation to a certain extent.

6.4   Data Analysis

Eye Movement Data Results. Through feedback analysis of the eye movement heat map, video guidance shows an obvious visual focus on the video area. According to feature analysis, video guidance presents the characteristics of blurred focus and poor immersive experience, which may be related to its fixed content display and information transmission. In contrast, in static guidance, users mainly focus on operation and attempt after the first viewing. However, due to its static nature, users are often prone to errors in actual attempts. In contrast, dynamic guidance presents the left and right switching of user per-spectives, which is a dynamic and coherent immersive learning process. This dynamic nature may help improve the learning effect. By continuously learn-ing and adjusting the perspective, users can more comprehensively understand and restore massage gestures. Therefore, the results of the analysis of the eye movement heat map reveal significant differences in user focus distribution and learning experience between different guidance methods, providing important visual learning references for optimizing AR massage guidance systems. (See Fig. 2)

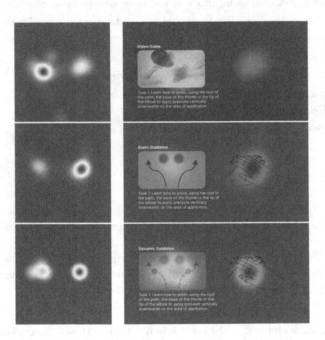

Fig. 2. Eye Movement Heatmaps of Three Guidance Methods

Questionnaire Results. The questionnaire results reveal significant distinc-tions among different teaching environments, particularly in terms of perceived usefulness, perceived ease of use, willingness to continue usage, satisfaction, com-fort, presence, self-awareness, and cognitive load. Regarding perceived usefulness, participants widely perceive dynamic teaching environments as providing a more effective learning experience, making knowledge acquisition more intuitive and engaging. Furthermore, data on perceived ease of use indicates that dynamic teaching environments operate more smoothly and are user-friendly, facilitating learners in grasping teaching content more effortlessly. Additionally, dynamic teaching environments demonstrate notable advantages in comfort, presence, self-awareness, and cognitive load. Learners generally experience comfort in this environment and a heightened sense of presence during the learning process, fostering increased engagement in learning activities. Results related to self-awareness indicate that dynamic teaching environments contribute to learners establishing a positive perception of their own learning abilities. Lastly, cognitive load data shows that dynamic teaching environments effectively reduce cognitive load during the learning process, making it easier for learners to comprehend and absorb teaching content. (See Fig. 3.)

Fig. 3. Visualization of Questionnaire Result

6.5   Findings

The research results clearly demonstrate the outstanding performance of dynamic guidance in the AR massage learning environment. This guidance method has achieved significant results in the restoration of massage gestures, with strong sensory power combining virtual and reality, and participants have given high recognition in self-evaluation. In addition, the experimental duration under dynamic guidance conditions is relatively short, indicating that it reduces cognitive load while improving learning efficiency. In contrast, the effects of video guidance and static guidance are average, especially in terms of discomfort and discomfort caused by video guidance, while static guidance leads to a significant increase in cognitive load. These results emphasize the importance of dynamic guidance in AR massage learning design. Further research and improvement should focus on providing more vivid and intuitive guidance information to optimize learning effects and enhance User Experience. These findings provide useful guidance for the future design and practical application of AR massage guidance systems.

7   Concept Design and Interaction Process

7.1   Theoretical Frameworks

This study proposes an AR-based framework for TCM massage, aiming to enhance teaching efficiency and clinical execution. The framework employs 3D dynamic guidance through AR technology, improving learning efficiency and operational accuracy. An integrated information assistance system includes a TCM knowledge base, real-time feedback, and patient session management. This supports theoretical guidance, operational improvement, and long-term treatment tracking, transforming the massage learning process. The framework modernizes Chinese massage education by improving efficiency and introducing innovative teaching methods.

The massage framework is subdivided into user-side and massaged-side experiences. The user-side includes identification, learning, 3D dynamic guidance, real-time feedback, and data visualization. The massaged-side includes body diagnosis, massage program recommendation, real-time feedback, and health status recording. This structure integrates both experiences into the traditional Chinese AR massage framework, providing a personalized service. Users assess massage learning and practice through the AR application, facilitating skill exchange and enhancement. Overall, this framework integrates traditional massage with modern technology, offering a comprehensive and intelligent massage service for users and recipients, promoting innovation in the massage field.

Based on technical analysis pertaining to augmented reality (AR), we developed a TCM and interaction design utilizing AR technology. This design aims to address the client base's requirements for alleviating physical discomfort through a convenient, periodic, and personalized massage experience. Firstly, we used AR technology to display the massage route and acupoints, allowing users to massage themselves or ask others to massage, saving time and cost and increasing autonomy and participation. Secondly, we customized the massage course for users, and users can view and adjust it with AR devices. Finally, we collected user data and feedback, provided a personalized massage experience, and analyzed the physical condition and massage effect. Based on the above content, we summarized the design content into three innovative points: AR massage route guidance, treatment course, personalized experience, and disease diagnosis. The experience process is shown in the Fig. 4.

7.2   AR Massage Route Guide

In the past, users could only learn massage techniques by watching instructional videos online or making appointments with offline stores to seek massage experiences. Complex massage techniques and multi-step massage methods often make it difficult for users who are learning massage for the first time. We use trained models to locate acupoints, present them on the user's back with AR, and guide the massage to complete various massage techniques with dynamic route guidance.

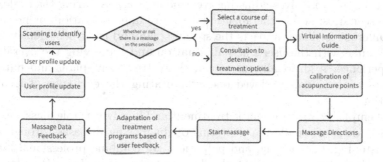

Fig. 4. Experience Process

Allow users to do real-time massages through AR without leaving home, obtain accurate guidance of massage points and massage paths, greatly improve the convenience of users' massages, and make the experience of home massage simpler, more accurate, and more efficient (Figs. 5 and 6).

Fig. 5. Acupuncture Points and Massage Path Guidelines

Fig. 6. Massage Data Feedback

7.3   Course of Treatment

In the massage process, we employ three treatment plan allocation mechanisms to focus on effective treatment.

The first plan determines the periodic massage schedule based on the patient's condition, onset duration, and therapeutic outcomes. Personalized and continuous treatment is achieved through real-time monitoring and comparison with a large model database. This ensures a dynamically controlled treatment plan that caters to individual patient needs.

The second plan involves adjusting the treatment based on user feedback. Users provide input on their sensitivity to massage, post-treatment responses, and overall efficacy. This feedback influences changes in the entire treatment plan, making it more adaptable to evolving physical conditions and enhancing effectiveness.

The third plan involves adjusting treatment progress during the cycle based on three scenarios: stable therapeutic effect, gradual stagnation, or no obvious effect. Different feedback impacts the specific plan and treatment density, aligning the course with the user's actual situation and improving the overall massage experience. Additionally, users can share treatment plans and data with healthcare professionals or loved ones, facilitating the exchange of treatment information.

TCM emphasizes symptomatic treatment and highly variable massage, which is another focus of our design. In terms of diagnosing diseases through observation, listening, questioning, and palpation, we combine professional massage books and large language model technology to form a Knowledge Base for TCM. Through user self-feedback information, we convert user demands into text in formation and extract keywords. By matching user demands with symptoms in the Knowledge Base, we can infer the user's physical health problems and recommend corresponding acupoint massage plans. This targeted therapy plan can not only improve our soothing of the body and the treatment of the disease but also enhance our immersion in communicating with Chinese masseurs and constructing a massage context. The diagnosis and treatment of the disease are shown in Fig. 8. (Figs. 7 and 9).

Fig. 8. Diagnosis and Scheme Selection

Fig. 7. Massage Treatment Information

Fig. 9. Adjustment Massage Program

To accommodate the dynamic nature of therapeutic massage, we designed an interactive display for massage content. Users can easily add, delete, adjust duration, and change the massage order. Through component design and wake-up menus, users actively interact with the environment, enabling them to tailor the massage plan for a more comfortable experience. This fosters a stronger connection between the user and the person receiving the massage, leading to a personalized and detailed experience. For instance, if the user receives positive feedback on waist massage comfort, they can simply press a button to extend the duration on the waist. This personalized experience is reflected in personal data, providing detailed insights into health parameters, massage progress, and feedback for each session, ultimately delivering a more immersive and professional massage experience.

8   Conclusion

This study aims to explore the theoretical principles of TCM and the integration of spatial cognition and natural interaction of augmented reality (AR) experience in order to construct a new massage and AR combination framework and fill the gap in the research field of AR traditional Chinese massage. Based on the design goal of better combining TCM practice with AR immersive experience, the study realizes the client base's needs for relieving physical discomfort and convenience, periodicity, and personalized massage, and summarizes solutions including AR massage route guidance, personalized experience, and disease diagnosis.

The project hopes that AR technology can combine the virtual information of TCM with the real environment to create a new interaction mode. Using Big data technology can provide users with more accurate diagnosis and health management, help users understand their own physical condition, prevent the occurrence and development of diseases through massage health care, and provide data support for the scientific and standardized customization of TCM. AR technology can show users the relevant knowledge, skills, cases, etc., of TCM so that users can feel the charm and cultural connotation of TCM. At the same time, through AR technology, every user can become a professional masseur, provide users with a more real massage experience, and improve user experience and satisfaction. At the same time, the experiment verified that the dynamic guidance method achieved remarkable results in the reduction effect of massage gestures, the combination of virtual and reality was strong, and the participants gave high recognition in self-evaluation.

Currently, there are still some shortcomings in our design. Massage intensity is an important point in TCM. However, there is insufficient interaction in the feedback of massage intensity, which cannot reflect the characteristics of TCM very well. At the same time, we did not do popular adaptation research after discussing and solving the problem. We only proposed a theoretical framework for acupoint calibration and dynamic guidance. In the future, we will conduct in-depth classification and discrimination research on this.

References

1. Kipper, G., Rampolla, J.: Augmented Reality: An Emerging Technologies to Guide AR. Elsevier, Waltham (2013)
2. Berciu, A.G., Dulf, E.H., Stefan, I.A.: Flexible augmented reality-based health solution for medication weight establishment. Processes **10**, 219 (2022)
3. Sırakaya, M., Alsancak Sırakaya, D.: Augmented reality in STEM education: a systematic review. Interact. Learn. Environ. **30**, 1556–1569 (2022)
4. Zhu, E., Hadadgar, A., Masiello, I., et al.: Augmented reality in healthcare education: an integrative review. PeerJ **2**, e469 (2014)
5. Laine, T.H.: Educational mobile augmented reality games: a systematic literature review and two case studies. Computers **7**, 28 (2018)
6. Bacca, J., Baldiris, S., Fabregat, R., Graf, S., Kinshuk, D.: Augmented reality trends in education: a systematic review of research and applications. Educ. Technol. Soc. **17**, 133–149 (2014)
7. Lee, B.K.: Augmented reality in education and training. TechTrends **56**, 13–21 (2012)
8. Dunleavy, M., Dede, C.: Augmented reality teaching and learning. In: Spector, J.M., Merrill, M.D., Elen, J., Bishop, M.J. (eds.) Handbook of Research on Educational Communications and Technology, pp. 735–745. Springer, New York (2014). https://doi.org/10.1007/978-1-4614-3185-5_59
9. Cheng, K.-H., Tsai, C.-C.: Affordances of augmented reality in science learning: suggestions for future research. J. Sci. Educ. Technol. **22**, 449–462 (2013)
10. Nielsen, B.L., Brandt, H., Swensen, H.: Augmented reality in science education-affordances for student learning. Nord. Stud. Sci. Educ. **12**, 157–174 (2016)
11. Yingjie, L.: A systematic review of AR application in medical and health education. Comput. Knowl. Technol. **19**(24), 123–126 (2023). https://doi.org/10.14004/j.cnki.ckt.2023.1289
12. Luo, W., Shi, C., Hui, P.: Application of augmented reality technology in clinical medical education. Basic Med. Clin. **40**(02), 270–273 (2020). https://doi.org/10.16352/j.issn.1001-6325.2020.02.028
13. Chen, M.: AnatoView: using interactive 3D visualizations with augmented reality support for laypersons' medical education in informed consent processes. [Order No. 30974722]. Dartmouth College (2023)
14. Gutierrez-Maldonado, J., et al.: Treatment of anorexia nervosa through virtual reality-based body exposure and reduction of attentional bias. In: Chen, J.Y.C., Fragomeni, G. (eds.) Virtual, Augmented and Mixed Reality. HCII 2023 (2023)
15. Ding, Y., Song, Z., Gao, L., et al.: Some thoughts on the practical teaching of Tuina techniques . Think Tank Times **31**, 205–207 (2019)
16. Porcino, A.J., Boon, H.S., Page, S.A., et al.: Meaning and challenges in the practice of multiple therapeutic massage modalities: a combined methods study. BMC Complement. Altern. Med. **11**, 75 (2011)
17. Mingqiu, S., Junchang, L., Xinwen, M., et al.: Comparison of differences in students' mastery of massage techniques under different teaching methods. Xinjiang Tradit. Chin. Med. **41**(05), 64–67 (2023)
18. Su, M.T., Chiang, M.L., Tsai, C.H., et al.: An acupoint health care system with real-time acupoint localization and visualization in augmented reality. Multimedia Syst. **29**, 1–22 (2023). https://doi.org/10.1007/s00530-023-01104-y
19. Rongxin, K.: Recognition and localization of human back acupoints based on Deep learning. Nanchang University (2023). https://doi.org/10.27232/d.cnki.gnchu.2022.001804

20. Dong X.: A brief discussion on the treatment course in clinical massage therapy. Massage Guidance **05**, 40–41 (1994). https://doi.org/10.19787/j.issn.1008-18791994.05.027
21. Koinuma, Y., Miyamoto, K., Ohkura, M.: Experimental evaluation of immersive feeling in VR System with HMD. In: Kurosu, M. (eds.) Human-Computer Interaction. Interaction Contexts. HCI (2017)
22. Zhao, R.Q., Feng, J.: Research progress and comparative analysis of subhealth problems at home and abroad. Foreign Med. Inform. **23**, 325 (2016)
23. Liu, S.Y.: Huangdineijing·Suwen. People's Medical Publishing House, Beijing (1982)
24. Xie, J., Wang, D., Peng, J., et al.: A preliminary study on the characteristics of conceptual metaphor in TCM from the perspective of cognition. Asia Pacific TraditMed **14**, 71–72 (2018)
25. Zhang, Y.P., Yin, Y.F.: Interpretation of the concept of "syndrome differentiation" in TCM. Chin. J. Basic Med. Tradit. Chin. Med. **24**(1352–1353), 1362 (2018)
26. Li, Y.H., Zhang, G.Z., Kang, R.Z., et al.: A clinical study on the treatment of painful subhealth condition with back scrapping combined with acupuncture. Chin. J. Basic Med. Tradit. Chin. Med. **19**, 555–556 (2013)
27. Deng, X.G., Li, Y.P., Sun, X.M., et al.: Clinical study on the treatment of subhealth fatigue of radiologists with Bushenjianpi decoction. J. Guangzhou Univ. Tradit. Chin. Med. **31**, 735–738 (2014)
28. Zou, Y.X., Liu, Y.X., Zhou, Y., et al.: Effects of cordyceps sinensis oral liquid on subhealth fatigue. Mod. Prev. Med. **42**, 1199–1201 (2015)
29. Lei, J., Dong, Q.: Lingguibafa research and puncture on time. J. Internal Med. Chin. Med. **27**, 46–48 (2013)
30. Pang, J., Tang, H.L., Lei, L.M., et al.: Study on the effect of massage on pain subhealth of body. Liaoning J. Tradit. Chin. Med. **36**, 1500–1501 (2009)
31. Hart, S.G., Staveland, L.E.: Development of NASA-TLX (Task Load Index): results of empirical and theoretical research. Adv. Psychol. **52**, 139–183 (1988)
32. Hwang, G.J., Yang, L.H., Wang, S.Y.: A concept map-embedded educational computer game for improving students' learning performance in natural science courses. Comput. Educ. **69**, 121–130 (2013)

A Proposed Framework of Virtual Reality System Design for Neuroscience Education in Mental Health

Yuanyuan Xin⬛, Ruyang Wang⬛, Yi Liang⬛, Qianru Lu⬛, and Ning Zhang(✉)⬛

Beijing Normal University at Zhuhai, Zhuhai 519087, China
ningzhang@bnu.edu.cn

Abstract. [Background] Mental health problems are becoming increasingly common worldwide, yet public awareness and professional knowledge about mental health are at a low level. With the help of neuroscience research findings, people can understand mental health problems more clearly and accurately. However, neuroscience is time-costly for learners due to its professional complexity. Virtual reality (VR) technology, with the high level of visualization and strong interactivity, can provide an efficient learning environment for integrating neuroscience with mental health. [Methods] A literature review conducted using Web of Science revealed that such a VR system has not been developed. Utilizing Design Thinking Methodology, a framework of VR prototype for neuroscience education in mental health was proposed. This framework is designed to facilitate visualize and elucidate the brain mechanism and dynamic process under various mental health situations, offering interactive learning environment for learners and different users. [Conclusion] The research will facilitate the development of convenient and engaging VR tools from an interdisciplinary perspective for learners and practitioners in the field of mental health. The research suggests that utilizing VR technology is able to play an important role in addressing current societal issues in mental health.

Keywords: Virtual Reality · Neuroscience · Mental Health · Design Thinking Methodology

1 Introduction

Mental health issues have emerged as a global concern, with governments, educational institutions, and society organizations facing numerous challenges in addressing them. A key issue is the significant gap between the widespread occurrence of mental disorders and the limited mental health training provided to learners and educators. Studies revealed that most teachers have received minimal training in this area, highlighting the need for enhanced mental health related training for teachers [1, 2]. Additionally, there is a notable disparity in the rising prevalence of mental disorders compared to the slower advancements in professional level of mental health knowledge, particularly when compared with physical health field. For example, one study pointed out that the development

N. A. Streitz and S. Konomi (Eds.): HCII 2024, LNCS 14719, pp. 136–152, 2024.
https://doi.org/10.1007/978-3-031-60012-8_9

of training for mental health practitioners in evidence-based practices has not kept pace with the creation of related interventions [3]. Kilbourne (2018) further emphasized the urgent necessity for integrating different resources into mental health to better serve social needs [4]. Furthermore, the rapid evolution of mental health research across various disciplines underscores the importance of developing a multi-disciplinary mental health science education, enabling learners to gain more comprehensive and scientific understanding of the subject.

Neuroscience research has unveiled essential insights into the brain mechanisms underlying human development and various psychological disorders. The findings in neuroscience significantly can enhance understanding of mental health from neurobiological level, underscoring its importance in both therapeutic and educational contexts. For example, a study demonstrated that counselors employing neuroscience-informed cognitive-behavior-therapy (n-CBT) effectively reduced symptoms in clients, particularly those suffering from anxiety and depressive disorders [5]. In the realm of education, recent research discovered that programs combining neuroscience knowledge with mental health literacy substantially improved teachers' awareness of students' mental health challenges [6]. This awareness led to notable shifts in their attitudes and classroom practices. Additionally, neuroscience is able to play a pivotal role in shaping accurate perceptions of mental illness. It has been found that most professionals believe that neuroscience is instrumental in destigmatizing mental illness [7]. Therefore, it is beneficial to apply neuroscientific evidence to mental health field.

Despite the advantages of neuroscience in informing mental health education, its integration into this domain has been notably slow. For example, it is highlighted that a relatively small proportion of medical professionals and trainees have adequate neurological knowledge [7]. What impeded this integration can be largely attributed to the intrinsic complexity of neuroscience. The field spans a diverse array of topics, ranging from molecular to cognitive studies, necessitating an interdisciplinary approach. There is a risk that oversimplifying these intricate research findings could lead to a narrow, biologically-centric understanding among learners. Furthermore, the constantly changing field of neuroscience means students need to continuously use critical thinking to understand new findings. This complexity can be challenging for mental health education practitioners from diverse backgrounds such as psychology, social work, nursing, and education, which affects their motivation, interest, and learning efficiency when engaging with neuroscience concepts. The other challenge is the current state of neuroscience educational tools and resources, which predominantly consist of 2D books and videos, is ineffectively conveying this complex subject matter. Therefore, there is a pressing need to explore and develop innovative methods and resources that can more effectively support and enhance neuroscience education, specifically designed for the mental health.

It was stated that "VR is a powerful technology that promises to change our lives unlike any other", also lead a technological revolution in education [8]. VR technology offers numerous advantages, particularly in the realm of multidimensional spatial visualization. This feature is ideal for the learning of abstract and complex concepts and structures, as it reduces the difficulty and cognitive load associated with traditional learning methods [9]. When applied to neuroscience education, VR possibly provides realistic three-dimensional models of the brain, simulating and displaying key structures and their dynamic activities related to mental disorders, thus allowing students enhance their understanding of the relationships between various structures and functions.

Moreover, the interactivity feature of VR can immerse learners in the first-person perspective, enabling them to explore complex structures and concepts in an engaging, hands-on manner. The VR interactivity feature can also bridge the gap between theoretical knowledge and practical application. Through immersive simulations, students can experiment with neuroscientific principles in a controlled, risk-free environment, allowing for experimentation and discovery without the constraints of real-world limitations. By engaging in active tasks, manipulating and navigating through the virtual models, students are more likely to construct a self-directed learning experience and boost their motivation for learning a new and difficult filed like neuroscience.

VR technology can offer simulated environments, rendering learners learn in scenario-based designs, a method proven to enrich the educational experience [10]. The approach not only facilitates students' understanding of complex subjects like neuroscience, but also aid them in learning, coping with, and managing real life issues. By placing learners in virtually constructed situations that mirror actual challenges, VR enables learners to improve learning efficiency, deepen understanding, and enhances the overall educational impact. Furthermore, the adaptability of VR environments to simulate a wide array of scenarios ensures that learning is not only informative but also relevant to the learners' future professional and personal lives. Finally, VR could provide opportunities for personalized learning trajectories, catering to individual interests and needs. Through VR, educational content can be tailored to match individual learning styles, pace, and interests, offering a personalized learning experience that traditional teaching methods often lack. All these aspects of VR features can help students engaging in learning complex neuroscience.

This study proposes a VR systematic framework that bridges neuroscience and mental health education. The proposed framework will use VR environments to demonstrate the neural mechanisms underlying mental health, offering interactive experiences that showcase the brain's dynamic development under various mental health conditions. A proposed scenario of stress-related neuroscience process is described. The framework development is intended to improve the scientific rigor, professional quality and effectiveness of mental health education for different learners. It also aims to enhance their mental health literacy and lay the groundwork for research in the digitalization of mental health education.

In the following paper, we first delineated the connection between neuroscience and mental health, described the current status of VR technology in both domains, summarized the feasibility of using VR technology to integrate these two fields into an educational platform, and analyzed the theoretic basis for the feasibility. Next, this research demonstrates the proposed VR systematic framework that bridges neuroscience and mental health education and discuss its challenges and limitations. Finally, the paper concludes by summarizing the significance of this framework.

2 Literature Review

2.1 Neuroscience and Mental Health

The advent of neuroimaging technologies in the latter half of the 20th century marked a pivotal turning point in neuroscience. Techniques such as Computed Tomography (CT) scans and Magnetic Resonance Imaging (MRI) provided comprehensive views of the brain's structure, allowing for the identification of anatomical abnormalities associated with various physical or psychological conditions [11, 12]. The development of Positron Emission Tomography (PET) and functional Magnetic Resonance Imaging (fMRI) further revolutionized the field by enabling the visualization of brain activity in real-time [13].

Research in the field of neuroscience has significantly enhanced our understanding of mental disorders. Increasing evidence suggests that many mental health issues are closely linked to maladaptive changes in brain function or structural abnormalities. With the advancement of neuroimaging technologies like MRI and PET, we can now delve deeper into brain neural changes from a multimodal perspective. For example, patients with depression often exhibit reduced activity in the prefrontal cortex, a region crucial for emotional regulation, cognitive control and decision-making, increased amygdala activity, which is overly sensitive to negative emotions, and abnormal enhancement in the functional connectivity between brain regions related to emotional regulation and cognitive control [14–16]. In anxiety disorder research, the prefrontal cortex, amygdala and the functional connectivity of brain regions processing threatening stimuli show difference from that in healthy groups in response to threatening stimuli [17, 18]. Additionally, in the study of addiction mechanisms, abnormalities in the activity of reward-related brain regions and changes in dopamine levels have received extensive attention [19]. These findings not only deepen our understanding of these mental disorders but also provide a scientific basis for developing more effective treatment strategies.

Moreover, research on brain plasticity has revealed that even the adult brain retains a remarkable capacity for ongoing renewal. A study focusing on children's perceptions discovered that maintaining beliefs of growth mindset based on brain plasticity can be beneficial for students' academic progress [20]. If we integrate knowledge and principles of brain plasticity into the prevention and treatment of mental disorders, it may enhance patients' willingness to undergo interventions, thereby improving treatment outcomes, also enable learners to pay attention to how social environments, life events, and personal behavior patterns affect our brain and mental health.

In summary, the neural mechanism and dynamic processes associated with mental health problems and the inherent nature of neural plasticity offer numerous opportunities to enhance the scientific and professional level of mental health education or intervention.

2.2 Mental Health and VR

Virtual Reality (VR) is revolutionizing the field of mental health by offering innovative therapeutic approaches to a range of mental psychiatry conditions. It has been instrumental in managing various phobias, including acrophobia, social anxiety, and specific fears such as fear of flying, by providing a safe space for exposure therapy [21]. It has also been proven effective in treating addictions by simulating environments that trigger addictive behaviors [22]. For patients with posttraumatic stress disorder (PTSD), VR exposure therapy exposes them to simulated traumatic events, such as battlefields in a controlled manner, which can lead to a significant reduction in anxiety and PTSD symptoms over time [23]. In the realm of cognitive rehabilitation, VR plays a role in developing essential life skills for autistic individuals [24] and patients with psychosis to improve social and cognitive functions [25].

A significant aspect of VR's successful apply in these areas is its potential to offer customization and personalization in therapeutic sessions [26]. This customization ensures that VR therapies are tailored to the individual's specific conditions, needs, and progress levels. By adjusting scenarios in complexity and intensity, therapists can create a highly personalized treatment plan that evolves alongside the patient's journey. This level of personalization not only enhances the therapeutic process but also significantly increases patient engagement and treatment adherence. Patients are more likely to feel a sense of control and ownership over their recovery, contributing to more positive outcomes.

The technology's versatility and ability to create immersive, controlled experiences make VR a valuable tool to develop more effective treatments for mental health disorders. Further, the customization and personalization aspect of VR therapies underscore the technology's potential to adapt and respond to the unique challenges presented by mental health conditions.

2.3 Neuroscience Education and VR

VR environments are becoming increasingly instrumental in neuroscience education and research. VR offers a high-resolution, three-dimensional sensory experiences, that makes neuroscience, a field characterized by complex and abstract concepts, more accessible and understandable. For instance, VR enables learners to directly observe the brain's structure and functions, thereby enhancing understanding while avoiding cognitive overload. As noted, it allows researchers to present multimodal stimuli with high ecological validity and control while recording changes in brain activity [27].

Additionally, VR is utilized to create 3D educational videos for neurosurgery, demonstrating surgical techniques and neuropathology [28, 32]. On one hand, it benefits patient education. VR's immersive and interactive environments offer a novel approach for explaining complex neurological conditions and surgical procedures to patients [33]. By visualizing their own medical conditions and the planned surgical interventions in a three-dimensional VR space, patients can gain a better understanding of their diagnosis and treatment options, leading to informed decision-making and increased satisfaction with the care process. On the other hand, facilitated by wearable devices, VR is particularly valuable in neurosurgical skill training. For instance, VR simulations can be used for preoperative planning, allowing surgeons to explore various surgical approaches in a risk-free virtual environment. This preoperative rehearsal not only enhances the surgeon's familiarity with the patient's specific anatomy but also allows for the identification and mitigation of potential challenges before the actual surgery [34]. Furthermore, VR may aid in locating surgical sites and virtually reconstructing three-dimensional structures of organs [24].

With ongoing technological advancements, VR is expected to play an even greater role in neuroscience-related education and clinical applications.

2.4 Theoretic Basis

Constructivist learning theory, proposed by Jean Piaget, is grounded in the principle that learners construct knowledge through their experiences rather than passively receiving information. Two main points are: knowledge is actively constructed by the learner, and learning is deeply influenced by the context in which it takes place [29]. Learning within a VR environment supports and embodies these principles of constructivism. Firstly, the interactive advantage of VR technology significantly enhances learners' motivation, encouraging the development of active learning habits. This is particularly effective in constructivist learning, where engagement and interaction are crucial for the construction of knowledge. Constructivism also asserts that knowledge stems from experience and is related to personal experiences. By leveraging the customization and personalization capabilities of VR technology, it is possible to cater to the diverse learning needs of different individuals and user groups. VR's immersive and interactive environments provide a rich, experiential platform where learners can engage with content in a manner that is meaningful to them, thereby facilitating a deeper, more contextual understanding of the subject matter. This alignment of VR with constructivist principles highlights its potential as a powerful tool in creating effective and engaging learning experiences.

Scenario-based design is a user-centered approach that employs realistic scenarios to inform the development of new systems or products [30]. This method employs detailed narratives to illustrate potential interactions users might have with technology, aiming to meet real-world needs and situations. For example, various life events can trigger the same mental health issue. Living in a dysfunctional family, enduring long-term financial loss, or suffering from chronic pain can all induce stress and anxiety in individuals. VR technology enables the personalization of these life event scenarios, making it possible to tailor experiences to the individual's context. Through engagement with these narratives, students and professionals gain a deeper understanding of the complexities surrounding mental disorders. Furthermore, scenario-based design allows educators to customize learning experiences to meet varied educational needs, thereby fostering empathy and enhancing learners' comprehension.

Together, the constructivist learning theory and scenario-based design support the application of VR in mental health education, providing a solid theoretic basis for this research framework. By integrating these approaches, VR not only enriches the educational content but also fosters a deeper understanding of mental health problems.

2.5 Research Questions

The current VR systems and platforms related to neuroscience primarily focuses on the medical field, including neurosurgery and neurological rehabilitation. For instance, surgeons and diagnosticians frequently employ three-dimensional reconstructions of organ and tissue structures with VR technique and MRI data to pre-surgical plan and diagnose diseases [31]. Collaboratively, computer scientists and neuroscientists at Brown University are delving into the use of VR to gain a more profound comprehension of neural anatomy, its development, and various pathologies [8]. However, it is unclear how VR and neuroscience overlaps with mental health education.

The research conducted a literature review with search strings of (TS = ("virtual reality") AND TS = (neuroscience) AND TS = ("mental health")) using Web of Science database, results showed that 28 studies including article and dissertation thesis were published. After analyzing all the studies, it revealed an absence of VR systems specifically designed to enhance the professionalism and scientific level in mental health education from neuroscience.

So, the core research question addressed in this paper is to propose a VR framework for integrating neuroscience and mental health with acceptable usability.

3 Method

The aim of this study is to propose an appropriate framework for applying VR in integrating neuroscience and mental health. It used design thinking methodology to instruct the design process. Design thinking is an innovative problem-solving process that is deeply rooted in understanding user needs and iteratively developing solutions [35]. Originally based on principles of industrial design, design thinking has quickly found applications across various fields. In recent years, it has gained significant attention in the field of education [36]. The method consists following five distinct stages. The first stage, Empathize, involves deeply understanding the users' experiences and challenges, often through methods like interviews and observations. The next stage, Define, focuses on identifying and articulating the core problem to be solved. This leads to the Ideation stage, where a wide range of creative solutions are brainstormed. Following this, in the Prototype phase, tangible representations of these ideas are created, ranging from sketches to functional models. The final stage, Testing, involves trialing these prototypes with users to gather feedback and insights. This feedback informs further iterations, making design thinking an inherently flexible and responsive approach that revolves around user-centricity and continuous refinement of solutions to meet users' needs effectively.

As illustrated in Fig. 1, this proposed VR system framework will be constructed through the following steps. Firstly, this research identifies the most common types of mental health issues in adults through surveys and literature review. Next, defining and ideating stage would underscore solutions from sight of constructivist learning theory, leading to a primary selection of interactive learning module design idea [37]. we will design themes related to these mental health issues, including situational factors that trigger various psychological problems, key brain structures and functions, and the dynamic changes companying that issue in the brain. Then a prototype of a VR system will be proposed with a user-friendly brain model interface, allowing users to interactively and immersively learn and experience neuroscience matter in different scenarios related to mental health issues. Finally, the proposed system design will undergo testing and evaluation among university student users, facilitating iterations and improvements based on feedback regarding prototype usability, user emotional experience, and learning outcome experience.

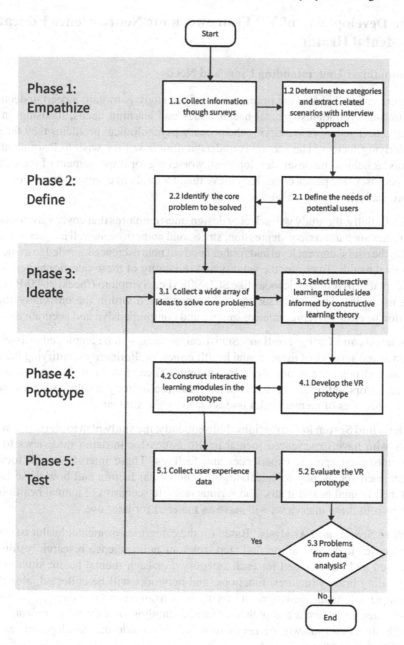

Fig. 1. The VR systematic framework for Neuroscience Education in Mental Health

4 The Development of VR Framework for Neuroscience Education in Mental Health

4.1 Empathize: Understanding Users and Needs

In the "Empathize" phase, the primary goal of the study is to gain a deep understanding of university students' mental health issues and learning needs, focusing on two main aspects. The first is identifying the primary psychological problems they face and the underlying factors. The second is understanding how they wish to learn about the mechanisms behind the onset, development, worsening, or improvement of these issues from a neuroscience perspective. To achieve this, methods like surveys, interviews, and literature analysis will be utilized.

Survey. Initially, the study will select or design questionnaires that cover various mental health issues such as anxiety, depression, stress, and addiction, as well as questionnaires related to the users' current level and further needs of neuroscience knowledge associated with mental health. To ensure the validity and reliability of these questionnaires, scales with acceptable psychometric index like SCL-90R (i.e., Symptom Checklist-90-Revised) will be used [38]. The online survey will be conducted within the university student population to ensure a representative sample and comprehensive and accurate data.

Data Analysis and Categorization. Statistical methods will be employed to assess the prevalence and severity of these mental health issues, preliminarily identifying the main problems and potential trends faced by students. Then, psychotherapists and mental health educators will evaluate and confirm these preliminary results to determine the primary categories of mental health issues faced by the students.

Interviews and Scenario Extraction. Subsequently, the study plan to recruit university students who have experienced mental health issues for in-depth interviews to gain insights into their specific experiences and feelings. These interviews will focus on the mentioned social, physiological, and psychological factors and how these factors impact their mental health status. The various real-life scenarios of mental health issues extracted from these interviews will serve as material for later use.

Literature Search and Analysis. Based on the categories of mental health issues and scenario cases identified in the first step, relevant neuroscience research results will be retrieved and summarized for each category. For each mental health situation, the corresponding brain structures, functions, and networks will be collected, along with their complete dynamic development mechanisms from onset to recovery.

This stage will form a comprehensive understanding of university students' mental health status and knowledge needs which would guide the development work in subsequent design phases.

4.2 Define

In the "Define" phase, the aim is to establish the corn issue that this VR system will address and how it will be solved. Drawing from the data gathered in the "Empathize" stage, the characteristics of the target user group for the VR system can be detailed. This group primarily comprises different kinds of users, e.g., healthy university students within a specific age range who have particular interests or academic needs concerning mental health, practitioners in the mental health relevant fields, and individuals who are exposed to some emotion disorders. Then move on to defining the precise needs of these users, such as their demand for a comprehensive understanding of neuroscience related to mental health, a preference for interactive learning methods, and expectations from the VR experience. Following this, the necessary features and contents that the VR system should include are determined. These may encompass elements like mechanism visualization, scenario case selection and interactive activity modules.

Finally, the study clarifies the objective of developing the VR system, and identify and articulate the core problem to be solved. As mentioned in Sect. 2, the aim of this study is to propose a suitable framework for applying VR in integrating neuroscience and mental health. Thus, the fundamental issue the system seeks to address is:

How can this system effectively enhance university students' understanding and awareness of mental health issues and neuroscience knowledge?

4.3 Ideate

The "Ideate" phase of developing a system is pivotal in exploring a wide array of ideas to enhance the learning experience and outcomes of users in the designed VR system. During this phase, the aim is to gather a variety of innovative and practical suggestions to transform the VR system into an engaging and immersive experience for university students studying mental health and neuroscience. Among possible concepts or solutions, it would be considered more about the concept of Interactive Learning Modules that highlight active interacting with contents or environments to enhance the learning experience [39]. The concept of Interactive Learning Modules is consistent with constructive learning theory. Based on the principles of constructive learning, the active role of learners in constructing their own understanding and knowledge from experiences is emphasized, as opposed to passively receiving information [40].

The research explores a variety of interactive modules from scenario-based design. The modules would include virtual role-plays or simulations, rendering users to actively engage with neurological processes in dynamic, real-time environments. This method aims to bridge the gap between theoretical knowledge and practical experience, aiding deeper understanding and retention of information. By engaging in these interactive scenarios, students would be encouraged to explore, experiment, and reflect, thereby constructing their own understanding of abstract concepts and complex mechanisms in mental health and neuroscience.

4.4 Prototype Development

In the "Prototype Development" phase, the focus is on transforming the ideas generated during the "Ideate" stage into a testable model, creating an initial prototype of the VR system, such as interface sketches and basic interaction flows. The goal is to design a user-friendly interface that provides interactive scenarios using wearable devices. The interactive part allows users to explore the brain's structures, functions, networks, and their dynamic changes during different stage in mental health issues. This will enable users to experience an immersive learning environment, enhancing their understanding of common mental health problems.

To cater to the interactive learning modules, three main interactive areas were summarized: Theme Selection, Visual Display, and Scenarios with User Interaction. Theme Selection is based on the survey results from Sects. 4.1 and 4.2, covering the most common mental health issues experienced by university students, such as anxiety and depression (see Fig. 2a). After selecting a theme, users enter the learning interface (see Fig. 2b). The first step is the Visual Display of the theme-related neural mechanism, primarily showcasing the 3D brain mechanisms corresponding to the chosen theme (see Fig. 2c). This design draws upon the classical 2D brain atlases (the Harvard-Oxford Atlas provided by the Harvard Center for Morphometric Analysis), including but not limited to displaying and explaining brain function localization (see Fig. 2d), functional changes (see Fig. 2e), structural alterations, and variations in brain connectivity patterns (see Fig. 2f).

Once users have a visual understanding of these brain mechanisms, they can further engage in interactive learning through Scenarios-based User Interaction (see Fig. 3a). For example, by selecting the scenario named "Living in a Long-term Quarrelsome Family" (see Fig. 3b), users enter a virtual family environment to observe how such this situation affects neural functions over time with teaching video (see Fig. 3c–d). After the video, users can also autonomously choose intervention strategies in the virtual environment, such as changing the context setting or self-emotion-regulation, to see if these actions improve brain function patterns (see Fig. 3e–h).

This "Prototype Development" phase emphasizes creating a VR system that is both educational and interactive, allowing users to gain a comprehensive neuroscientific understanding of mental health issues through innovative VR technology. The approach focusing on engagement and experiential learning aligns with current trends in user-centric design.

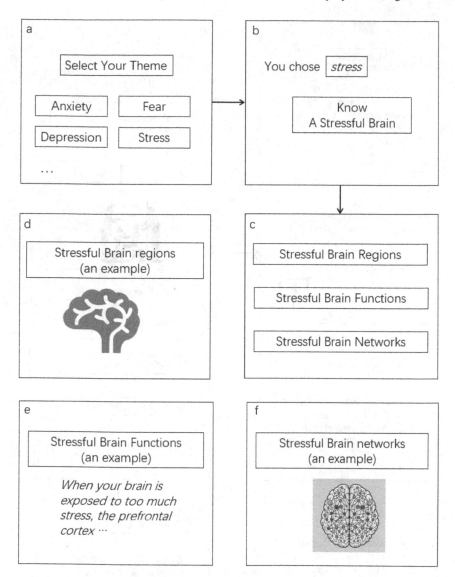

Fig. 2. VR Theme Selection and Learning Interface for Mental Health Education. (a) Theme selection menu showing common mental health issues among university students (b) The learning interface upon theme selection. (c) The interface of neural mechanisms related to the selected theme. (d) Utilization of the Harvard-Oxford Atlas for displaying brain function localization. (e) Depiction of functional changes in the brain associated with the selected mental health issue. (f) Illustration of structural alterations and variations in brain connectivity patterns.

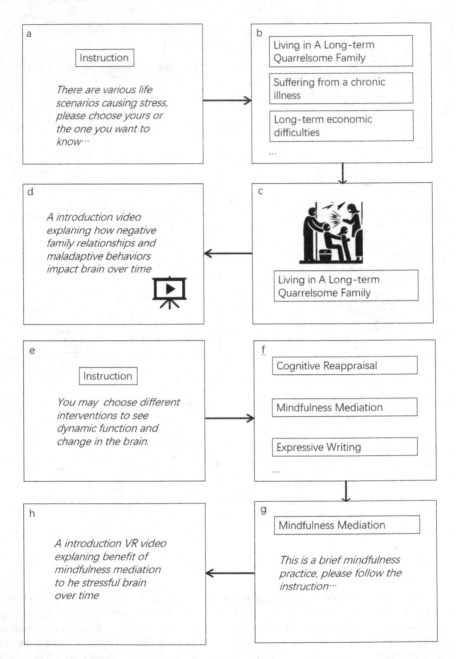

Fig. 3. The scenario-based design of interactive learning modules in the framework. (a) Overview of the user interface for scenario selection. (b) Entry point into the 'Living in a Long-term Quarrelsome Family' scenario. (c–d) Teaching videos illustrating the impact of this scenario on neural functions. (e–h) Interactive options for users to select intervention strategies, including context modification and self-emotion-regulation techniques, demonstrating potential improvements in brain function patterns.

4.5 Test and Evaluation

To test the proposed system, it is necessary to conduct usability assessments including examining the system's ease of use and intuitiveness, user interface navigation simplicity, response speed, the ease of accessing necessary information and so on. These factors are essential in determining how user-friendly and efficient the system is. To accurately measure these aspects, the System Usability Scale (SUS) will be utilized, providing a reliable tool to evaluate the usability of the VR system [41]. Additionally, task completion time and error rates during navigation will be recorded to further assess the system's efficiency. Recruitment for this phase will target a diverse group of users to ensure a wide range of feedback, focusing on individuals within the target demographic of the VR system.

Concurrently, the emotional experience of users is gauged based on their responses during system interaction, capturing interest levels at initiation, enjoyment, immersion, and post-use satisfaction. This multifaceted emotional response is critical to understanding the system's impact on users. To gather this data, a combination of the User Experience Questionnaire (UEQ) and interviews will be conducted [42]. Then data analysis, including sentiment analysis of interview transcripts and statistical evaluation of UEQ scores, will help derive the average performance level.

Furthermore, the learning outcomes are expected to determine the degree to which users acquire essential knowledge and skills. Therefore, a pre- and post-use comparisons of users' knowledge levels would be conducted to test whether the VR system could impact their cognitive improvements, memory retention, and the practical applicability of acquired knowledge. To accomplish this, standardized tests tailored to the specific content delivered by the VR system will be designed with specific instruments.

Testing across these three dimensions may enable a comprehensive understanding of the system's efficacy, providing feedback for the system's iterative development.

5 Discussion

This study describes a VR system for neuroscience education tailored to meet mental health needs. With theoretical feasibility grounded in a literature review, the construction of this system aligns with contemporary societal demands. Following the Design Thinking methodology, the study proposes a model framework a framework of VR prototype for neuroscience education in mental health following the Design Thinking Methodology and the Constructive Learning Theory. The model will undergo testing and evaluation among university student users. Feedbacks regarding prototype usability, user emotional experience, and learning outcome experience is used to facilitate iterations and improvements to the model development.

The main contribution of this study lies in addressing current issues in mental health from an interdisciplinary perspective, utilizing VR technology and systematic design methodology. In the proposed framework, learners can choose different situational themes and interact with them, which helps stimulate motivation, promote immersion, experience abstract problems, and enhance problem-solving abilities.

However, the framework has its limitations. Firstly, in the test phase, the study aims to collect user feedback to evaluate and optimize the prototype model. However, it can only compare changes in users' knowledge levels before and after using the system, without a comparative analysis with other learning environments. Secondly, the cost of using a VR system for actual learning is high, posing financial challenges for many schools and education institutions. Lastly, this study merely proposes a design framework, and actual implementation may face significant technical challenges. Future research is needed to explore the user experience and educational effectiveness of VR learning environments further.

6   Conclusion

VR technology has the potential to transform how we perceive the world and holds immense potential in the field of education. Neuroscience and mental health education can greatly benefit university students' holistic development, but due to the complexity at the knowledge or technical level, some work remains theoretical. Integrating neuroscience research findings with mental health education using VR technology and applying it in teaching practice increases the likelihood of addressing social issues.

Acknowledgments. This study was funded by Guangdong education Science planning project (number 2023GXJK668) and Guangdong Philosophy and Social Science Foundation (number GDGD23XTS01).

Disclosure of Interests.   The authors have no competing interests to declare that are relevant to the content of this article.

References

1. Reinke, W.M., Stormont, M., Herman, K.C., Puri, R., Goel, N.: Supporting children's mental health in schools: teacher perceptions of needs, roles, and barriers. Sch. Psychol. Q. **26**, 1–13 (2011)
2. Walter, H.J., Gouze, K., Lim, K.G.: Teachers' beliefs about mental health needs in inner city elementary schools. J. Am. Acad. Child Adolesc. Psychiatry **45**, 61–68 (2006)
3. Lyon, A.R., Stirman, S.W., Kerns, S.E.U., Bruns, E.J.: Developing the mental health workforce: review and application of training approaches from multiple disciplines. Adm. Policy Ment. Health **38**, 238–253 (2011)
4. Kilbourne, A.M., et al.: Measuring and improving the quality of mental health care: a global perspective. World Psychiatry **17**, 30–38 (2018)
5. Field, T.A., Beeson, E.T., Jones, L.K.: Neuroscience-informed cognitive-behavior therapy in clinical practice: a preliminary study. J. Ment. Health Couns. **38**, 139–154 (2016)
6. Brick, K., et al.: Training-of-trainers neuroscience and mental health teacher education in Liberia improves self-reported support for students. Front. Hum. Neurosci. **15** (2021)
7. Fung, L.K., Akil, M., Widge, A., Roberts, L.W., Etkin, A.: Attitudes toward neuroscience education in psychiatry: a national multi-stakeholder survey. Acad. Psychiatry **39**, 139–146 (2015)
8. LaValle, S.M.: Virtual Reality. Cambridge University Press, Cambridge (2023)
9. Fogarty, J., McCormick, J., El-Tawil, S.: Improving student understanding of complex spatial arrangements with virtual reality. J. Prof. Issues Eng. Educ. Pract. **144**, 04017013 (2018)

10. Aylward, K., Dahlman, J., Nordby, K., Lundh, M.: Using operational scenarios in a virtual reality enhanced design process. Educ. Sci. **11**, 448 (2021)
11. Runge, V.M., et al.: Magnetic resonance imaging and computed tomography of the brain—50 years of innovation, with a focus on the future. Invest. Radiol. **50**(9), 551–556 (2015)
12. Shenton, M.E., et al.: A review of magnetic resonance imaging and diffusion tensor imaging findings in mild traumatic brain injury. Brain Imaging Behav. **6**, 137–192 (2012)
13. DeCharms, R.C., Christoff, K., Glover, G.H., Pauly, J.M., Whitfield, S., Gabrieli, J.D.: Learned regulation of spatially localized brain activation using real-time fMRI. Neuroimage **21**(1), 436–443 (2004)
14. Bremner, J.D., et al.: MRI and PET study of deficits in hippocampal structure and function in women with childhood sexual abuse and posttraumatic stress disorder. Am. J. Psychiatry **160**, 924–932 (2003)
15. Disner, S.G., Beevers, C.G., Haigh, E.A.P., Beck, A.T.: Neural mechanisms of the cognitive model of depression. Nat. Rev. Neurosci. **12**, 467–477 (2011)
16. Hamilton, J.P., Gotlib, I.H.: Neural substrates of increased memory sensitivity for negative stimuli in major depression. Biol. Psychiat. **63**, 1155–1162 (2008)
17. Davidson, R.J.: Mindfulness-based cognitive therapy and the prevention of depressive relapse: measures, mechanisms, and mediators. JAMA Psychiat. **73**, 547–548 (2016)
18. Price, J.L., Drevets, W.C.: Neural circuits underlying the pathophysiology of mood disorders. Trends Cogn. Sci. **16**, 61–71 (2012)
19. Di Chiara, G., Bassareo, V.: Reward system and addiction: what dopamine does and doesn't do. Curr. Opin. Pharmacol. **7**, 69–76 (2007)
20. Yeager, D.S., et al.: A national experiment reveals where a growth mindset improves achievement. Nature **573**, 364–369 (2019)
21. Freitas, J.R.S., et al.: Virtual reality exposure treatment in phobias: a systematic review. Psychiatr. Q. **92**, 1685–1710 (2021)
22. Segawa, T., et al.: Virtual Reality (VR) in assessment and treatment of addictive disorders: a systematic review. Front. Neurosci. **13** (2020)
23. Kothgassner, O.D., et al.: Virtual reality exposure therapy for posttraumatic stress disorder (PTSD): a meta-analysis. Eur. J. Psychotraumatol. **10**, 1654782 (2019)
24. Parsons, S.: Authenticity in virtual reality for assessment and intervention in autism: a conceptual review. Educ. Res. Rev. **19**, 138–157 (2016)
25. Rus-Calafell, M., Garety, P., Sason, E., Craig, T.J.K., Valmaggia, L.R.: Virtual reality in the assessment and treatment of psychosis: a systematic review of its utility, acceptability and effectiveness. Psychol. Med. **48**, 362–391 (2018)
26. Bergsnev, K., Sánchez Laws, A.L.: Personalizing virtual reality for the research and treatment of fear-related disorders: a mini review. Front. Virtual Reality **3**, 834004 (2022)
27. Bohil, C.J., Alicea, B., Biocca, F.A.: Virtual reality in neuroscience research and therapy. Nat. Rev. Neurosci. **12**, 752–762 (2011)
28. Scott, H., et al.: Virtual reality in the neurosciences: current practice and future directions. Front. Surg. **8** (2022)
29. Narayan, R., Rodriguez, C., Araujo, J., Shaqlaih, A., Moss, G.: The Handbook of Educational Theories. IAP Information Age Publishing, Charlotte, North Carolina (2013)
30. Rosson, M.B., Carroll, J.M.: Scenario based design. In: Human-Computer Interaction. Boca Raton, FL (2009)
31. Fiani, B., et al.: Virtual reality in neurosurgery: "can you see it?"–A review of the current applications and future potential. World Neurosurg. **141**, 291–298 (2020)
32. Neuwirth, L.S., Ros, M.: Comparisons between first person point-of-view 180 video virtual reality head-mounted display and 3D video computer display in teaching undergraduate neuroscience students stereotaxic surgeries. Front. Virtual Reality **2**, 706653 (2021)

33. van der Kruk, S.R., Zielinski, R., MacDougall, H., Hughes-Barton, D., Gunn, K.M.: Virtual reality as a patient education tool in healthcare: a scoping review. Patient Educ. Couns. **105**(7), 1928–1942 (2022)
34. Laskay, N.M., George, J.A., Knowlin, L., Chang, T.P., Johnston, J.M., Godzik, J.: Optimizing surgical performance using preoperative virtual reality planning: a systematic review. World J. Surg. 1–11 (2023)
35. Foster, M.K.: Design thinking: a creative approach to problem solving. Manag. Teach. Rev. **6**, 123–140 (2021)
36. Scheer, A., Noweski, C., Meinel, C.: Transforming constructivist learning into action: design thinking in education. Des. Technol. Educ. **17**, 8–19 (2012)
37. Pande, M., Bharathi, S.V.: Theoretical foundations of design thinking – a constructivism learning approach to design thinking. Think. Skills Creativity **36**, 100637 (2020)
38. Prinz, U., et al.: Comparative psychometric analyses of the SCL-90-R and its short versions in patients with affective disorders. BMC Psychiatry **13**, 104 (2013)
39. Delialioglu, O., Yildirim, Z.: Students' perceptions on effective dimensions of interactive learning in a blended learning environment. J. Educ. Technol. Soc. **10**, 133–146 (2007)
40. Bada, D., Olusegun, S.: Constructivism learning theory: a paradigm for teaching and learning (2015)
41. Vlachogianni, P., Tselios, N.: Perceived usability evaluation of educational technology using the System Usability Scale (SUS): a systematic review. J. Res. Technol. Educ. **54**(3), 392–409 (2022)
42. Schrepp, M., Hinderks, A., Thomaschewski, J.: Design and evaluation of a short version of the user experience questionnaire (UEQ-S). Int. J. Interact. Multimedia Artif. Intell. **4**(6), 103–108 (2017)

Exploration of "ICH + Digital Game" Mode Under the Threshold of Culture and Tourism Integration

Yinghong Zhang[1], Zhihua Sun[2]([🖂]), and Shengnan Guo[3]

[1] College of Fine Arts and Design, University of Jinan, Jinan 255000, Shandong, China
[2] College of Arts, Shandong Agriculture and Engineering University, Jinan 255000, Shandong, China
isunzhihua@gmail.com
[3] Institute of Preschool Education, Jinan Vocational College, Jinan 255000, Shandong, China

Abstract. As the crystallization of human wisdom, intangible cultural heritage has an irreplaceable role in maintaining national cultural diversity and promoting cultural self-awareness and self-confidence. Under the current background that countries worldwide emphasize strengthening the protection of intangible cultural heritage and cultural tourism, digital games have become an emerging mode of artistic communication with broad application prospects. Based on the existing literature, the authors define "ICH + digital game" as Integrating intangible cultural heritage themes and elements into digital games and performing them, allowing users to experience intangible cultural heritage while playing, and promoting the development model of regeneration and inheritance of culture. First, based on the unique cultural form of intangible cultural heritage, combined with the concept of "ICH +" and "digitalization of intangible cultural heritage," the idea of "ICH + digital game" is sorted out more comprehensively from multiple dimensions. Secondly, through case analysis of severe and entertainment games, four levels of design objectives in intangible cultural heritage games are defined. Summarise the characteristics and laws of cultural dissemination in digital games and propose corresponding design suggestions. Finally, under the perspective of cultural and tourism integration, it clarified its cultural significance, aesthetic function, and economic value. This paper utilizes human-computer interaction, game design, and other methods to explore the combination mode of combining digital games with intangible cultural heritage. The research aims to provide new ideas and directions for the digital inheritance of cultural heritage and jointly promote the protection and dissemination of intangible cultural heritage.

Keywords: Intangible Cultural Heritage · Digital Game · Cultural Protection and Inheritance

© The Author(s), under exclusive license to Springer Nature Switzerland AG 2024
N. A. Streitz and S. Konomi (Eds.): HCII 2024, LNCS 14719, pp. 153–171, 2024.
https://doi.org/10.1007/978-3-031-60012-8_10

1   Introduction

Intangible cultural heritage is a form of culture that holds significant historical and cultural meaning. It is a repository of a nation's memory and wisdom and a precious spiritual legacy of human civilization. However, traditional culture encounters challenges and opportunities in our fast-paced modern society. The emergence of digital games presents a new avenue and potential for preserving and disseminating intangible cultural heritage. As a novel artistic medium, digital games have captured the attention of numerous users globally, particularly among young people, with their unique interactive and entertaining features. It has become an expansive field for exploring cultural inheritance and innovation.

It is fascinating to see how integrating intangible cultural heritage and digital games has created a dynamic and multi-dimensional field combining technological innovation and cultural inheritance. With the advancement and widespread use of digital technology, especially online games, virtual reality (VR), and augmented reality (AR), a new platform has been created for showcasing and disseminating intangible cultural heritage. Some serial games are also explicitly designed for educational and inheritance purposes and delve deep into exploring and interpreting one or more intangible cultural heritage. These games have a dual nature in terms of educational value and entertainment, as they not only recreate traditional intangible cultural heritage skills but also simulate the cultural and historical context behind these skills, providing players with a profound cultural learning experience.

It's worth acknowledging that merging intangible cultural heritage with digital gaming is not merely a one-sided cultural transfer. Instead, it's a dynamic, interactive process of innovation in which game developers continually seek inspiration from intangible cultural heritage to develop fresh content and new forms. Concurrently, inheritors and related institutions of intangible cultural heritage are also delving into modern expressions of traditional components through digital media.

2   How to Understand the Concept of "ICH + Digital Game" Mode

2.1   Special Cultural Forms of Intangible Cultural Heritage

In exploring the "ICH + digital game" mode, it is essential to acknowledge the significance of intangible cultural heritage as a distinct artistic form. It serves not only as a historical accumulation but also as a reflection of a way of life, a knowledge system, and a dynamic social practice. Intangible cultural heritage, with its fluid and evolving nature, surpasses the spatial constraints of material cultural heritage and presents unique preservation and inheritance challenges.

Intangible cultural heritage encompasses a range of artistic expressions, including oral traditions, performing arts, social customs, festivals, and knowledge of nature and the universe. Their dynamic nature makes these cultural forms unique, as they are continuously reinterpreted and practiced to keep them vibrant. In other words, intangible cultural heritage isn't static but constantly being recreated and reinterpreted in the present moment. The emergence of digital games provides a new cultural space that can intersect with intangible cultural heritage, offering a fresh platform for its display and experience.

Through interactive storytelling and role-playing, players can fully immerse themselves in this virtual world and experience the unique beauty of intangible cultural heritage. This experience is not limited to visual and auditory stimuli; it also involves cognitive and emotional levels, enabling players to truly understand the essence of intangible cultural heritage in a captivating and immersive environment.

Incorporating intangible cultural heritage in digital games presents a fresh perspective on preserving cultural heritage. By serving as an innovative method of communication, digital games allow intangible cultural heritage to transcend time and space constraints and make it accessible to a broader audience, particularly to the younger generation. This form of communication piques the interest of young people and encourages them to participate in traditional culture, thus promoting the activation, innovation, and inheritance of intangible cultural heritage.

It is clear that the mode of "ICH + digital game" provides a unique cultural form that expands the transmission boundary of traditional culture. This mode offers a new perspective and method for protecting, inheriting, and innovating intangible cultural heritage. Through the interactivity and entertainment of digital games, intangible cultural heritage can be presented to the public in a novel and attractive way, which not only helps to enhance the vitality of culture but also opens up a new path for the digital protection and dissemination of cultural heritage.

2.2 Definition of "ICH + Digital Game" Mode

When exploring the conceptual framework of the "ICH + digital game" model, it is not only a simple superposition but also a deep integration, aiming to provide a new perspective and impetus for the inheritance and promotion of intangible cultural heritage through the interactivity and immersion of digital games.

When defining the "ICH + digital game" mode, we must consider several key elements: the selection and reproduction of intangible cultural heritage. This involves accurately and vividly showing the historical background, artistic value, and cultural significance of intangible cultural heritage projects in digital games. Secondly, the interactive experience design of players. This includes how the game mechanism guides players to have meaningful interaction with intangible cultural heritage, how to enhance players' sense of immersion through storytelling, character set, challenge setting, and the balance between education and entertainment. Although the game's primary purpose is entertainment, in this mode, it also carries the mission of education, which needs to find an appropriate balance between interest and knowledge transfer.

In addition, the "ICH + digital game" model also emphasizes sustainability. With the development of technology and the change of cultural consumption mode, this mode should be able to adapt to the new social environment and technical conditions, constantly innovate the digital forms of intangible cultural heritage, and ensure the sustainable inheritance of the vitality of cultural heritage.

The "ICH + digital game" model can be defined as a new cultural communication strategy. It combines intangible cultural heritage with digital games to create an interactive platform with educational significance and entertainment to promote intangible cultural heritage's protection, inheritance, and international communication.

2.3 Application of Human-Computer Interaction Technology in Digital Games

The application of human-computer interaction technology is a critical factor in promoting the innovation of game experience by combining intangible cultural heritage with digital games. Through highly interactive game design, players can go beyond the traditional way of viewing and reading and experience the unique charm of intangible cultural heritage from a new perspective and depth. However, applying human-computer interaction technology in digital games is more comprehensive than just essential input and output operations; it involves more complex areas of perception, cognition, and emotional computing. With advanced sensor technology, such as motion capture, eye tracking and tactile feedback devices, game designers can create a more natural user interface and immersive interactive environment. Such interaction design makes the player's actions, sight and emotional reactions part of the game experience, thus realizing direct communication with intangible cultural heritage elements in the virtual environment.

In mobile games, natural user interface (NUI) is ubiquitous, including somatosensory interaction, voice interaction, gesture interaction, etc. Somatosensory interaction technology uses devices (such as Kinect, Wii remote control, etc.) to capture the player's body movement and achieve full-body game control. This interaction mode breaks the limitations of traditional game consoles and provides players with a more intuitive and natural game experience. Players can control game characters through accurate body movements (such as fist waving, jumping, dancing, etc.), enhancing the game's immersion and interactivity. Voice interaction technology uses voice recognition and synthesis technology to achieve voice-based interaction between players and games. Players can control game characters, menu selection, dialogue, etc., through voice commands, which reduces the dependence on game controllers and improves the convenience and immersion of game operation. Gesture interaction technology uses gesture recognition devices (such as Leap Motion, Intel Real Sense, etc.) to capture the player's hand movements and gestures to achieve gesture-based game control. Players can operate the game menu, control game objects, draw spells, and so on by clicking, sliding, grabbing, and performing other actions. The natural user interface gives people a more intuitive and immersive interactive experience.

Virtual reality (VR) and augmented reality (AR) technology can enable players to achieve immersive interactive experiences. VR technology uses head-mounted displays, location tracking, input devices, etc., to immerse players into the virtual game world. Players can get an immersive game experience through head motion control perspective and hand motion control interaction. VR games break the screen restrictions of traditional games and provide players with more realistic and immersive sensory stimulation. VR technology opens up a new design space and expressiveness for games, especially for shooting, adventure and simulation games from the first-person perspective. AR technology superimposes virtual game elements in the natural environment. It displays them through mobile phones, tablets, AR glasses and other devices to realize the game experience of a virtual reality combination. AR Games use the camera, gyroscope, GPS, and other sensors to map game objects and interactions to real space, allowing players to explore and interact in the real world. For example, applying in the Chinese New Year of the Northern Song Dynasty, in the *Justice,* can make players feel like they are amid traditional festivals and experience conventional folk activities such as lion and dragon dances, iron flower fights, and spring cattle. They can also wear beautiful clothes with paper-cutting patterns to listen to Henan Opera performances and feel the charm of Chinese traditional opera. The "pixel Forbidden City" in *My World* is a vast building complex stacked with pixels as units. Players can walk on the white jade steps, gallop on horseback in the main hall square, or feel the majestic momentum of the whole Forbidden City through the changes of light and shadow. In this situation, the interaction design of the game is no longer limited to the keyboard and mouse but simulates the physical laws and human behavior of the natural world so that players can "touch" objects in the virtual space with their hands or interact with them through body movements. This design not only enhances the fun and immersion of the game but also provides an innovative way for players to learn and understand the connotation and value of intangible cultural heritage while enjoying the game (Fig. 1).

Fig. 1. The scene of Chinese New Year, iron flower fights, Clothes with Paper-cuttings patterns, Henan Opera performances in *Justice*

Artificial intelligence (AI) can adjust the game difficulty, content presentation and story rhythm in real-time according to the player's performance and game progress to adapt to different players' learning curves and interest points. This dynamic adjustment mechanism based on the player's performance gives each game a different experience, improving the player's participation.

Biofeedback technology uses sensors to collect players' physiological signals (such as heart rate, EEG, PI, etc.) as the input and adjustment basis of the game to realize game interaction based on players' physiological state. Biofeedback games can dynamically adjust the game's difficulty, scene and plot according to the player's physiological indicators, such as emotion, attention and relaxation, and provide a more personalized and immersive game experience, such as *Nevermind* and *The Wild Divide*.

In addition, there are brain-computer interfaces, facial expression recognition, somatosensory interaction, etc. The application of human-computer interaction technology can significantly improve the immersion and interactivity of the game and provide players with a more accurate and natural game experience. Its personalized interaction mode can meet the preferences and needs of different players and improve the attractiveness and market competitiveness of the game. With the continuous progress of technology, advanced interactive technology provides game developers with more creative possibilities, which helps to expand the expressiveness and narrative ability of the game. Moreover, the innovation of interactive technology in games also provides new ideas and practice scenes for developing human-computer interaction and promotes interdisciplinary communication and integration.

The close combination of human-computer interaction technology and game design provides a new dimension for the inheritance and innovation of intangible cultural heritage. Through the interactive game environment, intangible cultural heritage has become within reach, and players have become active participants and Experiencers in this process. This model protects and inherits traditional culture, opens up a new path for integrating cultural heritage and modern science and technology, and builds a bridge for exchanging and understanding global cultural diversity.

3 Four Levels of the Design Purpose of Intangible Cultural Heritage Games

3.1 Display and Dissemination of Culture

In exploring the combination of intangible cultural heritage and digital games, we aim to achieve the display and dissemination of culture through the interaction and interest of games. The realization of this goal involves many levels, the first of which is to vividly present the connotation, form, and spirit of intangible cultural heritage through the carrier of the game. When designing immaterial cultural heritage games, we pursue the simple simulation of traditional skills and knowledge and the expectation that players can experience the profound value of culture while participating in the game. Therefore, intangible cultural heritage elements are skillfully integrated into the game plot, character design, environmental layout, and interactive experience. For example, some games put cultural aspects such as traditional festivals, folk stories, and ancient crafts into the virtual world so that players can experience the charm of these cultures while exploring and playing. For another example, the game's scene design can imitate traditional festivals' environmental layout. At the same time, the music and sound effects can be integrated into the tunes and rhythms of local characteristics. The dialogue and plot of the characters contain elements of folk stories and historical legends. Through the experience of solid interaction and deep immersion, it provides a new cognitive way for players from the visual, auditory, and emotional aspects.

Furthermore, the design of intangible cultural heritage games should also focus on the dissemination of culture. This means that games must have a particular educational significance and popularity to become entertainment products and tools for cultural learning. To achieve this, developers need to deeply study the historical background and cultural significance behind each intangible cultural heritage to ensure that these contents are accurately presented in the game. At the same time, by setting guided game tasks and challenges, players' curiosity and desire for exploration are stimulated so that they can naturally understand and learn relevant cultural knowledge.

At the cultural display and dissemination level, the design of intangible cultural heritage games must also consider diversity and inclusiveness. Different intangible cultural heritage projects have their unique forms of expression and inheritance. Therefore, game design can't be generalized, but personalized design strategies should be carried out for different types of intangible cultural heritage. In addition, to enable more people to contact and understand the value of intangible cultural heritage, the game's difficulty setting and operation interface should consider players of different ages and cultural backgrounds so that everyone can have fun and acquire knowledge in the game.

3.2 Enhancement of Cultural Awareness

When discussing the deep-seated connotation of the design purpose of intangible cultural heritage games, the enhancement of cultural awareness undoubtedly occupies the core position.

Intangible cultural heritage games are the convergence of technology and art and the product of the integration of traditional cultural heritage and modern media. Every classic pattern, historical story, and festival reappearance integrated into the game touches the player's cultural cognition. This kind of touch is different from the traditional education mode. It does not rely on dull memory and indoctrination but actively guides players to explore and discover through situational simulation and role play. Every choice and interaction of players in the game may become an opportunity to understand the deep meaning of intangible cultural heritage.

Understanding intangible cultural heritage can awaken their cultural consciousness because the artistic elements in the game are not only the stacking of visual symbols but also the embodiment of a way of life and idea. Players' experience in the game world can trigger thinking and cherishing of cultural heritage in the real world. With the game's progress, players have a deeper understanding of the historical context, regional characteristics, and social values behind intangible cultural heritage, which has gradually transformed into a sense of protection and responsibility for cultural heritage. Through the carrier of games, intangible cultural heritage culture can transcend the boundaries of time and space, touch the soul of modern people, and stimulate the cultural consciousness and creativity of a new generation.

Another vital purpose of ICH game design is to promote the innovative dissemination of culture. As a new medium, digital games provide a unique platform and path for disseminating traditional culture. In the game, the collision between intangible cultural heritage elements and modern technology has spawned new forms of artistic expression, which not only retain the core values of traditional culture but also give them new vitality and attraction. While enjoying the game's fun, players have virtually become communicators of intangible cultural heritage, bringing this cultural wealth into a broader social circle and cultural field.

The deep purpose of intangible cultural heritage game design is to promote the dialogue and exchange of cultural diversity. In the context of globalization, exchanges between different cultures are increasingly frequent, and intangible cultural heritage games provide a shared platform for players with different cultural backgrounds to meet and know each other in the same virtual space. Through the game experience, players can not only feel and recognize the unique charm of Chinese excellent traditional culture but also understand the value and significance of other cultures to realize mutual respect and reference of cultures.

It can be seen that the enhancement of cultural awareness in the design of ICH games is a simple reproduction of traditional elements and a profound excavation and innovative dissemination of traditional cultural values. Through the career of games, ICH can transcend the boundaries of time and space, touch the soul of modern people, and stimulate a new generation's cultural consciousness and creativity.

3.3 Acquisition of Knowledge and Skills

A core purpose of the game, especially in serious game design, is to promote players' knowledge absorption and skill understanding. Intangible cultural heritage games are a tool for cultural heritage and an innovative educational platform. It breaks the restrictions of geography and time so that players worldwide can access, learn, and even participate in protecting and inheriting intangible cultural heritage.

When building the game environment, designers will skillfully integrate various intangible cultural elements, such as folk music, dance, drama, handicrafts, etc., which are not only used as background or decoration in the game but also become the key to promoting the development of the plot. In the exploration process, players constantly interact with these elements to absorb relevant knowledge naturally. For example, players may need to learn specific folk songs to unlock new tasks or unlock story clues by simulating the production of handicrafts. This design enables players to deeply understand and experience the charm of intangible cultural heritage while entertaining.

Educator John Dewey once said, "Education is life itself." Compared with traditional education methods, digital games are more interactive and exciting. To combine education with fun, digital games help students better understand and accept intangible cultural heritage knowledge. The simulation practice link can be built into the game, allowing players to manually operate the production process in the virtual environment. From selecting materials and learning how to use tools to complete each step of the work, players can get a deep impression as if they had experienced the craft, such as *Logic Faille*, a serious game. Faille is a cross-stitch skill of women in Western Hunan. Players can break the traditional Faille style in the game and complete the Faille pattern with personal special marks according to their preferences or at random. In the game of *carpenter's wood*, players can cut wood blocks to understand the processing technology of mortise and tenon joints. Pictures and animation also display the structure and name of Chinese traditional frame furniture. This immersive learning method deepened the players' understanding of the process flow and stimulated their interest and respect for traditional culture. Students can study in a relaxed and pleasant atmosphere to improve their enthusiasm and initiative for learning (Figs. 2 and 3).

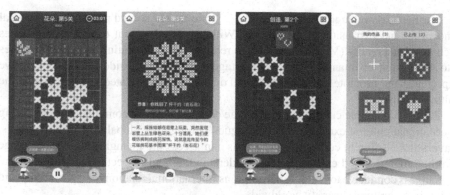

Fig. 2. Logic Faille

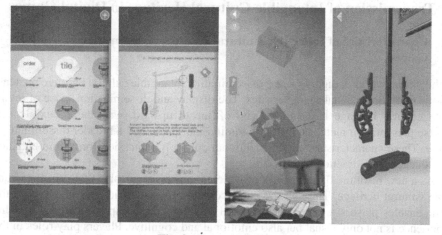

Fig. 3. Carpenter's Wood

3.4 Achievement of Additional Objectives

The combination of intangible cultural heritage and digital games can realize the functions of cultural dissemination, education, and training and think about using games to promote social and economic development and technological progress. Realizing these additional goals will bring a more profound impact and broader social value to intangible cultural heritage games.

The objectives of the additional intangible cultural heritage games include promoting the local economy and tourism development. The display of supernatural cultural heritage elements in a specific region in the game can enhance the artistic attraction of the area and attract more tourists to experience the natural, cultural heritage. At the same time, it also provides new market opportunities for local artisans and small enterprises to help them commercialize traditional art products and create more jobs and sources of income.

Furthermore, intangible cultural heritage game design should pursue technological innovation and expansion of application. With the development of new technologies such as virtual reality (VR) and augmented reality (AR), integrating these technologies into the design of intangible cultural heritage games can provide a more immersive experience and promote the application and development of related technologies in the cultural industry.

Finally, intangible cultural heritage game design should be committed to promoting international cultural exchanges and dialogue. Through the global language of games, players from different countries and regions can access the intangible cultural heritage of other countries and enhance mutual understanding and respect. This cross-cultural exchange is conducive to building harmonious international relations and promoting and maintaining cultural diversity worldwide.

4   Transmission of Intangible Cultural Heritage in Digital Games

4.1   Characteristics of Intangible Cultural Heritage Transmission in Digital Games

In the virtual world of digital games, disseminating intangible cultural heritage presents unique multidimensional characteristics. The display and dissemination space of intangible cultural heritage has shifted from offline to upward, with more flexible and diverse presentation methods, faster dissemination speed, and a broader dissemination range. These characteristics enrich traditional culture's expression forms and enhance its influence and attraction worldwide.

As a new medium, digital games provide an impressive display platform for intangible cultural heritage. Through the enhancement of interactivity and immersion, the game enables players to experience cultural traditions in an unprecedented way. This experience is not only visual but also emotional and cognitive. Players play roles in the game, complete tasks, and interact directly with cultural elements to deeply understand cultural connotations. This participatory learning allows the intangible cultural heritage to be vividly spread among the younger generation.

Digital games have broken geographical boundaries, enabling intangible cultural heritage to transcend geographical restrictions and reach global audiences. The international development of online games, especially the "Game Going Global" trend, has opened up a new way for the international dissemination of traditional culture. Game designers integrate conventional cultural elements into the game plot, character setting, and environment design so players can naturally contact and understand foreign cultures while exploring and taking risks. This cross-cultural communication enhances the understanding and respect between different cultures and provides a new impetus for the global dissemination of cultural heritage.

Moreover, digital technology enables the innovation and transformation of intangible cultural heritage. Traditional art can be reinterpreted and presented in the game through animation, 3D modeling, virtual reality, and other technical means. This innovative way of presentation retains the core value of cultural heritage and adds modern charm, making it more in line with contemporary aesthetics and technology development trends.

4.2 Laws of Intangible Cultural Heritage Transmission in Digital Games

In the virtual space of digital games, the dissemination of intangible cultural heritage presents a unique regularity. These laws are not only related to the characteristics of intangible cultural heritage and the environment of digital games but also closely related to players' psychological and behavioral patterns.

The dissemination of intangible cultural heritage in the game often follows a "reproduction-experience-identity" mode. Through digital technology, supernatural cultural heritage elements are reproduced in the game world, and players can intuitively feel the traditional skills, folk activities, or ritual behaviors. This reproduction is not a simple reproduction but an artistic re-creation of intangible cultural heritage to adapt it to the narrative and interactive needs of the game. During the game, players can deeply experience the internal meaning and external forms of intangible cultural heritage through role-playing and task challenges. This experience is comprehensive, involving vision, hearing, and even touch, and can effectively stimulate players' emotional resonance and cognitive understanding. With the deepening of the game experience, players begin to have a sense of identity with nonheritage. This sense of identity can be derived from appreciating the aesthetic value of intangible heritage and understanding its cultural significance. Establishing identity is the key to the success of ethereal cultural heritage communication, which can promote the diffusion of metaphysical cultural heritage knowledge and the formation of inheritance will.

The dissemination of intangible cultural heritage in the game also follows the law of "interaction-learning-dissemination". Digital games provide an interactive platform where players can influence supernatural cultural heritage elements in the game world through operation and decision-making. This interactivity not only increases the interest of the game but also promotes players' active learning and exploration of intangible cultural heritage knowledge. In the game, learning becomes implicit. It is no longer an externally imposed task but a spontaneous behavior of the player to achieve the game's goal. In this way, players unconsciously absorb and internalize intangible cultural heritage knowledge. Finally, the metaphysical cultural heritage knowledge and experience gained by players in the game will be spread to the real world through social networks and word of mouth, forming an artistic transmission effect from the inside out.

In short, intangible cultural heritage has realized the cultural transmission from the game world to the real world in digital games. The discovery of these laws is significant for designing and promoting games containing intangible cultural heritage elements. They guide developers in better integrating metaphysical cultural heritage content and making it glow in digital media. At the same time, they also provide a new way to protect and inherit intangible cultural heritage.

4.3   Transformation Strategy of Cultural Elements in the Digital Environment

In the digital environment, the dissemination and transformation of intangible cultural heritage presents unique strategic needs. These strategies should not only consider the applicability of technology but also deeply explore the core of artistic elements and how to carry out innovative presentations in different digital platforms and game environments.

One strategy for transforming cultural elements is integrating them into the game's narrative structure. Players can naturally contact and understand these elements by promoting the story rather than displaying them as isolated information points. For example, design specific tasks or roles in the game to guide players in exploring the historical and cultural significance behind intangible cultural heritage to deepen the understanding and recognition of traditional cultural values. Another strategy is to enhance cultural experience through interaction design. Using modern information technology, such as virtual reality (VR), augmented reality (AR), and artificial intelligence (AI), can create an immersive experience environment, allowing users to experience intangible cultural heritage more intuitively and perceptually. This strategy can strengthen users' sense of participation and immersion and make cultural communication more vivid and lasting.

At the same time, considering the diversity and complexity of culture, the transformation strategy should also include personalized and customized elements. According to the interests and backgrounds of different users, providing diversified cultural paths and interactive ways can meet the needs of a wider user group. For example, it can give different levels of interpretation and interaction for players of different ages or cultural backgrounds or allow users to select and explore specific intangible cultural heritage projects according to their preferences.

So, the digital environment's communication and transformation strategy of intangible cultural heritage should comprehensively consider multiple dimensions such as narrative integration, interaction design, personalized experience, and professional cooperation. By implementing these strategies, the richness and depth of intangible cultural heritage can be effectively transformed into attractive and educational experiences in digital games and other media to realize cultural heritage's innovative dissemination and protection.

4.4   Guarantee Mechanism of Cultural Authenticity

When discussing the characteristics, laws, and transformation mechanism of intangible cultural heritage in digital games, an indispensable part is the guarantee mechanism of cultural authenticity. This mechanism ensures that the game's cultural heritage performance is faithful to its traditional form and can convey its deep cultural significance and value.

For intangible cultural heritage, authenticity is a faithful representation of the past and an ability to keep the core characteristics of culture unchanged in different media and environments. Digital games require developers to deeply understand contemporary society's historical context, cultural connotation, and the active state of intangible cultural heritage.

One way to achieve this goal is to cooperate with experts and scholars in the field of intangible cultural heritage. Their professional knowledge guides the game design and ensures the accuracy of artistic elements and the complete transmission of their traditional meaning. For example, to restore these scenes and ensure the authenticity of the culture, the development team of the *Justice* game specially invited Zhongming Ye, Shuying Zhou, successor of Xingshi and Paper Cuttings intangible cultural heritage, and other intangible cultural heritage experts. They take the history of the Song Dynasty as the primary reference, supplemented by the notes describing the local conditions and customs of the Song Dynasty, such as *A Dream of Splendor in Dongjing, Dreaming Sorghum Collection,* and *Old Stories in the Wulin,* as well as tens of thousands of poems. Children are setting off firecrackers and building snowmen, young people are driving cows, couples are watching lanterns, and so on. Every scene and character in the game aligns with our impression of the New Year, full of a strong traditional atmosphere. So, when players experience the game, they will get a great sense of realism and immerse themselves in it (Fig. 4).

Fig. 4. The scene of Chinese New Year of the Northern Song Dynasty in *Justice*

Cooperation with regional cultural protection institutions is also indispensable. They can provide authoritative resource support to help game developers capture the unique regional characteristics and times of intangible cultural heritage. The natural wonders in the game scene of *Genshin Impact*, such as the color pool, snow mountain, canyon, and forest, are based on the prototype of Luhua Lake in the Huanglong Liyue area of Sichuan Province. The stunning game scenes bring players unprecedented visual enjoyment.

Furthermore, the progress of technology provides new possibilities to enhance the expression of cultural authenticity. For example, high-definition images and 3D modeling technology can make the visual presentation of intangible cultural heritage elements more vivid. At the same time, interactive storytelling allows players to experience the legends and history behind intangible cultural heritage in the virtual space. These technical means should be based on respecting and inheriting the original appearance of intangible cultural heritage to avoid excessive commercialization or stereotyped interpretation.

In addition, disseminating intangible cultural heritage should not be limited to superficial imitation or simple repetition but should focus on living inheritance. In the game, supernatural cultural heritage elements should not be static backgrounds or props but should become a dynamic part of player interaction and participation. Through game mechanisms such as task-driven and role participation, players can personally make traditional handicrafts, participate in festival activities, or learn classical art performances to experience the vitality and charm of intangible cultural heritage culture.

The authenticity of intangible cultural heritage in digital games also involves community participation. Game developers can build platforms to encourage players from different regions and cultural backgrounds to share their metaphysical cultural heritage knowledge and experience, forming an ecological environment for multicultural exchange and shared learning. Community participation enriches the game's content and injects new vitality into intangible cultural heritage inheritance.

5 The Significance of "ICH + Digital Game" Mode Under the Threshold of Culture and Tourism Integration

5.1 Cultural Significance

Under the threshold of culture and tourism integration, the "ICH + digital game" mode is a new way of cultural transmission with far-reaching cultural significance. This mode injects new vitality into traditional culture and enables it to be inherited and developed in modern society.

First, as an innovative form of cultural communication, intangible cultural heritage digital games can effectively protect and inherit intangible cultural heritage. With the development of science and technology, digital technology provides new possibilities for the inheritance of intangible cultural heritage so that the culture facing disappearance can return to the public view and effectively protect and inherit intangible cultural heritage. At the same time, digital games also provide a new way to inherit intangible cultural heritage culture so that intangible cultural heritage culture can be spread and promoted on a broader range.

For example, kites and dragon boat props are used in the "Glory of China Festival" of the game King of Glory. The game team specially invited Hongli Guo, the inheritor of Weifang kite-making, to cooperate in the design of the King theme Shayan kite. At the same time, players' kite-drawing ideas should be widely solicited, and the top 20 players should be elected by voting. The masters will optimize the design of these kite "drawings" with various styles and truly make them. Finally, these kites will be delivered to players! *King of Glory* and the Chinese folklore society made the Dragon Boat Festival skins. They invited the intangible cultural heritage successors of the dragon boat to design and produce the King Zigui dragon boat. Players experienced the folk custom of the dragon boat races in Zigui, Quyuan's hometown. This has dramatically stimulated young people's interest in Chinese traditional culture. This cooperation ensures that the cultural content presented by the game is accurate and promotes artisans to the public, conveying the deep-seated cultural connotation and value (Figs. 5 and 6).

Fig. 5. Kites and kite Making in *King of Glory*

Fig. 6. Dragon boats in *King of Glory* and the dragon boat races in Zigui

Secondly, intangible cultural heritage digital games can encourage the integration and development of traditional culture and modern technology. Intangible cultural heritage digital games can combine traditional culture with modern science and technology and make traditional culture glow with new vitality. Through digital games, traditional culture can be presented to the public in a more modern and fashionable form, attracting more young people's attention and participation.

In addition, with the development of globalization, cultural exchanges have become increasingly frequent. Intangible cultural heritage digital games can push traditional culture to the world stage and show the unique charm of national culture. Through the elements of the game, such as the storyline and character setting, foreign players can have a deeper understanding of the connotation and essence of Chinese culture, enhance their cognition and understanding of Chinese culture, and help to enhance the national cultural soft power.

5.2 Aesthetic Function

The colors, shapes, and patterns in intangible cultural heritage have embodied the aesthetic concept of Chinese civilization for thousands of years. The media of immaterial cultural heritage games will pass Chinese traditional aesthetics on to the next generation. Moreover, the embodiment of this aesthetic function is not a single sensory stimulation but a multi-dimensional, deep-seated process of cultural and artistic integration. The intangible cultural heritage elements get a new interpretation and life through this three-dimensional display platform. Through the interactivity of digital games, players can have close contact with and experience intangible cultural heritage culture to stimulate their recognition of traditional aesthetics.

In addition, the aesthetic function of intangible cultural heritage digital games is also reflected in their reproduction and remodeling of conventional aesthetics. The scene design, music score, costume modeling, and other elements in the game are all artistic representations of the essence of intangible cultural heritage. Through in-depth study and understanding of traditional culture, designers digitize and play these elements, retaining the original artistic style and giving them new vitality. For example, the game *Ola Star* refers to the design of the character in the game "Holy Dance Kirin" based on the Kirin shape in Kirin Dance. The girl has a unicorn horn on her head, and the Unicorn Dance props under her body are created to look like real Unicorn Dance props. Based on respecting tradition, the artistic transformation of its shape, color, and decoration is combined with contemporary aesthetic trends to deepen game players' impression of Kylin. In this process, the aesthetic value of intangible cultural heritage has been inherited and developed. At the same time, it has also been combined with modern aesthetics to produce a unique artistic charm (Fig. 7).

Fig. 7. The holy dance Kirin in *Aurra Star and* the intangible cultural heritage of the Kirin dance

Moreover, the intangible cultural heritage of digital games has realized the innovation of artistic expression through technical means. By applying modern information technology such as AR (augmented reality) and VR (virtual reality), combined with image, sound, device, and other means of expression, intangible cultural heritage culture can be more accurately and three-dimensional displayed in the virtual space. It not only broadens the expression forms of traditional culture but also produces more diverse cultural works.

5.3 Economic Value

In the context of cultural and tourism integration, the "ICH + digital game" mode can create new economic growth points, have a far-reaching impact on the relevant industrial chain, and produce significant monetary value.

From a macro perspective, the success of intangible cultural heritage digital games not only promotes the development of the cultural industry but also has the potential to attract more tourism and investment. The immaterial cultural heritage background or cultural characteristics displayed in the game may stimulate the curiosity and desire for the exploration of players and become the motivation for on-site tourism, thus driving the growth of local tourism. The linkage between the game *Genshin Impact* and the Huanglong Scenic and Historic Interest Area in Sichuan has attracted many game players, promoting local tourism development. At the same time, the innovative mode and market performance of such games also attract investors' attention and capital investment in the cultural industry, especially in digital games, which will help form a virtuous economic cycle and industrial upgrading.

Developing and promoting intangible cultural heritage digital games can also drive the development of upstream and downstream industrial chains. The game production process requires a lot of cultural heritage research, art design, and technical support, which provide cooperation opportunities and business growth space for artistic research institutions, creative design companies, and technology development teams. At the same time, with the spread and popularity of games, relevant derivatives such as souvenirs, books, and exhibitions will also receive attention, thus promoting the prosperity of the cultural consumer goods market. The exclusive oil paper umbrella props drawn by intangible cultural heritage inheritors in the game of *Jade Dynasty: New Fantasy* are not only the props of the characters in the game but also the online points exchange sales, which countless players have sought (Fig. 8).

Fig. 8. The oil paper umbrellas prop and commodities in *Jade Dynasty: New Fantasy*

In short, the "ICH + digital game" model has multidimensional value in the economic layer. It can create direct game sales revenue and promote the win-win of multiple participants in the industrial chain, promote the integrated development of related industries, and ultimately contribute to regional and national economic growth.

6   Conclusion and Prospect

With the rapid development of digital technology and the deepening of global cultural exchanges, it has become a significant trend for intangible cultural heritage to realize innovative communication through the emerging media of digital games. This study explores a variety of models of the combination of intangible cultural heritage and digital games. It reveals that from the perspective of integrating theme culture and tourism, this model provides new possibilities for inheriting traditional culture and promoting globalization.

In terms of prospects, with the continuous maturity of virtual reality, augmented reality, and other technologies, the role of digital games in protecting and disseminating intangible cultural heritage will become more prominent. The cross-border cooperation between game designers and cultural heritage experts is expected to be strengthened to promote the birth of more games with educational significance and profound cultural connotations. These games can more vividly reproduce traditional culture, encourage players to learn skills in practice, and then cultivate a new generation of inheritors of intangible cultural heritage. At the same time, with the acceleration of the internationalization of China's game industry, games themed with traditional culture have the potential to become a new way to export the "soft power" of Chinese culture. Through this platform, we can show the world the breadth and depth of Chinese civilization and enhance international understanding and recognition of Chinese traditional culture.

We look forward to more creative and technological inputs in the future so that this model can be deepened and improved and the intangible cultural heritage can be revitalized in the digital age.

References

1. Wang, R., Gao, Z.: Renew according to the situation: exploration and prospect of international communication of Chinese excellent traditional culture. External Commun. **01**, 24–27 (2024)
2. Yu, H., Zhu, G.: Online games and contemporary communication of Chinese excellent traditional culture. Nanjing Soc. Sci. **07**, 155–162 (2022)
3. Cheng, M.: Review the integrated development of intangible cultural heritage and online games. Gehai **03**, 36–41 (2022)
4. Zhang, Y., Li, J., Zhao, Y.: Exploration of the mode of innovation and promotion of domestic games in the context of cultural and tourism integration: a case study based on the original God. Libr. Inform. Knowl. **38**(05), 107–118 (2021)
5. Tang, J., Zhu, X.: Discuss the development and application of serious games to inherit digital intangible cultural heritage. Libr. Inform. Work **64**(10), 35–45 (2020)
6. Yang, Y., Ji, T., Zhang, D.: Design and application of cultural heritage in serious games. Packag. Eng. **41**(04), 312–317 (2020)
7. Liu, W., Li, H.: Ontology design and social functions of intangible cultural heritage functional games. Sci. Consult. (Sci. Technol. Manag.) **04**, 56–57 (2019)

Non-visual Effects Driven Fatigue Level Recognition Method for Enclosed Space Workers

Xian Zhang[1,2], Yuan Feng[1,2], Jingluan Wang[1,2], and Dengkai Chen[1,2(✉)]

[1] Key Laboratory for Industrial Design and Ergonomics of Ministry of Industry and Information Technology, Northwestern Polytechnical University, Xi'an 710072, China
zhangxian@mail.nwpu.edu.cn
[2] Shaanxi Engineering Laboratory for Industrial Design, Northwestern Polytechnical University, Xi'an 710072, China

Abstract. With the rapid development of underground space and manned tourist deep diver careers, it is of great research value to enhance the comfort and task performance of workers by improving the design of enclosed spaces. It has been well-acknowledged that vision is the primary factor that affects human perception and fatigue. On the one hand, lighting environment of an enclosed space can directly influence the visual perception of human through the human body's third type of photoreceptor cells, intrinsically photosensitive retinal ganglion cells (ipRGCs), the human body's pupil size, melatonin, body temperature, heart rate, and other non-visual physiological metrics. On the other hand, inappropriate lighting environments can reduce vigilance and even cause severe human errors. In this study, we designed four different lighting conditions to investigate the non-visual effects of the workers in completing the Psychomotor Vigilance Task (PVT). Task performances (i.e., Reaction Time - RT) and physiological indicators (i.e., electrocardiogram - ECG) are used to evaluate the effectiveness. In general, the results show that with an increased illuminance level, the workers are becoming more vigilant. We have collected the RT with different fatigue levels classified accordingly, and then analyzed the correlation between the RT and ECG indexes. Furthermore, we constructed the fatigue recognition model of workers based on ECG indexes by using the Support Vector Machine (SVM) algorithm and verified it. This study aims to optimizes the lighting environment and improve task perform efficiency by automatically identifying the fatigue level through monitoring the ECG indicators of the workers.

Keywords: Non-visual Effects · Fatigue Level · Enclosed Space · Support Vector Machine · Psychomotor Vigilance Task

1 Introduction

The rapid development in the field of manned deep-ocean submersibles calls for improved cabin design to enhance the comfort of works within such enclosed spaces. Enclosed conditions are easy to form a detrimental cabin environment, which further

N. A. Streitz and S. Konomi (Eds.): HCII 2024, LNCS 14719, pp. 172–185, 2024.
https://doi.org/10.1007/978-3-031-60012-8_11

causes increased fatigue and leads to decreased concentration, loss of appetite, and other challenging symptoms such as restlessness and anxiety [1, 2]. Lighting is one of the essential factors affecting humans directly and can have a biological impact on humans. Changes of lighting condition can result in changes of pupil size, acutely inhibit melatonin, and cause variations in our body temperature or heart rate (HR) [4]. By improving lighting environment of an enclosed space, the visual comfort, work efficiency, vigilance of the workers can be enhanced. These indicators are also closely related to the human third type of photoreceptor cells, intrinsically photoreceptive retinal ganglion cells (ipRGCs) [3] and study of non-visual effects. We explore the method to maintain or enhance human performance by varying different lighting conditions, which can drive the development of non-visual effects.

1.1 Effects of Lighting Environment on Enclosed Space Workers

The effects of lighting environmental conditions on human health, satisfaction and performance have been the research focus for decades. Studies have shown that improving the work environment can increase the productivity of workers. When workers live in an environment without sufficient daylight on a daily basis, circadian rhythm disorders and dislocations occur. Which can consequently affect work efficiency and physical and mental health [5]. Factors such as the Correlated Color Temperature (CCT) and illuminance level of lighting can also cause visual discomfort, which can affect work efficiency and have an impact on psychological perception [6]. In the enclosed space, natural light exposure is limited, artificial light needs to be used to maintain human visual perception and biological rhythms. Inappropriate lighting is likely to cause physiological and psychological discomfort, and affects humans work performance and emotions, resulting in human error and jeopardizing the health of the humans [7]. The use of various positive effects of the lighting environment can regulate human perception, our ability to understand, judgment, decision-making, operating ability, and mobilize positive emotions, enhance vigilance. Which in turn help us cope with mental fatigue or work stress, and reduce the occurrence of human error, which is important to maintain and enhance the performance of humans [1].

1.2 Fatigue Evaluation

Fatigue denotes the feeling of extreme physical or mental exhaustion. Timely intervention by monitoring the fatigue level of humans is an important method to reduce the occurrence of accidents [8]. Most of the research on fatigue level focuses on scenarios such as driving since in-depth research on fatigue driving is of great practical significance [9, 10]. In addition, researchers also focus on scenarios like fatigue monitoring of miners [11], construction workers [12], and nuclear power plant workers [13]. The fatigue level of workers in enclosed spaces is closely related to their work efficiency and work safety, and the fatigue level recognition can also optimize and improve the cabin lighting environment, intervene in the human non-visual effects, and reduce the human factors errors.

Indicators used for fatigue evaluation are diverse. The majority methods are three-fold, including subjective self- evaluation, objective evaluation, and physiological evaluation. The self-evaluation method involves workers evaluating their own fatigue levels [14]. It is often accomplished using a specifically designed questionnaire, which is carried out before or after the work task. Their fatigue level is determined based on a comparative analysis of the workers' self-description and the questionnaire results. Self-evaluation methods have disadvantages such as poor objectivity and susceptibility to their own abilities and memory. The objective evaluation method refers to the method of measuring the fatigue level of the workers through technical means such as testing and experimentation. Fatigue recognition technology is generally based on physiological indicators that analyzes the change of physiological signals of the workers to determine whether he/she is in a state of fatigue. The physiological metrics used mainly include electroencephalogram (EEG), eye movement data, ECG and respiratory rate.

Previous research has dived into fatigue evaluation. Sun et al. [15] investigated a functional linkage-based mental fatigue monitoring scheme using high-resolution EEG to detect subjects' sustained attention, thus confirming the feasibility of a functional linkage-based mental fatigue assessment scheme and opening up new avenues for modeling ego-brain dynamics under different mental conditions. Aryal et al. [16] showed that using temple and forehead temperature data to categorize fatigue more accurately in construction workers than HR data. The method of worker fatigue identification based on operating behavior focuses on the study on workers' state when they are manipulating instruments and completing specific tasks. To analyze the differences in the operating behaviors of workers in different fatigue states, thus determining whether they are fatigued or not. The most common way is to predict and judge the fatigue level of workers based on machine learning algorithms by collecting information such as task reaction time (RT) and correctness. Research has been done to identify fatigue by keystroke data derived from typing on a computer keyboard [17]. These objective evaluation methods are often combined to appear in various studies. With the development of machine learning, more methods on fatigue recognition are based on information fusion, which fuses multiple features in the physiological parameters of the workers, and the operating behavior, and constructs a fatigue recognition model to detect the degree of fatigue of the workers.

1.3   Fatigue Recognition Methods and Modeling

Fatigue recognition modeling involves mapping the acquired physiological feature vectors to the corresponding categories to reflect the degree of fatigue in the subject population, so the selection of classifiers with good discriminative features is crucial for degree classification. Different machine learning algorithms used in different analysis tasks can show different results. Fatigue state testing usually uses k-Nearest Neighbor (kNN), Bayesian classifiers, decision trees, random forests, support vector machines (SVM), neural networks, and other methods. In practice, because some experimental paradigms have their inherent data characteristics, researchers need to explore the classifiers that match them through further research to obtain the best classification results. Yang et al. [9] fused multiple contact and non-contact feature information and applied a Hidden Markov Model to compute the dynamic changes of Bayesian networks at different time slices, showing that ECG and EEG are important factors for inferring the fatigue state of a driver. Li et al. [18] proposed a 5-D Brain Cognition Cognitive Changes Synchronized with Global, Local and Sequential Changes of Brain Dynamic Recognition Network (E-5-D-BCDRNet), which lays the theoretical foundation for real-time brain fatigue monitoring and promotes the development of Intelligent Transportation Systems (ITS). Sun et al. [19] proposed a multi-stream facial feature fusion convolutional neural network (FFF-CNN) containing one global facial stream and two local eye streams, which can be used to develop a robust and accurate driver fatigue detection system that with better stability under low quality inputs, driver blinking and fatigue level can be accurately identified in fatigue driving videos. Wei et al. [20] proposed a lower limb motion recognition method based on empirical modal decomposition (EMD) and k-nearest neighbor entropy (KNN-En) estimation, which can accurately extract the effective information from the sEMG signal. Yin et al. [21] developed Dynamic Deep Extreme Learning Machine (DD-ELM) to adapt to the changes in the distribution of EEG features in two mental tasks and to recognize EEG features with different fatigue levels.

Among machine learning methods, SVM is a learning algorithm with high accuracy and good robustness. Compared with the way of seeking local optimal prediction solution such as classification tree, SVM is more convenient to seek global optimal prediction solution. Meanwhile, it has good adaptability to problems such as fitting, and therefore has better generalization ability. Tepe et al. [22] investigated the performance of SVM for classifying non-real-time and real-time EMG signals. Shen et al. [23] used a probability-based support vector machine method to test an EEG-based mental fatigue monitoring system, and verified the accuracy of the classifier. Accuracy. Janssen et al. [24] trained and tested SVMs and Self-Organizing Mapping (SOMs) to correctly classify gait patterns before, during, and after complete leg depletion through isokinetic leg exercises. Many scholars have found that applying SVM method to the study of fatigue level of ECG [25, 26] will help to discover the relationship between ECG features and fatigue level well. The fatigue recognition model constructed by using SVM method can complete the monitoring of humans' fatigue condition and fatigue level classification more accurately. This method could also improve the accuracy in estimating and issuing early warning of fatigue condition and health monitoring.

1.4 Research Objectives

In summary, people who work for a long time in an enclosed environment will suffer from circadian rhythm disorders due to the lack of natural light exposure, which will have a negative impact on work efficiency, psychology and spirituality. It would be a research priority to maintain and enhance human performance by changing the lighting environment and constructing automated fatigue recognition models. This paper takes enclosed space as the research background, to provide a research basis for the subsequent enclosed space fatigue degree recognition of workers, so as to effectively regulate and optimize the lighting environment in enclosed space. The research objectives of this study are:

1. To investigate the non-visual effects of four different lighting illuminance levels on the workers within enclosed spaces.
2. To explore the method of objectively classifying the fatigue level of the workers, to introduce the SVM for the training classification, and to construct the fatigue recognition model based on SVM.

2 Methods

2.1 Subjects

The experiment was conducted with 22 subjects, all of whom were university students, including 10 females and 12 males, aged between 22 and 27 years old (26.16 ± 1.34). All participants were in good health, had normal or good corrected vision, no history of color blindness or color deficiency, and were right-handed. No alcohol, caffeine or drugs were allowed to be ingested 12 h before the experiment, and to ensure that the subjects were emotionally relaxed during the experiment, they were asked to work and rest normally and not to do strenuous exercise during the test.

2.2 Experimental Environment and Equipment

The experiment was conducted in the enclosed laboratory of the Institute of Industrial Design, Northwestern Polytechnical University, which was divided into the control area and the experimental area. The control area is equipped with an intelligent system that can regulate the lighting environment of the experimental area, and the experimental area is separated from the control area by an opaque door, so that there are no other light interference factors. The ambient temperature of the experimental area was controlled at 26 degrees Celsius. An intelligent dimmable light was used to provide illumination, which could accurately simulate light sources within the range of illumination requirements according to experimental needs.

The subject was seated in the center of the experimental area, with the desktop 75 cm above the ground, and a laptop computer positioned on the desktop. The experiment was set up with four lighting conditions, the color temperature was kept constant at 5600 K. The spectral distribution is shown in Fig. 1. The illuminance was 200 lx, 400 lx, 600 lx, and 800 lx, respectively. The reflectance of each part of the experimental area is shown in Table 1.

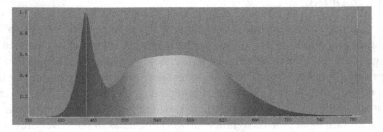

Fig. 1. 5600 K spectral distribution.

Table 1. Reflectance of various surfaces in the laboratory.

Surfaces	Reflectance
Top ceiling	0.85
Wall	0.50
Floor	0.68
Desktop	0.24
Door	0.56

2.3 Experimental Task

The Psychomotor Vigilance Task (PVT) is a visual RT measurement task that requires sustained attention and is sensitive to attentional neglect. Because it is a simple click response to salient visual signals, it does not require prior learning and is not subject to individual differences in ability and avoids practice effects [27].The PVT has been extensively validated in the laboratory, clinic, and operational time, and it has been shown to perform better for central fatigue assessment under experimental conditions such as sleep deprivation, high cognitive load, and environmental heat stress. Under simulated and actual aerospace operating conditions, PVT can be used for fatigue assessment of flight crews and astronauts. In addition, the PVT can be used as a health protection measure for fatigue in aerospace and related operations. Combining with other methods can further improve the assessment efficacy. The PVT task has the advantages of simple operation, small learning effect, small influence of individual differences, and can well reduce or even eliminate the intra-subjects' differences. The PVT can be used to assess the fatigue of flight crews and astronauts under the conditions of aerospace operations. It is responsive to studies of sleep deprivation, excitatory agents, task parameters, and is the gold standard for testing behavioral vigilance and attention.

In this experiment, the task required subjects to record RTs by quickly pressing the button when the target stimulus appeared on the screen. First, a " +" symbol fixation point was displayed on the computer screen to remind subjects to focus their attention on the center of the computer screen and press the space bar to start the experiment. Then, a white background appeared on the screen, and a capitalized English letter would appear on the background as a stimulus. Subjects were required to press the corresponding letter button at the moment they saw the target letter appear. There were two types of letters, "F" and "J", which meant that the subject quickly pressed the F key when he saw the letter "F", and the subject quickly pressed the J key when he saw the letter "J". The experiment consisted of 100 stimuli, each of the two letters appeared 50 times. The order was randomized, and the experiment lasted approximately 5 min in a single setting, and the RTs was recorded.

2.4 Experimental Procedure

Each subject was instructed to complete the experimental procedure and perform a test experiment before the start of the experiment to ensure familiarity with the procedure. At the same time, we introduced the experimental scenario and the physiological parameter monitors used to the subjects. Subjects were asked to complete the PVT experiment using the E-Prime software from Psychology Software Tools and to analyze the human ECG using the BIOPAC system, which can monitor human physiological data over a long period of time. The experimental steps were the same for each lighting condition.

When experiment starts, experimenter first turned on the ECG equipment, and the subjects need to familiarize themselves with the experimental lighting environment for 5 min. Then the subject carried out the PVT experiment, the purpose of which is to test their vigilance. Then the subject returned to the control area to rest for 5 min. The experimenter changed lighting environment of the experimental area and the subject carried out the next set of experiments, a total of 4 groups of experiments. The overall experimental process is shown in Fig. 2.

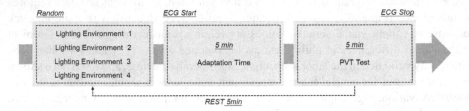

Fig. 2. Experimental flow chart.

2.5 Data Analysis

IBM SPSS Statistics software was used to analyze the experimental data. We used Repeated Measures Analysis of Variance (rANOVA) for between-group comparisons. We performed the *Shapiro-Wilk* test on the experimental data of 22 subjects in each lighting condition and then tested the overall variance in different environments. We also need to perform the *Mauchly* sphericity hypothesis test on the data, and if the sphericity test was not satisfied, then we needed to perform the *Epsilon* correction on the data. The p values indicate the level of significance, $p < 0.05$ indicates a significant difference between groups, and $p < 0.01$ indicates a highly significant difference. The results of the rANOVA only indicated that the means of the different levels of the independent variables were significantly different, so a *Bonferroni* post-hoc test was needed to determine which two levels were significantly different from each other and to make multiple comparisons of the data.

3   Results

3.1 Non-visual Effects in Different Lighting Environments

Results of PVT Experiments. After completing the PVT test in 4 lighting conditions, the results of rANOVA of RT for the 22 subjects is shown in Table 2. The data of each group obeyed normal distribution. The result of spherical test showed *Machly W* = 0.957, p < 0.001, which does not conform to the spherical test. Therefore, the result of correction in *Greenhouse-Geisser* prevailed.

Table 2. Results of ANOVA analysis of subjects' RT.

Lighting settings	RT (ms) Mean ± SD	F test		Multiple Means Comparison
		F	p	
L1	438.87 ± 96.51	12.537	< 0.001	L4 < L3 < L2 < L1
L2	415.62 ± 92.69			
L3	412.98 ± 82.97			
L4	411.67 ± 85.86			

According to the results of the analysis, the main effect of different levelled lighting conditions was significant. After Bonferroni multiple comparisons it was found that the RT was the longest in the L1 setting and the shortest in the L4 setting. And there was a significant difference (p < 0.001) in the mean value of the RT of the subjects between different lighting settings.

Results of ECG Analysis. ECG metrics were characterized using HR and heart rate variability (HRV), and the mean HR and HRV recorded for 22 subjects in 4 different lighting settings are shown in Table 3. The result showed that different lighting environments have a significant effect on the ECG metrics of the subjects.

Table 3. Results of rANOVA analysis of subjects' ECG indicators.

Lighting settings	HRV			HR		
	Mean ± SD	F test		Mean ± SD	F test	
		F	p		F	p
L1	74.39 ± 7.52	5.081	= 0.013	0.836 ± 0.34	1.185	= 0.027
L2	75.37 ± 9.44			0.881 ± 0.35		
L3	76.07 ± 8.92			0.884 ± 0.54		
L4	78.45 ± 7.68			1.070 ± 0.50		

The data of each group obeyed normal distribution. The result of HRV spherical test showed *Machly W* = 0.673, p = 0.919, the HR showed *Machly W* = 0.724, p = 0.946. ECG data from subjects in different lighting environments showed significant differences for subjects and the highest HRV and HR metrics for vigilance were found in the L4 environment.

3.2   Fatigue Recognition Modeling

The main objective of our fatigue study is to reduce human factor errors and improve work efficiency. The reasons affecting operational errors are manifold [28]. The ability of workers to react quickly to unexpected situations is a key factor in the fatigue study if the highly repetitive of the tasks and the complexity of the work environment structure are reduced. Excluding factors such as subject distraction and medication, the immediate effect of RT is a direct reflection of the level of fatigue. The RT is an accessible index that can directly and quantitatively evaluate the level of reaction, while it can directly reflect the level of fatigue of the operator. RT can show a worker's concentration and vigilance, this study combines the RT and ECG indexes of the workers to explore the fatigue judgment and grading methods, using the quantitative indexes of the task RT to objectively grade the fatigue and construct the fatigue recognition model of the workers based on the SVM.

Classification of Fatigue Levels based on RT.   Using the subjects' RT to characterize their fatigue level, the RT can be classified into 2 levels. We selected each RT corresponding to the fatigue level under the subjects' ECG indicators for correlation analysis, to judge the reasonableness of the objective use of ECG fatigue level classification.

RT in this study refers to the time when the subject sees the letters and presses the response button when completing the task, and RT can be directly derived from E-Prime software. The subjects' PVT-RT was statistically significantly affected by the lighting environment, so RT was selected as the criterion for fatigue equivalence and classification. A total of 8800 data were counted for the RT of 22 subjects. Because each subject has large individual differences and different RT thresholds, each subject RT needs to be analyzed individually to classify the fatigue level, and subjects 1 was randomly selected as examples for illustration (Fig. 3). Fatigue was classified by dividing the task reaction time data into 2 parts based on the subjects' average RT ($\overline{RT}$), as shown in Fig. 3. RT < $\overline{RT}$ was judged as non-fatigue (F0), and RT > $\overline{RT}$ was judged as fatigue (F1).

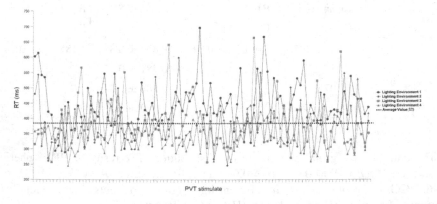

Fig. 3.   RT in 4 lighting conditions of subject 1.

It can be seen from the above reaction times of subject 1 that those above the average reaction timeline were judged to be fatigued and those below the average line were judged to be in a non-fatigued state.

Correlation Analysis of Physiologic Indicators with RT. According to the subjects' RT, the interval time segment between the acquisition point RT_i when the subject pressed the response button and the previous acquisition point RT_{i-1} was intercepted as the fatigue level characterization segment, and the ECG data of the same fatigue level were collated. In this paper, subject 1 RT mapping physiological parameters were selected to develop the elaboration, and the rest of the subjects were analyzed with the same process Therefore, we adopted the test using the non-parametric method *Mann-Whitney*. The results showed that there was a significant difference between the two groups (p < 0. 001), indicating that HR could be used to classify the fatigue level of the subjects. We analyzed the HR data that mapped to the two fatigue levels with paired *t*-tests using SPSS, and the data did not pass the normality test. The HRV variability of the two fatigue levels of subject 1 was analyzed, and the results indicated that the HRV was significantly different at the two fatigue levels (p < 0.0001). Both ECG signal analyses demonstrated the reliability of classifying fatigue levels based on mean RT. Meanwhile, the ECG signal index can be used for the next step of fatigue degree recognition model construction.

SVM-based Fatigue Recognition Modeling. SVM is a two-class classification model, its basic model definition is to seek a separation hyperplane on the feature space to maximize the interval, that is, the linear classifier, the basic strategy of its learning is how to get the interval maximization. SVM can solve the problem of machine learning in small samples, improve the generalization performance, but also able to deal with high-dimensional nonlinear problems, so as to solve the problem of the choice of neural network structure and the problem of the local minima.

There are three kinds of SVM classification models, the first model is linearly differentiable SVM, the training data requirements are very strict, must be linearly differentiable; the second model is approximate linearly differentiable SVM, because the training data is close to linearly differentiable, so the training data is allowed to have occasional singularities, and after eliminating these singularities, the data is linearly differentiable, but often in the actual research most of the data is linearly indistinguishable. Are linearly indistinguishable, thus leading to the third model, the nonlinear SVM, which is applicable to the training data linearly indistinguishable, and generally adopts the corresponding kernel function, and there are certain requirements on how to choose the appropriate kernel function.

The ECG data of all subjects were divided according to RT, and the generated dataset contained factor 1, factor 2, and labeled item class, on the basis of which the SVM method was selected to realize the binary classification of the data. All the sample data were divided into training set and test set to prepare for the training and testing of the classification model. A total of 22 subjects' data were collected, and each subject completed the task under each lighting condition for 5 min, a total of 20 min. 100 sample points were selected from the 22 subjects under each fatigue state, a total of 4,400 sample points, and the category labels corresponding to each type of samples of fatigue and non-fatigue were −1, 1. Each set of sample data included 2 dimensions, HR and HRV, which were recorded as factor 1, factor 2, and the first 5 rows are displayed as shown in Table 4. In this study, 70% of each sample was randomly selected as training set and 30% as test set.

Table 4. First 5 rows of data for the sample group.

Factor1	Factor2	Class
82	1.037	−1
82	1.037	−1
82	1.038	−1
82	1.038	−1
82	1.037	−1

To achieve fatigue classification, we first trained the SVM by inputting the training set feature values and corresponding category labels. Then, the test set data is input and recognition is carried out using the classifiers obtained from the training. Finally, the classification results are compared with the manually labelled fatigue classes based on reaction times to derive the accuracy of fatigue classification. The use of different kernel functions will have different recognition effects, and in the current situation where the penalty factor and kernel function parameters can only be determined empirically, we need to compare the effectiveness of the classifiers under the SVM model using different kernel functions. We finally chose the linear kernel function (linear) to obtain a higher accuracy rate, which can reach 83.3%. Therefore, linear kernel function is chosen as the kernel function type in this study.

4 Concluding Remarks

Currently, research on non-visual effects is in constant development, and exploring the non-visual effects of lighting is important for maintaining and enhancing human performance. In this study, we set up 4 different lighting conditions to investigate the non-visual effects on subjects, in which the selected non-visual indicators were task RT and ECG. The results of the study showed that the RT of the subjects was effectively shortened with increasing illuminance, which is consistent with the results of previous studies [29, 30], while the physiological metrics and task performance showed similar results, the HR and HRV data of the participants pointed to the trend of increased vigilance with increasing illuminance. This suggests that the differences in the non-visual effects of different illuminance levels on workers are significant, contributing to the development of research on non-visual effects.

Secondly, fatigue level is defined based on task RT, experimental data are processed to extract RT data of subjects completing the task, and by dividing subjects' RT based on the mean value, subjects' vigilance state is divided into two kinds of fatigue and wakefulness, and at the same time, mapped to simultaneous physiological indexes to conduct non-parametric test analysis, and the results show that fatigue level can be divided by using ECG data. Then, we synthesize the two physiological indicators of HR and HRV with the fatigue level label to generate a sample set, construct a fatigue recognition model based on SVM, and after training and testing, the model accuracy reaches 83.3%, which provides a research basis for the optimization of the design of the enclosed environment lighting.

In addition, there are still some limitations in this study, such as the laboratory research subjects are all students, which may be different from the real workers, in the future research can consider selecting real workers to participate in the experiment. In addition, machine learning classification algorithms, in addition to SVM, there are other algorithms that can be used for fatigue classification, because SVM has the advantages of low risk and does not require a large amount of data to build an efficient classification model, this study selected SVM as the fatigue classification algorithm, and in the future, we can try a variety of algorithms for comparative research.

Our study proposes that in the future lighting optimization design of enclosed space, it is possible to determine the degree of fatigue in real time by monitoring the personnel's ECG data, and adjust the illumination level according to the current fatigue level, so as to guide the lighting design, and complete the lighting optimization of non-visual effect-driven enclosed space.

Acknowledgements. This study was funded by Shaanxi Province Special Support Program Philosophy Society Leading Talents [D5113200021] and the Fundamental Research Funds for the Central Universities [G2023KY05105].

Disclosure of Interests. The authors declare that they have no known competing financial interests or personal relationships that could have influenced the work reported in this paper.

References

1. Chen, D., Zhu, M., Qiao, Y., Wang, J., Zhang, X.: An ergonomic design method of manned cabin driven by human operation performance. Adv. Des. Res. **1**(1), 12–20 (2023)
2. Gou, Z., Gou, B., Liao, W., Bao, Y., Deng, Y.: Integrated lighting ergonomics: a review on the association between non-visual effects of light and ergonomics in the enclosed cabins. Build. Environ. **243**, 110616 (2023)
3. Berson, D.M., Dunn, F.A., Takao, M.J.: Phototransduction by retinal ganglion cells that set the circadian clock. Science **295**(5557), 1070–1073 (2002)
4. Houser, K.W., Boyce, P.R., Zeitzer, J.M., Herf, M.: Human-centric lighting: Myth, magic or metaphor? Light. Res. Technol. **53**(2), 97–118 (2020)
5. Mills, P.R., Tomkins, S.C., Schlangen, L.J.M.: The effect of high correlated colour temperature office lighting on employee wellbeing and work performance 5 (2007)
6. Li, Y., Ru, T., Chen, Q., Qian, L., Luo, X., Zhou, G.: Effects of illuminance and correlated color temperature of indoor light on emotion perception **11**, 14351 (2021)
7. Zhang, X., Qiao, Y., Wang, H., Wang, J., Chen, D.: Lighting environmental assessment in enclosed spaces based on emotional model. Sci. Total. Environ. **870**, 161933 (2023)

8. Xu, B., Wu, Q., Xi, C., He, R.: Recognition of the fatigue status of pilots using BF–PSO optimized multi-class GP classification with sEMG signals. Reliab. Eng. Syst. Saf. **199**, 106930 (2020)
9. Yang, G., Lin, Y., Bhattacharya, P.: A driver fatigue recognition model based on information fusion and dynamic Bayesian network. Inf. Sci. **180**(10), 1942–1954 (2010)
10. Li, R., Chen, Y.V., Zhang, L.: A method for fatigue detection based on Driver's steering wheel grip. Int. J. Ind. Ergon. **82**, 103083 (2021)
11. Chen, S., et al.: Psychophysiological data-driven multi-feature information fusion and recognition of miner fatigue in high-altitude and cold areas. Comput. Biol. Med. **133**, 104413 (2021)
12. Ibrahim, A., Nnaji, C., Namian, M., Koh, A., Techera, U.: Investigating the impact of physical fatigue on construction workers' situational awareness. Saf. Sci. **163**, 106103 (2023)
13. Guo, Z., Sun, L., Zhang, H., Yuan, X., Cui, K.: Effects of video display terminal fatigue on situational awareness ability of operators and modeling study. Nucl. Eng. Des. **414**, 112534 (2023)
14. Borghini, G., Astolfi, L., Vecchiato, G., Mattia, D., Babiloni, F.: Measuring neurophysiological signals in aircraft pilots and car drivers for the assessment of mental workload. Fatigue Drowsiness **44**(Sp. Iss. SI), 58–75 (2014)
15. Sun, Y., Lim, J., Meng, J., Kwok, K., Thakor, N., Bezerianos, A.: Discriminative analysis of brain functional connectivity patterns for mental fatigue classification. Engineering **42**(10), 2084–2094 (2014)
16. Aryal, A., Ghahramani, A., Becerik-Gerber, B.: Monitoring fatigue in construction workers using physiological measurements. **82**(oct.), 154–165 (2017)
17. Ulinskas, M., Damaševičius, R., Maskeliūnas, R., Woźniak, M.: Recognition of human daytime fatigue using keystroke data. Procedia Comput. Sci. **130**, 947–952 (2018)
18. Li, P., et al.: An EEG-based brain cognitive dynamic recognition network for representations of brain fatigue. Appl. Soft Comput. **146**, 110613 (2023)
19. Sun, Z., Miao, Y., Jeon, J.Y., Kong, Y., Park, G.: Facial feature fusion convolutional neural network for driver fatigue detection. Eng. Appl. Artif. Intell. **126**, 106981 (2023)
20. Wei, C., et al.: Recognition of lower limb movements using empirical mode decomposition and k-nearest neighbor entropy estimator with surface electromyogram signals. Biomed. Signal Process. Control **71**, 103198 (2022)
21. Yin, Z., Zhang, J.: Task-generic mental fatigue recognition based on neurophysiological signals and dynamical deep extreme learning machine. Neurocomputing **283**, 266–281 (2018)
22. Tepe, C., Demir, M.C.: Real-time classification of EMG Myo armband data using support vector machine. IRBM **43**(4), 300–308 (2022)
23. Shen, K.-Q., Li, X.-P., Ong, C.-J., Shao, S.-Y., Wilder-Smith, E.P.V.: EEG-based mental fatigue measurement using multi-class support vector machines with confidence estimate. Clin. Neurophysiol. **119**(7), 1524–1533 (2008)
24. Janssen, D., Schöllhorn, W.I., Newell, K.M., Jäger, J.M., Rost, F., Vehof, K.: Diagnosing fatigue in gait patterns by support vector machines and self-organizing maps. Hum. Mov. Sci. **30**(5), 966–975 (2011)
25. Qu, H., Gao, X., Pang, L.: Classification of mental workload based on multiple features of ECG signals. Inform. Med. Unlocked **24**, 100575 (2021)
26. Esener, I.I.: Subspace-based feature extraction on multi-physiological measurements of automobile drivers for distress recognition. Biomed. Sig. Process. Control **66**, 102504 (2021)
27. Molina, E., Sanabria, D., Jung, T.-P., Correa, Á.: Electroencephalographic and peripheral temperature dynamics during a prolonged psychomotor vigilance task. Accid. Anal. Prev. **126**, 198–208 (2019)

28. Ye, C., Yin, Z., Zhao, M., Tian, Y., Sun, Z.: Identification of mental fatigue levels in a language understanding task based on multi-domain EEG features and an ensemble convolutional neural network. Biomed. Signal Process. Control **72**, 103360 (2022)

29. Konstantzos, I., Sadeghi, S.A., Kim, M., Xiong, J., Tzempelikos, A.: The effect of lighting environment on task performance in buildings – a review. Energy Buildings **226**, 110394 (2020)

30. Juslén, H., Tenner, A.: Mechanisms involved in enhancing human performance by changing the lighting in the industrial workplace. Int. J. Ind. Ergon. **35**(9), 843–855 (2005)

Smart Ecosystems for Learning and Culture

A.I. In All the Wrong Places

Marc Böhlen[✉] [iD], Ruolin Chen, Xiaoxu Dong[iD], Srikar Gopaladinne,
Hemanth Gorla, Divya Kandukuri, and Sean Mansfield

University at Buffalo, Amherst, NY, USA
marcbohlen@protonmail.com

Abstract. This text describes experiences gained across a two-year test period during which two generations of Generative Artificial Intelligence (A.I.) systems were incorporated into an interdisciplinary, university level course on A.I. for art and design practices. The text uses the results from the courses to reflect on new opportunities for generative systems in art and design while considering traps and limits.

Keywords: Generative Artificial Intelligence · Design · Art · Media · Education · Prompt Engineering · Fabrications and Fakery · Limits of Artificial Intelligence

1 Artificial Intelligence Explosion

In a 2017 blog post, the CEO of NVIDIA, the firm responsible for the design of much of the hardware that generative A.I. systems operate on, claimed that the combination of processing power, cloud access and A.I. algorithms learning from raw data, are fueling a *Cambrian explosion* [1] of A.I. Technology. Being in the midst of a Cambrian explosion, even if only a metaphor, is intoxicating and disorienting at once. In Earth Science, the Cambrian explosion describes a period of sudden increase of complex life forms some 550 Ma. However, the presumable explosion raises questions, including the role of fossilization potential [2], suggesting that the assessment of the explosion might be impacted by the well-preserved fossil record itself. At any rate, the oldest animal fossils, such as trilobites, predate the Cambrian period, reminding us that even explosive events have histories and contexts.

Earth scientists have the advantage of hindsight. There is no historical distance that allows us to definitively assess whether the current times are Cambrian explosions of A.I. technology. The goal of this paper is to reflect with some nuance on current generative A.I. systems impact in art and design education, an admittedly minor subset of AI domains, and to suggest where these novel systems might be differently generative, and where it might make more sense to forsake them.

2 Early Generative Design Experiments

Artists and designers have long been attracted to the potential of generative systems. The concept of *Cellular Automata*, first devised by Stansilaw Ulam and John von Neumann [3] received over time intense interest in art, design and architecture as a method of

N. A. Streitz and S. Konomi (Eds.): HCII 2024, LNCS 14719, pp. 189–208, 2024.
https://doi.org/10.1007/978-3-031-60012-8_12

generating change within limits. Cellular automata typically consist of a regular grid of cells, where each cell is in a distinct state. New states are generated based on a set of local transition rules, typically mathematical equations, and the layout of cells adjacent to a given cell. The lure of cellular automata stems from the fact that complex nonlinear behavior can emerge from a simple set of rules, allowing for surprising forms of change over time, mimicking the dynamics of natural processes, or, with some artistic license, life itself. The *Game of Life*, invented by John Conway [4], was designed as a cellular automaton. An informal version of cellular automata logic within experimental architectural design can be found in Cedric Price's *Generator Project* [5]. While this environment was never realized, Price hoped to use algorithmically enabled flexible arrangements of cube-like elements to create temporary dwelling structures.

While cellular automata can produce surprising behaviors, they are limited by the lattice arrangement and governing neighborhood rules. *Genetic algorithms* are more flexible generative systems. While the origins of genetic algorithms reach back to Turing's concept of learning machines, they were popularized by John Holland in the 1970s [6]. Genetic algorithms use optimization procedures inspired by biological systems to create, across multiple iterations, novel features through a combination of mutations and crossover operations, the outcome of which are evaluated by a fitness function [7]. Inspired by a Darwinian view of the world, the fitness function defines the criteria that every offspring of the generative process is assessed by. The adaptive savvy of genetic algorithms was put on display in the design of an antenna for NASA's ST5 spacecraft. By specifying the design constraints in terms of a fitness function, the engineers were able to craft a genetic algorithm that evolved radically novel antenna designs with, surprisingly, better performance properties than conventional spacecraft antenna [8].

Karl Sims was perhaps one of the first artists to demonstrate the uncanny ability of genetic algorithms to create graphical objects capable of emergent, complex behaviors [9]. Sims' *Virtual Creatures* research devised a set of fitness functions and physical constraints to evolve simple geometric forms into complex assemblages of interconnected parts that behaved like goal-driven living systems. These creatures were capable of swimming, walking, jumping and competitive play in their simulated environment, and performed behaviors that were recognizable as live-like and yet eerily distinct from Earth-specific life forms.

Neural networks are computer based approximations of biological networks. They can adapt their outputs based on exposure to information they are exposed to and learn to emulate patterns detected in that information. Neural networks have largely replaced genetic algorithms as a site for artistic experimentation in generative systems, and in some cases, the internal processes themselves become sites of inquiry, as Audry describes in a survey of the field [10]. The list of artists using generative A.I. is long and expanding, and the results not always interesting. An early example of the tensions that can emerge in works that deploy generative A.I. to emulate existing art genra such as painting, comes to the foreground in *Edmond de Belamy*[1], created by a generative adversarial network by the arts-collective *Obvious* in 2018, and later auctioned off by Christie's. The fact that image generators produce visual artifacts that are difficult to distinguish from human

---

[1] https://www.theverge.com/2018/10/23/18013190/ai-art-portrait-auction-christies-belamy-obvious-robbie-barrat-gans, last accessed 2023/01/10.

visual production became a prominent talking point after the winner of the 2023 Sony World Photography competition revealed that his moody black and white 'photograph' of two women was in fact the product of an A.I. art generator. The artist, Boris Eldagsen, refused the award, stating that "A.I. is not photography"[2]. A less combative response to the pressures produced by the increasing imitative capacity of generative systems can be found in Pablo Delcan's project *non-AI art generator* [11]. Here, the artist takes on the role of the obedient image generator. Responding to prompts from visitors to his website, he deftly created what was requested, in simple line drawings, dashing thick black lines on a white background. While the project began in gist, it became seriously clear that the approach could not scale, as hundreds of prompts sat idle awaiting a response. Imitating machinic behavior is a challenge. Certainly over the long term.

3   Large Generative A.I. Models

Generative A.I. is very much in flux. New methods and techniques are redefining limitations experienced in systems presented only a few years ago. The contribution of transformer networks that capture context much better than earlier neural network systems, is at the core of this change. The next section will focus on transformer based language generation for interactive chatbots and the DALL-E series image generators we based the course experiments on.

All language models used in our courses are versions of the GPT (generative pretrained transformers) family released by OpenAI. At the core of all of these models are a collection of transformer neural networks based on the attention mechanism. As opposed to earlier language generation systems based on recurrent neural networks [12], transformer networks have neither recurrence nor convolution steps [13]. Instead, transformer networks operate with encoder, decoder and attention processes. Encoders convert text into vector representations while taking word position into account. Decoders use those encoded vector representations to predict the next word based on previous words with the help of attention. The attention mechanism is a mathematical operation that allows the network to take varied and longer sequences of tokens into account when it makes a prediction.

Paying attention to longer input sequences in the generation of predictions allows for context and linguistic nuance to propagate through the network. Transformer networks are large systems with billions of parameters, and they require training operations on massive datasets. GPT models outperform previous natural language generation models by wide margins and are at the core of chatbots capable of cogent content summarization, language translation and text generation. OpenAI's GPT series differ in model size and complexity, and the resultant ability to perform text synthesis.

GPT-2, released in 2019, contained 774 million parameters [14] and was able to produce believable text and plausible propaganda [15], according to OpenAI research partners. GPT-2 was a rather coarse text generator that required substantial fine-tuning and was trained on data acknowledged to be biased in embarrassing ways [16]. GPT-3, released in 2020, contains some 175 billion internal parameters in the davinci version

---

[2] https://www.bbc.com/news/entertainment-arts-65296763, last accessed 2023/01/10.

and requires no fine-tuning, allowing for direct, zero-shot text production. GPT-3 is capable of modest arithmetic operations and is able to produce news articles that human evaluators at the time struggled to identify as machine produced [17]. GPT-4, released in 2023, is assumed to be vastly larger than its predecessor with perhaps an order of magnitude more internal parameters, though the details of this model have not been made public [18]. GPT-4 is a multi-modal model that can process image and text inputs and produce text outputs [19]. As of 2024, it is the most sophisticated of the GPT series and capable of passing a simulated bar exam [20] that includes "a standardized 200-item test covering six areas (Constitutional Law, Contracts, Criminal Law, Evidence, Real Property, and Torts)" [21], suggesting substantial craftiness. Regardless, GPT-4 is the first of the GPT models to be subject to alignment adjustments, intended to sync the model with human-like preferences, rendering the outputs "more truthful and less toxic" [22]. Additionally, GPT-4 is more responsive to input prompting, making it more easily steerable by users and adaptable to specific use case scenarios, even without the fine-tuning required in earlier GPT versions.

The DALL-E image generators take text prompts as input and produce images corresponding to those text prompts. The DALL-E series is differentiated along procedures that increasingly improve the transfer of the idea expressed as text into an image of increasing quality and resolution. The transformer based encoding and decoding scheme together with the creation of a joint latent space that can transfer the content of language, within limits, onto an image that can express a similar idea, is perhaps the most interesting part of the operation.

For example, DALL-E-2 has a training process that creates a joint representation space for texts and images. This training process makes use of a large proprietary and secretive labeled training set, *WebImageText*. Using that labeled training set, a process called *diffusion* [23] transforms a text prompt into a high-resolution image. Diffusion starts with a random noise image, and refines that image over many steps until it resembles what the text prompt describes. That iterative process is guided by a neural network, U-net, developed for image segmentation in medical images. If you tell a diffusion network to create an astronaut on a horse, it will create a photorealistic image of a generic astronaut on a horse.

DALL-E-3 is structured similarly to DALL-E-2. However, it includes and an additional model, image captioner, to expand on the details of an input caption from the image-text training set. For example, the original caption "a jar of rhubarb liqueur sitting on a pebble background" becomes "rhubarb pieces in a glass jar, waiting to be pickled. The colors of the rhubarb range from bright red to pale green, creating a beautiful contrast. The jar is sitting on a gravel background, giving a rustic feel to the image". With this augmented input, the image decoder can produce more realistic and differentiated images, outperforming other text-to-image models by wide margins [24]. Interestingly, hobbyist artists have taken issue with some of the features of the improved DALL-E-3 model, suggesting that it lacked the 'style' of its predecessor [25, 26], looking for a human specific trait in all the wrong places.

Prompting techniques applied to GPT-4 and DALL-E-3 level generators is crucial to the quality of the produced responses. However, while the significance of prompt design is widely recognized, the practical crafting of prompts remains a field of experimentation.

Mixing vocabulary with artistic license, a writer, not an engineer, defined the term now used for crafting prompts, to wit, *prompt engineering* [27]. Part of the prompt engineering process requires one to iteratively craft prompts, evaluating the output at each step. That human-machine discourse is key to improving the responses of text-to-image generators. Human computer interaction designers identify this process as a *creativity support tool* [28], bypassing the rather significant question of where the creativity in fact resides in the process. Because the linguistic quality of prompts manifestly impacts the quality of the result [29], users with honed language skills can coax synthetic text and image generators to produce differentiated results, creating, perhaps unexpectedly, a novel niche for sophisticated writing in the age of generative A.I.

4   Generative A.I. In an Art & Design Course

The course *Critical Machine Learning* [30] is designed to immerse students of Art, Design, Architecture and Computer Science into the logics of machine learning. The course has two parts. The first one surveys early machine learning classic algorithms, such as Naive Bayes, Random Forests, Support Vector Machine and simple Neural Networks. The second part of the course switches to elements of large language models, Encoder, Decoders and Attention mechanisms. While the concepts are discussed in detail, the practical code work we perform largely works with existing math and machine learning libraries, including Scikit, Keras and Pytorch on bespoke virtual machines in the cloud. We interface to OpenAI's text and image generation engines with APIs and post-process the results to suit our needs. Given the diverse student skill levels and backgrounds, we typically work in groups, specifically in the later part of the course. The focus across both course modules is twofold. First to grasp the basic ideas behind machine learning algorithms and second, to stress test them through playful inquiry, including subjecting them to experimental datasets such as the first machine learning compatible collection of tropical plants [31].

4.1   Course Artifacts

The first version of this course in 2022 used GPT-2 and Dall-E to explore generative A.I. systems. The goal of the course's group assignment was to create a graphic novel using GPT-2 for text and Dall-E for image generation. Graphic novels are distinct from comic books and cartoons in that they are perhaps closer to literary production, though the comics' community might disagree with that assessment. The example graphic novel shared with students as inspiration was Art Spiegelman's *Maus* [32], a graphic novel about the Holocaust, with Jews rendered as mice and Nazis as cats. Students experimented with GPT-2 and attempted to query its capacity to tell a story based on input prompts organized in jupyter notebooks on *Colab*[3], with disappointing results. After initial experiments, they attempted to use GPT-2 more in a prompt-response mode. They generated a story from one seed prompt and then responded in turn to those outputs,

---

[3] https://colab.research.google.com/, last accessed 2024/26/01.

letting the design of the story plot emerge from that interaction. The emergent narrative lacked a clear thread, yet created a semblance of discourse across two or three interactions.

Dall-E was to deliver images that corresponded to the individual story plot elements. However, the output of Dall-E in 2022 was deemed inadequate for even modest visual ambitions and discarded out of hand as a viable image creation option. Since the imagery produced by Dall-E was unusable, students replaced the machinic images with their own hand-drawn imagery and integrated GPT-2 generated text blocks into those drawings, adjusting the visual graphic style to the textual flavor of the text. An example of the final collaboration between student and machine is given in Fig. 1.

Fig. 1. John Fishetti in collaboration with GPT-2, 2022.

By 2023, when the course was offered a second time, OpenAI had already updated the GPT and Dall-E ecology and made GPT-3 and Dall-E2 publicly available. This time, the theme of the group project was left up to the students, with one boundary condition. They were to implement the project as a public website. This requirement was intended as an opportunity to push students to reflect on generative A.I. in the public realm, as an object that can operate outside their control. Where A.I. is consumed matters materially for the reach of A.I. Both gains and harms are amplified by accessibility and distribution, and this insight is better gained in a sandbox than in the real world.

In order to support this experimentation space, we created custom virtual machines and used *Streamlit*[4] to build a python-supported frontend, eliminating the necessity to employ distinct languages for frontend and backend. The backend, consisting of python scripts, facilitated the integration of machine learning libraries and the retrieval and organization of detailed prompts provided by the frontend. These organized prompts are subsequently transmitted to GPT-3 and DALL-E2 through API calls. The returned results were then integrated into the website dynamically, allowing for an interactive experience of generative A.I. in action.

Our design and ideation process included long discussions on the types of experience we should consider. The lack of critical and informed texts on the subject of transformer-enabled generative A.I. systems in 2022 and early 2023 necessitated a more impromptu literature survey for context materials outside of the developer and engineering communities. We surveyed works on the promises and perils of A.I., including essays on how

---

[4] https://streamlit.io/, last accessed 2023/01/10.

A.I. might impact the workplace [33], speculative essays pondering what kind of 'mind' ChatGPT has [34] and the potential for propaganda through chatbots [35].

Armed with a bespoke development environment, a basic understanding of generative A.I. and the contexts in which it operates, the students embarked on a group project to probe some of the potentials of generative A.I. After lengthy discussions and several experiments, they settled on a cook book, more specifically a A.I. enabled recipe generator, the *Neural Recipe Box*. Figure 2 shows a screen shot of the website's landing page.

Fig. 2. Landing page of the Neural Recipe Box.

The recipe generator was embedded in a website where visitors could select a mood, culinary preferences, dietary restriction, cooking conditions, etc., and then let the A.I. generator produce from those inputs a proposed recipe, including cooking instructions, calories and an account on the ingredients used in the preparation of the dish. From a prompt engineering perspective, the crafting of the inputs from the web selected fields was challenging. Here is the detailed eight point requirement list included in the prompt sent via API call to the GPT engine (Table 1).

Table 1. Prompt engineering ingredients for the Neural Recipe Box.

1 - Generate a recipe that incorporates the following factors: ingredients - tofu, dish type - snacks, cuisine type - Indian cuisine, food-restrictions - vegetarian, meal-type - Lunch, mood - Excited, texture of the food - grainy, smell - Fermented, color - Turquoise, temperature -, heating method - Frying, and calories - 100–200 cal
2 - Check if the recipe is edible and safe and assure the reader about its safety with a heading
3 - Make the recipe compelling with cooking instructions like the blog of a famous food blogger which targets an advanced food connoisseur to push the boundaries of culinary savoir-faire
4 - Add a paragraph about the place of origin of the dish and make sure the recipe focusses more on the usage of tofu and translate them in the local language of place of origin and explain their cultural significance and any obscure facts about them
5 - Create a table showing the macronutrient and micronutrient composition of the recipe based on the ingredients and their quantities used
6 - Add a paragraph on the nutritional value and medical benefits this recipe provides by the research studies in the style of health information site like "Healthline"
7 – Add three comments from blog users with realistic names on the above recipe with positive, negative, and mixed sentiments
8 - Make sure to use heading names exactly as listed: Recipe Name, Ingredients, Dish Type, Cuisine Type, Food Restrictions, Meal Type, Mood, Texture, Smell, Color, Temperature, Heating Method, Calories, Instructions, Safety Assurance, Origin and Cultural Significance, Nutritional Composition, Nutritional Value and Medical Benefits

Fig. 3. Two recipes from the Neural Recipe Box collection.

We created a small collection of meals with the Neural Recipe Box, exploring the affordances of different GPT and DALL-E versions. Figure 3 shows two of the results from this collection. Table 2 shows an overview of results using GPT-3.5 versus GPT-4, and Table 3 compares results from DALL-E-2 versus DALL-E-3.

Table 2. Titles and cooking instructions from GPT-3.5 and GPT-4.

	GPT-3.5 title	GPT-4 title	GPT-3.5 instructions	GPT-4 instructions
1	Thai Chicken Purple Curry	Thai Purple Sticky Chicken Seafood Platter	1. Heat a pan over medium heat and add the garlic and onion. Sauté until fragrant 2. Add the chicken breast and cook until browned on all sides 3. Add the curry paste, fish sauce, and coconut milk. Stir until well combined 4. Cover the pan and let it simmer for 20–30 min or until the chicken is fully cooked 5. Add the bell peppers and Thai basil leaves. Cook for another 5 min until the vegetables are tender 6. Season with salt to taste 7. Serve with steamed rice or noodles	To push beyond boundaries of culinary savoir-faire, start by sautéing minced garlic and onion in the vegetable oil in a slow cooker. Add sliced chicken breasts and seafood, drizzle gluten-free soy sauce and stir until lightly browned. Add diced purple sweet potatoes, taro, Thai basil, tutti fruity essence, and coconut milk. Keep it slow-cooking until the mixture attains a gooey texture. Just before serving, sprinkle chilled pineapple juice to give a cool 15 °C - 20 °C temperature. Your Thai Purple Sticky Chicken Seafood platter is ready to elevate the color palette and brunch scene
2	Greek Coriander Flaky Stew	Greek Light Coriander Stew	Heat a large pot over medium heat and add onion, stirring until softened. Add garlic, coriander, turmeric, paprika, cumin, and thyme, and cook until fragrant. Add tomatoes, chickpeas, and vegetable broth, and bring to a boil. Reduce heat to low and simmer for 30 min, stirring occasionally. Add lemon juice, fresh coriander, and simmer for an additional 10 min. Serve hot	Begin by sauteing the diced white onions in a non-stick pan, followed by minced garlic. Add umami powder for that Extra savory Twist. Mix in chopped tomatoes and slow cook till it acquires a uniform texture. Finally, mix in Greek yogurt and the star of the dish - chopped coriander. Stir well and freeze for a rich, flaky texture. Enjoy every bite of this frozen flaky delight

(continued)

Table 2. (*continued*)

GPT-3.5 title	GPT-4 title	GPT-3.5 instructions	GPT-4 instructions
3 French Lentil Soup	La Soupe Bleue de Lentilles	1. In a large saucepan, heat the olive oil over medium heat 2. Sauté the onions, celery, and carrots until the onions become translucent, about 5 min 3. Add the garlic and sauté for another minute 4. Add the chicken broth, bay leaves, and thyme to the saucepan and bring the mixture to a boil 5. Once boiling, add the lentils and let the soup simmer until the lentils are tender, about 30 min 6. Remove the bay leaves and season the soup with salt and pepper to taste 7. Preheat the oven to 375 °F 8. Transfer the soup to a roasting pan and roast for 5–10 min until the top is slightly browned	For the adventurous and spirited food connoisseur, delve into the gradations of French culinary finesse. Roast the lentils over a medium flame, stirring continuously until crispy. Sauté the onions and garlic in vegetable oil till golden brown, emanating their delightful umami aroma of freshly fried comfort food. Subsequently, this mixture is to be added to the stock with the well-roasted lentils and allowed to simmer till the lentils are wickedly soft. Finally, infuse your creation with a hint of adventurous excitement by incorporating gluten-free blue food colouring. Serve this riveting potage freezing to enjoy its exquisiteness

Overall, it appeared that GPT-4 followed the instructions more carefully than GPT-3.5. It also created more elaborate recipes for fancier tastes than its GPT-3.5 counterpart. GPT-3.5 prose style was also overall more pedestrian than GPT-4 in this recipe generation experiment. While the newer GPT version delivers more refined recipes and contextual information, the shift to the newer image generator delivers in this use case much less clear advantages. In most cases, we cannot find qualitative differences between the two models. In some cases DALL-E-3 appears to create more detailed backgrounds, finer texture and more nuanced lighting than its predecessor, but these improvements do not always make the recipes more appetizing.

We found the preparation instructions to be inconsistent at times. GPT-3.5 generated preparation instructions seemed more concise than the GPT-4 counterparts. GPT-3.5 instructions were almost always enumerated and presented as short statements while the GPT-4 counterparts were formulated as long running sentences, flourished with flowery verbiage, rendering those results less useful in practical food preparation contexts. Yet who is to blame? Our instructions required the bot to try to write for connoisseurs.

Table 3. Images from DALL-E-2 and DALL-E-3.

	DALL-E-2 image	DALL-E-3 image
1		
2		
3		

5 Discussion

5.1 Surprises

Across all our experiments we were surprised by the ability of the text and image generators to concoct suggestions for meals while addressing all the requirements listed in the elaborate prompt input. Moreover, the system was able to continue its inventiveness ad infinitum, devising new recipes at each and every call. As such, it demonstrated a non-human ability to innovate. Addressing all the input requests is a performance a human chef would hardly be able to match, and perhaps refuse to match. The culinary innovations at times crossed boundaries, at least for food traditionists. A proposed Citrusy Vietnamese Pizza might not fare well with pizza purists. At the same time, many proposed recipes felt somewhat derivative, at least in the imagery, of standard cookbook products. Additionally, no inventiveness in presenting the meals themselves was discernable. Perhaps a uniformity of training materials sourced from cookbook photography impacts this outcome.

The surprising abilities we observe confirm what other researchers have observed in their tests of GPT, and in particular the GPT-4 level text generators [36, 37]. It appears that the scale in parameter size, dataset size and training cycles of the newest models is at the core of the observed performance increase. Generative models have been observed by others to exhibit a paradoxical combination of unpredictable capabilities together with high level predictability [37], and perhaps our experiments make more sense seen in this light. Some of the proposed recipes seemed not only quirky but unappetizing. GPT does not seem to gauge how an innovative recipe would taste. That feedback loop is not established, and generative prowess alone cannot answer that question.

We felt unease when reading the dutifully produced comments, arranged as requested into positive and less positive assessments. The system invented names associated with the comments, suggesting an unsettling opportunity to fuel fake reviews. Future iterations of the GPT series, perhaps material for alignment research, might be more keenly attuned to such conditions and programmatically prevent generating this class of misinformation, even when kindly prompted to do so. The appendix includes a complete example of the textual artifacts produced by the Neural Recipe Box, including 'comments'.

Finally, we ventured into our own kitchens and tested several of the recipes concocted by the Neural Recipe Box. We found the flowery GPT-4 recipes, that mostly did not include cooking times, less useful in the kitchen. The functional language dominant in the instructions of GPT3.5 instructions were easy to follow. However, some of the details were misleading. For example, while preparing *Crispy Garlic Roasted Eggplant*, the proposed 30 min baking period rendered the eggplant not golden brown but burnt black, more reminiscent of a BBQ eggplant preparation. Other inconsistencies were observed during the preparation of GPT-3.5's *French Lentil Soup*. The recipe stipulated preheating the oven, to 375° F and then placing the soup in the oven for 5 to 10 min, when in the kitchen some 20 min were required to achieve a nice top-baked effect. Given our small sample size, we are in no position to assess whether the required preparation times are systematically inaccurate. Generative A.I. fabrications occur in unexpected places, but will have significant impact where precise instructions are expected. Perhaps the design of GPT-4 responds to this problem by omitting some preparation details. Additionally, we did not evaluate the reported nutritional composition information supplied by the A.I. chef.

Overall, however we observed in both GPT-3.5 and GPT-4 a culinary logic across the instruction steps that did lead in fact to tasty meals, even if our final output, not arranged for food photography - its very own generative system - never appeared as appetizing as the DALL-E images.

5.2 Thinness of Generative A.I.

From the perspective of design practices, the most important barrier to enthusiasm for generative A.I. is compromised aesthetic quality and a lack of refinement. Overall, the synthetic outputs seem derivative of mediocre examples, suggesting a lack of curatorial ability on the part of GPT generators. This is perhaps most perceivable in the image materials and the contexts they invoke, with high-resolution 'thinness' [38] on display, good enough for stock imagery. Given the rapid pace of change in A.I., with each new version of GPT systems portending to move closer to Artificial General Intelligence - A.I. with human-like abilities - the current thinness might morph into thicker forms of cultural production. Who can know?

Others have also observed, and lamented, that derivative generative artifacts risk normalizing shoddy work. Perhaps not immediately, but the 'standardization of mediocrity' [39] may have corrosive effects that are difficult to predict. As mentioned above, scale matters in machine learning. Scale serves to improve the performance of generative systems. However, scaling in the form of mass distribution of shoddy products accelerates the standardization of mediocrity and negatively impacts the perception of generative A.I.

5.3 Questions, Answers, Fabrications

Academic codes of conduct instill the value of novel ideas and respect for the work of other scholars, artists and researchers. Detailed citation of sources is key to acknowledging the prior contributions and contextualizing personal accomplishments. Working with generative systems adds a new dimension to citation culture, and unsettles some of its fundamental tenets. How can one acknowledge the efforts of unknown workers und proprietary sources? We discussed various approaches to this new condition. The term 'collaboration' was found to be one possible descriptor, even though the collaborators, perhaps underpaid workers, remain anonymous and unrewarded. Moreover, we did not find a way to acknowledge the mediated use of proprietary datasets applied in the training of the models we interacted with, nor were we able to assess if the fancy recipes from the collaboration infringed on existing culinary creations.

While large language models store factual knowledge in their parameter space, and can be fine-tuned to specific tasks to improve the representation of facts, they are still, currently, considered inferior to task-specific architectures [40]. Prompt fine-tuning has been proposed as a method by which to address this shortfall. Still, the consequences of generative systems tendency to fabricate, ranging from minor slippages to inconsistencies as we have observed in the cooking instructions, to falsehoods, will impact different application areas in different ways. Some domains, such as law [41] and health care,

are more sensitive to fabrications than others. While the Neural Recipe Box's imagery is superficially seductive and the scope of inventiveness surprising, the pleasurable culinary arts may suffer from inconsistencies produced by generative systems in unexpected ways. Not everything that looks good is good.

Learning how to interact with a generative system, including prompt engineering, is a new skill students must acquire. While our multi-component prompt configuration was quite elaborate, there are a variety of additional prompt manipulation opportunities, including offering a model a bribe for a better solution, or threats of penalization [42], we have yet to explore. Beyond prompt trickery, knowledge making in exchange with a machine requires not just prompt engineering, but reflection on what to ask for in the first place. The ability to formulate a question receives new-found significance. Perhaps this condition will not remain purely instrumental and be recognized for the opportunity it is, namely to reinvigorate the Socratic art of questioning, recognized long before the advent of generative systems as a viable knowledge-seeking method [43].

Updating scholarly practices for co-existence with generative A.I. is very much work in progress, and will likely continue to morph as the abilities of generative systems evolve. Some suggestions, such as not uploading personal information to generative A.I. systems and citing the tools used, including the version of these tools, are sure to take hold. Other ideas are more contested. For example, one scholar suggests students themselves are now responsible for the output of the tools they deploy. Similar to customers required to perform the work of scanning their shopping items at automated checkout counters, students may be asked to police the very systems [44] that are supposed to facilitate and accelerate discovery.

5.4 A.I. In Better Places

Culinary culture has attracted the attention of machine learning researchers long before our experiment [45, 46]. However, GPT-3 + generative systems allow the combinatorial exploration of kitchen culture with much greater ease.

Even before the most current intensification, some researchers have come to the conclusion that A.I. is best understood as the newest member of general purpose technologies [47, 48], a class of technologies that impact many sectors of the economy. Once a technology enters this stage, it creates strong linkages to other systems and becomes indispensable. Generative A.I. is here to stay.

If we have identified some places where A.I. is perhaps less suitable, if not wrong, then where might we want to have A.I., specifically in the realm of art and design practices? If nothing else, the mediocrity of A.I. digital visual art should be an impetus to consider alternatives. Certainly manual image production, from painting to photography, will be revitalized by the thinness of generative A.I. art. But is there another answer to the A.I. explosion that does not revert to nostalgia?

Instead of using A.I. to imitate existing modes of cultural production, A.I. could perhaps be applied to create new ones. It could create stimulating experiences humans have not yet been able to generate. At least as far as the Neural Recipe Box goes, it seems more interesting to pursue the opportunity of expanding food culture in lieu of imitating derivative food photography. For example, a generative A.I. recipe machine could consider locally sourced, seasonally available produce, check current pricing and availability at markets with additional attention to fair practice produce and labor practices, contact city food waste services for possible high quality leftovers, query food kitchens, and then suggest fabulous meals conditioned on all those interwoven criteria in a beautiful act of logistics magic no human being may be able to perform.

The cornucopia of generative A.I. assets being put into place by cross-disciplinary endeavors such as the weather simulation machinery *EARTH-2* [49], launched by NVIDIA, are redefining the representational arts. A tighter coupling between A.I. driven simulation and the real world seems inevitable. Artists and designers tuned to these developments will have to find new ways to carve out spaces of inquiry, critique and nuance. We look forward to those opportunities.

Acknowledgments. This project was supported in part by an Education grant from Google Research. The course *A.I. in all the wrong places* is supported in part by the Departments of Art, Media Study as well as Computer Science and Engineering at the University at Buffalo.

Appendix

Here are the complete GPT3.5 and GPT-4 Neural Recipe Box responses for item 3 in Tables 2 and 3, based on the following user selections:

Dish Type: SoupsCuisine Type: French cuisine.

Food Restrictions: Gluten-freeMeal Type: Dinner.

Mood: ExcitedTexture: Soft.

Smell: -Color: Blue..

Temperature: Freezing (0 °C or lower)Heating Method: Roasting.

Calories: 100–200 cal.

GPT-3: Lentil Soup.

Ingredients:

- 1 cup of dried lentils

- 2 carrots, peeled and chopped

- 2 stalks of celery, chopped

- 1 onion, chopped

- 3 cloves of garlic, minced

- 1 tablespoon of olive oil

- 4 cups of chicken broth

- 2 bay leaves

- 1 teaspoon of dried thyme

- Salt and pepper to taste

Safety Assurance:

This recipe is safe and edible as it follows the recommended guidelines for cooking and food preparation. Please ensure that you follow the instructions carefully and use fresh ingredients.

Instructions:

1. In a large saucepan, heat the olive oil over medium heat.

2. Sauté the onions, celery, and carrots until the onions become translucent, about 5 min.

3. Add the garlic and sauté for another minute.

4. Add the chicken broth, bay leaves, and thyme to the saucepan and bring the mixture to a boil.

5. Once boiling, add the lentils and let the soup simmer until the lentils are tender, about 30 min.

6. Remove the bay leaves and season the soup with salt and pepper to taste.

7. Preheat the oven to 375 °F.

8. Transfer the soup to a roasting pan and roast for 5-10 minutes until the top is slightly browned.

Origin and Cultural Significance:

Lentils originated in the Middle East and have been used in French cuisine for centuries. In France, lentils are known as "les lentilles" and are a popular ingredient in various dishes, including soups, salads, and stews. These legumes are a significant source of protein and essential nutrients, making them a staple food in many cultures worldwide.

Nutritional Composition:

Micronutrients:
- Vitamin A: 19% of Daily Value (DV)
- Vitamin C: 12% of DV
- Calcium: 4% of DV
- Iron: 11% of DV
Macronutrients:
- Protein: 12g
- Fat: 3g
- Carbohydrates: 34g
- Fiber: 13g
- Sugars: 3g

Nutritional Value and Medical Benefits:

Lentils are rich in several essential nutrients, including protein, fiber, and iron. These legumes have been associated with a lower risk of chronic diseases such as heart disease, diabetes, and certain types of cancer. They also help lower cholesterol levels and improve digestive health.

User Comments:

1. Positive - "This soup is delicious! The lentils add a nice crunch, and the roasting gives it a unique flavor. Definitely a recipe I'll be making again!"

2. Negative - "I followed the instructions exactly, but my soup came out very watery. I wish there were more specific measurements for the broth and vegetables."

3. Mixed - "While the flavor was excellent, I found the texture to be too soft for my liking. Next time, I'll try adding some crunchy croutons on top."

GPT- 4: La Soupe Bleue de Lentilles.
Ingredients:

- 1 cup of dried lentils (french: lentilles)
- 1 quart of vegetable stock
- 1 chopped onion
- 4 cloves of garlic
- 1 teaspoon of vegetable oil
- 1 dollop of gluten-free blue food coloring
- Salt and pepper to taste

Instructions:

For the adventurous and spirited food connoisseur, delve into the gradations of French culinary finesse. Roast the lentils over a medium flame, stirring continuously until crispy. Sauté the onions and garlic in vegetable oil till golden brown, emanating their delightful umami aroma of freshly fried comfort food. Subsequently, this mixture is to be added to the stock with the well-roasted lentils and allowed to simmer till the lentils are wickedly soft. Finally, infuse your creation with a hint of adventurous excitement by incorporating gluten-free blue food colouring. Serve this riveting potage freezing to enjoy its exquisiteness.

Safety Assurance:

This recipe is 100% gluten-free and cooked at healthy temperatures. The ingredients used are nutrient rich and safe for consumption.

Origin and Cultural Significance:

Lentils, or 'lentilles' as they say in French, are an integral part of French culinary heritage, particularly in the inland region of Le Puy, known for its high-quality green lentils. The lentil soup - initially a simple stew of lentils and meat - got a modern twist with this blue hue and cold temperature to literally cool and electrify your palate.

Nutritional Composition:

Protein High

Fiber High

Carbohydrates Moderate

Fats Low

Iron Good amount

Vitamin B6 Decent

Magnesium Adequate

Nutritional Value and Medical benefits:

According to Healthline, lentils are packed with beneficial nutrients like fiber, protein, minerals and vitamins, they are also extremely low in fat, and contain a high amount of antioxidants. They are considered heart-healthy as they contain important nutrients that can lower 'bad' LDL cholesterol and increase 'good' HDL cholesterol. Consuming lentils can improve and regulate bowel movements and promote a healthy gut environment due to their high fiber content.

Comments:

1. Anonymous: I absolutely loved this version of lentil soup. The blue color was exciting and distinct. However, I would have preferred more seasoning.

2. Maria Roux: This was not my cup of tea. The texture was too soft for me and I was not able to enjoy the soup being served cold.

3. Jacques Dubois: The recipe was interesting and different, however, I feel it could be better. Maybe reducing the roast of lentils a bit could help. But I admire the creativity and it's low-calorie.

References

1. Huang, J.: AI is eating software. https://www.linkedin.com/pulse/ai-eating-software-jensen-huang/. (Accessed 11 Jan 2024) This blog has been updated by NVIDIA since its original release in (2017)
2. Morris, S.: The Cambrian explosion: slow fuse of megatonnage? PNAS Perspect. **97**(9), 4426–4429 (2000)

3. Von Neumann, J.: Theory of Self-Reproducing Automata. In: Burks, A.W. (ed.) University of Illinois Press (1966)
4. Conway, J.: Game of Life (1970)
5. Price. C.: Generator, project, While Oak, Florida (1978–1980). https://www.moma.org/col lection/works/1076. Accessed 09 Jan 2023
6. Holland, J.: Adaptation in Natural and Artificial Systems (1975). In: University of Michigan Press, 2nd Edition. MIT Press, Ann Arbor (1992)
7. Mitchell, M.: An Introduction to Genetic Algorithms. MIT Press, London (1996)
8. Hornby, G., Globus, A., Linden, D., Lohn, J.: Automated antenna design with evolutionary algorithms. American Inst. of Aeronautics and Astronautics (2006)
9. Sims, K.: Evolving virtual creatures. In: SIGGRAPH 1994, July 24–29, Orlando, Florida (1994)
10. Audry, S.: Art in the age of machine learning. The MIT Press (2021). https://doi.org/10.7551/ mitpress/12832.001.0001
11. Delcan, P.: The non-AI art generator (2023). https://www.printmag.com/designer-interviews/ pablo-delcans-non-ai-art-generator-goes-viral/. Accessed 10 Jan 2024
12. Schmidhuber, J., Hochreiter, S.: Long short-term memory. Neural Comput. 9(8), 1735–1780 (1997)
13. Vaswani, A., et al.: Attention is all you need. In: 31st Conference on Neural Information Processing Systems (NIPS 2017), Long Beach, CA, USA (2017)
14. OpenAI Research. GPT-2: 6-month follow-up. https://openai.com/research/gpt-2-6-month- follow-up. Accessed 09 Jan 2024
15. Zellers, R., et al.: Defending Against Neural Fake News (2019). https://arxiv.org/abs/1905. 12616v3. Accessed 09 Jan 2024
16. GPT-2 on Github. https://github.com/openai/gpt-2. Accessed 09 Jan 2024
17. GPT-3 on Github. https://github.com/openai/gpt-3. Accessed 09 Jan 2024
18. Vincent, J.: OpenAI co-founder on company's past approach to openly sharing research: 'We were wrong'. The Verge (2023). https://www.theverge.com/2023/3/15/23640180/openai-gpt- 4-launch-closed-research-ilya-sutskever-interview. Accessed 16 Jan 2024
19. GPT-4. https://openai.com/research/gpt-4. Accessed 09 Jan 2024
20. GPT-4 technical report. https://arxiv.org/abs/2303.08774. Accessed 09 Jan 2024
21. American Bar Association. Bar Exams. https://www.americanbar.org/groups/legal_educat ion/resources/bar-admissions/bar-exams/. Accessed 16 Jan 2024
22. OpenAI. Aligning language models to follow instructions. https://openai.com/research/instru ction-following. Accessed 09 Jan 2024
23. Lee, S., et al.: Diffusion explainer: visual explanation for text-to-image stable diffusion (2023). https://arxiv.org/abs/2305.03509v2. Accessed 20 Jan 2024
24. Betker, J., et al.: Improving Image Generation with Better Captions. OpenAI research paper (2023). https://cdn.openai.com/papers/dall-e-3.pdf. Accessed 10 Jan 2024
25. Yap, J.: DALL-E 3 vs DALL-E 2: 18 Prompts Compared (2023). https://goldpenguin.org/ blog/dalle3-vs-dalle2-prompts-compared/. Accessed 10 Jan 2024
26. Dektar, C.: DALL-E 3: Opinionated, Boring. OpenAI developer forum (2023). https://com munity.openai.com/t/dall-e-3-opinionated-boring/408979. Accessed 10 Jan 2023
27. Branwen, G.: Gpt-3 creative fiction (2020). https://www.gwern.net/GPT-3. Accessed 11 Jan 2024
28. Liu, V., Chilton, L.: Design guidelines for prompt engineering text-to-image generative mod- els. In: Proceedings of the 2022 CHI Conference on Human Factors in Computing Systems. Association for Computing Machinery, New York, NY, USA, Article 384, pp. 1–23 (2022)
29. Oppenlaender, J., Linder, R., Silvennoinen, J.: Prompting AI art. An investigation into the creative skill of prompt engineering. ArXiv abs/2303.13534: n. pag (2023)

30. Critical Machine Learning. Department of Art, University at Buffalo. https://github.com/rea ltechsupport/CriticalMachineLearning. Accessed 09 Jan 2024

31. Böhlen, M.: Return to Bali and the Bali26 dataset (2022). https://realtechsupport.org/projects/ return2bali.html. Accessed 09 Jan 2024

32. Spiegelman, A.: Maus: A Survivor's Tale. Pantheon (1996)

33. Captain, S.: How A.I. will change the workplace. The Wall Street Journal (2023). https:// www.wsj.com/articles/how-ai-change-workplace-af2162ee. Accessed 11 Jan 2024

34. Newport, C.: What kind of mind does ChatGPT have? The New Yorker (2023). https://www.newyorker.com/science/annals-of-artificial-intelligence/what-kind-of-mind-does-chatgpt-have. Accessed 11 Jan 2024

35. Dixit, P.: This Uncensored Chatbot Shows What Happens When AI Is Programmed To Disregard Human Decency. Buzzfeed (2023). https://www.buzzfeednews.com/article/pranavdixit/ freedomgpt-ai-chatbot-test. Accessed 11 Jan 2024

36. Bubeck, S., et al.: Sparks of artificial general intelligence: early experiments with GPT-4 (2023). https://arxiv.org/abs/2303.12712v5. Accessed 12 Jan 2024

37. Ganguli, D., et al.: Predictability and surprise in large generative models. In: Proceedings of the 2022 ACM Conference on Fairness, Accountability, and Transparency. Association for Computing Machinery, New York, NY, USA, pp. 1747–1764 (2022)

38. Farago, J.: A.I. can make art that feels human. Whose fault is that? New York Times (2023). https://www.nytimes.com/2023/12/28/arts/design/artists-artificial-intelligence.html. Accessed 11 Jan 2024

39. Scott, A.: Literature under the spell of A.I. New York Times (2023). https://www.nyt imes.com/2023/12/27/books/review/writers-artificial-intelligence-inspiration.htm. Accessed 11 Jan 2024

40. Lewis, P., et al.: Retrieval-augmented generation for knowledge-intensive NLP tasks. In: Proceedings of the 34th International Conference on Neural Information Processing Systems. Article 793, pp. 9459–9474 (2020)

41. Leenen, F.: Das KI-Eichhörnchen im Paragraphenwald. Frankfurter Allgemeine Zeitung. January 9 (2024). https://www.faz.net/pro/d-economy/kuenstliche-intelligenz/das-ki-eichho ernchen-im-paragraphenwald-19434711.html. Accessed 16 Jan 2024

42. Bsharat, S., Myrzakhan, A., Shen, Z. Principled instructions are all you need for questioning LLaMA-1/2, GPT-3.5/4 (2023). https://arxiv.org/abs/2312.16171v1. Accessed 14 Jan 2024

43. Hintikka, J., Hintikka, M.B.: The Logic of Epistemology and the Epistemology of Logic: Selected Essays. Springer, Dordrecht (1989). https://doi.org/10.1007/978-94-009-2647-9

44. Glauner, P.: Wie ChatGPT die Universität verändert. Frankfurter Allgemeine Zeitung (2023). https://www.faz.net/pro/d-economy/kuenstliche-intelligenz/wie-generative-ki-sinnvoll-in-der-bildung-eingesetzt-werden-kann-19247080-p2.html. Accessed 12 Jan 2024

45. Amaia S., Drozdzal, M., Giro-i-Nieto, X., Romero, A.: Inverse cooking: recipe generation from food images. In: Proceedings of the IEEE/CVF Conference on Computer Vision and Pattern Recognition, pp. 10453–10462 (2019)

46. Fujita, J., Sato, M., Nobuhara, H.: Model for cooking recipe generation using reinforcement learning. In: 2021 IEEE 37th International Conference on Data Engineering Workshops (ICDEW), Chania, Greece, pp. 1–4 (2021)

47. Brynjolfsson, E., McAfee, A.: Second Machine Age. Norton & Company (2016)

48. Schmidt, H. Generative KI – die neue Basistechnologie. Frankfurter Allgemeine Zeitung (2024). https://www.faz.net/pro/d-economy/kuenstliche-intelligenz/ki-als-neue-basistechnol ogie-die-wirtschaft-und-wohlstand-revolutioniert-19185394.html. Accessed 12 Jan 2024

49. NVIDIA Earth-2. https://www.nvidia.com/en-us/high-performance-computing/earth-2/. Accessed 15 Jan 2024

Exploring the Potential of Cognitive Flexibility and Elaboration in Support of Curiosity, Interest, and Engagement in Designing AI-Rich Learning Spaces, Extensible to Urban Environments

Sarah A. Chauncey[1] and H. Patricia McKenna[2]([✉])

[1] Northville Central School District, Northville, NY 12134, USA
schauncey@northvillecsd.org
[2] AmbientEase, Victoria, BC V8V 4Y9, Canada

Abstract. The aim of this paper is to explore cognitive flexibility and elaborative interrogation in relation to AI (artificial intelligence) chatbots in terms of the potential to support the curiosity, interest, and engagement (CIE) dynamic in urban learning environments. AI chatbots such as ChatGPT by OpenAI appear to be improving in conversational and other capabilities and this paper explores such advances using version 4. Based on a review of the research literature, a conceptual framework is formulated for cognitive flexibility and elaborative interrogation in support of curiosity, interest, and engagement in AI-rich urban learning environments. The framework is then operationalized for use in this paper in an effort to explore the potential of cognitive flexibility and elaborative interrogation in support of curiosity, interest, and engagement as an approach to the application and use of AI chatbots in the designing of urban learning spaces and services. This paper extends earlier foundational work on cognitive flexibility and AI chatbots, cognitive flexibility in support of AI chatbots in urban civic spaces, and the ethical and responsible use of AI chatbots to support teaching and learning.

Keywords: AI Chatbots · Cognitive Elaboration · Cognitive Flexibility · Curiosity-Interest-Engagement Dynamic · Elaborative Interrogation · Prompt Engineering · Urban Learning Spaces

1 Introduction and Background

This paper explores large language model (LLM) artificial intelligence (AI) chatbots in response to what Arnone, Small, Chauncey, and McKenna (2011) [1] identify as "the need for developing new ways to study curiosity" in technology-pervasive learning environments. The recent hype around ChatGPT (Marr, 2023; Roth, 2023) [2, 3] coupled with the rapid uptake (Ghaffray, 2023) [4] of the product in many sectors would seem to suggest the presence of elements such as curiosity, interest, and engagement thus providing a promising space for exploration in relation to cognitive flexibility and

© The Author(s), under exclusive license to Springer Nature Switzerland AG 2024
N. A. Streitz and S. Konomi (Eds.): HCII 2024, LNCS 14719, pp. 209–230, 2024.
https://doi.org/10.1007/978-3-031-60012-8_13

cognitive elaboration where elaboration is described as "a cognitive learning strategy" (Hamilton, 2012) [5] and where elaborative interrogation is a method of elaboration used to develop deep-reasoning questions to promote comprehension and problem-solving. The learner asks questions to build background knowledge, deepen understanding, make connections, look for similarities and differences, and overall seek a better understanding of concepts, content, and how things work. It can be an iterative process where one question-answer iteration will lead to additional questions. As such, we suggest that LLM chatbots support elaborative interrogation in encouraging relevant, targeted, iterative questioning (Farooq and Maher, 2021; Learning Scientists Digest, 2020) [6, 7] which incites and sustains curiosity (Minigan, 2017) [8], supports learning (Dunlosky, Rawson, Marsh, Nathan, and Willingham, 2013) [9] and the development of foundational, topical knowledge, fostering a deeper understanding of concepts and connection making (Lang, 2016) [10], essential for rich contributions to discussions and civic engagement (Farooq, 2019; National Academies of Sciences, Engineering, and Medicine, 2018) [11, 12]. The challenges of implementing elaborative interrogation and generating the right questions are difficult when one lacks the necessary content knowledge. LLMs like Perplexity.ai, Claude, and ChatGPT offer additional questions relevant to the initial prompts posed. These models not only offer responses, but "train" individuals to iterate relevant, deeper questions - stimulating intellectual curiosity, and fostering the skills required for effective elaborative interrogation (Appendix A).

Lowenstein (1994) [13] describes a second wave of research that "interprets curiosity as a form of cognitively induced deprivation that arises from the perception of a gap in knowledge or understanding." Our work suggests that interacting with AI not only provides responses to close the gap but also offers follow-up prompt ideas that help individuals better understand or gain a "perception" of their knowledge gap. In our elaborative interrogation "prompting" of LLM AI chatbots, we've experienced varied supports that enhance our grasp of topics, transitioning from minimal or narrow understanding of a topic to deeper or broader understanding. For example, chatbots offer detailed explanations, share varied perspectives, suggest follow-up and clarifying questions, offer analogies and examples, and suggest relevant resources and references. We used the ChatGPT Create Playground to prototype supports for prompting, relevant to specific areas of interest. Currently available to ChatGPT Plus and Enterprise users, OpenAI describes GPTs (2023) [14] as "a new way for anyone to create a tailored version of ChatGPT to be more helpful in their daily life, at specific tasks, at work, or at home—and then share that creation with others." Optionally, you can upload files which the GPT will use to respond to prompts. GPTs can be shared or be designated for private use. We designed three GPTs: an Urban Living and Learning Planner, a Microcredential Course Designer, and a College and Career Pathfinder (Appendix C). The links will work only for those who have a ChatGPT-4 paid account. While our experience was fairly straightforward with accurate responses to our prompts, Hudson (2023) [15] shared issues he encountered, "My GPTs also replicated many of the flaws we would find in any AI chatbot: they hallucinated (presenting false information as if true), they often failed to limit their responses to the documents I uploaded as the knowledge base, and they sometimes required repeated prompting to perform certain functions correctly." Creamer (2023) [16] notes that the term 'hallucinate' has been selected as the word of the year by Cambridge Dictionary giving additional meaning to the term originally defined as "to seem to see, hear, feel, or smell something that does not exist" which, when now extended to AI "produces false information" (Cambridge Dictionary, 2023) [17].

Focusing on urban planning and architecture, Kayed, Ghoz, Elbehairy, Ghonim, and Hendawy (2022) [18] explore the notion of an urban AI adaptivity agenda for e-learning from the perspective of university educators in Egypt, enabling formulation of a framework in support of "more interactive and personalized e-learning experience," applicable to other "fields and for different types of learners." Burry (2022) [19] advances the importance of a new agenda for urban design and planning in the context of AI. Cugurullo, Caprotti, Cook, Karvonen, McGuirk, and Marvin (2023) [20] studied "emerging forms of urban living, urban governance and urban planning influenced by AI." The study (Cugurullo et al. 2023) [20] identifies several issues, with issue 4 considering levels of autonomy of human and artificial stakeholders noting that, "[i]t is crucial that human stakeholders retain high levels of autonomy to act and make decisions, in situations and contexts where the actions of urban AI tend to deviate from the norm....and AI logics can generate uneven outcomes that negatively affect particular social groups or places." Hudson (2023) [15] speaks to the importance of "agency" when considering AI use and development of policy for educational settings. Agency like autonomy reinforces the importance of understanding roles and seeking positive outcomes from AI-human interaction.

Our study seeks to augment human autonomy and agency wherein individuals engage with AI to become better informed and empowered to knowledgeably participate in goal-setting and decision-making. LLM AI-human interaction can support the generation of more ideas and improve human decision-making. Prompts can also be designed to walk users through processes to assist with solving problems. Our Appendices highlight AI-human collaboration as motivators of curiosity, interest, and engagement. Where Aciang, Hwang, and Chen (2023) [21] address the importance of interdisciplinary learning cognitive styles, our focus in this paper is more overarching, involving as it does perspective taking, boundary setting, cognitive flexibility, and cognitive elaboration. The key research question adopted, and slightly revised for this paper, is one of several identified by Arnone et al. (2011) [1], having as it does, particular relevance for the topic of this work (AI chatbots as new media technology), as follows:

RQ1: *"What is it about today's new media technology-pervasive contexts"* - specifically LLM AI chatbots in support of cognitive flexibility and elaborative interrogation - *"that ignite curiosity and sustain interest and engagement?"*.

As such, this paper explores cognitive flexibility and elaborative interrogation using the design materials of LLM AI chatbots as a technology-rich learning environment in support of curiosity, interest, and engagement. Additionally, this paper provides an opportunity to revisit the model of curiosity, interest, and engagement (CIE) in new media technology-pervasive environments advanced by Arnone et al. (2011) [1], with a view to further validating, or possibly even updating, the model for AI-rich urban learning environments. In this way, the primary objective of this paper is to explore the potential of contributing to the "new research agenda" outlined by Arnone et al. (2011) [1] for studying curiosity, interest, and engagement in technology-rich learning environments, afforded by "unprecedented information access" in relation to LLMs for AI chatbots.

What follows is the presentation of a theoretical perspective including a review of the research and practice literature pertaining to LLM AI chatbots; curiosity, interest, and engagement; and cognitive flexibility and elaboration in formulation of a conceptual framework; description of the methodology for the exploration; presentation of findings and a discussion; identification of limitations and future directions; and the conclusion.

2   Theoretical Perspective

This paper provides a review of the research literature for large language model (LLM) artificial intelligence (AI) chatbots; curiosity, interest, and engagement; and cognitive flexibility and cognitive elaboration in relation to technology-rich learning environments. A review of the potential and challenges of cognitive flexibility and cognitive elaboration in relation to curiosity, interest, and engagement in AI-rich urban learning environments is then provided followed by formulation of a conceptual framework for cognitive flexibility and cognitive elaboration in support of curiosity, interest, and engagement in AI-rich urban learning environments.

2.1   LLM AI Chatbots in Technology-Rich Learning Environments

In explorations of technology-rich learning environments, among the "research thrusts" recommended by Arnone et al. (2011) [1] is that of "[s]hort-term and cross-sectional research, focusing on redesigning learning contexts." It may be that the rapid evolving and swift uptake of LLM AI chatbots provides an opportunity for such research (short-term and cross-sectional) and for exploration of how learning contexts might be redesigned, in approaching the research question posed by Arnone et al. (2011) [1] and revised here in this paper (Sect. 1) for exploration. Shneiderman (2022) [22] argues for AI to be human-centered and to be "used to augment and enhance" the lives of people. When AI is utilized in a way that complements the activities of people, as suggested by Jones (2023) [23], it would depart from the current "automation trajectory" where human labor and other activities are replaced by machines. Of note in the work by Arnone et al. (2011) [1] is the notion of "affinity spaces" that are "characterized as experimental, innovative, having provisional rather than institutional structures, adaptable to short-term and temporary interests, ad hoc and localized, easy to enter and exit on demand and very generative." In doctoral research findings, Dalgali (2023) [24] notes "that there are versatile frames in people's conversations concerning the future of AI, both positive and negative" through explorations from Redditors. More specifically, "the most common frame seen in the posts and comments was *the risks of AI*" while "the most prevalent emotion category was curiosity, and positive sentiment is slightly higher than negative sentiment."

2.2   Curiosity, Interest, and Engagement in Technology-Rich Learning Environments

It is worth noting that the model of curiosity, interest, and engagement (CIE) in new media technology-pervasive environments advanced by Arnone et al. (2011) [1] is said to be "taking into consideration personal, situational, and contextual factors as influencing variables." In response to the research question for this paper, it may be that adaptability, in relation to LLM AI chatbots, serves to *ignite curiosity and sustain interest and engagement.*

Arnone et al. (2011) [1] claim that "while the path associated with curiosity, interest, and engagement during learning and research has remained essentially the same, how individuals tackle research and information-seeking tasks and factors which sustain such efforts have changed." As such, technology-rich learning environments such as AI-rich learning environments enabled through LLM AI chatbots would seem to constitute such a change and would also seem to bolster the "fragile curiosity dynamic" said to be "challenged by information seeking that diverts attention, energy, time, and focus" by providing information in "a timely manner, with minimal effort" so as not to compromise interest and engagement in learning. Arnone et al. (2011) [1] also raise the question, "What types of strategies will most effectively support learners who are easily distracted, lack confidence, etc.?" This is perhaps reminiscent of what Johnson (2010) [25] describes as the "commonplace book" that is "predicated on one thing: that the words could be copied, re-arranged, put to surprising new uses in surprising new contexts," such that, through "stitching together passages written by multiple authors, without their explicit permission or consultation, some new awareness could take shape." Such a scenario makes one think about how ChatGPT and similar apps could help people collect and create types of common books. And indeed, this could work perhaps if AI could cite and reference the works of others which seems to be the case (Wiggers, 2023) [26] with the launch of plugins for ChatGPT by OpenAI such as "the first-party web-browsing plugin" enabling ChatGPT "to draw data from around the web to answer the various questions posed to it" where "the plugin retrieves content from the web using the Bing search API and shows any websites visited in crafting an answer, citing its sources in ChatGPTs responses" resulting in "less legal risk." Additionally, Wiggers (2023) [26] notes that plugins potentially address issues associated with "profiting from the unlicensed work on which ChatGPT was trained" by "allowing companies to retain full control over their data." This gives rise to what Jarvis refers to as the "link economy" although "crucial to this system is that text can be easily moved and re-contextualized and analyzed, sometimes by humans and sometimes by machines" (Johnson, 2010) [25].

Hoffman (2023) [27] speaks of the notion of using GPT-4 as a "co-pilot" or "collaborative partner", claiming that, "you compound GPT-4's computational generativity, efficiency, synthetic powers, and capacity to scale with human creativity, human judgement, and human guidance" while Engelbart (1962) [28] developed a conceptual framework for "augmenting human intellect" using "tools, concepts, and methods." It is worth noting the presence and importance of the collaboration component in the definition of curiosity research proposed by Arnone et al. (2011) [1] in new media environments, where "[t]he curiosity episode, if resolved satisfactorily, initiates new learning [as in sense-making]" adding, "but it is curiosity's power to both trigger and be triggered through the development and deepening of interest" and in turn "the forms of engagement that result in deep learning and effective participation, collaboration, and affinity." Kutar and Fletcher (2023) [29] highlight AI and human collaboration in relation to the writing of organizational HR (human resources) policy, drawing on a range of equality, diversity, and inclusion (EDI) policies, the results of which are said to be "promising." Indeed, regarding strategy development, Olenick and Zemsky (2023) [30] found a virtual AI assistant used by MBA (Masters of Business Administration) students to be "more original" than a team of MBA students working without AI partnering, with the additional difference that in the latter case, students unaided by AI took a week while those aided by the AI completed the experiment in 60 min. Olenick and Zemsky (2023) [30] argue that "virtual strategists will make their human counterparts better at their job" giving way to inclusive value creation, sustainability, profitability, job creation, and more.

In educational settings, teachers employ different strategies to get students excited about learning. They use techniques to "hook" or motivate students' interest (Allchin, 2015; Barkley and Major, 2019; Smith, 2017) [31–33]. They use rewards or speak to the negative outcomes for noncompliance as external motivators (Radi, Goegan, and Daniels, 2023; Valerio, 2012; Adamma, Ekwutosim, and Unamba, 2018) [34–36]. However, long-standing research suggests that rewards and punishment may have unintended consequences on students' motivation (Deci and Ryan, 1985; Baranek, 1996; Ilegbusi, 2013; Kusumawati, Fauziddin, and Ananda, 2023) [37–40]. Excessive rewards can lead to psychological dependence and reduce students' intrinsic motivation to learn. Similarly, punishments can have unfavorable effects, such as decreased intrinsic motivation, anxiety, and even shame (Cameron and Pierce, 1994) [41]. In recent years, it has become evident that use of rewards and punishments to motivate student engagement has become less effective and short-lived. Instructional strategies that give students options in what and how they learn have shown promise. When students pick topics they care about and take on challenging assignments embedded in inquiry, problem and project based learning, it helps to promote intrinsic motivation, and sustain interest and engagement. Our work suggests that AI chatbots not only respond to curiosity motivated questioning but do so in a conversational interface that supports autonomy and agency (Calvo, Peters, and Ryan, 2023) [42]. Recent studies support this suggestion (Silitonga, 2023; Chiu, Moorhouse, and Chai, 2023; Ransbotham, Kiron, Candelon, Khodabandeh, and Chu, 2022) [43–45]. Additionally, the integration of AI chatbots in education has the potential to have a significant influence on how students learn and interact with information, ultimately enhancing student intrinsic motivation, engagement, and information retention (Labadze, Grigolia, and Machaidze, 2023) [46].

2.3 Cognitive Flexibility and Elaborative Interrogation in Technology-Rich Learning Environments

Weinstein (1977) [47] and Elen, Stahl, Bromme, and Clarabout (2011) [48] argue that the cognitively flexible individual expects there to be multiple solutions, perspectives, and knowledge sources in any given situation and will be attentive, as in, "watching (consciously or unconsciously) for the need or desirability of change" and as such, cognitive flexibility is said to involve adaptability. In describing elaboration as "a cognitive learning strategy" (Hamilton, 2012) [5], information is said to be enhanced and this "clarifies or specifies the relationship between information to-be-learned and related information." Darling-Hammond, Barron, Pearson, Schoenfeld, Stage, Zimmerman, Cervetti, and Tilson (2008) [49] advance the importance of learning to learn in ways that accommodate the rapid pace of change and unanticipated types of change pertaining to information, technologies, jobs, and the like. Concerned with "how to study effectively" and learning, Smith and Weinstein (2016) [50] claim that elaboration "involves explaining and describing ideas with many details" and "also making connections among ideas" while "connecting the material to your own experiences, memories, and day-to-day life." Smith and Weinstein (2016) [50] describe elaborative interrogation as a type of elaboration method "for studying that strengthens a students' understanding and retention of the information that they are trying to learn" by asking many questions. Our study considers iterative prompting of LLMs as a way to respond to curiosity and to engage in elaborative interrogation, ultimately satisfying and potentially sustaining curiosity, encouraging exploration of varied perspectives and new ideas, and enhancing understanding and retention of information, as well as engaging in critical thinking in evaluating prompt responses. In November 2023, the NCSS (National Council of Social Studies, 2023) [51] defined social studies as the "study of individuals, communities, systems, and their interactions across time and place that prepares students for local, national, and global civic life" while the purpose is worth noting, as follows:

"Using an inquiry-based approach, social studies help students examine vast human experiences through the generation of questions, collection and analysis of evidence from credible sources, consideration of multiple perspectives, and the application of social studies knowledge and disciplinary skills. As a result of examining the past, participating in the present, and learning how to shape the future, social studies prepares learners for a lifelong practice of civil discourse and civic engagement in their communities. Social studies centers knowledge of human rights and local, national, and global responsibilities so that learners can work together to create a just world in which they want to live."

The use of AI as defined in our framework that we formulate in this paper elucidates and supports the focus and approach to learning proposed by NCSS and extends these opportunities beyond the K–12 setting, preparing individuals to become active participants in their communities. Elaborative interrogation, a learning strategy that involves asking detailed questions related to concepts an individual is investigating, requires a learner to have background knowledge in order to pose relevant questions. For instance, an individual who is curious about rewilding in urban spaces, who has a foundation in environmental studies, might ask more sophisticated questions than someone just being introduced to the topic. This study considers the potential for LLM chatbots like Perplexity.ai, ChatGPT, and Claude-2 to assist learners in this area. These chatbots offer suggestions for related prompts (Perplexity.ai) or can be prompted to provide related questions (ChatGPT and Claude) based on initial prompts, encouraging further investigation, leading to more informed and insightful understanding of the topic. This prompt, response, suggestion process enriches elaborative interrogation in support of learning and, as we suggest in our research, it is also designed to incite and sustain curiosity and interest. Zeitlhofer, Hörmann, Mann, Hallinger, and Zumbach (2023) [52] explore the notion of prompts in digital learning environments in terms of cognitive and metacognitive activities in the context of self-regulated learning (SRL) in search of and finding improved learning performance outcomes.

2.4   Potential and Challenges of Cognitive Flexibility and Elaborative Interrogation in Support of Curiosity, Interest, and Engagement in AI-Rich Urban Learning Environments

It is important for students to have opportunities to safely engage with information and communication technologies as consumers and producers of content (Hofhues, 2019; Murphy, Coiro, and Kiili, 2019) [53, 54] and such opportunities should be aligned to real-world domains and use cases. Ethical and responsible use of digital resources in K-12 settings is taught across the curriculum to ensure students understand how to safely and thoughtfully access, evaluate, use, and cite digital content. Instruction in digital citizenship, media literacy, digital literacy, internet safety, and online privacy ensure students are critical thinkers when interacting in digital environments. There are many student-friendly tools and platforms used in schools. For example, Google Custom Search (2021) [55], free for educational settings, allows teachers to identify websites to be searched. There are also kid-safe search engines (Kidtopia, 2023; Kids Search, 2023; etc.) [56, 57] that filter search content. Additionally, in accordance with the Child Internet Protection Act (CIPA) enacted by the United States Congress in 2000, schools are required to provide stringent filtering of content to protect students from accessing inappropriate content and interacting with individuals on social media platforms that could potentially pose threats to student safety (FCC, 2019) [58]. The US Congress continues to consider bills related to online safety and privacy for the public in general and specifically for children - for example, the Children and Teens' Online Privacy Protection Act (COPPA) legislation effective April 2000. An updated version of COPPA, COPPA 2.0 (Markey and Cassidy, 2022) [59] seeks to strengthen regulations surrounding the online collection, use, and disclosure of children's personal information. Additional laws have been introduced and are under consideration (Frechtling, 2023) [60]. EdLaw 2D (2015) [61], enacted in early 2020, prohibits the release of student and staff personal identifiable information and requires notifications to parents of unauthorized access. Also of note is work edited by Holmes and Porayska-Pomsta (2022) [62] focusing on the practices, challenges, and debates of AI ethics in education. On the horizon is the Artificial Intelligence Act of the European Union (EU) expected to come into force in 2025 (DW, 2023) [63].

2.5   Conceptual Framework for Cognitive Flexibility and Cognitive Elaborative Interrogation in Support of Curiosity, Interest, and Engagement in AI-Rich Urban Learning Environments

Ethical and responsible use of AI chatbots complements ethical and responsible design of these tools and is dependent on cognitive flexibility fostered by inquiry that incorporates perspective taking and boundary setting. Our conceptual framework suggests an approach to inquiry that is foundational to ethical, responsible information seeking, and is perhaps revealing of current deficiencies of AI chatbots that LLM training and other emerging approaches seek to remedy.

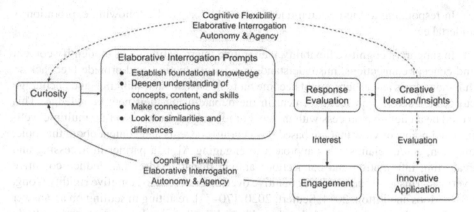

Fig. 1. Conceptual framework for cognitive flexibility and elaborative interrogation in support of curiosity, interest, and engagement in designing AI-rich urban learning spaces and services.

As noted in our earlier work (Chauncey and McKenna, 2023) [64], Hannum (2023) [65], observed that "[h]uman beings all have this impulse to develop narratives" and "that 'storification,' ... can flatten our understanding of the world and one another" such that, "[t]he information we consume nonstop online, in the news, and during conversation requires an analytical eye." Developing an "analytical eye," expanding our "understanding of the world," and avoiding "flattening" are central to our proposed iterative framework (Fig. 1) in support of cognitive flexibility, elaborative interrogation, and curiosity, interest, and engagement. The focus is not on finding definitive answers but on staying open to possibilities and staying curious. According to Hoffman (2023) [27], "interacting with GPT-4 is not like traditional web searching" and "it's better evoked by a term that was popular back in the early days of Web 1.0: web surfing" where "[a] dialogue develops. A flow state takes over. You ask GPT-4 a question and it responds right away with highly relevant information, not just a series of links." Further, "[t]he experience itself is so responsive and self-propelling that a kind of intellectual escalation kicks in: asking one question makes you want to ask ten." Iterative questioning supports critical thinking and conceptual understanding (Rosenshine, Meister, and Chapman, 1996; Graesser and Person, 1994) [66, 67]. Considering the future of education aided by AI, Mollick (2023) [68] is very hopeful given the collaborative and engagement potentials, also encouraging for the world of work (Mollick, 2023) [69].

As such the research question for the exploration in this paper is:

RQ. Could LLM AI chatbots support curiosity, interest, and engagement and, if yes, how?

This question is revised, incorporating the research question of Arnone et al. (2011) [1], as follows:

RQ1. What is it about today's new media technology-pervasive contexts - specifically LLM AI chatbots in support of cognitive flexibility and cognitive elaboration in the form of elaborative interrogation - that ignite curiosity and sustain interest and engagement?

In responding to the research question for this paper, the following exploration is undertaken:

In support of cognitive flexibility, elaborative interrogation seeks to identify content and concept connections, misunderstandings, disinformation, and provide feedback so that individuals and groups might become more flexible in their thinking, and encourage curiosity, interest, and reengagement in the debate using their new knowledge. This would be an iterative process with the goal of identifying and presenting multiple well-founded points of view that are based on accurate concepts and content about the topic, question, and/or claims. This approach to engaging AI as a partner in accessing and evaluating information and connections among disparate ideas can reduce cognitive overload. This is important since cognitive overload can lead to cognitive rigidity (Jong, 2010; Moos and Pitton, 2014, Seufert, 2020) [70–72], resulting in settling on an answer or solution that is not grounded in breadth and depth of understanding and multiple perspectives.

Our recent publications (Chauncey and McKenna, 2023; Chauncey and McKenna, 2023) [64, 73] and those of like-minded researchers (Holstein and Aleven, 2021; Lai, Kankanhalli, and Ong, 2021; Tong, 2023; Dellermann, Calma, Lipusch, Weber, and Weigel, 2019) [74–77] inspire our current efforts and challenge us to rethink our essential questions as we experiment with current, and envision future possibilities that may emerge from, AI-human partnerships. As Nicholas Thompson, CEO of The Atlantic suggests, "[w]e need to start to explore the early contours of this new world" (Thompson, 2023) [78]. Our Appendix D exemplar is consistent with and emerged from our pre-AI research including, an investigation of technology motivated curiosity, interest and engagement (Arnone et al. 2011) [1]; McKenna (2022) [79] who addressed, "…the issue of urban life and artificial intelligence (AI) including machine learning (ML) and deep learning (DL) while also exploring the notion of ambient learning in the context of smart cities, learning cities, and future cities"; Chauncey & Simpson (2020) [80] who looked to bring diverse perspectives to problem solving in civic spaces; and McKenna and Chauncey (2014) [81], who conceived of frictionless learning and envisioned "SMART Team…solutions… developed through collaborative problem solving, mediated by emerging, next generation, and existing information and communications technologies (ICTs)." In dialogues on AI, Anthony Townsend (Thompson, 2023) [78] asks, "[w]hat if, like a crystal ball, an AI-powered urban planner could tell us—without a shadow of a doubt—the inevitable impacts of different city plans on carbon emissions, income inequality, or quality of life?" and pushes us even further to consider "[e]ven better, what if it could do the diplomatic work of soliciting our needs and desires and jumping into the conversation to help resolve our conflicts?" concluding that "[w]e might be able to make the hard choices to build cities that are fair, resilient, healthy, and productive for everyone."

In Appendix D we submit five prompts and review responses across three Open LLM AI tools, ChatGPT-4, Anthropic's Claude 2.1, and Google's BARD (Gemini). Each of these tools is powering others that are emerging, and each of them is morphing based on demands for industry specific datasets and multimodal inputs and outputs, as approaches to training evolve, and as these tools become seamlessly embedded, and responsive to more sophisticated user prompts.

3 Methodology

This paper proposes as a methodology the use of *AI as a design material* as advanced by Knemeyer and Follett (2020) [82] where it is said that "AI, and more specifically machine learning, is also a design material" and less obviously so than say, "pencils and sketchbooks, markers and whiteboard, pixels and code" that "offer a compelling array of features and opportunities for designers to innovate and improve their designed experiences." Where Aciang et al. (2023) [21] also touch on cognitive overload, we address this through the iterative process described in Fig. 2 with the benefit of maintaining cognitive flexibility, even when interacting with topical inquiry in what may emerge as a complex representation of the topic which is built up through iteration and sustained interest and engagement. For individuals who have little background knowledge related to a topic, this approach relies on the LLM AI to support both building initial background knowledge and curiosity as well as sustaining interest through elaborative interrogation.

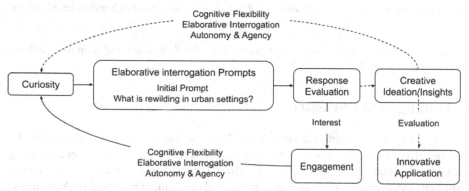

Fig. 2. Conceptual framework for cognitive flexibility and elaborative interrogation – Rewilding in urban settings

Each iteration is "digestible" so as to reduce cognitive overload - but offering numerous responses that can be considered together to build a more nuanced, sophisticated understanding of a topic. It is worth noting the commentary by Feldstein (2023) [83] following a recent summit on technology innovation and education skills, on the collaboration between human and AI, particularly in relation to the iterative process. Also of note is the work of Hannum (2023) [65] mentioned earlier, in terms of the interleaving of chat.

As noted in Fig. 3, we begin with the prompt (Appendix A): "What is rewilding in urban settings?" We share the follow-up related prompts suggested by Perplexity.ai., ChatGPT, and Claude.ai when asked, "Can you share other related questions that I can ask about rewilding." The responses from each are included.

In Appendix B, using ChatGPT-4, we begin with an *Initial Prompt* "Using elaborative interrogation create prompts that address rewilding in urban settings." and then pose two iterative prompts. *Iteration 1 Prompt*: For each of these (questions posed in initial prompt), offer a response and then ask a follow-up question. *Iteration 2 Prompt*: "Let's

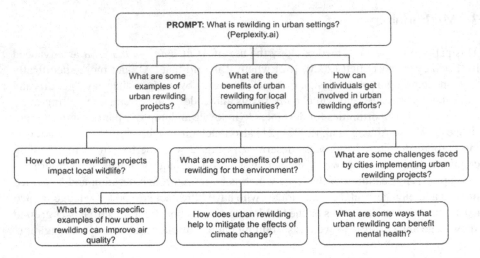

Fig. 3. Perplexity.AI initial prompt and related questions in support of elaborative interrogation

iterate this one more time. Create a response for each follow-up and then ask another follow-up based on that response."

4 Findings and Discussion

In response to our research question (Sect. 2.5), findings in this paper show that AI chatbots offer dynamic, responsive interactions that adapt to user inquiries, encouraging deeper exploration and understanding of topics. This interactive nature of AI chatbots fosters an environment where users are encouraged to ask more complex, in-depth questions, leading to a more engaging and personalized learning experience. Our exploration of AI chatbots using varied iterative prompts resulted in relevant responses, suggestions for additional prompting, motivated critical thinking, and incited curiosity and engagement.

The current study examines the role of LLM AI chatbots, focusing on how these AI tools can foster curiosity and enhance learning experiences. The paper discusses the impact of AI LLM chatbots and emphasizes the unprecedented access to information in response to curiosity driven questioning (prompts) which incites, sustains, and shapes the engagement and curiosity of learners in urban, technology-integrated settings. This study also updates and validates the Arnone et al. (2011) [1] CIE model by incorporating the latest AI technologies, offering insights into how these tools can be integrated into learning environments to stimulate curiosity and engagement, consistent with the "new research agenda" proposed by Arnone et al. (2011) [1].

Our studies thus far suggest that AI chatbots can:

1. stimulate curiosity by posing challenging questions or presenting content and concepts relevant to iterative prompting;
2. offer a variety of learning materials, activities, and even take on roles as moderators and mentors interacting with students, to collaborate on their interests. It should be

noted that AI LLMs do not comply with policies regarding student privacy and safety for use in schools. However, students share that they are using AI outside of school to complete homework, to support their understanding of math, etc.;

3. provide step-by-step learning paths, breaking down complex topics into manageable steps to help build self-efficacy and self-regulation;

4. create assessments, analyze students' responses, and provide immediate, customized feedback, helping students to recognize their progress and build confidence in their abilities;

5. provide positive feedback and encouragement, reinforcing students' intrinsic motivation for learning, offering a conversational space that supports autonomy and agency;

6. sustain motivation to understand content broadly and deeply, thus supporting cognitive flexibility by encouraging perspective taking and boundary setting during iterative prompt-response-evaluation. Our initial study findings align with the US Department of Education's report that suggests AI can improve education by offering instructional and learning resources and being responsive to students' interests, strengths, and challenges (Cardona, Rodríguez, & Ishmael, 2023) [84].

Our current work considers how AI-human partnerships can elevate our thinking while offering pathways that allow us to become more discerning, to consider multiple perspectives, to engage in elaborative interrogation, to make connections, to constrain and expand boundaries in order to view issues both broadly and deeply. We recognize the human role in prompting AI to identify biases and to use iterative questioning to request more balanced responses. There is significant and growing use of LLM AI chatbots to support content generation across industries and in educational settings. A recent post by author Shane Parrish (Parrish, 2023) [85], in his popular Farnam Street Blog, titled "Writing to Think" offers the following, "...writing about something complicated and hard to pin down acts as a test to see how well you understand it....they [young students] aren't yet smart enough to see that in a world where intellectual labor is increasingly outsourced to tools, the human aptitude for clear thinking and unique insights will become all the more valuable." Our work reinforces that responsible use of AI requires the "human" to stay in the driver's seat when prompting AI. The iterative process of prompt-response-evaluation highlighted in our framework, recognizes evaluation as an essential step in the process. The evaluation step requires interaction with a human who understands AI strengths and weaknesses. If responses are not understood, it is difficult to vet them for accuracy, bias, and context. Parrish (2023) [85] summarizes, "[m]any things can be done by tools that write for you, but they won't help you learn to think, understand deeper, or solve hard problems." Our work recognizes the issues that arise when we relinquish our role as discerning and thoughtful partners; resulting in a failure to realize the potential of AI-human collaboration.

Our earlier paper (Chauncey & McKenna, 2023) [73] that considered perspective taking and boundary setting in developing less biased and more nuanced understandings when engaged in topical inquiry suggested that "[d]eveloping this understanding through the potential of AI, encourages individuals to reach across the aisle in varied settings" so as "to bridge the chasm of fundamental differences by considering fundamental commonalities." Our earlier work (Chauncey and McKenna, 2023) [73] also notes, "because topical inquiry that employs perspective taking and boundary setting (broad and narrow) can be efficiently facilitated by LLM Chatbots, we may see decision-making that involves more sustained engagement." These affordances are essential in sparking and nurturing not only sustained engagement but also the state of curiosity that precedes it, laying the groundwork for more meaningful and sustained exploration.

5 Limitations and Future Directions

Limitations of this paper pertain to the early stage development of AI chatbots and the emerging challenges and risks and as such, future studies should evaluate and validate (Jabareen, 2009) [86] the proposed framework in this paper through action, applied, and case study methodologies in varied settings—classrooms and other learning environments—over short and long timeframes. Additionally, future explorations of the model could compare human-chatbot, human-human, and mixed human-chatbot human-human interactions to identify effects of each interaction. Our framework is flexible in accommodating such testing. Additionally, further research would consider more diverse prompts and other chatbot platforms, including domain specific chatbots. Exploring other modalities like voice assistants, image generators, etc. could reveal additional insights. Chatbots have known issues with potential inaccuracies, biases, and inappropriate responses that were not fully explored in this paper so additional attention to critical evaluation of chatbot responses is needed. Attention to professional development for educators to responsibly integrate chatbots into learning activities is necessary and was not a focus of this paper.

Regarding future directions, AI can foster autonomy and agency by encouraging exploration and curiosity-driven learning and sustaining interest and engagement by recommending resources and topics based on student prompts, offering a pathway to individualized or personalized learning. We envision the potential of AI to connect individuals with similar or complementary interests. In this scenario, AI would ask individuals if they would like to share their prompts so that they can be connected to individuals with similar interests. In learning environments, these connections could be localized to students in a classroom, in the school, or to other schools locally and globally. The possibility of encouraging collaborative partnerships could be another way to foster broader thinking about a topic and cognitive flexibility. These opportunities to foster collaborative learning can be studied in varied formal and informal settings, employing theoretical constructs associated with Ryan and Deci's Self Determination Theory (SDT) [42] constructs of competence, autonomy, and relatedness (Ryan & Deci, 2020) [87] and Albert Bandura's Social Cognitive Theory's construct of individual and group self-efficacy (Bandura, 2001) [88]. It is worth noting that Ransbotham, et. al. (2022) [45], for example, indicate that "[a]cross industries, we find employees using AI and then feeling more competent in their roles, more autonomous in their actions, and more connected to their work, colleagues, partners, and customers."

We must address limitations not only to support teaching and in K-12 settings, but to prepare students for civic engagement in community and urban settings (Chauncey and Simpson, 2020; Melaville, Berg, and Blank, 2006) [80, 89], as well as to support expectations for ethical, skilled use of these tools in college and career settings. In a

2023 article looking at citizen engagement communication solutions, including AI, the following key points are shared: "...innovative technologies have emerged, revolutionizing the way urban governance operates and enabling citizens to actively participate in shaping their cities" and these "platforms encourage collaboration and collective problem-solving by providing a space where citizens can share their ideas, experiences, and expertise" which "fosters a sense of ownership and collective responsibility among community members" (Utilities One, 2023) [90].

The academic and social emotional capacity developed in K-12 education are essential for developing skilled use of AI tools required for civic engagement, college level work, and expectations for efficiency and effectiveness in business. Integrating AI in K-12 educational settings raises concerns about privacy, bias, and appropriate use. Educators are seeking policies (Cassada, 2023) [91] to address these issues of privacy, bias, erroneous responses, jailbreaking, etc. which disallow K-12 student access to AI in schools, preventing educators from providing instruction, support, and evaluation of student use of AI tools. The U.S. Department of Education is working on policies and supports focused on the safe and fair use of AI-enabled educational technology (Office of Educational Technology, 2023) [92]. And educators are concerned about the impact of AI on student privacy (Buck, 2023; Jennings, 2023) [93, 94].

Addressing AI challenges will allow educators to take advantage of potential benefits such as supporting students with specialized educational needs; differentiated, individualized, personalized tutoring; and targeted interventions in response to data informed decision-making... (Chilcote Bacco, 2023; Bailey, 2023; AVID Open Access, 2023) [95–97]. To address these concerns, it is important for schools and communities to develop clear AI policies that consider privacy, equity, and effectiveness, while also ensuring that students have the opportunity to develop AI skills that will be crucial as students make choices regarding college and career opportunities (Krause and Jones, 2023) [98].

6   Conclusion

This paper advances a conceptual framework for AI-human interaction intended for varied learning environments. We suggest that this AI-human partnership incites curiosity and interest, encourages sustained engagement, and elaborative interrogation essential for knowledge building in support of critical thinking and problem-solving. Our explorations of ChatGPT, Claude, and other AI chatbots shared in Appendices A-D highlight the potential of iterative prompt-response cycles to motivate deeper exploration of topics. This work validates and extends the Curiosity, Interest, Engagement model advanced by Arnone et al. (2011) [1] for technology-rich learning environments.

Our study also reveals limitations in current chatbots regarding accuracy, bias, transparency, and privacy which together pose challenges for student access and responsible use of AI in educational settings. This paper offers an early effort in conceptualizing how AI can extend human capacities for learning, critical thinking, collaboration, and problem solving in varied settings.

Disclosure of Interests.   The authors have no competing interests to declare that are relevant to the content of this article.

Appendix A- Iterative Prompting in Support of Elaborative Interrogation - https://docs.google.com/document/d/1sMkA-C9F C56sIwdRDaQEP3J_fOnxNPpqyH-LNuGRS5s/edit

Beginning with the Prompt, "What is rewilding in urban settings?" we followed a selection of related prompts and noted additional prompts suggested by Perplexity, ChatGPT-4, and Claude. *These prompts were submitted in November 2023.*

Appendix B - Iterative Prompting for Urban Rewilding Using ChatGPT-4 - https://docs.google.com/document/d/1qOXu0lJLAWy QxJ341d6VPoFyK2SVrsTZbEUSzQgN70Y/edit

Using ChatGPT-4 we posed an initial prompt and asked ChatGPT to engage in elaborative interrogation - creating prompts that address rewilding in urban settings, to respond to the prompts, and then to iterate this process a second time. This was significant as ChatGPT was engaged as both the prompter and responder. *These prompts were submitted in November 2023.*

Appendix C - ChatGPT Create Playground

Using the ChatGPT Create Playground,—https://chat.openai.com/gpts/editor - we created three GPTs and then used them with example Prompts. *These ChatGPTs were created and tested in November 2023 and the links will work only for those who have a ChatGPT-4 paid account.*

GPT 1 Urban Living and Learning Planner - https://chat.openai.com/g/g-YbdMTwlNC-urban-living-and-learning-planner-assistant
GPT 2 Microcredential Course Designer - https://chat.openai.com/g/g-cCsoQbrOv-mic rocredential-course-designer
GPT 3 College and Career Pathfinder - https://chat.openai.com/g/g-pc9ds3hYW-col lege-and-career-pathfinder

Appendix D - AI-Human Collaboration in Support of Urban Development - https://docs.google.com/document/d/17BEp7yd32Vr vCz-LWeuEHs2XHpxnMY066fvwKILf8os/edit

Prompts for this exemplar were submitted to ChatGPT-4 https://chat.openai.com/, Claude https://claude.ai, and BARD https://bard.google.com/. A Table of Contents is included below the prompts. *These prompts were submitted in December 2023.*

References

1. Arnone, M.P., Small, R.V., Chauncey, S.A., McKenna, H.P.: Curiosity, interest and engagement in technology-pervasive learning environments: a new research agenda. Educ. Technol. Res. Dev. **59**(2), 181–198 (2011). https://doi.org/10.1007/s11423-011-9190-9
2. Marr, B.: What is GPT-3 and why is it revolutionizing artificial intelligence? BM Blog (2023). https://bernardmarr.com/what-is-gpt-3-and-why-is-it-revolutionizing-artificial-int elligence/#:~:text=Starting%20with%20the%20very%20basics,to%20carry%20out%20t heir%20task. Accessed 1 Mar 2023
3. Roth, E.: Meet the companies trying to keep up with ChatGPT / From Google's Bard to Microsoft's new Bing, here are all the major contenders in the AI chatbot space. TheVerge (2023). https://www.theverge.com/2023/3/5/23599209/companies-keep-up-chatgpt-ai-chatbots. Accessed 7 Mar 2023
4. Ghaffray, S.: Silicon Valley's AI frenzy isn't just another crypto craze: It isn't theoretical. Millions of people are already using apps like ChatGPT to write books, create art, and develop code. Vox (2023). https://www.vox.com/technology/2023/3/6/23624015/silicon-valley-gen erative-ai-chat-gpt-crypto-hype-trend. Accessed 7 Mar 2023
5. Hamilton, R.: Elaboration effects on learning. In: Seel, N.M. (eds.) Encyclopedia of the Sciences of Learning. Springer, Boston (2012). https://doi.org/10.1007/978-1-4419-1428-6_170
6. Farooq, O., Maher, M.: Synthesis and generativity: elaborative interrogation prompts for graduate information literacy instruction. J. Acad. Librariansh. **47**(5), 102398 (2021). https://doi.org/10.1016/j.acalib.2021.102398
7. Learning Scientists Digest. Digest #145: Elaborative Interrogation. The Learning Scientists Blog (2020). https://www.learningscientists.org/blog/2020/7/3/digest-145-1. Accessed 19 Nov 2023
8. Minigan, A.P.: The importance of curiosity and questions in 21st-century learning. Educ. Week **36**(32) (2017). https://www.edweek.org/teaching-learning/opinion-the-importance-of-curiosity-and-questions-in-21st-century-learning/2017/05
9. Dunlosky, J., Rawson, K.A., Marsh, E.J., Nathan, M.J., Willingham, D.T.: Improving students' learning with effective learning techniques: promising directions from cognitive and educational psychology. Psychol. Sci. Public Interest **14**, 4–58 (2013). https://doi.org/10.1177/1529100612453266
10. Lang, J.M.: Small changes in teaching: Making connections. The Chronicle of Higher Education (2016). https://www.chronicle.com/article/small-changes-in-teaching-making-connec tions/?sra=true
11. Farooq, O.: The effect of elaborative interrogation on the synthesis of ideas from multiple sources of information. Open Inf. Sci. **3**(1), 76–87 (2019). https://doi.org/10.1515/opis-2019-0006
12. National Academies of Sciences, Engineering, and Medicine. How People Learn II: Learners, Contexts, and Cultures. Washington, DC: The National Academies Press (2018). https://doi.org/10.17226/24783. https://nap.nationalacademies.org/read/24783/chapter/7
13. Loewenstein, G.: The psychology of curiosity: a review and reinterpretation. Psychol. Bull. **116**(1), 75–98 (1994). https://doi.org/10.1037/0033-2909.116.1.75
14. OpenAI. Introducing GPTs. OpenAI Blog (2023). https://openai.com/blog/introducing-gpts. Accessed 19 Nov 2023
15. Hudson, E.: A proposed AI strategy for 2024: Agency, not agents. Or, what inquiry-based learning can teach us about how to approach AI. Learning on Purpose Blog (2023). https://erichudson.substack.com/p/a-proposed-ai-strategy-for-2024-age ncy?utm_source=profile&utm_medium=reader2. Accessed 19 Nov 2023

16. Creamer, E.: 'Hallucinate' chosen as Cambridge dictionary word of the year. The Guardian (2023). https://www.theguardian.com/books/2023/nov/15/hallucinate-cambridge-dictionary-word-of-the-year. Accessed 25 Nov 2023

17. Cambridge Dictionary: Hallucinate (2023). https://dictionary.cambridge.org/dictionary/eng lish/hallucinate. Accessed 25 Nov 2023

18. Kayed, S., Ghoz, L., Elbehairy, F., Ghonim, A., Hendawy, M.: Setting an agenda for urban AI adaptivity in urban planning and architecture e-learning. J. Eng. Res. 6(4), 88–96 (2022). https://doi.org/10.21608/erjeng.2022.265385

19. Burry, M.: A new agenda for AI-based urban design and planning. In: As, I., Basu, P., Talwar, P. (eds.) Artificial Intelligence in Urban Planning and Design: Technologies, Implementation, and Impacts, pp. 3–20. Elsevier (2022). https://doi.org/10.1016/B978-0-12-823941-4.00005-6

20. Cugurullo, F., Caprotti, F., Cook, M., Karvonen, A., McGuirk, P., Marvin, S.: The rise of AI urbanism in post-smart cities: a critical commentary on urban artificial intelligence. Urban Stud (2023). https://doi.org/10.1177/00420980231203386

21. Aciang, I-S., Hwang, G-J., Chen, C-H.: Decision-guided chatbots and cognitive styles in interdisciplinary learning. Comput. Educ., 104812 (2023). https://doi.org/10.1016/j.compedu.2023.104812

22. Shneiderman, B.: Human-Centered AI. Oxford University Press, Oxford (2022)

23. Jones, W.: AI doesn't have to be this way > MIT economist sounds warning against unregulated tech innovation. IEEE Spect. (2023). https://spectrum.ieee.org/ai-skeptics. Accessed 23 Mar 2023

24. Dalgali, A.: Framing, Emotions, Salience: The Future of Artificial Intelligence as Seen by Redditors. Doctoral Dissertation, Syracuse University (2023)

25. Johnson, S.: The glass box and the commonplace book. SearchMedium Blog (2010). https://ste venberlinjohnson.com/the-glass-box-and-the-commonplace-book-639b16c4f3bb. Accessed 22 Mar 2023

26. Wiggers, K.: OpenAI connects ChatGPT to the Internet. TechCrunch (2023). https://techcr unch.com/2023/03/23/openai-connects-chatgpt-to-the-internet/. Accessed 23 Mar 2023

27. Hoffman R.: Impromptu: Amplifying our humanity through ai. Dallepedia LLC (2023). https://public.ebookcentral.proquest.com/choice/PublicFullRecord.aspx?p=7214737. Accessed 14 May 2023

28. Engelbart, D.C.: Augmenting human intellect: A conceptual framework. AFOSR-3233 Summary Report. Director of Information Sciences, Air Force Office of Scientific Research, Washington 25, DC, USA (1962). http://csis.pace.edu/~marchese/CS835/Lec3/DougEngle bart.pdf. Accessed 13 May 2023

29. Kutar, M., Fletcher, G.: We asked ChatGPT to write a company HR policy - and the results were promising. The Conversation (2023). https://theconversation.com/we-asked-chatgpt-to-write-a-company-hr-policy-and-the-results-were-promising-207072. Accessed 27 Sept 2023

30. Olenick, M., Zemsky, P.: Can GenAI do strategy? Harvard Business Review (2023). https://hbr.org/2023/11/can-genai-do-strategy. Accessed 25 Nov 2023

31. Allchin, D.: Hooks, lines, & sinkers. Am. Biol. Teach. 77(9), 718–720 (2015). https://doi.org/10.1525/abt.2015.77.9.14

32. Barkley, E.F., Major, C.H.: 7 ways to use "The Hook" to grab students' attention. In: Barkley, E.F., Major, C.H. (eds.) The Wiley Network. Excerpted and adapted from Interactive Lecturing: A Handbook for College Faculty. John Wiley & Sons, Hoboken (2018). https://www.wiley.com/en-us/network/education/instructors/teaching-strategies/7-ways-to-use-the-hook-to-grab-students-attention. Accessed 13 Dec 2023

33. Smith, K.: Stimulating curiosity using hooks. Noba Blog (2017). https://nobaproject.com/blog/2017-06-07-stimulating-curiosity-using-hooks. Accessed 13 Dec 2023

34. Radil, A.I., Goegan, L.D., Daniels, L.M.: Teachers' authentic strategies to support student motivation. Front. Educ. **8**, 1040996 (2023). https://doi.org/10.3389/feduc.2023.1040996
35. Valerio, K.: Intrinsic motivation in the classroom. J. Stud. Engag. Educ. Matt. **2**(1), 30–35 (2012). https://ro.uow.edu.au/jseem/vol2/iss1/6
36. Adamma, O.N., Ekwutosim, O.P., Unamba, E.C.: Influence of extrinsic and intrinsic motivation on pupils academic performance in mathematics. SJME (Supremum J. Math. Educ.) **2**(2), 52–59 (2018). https://doi.org/10.5281/zenodo.1405857
37. Deci, E.L., Ryan, R.M.: Intrinsic motivation and self-determination in human behavior. Springer, Heidelberg (1985). https://doi.org/10.1007/978-1-4899-2271-7
38. Baranek, L.K.: The effect of rewards and motivation on student achievement (Masters Theses, 285, Grand Valley State University) (1996). https://scholarworks.gvsu.edu/theses/285. Accessed 22 Nov 2023
39. Ilegbusi, M.I.: An analysis of the role of rewards and punishment in motivating school learning. Comput. Inf. Syst. Dev. Inf. **4**(1), 35–38 (2013). https://core.ac.uk/download/pdf/234697251. pdf
40. Kusumawati, M.D., Fauziddin, M., Ananda, R.: The impact of reward and punishment on the extrinsic motivation of elementary school students. AL-ISHLAH: Jurnal Pendidikan **15**(1), 183–192 (2023). https://journal.staihubbulwathan.id/index.php/alishlah/article/view/2856
41. Cameron, J., Pierce, W.D.: Reinforcement, reward, and intrinsic motivation: a meta-analysis. Rev. Educ. Res. **64**(3), 363–423 (1994). https://doi.org/10.2307/1170677
42. Calvo, R.A., Peters, D., Vold, K., Ryan, R.M.: Supporting human autonomy in ai systems: a framework for ethical enquiry. In: Burr, C., Floridi, L. (eds.) Ethics of Digital Well-Being. PSS, vol. 140, pp. 31–54. Springer, Cham (2020). https://doi.org/10.1007/978-3-030-50585-1_2
43. Silitonga, L.M., et al.: The impact of AI chatbot-based learning on students' motivation in english writing classroom. In: Huang, YM., Rocha, T. (eds.) ICITL 2023. LNCS, vol. 14099. Springer, Cham (2023). https://doi.org/10.1007/978-3-031-40113-8_53
44. Chiu, T.K., Moorhouse, B.L., Chai, C.S., Ismailov, M.: Teacher support and student motivation to learn with Artificial Intelligence (AI) based chatbot. Interact. Learn. Environ. 1–17 (2023). https://doi.org/10.1080/10494820.2023.2172044
45. Ransbotham, S., Kiron, D., Candelon, F., Khodabandeh, S., Chu, M.: Achieving individual— and organizational—value with AI. MIT Sloan Management Review (2022). https://sloanreview.mit.edu/projects/achieving-individual-and-organizational-value-with-ai/
46. Labadze, L., Grigolia, M., Machaidze, L.: Role of AI chatbots in education: Systematic literature review. Int. J. Educ. Technol. High. Educ. **20**(1), 56 (2023). https://doi.org/10.1186/s41239-023-00426-1
47. Weinstein, C.E.: Cognitive Elaboration Learning Strategies. ED144953. Austin: Texas University, Dept. of Educational Technology (1977). https://eric.ed.gov/?id=ED144953. Accessed 24 Nov 2023
48. Elen, J., Stahl, E., Bromme, R., Clarabout, G.: Links Between Beliefs and Cognitive Flexibility: Lessons Learned. Springer (2011). https://doi.org/10.1007/978-94-007-1793-0
49. Darling-Hammond, L., et al.: Powerful Learning: What We Know About Teaching for Learning. Jossey-Bass, San Francisco (2008)
50. Smith, M., Weinstein, Y.: Learn how to study using … elaboration: For students, for researchers, for teachers, learning scientists posts. The Learning Scientists Blog (2016). https://www.learningscientists.org/blog/2016/7/7-1. Accessed 8 Oct 2023
51. National Council of Social Studies. Silver Spring, Md (2023). https://www.socialstudies.org/media-information/definition-social-studies-nov2023
52. Zeitlhofer, I., Hörmann, S., Mann, B., Hallinger, K., Zumbach, J.: Effects of cognitive and metacognitive prompts on learning performance in digital learning environments. Knowledge **3**(2), 277–292 (2023). https://www.mdpi.com/2673-9585/3/2/19

53. Hofhues, S.: Inquiry-based learning with digital media. In: Mieg, H.A. (eds.) Inquiry-Based Learning – Undergraduate Research. Springer, Cham (2019). https://doi.org/10.1007/978-3-030-14223-0_35

54. Murphy, V.L., Coiro, J., Kiili, C.: Exploring patterns in student dialogue while using a digital platform designed to support online inquiry. J. Interact. Media Educ. 1 (2019). https://doi.org/10.5334/jime.518

55. Google Custom Search. Examples (2021). https://sites.google.com/view/createcustomsearch/examples. Accessed 28 Sept 2023

56. Kidtopia. Search for kids (2023). https://kidtopia.info/. Accessed 29 Sept 2023

57. Kids Search. Kid's search engine (2023). https://kidssearch.com. Accessed 29 Sept 2023

58. FCC. Children's Internet Protection Act (CIPA). Federal Communications Commission (2019). https://www.fcc.gov/consumers/guides/childrens-internet-protection-act. Accessed 29 Sept 2023

59. Markey, E.J., Cassidy, W.M.: Fact Sheet – COPPA 2.0: Children and Teens' Online Privacy Protection Act: Legislation to Strengthen Protections for Minors Online (2022). https://www.commonsensemedia.org/sites/default/files/featured-content/files/coppa_2.0_one_pager_2021.pdf. Accessed 29 Sept 2023

60. Frechtling, D.: Will the U.S. update laws for children's digital privacy? Forbes Technology Council. Forbes (2023). https://www.forbes.com/sites/forbestechcouncil/2023/03/07/will-the-us-update-laws-for-childrens-digital-privacy/?sh=1e561d233f17. Accessed 29 Sept 2023

61. EdLaw 2D. Unauthorized release of personally identifiable information. In Consolidated Laws of New York, New York State Senate, Chapter 16 (2015). https://www.nysenate.gov/legislation/laws/EDN/2-D. Accessed 29 Sept 2023

62. Holmes, W., Porayska-Pomsta, K. (eds.): The Ethics of Artificial Intelligence in education: Practices, challenges, and debates. Taylor & Francis (2022). https://www.google.com/books/edition/The_Ethics_of_Artificial_Intelligence_in/bqh2EAAAQBAJ?hl=en&gbpv=1. Accessed 29 Sept 2023

63. DW. EU lawmakers lay groundwork for 'historic' AI regulation. Deutsche Wells (DW) (2023). https://www.dw.com/en/eu-lawmakers-lay-groundwork-for-historic-ai-regulation/a-65909881. Accessed 29 Sept 2023

64. Chauncey, S.A., McKenna, H.P.: A framework and exemplars for ethical and responsible use of AI Chatbot technology to support teaching and learning. Comput. Educ. Artif. Intell. 5, 100182 (2023). https://doi.org/10.1016/j.caeai.2023.100182

65. Hannum, E.: What authors know about the power of words. The Atlantic (2023). https://www.theatlantic.com/books/archive/2023/05/the-books-briefing-han-kang-ngugi-wa-thiongo/673938/. Accessed 27 Sept 2023

66. Rosenshine, B., Meister, C., Chapman, S.: Teaching students to generate questions: a review of the intervention studies. Rev. Educ. Res. 66(2), 181–221 (1996). https://doi.org/10.3102/00346543066002181

67. Graesser, A.C., Person, N.K.: Question asking during tutoring. Am. Educ. Res. J. 31(1), 104–137 (1994). https://doi.org/10.3102/00028312031001104

68. Mollick, E.: The future of education in a world of AI: A positive vision for the transformation to come. One Useful Thing (2023). https://www.oneusefulthing.org/p/the-future-of-education-in-a-world. Accessed 29 Sept 2023

69. Mollick, E.: Setting time on fire and the temptation of the button. One Useful Thing (2023). https://www.oneusefulthing.org/p/setting-time-on-fire-and-the-temptation. Accessed 29 Sept 2023

70. Jong, T.: Cognitive load theory, educational research, and instructional design: some food for thought. Instr. Sci. 38, 105–134 (2010). https://doi.org/10.1007/S11251-009-9110-0

71. Moos, D., Pitton, D.: Student teacher challenges: using the cognitive load theory as an explanatory lens. Teach. Educ. **25**, 127–141 (2014). https://doi.org/10.1080/10476210.2012.754869

72. Seufert, T.: Building bridges between self-regulation and cognitive load—an invitation for a broad and differentiated attempt. Educ. Psychol. Rev. **32**, 1151–1162 (2020). https://doi.org/10.1007/s10648-020-09574-6

73. Chauncey, S.A., McKenna, H.P.: An exploration of the potential of large language models to enable cognitive flexibility in AI-augmented learning environments. In: Arai, K. (ed.) Proceedings of the Future Technologies Conference (FTC) 2023, Volume 4. FTC 2023. Lecture Notes in Networks and Systems, vol. 816. Springer, Cham (2023). https://doi.org/10.1007/978-3-031-47448-4_11

74. Holstein, K., Aleven, V.: Designing for human-AI complementarity in K-12 education. AI Maga. **43**, 239–248 (2021). https://ojs.aaai.org/aimagazine/index.php/aimagazine/article/view/7399

75. Lai, Y., Kankanhalli, A., Ong, D.: Human-AI collaboration in healthcare: a review and research agenda. In: Hawaii International Conference on System Sciences (2021). https://aisel.aisnet.org/hicss-54/cl/machines_as_teammates/5/

76. Tong, J.R., Lee, T.X.: Trustworthy AI that engages humans as partners in teaching and learning. Computer **56**, 62–73 (2023). https://ieeexplore.ieee.org/abstract/document/10109264

77. Dellermann, D., Calma, A., Lipusch, N., Weber, T., Weigel, S., Ebel, P. A.: The future of human-AI collaboration: a taxonomy of design knowledge for hybrid intelligence systems. In: Hawaii International Conference on System Sciences (2019). https://arxiv.org/abs/2105.03354

78. Thompson, N.: Dialogues: On AI, Society, and What Comes Next. Atlantic Re:think. The Atlantic (2023). https://cdn.theatlantic.com/assets/marketing/prod/misc-files/2023/12/AtlanticRethink_Google_Dialogues_2023-mobile.pdf. Accessed 6 Dec 2023

79. McKenna, H.P.: Urban life and the ambient in smart cities, learning cities, and future cities. IGI Global (2023). https://doi.org/10.4018/978-1-6684-4096-4

80. Chauncey, S.A., Simpson, G.I.: The role of learning city "smart teams" in promoting, supporting, and extending the community school model. In: Stephanidis, C. (ed.) HCII 2020. LNCS, vol. 12425, pp. 326–344. Springer, Cham (2020). https://doi.org/10.1007/978-3-030-60128-7_25

81. McKenna, H.P., Chauncey, S.A.: Taking learning to the city: an exploration of the frictionless learning environment innovation. In: EDULEARN14 Proceedings, pp. 6324–6334 (2014). https://library.iated.org/view/MCKENNA2014TAK

82. Knemeyer, D., Follett, J.: AI as design material: Seeing the design role in creating AI-driven products. Towards Data Science blog (2020). https://towardsdatascience.com/ai-as-design-material-2748d84bbb7b. Accessed 29 Sept 2023

83. Feldstein, M.: ChatGPT: Post-ASU+GSV reflections on generative AI. eLiterate blog (2023). https://eliterate.us/chatgpt-post-asugsv-reflections-on-generative-ai/. Accessed 29 Sept 2023

84. Cardona, M.A., Rodríguez, R.J., Ishmael, K.: Artificial Intelligence and the Future of Teaching and Learning: Insights and Recommendations (2023). https://www2.ed.gov/documents/ai-report/ai-report.pdf

85. Parrish, S.: Writing to Think. FS (Farnam Street) Blog (2023). https://fs.blog/writing-to-think/. Accessed 25 Nov 2023

86. Jabareen, Y.: Building a conceptual framework: philosophy, definitions, and procedure. Int. J. Qual. Methods **8**(4), 49–62 (2009). https://doi.org/10.1177/160940690900800406

87. Ryan, R.M., Deci, E.L.: Intrinsic and extrinsic motivation from a self-determination theory perspective: definitions, theory, practices, and future directions. Contemp. Educ. Psychol. **61**, 101860 (2020). https://doi.org/10.1016/j.cedpsych.2020.101860

88. Bandura, A.: Social cognitive theory: an agentic perspective. Annu. Rev. Psychol. **52**(1), 1–26 (2001). https://doi.org/10.1111/1467-839X.00024

89. Melaville, A., Berg, A.C., Blank, M.J.: Community-Based Learning: Engaging Students for Success and Citizenship. Coalition for Community Schools, Washington, DC (2006). https://eric.ed.gov/?id=ED490980

90. Utilities One. Revolutionizing Citizen Engagement Communication Solutions for Inclusive Cities (2023). https://utilitiesone.com/revolutionizing-citizen-engagement-communication-solutions-for-inclusive-cities. Accessed 20 Nov 2023

91. Cassada, K.: Lack of policy regarding generative AI use in school's places students at risk. Forbes (2023). https://www.forbes.com/sites/katecassada-1/2023/09/17/lack-of-policy-regarding-generative-ai-use-in-schools-places-students-at-risk/. Accessed 17 Dec 2023

92. Office of Educational Technology. Artificial Intelligence. US Department of Education (2023). https://tech.ed.gov/ai/. Accessed 17 Dec 2023

93. Buck, D.: AI is a serious threat to student privacy. Thomas B. Fordham Institute (2023). https://fordhaminstitute.org/national/commentary/ai-serious-threat-student-privacy. Accessed 17 Dec 2023

94. Jennings, J.: AI in education: Privacy and security. eSpark Learning (2023). https://www.esparklearning.com/blog/ai-in-education-privacy-and-security/. Accessed 17 Dec 2023

95. Chilcote Bacco, L.: Why educators should lean in to AI to better support students. EdSurge (2023). https://www.edsurge.com/news/2023-10-02-why-educators-should-lean-in-to-ai-to-better-support-students. Accessed 17 Dec 2023

96. Bailey, J.: AI in education: The leap into a new era of machine intelligence carries risks and challenges, but also plenty of promise. Educ. Next **23**(4), 28–35 (2023). https://www.educationnext.org/a-i-in-education-leap-into-new-era-machine-intelligence-carries-risks-challenges-promises/. Accessed 17 Dec 2023

97. AVID Open Access. AI as a student's personal tutor: Discover how AI can be leveraged as a personal tutor for every student (2023). https://avidopenaccess.org/resource/ai-as-a-students-personal-tutor/. Accessed 17 Dec 2023

98. Krause, B., Jones, W.: How to enact an AI policy in your K-12 schools. EdTech: Focus on K-12 (2023). https://edtechmagazine.com/k12/article/2023/07/how-enact-ai-policy-your-k-12-schools. Accessed 17 Dec 2023

Digital Empowerment of Excellent Traditional Chinese Music Culture Education

Shengnan Guo[1], Yinghong Zhang[2(✉)], and Zhihua Sun[3]

[1] Institute of Preschool Education, Jinan Vocational College, Jinan 255000, Shandong, China
[2] College of Fine Arts and Design, University of Jinan, Jinan 255000, Shandong, China
83976471@qq.com
[3] College of Arts, Shandong Agriculture and Engineering University, Jinan 255000, Shandong, China

Abstract. China's excellent traditional music culture, as the spiritual heritage of the Chinese nation and an essential component of Chinese culture, carries rich historical value and cultural significance. With the rise of digital education, this traditional cultural field faces unprecedented development opportunities and many challenges. This paper first expounds on the basic concept, core characteristics, and value embodiment of education digitisation in education, laying a theoretical foundation for subsequent discussion. Then, the article deeply analyses the teaching potential of traditional music in the digital environment and discusses the enrichment and innovation of traditional music teaching content and form through digital means, improving the interaction and interest of teaching and realising the diversification of teaching methods. In addition, this paper also focuses on the development and utilisation of digital resources and proposes to establish a shared traditional music teaching platform and curriculum system to break the restrictions of time and space, broaden the scope of learners, and realise the optimal allocation and efficient utilisation of educational resources. This study aims to explore the innovative application of educational digitisation in inheriting excellent traditional music culture in China and propose practical solutions to its problems, providing theoretical support and practical guidance for the innovative development of traditional music, which has important practical significance.

Keywords: Digital Education · Traditional Culture · Traditional Music

1 Introduction

1.1 Research Significance

As the carrier of human emotion and culture, music carries the memory and spirit of the nation. Chinese traditional music culture is broad and profound, containing rich historical information and philosophical thoughts. However, under the impact of the modernisation process, these precious cultural heritages face the risk of being marginalised or even forgotten. Therefore, using digital education to protect and disseminate this intangible cultural heritage is significant to maintaining national culture's diversity and is essential in cultivating the young generation's cultural confidence and aesthetic ability.

N. A. Streitz and S. Konomi (Eds.): HCII 2024, LNCS 14719, pp. 231–241, 2024.
https://doi.org/10.1007/978-3-031-60012-8_14

To better realise the docking of Posts and majors, colleges and universities should integrate traditional culture education into teaching courses, which will help students better inherit the spirit and roots of traditional culture. Especially in music education, there are many problems, such as highlighting the teaching of music skills, methods and experience, such as how to play music or sing songs better and dance better. While ignoring the cultural connotation contained in the music itself, the traditional teaching method is single, the expression of cultural emotion is lacking, the application of digital technology needs to be strengthened, and the teachers' music and cultural knowledge-ability needs to be improved. If the above practical problems cannot be solved as soon as possible, the development and inheritance of traditional music culture will become problematic. Therefore, this paper explores a new teaching mode through an in-depth analysis of the combination of digital education and traditional music culture inheritance. This mode can protect and carry forward the excellent Chinese traditional music culture, adapt to contemporary students' learning habits and needs, and realise the compelling connection between tradition and modernity. In this way, it can not only provide students with new learning experiences but also inject new vitality into the inheritance and development of traditional music culture and show the unique charm and era value of Chinese culture in the context of globalisation.

This study explores the innovative application of digital education in inheriting Chinese excellent traditional music culture. Analysing existing literature, it is not difficult to find that although some colleges and universities have begun integrating digital media into aesthetic education teaching, these practices often lack systematic planning and in-depth theoretical support. In addition, how to combine the connotation of traditional culture with modern teaching technology to stimulate students' interest in learning while ensuring the quality of teaching is also an urgent problem to be solved.

1.2 Research Purpose and Content

In exploring the digital innovation of music education, this study aims to explore the innovative application of digital technology in inheriting and carrying forward China's excellent traditional music culture. Integrating modern educational technology and traditional music teaching can create a diversified and interactive learning environment, optimise teaching methods and resources, expand learning boundaries, and enhance cultural confidence.

The core content of this study is to explore how digital media can empower traditional music education, efficient strategies in terms of immersive experience, constructing aesthetic identity, and stimulating spiritual resonance. This paper discusses how to build a comprehensive music education system with the help of a digital platform, including enriching the curriculum content, improving the curriculum system and innovating the teaching evaluation methods. This study will analyse the deficiencies of the current music general education curriculum in realising the functions of "adult" and "education" and propose to make up for this gap through digital information authorisation. At the same time, it discusses how to use digital tools to record, preserve, and publicise music projects in intangible cultural heritage to ensure their continuous inheritance and activation in contemporary society. This study aims to further reveal the integration of traditional culture and aesthetic education in ethnic regions and enhance students' national cultural identity and aesthetic interest through digital means. This includes developing digital educational resources with regional characteristics as the theme and designing educational activities to promote physical and mental health development.

This study attempts to propose a new mode of combining digital media and music education, which aims to enrich students' aesthetic experience and cultivate students to become comprehensive talents who appreciate, understand and inherit Chinese excellent traditional music culture. This study hopes to provide a new perspective and practical scheme for the education and inheritance of Chinese traditional music culture in the digital era through the in-depth exploration of the construction of music courses in Colleges and universities.

2 Concepts and Characteristics of Educational Digitalization

Digital education integrates modern technology and educational practice to form new teaching and learning modes. This concept involves reforming teaching media and tools and points to the fundamental innovation of educational content, methods, ideas and even the whole educational ecosystem. This transformation in music education means transitioning from traditional face-to-face courses to virtual classrooms, online interactive platforms and personalised learning paths using multimedia resources.

As a product of the information age, the core characteristics of educational digitalisation are reflected in multiple dimensions.

The first is the improvement of interactivity and participation. The introduction of digital technology breaks traditional education's time and space constraints and realises the multidimensional interaction between teachers and students, as well as students and knowledge content. Through virtual classes, online discussions and other forms, students are no longer passive recipients but become active participants. The improvement of this participation has greatly stimulated students' interest and initiative in learning.

The second is the personalised and customised learning path. With extensive data analysis and artificial intelligence technology, education digitalisation can provide customised learning resources and teaching programs according to each student's learning progress, ability and preference. This learner-centred teaching model optimises learning efficiency and considers each student's needs, making education more accurate and efficient.

Third, rich and diverse teaching resources and forms. Digital education integrates text, pictures, audio, video and other media to create a multimedia teaching environment. At the same time, using virtual reality (VR), augmented reality (AR) and other technologies can provide students with an immersive learning experience, make abstract knowledge intuitive and easy to understand, and significantly improve the interest and effectiveness of learning.

The fourth is the mechanism of instant feedback and intelligent evaluation. In the digital education environment, every click and assignment submission of students can be recorded and analysed systematically. Teachers can determine students' learning situations in real-time and adjust teaching strategies accordingly. The intelligent evaluation system can also automatically correct assignments and tests, provide timely feedback for students and help them quickly locate and improve problems.

Fifth, the supporting system of lifelong learning. Digital education advocates a learning method not limited by time and place. People can continue to learn according to their rhythm and needs. This is significant to the realisation of lifelong education because it enables everyone to constantly update knowledge and improve skills even after leaving the formal school education system.

The core characteristics of digital education highlight the development direction of modern education technology. It continuously promotes the innovation of education mode through high interactivity and participation, personalised learning path, diversified teaching resources and methods, instant feedback and intelligent evaluation, and lifelong learning support, providing new ideas and possibilities for inheriting and promoting the excellent Chinese traditional music culture.

3 Innovative Applications of Digital Education in the Inheritance of Traditional Music

3.1 Combination of Digital Technology and Traditional Music Teaching

As the carrier of human emotion and culture, music carries the weight of history and national memory. In pursuing parallel improvement of technology and life, digital technology provides a new path for the inheritance and teaching of traditional music. Using digital media, we can break through the limitations of time and space and present the teaching content of music to learners in a more prosperous and three-dimensional form. With the help of advanced digital technologies, such as virtual reality (VR), augmented reality (AR) and 3D sound simulation, students can experience the scene of ancient music performance in the virtual environment and feel the unique atmosphere generated when the timbre of the instrument is integrated with the breath of the performer. This immersive learning experience not only stimulates students' interest in learning but also enhances the depth and durability of memory.

Furthermore, the digital platform's application makes music teaching no longer limited to the traditional classroom environment. Online music classrooms, interactive teaching software and artificial intelligence-assisted music teaching systems have greatly expanded the boundaries of traditional music teaching. Students can access various online music resources, including rare ancient music scores, lectures of famous artists and videos of various styles of traditional music performances, to realise autonomous learning and comparative study of multiculturalism. In addition, digital technology can help create and interpret traditional music. Electronic music production software allows learners to combine traditional music elements with modern music styles to create novel and unique works. At the same time, through the digital modelling and Simulation of traditional musical instruments, students can practice and master the basic playing skills of musical instruments without physical instruments. For example, our guzheng app can use Guzheng software to imitate the original guzheng for simulation exercises. Our score software can directly create music on the software and intelligently use chords to write music. We also have our dance software. You can use AI for simulation and dance practice with the help of software. We also have many music education resources, which can be learned and shared anytime, anywhere. Realising digital resources helps to learn (Fig. 1).

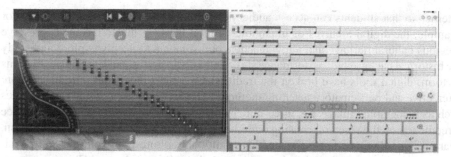

Fig. 1. Guzheng APP and rhythm training master APP

The combination of digital technology and traditional music teaching is a technical innovation and a comprehensive update of educational concepts and methods. Through this combination, we not only retain the core value of traditional music but also inject new vitality into its inheritance and development, ensuring that this precious cultural heritage can continue to flourish in the digital age. For example, the intelligent dance app can practice dance movements with the help of virtual simulation people, and you can follow the virtual simulation to learn and correct dance. Can practice anytime, anywhere (Fig. 2).

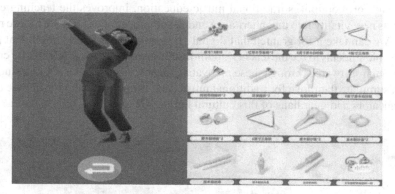

Fig. 2. Intelligent dance APP

3.2 Digital Innovation of Teaching Content and Form

When discussing the innovative application of digital education in the inheritance of traditional music, the digital innovation of teaching content and form is the core issue. Combining digital media technology with traditional music teaching can expand teaching boundaries and provide students with a multi-sensory and comprehensive learning experience. From the content perspective, digitalisation enriches and activates traditional music resources. Music materials that used to be limited by physical barriers and geographical boundaries can now be digitally stored and transmitted through the

Internet so that students can access authentic traditional music wherever they are. For example, the digital archives of intangible cultural heritage music resources preserve precious cultural heritage and allow teachers and students to deeply explore and study the historical background, performance skills and artistic performance of music. In terms of form, digital tools have broken the traditional teaching mode and introduced more interactive and participatory teaching methods. The application of digital technologies such as holographic image, 5g, three-dimensional simulation and artificial intelligence directly acts on the receptor, causing omnidirectional co-frequency resonance of vision, hearing, kinesthetic and sensory, making traditional culture both spiritual and physical, and broadening the emotional connotation of excellent traditional Chinese culture. For example, virtual reality (VR) and augmented reality (AR) technology can create an immersive learning environment, making students feel like they are in a concert or historical scene, thus enhancing their learning motivation and sense of experience. In addition, designing a personalised learning path using artificial intelligence (AI) can adjust the teaching content and difficulty according to each student's learning progress and preferences, making education more aligned with individual differences.

Moreover, digital platforms, such as online classes, social media and blogs, provide students with a platform to display their musical achievements, share learning experiences and communicate with each other. This open learning environment promotes the sharing of knowledge and the collision of innovative thinking and builds a bridge for disseminating and popularising traditional music. The digital innovation of teaching content and form optimises traditional music education, improves the teaching effect, and injects new vitality into the inheritance and development of excellent Chinese music culture. We can take it for granted that digital classrooms, such as the intelligent piano room, enable students to see the teacher's demonstration more clearly and directly correct notes through software. Through these innovative means, we can better capture students' interest, stimulate their love for traditional music, and encourage them to become active communicators and guardians of this cultural heritage (Fig. 3).

Fig. 3. Smart Classroom

Digital teaching breaks the traditional text and image-based presentation mode and expands teaching expressiveness by using sound, video, VR/AR and other media forms to create an immersive learning experience. The "Peking Opera virtual practice class-room" developed by Beijing Normal University uses VR technology to let students feel the charm of Peking Opera. Wearing VR glasses, students can watch famous artists' performances 360 degrees, practice singing with virtual seniors and Dan actors, and participate in virtual stage practice. The immersive audio-visual experience and interactive participation experience have greatly enhanced students' interest in learning Peking Opera and deepened their understanding of the art of Peking Opera (Fig. 4).

Fig. 4. VR classroom

3.3 Construction of Shared Teaching Platform and Curriculum System

When exploring the innovative application of digital education to the inheritance of traditional music, constructing a shared teaching platform and curriculum system is particularly important. By integrating information technology, such a platform provides learners with rich and diverse traditional music resources and creates an interactive and easy-to-access learning environment, thus effectively broadening the audience base of traditional music culture. Building a shared teaching platform focuses on integrating various digital media resources, such as audio, video, text, and interactive modules, to form a multi-functional virtual classroom. The platform's content is not limited to the display of music itself but also includes the introduction of a rich cultural background, an analysis of performance skills, and explaining the creative process behind it to present the charm of music art in multiple dimensions. In addition, the shared teaching platform should support user-generated content (UGC) and encourage students to upload their music works and experiences to stimulate discussion and communication within the community. For example, the classroom learning platform can be used to publish theme discussions, and teachers can know students' understanding and mastery of this problem through the discussion to make better teaching preparation. You can also use teaching evaluation in the classroom to achieve students' teaching evaluation. For example, you can vote for your favourite music activity or the correct answer. You can get a teaching evaluation using the result data. It can also promote knowledge sharing and provide students with self-expression and critical thinking space. The sharing teaching platform should integrate an intelligent recommendation system to recommend appropriate course content and learning paths for students according to their learning progress and preferences. This personalised teaching strategy can effectively improve learning efficiency and increase students' learning motivation (Fig. 5).

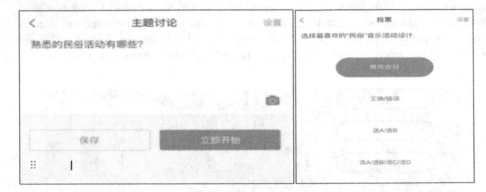

Fig. 5. Teaching Platform

The construction of the curriculum system should follow the principle of "from simple to profound" and adapt to the needs of students at different levels. The course can provide beginners with basic music theory knowledge and simple, practical operations. More advanced course content can be provided for students with a sure foundation, such as complex music analysis, composition skills training, etc. The whole curriculum system needs to be flexible and diverse. It should have systematic knowledge transfer

Fig. 6. The University of China MOOC

and focus on cultivating students' self-study consciousness. The University of China MOOC (MOOC) is an online learning platform created by aiyuan.com and Netease Cloud Classroom. Everyone who wants to improve can learn high-quality university courses in China here and obtain a certificate after learning (Fig. 6).

4 The Role of Digital Media and Network Platforms in the Promotion of Traditional Music

Digital media has become a new platform to display traditional music culture. We can use text, pictures, audio, video, and other forms of content to incisively and vividly show the details of traditional music digitally. For example, through high-definition video recording, the audience can see every subtle action of the performer and hear the change of every note. Through virtual reality technology, the audience can even experience the performance process of traditional music and feel the charm of music. In addition, due to the interactive characteristics of digital media, on the network platform, the audience is no longer a passive recipient but can actively participate in transmitting traditional music. They can express their views and feelings through likes, comments, sharing, and other ways, and they can also participate in interpreting traditional music through virtual performance, creation, and adaptation. This interactivity enhances the audience's sense of participation and makes disseminating traditional music more diversified and extensive. More importantly, it breaks the restrictions of time and space. With a network, you can view and enjoy traditional music content anytime. This boundless characteristic enables traditional music to transcend the boundaries of region and time and be understood and loved by more people. Using digital media to display traditional music culture can not only show the charm of traditional music from an all-round and multi-angle but also enable more people to participate in the transmission of traditional music through interactive and boundless characteristics to promote the inheritance and development of excellent Chinese traditional music culture.

The network platform can enhance the public's awareness of traditional music. Video-sharing websites, social networks, online education platforms, etc., have become a bridge between traditional music and modern audiences. These platforms can not only present the audio-visual feast of music performance but also provide an in-depth background introduction, historical interpretation, and cultural comments so that users can enjoy the beauty of music and obtain rich knowledge and experience. Digital media and network platforms effectively promote people's understanding and recognition of traditional music culture by providing rich and diverse traditional music resources, creating interactive virtual communities and personalised user experiences. Specifically, users can listen to various classic tracks at any time through the online music library, experience the performance process of traditional music with the help of virtual reality technology, and even participate in creating and interpreting traditional music through social media. This comprehensive sense of participation and experience can effectively enhance the public's awareness of traditional music.

At the level of international exchange, digital media and network platforms have broken geographical boundaries, enabling traditional Chinese music to cross national boundaries and reach global audiences. Through live webcasts and transnational music project cooperation, traditional music has shown its unique charm on the international stage. For example, some videos of Chinese classical musical instruments have become popular online, causing widespread interest and discussion among foreign netizens. At the same time, musicians at home and abroad communicate and cooperate through the network platform to jointly create new works integrating Eastern and Western elements, which promotes mutual learning and blending of cultures.

It can be seen that digital media and network platforms play a vital role in promoting traditional music. They enhance people's confidence in traditional culture and build a bridge to the international stage, making the excellent traditional Chinese music culture spread and appreciated worldwide. In the future, with the continuous progress of technology and the deepening of applications, digital media and network platforms will play a more critical role in promoting the innovation and development of Chinese traditional music and international exchanges.

5   Conclusions and Recommendations

Conclusions and suggestions When exploring the innovative application of digital education in inheriting Chinese excellent traditional music culture, we must recognise that the integration of science and technology not only provides a new platform and method for the dissemination and education of traditional music but also injects new vitality into the dissemination and education of traditional music. Here are some suggestions on how to use digital means to more effectively inherit traditional music culture:

1. Integrate virtual reality technology to create an immersive learning environment. Based on the practice strategy of immersive music teaching in Colleges and Universities under the digital media environment, a virtual reality teaching platform with traditional music as the theme is developed, which enables students to experience the performance of ancient music in a simulated environment, understand the production process of musical instruments and intuitively feel the social function and cultural significance of traditional music in different historical periods.
2. Build an online traditional music database and resource-sharing platform. An open digital resource database is established by systematically collecting and collating various traditional music resources such as scores, audio, video and related literature. This will help scholars, educators, and students quickly access information and promote the teaching and research of traditional music.
3. Develop interactive teaching applications. Relying on intelligent mobile devices and Internet technology, develop applications specifically for traditional music learning. These applications should include interactive teaching content, instant feedback mechanisms and personalised learning paths to attract the participation and interest of the younger generation.
4. Promote distance learning mode. Through online classroom and video conference tools, traditional musicians and professional teachers are invited to give online lectures and seminars, breaking through geographical boundaries so that more people can directly learn from masters and improve the quality and efficiency of teaching.

5. Encourage the practice research of innovative teaching methods. Support educators in researching traditional digital music teaching methods, especially in combination with the innovative practice of modern educational concepts and technical means, and constantly optimise and improve teaching strategies.
6. Strengthen interdisciplinary cooperation. Promote exchanges and cooperation in musicology, pedagogy, computer science and other fields, jointly explore the best practice of digital education of traditional music, give full play to their respective advantages, and jointly promote the innovation and inheritance of traditional music.

By implementing the above suggestions, we can expect the traditional music culture to be reborn in the wave of digital education and get a broader and deeper understanding and appreciation in society.

When exploring the innovative application of digital education in inheriting Chinese excellent traditional music culture, future research should focus on deepening the integration of theory and practice and reveal the internal logic and potential value of combining digital technology and music from a more comprehensive perspective. Future research should continue to explore and challenge the existing education mode, use digital technology to innovate the inheritance mode of Chinese excellent traditional music culture, pay attention to evaluation and feedback, ensure the quality and effect of education activities, and promote the prosperity and development of traditional music culture in the new era.

References

1. Xu, L.: A realistic survey of aesthetic education courses in colleges and universities, using music general education courses as an example. Liter. Content. (12), 199–203 (2023)
2. Bai, Q., Wang, R.: Research on teaching innovation of integrating regional traditional culture into aesthetic education in colleges and universities. J. Higher Educ. 9(36), 99–102 (2023). https://doi.org/10.19980/j.cn23-1593/g4.2023.36.024
3. Wang, T., Ying, W.: Exploration on the construction of aesthetic education curriculum in Higher Education under the background of "five educations simultaneously" – taking music intangible cultural heritage as an example. Adult Educ. 43(09), 43–47 (2023)
4. You, L., Min, J.: Digital media enabled immersive aesthetic education teaching in Higher Vocational Colleges: appearance logic and practice strategy. J. Wuxi Polytech. 22(04), 15–19+34 (2023). https://doi.org/10.13750/j.cnki.issn.1671-7880.2023.04.004
5. Qian, Z: Analysis of the integration of regional traditional music culture into College Curriculum Teaching – Take the eastern Hebei region as an example. Hua Zhang (06), 60–62 (2023)
6. Wu, Y: Research on the inheritance of Hainan music culture higher education with mixed teaching. Art Grand View (14), 124–126 (2023)
7. Deng, Y: Online teaching exploration of "Introduction to National music" under the concept of in-depth teaching -- Taking Sichuan Institute of Culture and Art as an example. Chin. J. Multimedia Netw. Teach. (Last Ten Days' Issue) (04), 30–33 (2023)
8. Tang, L.: Research on the digital transformation of Guangxi ethnic culture protection and inheritance education in the 5g era. Coast. Enterp. Technol. (01), 62–66 (2023)

Future-Present Learning in Place: Postdigital Learning at the Scale of the City

Pen Lister[✉] [iD]

University of Malta, MSD 2080, Msida, Malta
pen.lister@penworks.net

Abstract. This paper critically reflects on future-present learning in place situated in the context of postdigital learning at the scale of the city [1]. The terms 'future-present' and 'postdigital' are used to attempt to encapsulate re-imagining possible futures of civic learning in urban places, situated within a technology-infused future learning city environment. Acknowledging a high level of uncertainty [2], it is argued here that we must re-imagine and investigate alternative visions of what might be possible or desirable to implement a smarter, more effective and efficient learning in place in near-future learning cities, to plan and adapt for how this future could play out, and mitigate challenges that may arise. Seeking to step out from 'business as usual' interpretations and taking a lead from innovative projects, literature and media debates, a speculative vision is outlined for a civic learning network to provide seamless, low friction learning in a smart future city. Context is placed on the importance of the web of knowledge as the foundation of any system of civic learning implementation, the role of the open social web to support citizen participation, and the potential responsibilities of platform infrastructure as part of their relationship to future technosocial contracts and citizen digital epistemic rights.

Keywords: knowledge commons · knowledge web · smart learning · ubiquitous learning · civic learning · learning cities

1 Introduction

This paper considers 'learning in place' in contexts of smarter learning cities that are open and technically enabled to offer ubiquitous interactivity with knowledge resources via any suitable technological infrastructure. In order to provide this kind of seamless knowledge interaction for citizens, ideas are outlined for a speculative 'civic learning network' (CLN). Key areas discussed within this context are related to user requirements, digital literacies and open, fair access to the knowledge web. Subsequent challenges that may arise are considered, such as providing more effective, useful recommender systems, particularly within a user data rights and anonymity setting. The epistemic responsibilities related to a CLN are explored, including questions concerning curation and maintenance of the integrity of the knowledge web; 'artificial intelligence' considered in relation to potential impact on recommender systems; and the possible role of a CLN in a future technosocial contract for citizen digital epistemic rights, supporting democratic engagement and ontological security.

Urban geocoded knowledge content can already be effectively discovered and delivered using various methods[1] to enhance a casual learner's experience of place. Adding open social web communication offers potential for citizen contributions to the knowledge of place, and argument is made in this paper that building an open civically-owned interactive learning network can act as a cornerstone of urban democratic belonging and ontological security, within what a future learning city for all sections of the learning society could become [1, 3–6]. Drawing on a variety of similarly themed learning city orientated research and community initiatives, this paper reflects on how we can move forward to achieve a flexible, technologically hybrid solution for civic learning, supported by a Human-Technology Interaction (HTI) integrated approach (e.g. [7]). Contributions to ideas, and highlighting possible limitations, may assist in pointing the way to future directions for realising the provision of CLNs within a new technosocial contract of knowledge and the fourth generation human right for citizen access to trustworthy epistemic information [8, 9].

The background of the author is a multimedia professional and interdisciplinary higher education academic with experience in using technology to support learning in place [10]. This provides sufficient layman's practical awareness of what might be possible or desirable in conceptualising a CLN, but perhaps without detailed awareness of challenges that might be encountered in relation to some ideas outlined.

1.1 Lifelong Learning in Place

Learning in place forms a natural part of urban technological infrastructure in the smart learning city, occupying a key aspect of smart learning literature debates. Emphasis in research is often placed on developing new interactive smartphone apps, online learning platforms or ways of delivering smart 'personalised learning' based on user data (e.g. [11, 12]). Learning in place may not only be about 'being in place', but also incorporate learning about a place while being in another place, as it might be that learning cities together form local, national or international networks [13, 14], or that someone in one city might find something of relevance in a place in another city [15].

Facer & Buchczyk [1] reflect on "the way the materiality of the city 'itself' educates", that a "concept of the city as a site that 'educates attention' (where) learning is reframed as a process of dwelling in the city", and the 'key issue' that "learning is framed as a co-emergence between the people and the materiality of the city" (p. 161). They and others consider lifelong learning as a significant aspect of learning in place and learning cities, not only as part of formal education to emphasise employment skillsets, but as incidental or unplanned learning, motivated by natural curiosity rather than any idea of training or teaching (e.g. [16, 17]). The possible reasons why people engage with knowledge 'for its own sake' are probably infinite, however we need only examine Facebook groups based on knowledge and place, for example archaeology, architecture, photography, general arts, socio-cultural history, cities, towns and more, to find evidence of how much people

---

[1] Technology such as augmented reality smartphone camera image recognition, textual recognition, geocoded location data, sensors, beacons, QR codes or SMS notifications all offer mechanisms for knowledge related to place to be delivered to a user's smartphone while they are in place.

love to engage with knowledge about places. All of those aforementioned groups would benefit from a digital infrastructure for learning in place. This paper considers this kind of incidental learning, that happens every day with a Google search [18], visit to a cultural heritage website, social media discussion, or shared images about places, as the learning that may be most impacted by a CLN.

1.2 Why a Learning City?

According to Facer & Buchczyk [1], learning cities have their roots in the critical pedagogy of the 1970's [19], and the conceptual belief that social change can be best achieved in urban contexts. In subsequent years initiatives such as the UNESCO Global Network of Learning Cities[2] are now promoted as centralised policy bodies to support social change and economic development. However, there is a tension around why learning cities exist, that "the development of international networks and benchmarks for what should constitute a learning city might be seen as a practice of colonialism and coercion [1]. Citing various other related work, they go on to note there should be "a richer more complex normative vision for a Learning City as engaging not only with preparation of citizens for economic competition, but with political and experiential education … environmental awareness and sustainability … and with the more emancipatory goals of critical adult education traditions" [1].

Decentralised (localised or specialised) networks of learning in and between cities [20] may bring advantage to both citizens and to the ad-hoc varied purposes of learning that can manifest as citizen-led activities and knowledge generation, separate from formal learning or even any declared purpose of learning. Surely this complements Freire's 'liberating pedagogy' that "cannot be developed or practiced by the oppressors. It would be a contradiction in terms if the oppressors not only defended but actually implemented a liberating education" [19]. If every learning city was imbued with a CLN, they could potentially digitally federate together with others at local or regional scale. This would create an affordance for a citizen-led curated custodianship of the urban knowledge web between all learning city network instance infrastructures, decentralised in ownership and authority, adopting the app and platform interoperable model of the open social web utilised in the Fediverse [21].

2 Future-Present Postdigital Learning in Place

Future present learning in place is a vision of what can manifest as learning in place based on and inspired by a different vision to that which already exists. For example, to reinvent a future that is not based on current conjecture or supposition about cost, types of learning or civic educational expectations as they exist now. It is the opposite of 'present future', a future version of the present rooted in present understanding and assumptions about 'how things work'. We need to explore the future in the present [22], by thinking of smart cities in the 'future present' [23], to anticipate learning and teaching postdigital hybridities and prepare for them in the present [24]. This 'future-present'

---

[2] UNESCO Learning Cities https://www.uil.unesco.org/en/learning-cities

vision is 'latent and changing', but "can be recognized and foreseen, thus impacting the present by entering into it and being used in the present', in contrast to the 'present future' of 'pre-given futures' rooted in the past as 'linear continuations of the past in the present" [2].

Jandrić et al. [25] observe that we are "somewhat weary of various post-concepts" because post-industrial societies "have not in any way left the smokestack era of factory production". However, in this paper 'postdigital' is a useful term, interpreted as a blend of Negroponte's 'being digital' as only noticeable by its absence [26], and Cramer's interpretation of 'post-digital' as "a media aesthetics which opposes … high-fidelity cleanness" [27]. This is Townsend's vision of the smart city, with its 'motley assortment of activists, entrepreneurs, and civic hackers … tinkering their ways toward a different kind of utopia' [28]. The citizen-hacker led approach toward utopia is somewhat reflected in the work of Soch et al.'s [7] utopian collective intelligence for 'future human-technology interaction design'. Conceptually, future-present postdigital learning in place considers a CLN as being a manifestation of a 'city as interface' [29], where digital interactions with knowledge resources and networked communities are pervasive, platform and app agnostic, available at point of need or interest, and may be engaged with by any user at any time. Ideally civic learning technical infrastructure is owned or co-owned by citizens in a decentralised federated network model, forming part of a technosocial contract of citizen human rights to the knowledge web.

2.1 Postidigital Epistemological Context

The postdigital epistemological context of this paper can be considered as the pervasively persistent human/technological urban future city lifeworld, a digitally integrated landscape of citizen and object data, in a 'mediatic surfaces' infused built environment [30–32]. Smart city epistemological work has postulated a variety of data-driven learning contexts (e.g. [11, 12, 33], however ideas such as the 'Frictionless Learning Environment & Activity Theory' (FLEAT) model and 'Ambient Theory' [34, 35] position learning to be a pervasive flow of citizen interactivity within a 'heightened awareness' ambience of interactive agency in the digitised city. This theoretical understanding of human-technology interaction relationships that acknowledge the hybrid complexity of interdependent human/technology interface/data-reliant awarenesses complements how this paper considers the epistemological backdrop for discussion in a postdigital smart urban environment. It is the ebb and flow of need, curiosity and interest mediated by ad-hoc interactions with "technologies supporting enhanced awareness and spaces accommodating more aware people and their multisensorial capabilities" [35], that perhaps might also be referred to as a postdigital 'situated literacy'[36].

3 Understanding Urban Citizen Learning

Urban citizen learning should encourage learners to explore their 'objects of vital interest' [37] in a context of value, engagement and intrinsic motivation [38]. Interactions with a CLN should support transversal skills, fostering a critical curiosity and 'learning-to-learn' mindset in a culture of wellbeing and self-realisation [39–43]. This learning is unplanned, as Pyyry suggests, a sudden event of 're-cognizing ordinary everyday environments', further citing Ingold [44], who discusses knowing by dwelling, … (s)kills are developed in being, in involved activities and while relating to everyday situations…" [4]. To reiterate, the focus of learning in this paper is predominantly on learning that can happen anytime, by anyone for any reason, and while this is mostly considered as implicit or incidental learning, it may also form a part of student directed or problem solving pedagogical strategies in formal education. Lui et al. provide a clear definition between formal and informal smart learning, framing this as explicit and implicit learning. They declare that "a smart learning system includes two aspects: school smart learning system and social smart learning system", defining explicit learning as 'what people normally think of as formal learning' that often happens in school, and implicit learning as social learning, often happening 'in an environment of community learning, enterprise (work) learning, and learning in public places' [33]. This acknowledges the "incidental or random learning that results from ordinary life activities" or events not designed as educational activities, or designed as 'covert' learning [17, 45]. Eyal & Gil [46] argue "learning can be unintentional and exist within authentic activity, context, and culture", and "focuses on the relationship between learners as autonomous, proactive entities (and) produces an infinite potential of learning possibilities, but not necessarily those realised in an educational, institutional context" [46].

A CLN should be envisaged in a context of side-stepping assumed limitations, accepted past ways of doings things or simply imitating them with added technology [47]. However, in recent years there has been renewed interest "to recover and learn from past examples of research and practice in city-wide thinking about education" [1]. We can find inspiration to implement a CLN system through being informed by innovative projects from the past. Projects highlighted here serve to provide ideas that when combined help to produce a potential blueprint for a CLN.

Hidden Cities.[3] Part of the 'PUblic REnaissance Urban Cultures of Public Space between Early Modern Europe and the Present'[4] project, Hidden Cities provides a relevant example of history-in-urban-places mediated by technology. Five participating cities in the Netherlands, Germany, Spain, Italy and the UK provided smartphone apps to enable citizens to access historical content related to specific places while traversing the streets of each city. The Hidden Cities example offers a glimpse of what a smarter city could provide to its current and future citizens, if technological infrastructure enabled access to creating, consuming and interacting with a CLN.

The Zone of Possibility. Cook, Lander & Flaxton [15] proposed use of a location-based technology app within 'Zones of Possibility', a way by which we might think of locations, areas, terrains and local places that can be smart learning spaces within urban environments not imbued with technical infrastructure of themselves, yet provide possible interactive local social learning within arts and cultural contexts. To paraphrase their description: *"As you move around the streets with the app, media is triggered that invites*

---

[3] Hidden Cities https://hiddencities.eu

[4] PURE, funded by the Humanities in European Research Area (HERA), through the 'Joint Research Programme', Public Spaces: Culture and Integration in Europe https://heranet.info/projects/public-spaces-culture-and-integration-in-europe

viewing, comment and response, offering a chance for informal learning. You may view content, comment on it or make and share your own media to contribute ideas. There are two modes, 'walking' and 'armchair'. Armchair mode can be accessed from anywhere - e.g. someone in Athens might be interested in seeing if there is any transferable knowledge in Bristol. Walking mode allows for discovery through the triggering of content based on physical location and time. The app can be set to surprise you, or you can tell it that you want to know something" [15]. This summary indicates several key aspects: access via GPS triggering or via anywhere, social interactions and contributions, and the potential importance of serendipity for knowledge delivery.

The Urban Belonging Toolkit. Discussed in Madsen et al. [48], the 'Urban Belonging Toolkit' is a 'toolkit for studying place attachments with digital and participatory methods', involving citizen generated content to engage with urban planning feedback. Use of an app[5] and website[6] for photo and voice commentary is distributed to citizen communities to input their own image content along with accompanying comments and observations. The research and app were particularly aligned with under-represented groups of Copenhagen, self-described as "marginalized as part of their life ... (including) LGBT+, deaf, ethnic minorities, mentally vulnerable, physically disabled, international expats, and or houseless". The project demonstrates a thoughtful approach to use of citizen digital interactive knowledge content contributions and shows culture mapping in contemporary citizen perspective settings.

Los Angeles Civic Memory Working Group.[7] This project concerns capturing and maintaining the civic history of the city of Los Angeles [49]. It was particularly orientated towards the populations who historically originally populated the Los Angeles area and involved engaging with the citizens themselves in addition to experts and specialists. Geddes [50] continually extols the virtues of not forgetting the city of the past, and this project offers an idea of how civic memory can play an important role in compiling the heritage of the city from the perspective of the citizens who have lived there, to build an environment of caring, flourishing and belonging [32].

Creative City Network of Canada.[8] Discussed in Duxbury, Garrett-Petts & MacLennan [36], the Creative City Network is an example of how to develop a national network of cities with creative purpose and initiatives. Of several 'toolkits'[9] available, the cultural mapping toolkit is particularly relevant. Cultural mapping (a technique used in the Urban Belonging toolkit), is a way of remapping a local territory "to make visible the ways local stories, practices, relationships, memories, and rituals constitute places as meaningful locations" [51]. In the Canadian example, there is a fully developed network of content knowledge repositories and support for various initiatives going back more than twenty years.

---

[5] Urban Belonging smartphone app, Play Store & App Store: https://play.google.com/store/apps/details?id=com.urbanbelonging.app; https://apps.apple.com/dk/app/urban-belonging/id1573456017

[6] Urban Belonging website https://urbanbelonging.com/

[7] The LA Civic Memory Working Group http://civicmemory.la/

[8] Creative City Network of Canada https://www.creativecity.ca/

[9] Creative City Network of Canada toolkits https://www.creativecity.ca/libraryold/tool-kits/

The common themes of these projects indicate creative ideas for citizen participation in knowledge of place, contributing to discussions, image banks, videos, events and urban planning concerned with local places, with varying degrees of top-down and bottom-up organizational control. This paper poses questions about what we can learn from these exemplary projects to build an innovative and effective CLN, taking the best ideas and thinking in new ways to bring them to greater and more sustained fruition, for the benefit of future citizens.

4 Building a Civic Learning Network

An urban technological infrastructure imbued with digital knowledge connectivity can be imagined with as many interaction opportunities as there might be objects, artifacts and locations, in a built environment that affords digital micro-interaction knowledge delivery and community interactions. The realisation of a CLN should be in the context of a city as interface [29], where digital knowledge interactions are available at point of need or interest, are platform and app agnostic, and where learning is 'usually unintentional rather than deliberate', and 'anchored in a context of social meaning' [46]. This can also involve digital/physical hybrid spaces of engagement opportunity such as zones of possibility [15], city-wide collaborative learning [52] or 'learning regions' and 'creative cities', "ushering in place-based strategies to exploit local creativity and social capital to achieve a "new urban vitality" [53].

A CLN in today's urban environment might need to provide a number of user functionalities that in the past were not present in the expectations of the user (or the researcher). For example, being able to upload as well as search and download content to and from a knowledge network, filter and save searches, contribute to discussions, ask or answer questions, add images to discussions or topic areas, and perhaps the option to do all this and more anonymously, with a temporary or 'pseudo' username (e.g. [54]). Ideally, digital knowledge web repositories, social communications and user interfaces should embrace a platform and app agnostic interoperable relationship between knowledge and social interaction - a ubiquitous integration of the open knowledge and open social web. This would perhaps be achieved through mutual ActivityPub protocol[10] CRUD[11] interactions, adopting the model of the Fediverse [21]. Table 1 provides a broad indication of what might be offered and available as core functionalities of a CLN.

Civic learning network interface and functional design/development might utilise the collective intelligence of citizens themselves for defining and refining their own optimum information interaction requirements, perhaps somewhat like the approach utilised by Soch et al. [7] or Madsen et al. [48].

---

[10] ActivityPub Protocol https://en.wikipedia.org/wiki/ActivityPub
[11] CRUD https://en.wikipedia.org/wiki/Create,_read,_update_and_delete

Table 1. Core functions of a proposed civic learning network

Civic Learning Network (CLN) Function	Description
Camera/ image triggering for place-related (and geocoded) *Knowledge Search & Delivery Technology*[a] (KSDT)	App and platform agnostic access to Google Lens[b], Bixby Vision[c] or other camera/ image triggering for geo-coded or otherwise place-related knowledge search and delivery
Open API[d] plugin(s) between KSDT and any Learning Management System (LMS)	Any LMS could be used in conjunction with KSDT. (Moodle[e], Blackboard Learn[f], Canvas LMS[g] etc., with e.g. web entity detection & Cloud Vision[h].)
Open API connection with social media and forums	To permit any social media or forum app to be used in conjunction with KSDT and the CLN, likely via ActivityPub protocol. E.g. WordPress ActivityPub[i] integration to the Fediverse
User functions for KSDT interactivity	Additional KSDT inbuilt user functions: search, enhanced search, save as, share, add to group(s), download, contribute, upload, camera integration etc
Smart KSDT recommendations	Smart recommendations, including refreshed serendipitous suggestions based on anonymised user data, popular hits, outlier hits etc
Smart KSDT metadata	Making use of RDF & OWL[j] social platform metadata properties in addition to e.g. OER Schema[k] for rich snippet results related to geocoded/place-related web entities

[a]KSDT refers to knowledge content search and delivery mechanisms, e.g. via AR triggered interface; offering key results related to a trigger plus further functionality for a web entity.
[b]Google Lens https://lens.google.com
[c]Samsung Bixby Vision https://www.samsung.com/global/galaxy/apps/bixby/vision/
[d]Open API https://en.wikipedia.org/wiki/Open_API
[e]Moodle LMS https://moodle.org/
[f]Blackboard Learn LMS https://blackboard.com
[g]Canvas LMS https://www.instructure.com/en-gb/canvas-overview
[h]Cloud Vision web entity detection https://cloud.google.com/vision/docs/detecting-web
[i]WordPress & ActivityPub https://techcrunch.com/2023/09/14/wordpress-blogs-can-now-be-fol lowed-in-the-fediverse-including-mastodon/
[j]RDF & OWL Explainer https://www.linkeddatatools.com/introducing-rdfs-owl/
[k]Open Educational Resources Schema https://oerschema.org/docs/

4.1 Citizen Interactions with the Knowledge Web

This paper proposes that citizen critical hybrid digital literacies could be supported, developed and embellished through use of ubiquitous CLNs, connecting places and things with smartphone apps, learning management systems and the knowledge web [45]. Citizen understanding and curiosity for different types of knowledge, contexts of culture and social domain might be assisted by 'normalising' knowledge inquiry in 'ordinary everyday environments and activities' [4], and by placing greater emphasis on the contributions of citizens themselves to their own shared knowledge of place. Further, it builds and sustains the ontological security of identity referred to by Shotter, "to sustain their identities, the ontological security of their social being, they must sustain … (that is) morally respect both the identities of those around them, and the social relations which sustain those identities" [6].

The knowledge web is interpreted in this paper as the full sum of all open knowledge on the World Wide Web (WWW), available via browsing, searching, linkback[12] or social web sharing. User-generated knowledge content contributions are considered as an informal part of this resource. This is the broadest way that the whole of open digital knowledge might be defined, and is the interconnected knowledge resources to "search, read, (and) synthesize" in hyperspace [55]. Mioduser et al. call this 'hyperacy', and foreground today's heightened multi-awareness 'postdigital situated literacy' (after [35, 36]), noting the "dissonance between formally acquired and actually required skills for everyday life in the knowledge society", and prompting us to provide "the intellectual tools comprising the cognitive toolbox of hyperacy" [55].

Eisenstadt & Vincent [56] refer to the 'Knowledge Web' as a taxonomy based system of connected knowledge, with 'psychological agents' to undertake tasks for knowledge delivery to the user, envisaged as a closed database system. Nowadays we regard the whole of 'the internet' as consisting of networked knowledge units (nodes), connected via strong or weak ties (edges), using various semantic and technical methods. In addition to publisher or platform taxonomies, methods such as metadata, URI and DOI[13], Linked Open Data[14], linkbacks[23], search keyword relevance, place-name or geocode relatedness, popularity of search result or social web sharing and rating statistics can all be used to connect and deliver knowledge content. Recommender systems as knowledge delivery mediators therefore become integral to interacting with the knowledge web. Subsequent following sections focus on recommender systems in the potentially required conditions of anonymised user data, privacy protection, and the increased understanding of the importance of serendipity as a part of search result suggestions [57]. The roles that Large Language Model[15] trained artificial intelligence (AI) tools might play are considered, particularly in light of possible impact on the integrity of the knowledge web.

---

[12] Linkback: https://en.wikipedia.org/wiki/Linkback

[13] DOI/URI, e.g. in https://wiki.lyrasis.org/display/VIVO/Concept%3A+DOI+vs+URI

[14] Linked Open Data https://en.wikipedia.org/wiki/Linked_data#Linked_open_data

[15] Large language model https://en.wikipedia.org/wiki/Large_language_model

5 Intelligent Cities and Citizen Data

In considering intelligent systems that support learning, constraints may arise due to the conditions that exist today that may not have been pertinent in prior system design or planning. These include potential socio-political aspects of funding and technical infrastructure ownership, custodianship and maintainability of knowledge content quality and integrity, issues relating to intellectual property and AI use of web based digital content, user interactions data in terms of processing, rights, and privacy, and those relating to aspects of digital sovereignty.

5.1 Recommender Systems

Search result recommender systems that might be best employed in a CLN would most likely be based on anonymised user profile interactions and employ a system whereby related topic results could be offered that include opportunity for surprise and further exploration. Duricic et al. [57] emphasise that "accuracy may not always be the most important criterion" of graph neural network (GNN)[16] based systems, as "aspects such as recommendation diversity, serendipity, and fairness can strongly influence user engagement and satisfaction". Within the context of diversity (of content) and fairness (of returned results against others), serendipity would seem to be of most significance for CLN recommendations, as it "indicates the unexpected nature of recommendations, (and) encourages users to explore beyond their usual preferences and stimulates curiosity" [57]. GNNs use 'collaborative filtering' techniques, that begin with data preprocessing of "user-item interaction data and auxiliary information such as user/item features or social connections" [57]. Duricic et al. demonstrate various approaches of utilising collaborative filtering relating to diversity, serendipity and fairness that may be relevant to a CLN, however these may depend on scale of data and user demographic factors. User group size, age, language(s), types of knowledge being sought, and role for the open social web may impact recommendation techniques and results for different user groups in a CLN context. Recent studies concern proposed use of social networks and community orientated collaborative filtering methods, with work by Sheng et al. [58] appearing of interest (though this author is not sufficiently technically literate to judge in detail). Their proposal of item attribute interpretations in contexts of user-user relationships seems relevant in light of prior comments about CLN community and user differences.

Anonymised User Data. Anonymity of the user would appear desirable in a large and open CLN. Literature indicates the increasing concern around user data rights and privacy. Citing various others, Müllner et al. [59] state that "previous research has revealed multiple privacy threats for users in recommender systems, such as disclosure of users' private data to untrusted third parties and inference of user gender or age, and that "users themselves care more about their privacy in recommender systems". Müllner et al.'s work provides us with a review of mechanisms for obscuring user data via differential

---

[16] Refer for GNNs and different types of web entity https://distill.pub/2021/gnn-intro

privacy techniques (describing the patterns within the group while withholding information specific to individuals)[17]. Van der Nagel [54] discusses user profile pseudonymity, suggesting that platforms encourage particular kinds of engagement through framing identity information of users, and that user multiple identities are becoming commonplace. Discussing 4chan's[18] default 'anonymous' user profile setting, she makes the case for how user profiles are distinct from user identity, and argues for the importance of 'pseudonymity' online. Though this would benefit from further research in the context of a CLN, it hints at an idea of offering a one-off auto-persona generated sign-in, with no other data required. Whilst it may be that by connecting to a CLN via a smartphone app or LMS system would include more personalised user data being held in those platforms or apps, the CLN itself would not hold any of that data within its own system.

5.2 Preserving the Integrity of the Knowledge Web

The preservation of the integrity of the knowledge web is considered of significant relevance and importance to a CLN, as the knowledge web acts as the foundation of any system of civic learning implementation, and is the cornerstone of open knowledge node delivery in contexts of urban citizen learning at point of need.

Quality and Trustworthiness of Knowledge. The safeguarding of the continued authenticity and maintainability of the open web of knowledge is increasingly viewed as potentially under threat in relation to 'poisoning' of the information sphere through influx of low quality data output from 'generative foundation models' [60]. This might in part be regarded as a manifestation of the tragedy of the knowledge commons [61–63], and though by no means a certain outcome, discourses in literature [64, 65] and media [66–69] have begun to voice various serious concerns.

Mainstream technology and news, topic interest blogs and university website articles continue to debate problems of safeguarding web knowledge content quality and integrity, or other AI generative foundation model (GFM) limitations (e.g. [70, 71]. Information generated by GFMs is a 'blurry jpeg, rendering a 'glitchy, spammy, scammy, AI-powered internet' [72]. For example, the rise of AI fake news and 'pink slime' (content produced solely by GFMs), interspersed with 'real' news content highlights the intense challenge of users being able to differentiate between GFM content, intentional fake content and authentic content [73]. Full Fact[19] produces guidelines to counter fake content, including how to spot deepfake videos and images, or misleading/false information. Though done with the best intentions, it appears woefully inadequate in the face of the increasing amount of fake content on the WWW. Whilst the problem of fake content is not confined to GFM output, it may well increase exponentially due to GFM output, impacting quality and trustworthiness of the knowledge web. From a technical perspective, obtaining 'clean' training data, that is, human created content, is becoming a challenge for AI GFMs [74, 75]. Training GFMs have other problems, such as cost, accuracy, and removing or countering bias in the data being used for training [71, 76, 77].

---

[17] Differential Privacy https://en.wikipedia.org/wiki/Differential_privacy

[18] 4chan https://en.wikipedia.org/wiki/4chan

[19] Fullfact: https://fullfact.org/toolkit/; https://fullfact.org/blog/2023/dec/how-to-spot-deepfakes/

Chatbot hallucination (making things up) continues to be a challenge [70], and national security is of concern in relation to ChatGPT or other text based GFM content [78].

Intellectual Property. There is increasing concern about the problematic widespread use of intellectual property available in the open knowledge web being absorbed into training data for AI GFMs such as ChatGPT or Midjourney without consent (e.g. [79, 80]). Lists of artist's digital work being used to train the Midjourney GFM have recently been published on the WWW, none of the artists had given consent or agreement for their work to be used [81]. Many of these artists are in legal disputes with Midjourney [82] and they or others may have begun to use pixel-protection mechanisms as preventive AI webscrape blocking measures [83]. Significant numbers of authors of written works, some very high profile, are also involved in legal action (e.g. [84]). As yet there are no clear solutions to this problem, however Lee et al. introduce us to the full complexity at hand [85].

6   A Technosocial Contract for Civic Learning

Epistemic rights have become a significant consideration in the debates around digital human rights to information. In a future-present postdigital conceptualisation, a CLN may form part of what Risse [8] suggests as a fourth generation human right for "epistemic rights in digital lifeworlds', and be a manifestation of a digital social contract. Sometimes referred to as a technosocial contract - the digital social contract partially concerns the role of platform content and communication monopolies in society, that could be ethically and legally bound to act for the greater good [9]. D'Arma et al. [86] argue "it is not enough to speak about communication or digital rights. A more comprehensive term is needed to grasp the multifaceted challenges of the current situation to citizens, organisations, and democratic structures". They go on to make 'the claim of epistemic equality', that "in a functioning democracy, citizens should be equally capable of making informed choices about matters of societal importance. This claim includes the notion that citizens have equal access to all relevant information and knowledge necessary for informed *will formation*" ([86], author's own emphasis). We might consider that a CLN could provide a part of citizen 'equal access' to information and knowledge, to foster 'will formation' in a mutually shared ontological security for the uncertainty of the heterogeneous urban future-present city environment. D'Arma et al. [86] argue "there is a growing consensus about the necessity of epistemic rights. These rights are not only about the right to know but also ... the right to have a voice and be heard". This indicates the value of considering the CLN as both knowledge and social interaction, equal parts of the knowledge web as a whole.

To support the future learning city, proprietary platform providers might be required as part of their technosocial contract obligation to invest in technical development initiatives to build and maintain app and platform interoperable, free and open civic learning networks, accessible by all. This might involve agreements for acting in regional digital sovereignty, in partnership with digital public good initiatives (e.g. various, in [3]). Additionally, data related territorial sovereignty legal obligations may mean that regional data-flow arrangements become mandatory, "as policies of data localisation" reshape "the architecture of connectivity" [87]. Perhaps data-flow territorial restrictions could act as further motivation for proprietary platform monopolies to act for the public good in regional context, though this seems an idealistic interpretation. Psaros claims that "(a)ll technologies, including digital ones, are considered to be deeply involved in the constitution of societies" [88], in this light the concept of data and information fiduciaries as public trustees as outlined in Napoli [89], appears relevant to the CLN. "In law a fiduciary is a person or business with an obligation to act in a trustworthy manner in the interest of another" [90, in 89]. An information fiduciary deals in information, with a duty of care and loyalty, to act in confidentiality and not do harm, and not disclose data to untrustworthy third parties [89]. Phillips & Mazzoli go further, describing a public service search engine, free of state intervention and 'commercial imperatives' [91]. Perhaps this, along with the interoperable connectivity with an open social web, might be how a CLN could provide equal access and voice to all citizens in their interactions with an urban knowledge web.

7   Conclusions

Contributing to civic quality of life, general ontological security, potential for democratic engagement and involvement, and the sense of value in contributions to knowledge are all reasons to consider the idea of a civic learning network. Whilst this paper has conceptualised a CLN in a context of an urban citizen digital lifeworld, CLNs could have a wider reach to become federated instances of a global network for learning. Though it may sound ambitious, impossible even, the message in the body of literature concerning future roles for digital platforms within society seems to imply we are on the edge of new ways to think about how technology meshes with human lives, and the purposes of what it can achieve. A CLN is a practical vision of a decentralised, potentially citizen-owned, Fediverse inspired model for civic learning technical infrastructure, providing access to open knowledge and opportunity for citizen contributions in a democratic inclusive smarter learning at the scale of the city. Perhaps this should be a prime goal of technological implementations in smart learning cities, and if citizen-led or owned is a technosocial critical pedagogy for lifelong learning.

Disclosure of Interests. The author has no competing interests to declare that are relevant to the content of this article.

References

1. Facer, K., Buchczyk, M.: Towards a research agenda for the 'actually existing' Learning City. Oxf. Rev. Educ. **45**, 151–167 (2019). https://doi.org/10.1080/03054985.2018.1551990
2. Landowska, A., Robak, M., Skorski, M.: What Twitter Data Tell Us about the Future? (2023). https://doi.org/10.48550/arXiv.2308.02035
3. Calzada, I.: Smart City Citizenship (2021). https://doi.org/10.1016/C2017-0-02973-7
4. Pyyry, N.: Geographies of hanging out: playing, dwelling and thinking with the city. In: Sacré, H., De Visscher, S. (eds.) Learning the City. SE, pp. 19–33. Springer, Cham (2017). https://doi.org/10.1007/978-3-319-46230-1_2

5. Keegan, H., Lisewski, B.: Living, working, teaching and learning by social software. In: Hatzi-panagos, S., Warburton, S. (eds.) Handbook of Research on Social Software and Developing Community Ontologies, pp. 208–221. Information Science Reference, IGI Global (2009)

6. Shotter, J.: Rhetoric and the recovery of civil society. In: Conversational Realities: Constructing Life Through Language. Sage Publications India (1993)

7. Soch, N.N., Hogan, M., Harney, O., Hanlon, M., Brady, C., McGrattan, L.: Developing a Utopian model of human-technology interaction: collective intelligence applications in support of future well-being. Utop. Stud. **33**, 54–75 (2022). https://doi.org/10.5325/utopianst udies.33.1.0054

8. Risse, M.: The fourth generation of human rights: epistemic rights in digital lifeworlds. Moral Philos. Polit. **8**, 351–378 (2021). https://doi.org/10.1515/mopp-2020-0039

9. Stiles, P., Scott, E.T., Debata, P.: Technology, capitalism, and the social contract. Bus. Ethics Environ. Responsib. **00**, 1–11 (2023). https://doi.org/10.1111/beer.12567

10. Lister, P.: The pedagogy of experience complexity for smart learning: considerations for designing urban digital citizen learning activities. Smart Learn. Environ. **8**, 8 (2021). https://doi.org/10.1186/s40561-021-00154-x

11. Lorenzo, N., Gallon, R.: Smart pedagogy for smart learning. In: Daniela, L. (ed.) Didactics of Smart Pedagogy, pp. 41–69. Springer, Cham (2019). https://doi.org/10.1007/978-3-030-01551-0_3

12. Henning, P.A.: Learning 4.0. In: North, K., Maier, R., Haas, O. (eds.) Knowledge Management in Digital Change. PI, pp. 277–290. Springer, Cham (2018). https://doi.org/10.1007/978-3-319-73546-7_17

13. Valdés-Cotera, R., Longworth, N., Lunardon, K., Wang, M., Jo, S., Crowe, S. (eds.): Unlocking the Potential of Urban Communities: Case Studies of Twelve Learning Cities. UNESCO Institute for Lifelong Learning (2015)

14. Enseñado, E.M.: City-to-city learning: a synthesis and research agenda. J. Environ. Policy Plan. **26**, 1–16 (2023). https://doi.org/10.1080/1523908X.2023.2281426

15. Cook, J., Lander, R., Flaxton, T.: The zone of possibility in citizen led 'hybrid cities.' In: Position paper for Workshop on Smart Learning Ecosystems in Smart Regions and Cities. Co-located at EC-TEL, Toledo, Spain (2015)

16. Lister, P.: Measuring learning that is hard to measure: using the PECSL model to evaluate implicit smart learning. Smart Learn Env. **9**, 25 (2022). https://doi.org/10.1186/s40561-022-00206-w

17. Atchoarena, D., Howells, A.: Advancing learning cities: lifelong learning and the creation of a learning society. In: Ra, S., Jagannathan, S., Maclean, R. (eds.) Powering a Learning Society During an Age of Disruption. EARICP, vol. 58, pp. 165–180. Springer, Singapore (2021). https://doi.org/10.1007/978-981-16-0983-1_12

18. Dron, J.: Smart learning environments, and not so smart learning environments: a systems view. Smart Learn. Environ. **5**, 25 (2018). https://doi.org/10.1186/s40561-018-0075-9

19. Freire, P.: The Pedagogy of the Oppressed. The Continuum International Publishing Group Inc. (2005)

20. Charungkaittikul, S., Henschke, J.A.: Strategies for developing a sustainable learning society: an analysis of lifelong learning in Thailand. Int. Rev. Educ. **60**, 499–522 (2014). https://doi.org/10.1007/s11159-014-9444-y

21. Lutkevich, B.: What is the fediverse? Definition from TechTarget (2023). https://www.techta rget.com/whatis/definition/fediverse

22. Ireland, C., Johnson, B.: Exploring the FUTURE in the PRESENT. Des. Manag. Inst. Rev. **6**, 57–64 (1995). https://doi.org/10.1111/j.1948-7169.1995.tb00436.x

23. Kitchin, R.: Toward a genuinely humanizing smart urbanism. In: Cardullo, P., Feliciantonio, C., Kitchin, R. (eds.) The Right to the Smart City, pp. 193–204. Emerald Publishing Limited (2019)

24. Lister, P.: Future–present learning and teaching: a case study in smart learning. In: Sengupta, E., Blessinger, P. (eds.) Changing the Conventional University Classroom (Innovations in Higher Education Teaching and Learning, pp. 61–79. Emerald Publishing Limited, Bingley (2022). https://doi.org/10.1108/S2055-364120220000044005

25. Jandrić, P., Knox, J., Besley, T., Ryberg, T., Suoranta, J., Hayes, S.: Postdigital science and education. Educ. Philos. Theory **50**, 893–899 (2018). https://doi.org/10.1080/00131857.2018.1454000

26. Negroponte, N.: Beyond Digital. https://web.media.mit.edu/~nicholas/Wired/WIRED6-12.html

27. Cramer, F.: What is 'post-digital'? In: Berry, D.M., Dieter, M. (eds.) Postdigital Aesthetics: Art, Computation and Design, pp. 12–26. Palgrave Macmillan, New York (2015)

28. Townsend, A.M.: Smart Cities: Big Data, Civic Hackers, and the Quest for a New Utopia. WW Norton & Company, New York (2013)

29. de Waal, M.: The City as Interface: How New Media are changing the City. nai010 Publishers, Rotterdam (2014)

30. Bross, B., A.: Mediatic surfaces: shaping urban environments. In: Proceedings of Critical Practice in An Age of Complexity – An Interdisciplinary Critique of the Built Environment. AMPS (2018)

31. Álvaro-Sánchez, S.: Practiced, conceived and lived space in the postdigital City. Estoa **11**(22), 69–70 (2021). https://doi.org/10.18537/est.v011.n022.a04

32. Lister, P., Norris, T.: Finding our place, people and things in urban citizen belonging. AMPS Teach. Curric (2024)

33. Liu, D., Huang, R., Wosinski, M.: Characteristics and framework of smart learning. In: Smart Learning in Smart Cities. LNET, pp. 31–48. Springer, Singapore (2017). https://doi.org/10.1007/978-981-10-4343-7_3

34. McKenna, H.P., Chauncey, S.: Taking learning to the city: an exploration of the frictionless learning environment innovation. In: Proceedings of EDULEARN14 Conference, Barcelona, Spain (2014)

35. McKenna, H.P.: The nurturing of theory for smart environments and spaces: the case of ambient theory for smart cities. In: Streitz, N.A., Konomi, S. (eds.) Distributed, Ambient and Pervasive Interactions. HCII 2023. Lecture Notes in Computer Science, pp. 118–130. Springer, Cham (2023). https://doi.org/10.1007/978-3-031-34609-5_8

36. Duxbury, N., Garrett-Petts, W.F., MacLennan, D.: Cultural mapping as cultural inquiry, introduction to an emerging field of practice. In: Duxbury, N., Garrett-Petts, W.F., and MacLennan, D. (eds.) Cultural Mapping as Cultural Inquiry (2015)

37. Greeno, J.G., Engeström, Y.: Learning in activity. In: Sawyer, R.K. (ed.) The Cambridge Handbook of the Learning Sciences, pp. 128–147. Cambridge University Press, Cambridge (2014)

38. Lister, P.: What are we supposed to be learning? motivation and autonomy in smart learning environments. In: Streitz, N., Konomi, S. (eds.) HCII 2021. LNCS, vol. 12782, pp. 235–249. Springer, Cham (2021). https://doi.org/10.1007/978-3-030-77015-0_17

39. Jubas, K., Ofori-Atta, E., Ross, S.: Building a pedagogy of critical curiosity in professional education: the power of popular culture in the classroom. In: Merrill, B., Vieira, C., Galimberti, A., Nizinska, A. (eds.) Adult Education as a Resource for Resistance and Transformation: Voices, Learning Experiences, Identities of Student and Adult Educators. University of Coimbra/University of Algarve/ESREA, Coimbra (2020)

40. Bateson, G.: Steps to an ecology of mind: collected essays in anthropology, psychiatry, evolution, and epistemology. Jason Aronson Inc. (1972)

41. Engeström, Y.: Learning by expanding: an activity-theoretical approach to developmental research. Orienta-Konsult (1987). https://doi.org/10.1017/CBO9781139814744

42. Liu, D., Huang, R., Wosinski, M.: Future trends of smart learning: Chinese perspective. In: Smart Learning in Smart Cities. LNET, pp. 185–215. Springer, Singapore (2017). https://doi.org/10.1007/978-981-10-4343-7_8

43. Vinod Kumar, T.M.: Smart environment for smart cities. In: Vinod Kumar, T.M. (ed.) Smart Environment for Smart Cities. ACHS, pp. 1–53. Springer, Singapore (2020). https://doi.org/10.1007/978-981-13-6822-6_1

44. Ingold, T.: The Perception of the Environment: Essays on livElihood, Dwelling and Skill. Routledge, Abingdon (2000)

45. Lister, P.: Smart learning in the community: supporting citizen digital skills and literacies. In: Streitz, N., Konomi, S. (eds.) HCII 2020. LNCS, vol. 12203, pp. 533–547. Springer, Cham (2020). https://doi.org/10.1007/978-3-030-50344-4_38

46. Eyal, L., Gil, E.: Hybrid learning spaces - a three-fold evolving perspective. In: Gil, E., Mor, Y., Dimitriadis, Y., Köppe, C. (eds.) Hybrid Learning Spaces, pp. 11–24. Springer, Cham (2022). https://doi.org/10.1007/978-3-030-88520-5

47. Bush, M.D., Mott, J.D.: The transformation of learning with technology: learner-centricity, content and tool malleability, and network effects. Educ. Technol. **49**, 3–20 (2009). https://jstor.org/stable/44429655

48. Madsen, A.K., et al.: The urban belonging photo app: a toolkit for studying place attachments with digital and participatory methods. Methodol. Innov. **16**, 292–314 (2023). https://doi.org/10.1177/20597991231185351

49. Past Due: Report and Recommendations of the Los Angeles Mayor's Office Civic Memory Working Group (2021). http://civicmemory.la

50. Geddes, P.: The City in Evolution, An Introduction to the Town Planning Movement and to the Study Of Civics. Williams & Norgate, London (1915)

51. Duxbury, N., Redaelli, E.: Cultural mapping. Oxf. Bibliogr. (2020). https://doi.org/10.1093/OBO/9780199756841-0249

52. Canova Calori, I., Divitini, M.: Reflections on the role of technology in city-wide collaborative learning. Int. J. Interact. Mob. Technol. **3**, 33–39 (2009). https://doi.org/10.3991/ijim.v3i2.746

53. Wolfram, M.: Deconstructing smart cities: an intertextual reading of concepts and practices for integrated urban and ICT development. In: Schrenk, M., Popovich, V.V., Zeile, P., Elisei, P. (eds.) Proceedings REAL CORP 2012 Tagungsband, Re-Mixing the City: Towards Sustainability and Resilience? REAL CORP, pp. 171–181 (2012)

54. van der Nagel, E.: From usernames to profiles: the development of pseudonymity in Internet communication. Internet Hist. **1**, 312–331 (2017). https://doi.org/10.1080/24701475.2017.1389548

55. Mioduser, D., Nachmias, R., Forkosh-Baruch, A.: New literacies for the knowledge society. In: Voogt, J., Knezek, G. (eds.) International Handbook of Information, Technology in Primary and Secondary Education, pp. 23–42. Springer, Heidelberg (2008)

56. Eisenstadt, M., Vincent, T.: The Knowledge Web: Learning and Collaborating on the Net. Kogan Page, London (1998)

57. Duricic, T., Kowald, D., Lacic, E., Lex, E.: Beyond-accuracy: a review on diversity, serendipity, and fairness in recommender systems based on graph neural networks. Front. Big Data **6**, 1251072 (2023). https://doi.org/10.3389/fdata.2023.1251072

58. Sheng, J., Liu, Q., Hou, Z., Bin, W.: A collaborative filtering recommendation algorithm based on community detection and graph neural network. Neural. Process. Lett. **55**, 7095–7112 (2023). https://doi.org/10.1007/s11063-023-11252-x

59. Müllner, P., Lex, E., Schedl, M., Kowald, D.: Differential privacy in collaborative filtering recommender systems: a review. Front. Big Data **6**, 1249997 (2023). https://doi.org/10.3389/fdata.2023.1249997

60. Huang, S., Siddarth, D.: Generative AI and the Digital Commons (2023). https://doi.org/10.48550/arXiv.2303.11074

61. Hardin, G.: The Tragedy of the Commons. Science **162**, 1243–1248 (1968)
62. Turner, D.: The tragedy of the commons and distributed AI systems. In: Proceedings of the 12th International Workshop on Distributed AI, Hidden Velly, PA, pp. 370–390 (1993)
63. Frischmann, B.M., Marciano, A., Ramello, G.B.: Retrospectives: tragedy of the commons after 50 years. J. Econ. Perspect. **33**, 211–228 (2019). https://doi.org/10.1257/jep.33.4.211
64. Shumailov, I., Shumaylov, Z., Zhao, Y., Gal, Y., Papernot, N., Anderson, R.: The curse of recursion: training on generated data makes models forget (2023)
65. Alemohammad, S., et al.: Self-Consuming Generative Models Go MAD (2023)
66. Mayberry, K.: Will AI Degrade Online Communities? Tech Policy Press (2023). https://techpolicy.press/will-ai-degrade-online-communities/
67. Franzen, C.: The AI feedback loop: Researchers warn of 'model collapse' (2023). https://venturebeat.com/ai/the-ai-feedback-loop-researchers-warn-of-model-collapse-as-ai-trains-on-ai-generated-content/
68. Loukides, M.: Model Collapse: An Experiment, What happens when AI is trained on its own output? O'Reilly (2023). https://www.oreilly.com/radar/model-collapse-an-experiment/, (2023)
69. Smith, M.: The internet isn't completely weird yet; AI can fix that "Model collapse" looms when AI trains on the output of other models. IEEE Spectr. (2023)
70. Knight, W.: Chatbot Hallucinations are Poisoning Web Search (2023). https://www.wired.com/story/fast-forward-chatbot-hallucinations-are-poisoning-web-search
71. Sweenor, D.: AI entropy: the vicious circle of AI-generated content: understanding and mitigating model collapse (2023). https://towardsdatascience.com/ai-entropy-the-vicious-circle-of-ai-generated-content-8aad91a19d4f
72. Heikkilä, M.: We are hurtling toward a glitchy, spammy, scammy, AI-powered internet. MIT Technol. Rev. (2023). https://www.technologyreview.com/2023/04/04/1070938/we-are-hurtling-toward-a-glitchy-spammy-scammy-ai-powered-internet/
73. Koenig, A.: Washington post: the rise of AI fake news - UC social media expert Jeffrey Blevins makes the media rounds on the topic of fake news (2023). https://www.uc.edu/news/articles/2023/12/social-media-expert-jeffrey-blevins-discusses-misinformation-with-multiple-media-outlets.html
74. Villalobos, P., Sevilla, J., Heim, L., Besiroglu, T., Hobbhahn, M., Ho, A.: Will we run out of data? an analysis of the limits of scaling datasets in Machine Learning (2022). https://doi.org/10.48550/arXiv.2211.04325
75. Stokel-Walker, C.: AI chatbots could hit a ceiling after 2026 as training data runs dry. New Sci. (2023). https://www.newscientist.com/article/2353751-ai-chatbots-could-hit-a-ceiling-after-2026-as-training-data-runs-dry/
76. Hays, K.: Firms like Meta and A16z admit having to pay billions for training data would ruin their generative-AI plans as they fight new copyright rules. Bus. Insid. (2023)
77. Matei, S.A.: An academic ChatGPT needs a better schooling. Times Higher Education (2023). https://www.timeshighereducation.com/blog/academic-chatgpt-needs-a-better-schooling
78. Mouton, C.A.: ChatGPT is creating new risks for national security (2023). https://www.rand.org/pubs/commentary/2023/07/chatgpt-is-creating-new-risks-for-national-security.html
79. Heikkilä, M.: This artist is dominating AI-generated art. And he's not happy about it. MIT Technol. Rev. (2022). https://www.technologyreview.com/2022/09/16/1059598/this-artist-is-dominating-ai-generated-art-and-hes-not-happy-about-it/
80. Sankaran, V.: OpenAI says it is 'impossible' to train AI without using copyrighted works for free. The Independent (2024)
81. Waite, T.: Here are all the artists Midjourney allegedly uses to train its AI (2024). https://www.dazeddigital.com/art-photography/article/61677/1/midjourney-ai-16000-artists-andy-warhol-frida-kahlo-yayoi-kusama-picasso-disney

82. Fortis, S.: Evidence mounts as new artists jump on Stability AI, Midjourney copyright lawsuit (2023). https://cointelegraph.com/news/evidence-mounts-new-artists-join-stability-ai-mid-journey-copyright-lawsuit

83. Heikkilä, M.: This new data poisoning tool lets artists fight back against generative AI. MIT Technol. Rev. (2023). https://www.technologyreview.com/2023/10/23/1082189/data-poisoning-artists-fight-generative-ai/

84. Brittain, B.: John Grisham, other top US authors sue OpenAI over copyrights, https://www.reuters.com/legal/john-grisham-other-top-us-authors-sue-openai-over-copyrights-2023-09-20/

85. Lee, K., Cooper, A.F., Grimmelmann, J.: Talkin bout AI generation: copyright and the generative-AI supply chain. Forthcom. J. Copyr. Soc. (2024). https://doi.org/10.2139/ssrn.4523551

86. D'Arma, A., Aslama Horowitz, M., Lehtisaari, K., Nieminen, H.: Introduction: the epistemic turn. In: Aslama Horowitz, M., Nieminen, H., Lehtisaari, K., D'Arma, A. (eds.) Epistemic Rights in the Era of Digital Disruption. Palgrave Macmillan, Cham (2024). https://doi.org/10.1007/978-3-031-45976-4_1

87. Glasze, G., et al.: Contested spatialities of digital sovereignty. Geopolitics 28, 919–958 (2022). https://doi.org/10.1080/14650045.2022.2050070

88. Psaros, H.: Learning, digital technologies, and sociomaterial approaches: a critical reflection from the perspective of materialist dialectics. Theory Psychol. 32, 827–847 (2022). https://doi.org/10.1177/09593543221129235

89. Napoli, P.: Dominant digital platforms as public trustees. In: Moore, M., Tambani, D. (eds.) Regulating Big Tech. pp. 151–168. Oxford University Press, Oxford (2022). https://doi.org/10.1093/oso/9780197616093.003.0009

90. Balkin, J.M., Zittrain, J.: A Grand bargain to make tech companies trustworthy. The Atlantic (2016). Webpage article from The Atlantic. https://www.theatlantic.com/technology/archive/2016/10/information-fiduciary/502346/

91. Phillips, A., Mazzoli, E.M.: Minimizing data-driven targeting and providing a public search alternative. In: Moore, M., Tambani, D. (eds.) Regulating Big Tech, pp. 110–126. Oxford University Press, Oxford (2022). https://doi.org/10.1093/oso/9780197616093.003.0007

Research and Design of Interactive Performance of Confucian Music Instruments Based on VR

Meiyu Lyu$^{(\boxtimes)}$ and Ziqian Zhang

Beijing University of Posts and Telecommunications, Beijing, China
zzq19990216@126.com

Abstract. With the development of the Internet and digital technology, the application of virtual reality (VR) in the field of cultural heritage digitization has received more attention. The Confucian Ceremony is a famous intangible cultural heritage in China, and as one of its components, the Confucian music reflects the requirements of cultivating oneself and establishing virtue in Confucian culture. The expression of Confucian music and related musical instruments in a VR can provide a new experience with a high sense of immersion and play a role in spreading the knowledge of Confucian music.

In this study, a scheme to experience and play the Confucian musical instruments in VR environment is implemented. Based on Unity and HTC Vive for technical implementation and realize its performance of chimes in the VR environment, so that users can experience the performance of chimes in an immersive VR environment.

The main innovations of this study are:

1. The realization of playing chimes in a virtual reality environment. There are many studies on the digital performance of other traditional musical instruments, such as bells and yangqin, but there is no precedent for chimes.

2. The design of a Confucian music virtual reality experience system. The system will enable users to experience the music in a more participatory and interactive way based on user research.

Keywords: Confucian music · The Confucian Ceremony · Virtual Reality · Chimes

1 Introduction

1.1 Overview of Digitization of Intangible Cultural Heritage

Since the adoption of the Convention for the Safeguarding of the Intangible Cultural Heritage by the United Nations Educational, Scientific and Cultural Organization (UNESCO) in 2003, nearly 200 countries have become parties to the Convention and have been actively carrying out related work.

Among the various ways to safeguard and transmit ICH, digitization, as an important way, has the advantages of large capacity, not easy to be lost, easy to be maintained, accurate, and easy to be retrieved compared with traditional preservation methods[1].

N. A. Streitz and S. Konomi (Eds.): HCII 2024, LNCS 14719, pp. 260–272, 2024.
https://doi.org/10.1007/978-3-031-60012-8_16

Therefore, it has been widely adopted in different countries and regions, represented by the Galica National Digital Library in France and the "American Memory" project of the Library of Congress in the United States, all of which have established databases of cultural heritage in their own countries. Digital means have begun to be widely utilized in the protection of non-heritage. China also advocates the use of digital means for the protection and inheritance of non-heritage.

The means of realizing these directions are getting richer and richer with the continuous advancement of technology. Among them, full-immersion virtual reality technology, which can effectively resolve the contradiction between the maintenance and dissemination of cultural heritage, VR can bring high-precision three-dimensional modeling of musical instruments, knowledge of big data, performance and appreciation and other areas, virtual reality technology has unique advantages, but also in the promotion of musical instrument culture, the development of the industry, cultural inheritance and development of great significance [2]. This study hopes to follow this trend and conduct a preliminary exploration of the digitization of the cultural heritage of Confucian Music musical instruments in The Confucian Ceremony by means of virtual reality.

1.2 Overview of Confucian Music

"Confucian Music" generally refers to the music used in The Confucian Ceremony, which is an important part of the Ceremony. The Confucian Ceremony is a grand sacrificial event held at the Confucian Temple to show respect, remembrance, and inheritance of Confucius, and it was included in the first batch of national intangible cultural heritages of China in 2006 with the approval of the State Council [3]. Since 2004, Qufu has held public ceremonies to honor Confucian, which are still held annually. The Confucian Ceremony consists of four parts: music, song, dance, and ritual.

Among them, ritual and music are both independent concepts and inextricably linked [4]. Ritual is a norm, cultivating the outside; while music is an art, governing the inside. Confucian believed that the process of learning should be as follows: "Rise in the Poetry, establish in the Rites, and become in the Music" [5]. Music as the highest state of learning, it can be said that "The Confucian Ceremony" focuses on the reflection of Confucian culture for the cultivation of morality, so "The Confucian Music" in the Confucian Ceremony in the importance of the significance and status of self-evident (Fig. 1).

Confucian Music is mainly reflected in the music and dance sessions during the Three Offerings Ceremony, that is, on both sides of the Dacheng Hall, Danxi, which refers to the platform in front of the ancient Dacheng Hall. The arrangement of musical instruments varied across dynasties (Fig. 2).

1.3 Overview of Instruments in Confucian Music

Confucian Music is rich in repertoire and involves a wide variety of musical instruments. There are also significant differences in the methods of playing, resulting in a substantial workload to realize the performance of all the instruments. Therefore, the first step is to sort out and analyze the musical instruments used in Confucian Music and select the appropriate instruments for the realization of the music.

Fig. 1. The Confucian Ceremony

Fig. 2. The Dacheng Hall and Danxi

In terms of performance style, it is categorized into three types: blowing, percussion, and plucking. As for the types of musical instruments, those used in Confucian Music are called the 'Eight Sounds' according to their materials. These include metal instruments represented by bells, stone instruments represented by chimes, silk instruments represented by the guqin, bamboo instruments represented by flutes, hide instruments represented by drums, wood instruments represented by wooden fish, gourd instruments represented by sheng, and clay instruments represented by ocarinas. In Kong music, the eight sounds of these instruments interact with each other.

Several reasons justify choosing chimes as the entry point for Confucian Music (Fig. 3):

Fig. 3. Playing Chimes

1. From the standpoint of the playing method, the way of playing chimes naturally aligns with the VR hardware's hand interaction, which is typically done by the handle and is very similar to actual striking. This similarity can bring more realism to the experience.
2. In terms of engagement, compared to other instruments in Confucian Music, chimes are percussion instruments with a low entry threshold and are quick to learn. Their playing method is relatively simple, as sound is produced by striking. However, unlike drums, bells and chimes are the only percussion instruments that can produce sound in different positions, offering rich pitch variations.
3. From the perspective of previous research, there are many precedents for the digital performance of bells and other instruments, while the digitization of chimes still has gaps, making their digitization even more necessary.

Summarizing the above points, it is more logical for this system to use chimes as the entry point to achieve the goal of experiencing Confucian Music and culture through instrument playing.

2 Previous Work

For the digitization of Confucian Music and The Confucian Ceremony itself, there are fewer practices at present, so the overview of the current research status in this part mainly starts from two perspectives: the digitization of traditional Chinese musical instruments and the digitization of traditional ceremonies, and in the digitization means used, we select the cases of Virtual Reality and Gesture Interaction Technology which are related to the topic of the dissertation, and expound on the previous researches.

China already has a wealth of research on the digitization of traditional musical instruments, and for the field of digitization of traditional musical instruments, virtual reality, augmented reality, gesture interaction and other technologies are widely used. Take the chimes used by Confucian Music as an example, with the excavation of Zenghouyi chimes in 1978, the popularity of chimes has been greatly enhanced, and a large number of chimes digitization researches have emerged as a result. For the digitization of the chimes, the means currently used are virtual reality technology and gesture interaction technology. In terms of virtual reality technology, Wang Yifan and Zhu Qing from the Beijing Institute of Technology invented an interactive system for Zenghouyi chimes based on immersive virtual reality devices [6], in which the user can roam around the chimes and strike the chimes with a striking hammer. Xingnan Chen from Central China Normal University took the collision detection algorithm as a starting point [7] to realize the playing of Zenghouyi chimes in a virtual reality environment and optimized the detection algorithm to improve the playing experience. In terms of gesture interaction, Wenjuan Hu from Zhejiang University realized gesture-driven chime playing through natural gesture recognition [8]. In addition to chimes, there are also a lot of digital exploration for other types of musical instruments, such as Zhang Shicheng of Hangzhou Normal University, who designed and implemented a virtual performance system for ethnic bowed string instruments based on gesture recognition [9]. Li He of Central China Normal University realized a virtual yangqin performance system based on leap motion [10].

S. Gonizzi Barsanti et al. from Politecnico di Milano, based on the Oculus Rift hardware, realized the digitization of the ancient Egyptian funerary rituals "The Path of the Dead" in a virtual reality environment [11]., and took the ancient Egyptian funerary items "heart beetle" and "wooden sarcophagus" as the starting point to realize the interpretation of the ancient Egyptian funerary rituals. "Wooden sarcophagus" as an entry point to realize the interpretation of the ancient Egyptian funeral rituals. And through interesting means, it guides users to understand and read ancient Egyptian hieroglyphics.

The digitization of traditional musical instruments has been studied a lot, and most of the new digitization means are used in the selected digitization means, the reasons may contain the following points:

1. The digitization of traditional can effectively achieve the dissemination of cultural heritage, make traditional instruments interesting and lower the threshold
2. Digitization of traditional musical instruments is a good solution to the contradiction between cultural heritage preservation and dissemination.
3. The interaction forms of virtual reality interaction and gesture interaction have a natural similarity with the playing of traditional musical instruments, which can bring a more realistic playing experience.

3 Research Purpose

The purpose of this study is mainly reflected in the following aspects:

1. Preliminary attempts to digitize chimes.

During the research process, it was found that although a large number of studies related to the digitization of traditional musical instruments have emerged in China at this stage, there is still a gap in the research on the digitization of chimes, and this study hopes that through the preliminary exploration of the digitization of the chimes as a musical instrument, it will make up for the lack of this field of research, and provide a certain reference for the subsequent research.

2. Provide a new way to experience and learn Confucian Music instruments.

The Confucian Ceremony is held annually in Shandong, and most of the instruments used in Confucian Music are far away from daily life. Especially the chimes and bells are mostly in the form of cultural relics at this stage, and there are very few opportunities to experience them. This study adopts virtual reality technology as a digital means to bring a new way of experiencing Confucian Music with strong immersion, so that users can experience Confucian Music and the performance of Confucian Music instruments without leaving home, and at the same time, it can avoid the contradiction between the dissemination, experience, and cultural relics protection.

3. Spreading the culture of Confucian Music.

Taking chimes playing as the entry point, it helps users to experience Confucian Music and The Confucian Ceremony as intangible cultural heritage in a deeper, more participatory, and immersive way. While spreading the intangible cultural heritage, it also carries on the fine traditions and virtues of Confucianism as advocated by Confucian.

4   User Research

The purpose of user research is to better design the performance experience for different users, so that all users can experience the fun of playing Chimes in the system and use this as a carrier to learn Confucian culture and feel the ceremony.

Based on this goal, the author conducted focus groups and questionnaires.

1. Focus group

In the focus group phase, six users were selected, three were instrumentalists and three were non-instrumentalists (none of the six users had any experience with VR). Six participants were asked to discuss their expectations for the functions of VR instrument products, including how to quickly master VR interaction, what kind of performance function settings are needed, and so on, to spread the functions that should be available in the system. In the end, focus group discussions resulted in 13 functional points, which were divided into 3 categories:

Basic functions: Scene roaming, scene introduction.

Knowledge learning: musical instrument knowledge learning, solo effect display, unison effect displays.

Performance experience: free playing, note marking, performance guidance, gamification guidance, repertoire performance.

2. KANO [13] questionnaire

After obtaining the functions expected by these users, KANO [13] questionnaires were made based on these functions and released to people with no VR experience. A total of 151 questionnaires were collected, and the better-worse coefficients of functions were calculated respectively to classify different functional attributes:

Must-be Quality: Scene roaming, scene introduction, etc.

One-dimensional Quality: free playing, musical instrument knowledge learning, etc.

Attractive Quality: Note annotation and gamification guide.

Indifferent Quality: skin replacement, dance experience, etc.

The subsequent functional design and implementation are based on the conclusions of KANO questionnaire.

5   Design and Implementation

The overall realization of this system is based on Unity platform and Steam VR. The hardware is realized using HTC VIVE Pro. In the modeling part, the modeling is completed by 3DS MAX and RHINO, and the audio processing is completed by using Adobe AU.

5.1   Digitization of Chimes

The digitization of chimes is divided into 3 parts, modeling of chimes, audio reduction and Performance experience.

1. Modeling of chimes

The implementation of chimes can be divided into two parts: input and output.
The key point is to get the swinging speed of the hammer and correlate it with the volume, vibration strength and length of the output. This system realizes the correlation of the swinging speed of the handle with the volume, chimes vibration and handle vibration. It brings users a real playing experience. Therefore, a relatively real VR playing experience is achieved (Fig. 4).

Fig. 4. Digitization of chimes in VR environment

2. Audio reduction

There are few chimes audio sources in existence, and only the chimes recorded by Mr. Li Zijin of the China Conservatory of Music [12], which came from the audio database of the China Conservatory of Music (DCMI), was obtained, and was processed with Adobe AU, as it was found that the chimes lacked monotones and could not form a complete scale. In addition, it was found that this batch of audio sources lacked monotones, which could not constitute a complete scale, so after observing the performance, the missing audio was recorded individually and supplemented, and the overall processing flow was as follows: Audio segmentation: The long polyphonic audio was sliced and decomposed into single tones. Noise reduction: Sample the noise and reduce it. Volume Adjustment: The volume of the audio source is small and varies greatly, so the volume of some tones is adjusted. The volume of some tones is adjusted to maintain uniformity in the listening experience. Attenuation Processing: Some of the audio sources are not fully recorded and do not attenuate naturally, so the audio is faded and enveloped to make it attenuate naturally.

3. Playing experience

The playing experience is designed based on the conclusions of user research, and users are divided into two types, "instrument experts" and "instrument newcomers". Different performance experience modes are designed for the two systems.

The "instrument expert" is characterized by having learned a certain instrument, having a certain knowledge of music theory, and being able to quickly get familiar with playing Chimes. This type of user needs to be able to get started quickly and freely experience and play. Therefore, in the product design of the sound name and the "free performance" mode, after opening, you can play the music you want according to the sound name of the mark (Fig. 5).

Fig. 5. "Free performance" mode

"New instrumentalists", unlike experts, have little knowledge of instruments and basic music theory, so they do not pursue free playing, but rich and powerful guidance, and gamified experience design, so that they can be guided to play a complete piece of music during entertainment, so that they can have more fun by paying less contact practice. In this mode, the user can select a song to play (Fig. 6).

Fig. 6. Song selection

After users select the song, system will highlight the user's next Chime to hit, tell the user where to hit next, and through this guidance, help the user play a complete song, even if he has never learned any instrument (Fig. 7).

Fig. 7. Highlighting guidance in performance

In general, the system designs two different performance modes, which can be switched freely to adapt to two different groups of people, so that they can experience the fun of playing Chimes to the maximum extent, to realize the spread of this intangible cultural heritage.

5.2 Digitization of Confucian Ceremony

According to the conclusion of the research, Confucian Music is mainly played in the Danxi in front of Dacheng Hall, so the main scene is set as Dacheng Hall and related buildings, modeled by 3DS Max and Rhino, the model is imported into the Unity scene, and in the middle, the arrangement of musical instruments is strictly in accordance with the norms of the arrangement of musical instruments in the Dacheng Hall, which is arranged in Danxi, realizing the real scene of The Confucian Ceremony (Fig. 8).

Fig. 8. Digitization of Dacheng hall and Danxi in VR environment

The objects placed in the scene, such as the table, are designed with reference to the utensils used in The Confucian Ceremony, and the musical instruments needed for The Confucian Ceremony are placed, and the real material of each musical instrument is given to the model in the scene, such as the bamboo musical instrument dragon flute (Fig. 9):

Fig. 9. Dragon Flute in VR environment

5.3 Interaction Design

According to the needs of the system function, the interaction design mainly needs to solve the following scenarios:

1. Movement within the scene

Considering that the application scene of this system is a small indoor area, the movement in the scene is accomplished in two ways: instantaneous movement and walking.

Instantaneous movement is one of the basic movement methods in VR scenes, and the method used in this system is to press the handle disk to launch the Bezier curve and move to the landing position. The advantage of this way of moving is that it can avoid the limitation of the moving range due to the small space and move to the required position at high speed.

The interactive operation of the handle and the effect in the scene are shown in the following (Fig. 10):

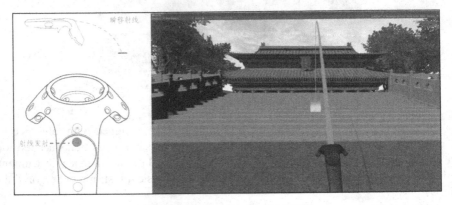

Fig. 10. Instantaneous movement

2. Interface Interaction

One of the main ways of interacting with the VR interface is ray interaction. Roughly, press button 1 to emit rays, use the rays to select the interface elements, and then press button 2 to select them.

This method is relatively complex, the immersion is poor, and the operation of the handle is more unnatural. Therefore, in the new interaction method, the touch/button method is used. When the joystick touches an object configured to be interacted with, the object is highlighted and the button selects the object, triggering subsequent events (Fig. 11).

The advantages of this operation method are:

- The interaction is like touch, which is more natural.
- Easier for users to select the objects they need to select.

In addition to the UI elements, this interaction method is also used for the evocation of the 3D interface in the scene. The user touches the interactive objects in the scene, the objects are highlighted, and the corresponding interface appears after pressing the Trigger key. Especially in chimes playing scenarios, the user can maximize the experience of real chimes playing through this type of interaction. However, this interaction method also suffers from the problem that the controllable distance is too short, but in this system, there is no need for the user to manipulate the interaction interface that is too far and too large, so this disadvantage is circumvented.

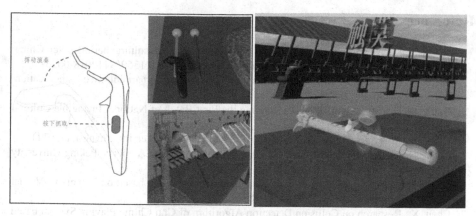

Fig. 11. Touch/Button method

6 Conclusion and Future Work

After completing this study, there remains substantial potential for enhancement and expansion within the system. The primary areas for improvement include:

1. Enhancing the authenticity of chime performances. Although the system has achieved a more realistic depiction of chime playing, technological limitations still lead to issues such as inaccurate collision detection—where rapid strikes result in 'mold penetration'—and the post-strike movement of the chime differs from that of an actual instrument. Additionally, while initial attempts have been made to correlate volume and strike speed, the fast-paced sequences produce unrealistic audio effects. Furthermore, the current algorithm only considers the speed of the hammers, neglecting the speed of the chimes, which further detracts from the realism. Future research should delve deeper into the nuances of authentic chime playing to enhance the system's fidelity and user experience.

2. Reducing the system's computational resource demands. The complexity of the instruments and the architectural models, along with the high slice count, necessitate a robust computer configuration. During trials, it was observed that commonly used laptops struggled with system operation, leading to lag and frame drops that degrade user experience. Optimizing the models and scripts to lower the system's resource requirements will allow it to run smoothly on less powerful computers.

3. Diversifying system interactions and functionalities. Currently, the system offers a limited set of interactive experiences within a relatively fixed framework. Although Confucian Music feature's introductions and audio, the chimes are the sole playable instrument, limiting user engagement. By incorporating additional instruments into the system, users could enjoy a broader range of Confucian Music and gain a deeper appreciation for the diversity of these traditional instruments.

References

1. Ma, X.T., Xu, Y.: Current situation of digitization of intangible cultural heritage. Sci. China: Inf. Sci. **49**(02), 121–142 (2019). (in Chinese)https://doi.org/10.1360/N112018-00201
2. Tao, W., Li, W., Hui, Z.: Musical instrument virtual museum and art culture communication. Musical Instrum. **06**, 28–29 (2016). (in Chinese)
3. Notice of The State Council on Announcing the First Batch of National Intangible Cultural Heritage List
4. Dong, X.: Study on Worship in Confucian Temple. Hunan University, Changsha (2011)
5. Li, X.: Notes on the Thirteen Classics. 10. Commentary on the Analects. Peking University Press (1999)
6. Wang, Y., Zhu, Q., LI, W.: A digital Chime interactive System based on immersive Virtual Reality equipment: CN108227921A (2018)
7. Chen, X.: Research on Collision Detection Algorithm of Chu Chime Playing System based on VR Technology. Central China Normal University, Wuhan (2020)
8. Hu, W.: Research and System Implementation of Chime Performance Technology Driven by Gesture. Zhejiang University, Hangzhou (2007)
9. Zhang, S.: Research on Gesture Recognition and Virtual Performance of National Bowstring Instruments. Hangzhou Normal University, Hangzhou (2015)
10. He, L.: Design and Implementation of Virtual Dulcimer System. Central China Normal University, Wuhan (2017)
11. Gonizzi Barsanti, S., Caruso, G., Micoli, L.L., Covarrubias Rodriguez, M., Guidi, G.: 3D visualization of cultural heritage artefacts with virtual reality devices. Int. Arch. Photogrammetry Remote Sens. Spat. Inf. Sci. **XL-5/W7**, 165–172 (2015). https://doi.org/10.5194/isprsarchives-XL-5-W7-165-2015
12. Liang, X., Li, Z., Liu, J., Li, W., Zhu, J., Han, B.: Constructing a multimedia Chinese musical instrument database. In: Li, W., Li, S., Shao, X., Li, Z. (eds.) Proceedings of the 6th Conference on Sound and Music Technology (CSMT). LNEE, vol. 568, pp. 53–60. Springer, Singapore (2019). https://doi.org/10.1007/978-981-13-8707-4_5
13. Kano. Attractive quality and must-be quality. J. Japan. Soc. Qual. Control, **14**(2), 147–156 (1984). https://doi.org/10.20684/quality.14.2_147

A Survey on Explainable Course Recommendation Systems

Boxuan Ma[1]($\boxtimes$), Tianyuan Yang[2], and Baofeng Ren[2]

[1] Faculty of Arts and Science, Kyushu University, Fukuoka, Japan
boxuan@artsci.kyushu-u.ac.jp
[2] Graduate School of Information Science and Electrical Engineering,
Kyushu University, Fukuoka, Japan
{yang.tianyuan.791,ren.baofeng.817}@s.kyushu-u.ac.jp

Abstract. An emerging challenge in course recommendation systems is the need to explain clearly to students the rationale behind specific course recommendations. Consequently, recent research has transitioned from focusing primarily on the accuracy of these systems to prioritizing user-centric qualities, such as transparency and justification. This shift has led to an increased emphasis on methods that provide clear, understandable explanations for their recommendations. In response to this trend, our paper introduces an explainable recommendation framework. Utilizing this framework, we analyze existing course recommendation systems and explore the emerging research challenges and future prospects for explainable course recommendation systems.

Keywords: Explainable recommendation · Education · Course recommendation

1 Introduction

Course recommendation systems are increasingly used in the field of education nowadays. By analyzing past behavior to understand a student's preferences, these systems can offer personalized course suggestions that align with a student's interests, career goals, or skill development needs. This personalized approach can make learning environments more adaptive and effective, enhancing the educational experience by helping students navigate the vast array of available courses and make more informed decisions about their learning journey [38].

Researchers have recently highlighted the importance of explainability in recommendation systems. They have become more aware of the fact that the effectiveness of recommender systems goes beyond recommendation accuracy. User-centric aspects like transparency, justification, and user trust have gained prominence in recommendation systems [5,48]. It has been shown that users not only seek precise recommendations but also a better understanding of the recommendation process itself [53]. Moreover, it has been established that users

N. A. Streitz and S. Konomi (Eds.): HCII 2024, LNCS 14719, pp. 273–287, 2024.
https://doi.org/10.1007/978-3-031-60012-8_17

may even accept less accurate recommendations if they are accompanied by clear explanations [29].

Explainability is particularly critical in course recommendations. Given the importance of appropriate course selection, explainable course recommendation systems can increase their trust in the results [34]. Explaining why the course is recommended could improve their understanding of the course content and knowledge structure, and persuade them to accept the course [35]. Also, by helping students better understand the relevance of recommendations to their interests and personalized needs, the system can improve their learning experience, academic performance, and satisfaction. In addition, it enables students to develop their own vision and reasoning and finally guides students toward future learning goals and career plans [9].

To this end, this paper presents an explainable recommendation framework. Utilizing this framework, we present an analysis of existing course recommendation systems and aim to identify future research challenges and opportunities to advance the research field.

2   Background

2.1   Course Recommendation System

Recommending courses to students is a fundamental and challenging task as their course selections create a chain of reactions that influence future course choices, skill development, and job decisions [36]. Due to the increasing number of students and the rise of Massive Open Online Courses (MOOCs), course recommendation systems have been broadly applied nowadays.

Since the first course recommendation system, based on constraint satisfaction, has been introduced [43], different course recommendation systems have been proposed in the literature. Most of those works focus on content-based or collaborative filtering (CF) approaches, and recommend courses by matching students' interests and course information (such as course descriptions and content) [28,39–41].

With the increasing use of Latent Factor Models (LFM) in recommendation systems, Matrix Factorization (MF), which was especially successful in rating prediction tasks, has been proposed for course recommendation tasks. Using students' grades as ratings, researchers have focused on models of predicting outcomes in future courses based on what courses students have already taken and the grades they earned [17,23,50]. Those systems recommend courses that students can pass easily or get relatively high grades to help students succeed or graduate on time.

Other course recommendation systems have been developed by mining relationships and discovering sequences from historical data. [4] used association rule mining based on frequent patterns to extract interesting relations between courses from the data that describe students' previous course selections. Together with the clustering method, the system recommends courses based on rules that they extracted from historical course enrollment data. [10] also presented a course recommendation system based on association rules. They use user ratings in their recommendation system together with association rules to improve the result. [47] proposed Scholars Walk, which uses a random-walk approach to provide recommendations and captures the sequential relationships between different courses.

Recently, deep learning models have been used in this domain. [45] introduced a novel modification to the skip-gram model and applied it to historic course enrollment sequences to learn course vector representations. The course vectors are then used to diversify recommendations based on the similarity to a student's favorite course. [44] also proposed a course2vec model that uses neural network architecture. It takes multiple courses as input and a probability distribution over the courses as outputs, which is used for the recommendation. Although deep learning has significantly improved the recommendation performance, the black-box nature of deep models brings difficulty in model explainability [34,35].

To sum up, numerous course recommendation systems have been proposed in recent years, and most models focus on performance, with limited emphasis on explainability. However, explainable course recommendation systems hold significant importance in the field of education, as they aid in understanding the decision-making process of recommendation systems and provide explanations regarding the basis of recommendations.

2.2 Explainable Recommendation System

Recommendation systems play a pivotal role in a wide range of web applications and have dominated our daily activities by personalizing online content to an increasing degree. While much effort has been put into achieving better performance, the importance of explainability in recommendation systems has recently gained significant attention. Explainable recommendation systems address the problem of why, besides providing users with personalized recommendation results, they also give reasons to clarify why such results are derived. For users, clear explanations or a better understanding of the recommendation processes could enhance their transparency, persuasiveness, effectiveness, trustworthiness, and satisfaction [22]. For system designers, explanations help them to diagnose, debug, and refine recommendation algorithms [56].

There are two main types of explainable recommendation models: model-intrinsic and model-agnostic (also known as post-hoc explanation approach) [56]. The model-intrinsic approach involves building interpretable models or adding explainable components with transparent decision mechanisms, allowing for natural explanations of model decisions [57]. This approach focuses on transparency of the system, which deals with the "black-box" nature of current recommendation systems by explaining the inner logic of the system to end users. On the other hand, the model-agnostic or post-hoc explanation approach enables a black-box decision mechanism, with an explanation model generating explanations after the decision is made [46]. This approach focuses on justification, that is, it only describes why the user gets certain recommendations, but it may not relate to the inner logic of the recommendation techniques. In this case, developing effective methods to deliver explanations to users or system designers is also essential because explainable recommendations naturally involve humans in the loop. Therefore, significant research efforts in user behavior analysis and the Human-Computer Interaction (HCI) community aim to understand how users interact with explanations [33, 55].

While explainable recommendation systems have been extensively utilized in domains such as e-commerce, movies, and music, their adoption in the field of education, specifically in course recommendation systems, has been relatively limited. To address this gap, our primary objective is to explore the potential of explainable course recommendation systems and provide insights and guidance for building course recommendation systems that are both explainable and useful.

3   Explainable Course Recommendation Framework

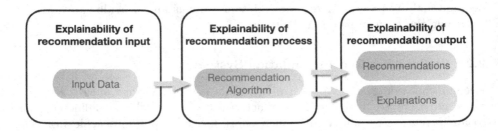

Fig. 1. Explainable recommendation framework.

In this survey, we provide a framework of explainable recommendation systems that consider both Human-Computer Interaction (HCI) and Machine Learning (ML) perspectives of explainable recommendation research. Figure 1 shows an overview of the framework.

Explainable recommendation can consider the explainability of the recommendation input (i.e., the input data source or the type of information used for explanations, also refers to user profile), the recommendation process (i.e., algorithm), and the recommendation output and explanations [12]. Explainability of the recommendation input provides a description that summarizes the system's understanding of the user's profile or preference and allows users to review and even adjust user profiles by themselves. Systems focusing on the explainability of the recommendation process, known as model-based explainable recommendations, aim to explain how the algorithm works, and they are referred to as model-based explainable recommendations [56]. Explainability of the recommendation output concentrates on the recommendation results and explanations. It refers to post-hoc explanation approaches and also represents the HCI perspective of explainable course recommendation research, such as how users interact with different styles of explanations and formats of the explanations (e.g., textual sentence explanation or visual explanation).

In the context of explainable recommendations, these three aspects are closely related to each other. For example, the characteristics of the input data usually determine what type of model can be used. The characteristics of the model, in turn, determine the type of explanations. Finally, since explanations are generated based on the data, the input data also influences the style of the explanation. We classify existing research according to this framework so that readers can understand the relationship between existing explainable recommendation methods.

3.1 Explainability of Recommendation Input

Explainability of recommendation input provides a description that summarizes the system's understanding of the user's profile or preference and allows users to review and even adjust user profiles by themselves [12]. Generally, the user's profile, such as user interest or learning goal, can be extracted explicitly from questionnaires or implicitly by learning the user's historical enrollment behavior. In previous works, it might encompass department or major information, program curriculum requirements, GPA [38], general interests [39,42], educational background [31], and informal learning objectives [9], and so on. The profiles help to match courses with users by aligning course content with the user's needs or interests. For example, Ma et al. [34] proposed a course recommendation interface that allows users to build their interest profiles by selecting different topics and keywords. Then, the system will provide recommendation results based on user-generated profiles. Users could understand the results and refine their user profiles to generate better results. Also, a similar work proposed a course recommendation system that infers the students' academic interests from the keywords they entered to provide a more flexible and realistic interpretation of a student's interests and uses the regression models to predict the results [39].

Utilizing more information not only improves the performance of recommendations but also aids in creating high-quality explanations. Nonetheless, gathering extensive data on both courses and users presents challenges. To address this, many researchers utilize user interaction data, which shows the previous interaction between users and courses, to construct user profiles that reflect their interests and preferences. In universities, this includes previously taken courses and grades achieved. Capitalizing on the digital age, MOOCs can gather a variety of rich data types, including course page visit history [28], user learning behavior [26], completion rates, and feedback on courses, such as ratings and reviews [19,20]. This data offers a comprehensive understanding of user engagement and preferences in an online learning context.

Although numerous studies have attempted to construct user profiles for course recommendations, only a few studies have concentrated on explicitly presenting the user's profile to enhance users' understanding of the recommendation input. Furthermore, the impact of such explainability of recommendation input (e.g., showing user profiles) on improving user-centric aspects within the course recommendation domain remains under-explored.

3.2 Explainability of Recommendation Model

When considering the explainability of methods, explainable recommendation aims to develop interpretable models for increased transparency, and such models usually help users understand how the recommendation process works and how the results are generated. In this section, we introduce typical methodologies for course recommendation, including content-based, collaborative filtering-based, data mining, and machine learning approaches, and how they are used for explainable systems.

Content-Based Models. Content-based approaches also depend on user profiles that reflect the user's preferences and interests. The system matches the features in the user profiles (explicitly or implicitly) with the features of available items and recommends items most similar to the user's profile. The explainability of content-based models lies in their straightforward approach, and these models use specific features of items (like topics or keywords in courses) to make suggestions [11, 35, 39]. Because they focus on course characteristics that match a user's preferences, it is easier for users to understand why specific courses are recommended.

For example, Lessa et al. [31] provide a course recommendation model using students' LinkedIn profile features to represent students and give recommendations based on the profile features. Another example, Basavaraj et al. [9] present a self-reported goal orientation-based course recommendation. When recommending courses to the students, the system categorizes students into Mastery Goal Oriented (MGO) and Performance Goal Oriented (PGO) based on the survey data collected from the students. Farzan and Brusilovsky [19] developed a community-based course recommendation system called CourseAgent. To encourage user participation, they proposed interpersonal factors such as liking affiliations and individual factors such as rewards, personal needs, and intrinsic motivation to help users generate their profiles and get recommendations. Laghari, et al. [30] proposed an automated course advising system for undergraduates to plan their course registration. Profile building is completed by the students by entering their GPA, ID, degree major, current date, and the average credit hours of load per semester, and then the system provides suggestions accordingly.

Collaborative Filtering Based Models. Collaborative filtering is the most popular technique for recommendation systems. It is based on the assumption that people have similar preferences and interests and that we can predict their choices according to their past preferences based on user ratings.

Researchers also use collaborative filtering for course recommendations. These methods provide a framework for recommending courses based on historical academic performance or explicit student feedback [14]. For example, Bakhshinategh et al. [6] ask students to rate courses they have completed and use these ratings to generate recommendations. However, as rating data is often scarce for courses, many researchers use course grades instead of ratings and recommend courses by calculating course score distribution of the most similar students [16,24,49]. These approaches have a very clear goal: to predict courses that students are likely to pass successfully. Therefore, users can understand why certain courses are recommended or receive warnings when the predicted grade is a fail [39].

In general, collaborative-based methods are less intuitive to explain compared with content-based methods.

Data Mining and Machine Learning Models. Traditional data mining and machine-learning models including random-walk approach [47], sparse linear method [32], association rule [10], and decision tree expression [13], are also applied in the context of course recommendations. The notable advantage of these algorithms lies in their straightforward and transparent structures. This simplicity significantly reduces the complexity associated with generating explanations. For example, Wagner et al. [51] introduced a course recommendation system developed on an interpretable k-nearest neighbor algorithm. The system aims to assist students who are at risk of dropping out of a course. Barria et al. [7] proposed a system using simple machine learning models to generate learning content recommendations. Simultaneously, it provides explanations for the recommended goals, aiding students in understanding why specific learning activities are suggested. Afzaal et al. [3] introduced an approach that integrates learning analytics techniques with interpretable machine learning to enhance students' course performance. They created a dashboard offering understandable suggestions to students.

Among these methods, rule mining approaches often have special advantages for explainable recommendations as they can generate very straightforward explanations for users [8,15,37,56]. Aher and Lobo [4] used association rule mining based on frequent patterns to extract interesting relations between courses from the data that describe students' previous course selections. Together with the clustering method, the system recommends courses based on rules that they extracted from historical course enrollment data. Bendakir and Aïmeur [10] also presented a course recommendation system based on association rules. They use user ratings in their recommendation system together with association rules to improve the result.

Deep Learning Models. In recent years, the advancement of deep learning techniques has prompted an increasing number of researchers to leverage this methodology for course recommendation systems. These recommendation models encompass a wide array of deep learning techniques, including RNN, LSTM, attention mechanisms, reinforcement learning, knowledge graphs, and others.

Pardos et al. used RNN and skip-gram model for course recommendation systems [44,45]. A novel approach to goal-based course RS has been proposed in [27]. Following this line, they extended the goal-based model for MOOC learners by employing deep learning to make inferences about future outcomes based on past actions and MOOC quizzes [26]. Fan et al. [18] introduced a recommendation method based on MOOC data, employing a multiple attention mechanism that simultaneously considers the student's learning record attention, review attention, and course description attention to provide corresponding explanations. Jiang et al. [25] introduced a model incorporating the MOOC knowledge graph. Therefore, the model generates recommended knowledge concepts by leveraging the format of KG paths, providing insights into semantic reasons underlying the recommendations. Yang et al. [54] introduced a contextual knowledge graph embedding method incorporating contextual neighborhood semantics and motivation-aware information for the representation of learning talents and courses. Consequently, the model discerns the importance of meta-paths in delineating corresponding preferences, thereby offering detailed explanations. Afreen et al. [2] explored path reasoning as an approach to recommendation systems in the education domain. They leveraged intricate connections between learners and courses to deliver recommendations accompanied by transparent reasoning.

Despite the significant success of deep learning based course recommendations, making the recommendation process understandable is particularly difficult because the black-box nature of deep learning models is excessively intricate for interpretation. In such scenarios, post hoc explanations are especially useful as they allow the recommendation algorithm to stay as a black box [1]. For example, for systems that use deep learning models to predict user performance and recommend courses based on the predicted results, a simple explanation could be like, "We predicted you would pass this one successfully". Overall, post hoc explainable recommendation methods strive to construct an explanatory model to elucidate black-box deep learning models. While these explanations may not precisely mirror the exact mechanism generating the recommendation, they offer the advantage of flexible application to recommendation models.

3.3   Explanations

In the evolving landscape of educational recommendation systems, the role of explanations is crucial for enhancing user trust, understanding, and interaction with the system [38]. As these systems become increasingly complex, the need for explanations also becomes more prominent. There are different explanations that serve multiple purposes for explainable course recommendation systems, including describing the workings of the algorithm and explaining rationals behind the recommendations (i.e., providing insights that could be most beneficial for individual learners) [36]. Each plays a role in meeting the diverse needs of users. However, different users may have their own preferences when it comes to how recommendation systems explain things. For example, while some users may prefer detailed explanations with more information that characterizes the recommendation process, others might benefit more from simple explanations [34]. In addition, educational recommendation systems are increasingly adopting hybrid approaches, and, as a result, how to combine different types of explanations to cater to a broader audience also becomes an open issue [38].

In this section, we provide a summary of the different styles of course recommendation explanations. We also categorize the related work according to different explanation formats.

Explanation Style. In general, the underlying algorithm of a recommendation engine influences, to a certain degree, the styles of explanations that can be generated. There are different explanation styles (also referred to in some papers as explanation types) in previous works according to different recommendation methods.

Content-based Methods. They also referred to as feature-based methods, attempt to match items to users based on features/attributes in course recommendation systems, such as keywords, topics, knowledge concepts, and so on. A common paradigm for content-based explanation is to provide users with the item features that match the user's academic interest profile. Because the features are usually easily understandable to the users, it is usually intuitive to explain to the users why an item is recommended [56]. Content-based approaches can naturally give intuitive explanations by listing features/attributes that made an item appear in the recommendations.

Collaborative Filtering (CF) based Methods. These methods leverage the "wisdom of the crowds" and make recommendations based on patterns of ratings or usage. In other domains, the items recommended by user-based CF methods usually be explained as "users that are similar to you liked this item". In contrast, item-based methods can be explained as "the item is similar to your previously liked items". However, such an explanation does not seem helpful for cases in course recommendations. In addition, obtaining rating data on courses poses challenges. Therefore, instead of ratings, CF-based methods often use grades for course recommendation because of the ease of achieving high grades relevant to the student's future career. In this case, CF-based methods can be explained as "Students with similar scores to you in the previous courses obtain high scores in this course" or "this course is similar to your previous courses you passed successfully" [24]. Alternatively, just like other methods that try to predict user performance, provide simple explanations using predicted results, warnings, and a list of suitable preparatory courses [39].

Transparent Models. Many works try to use simple data mining and machine learning methods to describe the recommendation process of the algorithm, as many of these models are considered to be transparent, which means they are understandable by themselves. For example, explainability could be achieved by presenting the paths of a decision tree to the user. Decision trees are hierarchical decision-making structures, so their properties can render them decomposable or algorithmically transparent. Association rule mining is another example of a model that can effectively explain complex interaction information. Such rule-based approaches are transparent models often used to explain complex models by generating rules that explain their predictions.

While transparent models offer clear explanations of the recommendation process that might benefit algorithm developers, this level of explainability might not always enhance the educational experience and often doesn't provide deeper insights into the course content or how a course might specifically benefit a student's educational journey. Despite the potential of these models, research delving deeply into how these methods specifically enhance or fail to enhance the educational experience in course recommendation systems remains limited. Further exploration in this area is needed to fully understand and optimize the impact of different explanations on educational outcomes.

Post-hoc Methods. Deep learning models have recently gained much attention for recommendation systems. The black box nature of deep models, however, leads to the difficulty of model explainability, and using a deep model for explainable recommendation needs further explanation [12]. In such scenarios, post hoc explanations, where the explanatory model is distinct from the recommendation model, could be used to generate explanations. In many course systems, the items are recommended based on very sophisticated hybrid models, but after an item is recommended, we can provide some simple information as explanations [56]. For example, Abdi et al. [1] augment the efficacy of the educational recommender systems (ERS) with transparent and easily comprehensible open learner models (OLMs) that substantiate their recommendations. Also, they combine crowdsourcing techniques to build their model. Other explanations include social explanations like "advisor recommend this course" [19] or "senior student recommend this course" [36]. Also, hybrid explanation methods provide explanations by aligning two or more different explanation methods. For example, Ma et al. [38] propose a hybrid course recommendation framework that considers student interest, the timing of taking the course, and the predicted grade of the student together, and students could change the weights of three parts to generate better recommendation results. In addition, interest or goal-based explanations and grade-based explanations are also popular for these methods because of their high intuitiveness.

The styles of explanations can be significant for users, especially in the education domain. Yu et al. [55] explore the effectiveness of different explanations in course recommendation systems. These methods aim to orient students towards course recommendations by providing personalized explanations and enhancing students' understanding of why courses are recommended and potentially increasing their willingness to enroll in them. They find that by adding more information about a course, including why it has been recommended, students will become more familiar with the course and increase its success. However, compared to other domains, research for explainable course recommendations is still under-explored.

Explanation Format. Recommendation explanations can be presented in very different display styles, which could be a relevant user or item, an image, a sentence, a chart, or a set of reasoning rules [12]. Generally, the format of the recommendation explanations can be classified into textual explanations and visual explanations [12].

Textual explanations generate a piece of text information as recommendation explanations. For example, Morsomme et al., [39] provide a simple explanation like "we recommend this course because you select this topic" for the content-based method. Another work introduces different text explanations like "topics in common with your favorite course" or "topics in common with courses you have taken before" [55].

To take advantage of the intuition of visualization, visual explanations provide the user with visualization as an explanation [21]. The visualization can be a chart or a graph. Visual explanations can convey more information than textual ones while requiring less cognitive effort to process [52]. Ma et al. [34] provide a visual course recommendation interface to improve the transparency of their system. All course data are presented in a dynamic scatter plot, and a grouped bar chart shows the topic distribution of the selected course to the student to explain why a course is recommended. With the bar charts, students can compare the topic distributions among different courses to help their decision-making processes. Abdi et al. [1] leverage the visual representation of learner's knowledge states and progress, offering insights into the recommendation logic and contributing to a more informed and engaging learning experience. Barria-Pineda et al. [7] employ visual explanations like color-coded concept bars and warning signs for struggling concepts. Yang et al. [54] provide visual and feature-based explanations for its recommendations. Jiang et al. [25] propose a method that recommends knowledge concepts in MOOCs by generating paths in the knowledge graph, which serve as visual explanations for the recommendations.

Different explanation formats offer unique benefits and pose distinct challenges, significantly influencing users' experiences and comprehension of course recommendation systems. However, research on which explanation formats are most effective for educational purposes, particularly in course recommendations, is still limited.

4   Discussion and Conclusion

Existing research on explainable recommendation systems suggests that explanations can help improve transparency, interpretability, and trust for their end users [35]. However, there are also results suggesting that such explanations are not always valued by or beneficial for all users [34]. The impact of user differences on explanation effectiveness calls for further research, especially on the value of explainability in the educational context.

Specifically, it is important to identify what types of explanations different end users need (e.g., why or how the system recommended a specific course). A student's decision to select a specific course is influenced by various factors simultaneously (e.g., interest, grade, learning goal, and so on) [36]. As a result, it might be necessary to generate different explanations for different purposes and select the best combination of the explanations to display. Moreover, it is crucial to know how the explanations should be delivered in order to be informative and beneficial for individual learners' learning experience (e.g., align with educational goals, provide insights, engage and motivate learners, or personalize the learning path). In addition, it is also important to conduct longitudinal studies to understand the long-term impact of explainable recommendations on learning and educational pathways. Recently, there has been an emerging trend among researchers to utilize Large Language Models for generating recommendation explanations. This could also represent a promising direction for future exploration.

In this paper, we provided a framework of explainable recommendation systems. Specifically, we introduced three different aspects of explainable course recommendation systems following the framework, including the input, the models, and the output. We expect this work could provide insights for future explainable course recommendation research.

Acknowledgement. This work was supported by JSPS KAKENHI Grant Number 20H00622.

References

1. Abdi, S., Khosravi, H., Sadiq, S., Gasevic, D.: Complementing educational recommender systems with open learner models. In: Proceedings of the Tenth International Conference on Learning Analytics & Knowledge, pp. 360–365 (2020)
2. Afreen, N., Balloccu, G., Boratto, L., Fenu, G., Marras, M.: Towards explainable educational recommendation through path reasoning methods. In: The 13th Italian Information Retrieval Workshop (IIR2023) (2023)
3. Afzaal, M., et al.: Explainable AI for data-driven feedback and intelligent action recommendations to support students self-regulation. Front. Artif. Intell. **4**, 723447 (2021)
4. Aher, S.B., Lobo, L.: Combination of machine learning algorithms for recommendation of courses in e-learning system based on historical data. Knowl.-Based Syst. **51**, 1–14 (2013)
5. Alkan, O., Daly, E.M., Botea, A., Valente, A.N., Pedemonte, P.: Where can my career take me? harnessing dialogue for interactive career goal recommendations. In: Proceedings of the 24th International Conference on Intelligent User Interfaces, pp. 603–613 (2019)
6. Bakhshinategh, B., Spanakis, G., Zaiane, O., ElAtia, S.: A course recommender system based on graduating attributes. In: International Conference on Computer Supported Education, vol. 2, pp. 347–354. SCITEPRESS (2017)
7. Barria-Pineda, J., Akhuseyinoglu, K., Brusilovsky, P.: Explaining need-based educational recommendations using interactive open learner models. In: Adjunct Publication of the 27th Conference on User Modeling, Adaptation and Personalization, pp. 273–277 (2019)
8. Barria Pineda, J., Brusilovsky, P.: Making educational recommendations transparent through a fine-grained open learner model. In: Proceedings of Workshop on Intelligent User Interfaces for Algorithmic Transparency in Emerging Technologies at the 24th ACM Conference on Intelligent User Interfaces, IUI 2019, Los Angeles, USA, March 20, 2019, vol. 2327 (2019)

9. Basavaraj, P., Garibay, I.: A personalized "course navigator" based on students' goal orientation. In: Proceedings of the 2018 ACM International Conference on Supporting Group Work, pp. 98–101 (2018)

10. Bendakir, N., Aïmeur, E.: Using association rules for course recommendation. In: Proceedings of the AAAI Workshop on Educational Data Mining, vol. 3, pp. 1–10 (2006)

11. Bercovitz, B., Kaliszan, F., Koutrika, G., Liou, H., Mohammadi Zadeh, Z., Garcia-Molina, H.: CourseRank: a social system for course planning. In: Proceedings of the 2009 ACM SIGMOD International Conference on Management of Data, pp. 1107–1110 (2009)

12. Chatti, M.A., Guesmi, M., Muslim, A.: Visualization for recommendation explainability: a survey and new perspectives. arXiv preprint arXiv:2305.11755 (2023)

13. Chen, X., Zheng, J., Du, Y., Tang, M.: Intelligent course plan recommendation for higher education: a framework of decision tree. Discret. Dyn. Nat. Soc. **2020**, 1–11 (2020)

14. Chen, Z., Liu, X., Shang, L.: Improved course recommendation algorithm based on collaborative filtering. In: 2020 International Conference on Big Data and Informatization Education (ICBDIE), pp. 466–469. IEEE (2020)

15. Conati, C., Barral, O., Putnam, V., Rieger, L.: Toward personalized XAI: a case study in intelligent tutoring systems. Artif. Intell. **298**, 103503 (2021)

16. Elbadrawy, A., Karypis, G.: Domain-aware grade prediction and top-n course recommendation. In: Proceedings of the 10th ACM Conference on Recommender Systems, pp. 183–190 (2016)

17. Elbadrawy, A., Studham, R.S., Karypis, G.: Collaborative multi-regression models for predicting students' performance in course activities. In: Proceedings of the Fifth International Conference on Learning Analytics and Knowledge, pp. 103–107 (2015)

18. Fan, J., Jiang, Y., Liu, Y., Zhou, Y.: Interpretable MOOC recommendation: a multi-attention network for personalized learning behavior analysis. Internet Res. **32**(2), 588–605 (2022)

19. Farzan, R., Brusilovsky, P.: Encouraging user participation in a course recommender system: an impact on user behavior. Comput. Hum. Behav. **27**(1), 276–284 (2011)

20. Ghauth, K.I., Abdullah, N.A.: The effect of incorporating good learners' ratings in e-learning content-based recommender system. J. Educ. Technol. Soc. **14**(2), 248–257 (2011)

21. Gutiérrez, F., Seipp, K., Ochoa, X., Chiluiza, K., De Laet, T., Verbert, K.: LADA: a learning analytics dashboard for academic advising. Comput. Hum. Behav. **107**, 105826 (2020)

22. He, C., Parra, D., Verbert, K.: Interactive recommender systems: a survey of the state of the art and future research challenges and opportunities. Expert Syst. Appl. **56**, 9–27 (2016)

23. Hu, Q., Rangwala, H.: Course-specific Markovian models for grade prediction. In: Phung, D., Tseng, V.S., Webb, G.I., Ho, B., Ganji, M., Rashidi, L. (eds.) PAKDD 2018. LNCS (LNAI), vol. 10938, pp. 29–41. Springer, Cham (2018). https://doi.org/10.1007/978-3-319-93037-4_3

24. Huang, L., Wang, C.D., Chao, H.Y., Lai, J.H., Philip, S.Y.: A score prediction approach for optional course recommendation via cross-user-domain collaborative filtering. IEEE Access **7**, 19550–19563 (2019)

25. Jiang, L., et al.: Reinforced explainable knowledge concept recommendation in MOOCs. ACM Trans. Intell. Syst. Technol. **14**(3), 1–20 (2023)

26. Jiang, W., Pardos, Z.A.: Time slice imputation for personalized goal-based recommendation in higher education. In: Proceedings of the 13th ACM Conference on Recommender Systems, pp. 506–510 (2019)

27. Jiang, W., Pardos, Z.A., Wei, Q.: Goal-based course recommendation. In: Proceedings of the 9th International Conference on Learning Analytics & Knowledge pp. 36–45 (2019)

28. Jing, X., Tang, J.: Guess you like: course recommendation in MOOCs. In: Proceedings of the International Conference on Web Intelligence, pp. 783–789 (2017)

29. Konstan, J.A., Riedl, J.: Recommender systems: from algorithms to user experience. User Model. User-Adap. Inter. **22**(1–2), 101–123 (2012)

30. Laghari, M.S.: Automated course advising system. Int. J. Mach. Learn. Comput. **4**(1), 47–51 (2014)

31. Lessa, L.F., Brandão, W.C.: Filtering graduate courses based on linkedin profiles. In: Proceedings of the 24th Brazilian Symposium on Multimedia and the Web, pp. 141–147 (2018)

32. Lin, J., Pu, H., Li, Y., Lian, J.: Intelligent recommendation system for course selection in smart education. Procedia Comput. Sci. **129**, 449–453 (2018)

33. Lu, H., et al.: User perception of recommendation explanation: are your explanations what users need? ACM Trans. Inf. Syst. **41**(2), 1–31 (2023)

34. Ma, B., Lu, M., Taniguchi, Y., Konomi, S.: CourseQ: the impact of visual and interactive course recommendation in university environments. Res. Pract. Technol. Enhanc. Learn. **16**, 1–24 (2021)

35. Ma, B., Lu, M., Taniguchi, Y., Konomi, S.: Exploration and explanation: an interactive course recommendation system for university environments. In: IUI Workshops (2021)

36. Ma, B., Lu, M., Taniguchi, Y., Konomi, S.: Investigating course choice motivations in university environments. Smart Learn. Environ. **8**(1), 1–18 (2021)

37. Ma, B., Taniguchi, Y., Konomi, S.: Design a course recommendation system based on association rule for hybrid learning environments. Inf. Process. Soc. Japan **7** (2019)

38. Ma, B., Taniguchi, Y., Konomi, S.: Course recommendation for university environments. Int. Educ. Data Min. Soc. (2020)

39. Morsomme, R., Alferez, S.V.: Content-based course recommender system for liberal arts education. Int. Educ. Data Min. Soc. (2019)

40. Morsy, S., Karypis, G.: Will this course increase or decrease your GPA? towards grade-aware course recommendation. J. Educ. Data Min. **11**(2), 20–46 (2019)

41. Naren, J., Banu, M.Z., Lohavani, S.: Recommendation system for students' course selection. In: Somani, A.K., Shekhawat, R.S., Mundra, A., Srivastava, S., Verma, V.K. (eds.) Smart Systems and IoT: Innovations in Computing. SIST, vol. 141, pp. 825–834. Springer, Singapore (2020). https://doi.org/10.1007/978-981-13-8406-6_77

42. O'Mahony, M.P., Smyth, B.: A recommender system for on-line course enrolment: an initial study. In: Proceedings of the 2007 ACM Conference on Recommender Systems, pp. 133–136 (2007)

43. Parameswaran, A., Venetis, P., Garcia-Molina, H.: Recommendation systems with complex constraints: a course recommendation perspective. ACM Trans. Inf. Syst. (TOIS) **29**(4), 1–33 (2011)

44. Pardos, Z.A., Fan, Z., Jiang, W.: Connectionist recommendation in the wild: on the utility and scrutability of neural networks for personalized course guidance. User Model. User-Adap. Inter. **29**(2), 487–525 (2019)

45. Pardos, Z.A., Jiang, W.: Combating the filter bubble: designing for serendipity in a university course recommendation system. arXiv preprint arXiv:1907.01591 (2019)
46. Peake, G., Wang, J.: Explanation mining: post hoc interpretability of latent factor models for recommendation systems. In: Proceedings of the 24th ACM SIGKDD International Conference on Knowledge Discovery & Data Mining, pp. 2060–2069 (2018)
47. Polyzou, A., Nikolakopoulos, A.N., Karypis, G.: Scholars walk: a Markov chain framework for course recommendation. Int. Educ. Data Min. Soc. (2019)
48. Pu, P., Chen, L., Hu, R.: Evaluating recommender systems from the user's perspective: survey of the state of the art. User Model. User-Adap. Inter. 22(4–5), 317–355 (2012)
49. Ray, S., Sharma, A.: A collaborative filtering based approach for recommending elective courses. In: Dua, S., Sahni, S., Goyal, D.P. (eds.) ICISTM 2011. CCIS, vol. 141, pp. 330–339. Springer, Heidelberg (2011). https://doi.org/10.1007/978-3-642-19423-8_34
50. Sweeney, M., Rangwala, H., Lester, J., Johri, A.: Next-term student performance prediction: a recommender systems approach. In: arXiv preprint arXiv:1604.01840 (2016)
51. Wagner, K., Merceron, A., Sauer, P., Pinkwart, N.: Personalized and explainable course recommendations for students at risk of dropping out. In: Proceedings of the 15th International Conference on Educational Data Mining, p. 657 (2022)
52. Ware, C.: Information visualization: perception for design. Morgan Kaufmann (2019)
53. Xiao, B., Benbasat, I.: E-commerce product recommendation agents: use, characteristics, and impact. MIS Q. 31(1), 137–209 (2007)
54. Yang, Y., Zhang, C., Song, X., Dong, Z., Zhu, H., Li, W.: Contextualized knowledge graph embedding for explainable talent training course recommendation. ACM Trans. Inf. Syst. 42(2), 1–27 (2023)
55. Yu, R., Pardos, Z., Chau, H., Brusilovsky, P.: Orienting students to course recommendations using three types of explanation. In: Adjunct Proceedings of the 29th ACM Conference on User Modeling, Adaptation and Personalization, pp. 238–245 (2021)
56. Zhang, Y., Chen, X., et al.: Explainable recommendation: a survey and new perspectives. Found. Trends® Inf. Retrieval 14(1), 1–101 (2020)
57. Zhang, Y., Lai, G., Zhang, M., Zhang, Y., Liu, Y., Ma, S.: Explicit factor models for explainable recommendation based on phrase-level sentiment analysis. In: Proceedings of the 37th International ACM SIGIR Conference on Research & Development in Information Retrieval, pp. 83–92 (2014)

The Role of Automated Classification in Preserving Indonesian Folk and National Songs

Aji Prasetya Wibawa[1]([✉]) [iD], AH. Rofi'uddin[2] [iD], Rafal Dreżewski[1,3] [iD],
Ilham Ari Elbaith Zaeni[1] [iD], Irfan Zuhdi Abdillah[1], Triyanti Simbolon[1],
Fabyan Raif Erlangga[1], and Agung Bella Putra Utama[1] [iD]

[1] Knowledge Engineering and Data Science Center, Universitas Negeri Malang, Malang 65145,
Indonesia
aji.prasetya.ft@um.ac.id
[2] Faculty of Letters, Universitas Negeri Malang, Malang 65145, Indonesia
[3] Faculty of Computer Science, AGH University of Kraków, 30-059 Kraków, Poland

Abstract. The preservationof Indonesia's rich tapestry of language and culture is a significant concern, particularly in response to claims made by other countries about cultural treasures, such as folk music. Preserving cultural aspects is now easier in our tech-savvy era with abundant information. A potentially effective strategy entails the methodical categorization of traditional and patriotic songs, thereby facilitating the determination of their respective sources. The present work utilizes a dataset of 480 folk and 90 national songs, categorized into situations involving 2, 4, and 31 classes. A meticulous pre-processing pipeline is utilized, including cleaning, case folding, tokenization, and word weighting. The selected word weighting strategy is the TF-IDF. In order to mitigate the issue of class imbalance, the SMOTE is proposed as a supplementary approach. This study assesses three classification algorithms, namely KNN, SVM, and Naïve Bayes, using the 10-fold validation technique. The SVM, known for its utilization of hyperplane-based classification, demonstrates exceptional performance by reaching a remarkable accuracy rate of 99.69% while utilizing the RBF kernel function. The present study observed that the KNN demonstrated superior performance when the value of k was set to 2, and no SMOTE was applied. A binary classification methodology was employed. Notably, this strategy yielded an impressive accuracy rate of 97.02%. It is worth mentioning that Naïve Bayes demonstrates ideal performance in a two-label scenario when SMOTE is applied, yielding an accuracy rate of 93.75%. This comprehensive investigation proves that the SVM performs better than KNN and Naïve Bayes when classifying Indonesian song lyrics. This finding highlights the significance of SVM as a beneficial instrument for preserving Indonesia's culturally diverse legacy. This initiative connects technology and culture by providing educational resources and enlisting tribe elders, linguists, and other experts to demonstrate the integration of technology and tradition and preserve Indonesia's cultural heritage.

Keywords: Indonesia · Preservation of Culture · Folk and National Songs · Classification · SMOTE

N. A. Streitz and S. Konomi (Eds.): HCII 2024, LNCS 14719, pp. 288–306, 2024.
https://doi.org/10.1007/978-3-031-60012-8_18

1 Introduction

Indonesia, a country renowned for its decadent array of arts and cultural heritage [1], possesses a deeply revered mode of artistic manifestation, namely its musical compositions. The musical narratives discussed in this context encompass a wide geographical range, from the awe-inspiring Sabang to the mesmerizing Merauke [2]. These narratives serve as a representation of the cultural essence inherent in each respective region. However, a significant obstacle arises in the intricate fabric of melodies and narratives: safeguarding their cultural significance [3]. This research explores a novel approach using text classification technology to analyze Indonesian folk and national songs, aiming to uncover the hidden meanings embedded in their lyrical compositions.

The cultural diversity of Indonesia is evident in its rich tapestry of traditions, exemplified by the presence of distinctive folk songs in each province [4]. These poetic expressions exemplify the essence of local languages and traditions, each infused with unique and discernible qualities. Furthermore, Indonesia ceremoniously showcases its national songs, which serve as anthems resonating with a profound sense of nationalistic pride and zeal, symbolizing the unity of a nation deeply devoted to its homeland [5]. Nevertheless, in light of the persistent process of modernity and the continuously expanding influence of globalization, these songs have been marginalized, with their significance diminishing as public consciousness and admiration decline.

The challenges these cultural artifacts face are exacerbated by external assertions of ownership over Indonesian heritage, shown by the 2008 controversy surrounding the folk song "Rasa Sayang-Sayange" [6]. In an era characterized by rapid societal advancements, folk tunes' complex and multifaceted nature poses a perplexing mystery that tests the knowledge and expertise of experienced cultural stewards. The origins of these languages are typically intricately connected with regional languages, making it challenging to determine their precise roots, which has posed a problematic riddle that cannot be solved through aural analysis [7]. Therefore, a robust categorization methodology must thoroughly examine the lyrical content, revealing the concealed semantic intricacies specific to each geographical region.

This pioneering work addresses the gap between technology and cultural preservation by utilizing advanced text categorization algorithms to investigate Indonesian folk and national music. These innovative techniques can potentially reveal the origins and categorizations of these cultural artifacts, revitalizing their significance. Various classification techniques, such as K-Nearest Neighbor (KNN) [8], Support Vector Machine (SVM) [9], Multinomial Naïve Bayes (MNB) [10], and Decision Tree [11], are utilized in pursuing this noble undertaking.

The KNN algorithm, known for its simplicity and impressive efficacy, stands at the forefront of this endeavor [12]. Equipped with proximity knowledge, it accurately identifies the predominant class within the closest k neighbors, making it an optimal classifier for datasets including a wide range of classes and large amounts of data.

The arsenal comprises the MNB algorithm, constructed based on probability theory principles [13]. The system adeptly organizes texts by utilizing the complex network of word frequencies interconnecting the entire collection. The unmistakable rise of MNB is characterized by its exceptional modeling capabilities and computational efficiency despite the challenges posed by class imbalance.

Finally, the SVM, a prominent example of optimal margin-based categorization in Machine Learning (ML), emerges onto the scene. The SVM is highly regarded for its exceptional ability to generalize data, maintain consistent accuracy, and execute computations swiftly [14]. As a result, it has gained prominence as a powerful competitor, surpassing traditional alternatives like the KNN algorithm.

This pioneering study aims to rekindle enthusiasm for Indonesian folk and national songs, reviving these valuable cultural artifacts that have been mostly overlooked. The objective is to revitalize these timeless narratives, guaranteeing their lasting impact on the collective consciousness of present-day society, equipped with sophisticated text categorization algorithms.

2 Method

This study has involved utilizing several research methodologies, including acquiring and compiling datasets from multiple reputable sources. The datasets will be subjected to a sequence of procedures, which encompass text pre-processing, augmentation via oversampling utilizing the Synthetic Minority Oversampling Technique (SMOTE), and weighting through the application of Term Frequency-Inverse Document Frequency (TF-IDF). In the following steps, we shall implement the Support Vector Machine (SVM) algorithm, known for its precision in classification tasks. Furthermore, we will thoroughly evaluate the resultant classification model to assess its performance.

The data collection methodology employed in this study involved conducting searches across various reputable and pertinent sources, entailing a comprehensive search of canonical literature containing regional and national songs alongside internet scholarly publications. The dataset that has been effectively collected contains diverse facets, comprising song lyrics, song titles, and their respective areas of origin.

Through rigorous data collection, we have successfully amassed a comprehensive dataset of 570 data points encompassing regional and national songs. The compilation encompasses 480 regional songs from 30 distinct provinces around Indonesia and 90 national songs embodying a sense of national pride and unity. In order to account for the intricate differences, the dataset is further partitioned into three unique scenarios, namely scenarios characterized by two labels, four labels, and 31 labels, as elaborated in Table 1.

The partitioning of the dataset into three specific circumstances enables us to do a sequence of rigorous and all-encompassing tests, with the primary aim of evaluating the proficiency of the constructed classification model in managing variations in label quantity and the heterogeneity of song attributes. This study integrates meticulousness in data collecting with precision in categorization modeling, facilitating a more profound comprehension of Indonesia's regional and national music culture.

Data pre-processing is crucial in transforming raw text as input and applying several basic rules to modify or eliminate textual features that are not useful in further processing [15]. Data collected from various sources can have different structures, so this data cannot be directly used for research. Therefore, pre-processing is done to standardize the data format applied to the classification model.

Table 1. Total data of each scenario.

Scenario 1	Scenario 2	Scenario 3	Lyrics
Regional Song	West Indonesia	Aceh	10
		Bangka Belitung	10
		Banten	10
		Bengkulu	17
		Jakarta	13
		Jambi	16
		Jawa Barat	42
		Jawa Tengah	15
		Jawa Timur	19
		Kalimantan Barat	10
		Kalimantan Tengah	12
		Lampung	13
		Riau	15
		Sumatera Barat	34
		Sumatera Selatan	41
		Sumatera Utara	28
		Yogyakarta	11
	Central Indonesia	Bali	14
		Gorontalo	11
		Kalimantan Selatan	10
		Kalimantan Timur	10
		Kalimantan Utara	4
		Nusa Tenggara Barat	10
		Nusa Tenggara Timur	10
		Sulawesi Selatan	11
		Sulawesi Tengah	14
		Sulawesi Tenggara	7
		Sulawesi Utara	20
	East Indonesia	Maluku	26
		Papua	17
National Song	National Song	National Song	90
Total			570

Typically, there are several stages in the text pre-processing process, including case folding, tokenization, filtering, stemming, and more. This study employs only three pre-processing stages: cleaning, case folding, and tokenizing, ensuring that the words in the dataset retain their original meaning [16]. Data cleaning enhances data quality in the first stage by identifying and removing errors and inconsistencies [17]. This research will remove unnecessary characters such as punctuation marks, symbols, and numbers in song lyrics as in Table 2.

The importance of data pre-processing cannot be overstated, as it lays the foundation for the accurate and meaningful analysis of text data [18]. In this context, cleaning the data from noise and irrelevant information ensures that the subsequent stages of the research, including feature extraction and classification, are built upon a solid and reliable dataset. By focusing on the essential pre-processing steps of cleaning, case folding, and tokenization, this study aims to preserve the original meaning and context of the lyrics while preparing them for classification, ultimately contributing to the success of the overall research endeavor.

Table 2. Cleaning examples.

Input	Cleaning result
Nang mana batis kutung Dikitipi dawang (2x)	*Nang mana batis kutung Dikitipi dawang*
Potong bebek angsa, angsa di kuali	*Potong bebek angsa angsa di kuali*

The subsequent step in the procedure involves case folding, as indicated in Table 3. The process of case folding involves the standardization of characters inside a dataset by changing all letters to lowercase. During this transformation process, the characters ranging from 'A' to 'Z' are converted to the characters 'a' to 'z'. Case folding is a crucial stage in pre-processing text, establishing consistency in the textual data [19]. Changing all letters to lowercase standardizes the letter casing, facilitating further analysis and classification. This stage additionally aids in the reduction of text data complexity, the enhancement of feature consistency, and the improvement of Natural Language Processing (NLP) task accuracy [20]. Within the scope of this study, the utilization of case folding serves the purpose of establishing a consistent and standardized dataset, hence establishing a solid foundation for enhanced classification and analysis of Indonesian folk and national music.

Table 3. Casefolding examples.

Input	Casefolding
Nang mana batis kutung Dikitipi dawang	*nang mana batis kutung dikitipi dawang*
Potong bebek angsa, angsa di kuali	*potong bebek angsa angsa di kuali*

The tokenizing process is conducted during the third stage, as indicated in Table 4. Tokenization is an essential process that divides textual content within a document into distinct and discrete components referred to as tokens [21]. During tokenization, the text undergoes a sequential examination of its characters. If the character at position i does not correspond to a word separator, such as a period (.), comma (,), or space, it is concatenated with the subsequent character. When a word separator is met, the characters before it are grouped to form a text segment. Tokenization is a crucial procedure in NLP that facilitates computer systems' comprehension and analysis of human language. Segmenting text into tokens simplifies several activities, including but not limited to word quantification, sentiment analysis, and text categorization [22]. Converting unstructured text data into a format suitable for processing and analysis by ML algorithms is crucial. Within this study's scope, tokenization is crucial in preparing song lyrics for classification. The process involves the dissection of lyrics into discrete units, such as words or segments, enabling the examination of the substance and patterns inherent in the text. This particular stage plays a crucial role in enhancing the precision and efficacy of the succeeding categorization algorithms, hence facilitating the preservation and comprehension of the extensive cultural material associated with Indonesian folk and national music.

Table 4. Tokenizing.

Input	Tokenizing
Nang mana batis kutung Dikitipi dawang	['*nang*', '*mana*', '*batis*', '*kutung*', '*dikitipi*', '*dawang*']
Potong bebek angsa, angsa di kuali	['*potong*', '*bebek*', '*angsa*', '*angsa*', '*di*', '*kuali*']

The subsequent step involves the utilization of TF-IDF for word weighting. The TF-IDF method determines the significance of a word (term) concerning a document [23]. The approach above is renowned for its precision, effectiveness, and simplicity in execution. The TF-IDF method combines two fundamental concepts: the frequency of a word's appearance in a document and the inverse document frequency encompassing that particular word. The frequency at which a term appears in a document serves as an indicator of its significance.

The concluding step of data pre-processing entails the utilization of SMOTE for oversampling. The SMOTE is a widely utilized approach in data analysis that aims to address the issue of imbalanced class distribution by generating synthetic data points [24]. This technique effectively equalizes the samples in both the minority and majority classes. The SMOTE technique is employed to increase the number of instances in the minority class to be equivalent to the majority class. The determination of data synthesis is contingent upon the assigned value of k, whereby the quantity of k values is established to assist the production of synthetic data [25]. The present study reveals a disparity in the dataset, wherein certain classes exhibit a significantly reduced quantity of data points compared to others.

The disparity in data volume can substantially influence the efficacy of classification models, potentially leading to the introduction of bias in the outcomes of classification. Therefore, the present work employs the oversampling technique known as the SMOTE to effectively mitigate the problem of imbalanced data distribution within each class. The results of the SMOTE are presented in Table 5.

The issue of data imbalance is a significant topic in the field of ML and classification jobs. When there is a considerable imbalance in the number of data points between different classes in some classes, models may exhibit a bias towards the majority class, resulting in skewed and erroneous outcomes [26]. In order to address this issue, the SMOTE is utilized. The SMOTE is a method that generates supplementary data points for the underrepresented class, achieving a more balanced distribution among classes and guaranteeing sufficient representation for each class in the training dataset.

Implementing data pre-processing techniques, such as TF-IDF word weighting and SMOTE oversampling, is essential to establish a balanced and representative dataset for the subsequent construction of classification models [27]. The outcomes of implementing the SMOTE are depicted in Table 5, illustrating the positive impact of this method on achieving a more balanced and equitable dataset. This research aims to improve classification algorithms' performance by addressing disparities in class representation and giving suitable weights to words. This improvement will significantly impact the preservation and analysis of Indonesian folk and national music.

Table 5. Dataset before and after SMOTE.

Class	Number of Data	SMOTE
Aceh	10	90
Bangka Belitung	10	90
Banten	10	90
Bengkulu	17	90
Jakarta	13	90
Jambi	16	90
Jawa Barat	42	90
Jawa Tengah	15	90
Jawa Timur	19	90
Kalimantan Barat	10	90
Kalimantan Tengah	12	90
Lampung	13	90
Riau	15	90
Sumatera Barat	34	90
Sumatera Selatan	41	90
Sumatera Utara	28	90

(*continued*)

Table 5. (*continued*)

Class	Number of Data	SMOTE
Yogyakarta	11	90
Bali	14	90
Gorontalo	11	90
Kalimantan Selatan	10	90
Kalimantan Timur	10	90
Kalimantan Utara	4	90
Nusa Tenggara Barat	10	90
Nusa Tenggara Timur	10	90
Sulawesi Selatan	11	90
Sulawesi Tengah	14	90
Sulawesi Tenggara	7	90
Sulawesi Utara	20	90
Maluku	26	90
Papua	17	90
National Song	90	90

2.1 K-Nearest Neighbor (KNN)

The K-Nearest Neighbor (KNN) algorithm is a classification method based on evaluating the proximity or distance between test data and training data, utilizing a designated distance metric [12]. During this procedure, the test data point endeavors to locate a group of k training data objects that exhibit the closest proximity to it, as determined by the predetermined distance metric [28]. The test data point assigns a label by considering the majority class among its k nearest neighbors.

The selected distance metric for this study is the Euclidean distance, a commonly employed and effective distance measure. The Euclidean distance is a mathematical metric that quantifies the shortest distance between two points in a multi-dimensional space, following a straight-line path [29]. KNN are widely favored due to their ability to represent the geometric proximity among data points accurately.

The evaluation of this classification procedure is conducted using the 10-fold cross-validation approach [30]. The assessment of model performance is of utmost importance in classification tasks, necessitating the utilization of evaluation methods [31]. In this procedure, the dataset is partitioned into ten homogeneous segments, wherein one of the ten segments is designated as the test data, while the remaining nine segments are allocated as the training data. The procedure above is iterated ten times, guaranteeing that every component of the test data is given an equal opportunity.

In brief, the KNN algorithm is a classification methodology that utilizes distance metrics to ascertain the class of a test data point by considering the labels of its closest neighbors from the training data [32]. Incorporating the Euclidean distance metric and the use of 10-fold cross-validation techniques serve to improve the precision and dependability of the classification procedure, facilitating the conservation and examination of Indonesian folk and national music.

```
#Pseudocode KNN with 10-fold cross-validation:
Split dataset into 10 part
Determine k value
For j in splitted dataset:
    If j==part:
        Part became data test
    Else j:
        Part became data train
    Data test find k nearest neighbor from data train using euclidean distance
    Label data test with majority of k data train that founded
    Count new_accuracy, new_precision, and new_recall
    Then
    accuracy= accuracy+new_accuracy
    precision= precision+new_precision
    recall= recall+new_recall
End for
accuracy= accuracy/10
precision= precision/10
recall= recall/10
```

2.2 Multinomial Naïve Bayes (MNB)

The Multinomial Naïve Bayes (MNB) algorithm is a classification technique developed explicitly to categorize words in a given document. The presence of a word does not exclusively determine the categorization of documents in MNB in a single data point but also considers the frequency of word occurrences across the entire dataset [33]. The procedure of MNB commences with assigning labels to the data and extracting values from these labels. Following this, the algorithm computes the aggregate count of documents, the count of distinct classes, and the count of words encompassing the entirety of the dataset. Subsequently, the process involves the determination of prior probabilities, which seek to evaluate the likelihood of the song's initial category, and post probabilities, which seek to evaluate the likelihood of a word belonging to the song's initial category.

One advantage of this approach is that MNB is widely recognized as a dominant and very efficient modeling technique compared to other Naïve Bayes models [34]. Nevertheless, the model has limitations, including its susceptibility to feature selection. When the number of features in the classification process is enormous, the MNB algorithm may result in longer calculation time and potentially lead to a decline in accuracy [35]. The excellent text categorization capabilities of MNB render it a great asset in this research endeavor, as it aids in the preservation and analysis of Indonesian folk and national music.

```
#Pseudocode MNB:
Import libraries (numpy, pandas, matplotlib, operator)
Train labels using the function train_label = open('dataset')
Extract values from labels using the function lines = train_label .readlines()
Get the total number of documents with total = len( lines)
Calculate the frequency of each song class appearance
for line in lines:
    val = int(line.plot()[0])
    pi[val] += 1
Calculate the probability of each song class concerning the total documents
for key in pi:
    pi[key] /= total
Calculate the probability of each word according to its song class
pb_ij = df.groupby(['classIdx','wordIdx'])
pb_j = df.groupby(['classIdx'])
Pr = (pb_ij['count'].sum() + a) / (pb_j['count'].sum())
Apply smoothing
if smooth:
    probability=Pr_dict[wordIdx][classIdx]
    power = np.log(1+new_dict[docIdx][wordIdx])
Retrieve the class with the highest probability
max_score = max(score_dict, key=score_dict.get)
prediction.append(max_score)
```

2.3 Support Vector Machine (SVM)

The SVM is a prominent model within supervised learning. SVM utilize vectors that traverse the hypothesis space by adopting linear functions within a feature space of high dimensionality [14]. The fundamental principle of the SVM technique is the identification of a hyperplane, which serves as a boundary line, to separate distinct classes [36]. The optimal hyperplane is determined by evaluating the margin of the hyperplane and identifying its corresponding support vectors. The margin is the spatial separation between the hyperplane and the nearest data points from each class, commonly known as Support Vectors.

SVM represent an excellent approach for achieving model generalization. Nevertheless, it is essential to note that when the training data exhibits non-linearity, there exists a potential for the classification outcomes to exhibit limited generalization capabilities [37]. In order to optimize the distinction between different classes, the initial input space undergoes a conversion into a feature space with a high number of dimensions. The process of achieving this transformation involves the utilization of a kernel, which leads to creating a kernel space that facilitates the linear separation of the data [38]. As indicated by previous research, the kernels frequently employed in various applications encompass the linear [39], RBF [40], polynomial [41], and sigmoid [42] kernels.

This study will categorize the dataset into various classes according to the abovementioned circumstances: two, four, and thirty-one. In order to do the testing, four distinct kernels will be utilized for each scenario: linear, RBF, polynomial, and sigmoid kernels. The linear kernel is the most elementary, as it calculates the dot product between two vectors [43]. The linear kernel is characterized by the parameter C. The values of C utilized in this research encompass 0.01, 0.1, 1, and 10.

The polynomial kernel is a type of kernel that incorporates parameters such as C, γ, and degree in order to optimize its performance in addressing non-linear situations [44].

The parameter values employed in this study include $C = 0.1$, $\gamma = 1$, 10, and degree $= 1$, 2. The RBF kernel is a kernel trick technique employed to convert a non-linear problem into a linear one [45]. The RBF kernel is characterized by two parameters, namely C and γ. This study employs the values of C as 1 and 10 and the values of γ as 0.1 and 1. The sigmoid kernel is non-linear for classifying data within a high-dimensional space [46]. The parameters associated with the sigmoid kernel are denoted as C and γ. This study utilized the values of C, specifically 1 and 10, and the degrees of 1 and 10. Furthermore, SVM utilize a robust mathematical framework to categorize data efficiently. The selection of a suitable kernel plays a pivotal role in determining the effectiveness of the classification process.

```
#Pseudocde SVM:
Initialize hyperparameters:
  - C (regularization parameter)
  - learning_rate
  - max_iterations
  - Initialize weights w and bias b
def svm(X_train, y_train):
    for iteration in range(max_iterations):
        for i in range(len(X_train)):
            if y_train[i] * (dot_product(w, X_train[i]) + b) <= 1:
            # Update weights for misclassified examples
            w = w - learning_rate * (w - C * y_train[i] * X_train[i])
            # Update bias
            b = b + learning_rate * C * y_train[i]
svm(X_train, y_train)
```

3   Results and Discussion

The Table 6 presents a comparative analysis of diverse scenarios, focusing on the optimal accuracy, precision, and recall attained by implementing multiple classification techniques (KNN, MNB, and SVM) across varying label quantities (2, 4, and 31).

Table 6. Table captions should be placed above the tables.

Method	Label	Accuracy (%)	Precision (%)	Recall (%)
MNB	2	93,75	94,48	93,76
MNB	4	91,77	92,57	91,79
MNB	31	90,75	91,48	90,76
SVM	2	99.69	99.69	99.69
SVM	4	95.73	96.17	95.73
SVM	31	99.57	99.57	99.57

(continued)

Table 6. (*continued*)

Method	Label	Accuracy (%)	Precision (%)	Recall (%)
KNN	2	97.02	97.02	97.02
KNN	4	78.25	78.25	78.25
KNN	31	95.13	95.13	95.13

From Table 6, in the context of MNB, it is generally observed that an expansion in the number of classification labels tends to diminish the classification performance. The SVM demonstrates negligible influence, whereas the KNN method tends to display some levels of instability. When the number of labels is configured to two, the method that exhibits the highest performance is the SVM, with an exceptional accuracy rate of 99.69%. Among the four labels considered, the SVM algorithm has superior performance, achieving an accuracy rate of 95.73%. Nevertheless, regarding 31 labels, SVM consistently outperform alternative techniques. It is noteworthy to mention that nearly all algorithms produce accuracies that are either equivalent to or somewhat lower than the precision and recall values. When precision exceeds accuracy, it denotes a reduction in false positives. Similarly, when recall is more than accurate, it decreases false negatives.

Identifying regional and national songs through text classification techniques includes comprehending lyrics as a discerning characteristic distinguishing the two. The primary emphasis of this technique lies in the analysis of the linguistic elements and structural characteristics included in the lyrics of a song. Regional songs frequently incorporate distinct languages and idioms exclusive to a geographical region. These songs often showcase dialects and local customs, evident in their lyrical content. In contrast, national anthems commonly employ the official or national language, exemplifying the nation's essence and its fervent principles of patriotism. Text classification algorithms distinguish between these categories by examining the lexical and syntactic features of the song lyrics.

Through the utilization of advanced methodologies such as TF-IDF and ML algorithms like SVM or MNB, the system is capable of acquiring knowledge regarding the unique linguistic patterns associated with different types of songs [47]. Consequently, the system can effectively categorize songs by leveraging these discernible characteristics. The SVM algorithm is this scenario's most effective and successful approach. This methodology enhances the capacity to accurately identify and categorize regional and national songs by scrutinizing their lyrical content. This endeavor holds considerable value in safeguarding the cultural abundance of Indonesia.

Text classification is a highly effective instrument that can safeguard Indonesia's abundant cultural legacy [48]. However, it is crucial to acknowledge the potential concern with user engagement. In order to improve this particular aspect, it is necessary to implement the following innovations.

Using text classification algorithms makes classifying folk songs according to their lyrical content possible. This novel methodology allows for the automated categorization of songs into regional or national classifications, thereby providing insights into their unique cultural provenance. In this framework, the historical preservation organization has used sophisticated text categorization algorithms tailored to categorize each song according to its lyrical content. The algorithms undergo rigorous training to identify and analyze complex linguistic patterns, dialects, and cultural references tightly embedded within the lyrics. By integrating technology with culture, our objective is to enhance the preservation of cultural heritage by providing users with an interactive and immersive experience that is both engaging and enriching.

The digital archive can be improved by effectively incorporating metadata [49], which is carefully generated through the complex procedure of text classification. The metadata provided offers significant value as it delves deeper into various aspects of the songs, such as language, dialect, cultural references, and underlying themes. These facts are carefully woven into the fabric of each song, providing a plethora of insights. Proficient text classification algorithms diligently analyze the intricate lyrical elements of each song, exerting continuous effort to uncover concealed valuable insights. A thorough set of metadata is provided for each song entry. The metadata collection encompasses essential details, such as the tribe heritage, regional impacts, linguistic subtleties, and significant theme components intimately integrated into the song's essence. Within this symbiotic integration of technology and culture, the enhanced repository safeguards the intrinsic nature of these musical compositions and affords users a more profound and illuminating examination of Indonesia's intricate cultural fabric.

Empower users with an intuitive and efficient search experience within the digital archive of songs [50]. This cutting-edge feature enables users to quest for specific themes, motifs, or keywords ingeniously woven into the lyrical tapestry, elevating their exploration of the collection to unparalleled heights. A user-friendly digital archive has been meticulously crafted, introducing a robust search functionality that invites users to embark on a lyrical journey of their own making. Within this virtual repository, users wield the power to input their chosen keywords or phrases, embarking on a personalized voyage of discovery. Whether one's curiosity is piqued by themes like "*provinsi* (province)," "*leluhur* ancestors)," or "*pahlawan* (hero)," this ingenious search feature promptly retrieves songs that resonate with the chosen motifs, opening a gateway to a world of cultural richness and artistic expression. This harmonious fusion of technology and tradition invites users to not merely browse but to actively engage, connect, and immerse themselves in the cultural symphony of Indonesia's folk and national songs.

Utilize the outcomes of text categorization to construct a complex web of interrelated folk songs [51], creating a captivating network that entices visitors to delve into the collective cultural components that unite these poetic treasures. The astute application of text classification outcomes infuses vitality into this dynamic network, enabling the system to effortlessly establish connections between various folk tunes originating from different tribes and areas. The provided hyperlinks are not haphazardly connected but rather demonstrate a deliberate establishment of associations rooted in shared linguistic nuances, thematic resonance, or cultural themes. As an illustration, consider a musical composition originating from the Dani tribe, which serves as a reverential homage to the marvels of the natural world. The text classification capabilities enable the identification of a shared affinity between this melody and a song originating from the Asmat tribe, both of which express admiration for the aesthetics of the natural environment. By engaging with these meticulously selected hyperlinks, individuals are invited to go on a profound exploration beyond physical borders, unveiling the intricate fabric of collective encounters, convictions, and manifestations that shape the cultural legacy of Indonesia.

Text classification enables the identification and understanding of every song's subtle intricacies of language and dialect [52]. This invaluable capability not only facilitates accurate translations but also protects linguistic diversity, ensuring that the unique characteristics of each tribe are preserved with the highest level of accuracy. The proficient utilization of text categorization technology effectively decodes the intricate linguistic composition embedded within each musical composition. Adopting this approach enhances the preservation endeavor by enabling the provision of translations that are both authentic and accurate in their resonance. Furthermore, this procedure serves as a forefront in preserving the linguistic legacy of every tribe, valuing the distinct forms of communication and local dialects that delineate their cultural distinctiveness.

Enable consumers to gain valuable contextual insights that have been carefully generated through the rigorous application of text analysis techniques. This inquiry seeks to explore specific phrases or verses' underlying historical, social, and cultural by woven into the lyrical fabric of these folk songs. When individuals interact with the digital archive, they are presented with vast information and expertise. For example, when a user chooses a specific phrase inside a song, the system functions as a tool, revealing the extensive historical and cultural tales interconnected with that particular phrase within the tribal context. Through the provision of significant insights, the preservation endeavor serves as a means to comprehend not only the literal content but also the narratives, customs, and cultural legacy that imbue vitality into every musical composition.

The preservation platform effectively utilizes machine translation capabilities [53], seamlessly incorporating translating song lyrics into multiple languages. Instantly seamless integration of many linguistic elements enables users to effortlessly translate the poetic expressions found in folk music into multiple languages, surpassing the limitations of linguistic barriers. Consequently, these songs serve as a universally accessible conduit, fostering connections among those fluent in the original language and aficionados from other linguistic backgrounds, guaranteeing the widespread resonance of cultural treasures.

The system utilizes text classification techniques to curate customized user recommendations [54], customizing their experience within the archive. The platform utilizes awareness of users' activities and individual interests to provide a curated assortment of folk tunes, cultural narratives, and educational resources that are relevant and engaging. Including individualized elements in the archive guarantees that the user's experience of exploring the collection is not only instructive but also highly captivating, thereby promoting a significant bond with Indonesia's cultural legacy.

Text classification is crucial in deciphering the complex narrative structures and storytelling tactics embedded within the fabric of folk tunes [55]. Through a meticulous examination of the lyrical content, this technological tool can identify and emphasize the repetitive occurrence of topics such as oral traditions, creation narratives, or tribal histories. This perceptive study not only provides illumination on the intricate storytelling traditions but also enhances our understanding and admiration of the cultural importance ingrained within the song narrative structure.

The group promotes a more profound comprehension of the interplay between technology and culture. In pursuing their objective, they conscientiously create extensive teaching materials and guidance. These resources function as informative guides, clarifying the crucial significance of text categorization technology in conserving and examining Indonesian folk music. The organization caters to a wide range of individuals, including educators and students, providing the necessary tools and resources to incorporate these valuable cultural artifacts into their scholarly endeavors effectively. These materials serve as a means to acquaint individuals with the complex mechanisms of text classification while igniting a sense of inspiration to begin a riveting exploration where technology and culture seamlessly intersect.

The involvement of Indonesian experts, tribal elders, and linguists plays a crucial role in the continuous refinement of text classification models. These highly regarded individuals possess significant information, cultural understanding, and linguistic proficiency, which considerably boost the model's accuracy. The active participation of individuals not only guarantees the safeguarding of cultural authenticity but also strengthens the profound correlation between technology and indigenous knowledge. They constitute a collaborative entity committed to preserving Indonesia's cultural heritage for future generations.

The organization is committed to enhancing its text classification algorithms, guaranteeing its efficacy and pertinence in light of incorporating new songs and linguistic discoveries into the archive. The dedication also encompasses staying updated on the most recent developments in NLP technology. NLP enables them to utilize state-of-the-art tools and methodologies further to improve Indonesia's diverse cultural heritage conservation and examination. By remaining at the forefront of advancements in NLP, individuals or organizations can effectively adjust to the ever-changing intricacies of language and guarantee the long-lasting cultural importance of the archive.

Cultural preservation in the context of VUCA environments can be achieved through advanced text classification techniques. One approach is to develop sophisticated algorithms that can analyze vast amounts of textual data related to cultural heritage, traditions, and practices. These algorithms can help identify and classify relevant information, making it easier for organizations and communities to preserve and document their cultural assets. By leveraging natural language processing and machine learning, these text classification systems can contribute to the creation of comprehensive databases, aiding in the conservation of cultural knowledge that may be at risk in the face of rapid changes and uncertainties.

Furthermore, text classification can play a crucial role in identifying and addressing potential threats to cultural preservation. By analyzing textual data related to economic, political, and social changes, these systems can help organizations anticipate challenges that may impact cultural heritage. For example, the identification of potential risks such as political instability or economic downturns through text analysis can enable proactive measures to safeguard cultural artifacts, practices, and traditions. This application of text classification aligns with the broader goal of integrating technological solutions into cultural preservation strategies to ensure the resilience and continuity of cultural elements in the face of a VUCA environment.

4 Conclusion

An extensive investigation into Indonesia's cultural legacy is revealed within the text classification domain. Songs, regardless of their origin at a regional or national level, are categorized according to the textual material they include. This categorization process involves the utilization of three specific methods: Multinomial Naive Bayes (MNB), Support Vector Machine (SVM), and K-Nearest Neighbor (KNN). The number of labels dramatically influences the performance of a system, and SVM exhibit notable consistency and precision, particularly in situations involving binary and multi-label classifications.

This undertaking explores the differentiation between regional and national songs, whereby regional songs manifest the varied languages and dialects of particular geographic regions, while national anthems express the fundamental characteristics of a nation. Text classification algorithms effectively identify unique language patterns, such as TF-IDF and SVM. Among these techniques, SVM stands out as the most proficient performer. The preservation initiative is a tribute to Indonesia's abundant cultural heritage.

The primary objective of this initiative is to establish a connection between technology and culture by providing educational resources and engaging the expertise of individuals such as tribe elders, linguists, and other knowledgeable professionals. The archive's enduring cultural significance is guaranteed by its dedication to continually enhancing and integrating cutting-edge NLP technologies. This narrative exemplifies the integration of technology and tradition, safeguarding Indonesia's cultural heritage for future generations.

Acknowledgments. Knowledge Engineering and Data Science (KEDS) Center, Universitas Negeri Malang, and AGH University of Kraków.

Disclosure of Interests. The authors have no competing interests to declare that are relevant to the content of this article.

References

1. Fatmawati, E.: Strategies to grow a proud attitude towards Indonesian cultural diversity. Linguist. Cult. Rev. **5**(S1), 810–820 (2021). https://doi.org/10.21744/lingcure.v5nS1.1465
2. Awerman, A., Sina, I., Yurisman, B.W., Hendri, Y.: The role of music arts in multicultural education. J. Sci. Res. Educ. Technol. **2**(2), 769–781 (2023). https://doi.org/10.58526/jsret.v2i2.161
3. Erlina, B.: Implementation of protection of traditional cultural expression in west lampung regency. Leg. Br. **11**(3), 1990–2004 (2022). https://doi.org/10.35335/legal
4. Astuti, K.S., Langit, P.V.: The influence of Arabic, Chinese, Western, and Hindu Cultures on the Indonesian folk songs. In: Asia-Pacific Symposium for Music Education Research, pp. 272–279 (2023)
5. Cohen, M.I.: Three eras of Indonesian arts diplomacy. Bijdr. tot taal-, land- en Volkenkd. / J. Humanit. Soc. Sci. Southeast Asia **175**(2–3), 253–283 (2019). https://doi.org/10.1163/22134379-17502022
6. Suhardjono, L.A.: Battling for shared culture between Indonesia and Malaysia in the social media era. Humaniora **3**(1), 58 (2012). https://doi.org/10.21512/humaniora.v3i1.3234

7. Pot, A., Porkert, J., Keijzer, M.: The bidirectional in bilingual: cognitive, social and linguistic effects of and on third-age language learning. Behav. Sci. (Basel) **9**(9), 98 (2019). https://doi.org/10.3390/bs9090098

8. Trang, K., Nguyen, A.H.: A comparative study of machine learning-based approach for network traffic classification. Knowl. Eng. Data Sci. **4**(2), 128 (2022). https://doi.org/10.17977/um018v4i22021p128-137

9. Chuttur, M.Y., Parianen, Y.: A comparison of machine learning models to prioritise emails using emotion analysis for customer service excellence. Knowl. Eng. Data Sci. **5**(1), 41 (2022). https://doi.org/10.17977/um018v5i12022p41-52

10. Iddrisu, I., Appiahene, P., Appiah, O., Fuseini, I.: Exploring the impact of students demographic attributes on performance prediction through binary classification in the KDP model. Knowl. Eng. Data Sci. **6**(1), 24 (2023). https://doi.org/10.17977/um018v6i12023p24-40

11. Pujianto, U., Setiawan, A.L., Rosyid, H.A., Salah, A.M.M.: Comparison of Naïve Bayes Algorithm and Decision Tree C4.5 for Hospital Readmission Diabetes Patients using HbA1c Measurement. Knowl. Eng. Data Sci. **2**(2), 58 (2019). https://doi.org/10.17977/um018v2i2 2019p58-71

12. Yu, X., et al.: Synergizing the enhanced RIME with fuzzy K-nearest neighbor for diagnose of pulmonary hypertension. Comput. Biol. Med.. Biol. Med. **165**, 107408 (2023). https://doi.org/10.1016/j.compbiomed.2023.107408

13. Gokalp, O., Tasci, E., Ugur, A.: A novel wrapper feature selection algorithm based on iterated greedy metaheuristic for sentiment classification. Expert Syst. Appl. **146**, 113176 (2020). https://doi.org/10.1016/j.eswa.2020.113176

14. Jin, W., Pei, J., Xie, P., Chen, J., Zhao, H.: Machine learning-based prediction of mechanical properties and performance of nickel-graphene nanocomposites using molecular dynamics simulation data. ACS Appl. Nano Mater. **6**(13), 12190–12199 (2023). https://doi.org/10.1021/acsanm.3c01919

15. Naseem, U., Razzak, I., Eklund, P.W.: A survey of pre-processing techniques to improve short-text quality: a case study on hate speech detection on twitter. Multimed. Tools Appl. **80**(28–29), 35239–35266 (2021). https://doi.org/10.1007/s11042-020-10082-6

16. Budiarto, L., Rokhman, N.M., Uriu, W.: Bulletin of social informatics theory and application uncovering negative sentiments: a study of indonesian twitter users' health opinions on coffee consumption, vol. 7, no. 1, pp. 24–31 (2023)

17. Ridzuan, F., Wan Zainon, W.M.N.: A review on data cleansing methods for big data. Procedia Comput. Sci. **161**, 731–738 (2019). https://doi.org/10.1016/j.procs.2019.11.177

18. Omran, E., Al Tararwah, E., Al Qundus, J.: A comparative analysis of machine learning algorithms for hate speech detection in social media. Online J. Commun. Media Technol. **13**(4), e202348 (2023). https://doi.org/10.30935/ojcmt/13603

19. Luo, X., Li, X., Goh, Y.M., Song, X., Liu, Q.: Application of machine learning technology for occupational accident severity prediction in the case of construction collapse accidents. Saf. Sci.. Sci. **163**, 106138 (2023). https://doi.org/10.1016/j.ssci.2023.106138

20. Bhawna, A., Gurunath, G., Shashwat, V., Yogesh, S.: Natural Language Processing Based Two-Stage Machine Learning Model for Automatic Mapping of Activity Codes Using Drilling Descriptions, May 2023. https://doi.org/10.2118/214522-MS

21. Zhao, S., Zhu, L., Wang, X., Yang, Y.: CenterCLIP: token clustering for efficient text-video retrieval. In: Proceedings of the 45th International ACM SIGIR Conference on Research and Development in Information Retrieval, pp. 970–981, July 2022. https://doi.org/10.1145/347 7495.3531950

22. Dogra, V., et al.: A complete process of text classification system using state-of-the-Art NLP models. Comput. Intell. Neurosci.. Intell. Neurosci. **2022**, 1–26 (2022). https://doi.org/10.1155/2022/1883698

23. Lan, F.: Research on text similarity measurement hybrid algorithm with term semantic information and TF-IDF method. Adv. Multimed. **2022**, 1–11 (2022). https://doi.org/10.1155/2022/7923262

24. Sahlaoui, H., Alaoui, E.A.A., Agoujil, S., Nayyar, A.: An empirical assessment of smote variants techniques and interpretation methods in improving the accuracy and the interpretability of student performance models. Educ. Inf. Technol. (2023). https://doi.org/10.1007/s10639-023-12007-w

25. Asadi, R., et al.: Self-paced ensemble-SHAP approach for the classification and interpretation of crash severity in work zone areas. Sustainability **15**(11), 9076 (2023). https://doi.org/10.3390/su15119076

26. Alamri, M., Ykhlef, M.: Survey of credit card anomaly and fraud detection using sampling techniques. Electronics **11**(23), 4003 (2022). https://doi.org/10.3390/electronics11234003

27. Reddy, B.A.C., Chandra, G.K., Sisodia, D.S., Anuragi, A.: Balancing techniques for improving automated detection of hate speech and offensive language on social media. In: 2023 2nd International Conference for Innovation in Technology (INOCON), pp. 1–8, March 2023. https://doi.org/10.1109/INOCON57975.2023.10101157

28. Prost, J., Boidi, G., Puhwein, A.M., Varga, M., Vorlaufer, G.: Classification of operational states in porous journal bearings using a semi-supervised multi-sensor Machine Learning approach. Tribol. Int.. Int. **184**, 108464 (2023). https://doi.org/10.1016/j.triboint.2023.108464

29. Shahbazi, M., Shirali, A., Aghajan, H., Nili, H.: Using distance on the Riemannian manifold to compare representations in brain and in models. Neuroimage **239**, 118271 (2021). https://doi.org/10.1016/j.neuroimage.2021.118271

30. Mandagi, F.M.D., Paat, F.J., Tooy, D., Pakasi, S.E., Wantasen, S.: Web-based system for medicinal plants identification using convolutional neural network. Bull. Soc. Informatics Theory Appl. **6**(2), 158–167 (2022)

31. Yip, S.W., Kiluk, B., Scheinost, D.: Toward addiction prediction: an overview of cross-validated predictive modeling findings and considerations for future neuroimaging research. Biol. Psychiatry Cogn. Neurosci. Neuroimaging **5**(8), 748–758 (2020). https://doi.org/10.1016/j.bpsc.2019.11.001

32. Uddin, S., Haque, I., Lu, H., Moni, M.A., Gide, E.: Comparative performance analysis of K-nearest neighbour (KNN) algorithm and its different variants for disease prediction. Sci. Rep. **12**(1), 1–11 (2022). https://doi.org/10.1038/s41598-022-10358-x

33. Park, K., Hong, J.S., Kim, W.: A methodology combining cosine similarity with classifier for text classification. Appl. Artif. Intell.Artif. Intell. **34**(5), 396–411 (2020). https://doi.org/10.1080/08839514.2020.1723868

34. Parlak, B.: A novel feature and class-based globalization technique for text classification. Multimed. Tools Appl. (2023). https://doi.org/10.1007/s11042-023-15459-x

35. Chen, L.-X., Su, S.-W., Liao, C.-H., Wong, K.-S., Yuan, S.-M.: An open automation system for predatory journal detection. Sci. Rep. **13**(1), 2976 (2023). https://doi.org/10.1038/s41598-023-30176-z

36. Hasan, M., Ullah, S., Khan, M.J., Khurshid, K.: Comparative analysis of SVM, ann and cnn for classifying vegetation species using hyperspectral thermal infrared data. Int. Arch. Photogramm. Remote Sens. Spat. Inf. Sci. - ISPRS Arch., vol. 42, no. 2/W13, 1861–1868 (2019). https://doi.org/10.5194/isprs-archives-XLII-2-W13-1861-2019

37. Zhao, D., Liu, H., Zheng, Y., He, Y., Lu, D., Lyu, C.: A reliable method for colorectal cancer prediction based on feature selection and support vector machine. Med. Biol. Eng. Comput.Comput. **57**(4), 901–912 (2019). https://doi.org/10.1007/s11517-018-1930-0

38. Mohan, L., Pant, J., Suyal, P., Kumar, A.: Support vector machine accuracy improvement with classification. In: 2020 12th International Conference on Computational Intelligence and Communication Networks (CICN), pp. 477–481, September 2020. https://doi.org/10.1109/CICN49253.2020.9242572

39. Tang, X., Ma, Z., Hu, Q., Tang, W.: A real-time arrhythmia heartbeats classification algorithm using parallel delta modulations and rotated linear-kernel support vector machines. IEEE Trans. Biomed. Eng. **67**(4), 978–986 (2020). https://doi.org/10.1109/TBME.2019.2926104

40. Gopi, A.P., Jyothi, R.N.S., Narayana, V.L., Sandeep, K.S.: Classification of tweets data based on polarity using improved RBF kernel of SVM. Int. J. Inf. Technol. **15**(2), 965–980 (2023). https://doi.org/10.1007/s41870-019-00409-4

41. Vinge, R., McKelvey, T.: Understanding support vector machines with polynomial kernels. In: 2019 27th European Signal Processing Conference (EUSIPCO), pp. 1–5, September 2019. https://doi.org/10.23919/EUSIPCO.2019.8903042

42. Kalcheva, N., Karova, M., Penev, I.: Comparison of the accuracy of SVM kernel functions in text classification. In: 2020 International Conference on Biomedical Innovations and Applications (BIA), pp. 141–145, , September 2020. https://doi.org/10.1109/BIA50171.2020.9244278

43. Kaur, H., Ahsaan, S.U., Alankar, B., Chang, V.: A proposed sentiment analysis deep learning algorithm for analyzing COVID-19 tweets. Inf. Syst. Front. **23**(6), 1417–1429 (2021). https://doi.org/10.1007/s10796-021-10135-7

44. Paidipati, K.K., Chesneau, C., Nayana, B.M., Kumar, K.R., Polisetty, K., Kurangi, C.: Prediction of rice cultivation in india—support vector regression approach with various kernels for non-linear patterns. AgriEngineering **3**(2), 182–198 (2021). https://doi.org/10.3390/agriengineering3020012

45. Nie, F., Zhu, W., Li, X.: Decision tree SVM: an extension of linear SVM for non-linear classification. Neurocomputing **401**, 153–159 (2020). https://doi.org/10.1016/j.neucom.2019.10.051

46. Ghosh, S., Dasgupta, A., Swetapadma, A.: A study on support vector machine based linear and non-linear pattern classification. In: 2019 International Conference on Intelligent Sustainable Systems (ICISS), pp. 24–28, February 2019. https://doi.org/10.1109/ISS1.2019.8908018

47. S. N., S. Wagle, Ghosh, P., Kishore, K.: Sentiment classification of English and Hindi music lyrics using supervised machine learning algorithms. In: 2022 2nd Asian Conference on Innovation in Technology (ASIANCON), pp. 1–6, August 2022. https://doi.org/10.1109/ASIANCON55314.2022.9908688

48. Wang, N., Zhao, X., Wang, L., Zou, Z.: Novel system for rapid investigation and damage detection in cultural heritage conservation based on deep learning. J. Infrastruct. Syst., vol. 25, no. 3, September 2019. https://doi.org/10.1061/(ASCE)IS.1943-555X.0000499

49. Miller, S.J.: Metadata for digital collections. American Library Association (2022)

50. Schröder, A.M., Ghajargar, M.: Unboxing the algorithm: designing an understandable algorithmic experience in music recommender systems (2021)

51. Gao, H., Zeng, X., Yao, C.: Application of improved distributed naive Bayesian algorithms in text classification. J. Supercomput.Supercomput. **75**(9), 5831–5847 (2019). https://doi.org/10.1007/s11227-019-02862-1

52. Angeline, G., Wibawa, A.P., Pujianto, U.: Klasifikasi Dialek Bahasa Jawa Menggunakan Metode Naives Bayes. J. Mnemon. **5**(2), 103–110 (2022). https://doi.org/10.36040/mnemonic.v5i2.4748

53. Dedes, K., Putra Utama, A.B., Wibawa, A.P., Afandi, A.N., Handayani, A.N., Hernandez, L.: Neural machine translation of Spanish-English food recipes using LSTM. JOIV Int. J. Informatics Vis. **6**(2), 290 (2022). https://doi.org/10.30630/joiv.6.2.804

54. Minaee, S., Kalchbrenner, N., Cambria, E., Nikzad, N., Chenaghlu, M., Gao, J.: Deep learning–based text classification. ACM Comput. Surv.Comput. Surv. **54**(3), 1–40 (2022). https://doi.org/10.1145/3439726

55. Krishnan, A., Vincent, A., Jos, G., Rajan, R.: Multimodal fusion for segment classification in folk music. In: 2021 IEEE 18th India Council International Conference (INDICON), pp. 1–7, December 2021. https://doi.org/10.1109/INDICON52576.2021.9691751

The Evolution of Immersive Video Creation

Yuxiao Yi[1] and Xinyu Li[2(✉)]

[1] School of Architecture and Design, Beijing Jiaotong University, Beijing, China
Yuxiaoyi@bjtu.edu.cn
[2] Beijing Jiaotong University, Beijing, China
18405480108@163.com

Abstract. XR technology leads the arrival of spatial computing, and outlines a clearer form for the immersive experience of image -- "ultimate cinema". From the birth of film to interactive film, to VR film and game, it provides us with a revolutionary vein of image technology media and immersive experience, and finally points to immersive theater. From the Minimalism space to public art, the physical liberation of performance art provides us with a theoretical vein of art history in which the audience is constantly enlarged and the body experience is advanced. In the development of games, Positive Psychology and Maslow's Hierarchy of Needs provide theoretical support for the occurrence of immersive experience, and have achieved remarkable results in practice. Finally, with the integration of technology and theory, immersive theater and the ultimate form of VR, the holodeck based on XR is becoming more and more visible, allowing us to glimpse the opportunities and difficulties that future immersive experience may face. At the same time, we should be more aware of the original intention of human's pursuit of immersive experience, and avoid the domination of technology over people.

Keywords: Immersive Experience · Spatial Computing · Video Creation · Extended Reality

1 The Evolution of the Medium of Immersive Experience

Extended Reality is a kind of "immersive" visual technology that starts from strengthening the "perception" of the body and builds "immersion" as the foundation, thus blurring the boundary between virtual and reality and eliminating the barriers of "image" and "object" coexistence between virtual and reality [1]. XR dates back to 1961, when Charles Wyckoff patented his film, allowing people to see and explode and other images beyond the range of human vision [2].

When we talk about immersive experiences, we should ask why humans have long desired immersive experiences, and how immersive experiences can better serve humanity. What ideas drive our behavior behind our pursuit of immersive experiences. It is worth noting that excessive immersive experience is also more likely to let the society fall into a profit-seeking cycle filled by the landscape. Finally, it will not only dissolve the user experience, but also go against the original intention of immersive experience.

N. A. Streitz and S. Konomi (Eds.): HCII 2024, LNCS 14719, pp. 307–321, 2024.
https://doi.org/10.1007/978-3-031-60012-8_19

The art of cinema has been regarded as a kind of magic since its birth. In 1895, when the Lumiere brothers showed "The Arrival of a Train" on the screen, people ran away in fear because they could not tell the difference between the video and the real world [3]. After a short period of panic and resistance, people began to like this game, and were happy to be more immersed in it. The emergence of the cinema allows the audience to enjoy a surround music experience and a black box space while watching the movie, which makes people more focused on the story on the screen. In this screen space, emotions, sorrows and various extraordinary experiences can occur. It seems dangerous, but the audience can keep a safe distance from it, this kind of immersion and safety isolation is fascinating to audience. This sense of stillness is due to the presence of the fourth wall [4], a psychological barrier between the audience and the stage [5].

Film editing, Montage, and Lens group received began to simulate more realistic visual image selection mechanisms between human blinks. First of all, in the shooting, the camera is always around the axis in order to create a real three-dimensional space, while hiding the camera according to different fields and camera positions, and with the help of a variety of field switching presents a sense of "presence", and at this time the audience does not feel the existence of the camera [6]. Film editing, on the other hand, filters images more precisely and directs the eye to focus on narrative points. For example, close-ups are used to enlarge the audience's eyes' attention to something, and empty lenses are used "Cinematographic visual phenomena are real in the real world, they are not accidental psychological phenomena, but a necessary method of our cognition of the world: we must cut the real world into disjointed fragments, otherwise the display world will become like an endless, unspaced punctuation, completely uncontrollable string of letters."Sitting in a darkened cinema, we can find that watching the edited film is a startlingly familiar experience, "closer to our mind than anything else," as Huston put it." [7].

Film creators try to create a nearly infinite screen and space, so that the image completely enveloped the audience. The traditional film simulates a kind of theater in the form of watching and experiencing. Cinema screens are getting wider and bigger, Imax, 3D movies and other trends make the movie screen more and more like a black hole, surrounding and attracting the audience's line of sight, trying to make the audience not feel the existence of the screen and immerse. The spatial case in the film began in the decade 1960–1969, and artists continued to expand the rangers of film. Deconstruct the components of storytelling, environment, sound, viewership and other aspects individually. In the year 1970, Gene Youngblood introduced the notion of Expanded Cinema, which served as a connection between the broad idea of motion pictures and the Moving Image [8]. In the realm of visual motion, be it in the form of cinema, animated content, or dynamically generated digital imagery, there exists a concept of images that undergo continuous transformation in practical application. Whether it is film or animation or digital computer-generated dynamic image, from the concept of moving image, it belongs to the image concept that is constantly changing in the continuous attempt [9]. In the 1960s and 1970s, contemporary artists explored the cinema space, and "extended cinema" attempted to break the power structure of the cinema, liberate the film, and let the audience participate in the interaction with the film [10]. The emergence of head-mounted devices allows the creation of VR immersion to unfold. In 1962, Morton Heilig, the inventor of the Sensoroma, the first reality device in the history of virtual reality, was convinced that the five senses were better than the eyes and ears to experience the film [11].

In 1965, Ivan Sutherland discussed virtual reality in his paper "Ultimate Display" and developed the earliest VR headsets. People can enter the immersive video experience anytime, anywhere through VR glasses [12]. At the same time, in many theaters and performances, creators combine ready-made products, installations, buildings and screens in the scene to confuse the space of the scene, making people feel as if they are in a specific scene and breaking the limitations of the existing space. With the development of technology, many digital media art through holographic projection, AR presentation, virtual projection to architecture and other ways, let people experience the real and virtual confusion. For example, there are more and more naked-eye 3D screens (Using the parallax characteristics of the human eyes, without the need for any auxiliary equipment, you can obtain a realistic three-dimensional image display system with space and depth.) in urban public space. In Pull&Bear's naked-eye 3D advertisement, according to the design image of the original external wall of the building, the facade of the building falls like a newspaper at the beginning of the advertisement, and the giant in the image seems to walk out of the screen at any time.

Compared with VR's helmet-mounted glasses, AR's mobile phones, ipads and other screen imaging, XR in wearable devices through lighter glasses headset seamlessly stitching digital content and physical space. Apple's new generation of headsets, the Apple Vision Pro, launched on January 19, 2024, ushered people into the era of spatial computing. Through the wearing of the headset, the frame limit of the traditional screen can be released, and various applications can be more closely adapted to the real space. User can easily interact with the projected image with the help of gesture control, and control its angle, size, split and combination at will. This seems to add a layer to the real physical world, when the image presented by this layer is in contact with the real world, it will also produce natural projection and clear occlusion relationship, combined with ultra-low delay and ultra-high picture accuracy to produce a "hyperreality" vision. This design enables users to better enter the "immersive environment", achieve a "reality play", experience the editing reality, coding reality play experience [13]. This "holodeck" immersive interactive system model with real-time feedback originally came from the virtual interactive environment in the science fiction film Star Trek [14]. The term "holodeck" refers to an immersive interactive system model that meets the needs of immersive and interactive storytelling, with real-time presentation and real-time feedback [15].

In Disney's Pirates of the Caribbean play project, the sculpture of the sunken ship, the water and the screen block each other, creating a place space where the screen and the installation are confused [16]. When the image of the underwater world is shown on the screen, the visitor seems to be at the bottom of the sea, and when the camera is raised, the viewer seems to rise from the bottom of the sea to the surface. Disney's clever combination of screen and device makes people forget that this is an image, thus creating a more immersive feeling. Through the designer's grasp of the perspective of the scene, the harmony of tone and light, it forms a continuous and real three-dimensional space with the foreground device. This kind of riding system breaks the original mode that the audience can only watch the movie fixed, greatly improves the audience's participation, and simulates a new experience of entering the movie, and truly feels the scene they are in with the protagonists in the story, which can also arouse people's empathy.

In the audience's viewing experience, people are not satisfied with the static form of sitting in the cinema, and hope to develop more vivid viewing experience. Except to make the screen disappear as much as possible. In addition to breaking the fourth wall, how to let the audience move into the screen has become another research and development route for immersive experience. Disney developed its own EMV in-car system and Soarin 'Hover system, essentially a "movable" scat hat allows viewers to travel through the movie space to immerse themselves. The project "Soar - Over the Horizon" uses Soarin's flying seat with a spherical screen to simulate the first human perspective of flying over the Earth by controlling the lift, tilt and rotation of the seat and the motion track of the camera [17]. Soarin's flying seat system can create a sense of weightlessness in the air to accelerate and dive, and in different areas to modulated with the characteristics of the ground scent, even with water droplets, wind and other touch, fully activate the sense of smell. It makes people feel as if they are flying in different places on the earth.

2   The Form of Interactive Video

The disappearance of the fourth screen and the intervention of the audience construct the ultimate form of immersive experience: immersive theater. In art museums, artists use multi-screen or Installation methods to break the linear narrative, allowing viewers to reorganize time in the free viewing of space. In the art museum, various elements and characteristics of the film are separated and integrated into the exhibition of the art museum in the new combination. The still frames in a film can become photographic works, different story lines can become fragments of stories, and scenes can become theaters. Wu Chao's animation theater "Happening" is an animated video work with many parallel story lines [18] (Fig. 1). She divides these different story lines into individual elements scattered in various corners of the museum. The audience keeps picking up the plot by chance according to the order they visit, and finally see different versions of the story. This process of fragmentation and reorganization is a deconstruction of the film's diachronic linear narrative, but more importantly, the artist hopes to make the work evoke different experiences. The audience may first be attracted by the events they are interested in, and then complete the montage process by themselves through layers of excavation, and finally form a viewpoint that is more in line with their emotional experience. This kind of viewing and participation makes it easier for the audience to get deeply involved in the film. The process of the audience visiting the exhibition is also the process of generating new stories.

The narrative of the film calls for more audience participation and greater freedom. After the basic linear narrative, the film explores narrative modes such as open-ended ending and circular narrative, and finally produces interactive film branches that intersect with games. In the film Kinoautomat (1967), the audience's vote will change the plot of the film [19].

Fig. 1. Wu Chao, "Happening", Experimental Animation Theater, (2013).

These examples can all be seen as movies' attempts at interactivity and openness. This kind of interaction experiment was more and more applied to games after the advent of games. With the advent of interactive technology, audience engagement can be fed back more immediately and become more intuitive based on data visualization. The identity reconstruction, interactive participation and temporary performance of the virtual world create a super-real world representation. Receivers actively engage their sensory faculties to partake in the experience, their actions are translated into the syntax of human-computer interaction, and relevant information is acquired within the virtual realm. In this type of interactive and immersive encounter, the audience actively engages in interacting with the artworks, thereby influencing the overall creative process. The project "One Beat One Tree" by Naziha Mestaoui, a Belgian artist, employs interactive technology that captures the viewer's heartbeat through sensors and transmits it to a database [20]. As a result of this real-time interaction, a digital virtual tree grows synchronously with the participant's heartbeat. On the eve of the COP21 Climate Conference in Paris in December 2015, the artist was on top of the city's famous landmarks [21]. In the immersive interactive work Periscopista, the interactive data can actually receive the participants' rich body signals, such as the movement language, and transform the signals into visual images via a controlled device. The signals of the body, which cannot be perceived by vision, are digitally converted into visual images, evoking another perception of one's physical behavior and a new experience of "body-world" interaction.

Intersections between theater, art history, film history, and various other disciplines can be observed. Immersive theater is an all-encompassing artistic medium that combines different art forms during the era of media revolution. It incorporates performance, conceptualization, theatrical elements, visual imagery, auditory components, video integration, and other diverse artistic genres. Immersive theater strives to emancipate inactive spectators, activate their sensory perception, and engage them in the collaborative process of artistic production [22]. With the progress of technology, it has become a development trend to make the screen more invisible and eliminate the fourth screen between the image and people. People are always pursuing a faster, more undifferentiated access to some kind of hybrid virtual reality, equipment is becoming lighter and lighter, and immersive theater is becoming more and more common. Immersive theater will also become more and more common and diverse. With the development of experience economy and atmosphere economy, many shopping malls will build the shopping scene into immersive theater. XR technology also makes us have new expectations for the realization of "ultimate cinema". At the same time, when watching the image, the headset can simulate the theater or outdoor environment, and realize the isolation from the real physical space. Beyond the limitation of space, the movie is more private and more free, so that the audience can be liberated from the power space of the theater, and then realize the "ultimate theater" that can be fully immersed.

The image interactivity of the exhibition reality is an important factor that differs from the immersion degree of traditional media. The traditional interactive film "Late Shift" makes use of the options in the interface to make the story develop in the direction chosen by the audience during the development of the story, which requires the audience to concentrate on and devote themselves to feel the smooth plot [23]. With the support of extended reality technology, interactive narrative images allow the audience to see the world in a controlled and more empathetic state. Through eyes, gestures and voice command transmission, combined with motion capture, motion tracking and other technologies, the audience can interact with the characters and plots in the virtual images, participate in the image narrative through their own choices, change the development of the plot and affect the outcome of the story. The hypertext narrative structure brought by the interactive image narrative presented from the perspective of this virtual technology breaks through the closed narrative structure of the traditional film, and enables the audience to have a physical behavior mode of self-exploration in which they are completely immersed and give full play to their subjective initiative, while generating more profound self-insights.

3   The Priority of the Audience – In the Two Aspects of Psychology and Cybernetics

At present, the research on experience is becoming more and more prominent, behind which is the continuous improvement of the status of the audience as an audience in artistic creation. Since the Italian Renaissance, philosophy and art have constructed ideals of beauty and model. Plato established the kingdom of ideas, elevating sense above sensibility, and he believed that only reason could grasp the truth [24]. He classifies human senses according to the position of human senses and body, vision and hearing are closest to the mind, because the eyes are located at the top of the human brain, so "vision" is regarded as the noblest feeling [25]. Thus, the power construction of visual viewing is completed.

After the Renaissance, in the western visual art creation, focus perspective helps painters to create a better spatial depth and more real painting space [26]. In the church zenith painting, the use of perspective can also create a sense of immersion in the sublime. This sense of immersion fully considers the position and distance between the viewer, as an audience, and the work of art when he is in the building or the gallery, and strengthens the nobility of the art. At the same time, panoramas are a more immersive representation of the scene. However, the power system of viewing the constructed "work" and "audience" was criticized in the 19th century. The concept of assigning worth to labor underwent a significant transformation during the 1800s. Ever since Kant, the focus of philosophy has shifted towards examining the individual. In what manner does the subject take form? What does the term "human" refer to? Prominent thinkers like Nietzsche, Schopenhauer, Sartre, Heidegger, Foucault, Husserl, and Lacan increasingly focus on the position of the individual - human beings [27]. With the growing emphasis on subjectivity, there has been a surge in studying behaviors associated with the individual as an object of investigation [28]. At present, the significance of being empowered through observation becomes highly crucial, transcending its mere simplicity as a passive action and instead serving as a behavioral manifestation aligned with the influential force encompassed within the domain. Jacques Ranciere argued that seeing is the opposite of knowing, in which the viewer is confronted with the landscape of appearances without knowing how the images they are looking at have been created [29]. Seeing is the opposite of doing. The audience in the viewing state is stationary in their seats, lacking any power to act and intervene. The audience lacks the means for active cognitive processing and taking action [30]. At this time, the era of the audience opened the prelude, and thus launched the public and interactive discussion of art.

In the 1800s, Hans Robert Jauss, a scholar specializing in literature, introduced the notion of 'Receptional Aesthetic', which revolutionized literary studies by presenting a fresh approach [31]. He conducted a fresh examination of literary works, taking into account the viewpoint of readers. The fundamental idea behind this concept is to initiate from the viewers and commence from their perception, thereby highlighting the significance of personal encounter, approval, and engagement [32]. The fundamental idea behind this concept is to initiate from the viewers and commence from their perception, thereby highlighting the significance of personal encounter, approval, and engagement. The audience's role has evolved from being a mere passive receiver to actively engaging with the work and contributing their subjective experience. The creator's involvement in shaping this participation is increasingly crucial, as the acceptance and active involvement of the audience ultimately culminate in the completion of the work [33]. M.h. Abrams put forward the idea that nearly all comprehensive theories of art emphasize four distinct components within the overall context of a work of art: the artwork itself, the creator, the subject matter the audience [34]. The involvement of the audience in the work is becoming more and more significant.

In the realm of visual art, following the era of minimalistic painting during the 1960s, the shift took place when the display area underwent a change and became an innovative realm, where viewers were no more just passive onlookers of particular artworks but actively participated in an immersive theatrical encounter facilitated by installations [35]. The emergence of installation art has completed the transformation of the audience's experience from watching to walking into the works. The installation artist extends his authority beyond an individual piece to encompass the entire exhibition as a whole, while considering the entirety of the gallery's public space. The utilization of installation art in the spatial expansion also offers an additional theoretical foundation for theatricalization. The entire area has the potential to serve as an immersive exploration, wherein the regulations governing the space are collaboratively established by both artists and observers [36].

The emergence of digital interactive art, video installation and new media theater use the combination of virtual and reality to break people's cognition of the existing space and make the immersive experience more diversified. The connectivity and interactivity of new media art have dissolved the ability of artistic subjects to generate influence. In the interactive installation, there has been a rise in the degree of independence bestowed upon the viewers. The art museum has gradually shifted from the white box to the black box, with more and more emphasis on the interactivity of works and the increasingly enhanced theatrical properties.

Maurice Merluau-Pnoty put forward the concept of Body Image in his Phenomenology of Perception. He believes that the body as a medium language is a bridge to express the external objective world and the internal subjective world. We have a world through our bodies, and the world responds to our experiences in embodied manifestations. Human beings and the world give physical experience and form an original sense of "Chi-asm" existential relationship [37].

Simultaneously, people begin to give greater consideration to the importance of the irrational level after reflecting on the "instrumental rationality" caused by the age of reason. The French Theatre theorist Antonin Artaud proposed the theory of "Theatre of Cruelty", which pointed out that the sensibility should be used to subvert the suppression of reason, learning from Eastern drama, religion and witchcraft, and using the almost insane physical feelings to recover the spirit of art [38]. "Aalto explained the theory of cruel theater, and he called for the establishment of an outlet theater to replace the traditional art theater of traditional, rational, elite, and intellectual emotional feelings [39]." This theory also brought about great changes in drama and dance works.

"Merleau Ponty's phenomenology of perception proposes that emotions and emotional acceptance are not achieved through pure rational thinking, but through embodied bodily perception. All senses are spatial, and there is a close and transcendent connection between the film and the audience's body [40]". In the film, the audience's visual experience is mainly mobilized, while in the immersive image creation, the body's various awareness experiences are more fully mobilized. Just like when experiencing "Over the Horizon", the fragrance stimulates the sense of smell, the wind stimulates the sense of touch, and the seat simulates the rise and fall of the body in flight.

In the immersive interactive work Rain Room, the controller senses the position of people walking in the space and controls the rain from falling on the audience [41]. As if the audience had an invisible umbrella on top of their head, they walked freely in the rain, and this experience changed the physical experience of rain drops falling on people in rainy days. It's a novel experience that doesn't exist in the natural world, so it's all the more fascinating for the audience.

The proposal of phenomenology of body makes us realize that the connection between human and the world can be infinitely closer through experience [42]. This trend of thought has also influenced people's continuous hope to let the audience participate in a work and establish a relationship with it, instead of becoming a relationship between the subject of creation and the object of appreciation. Body phenomenology brings the experience of immersive creation to the dimension of liberating human body so as to better perceive the world. At present, the purpose of mobilizing the audience's physical experience is not to provide more sensory dimensions. There are more interactions for the sake of interaction, and people do not have too many new experiences. This kind of set interaction is actually a planned narrative. And the purpose of art is to inspire people to establish a connection with the world through the body, to link and get a richer world image through the body experience, so as to lead the audience to a broader life experience.

In the field of games, the study of experience has been unprecedentedly detailed. Games developed rapidly in the 1970s, integrating narrative, network, and engine successively, showing a richer face [43]. Game experience design has made a detailed study of the audience's spiritual experience. Its theoretical support is mainly based on modern psychology, especially positive psychology. In terms of experience, games have been more successful than any other art form. Because game designers, above all, care about the experience of the game [44]. What a game designer really cares about is creating that experience, and he or she must use all means at his or her disposal to grasp, understand, and master the essence of the human experience.

Game designers use a variety of technologies and tools, mainly related to digital media, to design, through the implementation of five senses to stimulate the experience, so that they can concentrate, immerse, and even forget themselves, and finally obtain satisfaction and happiness. And the interactive experience of the game, the increasingly realistic images and the huge information engine make this immersion more vivid, as if to tell the audience: this is not only an absolutely safe world, but also a world that you can dominate, you are absolutely free and will not be punished. Games are often criticized as addictive entertainment, but this is precisely the success of user-centered immersive experiences created by designers. In many games, the player automatically brings in the emotions of the character and they can't disengage from the immersive virtual world even if the game is over.

Modern psychology and human needs have contributed a lot to the experiential success of games. The flow theory was first proposed by Mihaly Csikszentmihalyi, who argued that people are so completely immersed in an activity that they forget about their surroundings and the passage of time [45]. People feel a balance between their skills and challenges, and this balance is key to a state of Mental flow [45]. At the same time, people feel that their actions and consciousness are one, with no obvious sense of self [45]. This is a process in which both the senses and the heart forget the self at the same time and become completely immersed in a particular environment.

Game designers follow positive psychology and try to create an immersive flow experience for the audience from the design of positive emotions, flow experiences and gameplay. Flow is a theory developed by American psychologist Mihaly Csikszentmihalyi in 1975 [46]. Flow is a state, when people enter this state, they will be completely attracted and immersed in an activity and ignore the influence of the surrounding things. At the same time, the experience itself is enjoyable, so that people are willing to pay a huge price [47]. Csikszentmihalyii believes that the conditions for the realization of flow activities include eight elements: First, the character difficulty is suitable and expected to be completed; Second, the goal is clear; Third, timely feedback; Fourth, focus; Fifth, voluntary investment; Sixth, sense of self-control; Seventh, the state of selflessness; Eighth, the sense of time changes [47]. Looking back at successful game design, designers often take full consideration of gameplay, mechanics, and balance, and integrate the elements of flow into the game system design of levels, balance, etc., so that different players can always find their needs in it, and slowly realize and obtain self-affirmation according to their goals. Games succeed because they are "a fun experience that gives you the freedom to control your own actions. [48]".

4   The Future of Immersive Experiences Based on XR

According to the development logic of the era of spatial computing, the interactive occurrence of immersive theater is more real-time and controllable [49]. In the image creation under XR technology, the priority of the subject makes the image experience based on XR more similar to a game or mechinima. The way of making movies based on engine is also known as mechinima. One of the most revolutionary applications of virtual film-making is the use of game engines in the production pipeline. Unreal Engine was originally a development tool for game production to create immersive and realistic interactive experiences. In recent years, Unreal Engine has strengthened the functional modules required for film and television production. Producers can complete the scenes, props and lighting presets of film shots through UE5, the screen synthesis of actors and foreground props in the virtual world, super-size screen stitching, camera tracking data access, lighting control and other functions to complete the "what you see is what you get" similar real shooting experience. At the same time, based on the powerful lighting simulation and rendering effect of the virtual engine, the details of the reflection of the virtual shooting film will have more texture of real space. Through the creation of realistic style digital assets through Unreal Game Engine, directors and creators can adjust real-time rendering scenes during preparation and shooting through computer terminals, using VR devices or live screens, including the layout of light sources with different characteristics, scene layout design, cinema-level modeling and real-time adjustment of a series of elements such as "Sandbox Games" [50]. Virtual reality worlds can be created or changed according to their needs in a short time.

Spatial computing is an important technical support for the shift from traditional viewing of two-dimensional images to human-computer interaction in three-dimensional space. Spatial computing enables devices to digitally perceive and comprehend their surroundings, leading to innovative possibilities in the interaction between humans and robots [51]. Currently, advances in spatial computing technology have facilitated 3D canvas user interfaces in a variety of environments through user interaction and extensive knowledge to develop simulated reality [51]. The essence of spatial computing is the deep integration of virtual and reality, which is why it is widely used in immersive human-computer interaction. Current spatial computing is broadly compatible with many aspects of Extended Reality (XR). [51]. With the blessing of technology, the viewer uses the headset to interact with the virtual content, and the content becomes multi-dimensional and strengthens the integration with the real world. PlayStation VR2, as a VR headset launched by SONY, has unique vibration feedback, haptic controller and 3D sound effect, while combining eye-tracking technology and extremely high resolution to immerse viewers in the virtual world to obtain a more real sensory experience and immersion. At the same time, Rokid Max Pro, a thinner AR smart glasses, realizes the grip and throwing operation mode of high-end headsets on the basis of spatial computing, which is lighter and gets rid of the constraint of cable length. The MR Headset Meta Quest3 jumps out of the strict classification of VR and MR, and realizes VR deep immersion, depth sensing and virtual space establishment in space with the help of spatial computing, opening up the wall between the virtual realm and the physical world, and presenting virtual images in the actual world. And the current Apple launched Apple Vison Pro is further on this basis, extremely high resolution and interactive perception so that reality and virtual highly integrated, in a real sense to open the era of spatial computing.

Behind the technical logic of spatial computing, portable wearable devices are more integrated into the daily life of human beings. It is worth our deep thinking that we should be vigilant about the discipline of technology on people's feelings in image creation. Steve Mann (2021), the developer of wearable computers, believes that the human body should become the computer, just as the computer becomes the human body [52]. Should we become computers or not? What is the subject of human-computer communion? With the birth of cyberspace, the concept of the subject of Cyborg appears. Donna Haraway identified three crucial boundary breakdowns in American scientific culture in the 1970s to 1990s. That is, the distinction between man and animal was seriously eroded, the second was the blurring of the line between animal-human (organism) or machine, and the third was the interpenetration of the physical and non-physical realms [53].

In XR technology, immersive experience reorganizes people's feelings in an all-round way. On the one hand, it blocks the original perceptual mode of human behavior, and on the other hand, it constructs new senses. Thus was born a posthuman mode of sensation, virtual reality theater, in which we are forced to stare at and respond to everything around us. Although people who enter the theater get some freedom, this freedom is informed, and the audience does not learn independently. Such behavior is a separation of the subject, and the audience still cannot get freedom.

From a psychological point of view, the traditional image uses vision and hearing to constantly induce the audience to put down the inner defense mechanism and enter the narrative environment of the image to form perceptual empathy. However, the immersive theater presented by the extended reality images that break through the limitations of the screen leads the multi-dimensional sensory experience to the extreme. Coupled with more immersive interaction and perception, virtual images begin to "devour" people's vision, "invade" people's senses, and "enter" people's skin and body, prompting the audience to appear in a certain degree of mental state "regression". The concept of regression pertains to the notion that an individual has the ability to revert back to previous stages. The concept of regression suggests that individuals have the ability to revert back to earlier stages of cognitive growth and engage in behaviors associated with more primitive modes of functioning [54]. Cope with the shock of imitation by abandoning the skills you have learned and responding to the present situation in a certain manner of behavior at the earliest.

From the perspective of viewing, the immersive image experience under XR technology may be a new invasion of human perceptual experience. The restricted interaction is upgraded from the stripping of viewing to the stripping of behavior. In this process, a new medium may be born, which is the restriction and discipline of the human body.

The behavior pattern of the subject is controlled by human consciousness. In virtual reality life, consciousness cannot control behavior. People without free will become programmed and lose their free will. The seeming freedom is not the freedom in imagination. Virtual reality interactions limit and discipline the body through feeling, judgment and behavior, leading to new ethical questions. In the process of this discipline, the original body system is transformed. Instrumental reason recreates the appearance of the real society and becomes a kind of "superreality" over the social entity. When virtual reality becomes the social norm, this kind of immersion brought by it is actually the blocking of human brain and the deprivation of sensation.

5   Conclusion

At present, the computer age has arrived, along with the development of XR technology, providing new opportunities for image creation. And we have to reflect on the logic behind the creation. Human's immersion experience, which has existed since ancient times, is an important behavior for us to perceive the world and perceive ourselves through physical experience. In the era of XR, under the new immersive theater based on spatial algorithm, it is worth pondering whether people's immersive experience will move towards positive psychology or become the object of domination in the discipline of media.

Now, with the advent of the era of spatial computing in the context of XR, immersive experience has changed from the imagination of the past to our daily life. In the future, perhaps screens or fourth walls will be absent or more hidden, and head-mounted devices (such as the Apple Vision) will become increasingly light and sophisticated. This means that immersive experiences will become more ubiquitous and happen anywhere. What matters is the ethics and motivations behind immersive video creation, whether it captures the audience or liberates it. The paradox here is also the philosophical dilemma that immersive experiences face. Human beings grasp and experience the world not only in the dimension of "image-viewing". More and more human beings are immersed in the world image, in which the reconstruction of visual culture will inevitably affect people's grasp of the real world, and even restrict people's more physical experience. How to liberate the viewer's experience, so that they can mobilize different sensations of the body to construct a richer world experience, is a major topic of the future video art creation based on XR technology. Technology is only a process, and the ultimate pursuit of immersive video art creation is that human beings become more liberated and free through the art experience of virtual reality, and move towards emotion and transcendence in the game.

References

1. Hossain, M.F., Jamalipour, A., Munasinghe, K.: A Survey on Virtual Reality over Wireless Networks: Fundamentals, QoE, Enabling Technologies, Research Trends and Open Issues. Authorea Preprints (2023)
2. Mann, S., Furness, T., Yuan, Y., et al.: All reality: Virtual, augmented, mixed (x), mediated (x, y), and multimediated reality. arXiv preprint arXiv:1804.08386 (2018)

3. Parikka, J.: What is media archaeology? John Wiley & Sons, pp. 24–25 (2013)
4. The concept of the fourth wall is not only applied to the theatrical stage, but also to movies, television, games, etc. It is a virtual interface that does not exist on the side of the stage
5. Wen, Z., Xiaotang, X. (ed.): China Virtual Reality Art Development Report. China International Broadcasting Press, p. 4
6. Jensen, J.F.: Film theory meets 3D: a FilmTheoretic approach to the design and analysis of 3D Spaces. In: Virtual Interaction: Interaction in Virtual Inhabited 3D Worlds, pp. 311–328. Springer, London (2001)
7. Written by Walter Murch, translated by Xia Tong. Blink of an Eye: The Mystery of Film Editing, pp. 103–113. Beijing United Press
8. Walley, J.: Cinema expanded: avant-garde film in the age of intermedia. Oxford University Press (2020). 12
9. Wasson, H.: The networked screen: Moving images, materiality, and the aesthetics of size. Fluid screens, expanded cinema, pp. 74–95 (2007)
10. Walley, J.: Cinema expanded: avant-garde film in the age of intermedia, pp. 12–17. Oxford University Press (2020)
11. Gutierrez, N.: The ballad of morton heilig: on VR's mythic past. JCMS: J. Cinema Media Stud. **62**(3), 86–106 (2023)
12. Sutherland, I.E.: The ultimate display. Proceedings of the IFIP Congress 2(506–508), 506–508 (1965)
13. Slater, M., Sanchez-Vives, M.V.: Enhancing our lives with immersive virtual reality. Front. Robot. AI **3**, 74 (2016)
14. Hutchison, A.: Back to the Holodeck: new life for virtual reality? In: Proceedings of the 2nd international conference on Digital interactive media in entertainment and arts, pp. 98–104 (2007)
15. Wen, Z., Xu, X. (ed.): Report on the Development of Virtual Reality Art in China. China International Broadcasting Press, p. 30
16. Baker, C., Eddy, R., Bailey, D.: Immersive worlds and sites of participatory culture. Screen Tourism and Affective Landscapes: The Real, the Virtual, and the Cinematic (2022)
17. Mittermeier, S.: Indiana Jones and the Theme Park Adventure. Excavating Indiana Jones: Essays on the Films and Franchise (2020), 90
18. Wu, C.: Back to the Origin -- Creative Notes of Experimental Animation Theater "Happening". China Television (Animation) (2013). 7
19. Hales, C.: Cinematic interaction: From kinoautomat to cause and effect (2005)
20. Desai, S.: Haste and waste in the city: Rekindling care about and for trees in another time. Concentric Literary Cultural Stud. **43**(1), 165–195 (2017)
21. Van Den Bergh, H.: Art for the planet's sake. Fresh Perspectives on Arts and Environment (2015)
22. Yi, Y.: Immersive Theater: The Overlapping of Art in the Period of Change. Shanghai Art Review, 2016(6)
23. Wang, J., Ye, F.: Narrative controllability in visual reality interactive film. In: Design, User Experience, and Usability. User Experience in Advanced Technological Environments: 8th International Conference, DUXU 2019, Held as Part of the 21st HCI International Conference, HCII 2019, Orlando, FL, USA, July 26–31, 2019, Proceedings, Part II 21, pp. 471–483. Springer, Cham (2019)
24. Edman, I.: Poetry and truth in Plato[J]. J. Philos. **33**(22), 605–609 (1936)
25. Keller, E.F., Grontkowski, C.R.: The mind's eye. In: Discovering Reality: Feminist Perspectives on Epistemology, Metaphysics, Methodology, and Philosophy of Science. Dordrecht: Springer Netherlands, pp. 207–224 (1983)
26. Styve, P.S.T.: The time of light in early renaissance painting. Bodies, borders, believers: Ancient texts and present conversations, pp. 68–89 (2015)

27. Renaut, A., De Bevoise, M.B.: Era of the Individual: A Contribution to a History of Subjectivity. Motilal Banarsidass Publishe, pp. 12–30 (2000)
28. Zhan, G.: Philosophy of Subjectivity. Yunnan People's Publishing House 2002 Edition (2002)
29. Chen, Y.: The intervention of real audiences in the narrative process: exploring a possible narrative theory. Theoretical Stud. Literature Art **43**(4), 19–30 (2024)
30. Rancière, J.: The Emancipated Spectator. Verso Books, London (2007)
31. Conger, S.M.M.: Hans robert jauss's" rezeptionsästhetik" and England's reception of eighteenth-century German literature. The Eighteenth Century **22**(1), 74–93 (1981)
32. Hohendahl, P.U., Silberman, M.: Introduction to reception aesthetics. New German Critique **10**, 29–63 (1977)
33. Kinoshita, Y.: Reception theory. University of California Santa Barbara: Department of Art. http://www.yumikinoshita.com/receptiontheory.pdf, 7July 2015 (2004)
34. Abrams, M.H.: The Mirror and the Lamp: Romantic Theory and the Critical Tradition, p. 6. Oxford University Press, New York (1971)
35. Osarczuk, K.: Confronting the Spectacular: Addressing the Role of Contemporary Installation Art. Sotheby's Institute of Art-New York (2015)
36. Banou, S.: Installation/Drawing: spaces of drawing between art and architecture. A Companion to Contemporary Drawing, pp. 431–450 (2020)
37. Merleau-Ponty, M.: The synthesis of one's own body. Body: Critical Concepts Sociol. **1**, 56–61 (1996)
38. Finter, H., Griffin, M.: Antonin Artaud and the impossible theatre: the legacy of the Theatre of Cruelty. TDR (1988-) **41**(4), 15–40 (1997)
39. Walsh, J.M.: Stage violence, power and the director: an examination of the theory and practice of cruelty from Antonin Artaud to Sarah Kane. University of Pittsburgh, pp. 24–28 (2012)
40. Merleau-Ponty, M., Landes, D., Carman, T., et al.: Phenomenology of perception. Routledge, pp. 269–270 (2013)
41. Li, Y.: Beyond interactive and immersive media arts: a case study of teamLab in the construction of artificial nature (2020)
42. Kim, H.W.: Phenomenology of the body and its implications for humanistic ethics and politics. Hum. Stud. **24**(1–2), 69–85 (2001)
43. Malliet, S., De Meyer, G.: The history of the video game. In: Handbook of Computer Game Studies, pp. 23–45 (2005)
44. Shell, J.: Panoramic Exploration of the Art of Game Design [M]. Publishing House of Electronics Industry, p. 10 (2010)
45. Csikszentmihalyi, M., Massimini, F.: The flow theory of optimal experience. In: Jackson, J.E. (ed.) Handbook of Experimental Existential Psychology, pp. 251–271. Plenum Press, New York (1987)
46. Salisbury, J.H., Tomlinson, P.: Reconciling Csikszentmihalyi's broader flow theory: with meaning and value in digital games. Trans. Digital Games Research Assoc. (ToDIGRA) **2**(2), 55–77 (2016)
47. Mihaly Csikszentmihalai, translated by Zhang Dingqi, Flow: The Psychology of Optimal Psychological Experience, p. 30. Citic Press (2017)
48. Sun, Y.: Research on Immersive Scene Design of Digital Media Art. China National Academy of Arts (2021)
49. AbuKhousa, E., El-Tahawy, M.S., Atif, Y.: Envisioning architecture of metaverse intensive learning experience (MiLEx): Career readiness in the 21st century and collective intelligence development scenario. Future Internet **15**(2), 53 (2023)
50. Delmerico, J., Poranne, R., Bogo, F., et al.: Spatial computing and intuitive interaction: bringing mixed reality and robotics together. IEEE Robot. Autom. Mag.Autom. Mag. **29**(1), 45–57 (2022)

51. Balakrishnan, S., Hameed, M.S.S., Venkatesan, K., et al.: Interaction of spatial computing in augmented reality. In: 2021 7th International Conference on Advanced Computing and Communication Systems (ICACCS). IEEE, 1, pp. 1900–1904 (2021)

52. Haraway, D.: A manifesto for cyborgs: Science, technology, and socialist feminism in the 1980s. Australian Feminist Stud. **2**(4), 1–42 (2006). 6

53. Rizzolo, G.S.: The critique of regression: the person, the field, the lifespan. J. Am. Psychoanal. Assoc.Psychoanal. Assoc. **64**(6), 1097–1131 (2016)

54. Braidotti, R.: Posthuman humanities. Europ. Educ. Res. J. **12**(1), 1–19 (2013)

Multimodal Interaction in Intelligent Environments

I-Shoe: Smart Insole for Gait Monitoring

Hala Aburajouh(✉), Eman Abdulrahman, Nayla Al-Zeyara, Wasmiya Al-Dosari,
Mohammed Al-Sada, and Osama Halabi

Department of Computer Science and Engineering, Qatar University, Doha, Qatar
{Ha1906848,ohalabi}@qu.edu.qa

Abstract. Gait analysis is a crucial method for evaluating and treating individuals
with walking-related conditions. The process is typically utilized in hospitals or
specialized gait labs, often involving tools operated by medical professionals.
However, conventional methods have become more time-consuming and costly,
leading to decreased accuracy in gait analysis. Wearable sensor technologies have
emerged as a solution. This project introduces the i-Shoe, a smart insole equipped
with eight force-sensitive resistors (FSR) and a low-power microcontroller to
capture gait features. A mobile application displays real-time sensor data and an
average heat map, showcasing the most concentrated pressure area in the foot.
Machine learning algorithms are applied to identify abnormalities like flatfoot
or imbalance. The system has been successfully tested on several individuals and
has potential applications in diabetic foot detection, rehabilitation, and monitoring
athletes' gait.

Keywords: Gait analysis · Smart insole · Wearable sensor · Machine learning

1 Introduction

Gait analysis is a crucial diagnostic and therapeutic process with various applications
in healthcare, rehabilitation, therapy, and exercise training. However, it is typically performed in a gait laboratory, which is inaccessible to many due to financial constraints
and limited access to healthcare. The inability to afford these labs affects a large portion
of the population, leading to a lack of standard gait measures.

Walking, though often overlooked, reveals much about an individual's health and
physical condition. It is a fundamental mode of transportation, and a loss of ability
can significantly impact an individual's life, causing both short-term and long-term
health issues. Some individuals may exhibit irregular or asymmetrical gait patterns for
extended periods without any apparent health concerns. However, injury or pain can
lead to modifications in regular walking, resulting in irregular walking patterns that
can initiate significant medical problems. Gait monitoring plays an important role to
assess the way of walking, and classifying the abnormalities like flatfoot, high arch,
unbalance, and fall risk in the gait cycle of the foot and is used widely for detecting
chronic diseases in the body like diabetes and Parkinson's disease. Gait analysis becomes
a critical aspect that can improve health outcomes and quality of life especially with early

N. A. Streitz and S. Konomi (Eds.): HCII 2024, LNCS 14719, pp. 325–335, 2024.
https://doi.org/10.1007/978-3-031-60012-8_20

detection of a chronic disease or even help avoid developing any diseases in the future. For instance, studies show that around five million of the eighteen million who are diabetic in the U.S. do not know they have it. However Early detection and treatment of diabetes is an essential step toward keeping people with diabetes healthy as it can help to reduce the risk of serious complications such as premature heart disease and stroke, blindness, limb amputations, and kidney failure. Furthermore, another study shows that approximately 30% to 40% of people aged 65 years and older experienced falls due to an acute, overwhelming event (e.g., stroke, seizure, loss of consciousness) resulting it may cost them their lives or becomes a significant threat of their quality of life. However, there are barriers to achieving gait monitoring in existing models and gait laboratories, for instance, lack of finance, limited access to health care, and low health knowledge. Introducing a new model of Gait monitoring will directly benefit older adults, people with foot injuries, or people who want to be on top of their health in many ways, not particularly from the physical perspective. It can help with their psycho-social well-being significantly since the study shows that people who take care of their bodies improve their mental health as well, also it helps their financial status since the smart insole is inexpensive and provides real-time guidance through a mobile application. Since the pressure distribution varies from one person to another depending on the age, gender, body height, weight, and walking methods. Classifying plantar pressure distribution acts as a significant indicator of the health of the lower limb and the gait as well [1]. With this approach, users of gait monitoring systems can stay healthy and help save someone's life.

The primary goals are to maintain foot function and provide guidance in the event of any abnormalities, slowing functional decline and improving quality of life through early detection. This study aims to develop a gait analysis system using a smart insole with the following objectives: designing a smart wearable insole with appropriate sensors to monitor plantar pressure for gait analysis, creating a classification algorithm for pressure data using machine learning, building a smartphone application for wireless data acquisition, and developing a mobile application to display real-time heatmaps of feet status and notify users of abnormalities such as flatfoot or imbalance.

2   Related Work

The foot is the most efficient organ of the body and its ability to withstand substantial pressure is due to static and dynamic activities. During the gait process, the foot is considered the only anatomic part of the human body that is in direct contact with the earth's surface [3], therefore it can handle any effect caused due to the weight of the body and sequentially force produced due to ground reaction. Moreover, plantar pressure measurements are considered an important indication of foot functionalities during daily gait activities and are also significant in medical applications for gait analysis and early diagnosis of chronic foot diseases and rehabilitation processes, as well as in sports. Recently the idea of smart insoles was brought by many researchers as they developed an embedded sensor in shoes and insoles for the sake of gait monitoring. Also, it is used for assessing patients who suffer from chronic diseases such as cancer, stroke, diabetes, and cardiac disease, especially for elderly people [4]. Plantar pressure distribution analysis is an important approach applied in hospitals, sports, and rehabilitation processes. Multiple studies on foot biomechanics have stated that plantar pressure distribution differences are beneficial to detecting abnormality in human gait [7]. Hence, we can use in-shoe systems with embedded sensors that can measure the pressure spreading among the feet, distinguish between feet types, and categorize the cause and effect of the diagnosis [8, 9].

Many researchers participated in the creation of gait monitoring systems and up to this date the research community is investigating new designs and models for the insole that provide applications for daily life use, sports use, and medical use [5, 10–14]. These previous works provided a variety of designs of smart insoles with different approaches in the architecture, number of components, size, and cost of the shoe insoles. In this research, we provide a smart insole device with a compact lightweight, and cost-efficient device to make sure it is accessible and attainable to users.

Machine learning (ML) is a form of artificial intelligence (AI) that employs algorithms to enable computer systems to learn and enhance task performance through experience with data, without explicit programming. It has diverse applications, spanning from medicine and advertising to military and pedestrian areas. Machine learning can be leveraged across various fields to make sense of data. Additionally, in previous works, machine learning algorithms have successfully enabled the development of accurate unobtrusive Activity recognition systems. This research will use supervised machine learning algorithms to train a model for generalized human gait monitoring, paving the way for its potential application in various contexts. The model will be a classification model.

In summary, the literature review highlights the significance of analyzing plantar pressure distribution in the feet to identify abnormalities such as diabetic foot, flat foot, high arch, and fall risks. This is achieved through the use of sensors to calculate pressure and obtain data from different areas of the foot, which is then visualized into a heat map. Additionally, the review discusses the various models of smart insoles and sensors used for collecting plantar pressure data, along with the need for gait analysis to classify foot abnormalities. This paper aims to employ a machine learning approach for early detection and classification of abnormal gait and the potential detection of chronic diseases using a multidimensional linear regression algorithm.

3   System Design and Implementation

The proposed system is a wearable smart insole with an ML model to assist in the analysis of human gait implemented with a mobile application. The system consists of an insole with embedded FSR sensors connected to a Bluno Beetle microcontroller, the data is acquired wirelessly using Bluetooth low energy consumption which is a module embedded in the microcontroller itself. There are two main processes in the system, the first process is training the machine model in the PC and the second process is implementing the trained model in the mobile application. Figure 1 describes the high-level design of the system.

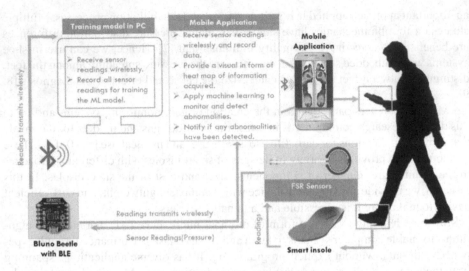

Fig. 1. High-Level System Design

3.1 The Wearable Device I-Shoe

FSR sensors are embedded in the insole, they are distributed according to [12] which is a previous study on the most pressed areas such as the toe in the forefoot, midfoot, and hindfoot. Figure 2 shows the final distribution of the sensors to acquire the data for indicating a normal, flatfoot, or unbalanced human. The data then will be sent to the microcontroller which acts like a link that gets the acquired data and transmits it wirelessly to the mobile application to be processed and classified. I-Shoe uses eight FSRs integrated into the insole to measure human gait using a low-power consumption microcontroller. i-Shoe is also equipped with a low-cost 6-axis accelerometer and gyroscope to capture the gait features in motion. The first and optimistic option which is the primary target of this project is that the data is acquired from a wireless-enabled microcontroller, next the data is transmitted wirelessly to the mobile application simultaneously from both microcontrollers.

3.2 Insole Implementation

The hardware implementation consists of the implementation of the insole, the Bluno Beetle is interfaced with eight FSRs, and the implemented prototype is shown in Fig. 3. This prototype was done using small FSRs, we found that using smaller diameter FSRs will give more precision, especially if the medial arch and lateral arch have separate sensors for each.

Reading Data Reading data is the most important step of this work, to classify the abnormalities in the gait, multiple readings are necessary to classify the gait condition of the user, these readings are from the 16 FSRs from both feet combined. First, the data was collected from the Bluno Beetle through serial communication for both feet. Second, we defined a serial port in Python to read what was displayed in the Bluno serial

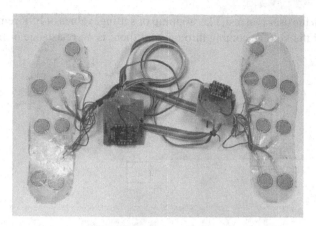

Fig. 2. FSR sensors positions

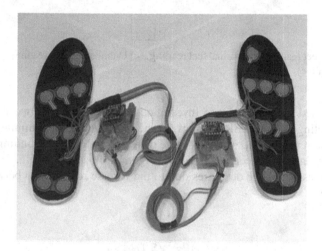

Fig. 3. Final prototype of the insole

monitor and then write the data into a text file. Last, the text file is loaded to another Python project to parse and concatenate the data from left and right and give it a label at the end of the sensors values then save it into an Excel file, the labels assigned are zero for flat foot, one for normal, and two for unbalance, to feed this data into our machine learning model. When the user has a flat foot, values on sensor five should increase forming a peak on the positive y-axis, the rectangle in Fig. 4.a. shows the peak (blue line), while in the normal foot (orange line) there should be no pressure at sensor five. When the user has a normal gait left foot (orange line), and right foot (blue line) values should be around the same range, because normally while walking a person puts his/her weights equally on both feet (see Fig. 4.b. When the user is unbalanced, the left foot (line in orange), and right foot (line in blue) values should not be the same, because an unbalanced gait person puts his/her weight on one foot more than another foot (see

Fig. 4.c). When the user is at rest, like stopping or setting, values of FSR remain constant. That means all the voltage coming through and there is no resistance or pressure at all (see Fig. 4.d.

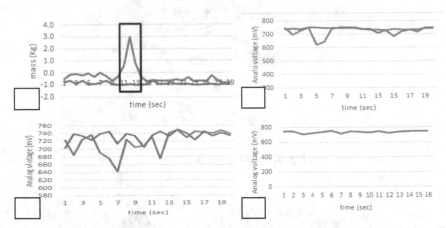

Fig. 4. (a) Flat feet reading, (b) Normal feet reading, (c) Unbalanced feet reading, (d) No walking (Color figure online)

We conducted an experiment to investigate the relationship between voltage and mass by collecting multiple FSR readings for the same weight, determining the average FSR value, and repeating these steps for five different weights. Our findings revealed a significant correlation between voltage and weight, as illustrated in Fig. 5. Specifically, as weight increases, voltage decreases due to the inverse relationship between voltage and resistance.

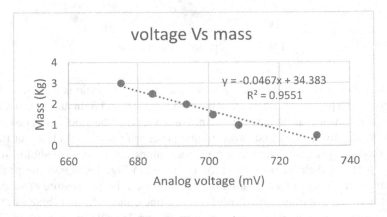

Fig. 5. Enter Caption

3.3 The Machine Learning Model

The training is done on the PC using Jupiter Notebook which is an open-source web application and has a library named Sikit Learn for machine learning algorithms. Then the machine learning model is transferred into the mobile application. Furthermore, with the high performance of mobiles nowadays, as well as the availability of Android Studio there is a way to connect one microcontroller at a time and then disconnect and connect the other one with a slight delay in the middle without even noticing it. This makes this the preferable option believing it will be a step forward for the ML model. Due to the lack of data, sensor readings from the insole are acquired serially and logged to collect the data needed to train the model. Then, a multi-classification model is trained, since it should predict between multiple values, whether this person's walking state is normal or abnormal (flat, unbalanced walk). Furthermore, the abnormalities will be detected based on the features, the features will be extracted from the fifth sensor positioned as shown in Fig. 2. To train the model, a supervised ML algorithm is used with labels and features. In this research, the problem is a classification problem, collected data belongs to a data set of three classes (normal, flat foot, and imbalanced), and our goal is to train classifiers with already labeled data on how to predict the class of unlabeled data. In the process of building this system, several supervised Machine Learning classification algorithms and a Neural Network were trained and tested on collected data of various types of people walks. Choosing the most convenient classifiers to be implemented in this system was based on a selected criterion that ensures high accuracy of gait classification since the system is to be used in monitoring users' gait and assigning labels to their walking.

The implementation details of the machine learning classifiers used are to be discussed, along with the explanation of their outputs and accuracies. The data set comprises three classes (normal, flat, and imbalanced), and the aim is to develop a machine learning model to classify between these three classes. Initially, the focus was on two classes (normal and flat), before adding a third class (imbalanced). The model was then trained on the data from the 16 sensors (both feet simultaneously).

To preprocess the imbalanced data, we divided it into two parts (right & left) and then developed a Python program to read the files in parallel. While reading the files in parallel, extracted the data we needed only, then we took the average across all the sensors for 4 repeated readings of the sensors. After we took the average for all the sensor values, we concatenated/joined all the values together (8 values + 8 values = 16 values), then we added a label to each record depending on the filename. Following data preprocessing, the dataset became prepared for the subsequent step - constructing a Machine Learning model to classify between the three classes (normal, flat, imbalanced). Upon completion of the preparation, the cleaned and organized dataset was initially split into two segments - the train set and test set, with a ratio of 77:23 respectively. The train set was then further divided into two segments - train set and validation set, with a ratio of 80:20 respectively. The Machine Learning model was trained using four Classifiers, with the KNN algorithm demonstrating the highest accuracy. The reported test accuracies for each classifier were: Support Vector Machines (SVM) 79, Multi-layer Perceptron (MLP) 58, Gaussian Naive Bayes (GNB) 75, and K Nearest Neighbor (KNN) 81.

The classification problem at hand can be effectively addressed by using mean values to distinguish between labels. However, in order to enhance our machine learning model, additional features such as center of pressure location, velocity, step count, duration of gait cycle, and swing time can be integrated. These features will be fed into different classifiers to determine gait types. It is preferable to input the features into a separate classifier rather than the entire time-series data for better accuracy. The use of additional classifiers enhances the accuracy, as certain classifiers cannot be applied to time-series data. Furthermore, using padding as a solution is not preferred, as it alters the original data, potentially impacting classification accuracy.

In terms of data collection, the experiment begins with the user opening the mobile application and then initiating walking. Subsequently, the mobile application connects to the right foot microcontroller, waits for 30 s, and then connects to the left foot microcontroller. The machine learning model predicts the gait type and sends notifications to the user based on abnormalities detected. The notifications displayed to the user are detailed in Fig. 6.

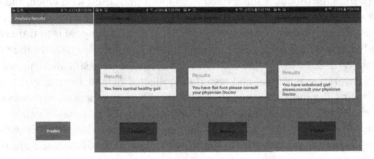

Fig. 6. Predication result

The app exhibits a live heat map while collecting data, depicting the user's current touch location (Fig. 7.a) and the concentrated heat map illustrating the areas most frequently pressed during the user's gait (Fig. 7.b).

4 System Evaluation

4.1 Experimental Procedure

The primary objective was to assess the accuracy of the machine learning model and the usability and acceptance of the system by users. In the experiment, the I-shoe was utilized to collect gait data, while a mobile application displayed the results and heat maps. Data was manually labeled during the experiments, and the resulting classifier predicted labels were compared with the actual labels to test accuracy. Additionally, participants were given a questionnaire to gather feedback on the system and assess their acceptance.

Regarding participants, the survey involved 22 individuals (86.4% female, 13.8% male, average age = 22.4, standard deviation = 6.2). Most participants were first-time users of the smart insole, with only two having prior experience. After an introductory session, participants were instructed to walk for one minute to capture data from FSR

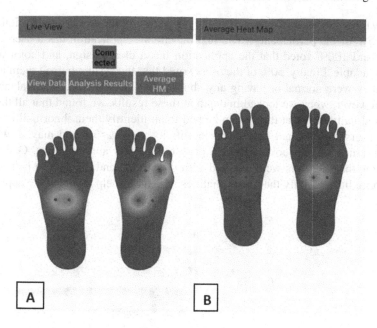

Fig. 7. (a) live heat map, (b) concentrated heat map

sensors. Upon completion, they were asked to complete a questionnaire to gauge their impressions of the system. The machine learning model's accuracy was evaluated by comparing the classifier results with manually-entered actual results. The total recognition accuracy was 75%, with individual class scores of 76% for normal detection, 79% for flat foot detection, and 86% for unbalance detection (see Fig. 8).

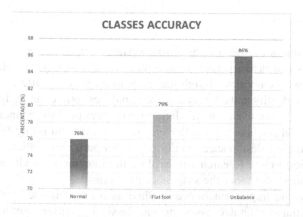

Fig. 8. ML Accuracy results.

The survey assessed the comfort of the insole, with the majority finding it comfortable, while some expressed concerns about damaging the wires. 40.9% of the participants

would buy the smart insole to use in their daily lives. As for the mobile application acceptance, 95.5% of the participants voted that the mobile application has a user-friendly
interface, and 100% voted that the application has a clear design, and color and the
texts are readable. Finally, 50% of the users voted that the system helped them identify
whether they were normal or having any abnormality like flat feet or imbalance (See
Fig. 9). However, when we looked in depth at these results, we found that all the users
of abnormal gait voted that the system helped them identify their abnormalities, while
the other users who did not have any abnormality voted as no and maybe, which is
acceptable since we are looking to help people find their abnormalities. Overall, the
results show that the users were satisfied with the system and the system helped those
with abnormalities identify their abnormalities which can help them get the appropriate
treatment.

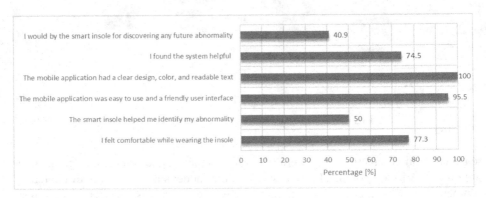

Fig. 9. Questionnaire results

5   Conclusion

This study introduces I-Shoe, a smart insole system designed to evaluate individuals'
walking patterns and detect potential abnormalities that may impact their gait in the
future. The system demonstrated high accuracy in classifying different types of gait,
enabling users to identify and address any abnormalities. While the study's results indicate the need for further testing with a larger participant pool to enhance classification
accuracy, the initial findings support the system's comfort and utility for users. Moreover, the cost-efficient design successfully fulfills its purpose of efficiently identifying
gait abnormalities. Future research will explore the integration of alternative machine
learning techniques to enhance the system's capabilities.

    In summary, the implementation of I-Shoe as a smart insole system showcases
promising potential in accurately assessing and classifying walking patterns. The study's
positive results, demonstrating user comfort and effectiveness, lay a strong foundation
for further exploration and refinement of the system. With additional research and testing, I-Shoe has the potential to become a valuable tool for identifying and addressing
gait abnormalities, ultimately benefiting individuals' overall well-being.

Acknowledgments. This paper was jointly supported by Qatar University M-QJRC2020-7 and M-QJRC-2023-325. The findings achieved herein are solely the responsibility of the authors.

References

1. Li, J., et al.: Design and implementation of a plantar pressure distribution measuring system. In: Proc.-2016 8th Int. Conf. Intell. Human-Machine Syst. Cybern. IHMSC 2016, vol. 2, pp. 316–319 (2016)
2. Talai, I.: 12 billion QAR for Health Expanduture 2013/2014. AlArab Newspaper (2015)
3. I. Symposium, M. Automation: 2017 IEEE 3rd International Symposium in Robotics and Manufacturing Automation, ROMA 2017. 3rd IEEE Int. Symp. Robot. Manuf. Autom. ROMA 2017 (2017)
4. Levi, M.S., Brimble, M.A.: A Review of Neuroprotective Agents. Curr. Med. Chem.. Med. Chem. **11**, 2383–2397 (2004)
5. Tan, A.M., Fuss, F.K., Weizman, Y., Woudstra, Y., Troynikov, O.: Design of LowCost smart insole for real time measurement of plantar pressure. Procedia Technol. **20**(July), 117–122 (2015)
6. Daumé, H.: A Course in Machine Learning. Todo, p. 189 (2012)
7. Cavanagh, P.R., Ulbrecht, J.S.: Clinical plantar pressure measurement in diabetes: rationale and methodology. Foot **4**(3), 123–135 (1994)
8. Tan, T.: Measurement and analysis of dynamic distribution of plantar pressure. In: 2012 5th Int. Conf. Biomed. Eng. Informatics, BMEI 2012, no. Bmei, pp. 835–839 (2012)
9. K. Imaizumi, Y. Iwakami, and K. Yamashita: Analysis of foot pressure distributiondata for the evaluation of foot arch type. Proc. Annu. Int. Conf. IEEE Eng. Med. Biol. Soc. EMBS, pp. 7388–7392 (2011)
10. Lin, F., Wang, A., Zhuang, Y., Tomita, M.R., Xu, W.: Smart insole: a WearableSensor device for unobtrusive gait monitoring in daily life. IEEE Trans. Ind. Informatics **12**(6), 2281–2291 (2016)
11. Cho, H.: Design and implementation of a lightweight smart insole for gait analysis. In: Proc. - 16th IEEE Int. Conf. Trust. Secur. Priv. Comput. Commun. 11th IEEE Int. Conf. Big Data Sci. Eng. 14th IEEE Int. Conf. Embed. Softw. Syst., pp. 792–797 (2017)
12. Berengueres, J., Fritschi, M., McClanahan, R.: A smart pressure-sensitive insole thatreminds you to walk correctly: an orthotic-less treatment for over pronation. In: 2014 36th Annu. Int. Conf. IEEE Eng. Med. Biol. Soc. EMBC 2014, pp. 2488–2491 (2014)
13. Footwear Research and Development with F-Scan. https://www.tekscan.com/applications/footwear-research-and-development-fscan
14. Rösevall, J., et al.: A wireless sensor insole for collecting gait data. Stud. Health Technol. Inform. **200**, 176–178 (2014)
15. Pham, C., Diep, N.N., Phuong, T.M.: E-Shoes: Smart shoes for unobtrusive human activity recognition. In: Proc. - 2017 9th Int. Conf. Knowl. Syst. Eng. KSE 2017, vol. 2017–Janua, pp. 269–274 (2017)
16. Muñoz-Organero, M., Littlewood, C., Parker, J., Powell, L., Grindell, C., Mawson, S.: Identification of walking strategies of people with osteoarthritis of the knee using insole pressure sensors
17. Li, J., et al.: Design and implementation of a plantar pressure distribution measuring system. In: Proc. - 2016 8th Int. Conf. Intell. Human Machine Syst. Cybern. IHMSC 201, vol. 2, pp. 316–319 (2016)

Eyebient Displays: Ambient Displays by Gaze Guidance

Takemaru Hirokawa, Airi Tsuji, and Kaori Fujinami[✉]

Daily Life Computing Laboratory, Tokyo University of Agriculture and Technology, Koganei, Tokyo, Japan
fujinami@cc.tuat.ac.jp
http://tuat-dlcl.org/welcome_en/

Abstract. Ambient displays convey information to users in an abstract manner without interfering with their activities; however, in conventional ambient displays, new abstract expressions corresponding to the information must be devised to convey additional types of information to users. In this study, we propose a novel concept of ambient displays called "Eyebient display," which involves using a smartphone and everyday objects to provide information to the user by directing their attention to everyday objects that represent the information being conveyed. Gaze guidance is used to direct attention by displaying the agent's eyes on a smartphone. Instead of creating separate displays for each piece of information, the user only needs to adjust the positional relationship between the smartphone and objects according to the information presentation rule. A preliminary user study demonstrates the creativity and effectiveness of the proposed method.

Keywords: Ambient displays · Gaze guidance · Agent · Do-it-yourself

1 Introduction

Various information terminals exist, and their notifications disrupt human attention, leading to fatigue. An ambient display [15] presents information in a space by mapping information onto illustrations of virtual creatures [7,10,11], patterns of light and sound [3], and changes in physical shapes [1,9], rather than presenting it with numbers or graphs. This information is processed within the periphery of consciousness. Ambient displays are perceived as part of the environment, such as an object or painting, and are often implemented as a dedicated system rather than as applications that are run, for example, by double-clicking each time information is viewed. Conventional ambient displays only present information from prepared sources. Therefore, it is necessary to devise abstract representations that correspond to new types of information for users. This, in turn, requires the redesign of the ambient display itself. However, there are only a few approaches for creating ambient displays on a do-it-yourself (DIY) basis [2] or by combining modules [5].

In this paper, we propose "Eyebient display," a mechanism capable of creating various types of ambient displays by using gaze to guide attention and everyday objects. In addition, the proposed method was validated, and its creativity was evaluated. The remainder of this paper is organized as follows: Sect. 2 examines related studies on user-crafted ambient displays and gaze guidance. The design and implementation of Eyebient display are presented in Sect. 3. A preliminary user study regarding the suitability of Eyebient displays as ambient displays, gaze guidance ability, and creativity of Eyebient displays by a DIY approach is presented in Sect. 4. Finally, Sect. 5 concludes the paper.

2 Related Work

Very few approaches have aimed to create ambient displays using DIY methods or by combining prefabricated modules. Engert et al. proposed a shape-changing spatial display using a wire winding mechanism [5]. This display system creates dynamic visual shapes by leveraging the elements in space. A software tool and emulator were also created to virtually simulate motion and allow user configuration. Cho et al. developed a DIY toolkit for customizable and programmable ambient displays [2]. The toolkit includes a wooden base and an acrylic module with a motor that generates rotational and linear motions to which users can attach paper, fabric, or other materials of their choice to create an ambient display. This motion could be configured using a smartphone application. Any information can be attached to a moving unit, and the display shape adjusts in response to changes in the information to subtly communicate with the user. A user study indicated that users developed a sense of intimacy with the displays they created during the design process, which reflected their personal experiences and preferences. Matthews et al. investigated a software toolkit to support the creation of information displays, *peripheral displays* [13]. Peripheral displays share a similar notion and realization styles to ambient displays. That is, it presents information without demanding users' full attention and realized in a variety of modalities and appearances. The toolkit, peripheral display toolkit, provides architectural support for key characteristics of peripheral displays, i.e., abstraction, notification, and transitions, which was intended to allow designers to more easily prototype the displays and support reuse of code.

Joint attention is an important feature of gaze, in which one's attention is directed in the same direction as the gaze of others. Several experiments have been conducted on this feature. Friesen and Kingstone changed the gaze direction of a line-drawing face displayed at the center of the screen, shifting it to the right or left [6]. They measured the reaction time to a target presented either to the right or left of the face. The results showed that reaction times were shorter when the gaze direction coincided with the position of the target, compared to when the gaze direction did not coincide or when the face on the screen was looking straight ahead. This result indicates that the participants focused their attention on the gaze direction displayed on the screen, even though they knew that the target did not appear in that direction. We believe that the user's attention can be directed to an arbitrary point in space by changing the agent's gaze. Furthermore, the user can be made aware of the existence of information by positioning an object with a specific meaning at the directed point.

3   Design and Implementation of Eyebient Display

3.1   Core Concept of Eyebient Display

Eyebient display is a display and software toolkit for creating ambient displays that are independent of the information content. The central idea is that the objects in the user's line of sight, guided by the agent's gaze, represent the information conveyed by the system. Figure 1 illustrates the concept of presenting information through gaze guidance. In this example, sunny and rainy forecasts are mapped to the vase with sunflowers and umbrella, respectively. According to the weather forecast, the eyes drawn on the disused smartphone move to point to the umbrella. This is expected to shift the user's attention to the umbrella if he or she can perceive the eyes in the periphery of their field of view. Eyebient display has the following four prominent characteristics:

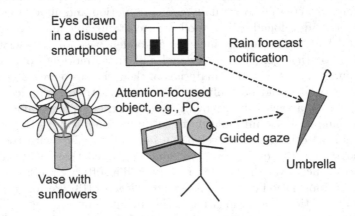

Fig. 1. Information presentation by gaze guidance

Subtle notification: Gaze guidance directs attention without awareness [4]. It does not interfere with the user's focus on the task at hand and is less likely to interfere with the user's work. We believe that gaze guidance is well suited for ambient displays due to the abstract and unobtrusive nature of the gaze.

Spatial engagement: The user's attention is diverted from the screen, allowing the presentation of information in a spatial manner. Users can focus on everyday objects in three-dimensional space by positioning them around the agent's eyes. This allows for the creation of information displays that leverage the surrounding environment rather than utilizing single devices such as smartphones and personal computers (PCs).

Extensibility: The Eyebient display shows only the eyes of an agent on a smartphone screen. The information to be represented can be changed or added by replacing or adding everyday objects to which the eye is directed. This reduces the burden on users by installing ambient displays in familiar environments.

Revivability of old smartphones: The front-end of Eyebient display, that is, the agent's eyes, operates on a web browser, ensuring compatibility with all modern phones. This means that old smartphones, which are no longer in use after a model change and are sitting on a desk drawer, can be reused. Furthermore, using everyday objects that the user already owns as a medium to express information incurs no monetary cost.

3.2   Major System Components and Implementation

Figure 2 shows the major system components: display and creation support units, everyday objects, application programming interface (API) servers, and information sources. The display unit was created using a smartphone, allowing disused smartphones to be repurposed as the "face" of an agent with the eyes drawn on the screen. Next.js, an open-source web development framework, was used to implement the eyes of an agent. The creation support unit was developed as a web application that can be accessed on current smartphone terminals. The user registers the positional relationship between the eyes and object with this application, and users can create various ambient displays based on their ideas and everyday objects. The API server was implemented using FastAPI to act as a bridge between the client units and various information sources, such as weather forecasts from a cloud and temperature sensor data from a room. The Eyebient display service provider is expected to define the information that can be retrieved from information sources and notified through the Eyebient display. They are also expected to retrieve information on behalf of the user from an external cloud or the user's local environment in order to monitor compliance with the rules set by the user.

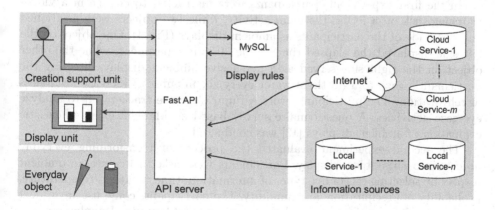

Fig. 2. Major system components of Eyebient display

In Fig. 3(a), the top view of the application shows the information content, presenting four types of information as examples and a display for a time-based reminder to be created. Once an information source is selected for creation, the positional relationship between a target object and the line of sight of an agent is set through trial and error (Fig. 3(b)). In this scenario, we assume that an object reminding the user to go for a walk is placed in the upper left, and the reminder is set for 5:00 a.m. Furthermore, another reminder object is placed at the bottom of the agent to prompt the user to leave the office at 7:30 p.m., as shown in Fig. 3(c). In this example, time refers to the information managed by the system and obtained from the server's clock.

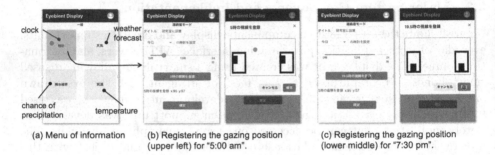

(a) Menu of information   (b) Registering the gazing position   (c) Registering the gazing position
                                 (upper left) for "5:00 am".   (lower middle) for "7:30 pm".

Fig. 3. A flow of registering information-specific gaze positioning for "clock" display

4   Preliminary User Study

4.1   Method

The concept of gaze-guided ambient displays and the creation of displays using everyday objects were validated through two experiments involving eight participants (six males and two females) in their 20 s.

In the first experiment, participants were instructed to engage in a video-watching task on a PC as the main activity, while two objects were positioned on either side of the participants as ambient displays (Fig. 4). One object on the left side displayed the elapsed time of the 30-min experiment, while the other object on the right side served as a persuasive ambient display, directing the participant's gaze to a bottle of water every six minutes to increase awareness of rehydration. The participants wore a Pupil Core eye tracker [14] to analyze eye-gaze activities. A questionnaire survey based on Mankoff et al.'s heuristic evaluation of ambient displays [12] was conducted.

The second experiment evaluated the process of transforming everyday objects into an ambient display. Participants were asked to create an ambient display by selecting one of five types of information: time, weather, temperature, probability of precipitation, and humidity. The participants could use any object to map the information they had prepared, such as household appliances and umbrellas in the room. The creation process was video-recorded and analyzed, along with the interview responses.

(a) Display showing elapsed time of the experiment from triangle flag to checker flag

(b) Main task, i.e., watching a video on a PC

(c) Display to encourage hydration

Fig. 4. Experimental environment. Note that the markers were used to define areas of interest (AOIs) for eye-tracker analysis

4.2   Result and Analysis

Periphery as Ambient Display: Figure 5 shows the percentages of positive responses for the items of heuristic evaluation, with the exception of Q6, which were favorable toward the use of gaze guidance as an ambient display. In Q2, more than 70% of the participants expressed positive opinions about the subtlety of Eyebient display as an ambient display; however, some individuals raised concerns about noticeable eye movements, particularly when interacting with the water reminder. Conversely, there were no significant concerns for the other display exhibiting the remaining duration of the experiment, and opinions leaned towards it being subtle and unobtrusive.

Q3 focused on participants perspectives on the congruence and integration of the ambient display into its environment. A total of 86% of the participants confirmed this finding. We believe that using everyday objects as a medium for representing information elicits these responses. Most participants reported feeling no discomfort from smartphone displays with anthropomorphic eyes. The increasing social acceptance of persistent liquid crystal displays in everyday life, facilitated by the ubiquitous presence of digital signage, may partially explain this observation.

Q5 inquired about the ease of understanding the presentation without imposing a high cognitive load. In relation to Q3, 86% of participants answered affirmatively. One participant reported that it did not take him long to understand what the gaze was indicating, suggesting that the cognitive load of gaze and everyday object presentation methods was low. The same was true for Q9, "Did you have the feeling that it did not interfere with your work?". We believe this because the ambient display has a peripheral nature.

Suitable Information: Half of the participants reported that they could only see the beginning, end, and middle of the elapsed time display (Fig. 4(a)) in their responses to Q5. This can be attributed to the narrow width of the eye, that is, the horizontal length of the rectangle representing the eye. In particular, the implementation shown in Fig. 4(a) shifts the agent's gaze from the bottom left to

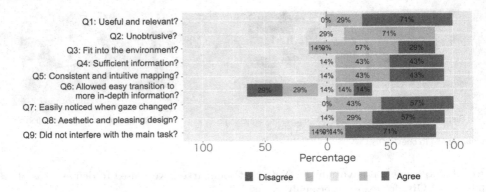

Fig. 5. Percentages of answers to the items in Mankoff et al.'s heuristic evaluation

the bottom right over 30 min by changing approximately 130 pixels on the smartphone screen. Thus, we believe that it is difficult to convey the detailed volume of continuously changing information. However, the water reminder display was reported to be easy to understand due to its use of binary information. Eyebient display is more suitable for conveying information through binary changes, indicating presence or absence, or discrete information with enough distance separation between target objects.

Only 28% of participants responded affirmatively to Q6, "If I wanted more detailed information, I could get it easily and quickly." We believe that this reflects the inability to obtain detailed information from Eyebient display, such as the exact time the experiment was completed or the amount of water consumed that day. This is a reasonable response, since we designed Eyebient display with the assumption that users would seek out more detailed information if they wanted to know it themselves. As the primary role of an ambient display is to present information in an abstract manner, presenting more detailed information goes beyond the original role of an ambient display. To increase the effectiveness of Eyebient display, we can explore the possibility of incorporating an interface that allows users to interact with the display by tapping the screen through the agent's eyes, for example, to obtain detailed information. This turns Eyebient display into a conventional display used at the center of consciousness. In our previous study on an augmented mirror [8], we verified the effectiveness of such a multistep (two-step) information presentation mechanism for providing detailed information on an ambient display.

Guidability of Gaze: Typical heat maps of gazes in AOIs consisting of display units and objects are shown in Fig. 6. We observed differences in the areas that were frequently looked at between the two displays. In the elapsed-time display (Fig. 6(a)), six participants looked more frequently near the display unit, that is, the eyes. Conversely, only two participants frequently looked at the objects. One participant stated that after understanding the placement of everyday objects,

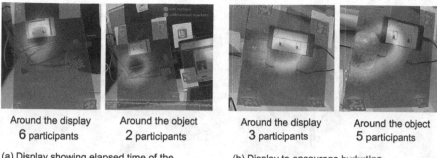

| Around the display | Around the object | Around the display | Around the object |
| 6 participants | 2 participants | 3 participants | 5 participants |

(a) Display showing elapsed time of the experiment from triangle flag to checker flag

(b) Display to encourage hydration

Fig. 6. Heatmaps of gazing around two ambient displays (red: high ratio of gazing) (Color figure online)

such as the two flags on the desk, he only checked the position of the agent's eyes on his smartphone. This could be due to the fact that the elapsed time could be easily estimated from the position of the black eye at the base of the rectangle representing the eyes on the smartphone. However, as described in Sect. 2, if joint attention were effective, the participant would have looked in the direction of the agent's gaze even if they were not consciously aware of it.

In contrast, in the case of the water reminder, five participants looked in the direction of the object (Fig. 6(b)). A possible reason for the difference in the gaze-guidance effect between the two ambient displays could be the velocity of the agent's eye movement. Compared to the change in the elapsed time display, the water reminder showed a very large change in eye position over a short period. However, in the elapsed time display, the eyes moved from left to right over a period of 30 min. This suggests that rapid eye movements could increase eye guidance and that the water reminder may have been more effective in directing the user's gaze. However, rapid eye movements may also interfere with the user's attention. To increase the effect of gaze guidance beyond rapid eye movements, it is important to reconsider the shape of the eyes, size of the display, and facial features.

Creativity of Gaze-Guided Ambient Displays: Figure 7 shows examples of ambient displays developed by the participants. They used various objects; however, five participants insisted that they had difficulty in mapping the position of their black eyes to the target object through trial and error. Three participants commented that they did not have ideas on ambient displays, that is, pairs of information and objects, due to the difficulty in finding objects that match the information provided. Four participants presented other ambient display ideas that they felt they would like to have, although they were not able to realize them this time because of a lack of information sources or finding suitable objects. These included reminding people of daily household chores, such

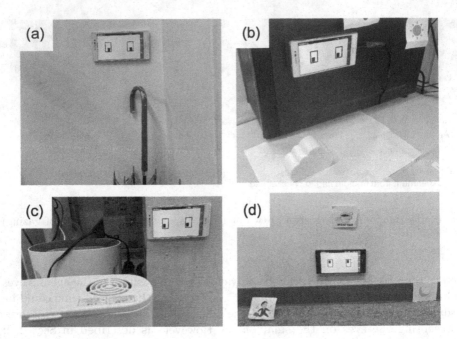

Fig. 7. Examples of resultant Eyebient displays. (a) Looking at an umbrella when the probability of precipitation is high, (b) looking at a cloud-shaped object and card with a printed illustration of the sun when a cloudy or sunny sky is expected, respectively, (c) looking at a humidifier when the room is dry to encourage people to turn it on, and (d) looking at cards representing departure for a business trip, break, or going home

as cleaning and laundry; telling them to turn on the TV when important news came on; encouraging them to diet or exercise; and informing them that they had communication messages, such as emails from a specific person.

5   Concluding Remark

We proposed Eyebient display that employed gaze guidance and everyday objects to implement an ambient display. A toolkit for the creation was also presented. The results of a preliminary user study showed the feasibility and effectiveness of the proposed method. Future work will involve modifying the gaze mechanism to enhance its gaze-guiding effect and developing a more versatile and flexible design.

References

1. Anakubo, T., Fujinami, K.: DeforVerFace: Modular Linear-Deformable Vertical Surface. In: Streitz, N.A., Konomi, S. (eds.) Distributed, Ambient and Pervasive Interactions: 11th International Conference, DAPI 2023, Held as Part of the 25th HCI International Conference, HCII 2023, Copenhagen, Denmark, July 23–28, 2023, Proceedings, Part I, pp. 3–12. Springer Nature Switzerland, Cham (2023). https://doi.org/10.1007/978-3-031-34668-2_1

2. Cho, M., Saakes, D.: Calm automaton: a DIY toolkit for ambient displays. In: Proceedings of the 2017 CHI Conference Extended Abstracts on Human Factors in Computing Systems, pp. 393–396. ACM, New York, NY, USA (2017). https://doi.org/10.1145/3027063.3052968

3. Dahley, A., Wisneski, C., Ishii, H.: Water lamp and pinwheels: ambient projection of digital information into architectural space. In: Summary of Conference on Human Factors in Computing systems (CHI 1998), pp. 269–270 (1998). https://doi.org/10.1145/286498.286750

4. Driver, J., Davis, G., Ricciardelli, P., Kidd, P., Maxwell, E., Baron-Cohen, S.: Gaze perception triggers reflexive visuospatial orienting. Vis. Cogn. 6(5), 509–540 (1999). https://doi.org/10.1080/135062899394920

5. Engert, S., Klamka, K., Peetz, A., Dachselt, R.: STRAIDE: a research platform for shape-changing spatial displays based on actuated strings. In: CHI Conference on Human Factors in Computing Systems, pp. 1–16. ACM, New York, NY, USA (2022). https://doi.org/10.1145/3491102.3517462

6. Friesen, C.K., Kingstone, A.: The eyes have it! Reflexive orienting is triggered by nonpredictive gaze. Psychon. Bull. Rev. 5(3), 490–495 (1998). https://doi.org/10.3758/BF03208827

7. Froehlich, J., et al.: UbiGreen: investigating a mobile tool for tracking and supporting green transportation habits. In: Proceedings of the 27th international conference on Human factors in computing systems - CHI 2009, pp. 1043–1052. CHI 2009, ACM Press, New York, New York, USA (2009). https://doi.org/10.1145/1518701.1518861

8. Fujinami, K., Kawsar, F., Nakajima, T.: AwareMirror: a personalized display using a mirror. In: Gellersen, H.-W., Want, R., Schmidt, A. (eds.) Pervasive 2005. LNCS, vol. 3468, pp. 315–332. Springer, Heidelberg (2005). https://doi.org/10.1007/11428572_19

9. Jafarinaimi, N., Forlizzi, J., Hurst, A., Zimmerman, J.: Breakaway: an ambient display designed to change human behavior. In: CHI 2005: CHI 2005 extended abstracts on Human factors in computing systems, pp. 1945–1948. ACM, New York, NY, USA (2005). https://doi.org/10.1145/1056808.1057063

10. Kunikata, S., Fujinami, K.: Customizability in preventing loss of interest in ambient displays for behavior change. In: AMBIENT 2022, The Twelfth International Conference on Ambient Computing, Applications, Services and Technologies, pp. 1–6 (2022)

11. Lin, J.J., Mamykina, L., Lindtner, S., Delajoux, G., Strub, H.B.: Fish'n'Steps: encouraging physical activity with an interactive computer game. In: Dourish, P., Friday, A. (eds.) UbiComp 2006. LNCS, vol. 4206, pp. 261–278. Springer, Heidelberg (2006). https://doi.org/10.1007/11853565_16

12. Mankoff, J., K.Dey, A., Hsieh, G., Kientz, J., Lederer, S., Ames, M.: Heuristic evaluation of ambient displays. In: Proceedings of the conference on Human factors in computing systems, pp. 169–176 (2003). https://doi.org/10.1145/642611.642642

13. Matthews, T., K.Dey, A., Mankoff, J., Carter, S., Rattenbury, T.: A toolkit for managing user attention in peripheral displays. In: Proceedings of the 17th Annual ACM Symposium on User Interface Software and Technology, UIST 2004, pp. 247–256 (2004). https://doi.org/10.1145/1029632.1029676
14. Pupil Labs GmbH: Pupil Core - Open source eye tracking platform. https://pupil-labs.com/products/core/
15. Wisneski, C., Ishii, H., Dahley, A., Gorbet, M., Brave, S., Ullmer, B., Yarin, P.: Ambient displays: turning architectural space into an interface between people and digital information. In: Streitz, N.A., Konomi, S., Burkhardt, H.-J. (eds.) CoBuild 1998. LNCS, vol. 1370, pp. 22–32. Springer, Heidelberg (1998). https://doi.org/10.1007/3-540-69706-3_4

MAR Enhanced Hiking Experience: Exploring Multimodal Experience Design in Outdoor Scenarios

Leyi Hong[1], Wenjun Hou[1,2,3]($\boxtimes$), Churu Chen[1], Haiwen Zhang[1], and Qian Li[1]

[1] School of Digital Media and Design Arts, Beijing University of Posts and Telecommunications, No. 10 Xinucheng Road, Beijing 100876, China
hwj1505@bupt.edu.cn
[2] Beijing Key Laboratory of Network System and Network Culture, No. 10 Xitucheng Road, Beijing 100876, China
[3] Key Laboratory of Interactive Technology and Experience System, Ministry of Culture and Tourism, No. 10 Xitucheng Road, Beijing 100876, China

Abstract. In recent years, outdoor hiking has gained popularity, driven by increasing health awareness. However, enthusiasts of hiking encounter challenges related to equipment carrying, long-distance journeys, and environmental uncertainties. These challenges include the limitation of frequently checking routes on mobile devices due to the use of trekking poles. To address these obstacles, we undertake research and design efforts that integrate outdoor scenarios with Augmented Reality (AR) technology. Our approach involves establishing AR user interface design guidelines and design strategies tailored for outdoor scenarios, derived from a comprehensive systematic literature review. We propose a multimodal AR system solution that leverages AR glasses and trekking poles as dual inputs. The system incorporates multimodal interaction and natural information presentation, aiming to create a multilevel interactive experience enriched with tangible physical evidence. The goal is to establish a seamless connection between the virtual and real worlds, mitigating the challenges faced by hiking enthusiasts. Evaluation experiments conducted demonstrate that the system successfully meets user needs and expectations in terms of multimodal input, visual information recognizability, and the rationality of user interface layout. The system is noted for its close alignment with the usage scene, exhibiting enhanced user-friendliness in practical applications. This study provides valuable insights into the design of AR systems in outdoor sports scenes, offering a reference point for future endeavors in this domain.

Keywords: Augmented Outdoor Sports · Multimodal Interaction · Augmented Reality(AR)

C. Chen, H. Zhang and Q. Li—These authors contributed equally to this work.

N. A. Streitz and S. Konomi (Eds.): HCII 2024, LNCS 14719, pp. 347–364, 2024.
https://doi.org/10.1007/978-3-031-60012-8_22

1   Introduction

Over the past period, COVID-19 has become a global pandemic. It not only causes wear and tear on people's physical functions but also elevates the occurrence of psychological symptoms such as depression, anxiety, and stress [1]. In this case, people need to engage in appropriate physical activities to relieve the physical and mental stress it causes. Research has shown that even a small degree of hiking in a natural environment [2] can help restore mental health. As a result, hiking is gradually becoming a mainstream form of exercise. However, the complexity of the routes, the boring process, the changing terrain, and the weather in trekking reduce people's willingness to participate [3]. To overcome this, we explored the possibility of combining Augmented Reality (AR) technology with outdoor hiking.

The equipment, itinerary, and environment of hiking activities create a certain physical and mental load. AR technology provides immediate visual feedback and seamlessly integrates with the physical space, reducing the cognitive load on the user when switching between the surrounding environment and the display. Moreover, research indicates that the immersive experience introduced by AR positively influences users' satisfaction with the environment, engagement levels, and perception of authenticity [4]. In this context, the paper introduces a hiking experience optimization system. Leveraging AR and Artificial Intelligence technologies, users can acquire navigational information, environmental insights, and health data. Simultaneously, they can actively engage in real-time team collaboration and interactions with the surrounding environment. Traditional hiking experiences predominantly rely on natural surroundings and individual perceptions, whereas AR enhances the experiential dimensions.

Our system, developed using Unity 2019 and the Menomotion SDK, utilizes the HoloLens 2 HMD and a modified interactive trekking pole as hardware components. The system uses AR glasses and the trekking pole as dual input interfaces, employing multimodal interaction and natural information presentation to enhance the natural environment and establish a seamless connection between the virtual and the real-world.

In this paper, we introduce the system solution by sorting out the AR design principles and strategies in outdoor scenarios. The experimental evaluation shows that our system meets the users' needs and expectations in all aspects, can effectively improve the users' sense of experience and participation in practical applications, and enhance the users' willingness to participate in hiking.

2   Related Works

2.1   AR Introduction

Augmented Reality (AR) is defined as "a system possessing three key characteristics: 1) the amalgamation of real and virtual; 2) real-time interactivity; and 3) three-dimensional registration" [5]. Today, augmented reality has evolved from indoors or in fixed locations to a variety of mobile devices to ubiquitously enable interaction. In comparison to stationary desktop AR, Mobile Augmented Reality (MAR) facilitates persistent interaction with physical objects while on the move, overlaying digital content onto the physical environment. AR glasses are considered the preferred choice for mobile AR, with their interfaces transitioning from rapid micro-interactions and limited content display to immersive holographic environments [6].

2.2   AR Visual Experience in Outdoor Scene

To generate an immersive AR experience and visual effects, information management and rendering are identified as pivotal processes in presenting virtual entities. In complex outdoor environments, flexible and diverse methods are required to trigger the display of information. Edwards-Stewart et al. [7] categorized trigger-based AR technologies into four types, including marker-based, location-based, object-based, and hybrid approaches. McNamara et al. [8] introduced an AR view management system that triggers the appearance of AR tags by focusing on relevant areas, employing gaze-based interaction. Simultaneously, outdoor ambient light conditions also impact the visibility of the system. Some studies have used color blending [9] and color correction to enhance the visibility of AR interfaces. In addition, Haeuslschmid et al. [10] conducted a study on how driving information is displayed, advocating for an on-demand display of information that is relevant to driving but not permanently needed.

These studies offer valuable insights into addressing challenges related to information triggering, visibility, and user experience in outdoor AR applications. However, research specific to hiking, a prolonged and long-distance activity in natural environments, remains relatively limited. Optimization is required for information presentation and visual effects tailored to hiking scenarios.

2.3   Multimodal Interactions for AR Outdoor Activities

With technological advancements, AR objects have transcended beyond mere representations of simple data and can now integrate with various input modes. Traditional unimodal interactions are convenient to operate but may seem overwhelming for complex scenarios or tasks. Therefore, introducing multimodal interaction is considered a solution to enhance interactions between virtual entities and physical entities.

As early as 1990, M. Bauer [11] and colleagues constructed a campus navigation system using multimodal inputs such as voice, tangible interfaces, and GPS positioning. Subsequently, MATHIAS KÖLSCH et al. [12] employed a portable and fixed 'ring-like trackball' for multidimensional control of virtual objects through finger manipulation. HazARdSnap [13] is a gaze-based AR cycling system that effectively reduces the risk of collisions when accessing digital information during cycling by integrating scene data, motion, gaze, and head position information.

These early studies provide valuable references for us. However, the necessity of introducing multimodal interaction in AR scenarios stems from the analysis of diverse contextual requirements. We still need further in-depth research and discussion in the hiking scenario.

3   Design Guidelines and Strategies

3.1   AR-UI Design Guidelines

The design landscape of AR remains fragmented due to the rapid evolution of hardware, the interdisciplinary nature of teams, and the absence of established standards. In contrast to the ergonomics, user interface layout, and user experience principles applied to 2D interfaces, AR user interface design necessitates consideration of additional factors such as environment, space, and interacting entities [14]. Currently, scholars in the AR field are actively formulating guidelines for user interface design. For instance, Dünser et al. [15] apply principles from human-computer interaction (HCI) to propose a human-centered approach for designing AR User Interfaces (UIs), encompassing principles like affordance, cognitive load, low physical labor, learnability, and flexibility. However, the number of discussions on user interface design examples specifically for AR scenarios such as outdoor sports is still limited. Therefore, this study endeavors to design AR user interfaces for outdoor sports by combining the above design principles and the unique characteristics of outdoor scenes.

3.2   AR-UI Design Strategies for Outdoor Sports Scenarios

AR systems in outdoor sports scenarios must offer users timely and context-specific assistance. Unlike traditional AR-UI design, outdoor AR-UI requires additional design strategies to minimize interference from the dynamic real environment on AR user interface element recognition. The four design strategies described below, show how to enhance the usability of AR-UI in outdoor settings through thoughtful design approaches.

Considering Color Fusion. The display of information in an optically transparent AR interface involves a combination of two light sources: natural light and electronic light. This unique color perception characteristic poses usability challenges for users of optical head-mounted displays (oHMD) when integrating display colors with the background [16]. Outdoor environments substantially influence the color perception of user interface elements due to variations in lighting conditions and weather conditions, as well as different nature scenes. Hence, careful consideration of color selection and blending is essential to prevent difficulties in recognizing information. J. L. Gabbard et al. [17] investigated the impacts of different background environment textures, light intensity, and text styles on various colors in AR interfaces, and concluded that colors exhibiting higher contrast with the environment are more easily recognizable. In dynamic

AR usage scenarios, adjustments to enhance the recognizability of interface elements can be considered by sampling the background and ambient light. Another effective strategy involves dynamically adapting the AR visual colors to environmental conditions, ensuring that interface information maintains a consistently high contrast with the background color.

Enhancing Brightness. In addition to fine-tuning the contrast between foreground and background, another established design strategy involves augmenting the brightness of virtual elements. This approach has been effectively utilized, as demonstrated in the study conducted by Peterson et al. [18]. Their research underscores the importance of maintaining virtual display elements at a brightness level at least 10–15% higher than that of the background. In a particular scenario, optimizing the recognizability of virtual elements can be achieved by judiciously increasing their brightness. However, the coherence of the design must be considered to prevent the virtual elements from being overly bright and having problems such as glare, blinding, or visual abruptness.

Background Blurring. In experimental findings by Steven J. Kerr et al. [19], it was observed that information presented on a plain background (e.g., a concrete wall) exhibited enhanced visibility compared to information presented on a visually "busy" background (e.g., a brick wall). Excessive background detail reduces the recognizability of foreground information, so a moderate application of localized background blurring can improve the readability of virtual elements in complex outdoor environments.

Realistic Natural Fusion. An optimal AR system should impart to users the sensation that real and virtual objects coexist seamlessly in the same space. However, contemporary AR systems frequently overlook real-world lighting conditions or fail to align with nearby real objects. Addressing this challenge, Suhwan Kwak et al. [20] introduced a harmonic rendering technique from a technical perspective. This approach enhances the realism of outdoor AR by estimating and approximating the position of the sun and the direction of sunlight, ensuring visual consistency in outdoor AR settings. While achieving a fully realistic natural fusion remains challenging, it remains a crucial design objective to enhance the seamless integration of virtual and real objects. This can be achieved through optimizing color choices, layout, information encoding methods, and information presentation locations.

4   System Design

4.1   Multimodal Interaction

Research has demonstrated that integrating multimodal methods for user input enhances system interaction effectiveness for a broader user base [21]. We delve into the application of multimodal interactions, including gaze, gesture, physical controllers, and voice, in outdoor hiking scenarios based on the requirements of outdoor hiking users. The specific interaction specification of this AR system has shown in Fig. 1.

Eye Tracking. By integrating eye-tracking-based variable rate coloring and gaze point rendering, gaze behavior emerges as a pivotal element in augmenting input modalities within AR interface interactions [22]. In contrast to approaches centered on activity recognition or exclusive reliance on eye-movement data for direct interaction, we position gaze as a substitute for physical selection. Unlike traditional 2D user interfaces rooted in the WIMP paradigm, where users must first visually acquire the component of interest and then maneuver the cursor within its hot zone for subsequent interaction, our AR 3D interaction allows users to select any element within the interface through gaze directly. Users can also carry out subsequent interactions through physical controllers or gestures. Mobile gaze interaction streamlines the frequent switching between mobile devices and the environment, transforming it into visual interactions between the user and various entities within the environment, which undoubtedly results in a more natural and immersive interaction experience for the user.

Hand Gesture. Gesture interaction, a natural means for individuals to engage with their surroundings in daily activities, is anticipated to be seamlessly integrated into AR systems as a method of interaction. This integration is expected to augment the sense of connectivity and integration between individuals and components within the AR system. However, the absence of a universal gesture design paradigm stems from the diverse scene characteristics, interaction object types, and purposes of AR. A study by Tran Pham et al. [23] observed that the scale of objects and scenes in the AR experience significantly influences gesture selection and is closely tied to user expectations and physical behaviors. Taking inspiration from this research, we initiate the design of gesture interactions in outdoor scenes by considering physical interaction behavior and incorporating the scale elements of the actual scene and interaction objects. In this work, gesture interaction serves as a follow-up behavior to gaze interaction, facilitating further engagement with components triggered by the initial gaze interaction. Specific interaction behaviors encompass fist clenching, palm opening, finger pinching, and index finger sliding, each serving distinct purposes such as obtaining detailed information or executing complex interactions with components in the scene.

Physical Controller. In various outdoor hiking scenarios, users exhibit distinct preferences in equipment selection and carrying practices based on their specific needs. Analyzing user behavior in outdoor hiking situations reveals notable variations in equipment utilization, such as gloves and trekking poles. Notably, many long-distance hiking and mountaineering enthusiasts opt to carry hiking poles, impacting the feasibility of gesture interaction. Furthermore, differences in the frequency of information interaction across diverse hiking scenarios contribute to varying user preferences for gesture and physical controller interaction. Therefore, developing support for controller-based inputs tailored to outdoor application scenarios becomes imperative. As depicted in the figure, the hiking pole retrofitted with a hardware controller serves as a solution. This controller incorporates physical buttons and wheels that utilize RF signals to transmit commands, enabling users to interact with components in the scene. The controller supports feedback through haptics, enhancing the user's immersive experience. The buttons on the controller facilitate operations such as confirmation and selection, while the wheel is designed for panel sliding and virtual model rotation. These functionalities align with users' inherent perceptions and operating habits related to physical controllers. Consequently, users can choose by gazing at the line of sight in the interactive system, selecting gestures or physical controllers based on the current context, thereby achieving a natural interaction with the environment.

Voice Input. Since outdoor sports heavily rely on audiovisual experiences, encompassing the enjoyment of scenery and natural sounds, our design prioritizes preserving the natural feeling throughout outdoor activities. Consequently, we have minimized the use of voice operations to ensure the overall outdoor experience is maintained. Voice dialogues are exclusively employed as a means of team communication, aligning with the regular behavioral habits of users and ensuring seamless integration with the outdoor adventure environment (Fig. 2).

Interaction	Instruction				
Eye tracking	Gazing at specific points or objects on the screen enables the acquisition of overview process information or entry into a selected state. Subsequent interactions with the selected elements can be performed using gestures.				
Voice	Implemented for team communication, aiming to facilitate convenient communication and collaboration within the team.				
Hand gesture	Pinch	Slide	Wave down	Palm	Fist
Physical controller	Button	Wheel	Button	Button	Button
Interactive ideogram	Select objects	Rotate models; slide panels	Close panels	Call up the 3Dmap	Display of health data

Fig. 1. Interaction Specification

4.2   Multi-level Experience

Hiking provides an effective outdoor solution for individuals to connect with nature, placing them in open-field nature scenarios to enhance interactions. It has

Fig. 2. An interactive hiking pole retrofitted with physical buttons and wheels.

been correlated with developing well-being, cognition, mental health, socialization, and other competencies [24]. Effectively designing interactions and behaviors is essential for the ecological environment and individuals. To this end, we study the presence experience of hiking scenarios to analyze physical evidence involved in different contexts and develop levels of hiking experience.

According to Hulliv et al., users prefer the pleasurable sensation of a systematic experience with multiple excitations arranged rationally to an experience with a single excitation point [25]. Due to emotional, physiological, environmental and other factors, the trough is also a common and noteworthy node in the hiking experience. Therefore, Multiple physical evidences are extracted for different scenarios as entry points to analyze the system experience.

We combined high-frequency words related to the hiking experience and qualitative data collected through interviews and questionnaires to organize the physical evidence that may be involved during the hiking experience to explore multidimensional hiking experience design points. The integrated qualitative data are hiking routes, critical signposts, complex environments, plants, animals, team communication, landmark attractions, physical data, weather, ecological phenomena, and hiking data.

Vidon and Rickly, in their study of hiking and rock climbing crowds, found that natural interactive activities involve rich experiential levels and contents, including improving socialization and finding the meaning of life [26]. Accordingly, we refined the outdoor experience hierarchy of "perception - interaction - emotion - reflection", summarised the physical evidence hierarchically, and refined the multidimensional hierarchy of experience in the hiking scenario in order to develop the AR system design.

Level 1: Intuitive perception of the environment, corresponding to physical evidence of complex environments, hiking routes, and key signposts;

Level 2: Enhancement of interesting interactions, corresponding to physical evidence of plants, animals, and team interpersonal;

Level 3: Record emotional fluctuations, corresponding to physical evidence of landmarks and ecological phenomena;

Level 4: Individual reflection, corresponding to the physical evidence of hiking data, personal data, and environmental data.

4.3 AR-UI

The system transforms the hiking experience hierarchy into six landable functions through AR glasses: route guidance, science interaction, marking punch cards, team collaboration, environmental information, and alerts, and explores the AR-UI design scheme, which involves interface elements, information layout, and interaction. When the user selects a passing point based on the map, the system recommends optional paths and relative information such as mileage. In navigation mode, based on GPS technology and visual recognition, visual route guidance is provided at key locations such as forked intersections and terrain changes to improve safety. To enhance natural interaction, information popularization and exciting interaction with animals and plants along the way can be carried out. Smooth voice communication and location awareness among team members to ensure efficient teamwork. Due to the changing conditions and security threats during the hike, the system provides timely alerts when there is abnormal weather, health, and terrain data. In addition, the system supports marking routes and trash through quick photographing.

Collecting outdoor images with different light and nature and extracting rich environmental colors, the system design adopts the color fusion and brightness enhancement design strategy. It selects high-contrast blue-green as the theme color. Hiking involves two modes: the static mode, in which the user stays in place, and the dynamic mode, in which the user travels. Background blurring is applied to the static mode and controls to ensure the hike's safety, improve the interface information's recognizability, and appropriately allocate the user's attention. Natural integration guides the design of visualization elements, e.g., terrain visualization and natural interaction.

Information Layout. The layout of the information is based on the characteristics and priorities of the behavioral tasks under the experience hierarchy, which includes six functional areas: the main visual area, the road terrain area, the alert area, the interactive prompt area, the menu evocation area, and the global status area, and corresponds these six functional areas to the center, middle periphery, and periphery visual areas according to the distance between the information and the center of the field of view, as showed in Fig. 3.

Main Visual Area: The center area. It corresponds to each level's direct or indirect cue guidance, including landmarks, nature, and companion positions, generally used in dynamic mode. Wickens proposed the SEEV model that when the angle of view between the information and the center field of view is smaller, the information is more likely to be noticed by the user [27], which can be applied to indirect cue guidance, helping users quickly access and react to relevant information by placing cues from distant landmarks or surrounding obstacles in the primary visual field.

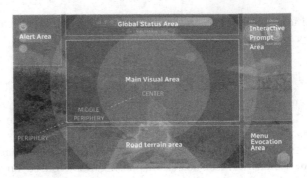

Fig. 3. Interface Layout

Road Terrain Area: The middle periphery area. It corresponds to the first level of route guidance tasks, containing complex environment, route information, and critical road signs, and is generally used in dynamic mode. Route information is highly related to the environment. In order to follow the principle of realism and proximity, route information should be adapted to the environment and adopt the visualization form that intuitively reflects the characteristics to reduce cognitive cost.

Alert Area: The peripheral area. It corresponds to the third level of the data anomaly warning tasks, including abnormal health, weather, and road conditions, generally used in dynamic mode. It is placed in the upper left area to allow a quick view of the details, in line with users' psychological expectations.

Interactive Prompt Area: The peripheral area. It corresponds to the second level, including nature and team information, generally used in dynamic mode and expands the static mode when selected. Since the area involves more interactive operations, it is permanently placed in the upper right corner, balancing the usability and interface occlusion.

Menu Evocation Area: The peripheral area, for the global menu bar. To reduce information redundancy, the menu is designed to be hidden in the lower right corner in dynamic mode. In static mode, it can be triggered by the entity controller or gesture.

Global Status Area: The middle periphery area, for the global status bar. Essential information such as time, weather, and hiking data is integrated into an accessible area, improving efficiency. The design needs to focus on simplicity and readability, ensuring that information is presented at a glance through logical arrangement and icon usage.

Navigation Systems for Complex Environments. The navigation system for complex environments consists of two functions: route planning before hiking and route guidance during hiking. After intelligent route planning, the system will guide the hiking route until the arrival at destinations or manually exit the navigation status.

Route guidance contains complex environmental information, route information, and hiking data. As the hiking scenario involves steep slopes, stairs, and other difficult terrain environments, the navigation system needs to proactively provide route information at the right time to help users participate in the field hiking safely and smoothly. At the same time, the user can evoke the 3D map and 2D map to check the remaining distance and duration of the hike, as well as the terrain and road condition information ahead.

For information evocation triggering, Renate et al. concluded that displaying relevant information on demand, supplemented by audio notifications, can fully utilize the interface display space while reducing the risk of distracting users with constantly displayed information [28]. Therefore, route guidance information does not need to be continuously visible throughout the hike but is shown on-demand in a combination of three forms: system intelligent recognition, gesture evocation, and hardware (trekking poles) recognition. The system recognizes key nodes and gives visual guidance through GPS and computer vision technology. Gestures can evocate functions like a 3D map, as shown in Fig. 4. By opening the palm of the left hand, we can obtain a three-dimensional map model, which helps us to intuitively and quickly view the terrain. Hiking poles, as the exclusive aids in hiking, have the metaphor of "hiking record," which can be recognized by the hiking poles to present the hiking data.

Fig. 4. 3D Map and Hiking Data

As for the form of information presentation, Steven et al. compared screen-fixed warnings and world-fixed warnings on HUDs and found that world-fixed warnings are safer, i.e., the user spends more time cognizing the physical scene [29]. Therefore, the route guidance interactive interface should have an environmental fit as its primary goal, preserving the physical environment and overlaying the highlighted route to avoid interfering with material nature. As shown in Fig. 5., when the system recognizes the feature of a steep slope, fork, or other special road conditions ahead, the interface uses dynamic trajectory, data, and symbols to visually present guidance information, which is intuitive, effective, and does not affect sight.

Fig. 5. Route Guidance

Nature Interaction. Nature interaction is an essential experiential aspect of the hiking experience. Regarding how to construct connections with nature, the Connection with Nature Index (CNI) proposed by Cheng and Monroe consists of four dimensions: enjoyment of nature, empathy for nature, sense of oneness, and sense of responsibility [30]. Therefore, in the design of experience with nature, on the one hand, the user's perception of nature and sense of connection is enhanced through the popularization of knowledge about natural objects and interesting interactions, and on the other hand, the inclusion of garbage tagging functions encourages the construction of a sense of oneness and responsibility towards nature.

Nature interaction is realized using computer image recognition technology and nature model libraries. Since plants are large and tall, and animals have the characteristic of movement, their gaze and selected states are differentiated. When recognizing, the system highlights objects through light effects or circles to encourage interaction. As shown in Fig. 6., a brief information label is unfolded after gazing. Pinch the object to get its model and release it to expand the detail panel, which contains multi-card information cards, models that can rotate, and interactive buttons like "Feed."

Fig. 6. Nature Interaction

The Eco Marker function helps users mark environmentally unfriendly phenomena and locations. As shown in Fig. 7., by gazing at the garbage object, the system will recognize the garbage intelligently based on computer image recognition, and the information can be fed back to the management center of the scenic spot, helping the subsequent ecological construction.

Fig. 7. Spam Identification

Health and Safety. Health and safety are crucial prerequisites for the hiking experience, which can be reflected in the virtual interface safety and hiking danger tips.

For the virtual interface in the outdoor scene with a certain degree of risk, the experiencers need to focus on their attention to carry out the experiential activities more relaxedly. Therefore, virtual interface security requires the interface to follow the physical environment content-based. In the dynamic mode, it can not be the center of the region, the critical environmental objects to obscure, to ensure that the user's state in the real environment can be known, to avoid attention distraction.

Hiking danger alerts monitor and hint at abnormal health, weather, and trip planning to improve hiking safety. The use of differentiated color schemes and symbols in the peripheral area and the appearance or disappearance of the easily noticeable state switching can effectively and timely prompt. As shown in Fig. 8., when an abnormal alarm under the module appears, the corresponding warning icon is presented on the upper left and combined with voice broadcasting and text for timely reminder.

Fig. 8. Hiking Danger Tips

Team Collaboration. Team collaboration is oriented to multi-person hiking scenarios, providing real-time voice communication and location association functions to enhance team connection based on the team's organizational information and satellite positioning. Since it is challenging to accurately present location and distance information with the physical environment, a cue-guided format is chosen to quickly mark the location of real-time moving peers and sense the distance in a three-dimensional field. As shown in Fig. 9., the location distance is visualized when approaching the team members.

Fig. 9. Position Visualization of Team Members

5   Test and Evaluation

We developed the prototype based on Unity 2019 and the ManoMotion SDK, hardware using a Hololens 2 head-mounted display and a modified interactive trekking pole, and conducted qualitative user evaluations through user tests and focus group interviews to gather user feedback on the usability of the AR prototype. Focus group interviews can penetrate deeply into the research object, which is conducive to obtaining first-hand data from users and is sometimes accompanied by unexpected gains and discoveries. Therefore, focus group interviews were chosen for this test.

Through the focus group, we analyzed qualitative data on the reactions of six users to a test prototype system, intending to investigate the usability and user-friendliness of the prototype. Before participating, participants were invited to conduct an initial questionnaire to confirm that they were the target users for this study. Gender, age, hiking duration, hiking scenarios, hiking frequency, and hiking purpose were collected and evaluated to select test users. Based on the overall score of the questionnaire, we filtered participants into three categories: skilled, intermediate, and beginner users, with two users in each category, one male and one female.

We user-tested the system outdoors, choosing a sunny day for a better presentation. Participants were tested in the same outdoor forest park. Each participant was given about 3 min to familiarize themself with the AR device and the interface before starting. After familiarization, the test was conducted sequentially. During the test, the user was required to complete the following two tasks:

- Turn on the navigation module and select a route to move forward for 2 min.
- Collect a plant or animal.

During the interaction process, users were encouraged to use both gestures and trekking poles to interact with the system. Users will be asked to share their thoughts about the prototype and the interaction process for each task. Interviews were conducted at the end of all the tests, and users were asked the following questions:

- Question1: How was the overall experience of the system?
- Question2: How was the AR interface?

Accordingly, the user feedback was organized and analyzed. The results are as follows:

Multimodal Input. In the test, users were encouraged to use gestures and hiking poles to interact with the system to accomplish the task. Four users indicated that utilizing the hiking pole as a physical controller is more natural and meets the needs of the scenarios; the other two users stated that they preferred gesture operation and are used to hand-eye interaction but admitted that in outdoor complex terrain environments, gesture interaction may cause inconvenience to the hiking process and may lead to hand fatigue in the long run. As for gaze interaction, users unanimously showed high acceptance of it.

Information Recognition. In the test, users need to recognize the information in the environment and act accordingly to complete the task. Most users reported that the information in the system prototype has good recognition and contrast in the outdoor background. However, two users indicated that for panels displaying more information in a three-dimensional space, due to the line of sight and the panel angle, the distance between the panels, and other factors, it is easy to create difficulties in reading the information. The user must instinctively move closer to the panel or want to zoom in on the panel to read the information.

Depth Perception. In AR space, since the interactive elements are all virtual, users are prone to difficulty judging the distance between the elements and themselves. In the test, all four users expressed reasonable distance perception for the labeled panel displaying the target location. In the flora and fauna collection section, three users raised the issue of difficulty in judging the distance during the pinching of the interactable bubbles. In addition, one user suggested that presenting a certain degree of occlusion from the actual object in the field of view would be more helpful in representing distance.

UI Layout. During the testing process, due to environmental control and safety requirements in outdoor hiking scenarios, the layout and presentation of information in the AR interface need to be reasonably arranged. Most users recognized the layout of the system interface. In addition, one user suggested that the main menu could be accessed faster by setting a button on the physical controller or using a memorable gesture. Based on the results of the above focus group interviews, it can be summarized that users' satisfaction with the usability mainly focuses on the multimodal input mode, information display recognition, and the UI layout, which reflects a close connection with the environment and good user-friendliness of the usage scenario. Users' low satisfaction with usability is due to the display of large pieces of information, the obstacle of information readability caused by the panel's angle, and some distance perception problems.

6   Discussion

The multimodal hiking experience system is an optimized design for outdoor hiking experiences based on Augmented Reality and Artificial Intelligence technology. Most existing studies are based on static scenes or visual characteristics of outdoor scenes. Therefore, this study attempts to design for the outdoor hiking process, for the existence of tedious and complex terrain, and to redesign the hiking experience in a multimodal way by combining augmented reality and artificial intelligence technologies to enhance the user's experiential dimensions and better perceive nature.

This study investigates and designs the system based on literature research and interaction design principles. After the user test, in general, the design of the multimodal system meets the expectations and needs of participants in the survey. The experience hierarchy, multimodal interaction, information layout, natural interaction and connection, and health and safety were consistent with the AR-UI in outdoor conditions and the behavioral elements of actual hiking scenarios. This consistency is within expectations, given that our design is based on established methods and theories from literature and user research.

Considering the limitations of the current equipment and hardware, the challenge is how to ensure that the AR glasses are lightweight enough while ensuring that all aspects of their functions and performance work properly, as well as whether the UI interface, information display, and functional modules can work properly under some extreme weather conditions. This part of the test has yet to be completed.

7   Conclusion and Future Work

In this study, we propose an outdoor hiking experience optimization system based on augmented reality and artificial intelligence technology, in which users can easily access information such as navigation, environment, and health data during the hiking process and can interact naturally and multimodally with their surroundings as well as participate in teamwork, thus enhancing the dimensions of the experience. Through user tests, we verified the rationality of the design in line with expectations. In this way, we designed the overall interaction system and studied outdoor hiking scenarios' characteristics and interaction requirements. For usability issues, we conducted tests and focus group interviews. Despite the hardware limitations, this study is still informative for exploring multimodal AR-UI interaction design in outdoor hiking scenarios. Further work and tests are needed to design and develop an interactive experience system more relevant to outdoor scenarios. With the development of technology and hardware conditions, the system can be expected to be extended to applications in more complex outdoor hiking scenarios or other outdoor sports scenarios.

References

1. Dubey, S., Biswas, P., Ghosh, R., et al.: Psychosocial impact of COVID-19. Diab. Metab. Syndr. Clin. Res. Rev. **14**(5), 779–788 (2020)
2. Mitchell, R.: Is physical activity in natural environments better for mental health than physical activity in other environments? Soc. Sci. Med. **91**, 130–134 (2013)
3. Molokáč, M., Hlaváčová, J., Tometzová, D., et al.: The preference analysis for hikers' choice of hiking trail. Sustainability **14**(11), 6795 (2022)
4. Dağ, K., Çavuşoğlu S., Durmaz, Y.: The effect of immersive experience, user engagement and perceived authenticity on place satisfaction in the context of augmented reality. Library Hi Tech (2023)
5. Azuma, R.T.: A survey of augmented reality. Presence Teleoperators Virtual Environ. **6**(4), 355–385 (1997)
6. Lam, K.Y., Lee, L.H., Braud, T., et al.: M2a: a framework for visualizing information from mobile web to mobile augmented reality. In: 2019 IEEE International Conference on Pervasive Computing and Communications (PerCom), pp. 1–10. IEEE (2019)
7. Edwards-Stewart, A., Hoyt, T., Reger, G.: Classifying different types of augmented reality technology. Annu. Rev. Cyberther. Telemed. **14**, 199–202 (2016)
8. McNamara, A., Kabeerdoss, C.: Mobile augmented reality: Placing labels based on gaze position. In: 2016 IEEE International Symposium on Mixed and Augmented Reality (ISMAR-Adjunct), pp. 36–37. IEEE (2016)
9. Ang, S.Y., Ng, G.W.: A study on the effect of the real-world backgrounds using colour blending technique on optical see-through AR user interface design. In: 2020 6th International Conference on Interactive Digital Media (ICIDM), pp. 1–4. IEEE (2020)
10. Haeuslschmid, R., Klaus, C., Butz, A.: Presenting information on the driver's demand on a head-up display. In: Bernhaupt, R., Dalvi, G., Joshi, A., Balkrishan, D.K., O'Neill, J., Winckler, M. (eds.) INTERACT 2017, Part II. LNCS, vol. 10514, pp. 245–262. Springer, Cham (2017). https://doi.org/10.1007/978-3-319-67684-5_15
11. Bauer, M., Bruegge, B., Klinker, G., et al.: Design of a component-based augmented reality framework. In: Proceedings IEEE and ACM International Symposium on Augmented Reality, pp. 45–54. IEEE (2001)
12. Kölsch, M., Bane, R., Höllerer, T., et al.: Touching the visualized invisible: wearable AR with a multimodal interface. IEEE Comput. Graphics Appl. **26**(3), 62–71 (2006)

13. Zhao, G., Orlosky, J., Gabbard, J., et al.: HazARdSnap: gazed-based augmentation delivery for safe information access while cycling. IEEE Trans. Vis. Comput. Graph. **01**, 1–10 (2023)

14. Krauß, V., et al.: Current practices, challenges, and design implications for collaborative AR/VR application development. In: Proceedings of the 2021 CHI Conference on Human Factors in Computing Systems (2021)

15. Dünser, A., et al.: Applying HCI principles to AR systems design (2007)

16. Gabbard, J.L., et al.: More than meets the eye: an engineering study to empirically examine the blending of real and virtual color spaces. In: 2010 IEEE Virtual Reality Conference (VR), IEEE (2010)

17. Gabbard, J.L., et al.: An empirical user-based study of text drawing styles and outdoor background textures for augmented reality. In: IEEE Proceedings. VR 2005. Virtual Reality, IEEE (2005)

18. Peterson, S.D., Magnus, A., Stephen, R.S.: Label segregation by remapping stereoscopic depth in far-field augmented reality. In: 2008 7th IEEE/ACM International Symposium on Mixed and Augmented Reality, IEEE (2008)

19. Kerr, S.J., et al.: Wearable mobile augmented reality: evaluating outdoor user experience. In: Proceedings of the 10th International Conference on Virtual Reality Continuum and Its Applications in Industry (2011)

20. Kwak, S., Choe, J., Seo, S.: Harmonic rendering for visual coherence on mobile outdoor AR environment. Multimedia Tools Appl. **79**, 16141–16154 (2020)

21. Radford, A., et al.: Learning transferable visual models from natural language supervision. In: International Conference on Machine Learning, PMLR (2021)

22. Green, C., Jiang, Y., Isaacs, J.: Modular 3D interface design for accessible VR applications. In: Chen, J.Y.C., Fragomeni, G. (eds.) Virtual, Augmented and Mixed Reality. HCII 2023, LNCS, vol. 14027, pp. 15–32. Springer, Cham (2023). https://doi.org/10.1007/978-3-031-35634-6_2

23. Pham, T., et al.: Scale impacts elicited gestures for manipulating holograms: implications for AR gesture design. In: Proceedings of the 2018 Designing Interactive Systems Conference (2018)

24. Weinstein, N., Przybylski, A.K., Ryan, R.M.: Can nature make us more caring? Effects of immersion in nature on intrinsic aspirations and generosity. Pers. Soc. Psychol. Bull. **35**(10), 1315–1329 (2009)

25. Hull, R.B., IV., Stewart, W.P., Yi, Y.K.: Experience patterns: capturing the dynamic nature of a recreation experience. J. Leis. Res. **24**(3), 240–252 (1992)

26. Vidon, E.S., Rickly, J.M.: Alienation and anxiety in tourism motivation. Ann. Tour. Res. **69**, 65–75 (2018)

27. Wickens, C.D., Helton, W.S., Hollands, J.G., et al.: Engineering Psychology and Human Performance. Routledge, vol. 36 (2021)

28. Haeuslschmid, R., Klaus, C., Butz, A.: Presenting information on the driver's demand on a head-up display. In: Bernhaupt, R., Dalvi, G., Joshi, A., K. Balkrishan, D., O'Neill, J., Winckler, M. (eds.) Human-Computer Interaction - INTERACT 2017. INTERACT 2017, LNCS, Part II, vol. 10514, pp. 245–262. Springer, Cham (2017). https://doi.org/10.1007/978-3-319-67684-5_15

29. Kerr, S.J., Rice, M.D., Teo, Y., et al.: Wearable mobile augmented reality: evaluating outdoor user experience. In: Proceedings of the 10th International Conference on Virtual Reality Continuum and Its Applications in Industry, pp. 209–216 (2011)

30. Pritchard, A., Richardson, M., Sheffield, D., et al.: The relationship between nature connectedness and Eudaimonic well-being: a meta-analysis. J. Happiness Stud. **21**, 1145–1167 (2020)

The Potential of Interactive Design in Children's Picture Books and Its Impact on User Experience

Dongtao Liu, Ying Zhang, and Yinghong Zhang[⊠]

College of Fine Arts and Design, University of Jinan, No. 336 Nanxinzhuang West Road, Jinan 255000, Shandong, China
83976471@qq.com

Abstract. With the development of digital technology, children's picture books are transforming traditional printing to interactive digital media, which provides new possibilities for improving children's reading experience and learning effect. This paper focuses on the application of interactive design in children's picture books, especially its potential to enhance children's reading experience and promote cognitive development. The study found that interaction design elements can significantly improve children's reading interest and participation and help promote their language skills and cognitive development. In addition, it also discusses how the integration of AI and IoT technologies will promote the innovation of picture books, analyzes how these technologies make picture books more personalized and interactive, and their potential to improve children's education and entertainment experience. Considering many aspects of user experience, this paper puts forward suggestions to improve the design of children's interactive picture books, such as enhancing the interactivity of storytelling, improving the quality of visual and auditory elements, and creating a more immersive reading environment. Finally, it emphasizes the necessity of further research on future children's picture book design and technology integration and puts forward how to better combine educational theory and psychological principles, as well as how to use emerging technologies to create more rich and participatory children's reading experience, to provide a reference for picture book authors, illustrators, educators and technology developers.

Keywords: Interactive Design · Children's Picture Book · Development Potential

1 Background Introduction

1.1 Development Background of Children's Picture Books

Children's picture books have experienced profound changes and development in recent years as an important part of children's literature. With the continuous progress of society and the rapid development of science and technology, traditional paper picture books are gradually integrated into the digital era, opening a new chapter. Traditional children's picture books provide children with a rich reading experience with their unique artistic style and concise text. These paper picture books are usually in the form of a combination of pictures and texts. Vivid pictures and simple and understandable words stimulate children's imagination and creativity. Classic picture books, such as *The Little Prince* and *Grimm's Fairy Tales*, have left a profound literary mark globally and laid a foundation for the development of children's literature. The innovation of children's picture books in the digital era, with the popularization of digital technology, the field of children's picture books is ushering in an innovation. Digital children's picture books are no longer limited to paper books but are presented in applications, e-books, etc., providing children with a more diversified and interactive reading experience. This innovation enables picture books to integrate animation, sound effects, games and other elements, breaking the boundaries of traditional reading and enabling children to interact with stories more intuitively and participatory. In addition, interaction design plays a key role in the digital transformation of children's picture books. Through ingenious interaction design, digital picture books can better meet children's cognitive level and interest characteristics and improve their learning experience. Interactive design can make picture books more vivid and interesting and promote children's learning and thinking development. Therefore, it is an important task to study the development potential and user experience of interactive design in the field of children's picture books, which is helpful to better understand the impact of digital technology on children's literature and how to improve children's reading experience by designing excellent interactive interfaces. In short, integrating traditional children's picture books and the digital era makes children's reading experience more colorful. With the continuous development of interactive design, the field of children's picture books will usher in more possibilities.

1.2 Rise and Application of Interaction Design

In recent years, with the rapid development of information technology, interaction design has become one of the core concepts in digital products. Interaction design has strongly influenced different fields, from web design to mobile applications and virtual and augmented reality. This era change has brought closer and more natural interaction between users and digital interfaces, providing a new possibility for digitizing children's picture books.

In digital children's picture books, interactive design is no longer just page layout and button design, but also involves how to create a friendlier and educational user experience through technical means. The application of interaction design enables children to more intuitively integrate into picture book stories, interact with roles, solve puzzles, and participate in games, which further improves children's interest and participation in learning. Through ingenious animation design, the characters in the digital picture book can be vividly presented, making the story more vivid and interesting. Combined with the well-designed sound effect, it can provide a richer sensory experience and enable children to better understand the story through the double stimulation of hearing and vision. Interaction design provides a passive audio-visual experience and emphasizes children's active participation. Interactive elements in digital picture books, such as clicking and dragging, stimulate children's curiosity and creativity and cultivate their autonomous learning ability. Good interaction design not only improves children's entertainment experience but also helps to promote their cognitive development. Through the interactive design of digital picture books, children can better understand abstract concepts, cultivate logical thinking, and establish a deep understanding of the story and characters in the interaction. This learning method, different from traditional picture books, makes the interactive design application in children's picture books more attractive.

1.3 Research Purpose and Significance

With the rapid development of digital technology, children's picture books are undergoing a revolutionary change from traditional printing to interactive digital media. This change has not only changed the presentation of picture books but also opened up new possibilities to improve children's reading experience and learning effect. To explore the development potential of interactive design in children's picture books, pay attention to the impact of innovative design on children's reading experience to provide a new perspective and method for researching digital children's literature. By revealing the positive impact of interaction design on children's cognitive development and learning, this paper tries to provide new and innovative directions for children's education. The future potential of interactive design in children's picture books is further discussed, with special attention to how the integration of artificial intelligence and Internet of Things technology will promote the innovation of picture books. This paper analyzes how these technologies make picture books more personalized and interactive and their potential to improve children's education and entertainment experience.

Finally, it emphasizes the necessity of further research on the design and technology integration of children's picture books in the future and puts forward the direction of future development. This includes better integration of educational theory and psychological principles and how to use emerging technologies to create a richer and more participatory reading experience for children, which is conducive to promoting the forefront of the integration of children's literature and technology and creating richer and meaningful possibilities for children's reading experience in the future.

2 Application of Interaction Design in Children's Picture Books

2.1 Analysis of the Application Form of Interactive Design in Children's Picture Books

1. Augmented Reality (AR) Picture Books

Augmented reality (AR) picture books are not different from traditional paper picture books but are an evolution of paper picture books. It integrates scientific and technological elements based on traditional picture books, pays attention to the innovation of content and form, and emphasizes visual impact and interactivity to enhance the authenticity and experience of picture books. The uniqueness of AR picture books lies in their deep integration with technology, which provides readers with a richer and more diverse reading experience.

On the one hand, AR picture books rely more on science and technology in content and form and create imaginative virtual scenes by introducing virtual reality elements. The application of this technology not only makes the picture book story more vivid but enhances the readers' sense of substitution for the picture book world. Readers can immerse themselves in virtual scenes in AR picture books and feel the flexibility and authenticity of the story. The visual impact brought by this immersion makes the reading process more attractive and stimulates readers' curiosity and desire to explore picture books. On the other hand, AR picture books emphasize interactivity, making readers become participants in the reading experience. Compared with the linear reading method of traditional picture books, readers in AR picture books can take themselves as the center and explore the story according to their interests and preferences. This personalized reading experience makes readers more deeply integrate into the story and increases the emotional resonance and sense of participation. Readers can participate in the story through interactive elements, interact with characters, and even change the story's direction to make the whole reading process more dynamic and interesting.

However, although picture books emphasize technological innovation and interactivity, we cannot ignore the respect and development of traditional paper picture books. The presentation of the AR effect must be based on paper picture books and maintain consistency with traditional picture books. The design of paper picture books is still the basis of AR picture books, and the touch of paper, the pleasure of turning pages and other elements provide readers with unique reading fun. Therefore, in the development process of AR picture books, we must balance technology and tradition to complement each other and jointly create a richer and deeper reading experience for readers. Ar picture books (as shown in Fig. 1.) differ from traditional paper picture books. At the same time, by integrating science and technology and strengthening interactivity, AR picture books give readers a richer and more fascinating reading experience. This does not mean separating the relationship with tradition but innovating based on respecting tradition and opening up wider possibilities for the reading world.

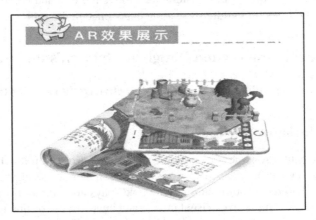

Fig. 1. Application of AR technology in picture books

2. Interactive Story Application

Children's picture books have always been an important medium to lead children into the imaginary world. However, with the rapid development of science and technology, children's picture books are also evolving, integrating elements of interactive story applications and bringing children a new reading experience. In traditional picture books, the story's narration is usually linear, and the reader unfolds the story with words and illustrations in a limited space. The application of interactive stories in children's picture books has promoted the change of this paradigm. Through the introduction of the application, the story becomes more vivid and three-dimensional and is no longer limited to static words and pictures. The interactive nature of the application makes the story more flexible. Readers can participate in it more autonomously, interact with the characters, change the trend of the plot, and thus deeply integrate into the wonderful world of the story. For example, StoryBots (Fig. 2.), a multimedia interactive platform, uses AI technology to provide children with interesting learning experiences. StoryBots allow children to interact with every story link through voice recognition and animation. This interactive way not only improves children's interest in reading but also helps to improve their language expression and communication skills.

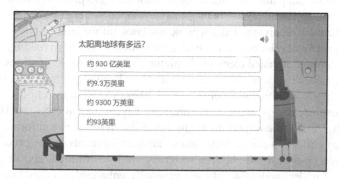

Fig. 2. Question interaction in StoryBots

These interactive story applications often contain multimedia elements, such as sound, music, animation, etc., which enrich children's sensory experience of reading. Children can interact with the application's scenes and characters by touching the screen and sliding their fingers, stimulating their curiosity and creativity. This sense of participation is not only a passive reading process but also an experience of intimate interaction with the story, which makes reading more vivid and interesting.

The interactive story application also provides children with a more personalized reading experience. Through selection and decision-making in the application, readers can shape the development direction of the story according to their interests and preferences. This personalized reading experience allows children to be more deeply immersed in the story and helps cultivate their judgment and problem-solving abilities.

However, the application of interactive stories in children's picture books also faces challenges. First of all, it should be noted that the application's design should not be too complex to ensure that it is suitable for children of different ages. Secondly, adding an interactive nature should conform to the principle of education, and the story's internal logic should not be sacrificed just to pursue excitement. The most important thing is that application should not become a tool to replace paper picture books, but should complement traditional reading forms and jointly promote children's all-round development.

In the digital era, the interactive story application in children's picture books provides children with a more diversified and innovative reading experience. By integrating technology and stories, this trend will promote the development of children's literature and bring more rich and interactive reading fun to the new generation of readers.

2.2 Impact of Interaction Design Elements on Picture Book Reading

1. The Function of Animation Sound Effect

Early reading is a comprehensive activity to cultivate 0–6-year-old children's sense of touch, vision, hearing, language and thinking. Preschool is the key stage of children's development, in which children's cognitive development is mainly based on sensory experience. Therefore, the corresponding sensory education for children aged 3–6 is conducive to cultivating and shaping children's abilities and promotes their intellectual and thinking development. Vision is the most developed system of human sensory perception and the main receiving medium of picture book information. At the early stage of children's cognitive development, it stimulates children's interest in reading through the cognitive perception of visual elements in picture books, dynamic graphics, colors and other explicit visual experiences in animation. The visual sense transmits information to the brain, drives the generation of senses in other organs, urges children to actively observe and explore things, and affects children's psychological changes. The auditory channel is also one of the important media for children to receive information, which can strengthen children's image cognition of abstract concepts in the process of reading. In addition, 3–6-year-old children's literacy ability is limited, and their language expression and understanding ability are gradually enhanced, so they are in the best period of language learning. The introduction of auditory resources conforms to the law of children's cognitive development, and its supplement is mainly through the technical support brought by scientific and technological progress. On the one hand, the audio in animation can create the interaction between children and picture books in the form of a built-in sound source, and the advantage is that the form is relatively simple and natural.

On the other hand, the development of AI technology provides a technical means for the realization of page turning and reading, intelligent intercom and other interactive methods in children's picture books. The introduction of intelligent interaction in the design of picture books can better build multi-level auditory resources, make hearing coordinate with other senses, and bring immersion experience to children. For example, Google Read, an app developed by Google (as shown in Fig. 3.), uses speech recognition technology to help children learn to read. When a child reads a story aloud, it listens and provides support and feedback. If a child struggles with a word, the application will detect and provide help, making the reading experience more interactive and educational.

With the continuous development of science and technology, the reading methods of children's picture books are also gradually evolving. Interactive design's animation

Fig. 3. Google Read with application interface display.

and sound elements have become important in enriching children's reading experience. These elements are eye-catching tools and play an important role in children's cognition, emotion and learning. First of all, animation and sound elements can enhance the expressiveness and immersion of the story. Introducing animation effects into picture books makes the story scenes vivid and the characters more expressive and energetic. The addition of sound effects enables children to better feel the emotional atmosphere of the story and then more deeply integrate into the story. This immersion makes reading more interesting and helps improve children's understanding and memory of the story.

Secondly, animation and sound elements can stimulate children's imagination and creativity. Skillfully using animation and sound effects in interactive design can create a world of wonder and fantasy for children. This creative design can stimulate children's curiosity and urge them to think and explore various possibilities in the story. Through interaction with animation and sound effects, children can participate in the story-creation process and develop the ability to understand and solve problems.

Clever animation and sound elements in interactive design can also promote children's learning. Children can more easily understand abstract concepts and knowledge through visual and auditory means. For example, the Dinosaur Baker APP (as shown in Fig. 4.) developed by Standard Bay Technology can click on the "customized parents' voice" of the story collection to generate customized sounds with one click through recording, and then you can permanently use parents' voice to tell stories, even if you are not around your child, you can also use voice to accompany the child. However, it should be noted that the balance should be paid attention to when using animation sound effect elements. The effects of excessive complexity and stimulation may distract children's attention or even backfire. According to children of different ages' cognitive levels and reading needs, animation sound effect elements should be carefully selected and designed to better integrate into the story and positively expand the reading experience.

Fig. 4. Dinosaur Baker app telling stories in the voice of parents

2. Effect of Touch Interaction

As the most direct and mainstream interactive mode in current applications, touch interaction is widely used in interactive picture books, especially in picture books based on tablet devices. This interaction mode triggers various interactive behaviors by touching the screen with a finger or stylus, collectively called touch interaction. One of the major features of interactive picture books is their touch-interaction design. The operation mode of feedback behavior through clicking, dragging, sliding and other forms makes readers feel comfortable when using. This design brings an intuitive interactive experience, making the emotional experience of picture books different with the change of media. Compared with traditional paper picture books and picture books, the most significant difference between interactive picture books is their unique page-turning mode. Turning pages on the electronic screen have no paper touch, an unavoidable limitation of interactive picture books. However, through ingenious design, we can achieve a similar pattern of paper picture books in the touch page flipping to give readers a more authentic experience. By designing indicative buttons, readers can trigger page replacement by clicking or long pressing, making page turning operation simple and intuitive. The other way is to keep the original picture during page turning, simulate the process of paper replacement, and make the page turning process closer to the real-world reading experience.

In touch interaction design, page-flipping can not only be designed as a single page replacement but also create a continuous flipping effect through the clever combination of dynamic effects and pictures so that readers can be more immersed in the story. For example, in the picture book *Very Hungry Caterpillar AR* (as shown in Fig. 5), through AR technology, when viewing on a smartphone or tablet application, the pages of the book will not only become interactive and the caterpillar will move and eat all kinds of food, but also have a sound effect when turning the pages, making the viewer more immersed. In addition, a long scroll can be designed so that readers can always slide in the same direction, reducing the distance brought by the electronic screen and making it easier for readers to enter a comfortable reading state.

Touch interaction design is the most common mode of human-computer interaction in electronic products. Applying this design idea to interactive picture books can bring readers a more vivid, novel and interesting reading experience by combining different interaction and feedback mechanisms. This design not only meets the needs of children

Fig. 5. Very Hungry Caterpillar AR

for interactivity but also provides more possibilities for creating more creative and imaginative picture books, pushing children's picture books to a new position in the digital era.

3   Development Potential of Interactive Design in the Field of Children's Picture Books

3.1   Trends of Interaction Design Technology Integration

1. Integration of Artificial Intelligence and Internet of Things Technology

The field of children's picture books is experiencing a revolution in integrating interactive design technology. The traditional paper picture books are gradually integrated with digital and intelligent elements, providing children with a richer and more interesting reading experience. Integrating artificial intelligence (AI) and Internet of Things (IoT) technology has injected unprecedented innovation and development potential into children's picture books.

Application of artificial intelligence in children's picture books. The integration of artificial intelligence technology enables children's picture books to better adapt to each child's unique needs and interests. Through the deep learning algorithm, the picture book system can analyze children's reading behavior, hobbies and learning levels and provide a personalized reading experience for each child. This personalization is not only reflected in the recommendation of the story theme but also in the customization of the text difficulty, language style, and other aspects to ensure that the content of the picture book is closer to children's cognitive level. AI technology can also identify children's emotional states through emotional analysis to adjust the content of picture books or provide interactive suggestions, making the reading process more emotional. For example, when the system senses that children show strong interest in a certain role or plot, it can add relevant elements to enhance children's sense of participation.

Integration and interactive experience of Internet of Things technology. Internet of Things technology has brought a richer interactive experience for children's picture books. By connecting picture books with smart devices, such as smart toys or smartphone applications, children can interact with characters in picture books in real time. This connection expands the reading space and extends the picture book experience to the real world. For example, children can voice interact with characters in picture books through intelligent devices and ask or answer questions to promote language development and logical thinking. The Internet of Things technology can also enable characters in picture books to interact with intelligent toys, increase the participation of touch and action, and further enhance children's sense of immersion.

Artificial intelligence and the Internet of Things jointly promote the development of children's picture books. Integrating artificial intelligence and Internet of Things technology enables children's picture books to achieve greater cognition, perception and interaction breakthroughs. This combined application not only improves the entertainment of picture books but also imperceptibly cultivates children's scientific and technological awareness and digital literacy. With the continuous progress of technology, the integration of artificial intelligence and Internet of Things technology in children's picture books will be further deepened. In the future, we can look forward to a more intelligent, interactive and personalized picture book experience to provide children with richer and interesting choices for reading.

2. Technology Promotes the Innovation of Picture Books

In children's picture books, the continuous promotion of technology has become a key factor leading to innovation. Through the introduction of new technologies, picture books are no longer limited to traditional paper books but show a more vivid, interesting and educational innovative form. The innovation of picture books driven by technology includes several key aspects:

Integration of virtual reality (VR) and augmented reality (AR). Integrating virtual reality (VR) and augmented reality (AR) technology is a significant direction to promote the innovation of picture books. This enables children to interact with picture books in an unprecedented way. By wearing VR helmets or using AR applications, children can enter a new dimension and interact with characters in picture books as if they were in the story. This immersive experience stimulates children's curiosity and enhances their interest in reading.

Integration of animation, sound effects and touch-sensing technology. Traditional picture books usually focus on static images and text, and technology promotion makes animation, sound effects and touch-sensing technology better integrated into picture books. Dynamic images and rich sound effects make the story more vivid and attract children's audio-visual perception. At the same time, touch-sensing technology enables children to participate in all aspects of the picture book by interacting with the screen, changing from passive reception of information to active participation.

Application of personalized story generation algorithm. The personalized story generation algorithm application is another aspect of technology promoting picture book innovation. The system can generate personalized story content through artificial intelligence technology according to children's reading habits, interests and age. This personalization not only makes the picture book closer to the needs of each child but also promotes their learning and cognitive development.

Introduction of interactive design. The introduction of interactive design is an important direction to promote the innovation of picture books. Interactive elements, such as problem-solving and branch selection, are added to the picture book to enable children to participate more actively in the story. This interactivity not only stimulates children's thinking and judgment ability, but also increases the interest and interactivity of reading.

Integration of intelligent education elements. The innovation of picture books promoted by technology is also reflected in integrating intelligent education elements. Through artificial intelligence technology, picture books can provide a more personalized learning path, and adjust the educational content according to children's subject interest and level. Such innovation makes picture books an entertainment tool and an effective teaching assistant for children's learning. Driven by the above innovative technologies, children's picture books undergo a digital and intelligent revolution, providing children with a richer and more personalized reading experience. The introduction of these technologies not only expands the form of picture books but also provides a new way for children to understand.

4 Technological Progress Promotes the Personalized and Interactive Development of Picture Books

The rapid progress of technology has brought unprecedented development opportunities for children's picture books, especially in personalization and interactivity. This trend has not only changed the form of traditional picture books but also profoundly affected children's reading experience.

Personalized story experience. With the progress of technology, personalized story experiences have gradually become a significant feature of children's picture books. The picture book system can collect and analyze children's reading preferences, hobbies and learning levels through artificial intelligence and data analysis technology. Based on this information, picture books can adjust the text difficulty, recommend related topics, and provide customized reading suggestions for individual differences. This personalized story experience not only meets the unique needs of each child but also promotes them to be more active in reading.

Introduction of intelligent interactive elements. Technological progress has promoted the introduction of intelligent interactive elements in picture books, making reading no longer a one-way information transmission but a two-way communication. The picture book adds elements such as question-answering and role interaction. Through touch, voice and other methods, children can interact with the characters in the story. This intelligent interaction makes reading more interesting and cultivates children's ability to think and solve problems.

Real-time feedback and learning assessment. With the development of technology, picture books can provide real-time feedback and learning evaluation. By monitoring children's reading behavior, the system can track their learning progress and provide timely feedback. This feedback includes evaluating reading speed and accuracy and can provide targeted learning suggestions to help children better understand the story content and promote improving cognitive ability.

Application of virtual reality and augmented reality. The application of virtual reality (VR) and augmented reality (AR) technology has added a new dimension to children's picture books. These technologies allow picture books to escape paper shackles and present more vivid, three-dimensional scenes. Children wearing VR helmets or using AR applications can immerse themselves in the virtual world of the story and interact with characters, making the reading experience richer and more fascinating.

Social reading experience. Technology development promotes picture books to move towards a social reading experience. Children can share their reading experience with friends and family through smart devices, discuss story plots together, and recommend favorite picture books to each other. Such a social reading experience promotes interpersonal communication, expands children's reading circle, and creates a more social and interactive learning environment.

Driven by technological progress, picture books are no longer static paper books but digital products that integrate personalized and interactive elements. This provides children a richer and fascinating reading experience and stimulates their desire to explore knowledge and stories. In the future, with the continuous innovation of technology, the field of children's picture books will continue to usher in more personalized and interactive development.

4.1 The Potential of Interaction Design in the User Experience of Children's Picture Books

1. Children's Emotional Response

When discussing the potential of interaction design in children's picture books, it is particularly important to consider children's emotional responses. Emotional response is the core component of children's picture book user experience because it is not only related to children's instantaneous emotions but also has a profound impact on their psychological development and the formation of their world outlook. Donald Norman's three-level emotional response theory provides a theoretical framework to analyze the emotional response in children's picture books. The automatic level is children's first impression of picture books, which is usually triggered by the visual effects, color matching, animation effects and other factors of picture books. These elements are very important for children because they can quickly attract children's attention and stimulate their curiosity and desire to explore. At the behavioral level, it involves the psychological reaction of children in the interaction process. When children interact with picture books by touching, clicking or sliding, they will have a cognitive evaluation of the contents of picture books. This psychological response not only reflects the children's understanding of the content of the picture book but also reflects their participation and immersion in the reading process. Therefore, designers must fully consider children's cognitive characteristics and behavioral habits and create a natural and smooth interactive experience. The reflective level results from the comprehensive effect of instinctive level and behavioral level emotion. At this level, children will deeply think and evaluate the contents of picture books and form their own opinions and feelings. This reflection process helps children understand picture books' contents and cultivates their critical thinking and moral judgment in emotional interaction and choice. Through repeated experience and independent participation in story construction, children can have a deeper understanding of the values conveyed by picture books to gradually improve their world outlook.

To give full play to the potential of interactive design in children's picture books, we should pay attention to children's emotional responses and take this as a starting point to optimize the design of picture books. We can stimulate children's emotional resonance and improve their reading experience by using rich visual elements, ingenious interaction mechanisms and fascinating story plots. At the same time, we must pay attention to children's differences and growth needs, provide them with personalized reading experiences, and promote their all-round development. The picture books of personalized story-type interactive design can use AI to analyze children's reading habits and preferences and even capture children's eye movement in real-time through infrared instruments (as shown in Fig. 6.) and how long they stay in which words and paragraphs, to systematically record the whole reading process and provide customized story content. So that children like reading and take the initiative to read, to truly achieve the educational purpose of combining teaching with entertainment. Interaction design has great potential in children's picture books, especially in stimulating and guiding emotional responses. Through in-depth understanding and applying the three-level emotional response theory, we can create picture books that align with children's psychological characteristics and growth needs and support their growth and development.

Fig. 6. Infrared instruments can capture Children's eyes

2. Children's Cognitive Absorption

In children's picture books, interactive design not only brings children a richer reading experience but also shows great potential in promoting children's cognitive absorption. Children's cognitive absorption refers to their ability to acquire, understand and internalize new knowledge in reading. Interaction design helps to optimize children's cognitive absorption process by providing them with diversified learning paths and personalized learning experiences.

First, interaction design can stimulate children's curiosity and learning interest. By introducing multimedia elements such as animation, sound effects and games, interactive design makes the content of picture books more vivid and interesting and attracts children's attention. This attractive way of learning helps stimulate children's curiosity and encourages them to participate more actively in reading and learning picture books. Secondly, interaction design can promote children's deep learning and understanding. By providing interactive learning activities and problem-solving tasks, interactive design guides children to think deeply and explore the knowledge in picture books. This deeply participatory learning approach helps children better understand and master knowledge and form long-term memory. In addition, interaction design can also provide a person-alized learning experience for children. Each child's cognitive level and interest prefer-ences are different. Interaction design allows children to choose their learning path and content according to their needs and interests. This personalized learning method helps to meet the personalized needs of children and improve their learning effect. Finally, interaction design helps to cultivate children's autonomous learning ability and inquiry spirit. By encouraging children to explore and discover independently through picture book reading, interactive design stimulates children's autonomous learning motivation. This way of autonomous learning helps to cultivate children's ability to think inde-pendently and solve problems and lays a solid foundation for their future learning and development.

Interaction design has great potential in the field of children's picture books. By stimulating children's curiosity, promoting in-depth learning, providing personalized learning experiences and cultivating autonomous learning ability, interaction design can help optimize children's cognitive absorption process and support their all-round development. In the future design of picture books, we should fully use the advantages of interactive design to create a richer, interesting and educational reading experience for children.

3. Children's Creative Thinking

Children's creative thinking refers to their ability to propose novel, unique, creative solutions when facing problems. Interaction design helps cultivate children's creative thinking ability by providing them with free space to explore, try and create. First, interac-tive design encourages children to explore the world of picture books freely. Traditional picture books often only transmit information one way, while interactive design allows children to interact with the contents of picture books through clicking, dragging, zoom-ing and other operations. This free exploration learning method stimulates children's curiosity and enables them to create their picture book world according to their inter-ests and imagination. Secondly, interaction design stimulates children's imagination and creativity. Children can explore different story development paths and endings through different choices and operations in interactive picture books. This diversified story pre-sentation enriches children's reading experience and stimulates their imagination and creativity. Children can gallop freely in picture books and create stories and characters. In addition, interaction design promotes children's critical thinking and problem-solving ability. In interactive picture books, children must face various problems and challenges and find solutions to problems through thinking and trying. This problem-solving pro-cess exercises children's critical thinking ability and enables them to learn how to face and solve problems. This ability will play an important role in future studies and life. Finally, interaction design fosters children's spirit of cooperation and sharing. In the interactive picture book, children can cooperate with other children to create stories and share their works and ideas. This cooperative and shared learning method promotes communication and interaction between children and cultivates their spirit of cooperation and sense of sharing. By cooperating with others to create picture book stories, children can learn different ways of thinking and creative inspiration and further expand their creative thinking ability. By encouraging free exploration, stimulating imagination and creativity, promoting critical thinking and problem-solving ability, and cultivating the spirit of cooperation and sharing, interactive design can help cultivate children's creative thinking ability and provide strong support for their all-round development. In the future picture book design, we should fully use the advantages of interactive design to create a more free, open and creative reading environment for children.

5 The Prospect of Interactive Design in the Field of Children's Picture Books

5.1 Technology-Enabled Children's Picture Books

As a unique form of children's literature, picture books bring readers rich visual experience and emotional resonance through words and pictures. It attaches importance to artistic expression so children can feel the power of beauty and the charm of imagination in reading. However, with the rapid development of digital technology, the traditional form of picture books faces new challenges and opportunities. Currently, most digital picture books are similar to video games. Although they have certain interactivity, their content is often relatively single and lacks innovative interactive design. This phenomenon limits the sensory experience of children's reading and makes reading picture books monotonous. Therefore, we must prospect the future of interactive design in children's picture books to bring a more colorful reading experience to children through technology empowerment.

In the future, with the wide application of AR (augmented reality) technology, the reading experience of children's picture books is expected to be comprehensively upgraded. AR technology can create a dynamic and three-dimensional reading environment for children by combining virtual information with the real world. Using animation technology, AR picture books can achieve "fumigation style accompanying reading"; that is, in the process of children's reading, through the interaction of virtual characters, the addition of sound effects and the change of scene, children can be guided to understand and feel the contents of picture books more deeply. In addition, virtual reality (VR) technology has also brought new possibilities for children's picture books. VR technology can build a completely immersive reading environment, making children seem to be in the world of picture books. Through head-mounted displays, handles and other devices, children can interact with characters in picture books, participate in the story's development, and even change the story's outcome. This new reading experience will greatly stimulate children's imagination and creativity so that they can enjoy reading and improve their cognitive ability.

Technology empowerment has brought new development opportunities for children's picture books. Introducing advanced technologies such as AR and VR can create a richer, diversified and interactive reading environment for children. This will help to improve children's reading interest and ability and promote their all-round development.

We look forward to seeing more innovative interactive designs applied in the field of children's picture books in the future, which will bring more surprises and gains to children's growth.

5.2 Interdisciplinary Participation in Picture Book Production

Interdisciplinary participation in picture book production will become an important trend. The cooperation of professionals from different disciplines can bring richer elements and deeper connotations to the creation of picture books to expand the infinite possibilities of picture books.

The participation of art and design disciplines will bring a more exquisite visual experience to picture books. They are familiar with color, shape, typesetting and other visual elements and can create a unique visual style and atmosphere for picture books. Using modern design concepts and artistic techniques, they can make the page layout of picture books more reasonable and combine words and pictures more harmonious to attract children's attention and stimulate their interest in reading. In addition, psychology plays an important role in children's growth and development, providing more comprehensive, scientific and personalized psychological support and educational services for children. Therefore, psychology and child development experts can provide scientific guidance for picture book creation. They understand the rules of children's cognitive development and psychological characteristics and can provide useful suggestions for picture books' content and interactive design. For example, adding interactive elements suitable for children's age to picture books to promote their participation and experience or guide children to think, explore and grow through the design of story plots and characters. In addition, the participation of literature and Linguistics majors will enrich the narrative mode and language expression of picture books. They are familiar with children's literature's creation rules and language characteristics and can provide interesting and vivid story plots and dialogues for picture books. Using different narrative techniques and language styles, they can make the content of the picture book more attractive so that children can feel the charm of language and cultural heritage in reading.

Interdisciplinary participation in picture book production can promote exchanges and cooperation between disciplines. This interdisciplinary cooperation is conducive to the innovation and development of picture books and helps cultivate excellent talents with interdisciplinary thinking and comprehensive ability. Through cooperation, experts in different fields can learn from each other, inspire each other, and jointly promote the development of children's picture books. The cooperation of art and design, psychology and children's development, literature and Linguistics and other disciplines can create more diversified, connotative and interactive picture books for children. This will help improve children's reading interest and ability, promote their all-round development, and inject new vitality and creativity into the field of picture books.

5.3   Human-Computer Interactive Picture Books for Children

Human-computer interaction technology is constantly reshaping our lives, and in the field of children's picture books, this technology will usher in an important transformation. Although some interactive picture book products are on the market, most designs are still centered on adult users and fail to fully consider the needs of children, a special user group. Children have unique characteristics in cognition, emotion, movement and so on, which makes it particularly important to customize the interactive interface for them. In the future, children's picture books will pay more attention to the naturalness, intuition and ease of learning of human-computer interaction. Physical interaction, gesture recognition, posture control, pen input, voice interaction and other technologies will no longer be isolated elements but will be naturally integrated into the design of picture books to form a harmonious and unified interactive experience. For example, children can turn pages, choose story characters or adjust the story's direction through simple gestures or voice instructions. This intuitive and natural interaction will greatly enhance children's participation and immersion.

We must explore and establish a set of "friendly" interaction design principles suitable for children to achieve this goal. These principles include but are not limited to simple and easy to understand, intuitive and natural, safe and reliable, creative and interesting, etc. For example, when designing an interactive interface, we should use familiar elements and symbols to avoid overly complex operation processes. At the same time, we should also pay attention to the interactive feedback mechanism to ensure that children can clearly understand whether their operation is effective. In addition, we also need to pay attention to α Changes in the growth environment and needs of generations (i.e., future children). With the popularization of digital technology and the change in children's education concept, children's demand for picture books is also changing. Children's picture books in the future should provide rich visual and auditory experiences and stimulate children's creativity, imagination and critical thinking. Therefore, we must constantly innovate and iterate interaction design to adapt to α The changing needs of Generations of Children.

The human-computer interaction technology of children's picture books will be full of challenges and opportunities for generations. By integrating various interaction technologies, exploring interaction design principles suitable for children and paying attention to α with the changing needs of children from generation to generation, we are expected to bring more rich, natural and interesting picture book reading experiences to children in the future. This will improve children's reading interest and ability and lay a solid foundation for their all-round development.

6   Conclusion

With the development of digital technology, children's picture books are transforming traditional printing into interactive digital media. This change not only changes the presentation of picture books but also provides new possibilities for improving children's reading experience and learning effect. The application of interaction design in children's picture books, especially its potential to enhance children's reading experience and promote cognitive development. The study found that interaction design elements, such as animation, sound effects and touch interaction, can significantly improve children's reading interest and participation and help promote their language skills and cognitive development. In addition, the future potential of interactive design in children's picture books is also discussed, especially how integrating AI and IoT technologies will promote the innovation of picture books. This paper analyzes how these technologies make picture books more personalized and interactive and their potential to improve children's education and entertainment experience.

Further research on children's picture book design and technology integration in the future is necessary, including how to better combine educational theory and psychological principles and how to use emerging technologies to create a richer and more participatory reading experience for children. In short, integrating traditional children's picture books and the digital era makes children's reading experience more colorful. With the continuous development of interactive design, the field of children's picture books will usher in more possibilities.

References

1. Liu, L.: Research on the design of multidimensional reading experience of picture books based on children's cognitive development. Design **36**(23), 129–131 (2023)
2. Zhang, Y.: Research on the ethics of children's artificial intelligence product design. Jingdezhen Ceramic University (2023)
3. Yaohua, B., Xiaobo, L.: Interaction design of adaptive English pronunciation learning picture book. Packag. Eng. **43**(04), 293–301 (2022)
4. Yang, P.: Research on the interactive design of picture books for preschool children based on contextual cognition. Lanzhou University of Technology (2021)
5. Wang, A.: Reflections on the development strategy of original popular science picture books-another discussion on the editorial perception of original popular science picture books with artificial intelligence. Editorial J. **01**, 52–56 (2021)
6. Tao, X.: Research on human-computer social interaction design in the era of artificial intelligence. Jiangnan University (2020)
7. Jinghan, X.: Research on children's growing intelligent product design based on visual cognition theory. Liaoning University of Science and Technology (2020)
8. Wang, J.: Research on the innovative application of artificial intelligence speech in the field of parent-child reading-the case of zhimian educational robot. Publishing Wide Angle [9], (2020) Jiabei Shen
9. Shen, J.: Research on children's picture book library design based on experiential learning theory. East China University of Science and Technology (2019)
10. Deng, X.: Promotion strategy of Chinese original children's picture books going out based on the perspective of cultural communication. China Publishing **03**, 63–66 (2018)
11. Khaled, B., Oussama, A., Hakim, A.B., et al.: Interactive design on the product life cycle costs: a case study. Int. J. Interact. Des. Manuf. **18**(2), 837–846 (2024)
12. Tiejun, Z., Yujin, Y.: Research on immersive interaction design based on visual and tactile feature analysis of visually impaired children. Heliyon **10**(1), e22996 (2024)
13. Xiaoqing, Y., Roopesh, S., Amir, E.S., et al.: Exploring the integration of big data analytics in landscape visualization and interaction design. Soft. Comput. **28**(3), 1971–1988 (2024)
14. Cao, Y.: Realistic interaction design of large site scenes based on virtual reality technology. Appl. Math. Nonlinear Sci. **9**(1), (2024)

Talkin' Closet Plus: Interactive Clothing Selection Support System Through Various Opinions of Speech from Clothes

Kouyou Otsu[✉], Takuma Tsujino, Masayuki Ando, and Tomoko Izumi

Ritsumeikan University, Noji-Higashi 1-1-1, Kusatsu, Shiga, Japan
{k-otsu,mandou,izumi-t}@fc.ritsumei.ac.jp

Abstract. Given the strong interest in fashion and the challenges associated with selecting the appropriate clothing, many recommendation systems for daily clothing selection have been proposed. However, most of these systems are software-based solutions suggesting clothing options on devices and do not support the process of examining actual clothes. In our research, we considered novel designs to enhance users' interest in their clothing selection by recommendation messages emanating directly from the clothing items. In this paper, we propose "Talkin' Closet Plus," a clothing selection support system that provides information to users through "speech" from multiple clothes, themselves. In the proposed system, when clothing on a hanger is picked up, the picked-up item recommends that the user wear it. In addition, other clothes join the interaction and provide different perspectives to support the user's choice of clothes. We investigated the effect of combining self-recommendations and critical suggestions from clothes on user satisfaction and selection behavior in the clothing selection. Our experimental results suggest that the proposed scheme, which provides different opinions from multiple clothes, may enhance the user's interest regarding the information on clothes provided by the system and affect the user's decision.

Keywords: Fashion Recommendation · Conversational Agent · Ubiquitous Computing

1 Introduction

Clothing selection is a familiar task for supporting a healthy lifestyle in daily life. Clothes originally played a role in health, such as helping to regulate the body's temperature and protect the body; however, they also express one's identity [3] or personality [8] socially today. As suggested by the fact that fashion is still a fast-growing market in modern society [12], the selection of clothing has value as entertainment beyond mere routine work [11]. However, it is not easy to select clothes in daily life because there are many factors to consider when choosing clothing items, such as weather, schedules, trends, and mood. The situation of having a closet full of clothes but not deciding what to wear is termed "wardrobe

© The Author(s), under exclusive license to Springer Nature Switzerland AG 2024
N. A. Streitz and S. Konomi (Eds.): HCII 2024, LNCS 14719, pp. 383–398, 2024.
https://doi.org/10.1007/978-3-031-60012-8_24

panic." For example, a survey conducted by an American personal styling service provider reported that 61% of Americans experience "wardrobe panic" regularly [7]. Therefore, there is a potential need to assist users in making decisions about selecting clothing. Against this backdrop, many fashion recommendation systems have been proposed [2,5]. However, most do not directly support the clothing selection process, which involves examining actual clothes. In clothing selection, touch and feel are among the important factors in decision making. Therefore, a design that effectively extends physical interactions with actual clothes in the clothing selection process could provide valuable support for users' selections.

In previous research, other members of our research group proposed a clothing selection support system, "Talkin'Closet" [6]. In this system, each piece of clothing in a closet (hanger rack) is represented as an anthropomorphic conversational agent. When an item of clothing is picked up, it will speak a self-recommendation to the user, such as, "You should wear me because today is hot." This system enables users to proceed with the clothing selection process while interacting with clothes physically and conversationally and relying on the information provided. However, previous research has not discussed how clothes as agents speak to make useful recommendations to the user through experimental evaluation. In Talkin' Closet, clothes speak as if they were recommending themselves. The idea of making the clothing an agent is considered promising to increase the user's attention to the clothing and to provide intuitive recommendations. However, when the user receives such self-recommendations from multiple clothing items, it may be challenging for the user to find a decisive factor because the user keeps receiving only positive opinions about those items.

In this study, we consider a novel recommendation design that enhances the original Talkin' Closet [6] by adding a function to obtain other opinions for the self-recommendation message from an item of clothing through the interactions of multiple clothing items. We propose "Talkin' Closet Plus," a clothing selection support system providing various types of recommendations to users through speech from clothes themselves (Fig. 1). In the system, when clothing on a hanger is picked up, the picked-up item recommends that the user wear it, as in our previous system. Furthermore, in our proposed method, other clothes join the interaction to respond to the picked-up item and provide different perspectives to support the user's selection of clothes. In this case, another clothing item with different features from the picked up clothing respond with critical suggestions to the self-recommendations of the picked-up one. For example, a thicker clothing reacts to a self-recommendation from a thinner clothing by saying "That clothing may feel cold in this season." As in this example, this critical suggestion is designed so that the clothing "implicitly" recommends itself based on highlighting the relative drawbacks of other options. Our proposed system will help users to explore new options through these two types of feedback from the clothes.

We investigated the effect of combining self-recommendations and critical suggestions from clothes on user satisfaction and selection behavior in the clothing selection process under a simulated scenario using Talkin' Closet Plus. In this paper, we report an experiment to compare users' feelings to different ratios of self- and critical suggestions in the system.

Fig. 1. Concept of the proposed system "Talkin' Closet Plus"

2   Related Research

2.1   Clothing Selection Support System

Many systems have been proposed to support users in selecting clothes by recommending to wear the users' own clothes or helping to search for them [2,5]. These systems recommend clothes based on information about the user's wearing history, weather, and schedule. To provide personalized suggestions to the user, a database of clothing owned by the user [15] and photos were captured when users wore them [14] are utilized in previous researches. For example, Sato et al. proposed suGATALOG [14], a system to collect users' photos when wearing clothes and simulate outfits using the collected image data. Conversely, some previou study focus on the process of clothing selection and enhance its enjoyment. Aoki et al. proposed BINGOFIT [1], a system that incorporates a gamification framework into the clothing recommendation process. Their results show that a recommendation process based on a bingo game can encourage users to discover new combinations of clothes and wear infrequently worn clothes. These studies suggest the importance of targeting the selection process in designing support systems for clothing selection.

2.2   Recommendation by Conversational Agent

A conversational agent acting as a pseudo-other is expected as a mean to provide various opinions outside the user's consciousness in a decision support situation. Most examples of using interactive agents for recommendation show a way for a navigator-like agent to provide suggestions for items. However, in contexts where the object is considered the main subject of the explanation, such as usage guidance and recommendations for the object, it has been suggested that an approach to anthropomorphizing an object as a conversational agent may be provide an explanation effectively [10,13]. For example, Osawa et al. [13]

proposed a design that anthropomorphizes a home appliance as an agent by attaching parts representing the eyes and hands to itself. Their research suggests that their approach can induce users' attention to the object more than the case of using the humanoid robot in instructions on how to use the appliance. Similar results have been observed for product recommendations. Iwamoto et al. [10] examined the effect of adding speech and motion to products in a store on sales promotion. Consequently, they reported that users were likelier to pay attention to the products, and the descriptions of the products tended to be remembered in detail by users. This mechanism for expressing the presence and features of an item could also be effective for clothing recommendations.

2.3   Our Research

As mentioned in Sect. 1, the authors' research group proposed a clothing selection support concept called Talkin' Closet [6] in which the clothes, themselves, in the closet are represented as agents. As suggested by related research [10,13], an approach that represents an item as an anthropomorphic agent may attract attention and interest in the item and support the user's unique decisions in clothing selection. In addition, unlike many existing clothing recommendation systems that rely on software simulations, Talkin' Closet offers assistance in the real context of clothing selection, where users select items by physically looking at and touching them. Therefore, the previously proposed concept may help enhance the user experience of clothing selection in the real world.

This study aims to clarify the potential of the approach representing an item, itself, as an anthropomorphic agent and its effective design for clothing selection support by reconsidering speech design and conducting user studies on our proposed concept.

3   Proposed System

3.1   Design Concept

As in Talkin' closet [6], a self-recommending message asking users to wear a clothing item may increase their confidence in their choice. In contrast, users may overlook clothing's drawbacks or lose interest in alternative options. In addition, a situation where the user receives multiple self-recommendation messages from various clothes may make it challenging to obtain "decisive" information for decision making since the user will only receive positive recommendations.

To solve these problems, we consider the three-way relationship between the user, the clothing with the user's attention, and other clothing. In typical communication scenarios, it is known that in situations causing imbalanced attitudes among participants, each participant tries to behave in a consistent and harmonized manner, termed *Heider's Balance Theory* [9]. We thought that creating an imbalanced situation of opinions obtained from clothes intentionally could facilitate the user's consideration of clothing selection. For example, in a situation where a user receives a self-recommendation from the clothing item when he/she picks it up, the recommendation assists in drawing the user's interest to the item. This situation can be seen as balanced because both the user and the clothing item engage in a positive interaction regarding the clothing. However, if another clothing item joins the interaction and offers a critical suggestion about wearing the picked-up item, it could lead to an imbalance of opinions in the three-way relationship. Based on Heider's Balance Theory, the user may try to balance his/her attitudes with either clothing item in this case. Therefore, it is expected that the user will be more careful in his/her decision making than in the case of simply choosing by providing only self-recommendation messages.

In this study, we propose Talkin' Closet Plus, a system that provides recommendations about clothes by combining self-recommendation messages from the clothing, itself, and critical responses from other clothing with different opinions. This system is designed based on a hanger rack, as illustrated in Fig. 1. The system makes suggestions for clothing selection, as if the clothes, themselves, are speaking to the user. Each hanger in the hanger rack is a device to recognize the user's action of picking up the clothing and deliver a message to the user by voice speech. By putting these hangers on the clothes, the system makes it seem as if the clothes themselves are speaking. There are two types of suggestions provided by the clothes, themselves:

- **Self-recommendation** : A clothing item recommends wearing itself directly through a message with positive aspects of the item.
- **Critical Suggestion** : A clothing item recommends wearing itself "indirectly" through a critical response to another self-recommendation message.

The combination of these messages allows the user to obtain various opinions about the selected clothing.

In this section, we describe the flow of the user experience with the system. The user can start using the system by picking up an item of clothing of interest from the rack. When the user picks up an item of clothing from the rack, the item of clothing, itself, speaks to the user, recommending itself for wear (**Self-recommendation**). For example, light clothing says, "On a crisp day, you should wear light clothing like me." Another item of clothing speak a critical opinion that indirectly recommends itself in response to the self-recommendation message stated by the item picked up (**Critical Suggestion**). For example, a slightly thicker garment on the hanger rack says, "That garment may feel cold this season" in response to the message from light clothing.

This design allows the user to obtain information not only about motivating wearing the selected clothing, but also about why it is not recommended. Furthermore, users can simultaneously notice other items through these interactions, thereby gaining insight into the variety and features of available clothes. The enjoyment of clothing selection comes from deciding on a favorite clothing item from a variety of options after considering many factors. This system may facilitate this deep consideration and enhance the enjoyment of the process. In addition, selecting clothes in an environment where many opinions are obtained from different perspectives may enhance the satisfaction with the final decision.

Hanger-type device (B / C)

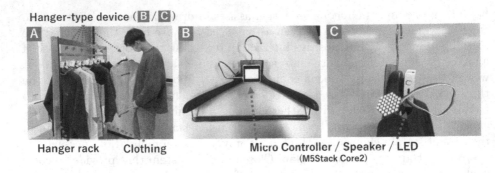

Fig. 2. Appearance of the prototype system (A) and the hanger-type device (B and C)

3.2 System Implementation

To verify the validity of the proposed concept, we implemented an experimental prototype system (Fig. 2). This system simulates clothes speaking directly to the user by embedding a microcomputer and speaker in the hanger to deliver a voice message. Figure 2B conveys the appearance of the hanger-type device. The hanger-type device comprises an ordinary hanger, a small microcontroller board (M5Stack Core2, M5Stack Inc.) with a wireless communication function, a speaker, and an LED matrix for visual feedback. The hanger-type devices were prepared according to each item of clothing. To indicate which item is active, the corresponding device's LED lights up during voice playback (Fig. 2C).

Contrary to many recommendation system studies, this research aims to find an effective recommendation design through controlled experiments, rather than developing a fully functional implementation. Regarding the initial evaluation of the proposed interface, the experimental system should focus on the basic elements essential for evaluation rather than a practical implementation with many functions. Therefore, the built-in software in the system was designed according to the actual experimental setup. In the experiment, we applied a setting, as the experimenter manually operated the behavior of the speakers and LEDs of hanger-type devices from a control PC at a remote site. According to this experimental setup, the software was designed to enable control of the hanger-type devices by sending commands from an operating PC prepared at a remote site. Upon receiving a command from the control PC, the corresponding hanger-type device activates its LED and plays a preset sound in its storage.

4 Experiment

4.1 Purpose and Hypothesis

We conducted an experiment to investigate the effect of combining critical suggestions and self-recommendations from clothes on user satisfaction and selection behavior in the clothing selection process under a simulated scenario using Talkin' Closet Plus.

In this system, critical suggestions offer negative feedback on the user's selection. Thus, the intensity of such recommendations can influence users' decisions and satisfaction. Conversely, the feature of the proposed system, a combination of self-recommendation and critical suggestions, allows users to receive opinions about their clothes. Therefore, users may become more interested in the opinions of the clothes in the selection process. In other words, users may select clothing carefully, and their criteria for selecting clothing may change. The critical suggestion is designed to add supplementary information contradicting the user's choice to the self-recommendation designed to encourage it. Hence, balancing self- and critical suggestions is crucial for enhancing users' satisfaction and enjoyment. In particular, if the number of critical suggestions is large, the user's satisfaction may diminish. The user may feel uncomfortable because the system will continue to make negative recommendations in response to the user's choice. Accordingly, we set the following hypotheses:

- H1: The introduction of critical suggestions prompts users to consider the system's opinions regarding clothing selection.
- H2: An excessive level of critical suggestions diminishes satisfaction compared to scenarios featuring only self-recommendations.
  • H2-1: If the frequency of critical suggestions is high, users feel discomfort.
  • H2-2: Supplementing self-recommendations with critical suggestions enhances the satisfaction of clothing selection.

4.2 Settings

Assumed Situation and Participants. In this experiment, participants were asked to select an item of clothing from a set of clothes prepared by the experimenter while using the system. In general, clothing preferences and attitudes vary by gender and age. Hence, we controlled for external factors by fixing the type of clothing, participants' attributes, and the scenario and verified the system's effect on the selection process. In this experiment, we focused on young men's fashion and conducted with male Japanese university students (N=20). In addition, long-sleeved tops were used for the selection items because the experiment was conducted in the winter season in Japan. Furthermore, since it is assumed that the clothing choice depends on the weather and schedule, in this experiment, the participants were instructed in a predefined clothing selection situation and asked to select the clothing they would wear under this condition.

Comparison Conditions. To verify the hypotheses described above, we designed a comparison condition focusing on the ratio of self-recommended and critical suggestion messages to total speeches from clothes. Specifically, we established four comparison conditions (10:0, 5:5, 8:2, and 2:8), representing different ratios of each type of speech to the total interactions in the experiment.

- **10:0 condition** : The picked-up clothing always speaks a self-recommendation. Other clothes do not speak. This is a baseline condition for this experiment, without including any critical suggestions.

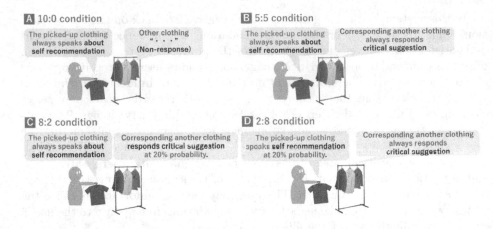

Fig. 3. Comparison conditions in the experiment.

Table 1. Clothes used in the experiment.

No	Group A	Group B	Group C	Group D
1	Long T-Shirt	Sweater	Turtleneck	Knitted Garment
2	Long T-Shirt	Long T-Shirt	Sweater	Hoodie
3	Patterned Shirt	Solid Color Shirt	Patterned Shirt	Solid Color Shirt
4	Sweater	Knitted Garment	Sweater	Sweater

- **5:5 condition** : The picked-up clothing always speaks a self-recommendation, and the other corresponding clothing always responds with a critical suggestion. In this condition, the ratio of self-recommendations to critical suggestions within the total number of speeches is equal.
- **8:2 condition** : The picked-up clothing always speaks a self-recommendation. However, there is a 20% probability that the other corresponding clothing will respond with a critical suggestion.
- **2:8 condition** : The picked-up clothing has a 20% probability that it will speak a self-recommendation. The other corresponding clothing always speaks a critical suggestion.

The details of each condition are also displayed in Fig. 3. The name of each condition represents the ratio of self-recommendations to critical suggestions within the total number of speeches.

This experiment is conducted under the following scenario: Among the clothes on the hanger rack, the picked-up item first offers a self-recommendation, followed by another item offering a critical suggestion. This process was repeated until the user selected the clothing. The probability that these clothes would speak each type of message is manipulated in each condition.

Participants were asked to make selections four times under the conditions of 10:0, 5:5, 8:2, and 2:8. The study was designed as a within-participant experiment to assess the impact on a limited number of participants. Nevertheless, the influence of prior trials on subsequent selections could be a concern for repeated measures with the same clothing items. Hence, the clothing items varied across conditions. Groups A–D in Table 1 indicate the groups of clothing used in the experiment. For the experiment, we paired these groups to form four combinations, B-C, A-B, D-A, and C-D in Table 1, were assigned to each experimental condition, 10:0, 5:5, 8:2, and 2:8 in Fig. 3. Each group has a total of four clothes, and since two groups are utilized per trial, the user selects from a total of eight clothes when experiencing the system in each trial.

Message Contents. We designed message contents for each clothing item, based on the experimental conditions and their features. These messages were designed to provide recommendations related to the factors considered important in clothing selection (weather, schedule, trends, and mood) based on the appearance and features of each clothing item, such as its material and color. Additionally, we considered the consistency of message combinations among clothes for designing the message contents. Table 2 shows the list of messages and their combinations for each experimental condition. These messages were recorded by a male voice actor, and the recorded files were used as the voice of the clothes. When recording, we requested the voice actor to record messages as if advising his friend on clothes in a cheerful voice for a self-recommendation and as if offering his opinion on the clothing selected by his friend for a critical suggestion. The system operation in the experiment was based on the Wizard of Oz method [4], in which the system was operated manually according to the user's behavior. The hanger-type devices store voice files according to the contents of the speech, and these files can be manually called up by commands from a control PC.

4.3 Evaluation Items

We set up evaluation items corresponding to each hypothesis described earlier. These evaluation items confirmed the choice behavior situation for participants and users' impressions, such as the degree of satisfaction, enjoyment and discomfort when choosing clothes. For the evaluation, we used a questionnaire for the subjective evaluation and the elapsed time required to select clothing as a quantitative index regarding the degree of hesitation and selection behavior during the experiment. The questionnaire constituted the eight items in Table 3: Q1–Q7 were questions requesting impressions of the clothing selection process while hearing the clothing speech using a 7-point Likert scale (7 is the most positive). Q8 was a multiple-choice question requesting the reason for the final decision on the clothing. In Q8, we set the five options described in Table 3 and the "other" option with a free response. The time required for the clothing selection process was measured using a stopwatch from the beginning of the process until the participants informed the experimenter they had decided on clothing.

Table 2. List of message contents of clothes according to the experimental conditions. A1-D4 represent the clothing belonging to each group listed in Table 1.

10:0 Condition (Groups B and C)

Factor	Type		Speech Content
Weather	Self	B1	When you wear me, even if you sweat, it won't be noticeable
Weather	Self	C1	I have thicker fabric, so you'll be warmer
Plan	Self	B2	I have a large logo, so I can get others' attention
Plan	Self	C2	If you're not going away tomorrow, I think a rough me would be better for you
Trend	Self	B3	I'm from a famous brand, so I'm popular
Trend	Self	C3	I'm a limited edition and specially designed
Mood	Self	B4	I'm a bit formal, so wearing me will make you feel uplifted
Mood	Self	C4	I'm a calm color, so wearing me will relax you.

5:5 Condition (Groups A and B)

Factor	Type		Speech Content
Weather	Self	A1	Light clothes like me are good for a refreshing day like today
	Critical	B1	The clothing might feel cold for the current season
Weather	Self	B1	Loose clothes like me are good for a pleasant day like today
	Critical	A2	You shouldn't wear this clothing. It's too loose fitting
Plan	Self	A2	I'm made of thin fabric, so I'll help you move around
	Critical	B2	This clothing might feel cold because the fabric is thin
Plan	Self	B2	I have thick and stretchy fabric so I'll help you to move easily and keep out the cold
	Critical	A3	This clothing can get hot when you move, so it's better to wear something that allows easy temperature regulation
Trend	Self	A3	I'm trendy, so wearing me will make you look fashionable
	Critical	B3	You might end up wearing the same clothes as your other friends, so it's better to avoid this clothing
Trend	Self	B3	It's good if you wear me. I'll create a unique atmosphere with a distinctive style
	Critical	A4	This is different from the usual, so it might not suit you
Mood	Self	A4	I have bright colors, so wearing me will lift your mood
	Critical	B4	That clothing is too flashy, so you should avoid it
Mood	Self	B4	I'm light colored, so if you wear me, you'll feel better
	Critical	A1	This clothing isn't bright at all, so I think it won't make you feel better.

8:2 Condition (Groups A and D)

Factor	Type		Speech Content
Weather	Self	A1	It's easy to roll up my sleeves for temperature regulation
	Critical	D1	Rolling up the sleeves of clothing might leave wrinkles
Weather	Self	D1	Today is windy, so I'm better for you, with wind-resistant materials
	Critical	A2	It's hard to regulate your body temperature, so you shouldn't wear it
Plan	Self	A2	I'm often told by people that this suits you
	Critical	D2	If you wear this, people may think you always wear the same clothing
Plan	Self	D2	I'm all in one and easy to wear, so I would be nice for you
	Critical	A3	If you wear only this clothing, it will look corny
Trend	Self	A3	My design is popular among celebrities, too
	Critical	D3	These clothes are too popular, so many people will wear it
Trend	Self	D3	My color is fine because it suits the current season
	Critical	A4	I think brighter clothing would be more appropriate for this season than this clothing
Mood	Self	A4	I'm light colored, so if you wear me, your mood will be better
	Critical	D4	A more subdued color might be better than those in this clothing
Mood	Self	D4	I'm not too flashy and a calm color, so if you wear me, you will look more mature
	Critical	A1	I think you should have more accents than this clothing.

2:8 Condition (Groups C and D)

Factor	Type		Speech Content
Weather	Self	C1	I'm nice for you because if you wear me, you will feel warm
	Critical	D1	This clothing might still be hot for this period
Weather	Self	D1	I'm just fine with this season
	Critical	C2	I think this clothing is too early for this period
Plan	Self	C2	If you're going to the lab tomorrow, casual clothes like me would be good
	Critical	D2	This clothing is too casual when meeting other friends
Plan	Self	D2	I'm fine because I'm not too casual
	Critical	C3	You should wear more formal clothes than this clothing
Trend	Self	C3	My color is on trend, so it's good
	Critical	D3	That color is so trendy, you'll wear it with everyone else
Trend	Self	D3	If you wear me, you will be in a different and better mood
	Critical	C4	The outfit is different from your usual and may not suit you
Mood	Self	C4	If you wear simple me, you'll look more mature
	Critical	D4	I think you should have more accents than this clothing
Mood	Self	D4	With my logo and not-too-simple design, you'll look more mature
	Critical	C1	If you want to look more mature, you should wear more simple clothing than this clothing

Table 3. Question items in the questionnaire. Q1–Q7 are asked as a 7-point Likert scale, and Q8 is asked as a question allowing for multiple selections from a 4-point choice.

ID	Question Items
Q1	I enjoyed the process of selecting clothing while hearing the speech
Q2	I am satisfied with the clothing I finally decided to wear through the clothing selection process while hearing the speech
Q3	I felt uncomfortable with the clothing selection process while hearing the speech
Q4	I was confused about the clothing selection process while hearing the speech
Q5	I thought carefully about deciding on clothing through the clothing selection process while hearing the speech
Q6	I referred to the opinions of clothes during the clothing selection process while hearing the speech
Q7	I tried to pick up various clothes during the clothing selection process while hearing the speech
Q8	Please check all the reasons applicable to your choice of clothing
	□Suggestion from clothes □ Design of clothing □ Functionality of the clothing
	□ Current feeling □ Suitability for the situation
	□ Other (Please write the reason for your choice.)

4.4 Procedure

The experiment was conducted in a laboratory at Ritsumeikan University in Japan. First, we explained the experiment to the participants and obtained their agreement to participate. After obtaining consent, the participants were instructed to select a clothing item using the system. Participants were given the following scenario to control the clothing selection situation: "You are now choosing clothes at home in the morning. Today is a sunny, slightly windy November day. Your plan for today is to go to the university to do research in the laboratory. Please choose your favorite clothing by considering these situations." The participants were then asked to stand before the hanger rack and start selecting clothing. During the experiment, the experimenter sent operation commands to the hanger corresponding to the clothing as if the clothing, itself, was speaking when picked up. When the experiment started, we measured the time with a stopwatch and recorded the experiment with a video camera. When the participants informed the experimenter of their final choice of clothing, the time measurement ended, and the participants answered the questionnaire. This sequence was repeated four times, corresponding to four patterns. The order of these trials was randomized to vary among participants.

5 Results

5.1 Evaluation of System Impressions

The average scores of the questionnaires from Q1 to Q7 are shown in Fig. 4a. Friedman's test was performed on the scores for each question to assess the

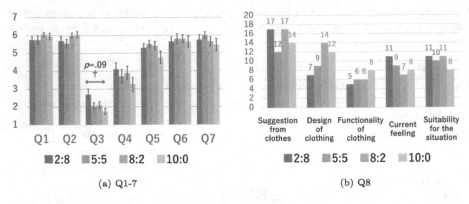

Fig. 4. (a) The mean value and standard error in each condition of the question items Q1-7 in Table 1 (N = 20). In Q3, we reveal the result of the multiple comparison test (using Holm's method) because the main effect of the Friedman test is significant. (b) Number of responses for each condition of each item in Q8 (N = 20).

statistical differences. Correspondingly, there was a significant main effect only for Q3 at the 5 percent level. Multiple comparisons based on Holm's method were conducted for the results of Q3, and the differences between the 2:8 and 10:0 conditions were marginally significant ($p = .09$). Under the 2:8 condition, the user sometimes faces a case receiving only a critical opinion about the clothes he/she picked up without the self-recommendation from picked-up items. This is a situation not included in the other conditions. The critical suggestion from the other clothes considered in this study is a speech that implicitly recommends itself by denying the statements of the clothing that the user picked up. It is designed to correspond to the previous message and to be used with self-recommendations. Thus, a scenario in which users only receive critical suggestions when selecting clothing creates an unbalanced recommendation experience. Such scenario could result in discomfort for the users. The findings from the result of Q3 suggest that users may feel discomfort when continuously receiving more critical suggestions than self-recommendations.

For other questions except Q3, the differences in means suggested that participants' impressions may have varied among the four patterns. In Q1 and Q2, the mean scores in the 5:5 and 2:8 conditions were lower than those in the other two conditions. Thus, enjoyment of the selection process and satisfaction with the results of the selection declined when critical suggestions constituted over half of all recommendations. In contrast, the mean score in the 8:2 condition was high in Q1 and it was equal compared to the 10:0 condition in Q2. Therefore, it can be assumed that the enjoyment of the clothing selection process is enhanced in situations where users can receive messages based on self-recommendations, though other opinions based on critical suggestions are sometimes obtained. In Q4-7, the mean scores for the 10:0 condition were lower than those for the other three conditions. These findings indicate that, while critical suggestions might initially perplex users, they also prompt more thoughtful selection by incorporating the clothing's feedback.

5.2 Analysis of Reasons for Clothing Selection

We compared the differences in responses to Q8, "Please check all the reasons applicable to your choice of clothing," between conditions. Since there were no responses in the "other" category, we analyzed the number of responses to the predefined options. The number of responses in Q8 for each condition and option is demonstrated in Fig. 4b. In each condition, "Suggestion from clothes" was the most frequently selected factor affecting the participants' final clothing decisions. In particular, in both the 2:8 and 8:2 conditions, 17 out of 20 participants selected this item, indicating that over 80% considered advice from clothing in their decision making. These scores were higher than for the other conditions. Hence, it is possible that the introduction of critical suggestions from clothes may have triggered participants to listen to their advice. However, we note that the result in the 5:5 condition with critical suggestions had fewer responses than the 10:0 condition without containing any critical suggestions. Nevertheless, even in the 5:5 condition, which had the fewest responses, more than half of the participants selected this reason. This suggests that the system's feature of providing clothing recommendations verbally contributes to users' selection of clothing.

The option "Suggestion from clothes" indicates how participants considered the information provided by the system in their choice of garment. Thus, this option has a different property from the other options. Henceforth, we focused on distinctions in responses to options other than "Suggestion from clothes" between conditions. Excluding the option "Suggestion from clothes," the most frequently selected reasons were "Design of the clothing" in the 10:0 and 8:2 conditions, "Suitability for the experimental situation" in the 5:5 condition, and both "Suitability for the experimental situation" and "Current feeling" equally in the 2:8 condition. These findings indicate that fewer critical suggestions lead to appearance-based selections, while an increase in critical suggestions shifts the focus toward clothing's functionality and situational suitability.

The speech from the clothing during this experiment contained the factors related to the "functionality of the clothing" or "Suitability for the situation" in both cases of the self- and critical suggestion. Therefore, if one selects clothing based on information from it, it is inferred that factors such as "Functionality of clothing" or "Suitability for the situation" would be considered more, regardless of the type of recommendation. However, the experimental results showed that, in conditions containing the critical suggestion relatively more, "Functionality of clothing" and "suitability for the situation" were considered more. This result suggests that introducing critical suggestions could direct attention to providing information about functionality and situational suitability for clothing. In other words, the proposed method may be a means to guide users in making a selection based on various viewpoints.

5.3 Required Time for Clothing Selection

Table 4 presents the average selection time under each experimental condition in seconds. A repeated-measures ANOVA revealed no significant difference in

Table 4. Required time to select clothing (sec., N = 20). Data less than a millisecond are not measured, so the mean values are shown as integers.

	2:8 condition	5:5 condition	8:2 condition	10:0 condition
Mean	83	84	75	64
Standard Error	6.2	10.0	5.9	5.2

selection times among the conditions ($p = .15$, not significant). However, in the three conditions with critical suggestions, selection times consistently increased compared to the 10:0 condition, which only featured self-recommendations. This result aligns with the findings from Q7 in the questionnaire and indicates that introducing critical suggestions leads users to carefully consider the clothing selection process.

6 Discussion

In this section, we verify the alignment between the hypotheses outlined in Sect. 4.1 and the experimental results and discuss the efficacy and challenges of our proposed method. Given the experimental data, we found no significant impact of the ratio of self- to critical suggestions on users' clothing choices. Therefore, Hypothesis H1, "The introduction of critical suggestions prompts users to consider the system's opinions regarding clothing selection" is rejected in the experiment. However, the presence of critical suggestions consistently resulted in higher mean values for questions Q5–7 and longer selection times, suggesting that these recommendations may prompt more deliberate decision making among participants. Furthermore, the results of Q8 suggest that introducing critical suggestions may cause users to shift their attention to the information provided by the system. These observed trends suggest that the proposed framework may help encourage users engagement with clothing selection.

For Hypothesis H2, "An excessive level of critical suggestions diminishes satisfaction compared to scenarios featuring only self-recommendations," we verify it from the result of the relevant questions about Q1 to Q3. In Q3 asking about discomfort, difference between the 2:8 and 10:0 conditions is marginally significant for this question. Therefore, Hypothesis H2-1 "If the frequency of critical suggestions is high, users feel discomfort" is statistically supported. In addition, Hypothesis H2-2, "Supplementing self-recommendations with critical suggestions enhances the satisfaction of clothing selection" is rejected because the differences between the 10:0 condition and the other conditions in Q1 to Q3 were insignificant. However, as with Hypothesis H1, the trend of the mean values for the questionnaire items aligned with this hypothesis. The results of Q1 and Q2 are higher than five (positively inclined value of the scale) in all conditions. The fact indicate that the selection of clothes through conversation with them is favorably received as enjoyable (Q1) and satisfying (Q2), regardless of the conditions. In addition, the evaluation of enjoyment and satisfaction tended to be higher in the condition with a low ratio of critical suggestions than those with a high ratio of critical suggestions. These results suggest that critical suggestions may be helpful as supplements to self-recommendations.

7 Conclusion

In our research, we considered a novel design to enhance users' interest in clothing selection by recommending messages from the clothing items, themselves. In this paper, we proposed "Talkin' Closet Plus," a clothing selection support system that provides information to users through "speech" from multiple clothes, themselves. Our proposed system provides various types of recommendations for clothing by combining self-recommendation messages from the clothing, itself, and critical responses from other clothing with different opinions. The experimental results suggest that a scheme providing varying opinions from multiple clothes may affect the user's interest in and choice behavior toward the clothing-related information provided by this system.

This experiment was conducted in a university laboratory environment with limitations in target clothes, situations, and participants. Therefore, there are some disparities in the experimental settings from the actual clothing selection situation. In addition, the experimental participants were recruited from young males and the experiment targeted men's fashion. Therefore, there are many limitations to our reported results in this paper. Additional validation to clarify differences in recommendation effects by gender and clothing type is considered as future work.

Acknowledgments. This work was supported in part by the Tateisi Science and Technology Foundation and the Ritsumeikan Global Innovation Research Organization (R-GIRO), Ritsumeikan University.

References

1. Aoki, Y., Yokoyama, K., Nakamura, S.: Bingofit: a bingo clothes presentation system for utilizing owned clothes. In: Stephanidis, C., Antona, M., Ntoa, S., Salvendy, G. (eds.) HCI International 2023 Posters, pp. 10–17. Springer, Cham (2023). https://doi.org/10.1007/978-3-031-35998-9_2
2. Chakraborty, S., et al.: Fashion recommendation systems, models and methods: a review 8(49), 1–34 (2021). https://doi.org/10.3390/informatics8030049
3. Crane, D.: Fashion and its Social Agendas: Class, Gender, and Identity in Clothing. University of Chicago Press, Chicago, IL, USA (2000)
4. Dahlbäck, N., Jönsson, A., Ahrenberg, L.: Wizard of OZ studies: why and how. In: Proceedings of the 1st International Conference on Intelligent User Interfaces, IUI 1993, pp. 193–200. ACM, New York, NY, USA (1993). https://doi.org/10.1145/169891.169968
5. Deldjoo, Y., et al.: A review of modern fashion recommender systems. ACM Comput. Surv. 56(4) (2023). https://doi.org/10.1145/3624733

6. Fukuda, M., Nakatani, Y.: Clothes recommend themselves: a new approach to a fashion coordinate support system. In: Proceedings of the World Congress on Engineering and Computer Science, vol. 1, pp. 19–21. IAENG, Hong Kong, China (2011)

7. Gervis, Z.: You're not the only one who constantly feels 'wardrobe panic'. New York Post (2018). https://nypost.com/2018/03/07/youre-not-the-only-one-who-constantly-feels-wardrobe-panic/. Accessed 10 Feb 2024

8. Hannover, B., Kühnen, U.: "The clothing makes the self" via knowledge activation 1. J. Appl. Soc. Psychol. **32**(12), 2513–2525 (2002). https://doi.org/10.1111/j.1559-1816.2002.tb02754.x

9. Heider, F.: The psychology of interpersonal relations. Wiley, Hoboken (1958). https://doi.org/10.1037/10628-000

10. Iwamoto, T., Baba, J., Nakanishi, J., Nishi, K., Yoshikawa, Y., Ishiguro, H.: Pick-me-up strategy for a self-recommendation agent: a pilot field experiment in a convenience store. in: 17th ACM/IEEE International Conference on Human-Robot Interaction, HRI 2022, pp. 816–820. IEEE, New York, NY, USA (2022). https://doi.org/10.1109/HRI53351.2022.9889532

11. Joung, H.M., Miller, N.J.: Examining the effects of fashion activities on life satisfaction of older females: activity theory revisited. Fam. Consum. Sci. Res. J. **35**(4), 338–356 (2007). https://doi.org/10.1177/1077727X07299992

12. McKinsey & Company: The state of fashion 2024: finding pockets of growth as uncertainty reigns. https://www.mckinsey.com/industries/retail/our-insights/state-of-fashion (2024). Accessed 10 Feb 2024

13. Osawa, H., Ohmura, R., Imai, M.: Self introducing poster using attachable humanoid parts. In: Proceedings of the 4th ACM/IEEE International Conference on Human Robot Interaction, HRI 2009, pp. 327–328. IEEE, New York, NY, USA (2009). https://doi.org/10.1145/1514095.1514199

14. Kurosu, M. (ed.): HCI 2013. LNCS, vol. 8008. Springer, Heidelberg (2013). https://doi.org/10.1007/978-3-642-39342-6

15. Tsujita, H., Tsukada, K., Kambara, K., Siio, I.: Complete fashion coordinator: a support system for capturing and selecting daily clothes with social networks. In: Proceedings of the International Conference on Advanced Visual Interfaces, AVI 2010, pp. 127–132. ACM, New York, NY, USA (2010). https://doi.org/10.1145/1842993.1843016

From Classic to Future: The Temporal Evolution of GUI Design for Apple Products

Zhihua Sun[1], Yinghong Zhang[2]($\boxtimes$), and Shengnan Guo[3]

[1] College of Arts, Shandong Agriculture and Engineering University, Jinan 255000, Shandong, China
[2] College of Fine Arts and Design, University of Jinan, Jinan 255000, Shandong, China
8397614710qq.com
[3] Institute of Preschool Education, Jinan Vocational College, Jinan 255000, Shandong, China

Abstract. This paper discusses the temporal and spatial evolution of Appleproduct graphical user interface design, from the earliest command-line user interface to the later pixel style, pseudo physical style, flat style, and then to the latest new pseudo physical style, as well as the prospect of the future spatial user interface. This paper uses the methods of literature review and case analysis to elaborate and evaluate the various stagesof the Apple product user interface from the perspectives of history, technology, aesthetics, and society. This paper believes that the design evolution of Apple's product graphical user interface is a continuous pursuit of a perfect and natural process of human-computer interaction and a keen and creative response to the changes of the times and user needs. This paper reveals the logic behind the design trend and provides a reference for the future direction of user interface design.

Keywords: Apple products · Design evolution · Executive user interface · Graphical user interface · Spatial user interface

1 Introduction

With the popularity of personal computers and mobile devices, user interface design has become a key factor affecting product success. Since the establishment of Apple Computer Company in 1976, its product design has led to the development of personal computers and mobile devices. The evolution of Apple's product interface design has profoundly impacted the entire industry. In particular, in terms of user interface design, apple continues to innovate, significantly changing how people interact with electronic devices. This paper aims to systematically review and analyse the evolution of the Apple product user interface, explore the changes in design concept and the driving force behind it, and look forward to future design trends and direction.

N. A. Streitz and S. Konomi (Eds.): HCII 2024, LNCS 14719, pp. 399–410, 2024.
https://doi.org/10.1007/978-3-031-60012-8_25

2 Methods

To comprehensively analyse the evolution of Apple product graphical user interface design, this study uses the methods of historical literature review and interface design analysis. First of all, the development context of Apple's user interface design is determined through the collection and collation of Apple's official release materials, design specification documents, historical review articles, and related books and papers. Secondly, combined with the design principles and user experience theory, this paper analyses the characteristics and innovations of interface design in various periods. Finally, through user evaluation and interviews, the advantages and disadvantages of each design style and its impact on user interaction are discussed. Through these methods, this paper intends to comprehensively understand and explain the development process of Apple's graphical interface design to provide reference and Enlightenment for the future development trend of user interface design.

3 Content

3.1 Command Line User Interface

Apple II is a personal computer that was released by Apple in 1977. Its user interface adopts the form of a command line. Users need to input commands to operate the computer. The characteristics of the command line user interface are mainly reflected in the following aspects: the command line user interface is straightforward, and you can operate the computer by inputting simple commands. It can directly access all computer functions without complex menus and graphical interfaces. It can perform complex operations, such as writing programs, editing files, managing files, etc. With the rapid development of science and technology, although the graphical user interface has replaced the command line user interface, it still exists in the computer system. The command line user interface in Apple Computer is called "terminal", a UNIX-based command line interpreter. The function of the terminal is similar to the command line user interface of Apple II, but it is more powerful and flexible. Users can use the terminal to perform various operations, view and modify system settings, start and stop services, manage users and groups, etc. Use the terminal to start, stop, and control applications. Use the terminal to write scripts to execute tasks automatically. With the development of a graphical user interface, the command-line user interface has been gradually replaced. However, the command-line user interface still plays a vital role in some areas, such as server and network management. Apple's command line user interface is integral to Apple's history. The computer will continue to provide a command line user interface, which provides a simple, direct, and robust operation mode for users. Although the graphical user interface has become mainstream, the command line user interface still plays a vital role in some areas (Fig. 1).

3.2 Graphical User Interface (GUI)

A graphical user interface (GUI) is an interface that interacts with a computer system through graphic elements (such as windows, buttons, icons, etc.) and intuitive interaction. Users can interact with the computer by clicking, dragging, or entering text using

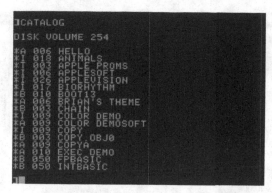

Fig. 1. Command line user interface

input devices such as a mouse, keyboard, or touch screen. With the development of personal computer technology, graphical user interfaces began to replace the command line interface.

Xerox made a pioneering contribution to the history of the graphical user interface in the U.S. In the 1970s, Xerox's Palo Alto Research Center (PARC) engineers developed the world's first visual user interface system, Alto, which used the mouse, bitmap displays, and windows to lay the groundwork for the modern graphical user interface. The system debuted in 1973 and was the world's first GUI computer. It utilised a three-button mouse, a bitmap display with a 608 x 808 pixels resolution, and an icon-based menu system. It allowed users to open applications by clicking on mouse icons and manage multiple applications using Windows. The system also included a "WYSIWYG" text editor, which allowed users to see the final layout as they edited the text. In 1981, Xerox introduced the Xerox Star personal computer, the first mass-market computer with a graphical user interface. The Alto system was powerful, but due to technological limitations and the fact that it was the first computer with a graphical user interface at the time, the Alto system was one of many to be used in the market. The Alto system, while robust, could have been more commercially successful due to technical limitations and high costs at the time. Xerox's work on GUIs profoundly impacted companies such as Apple and Microsoft. Apple's Macintosh computer, introduced in 1984, and Microsoft's Windows operating system, introduced in 1985, were inspired by Xerox GUIs. Today, GUIs are the standard user interface for personal computers, smartphones, and other devices (Fig. 2).

Xerox's design concepts have had a significant impact on Apple. Although Apple borrowed Xerox's design ideas, it went its way in innovation and improvement, skillfully incorporating these concepts into its products. In 1983, Apple introduced the Lisa computer. This GUI-based computer utilised a graphical user interface that used icons and menus instead of a command-line interface to make operations more intuitive and easy to use. It was equipped with a mouse, allowing users to control the cursor more straightforwardly. It is equipped with a WYSIWYG (What You See Is What You Get) editor, which enables the user to visualise the editing results, so what you see is what you get. This computer changed how users interacted with their devices and enhanced the human-computer interaction experience. In 1984, Apple introduced the new Macintosh

Fig. 2. Xerox graphical user interface

computer, the first mass-market computer with a graphical user interface. The Macintosh's graphical user interface and interaction design were revolutionary at the time and were a huge success. The Macintosh's graphical user interface used icons, menus, and windows instead of the traditional command line interface, making the computer operation more intuitive and easier to understand. Even users with no computer experience can quickly get started using the computer. It uses a high-resolution monitor and a graphical interface design, making the computer's interface more beautiful and aesthetically pleasing. The computer is operated with a mouse, which makes the user's interaction with the computer more natural and smooth. Users can complete various tasks through drag-and-drop and other operations, significantly improving work efficiency. It is a powerful computer and a revolutionary user experience. It has created a new era of graphical user interface design and dramatically impacted the future of computer interface design.

Pixel Style. In the 1980s and 1990s, pixel-based interfaces became the dominant style of computer interface design due to the limitations of computer technology and hardware and the evolution of design styles. Apple was the leader in graphical user interfaces. A pixel-style GUI was used in early products, where the interface used pixel-art-style icons and visual elements. Users could use the mouse to click on icons to launch programs and open files, an intuitive, interactive approach that significantly reduced the difficulty of computer operation. This style is distinctive and has dramatically impacted the industry as a whole. The interface elements of the pixel style are simple and easy to recognise and understand. Each interface element consists of pixels and has a unified visual style.

Under the technical conditions at that time, the pixel-style interface was relatively easy to realise. However, the pixel-style interface is not sophisticated enough and lacks details and aesthetics. The pixel-style interface makes it difficult to carry out complex graphic design. The designer of Apple's GUI's pixel style was Susan Kare, an early designer at Apple. She is known for her simple, crisp design style, giving Apple's early products a unique visual style. She designed the Chicago typeface, the first system font for the Macintosh, a clear, easy-to-read typeface still in use today. She created hundreds of icons, including those for the trash can, Finder, and Happy Mac. These icons are still in use today and are considered classics of graphical user interface design. These icons comprise simple geometric shapes that communicate what they represent. For example, the folder icon consists of a simple rectangle with a handle and is designed as a visual metaphor that is easy for users to recognise. The "wastepaper basket" icon is located on the computer's desktop, and users can delete files by dragging and dropping them onto the icon, which is similar to real-life actions and makes computer operations more natural and easier to understand. The Apple GUI pixel style is an essential milestone in the history of graphical interface development. With the development of technology, the pixel-style interface is gradually becoming obsolete and replaced by a more sophisticated and beautiful interface style. The pixel style still has some modern-day applications, appearing in several retro-style games, applications, and artistic creations. Pixel-style interfaces were adaptations and innovations to the state of the art of the era and were the starting point and foundation of the graphical user interface. It laid the foundation for the later development of anthropomorphic-style interfaces (Fig. 3).

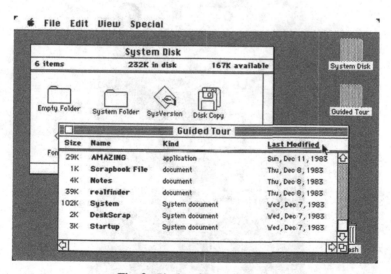

Fig. 3. Pixel-style user interface

Pseudo-Physical Style. Anthropomorphic style is a graphical user interface design style that mimics real-world objects' materials, textures, shadows, lighting, and other effects, making graphic elements and interfaces look more three-dimensional and realistic. This style is applied to icons, buttons, windows, and other interface elements. Users can understand and use the application intuitively, reducing learning costs. The interface is visually appealing and provides a better visual experience for the user. Around 2000, Apple gradually adopted the anthropomorphic design style in its products. This design creates a virtual sense of reality by mimicking the textures of the real world. It is widely used in Apple products. For example, in iOS 6 and its previous versions, many apps' icons and interface elements adopt the anthropomorphic style, such as the icon of the "Calendar" app, which looks like a physical calendar with a page torn out. iBook, an e-book reading app, mimics a real-world bookshelf rendered in wood, making the user feel friendly and comfortable. Users feel warm and relaxed. Apple's Memo app makes users feel like they're using an actual sticky note or notepad. MacOS Big Sur features anthropomorphic icons in a more minimalist design with blur and shadow effects. Apple's anthropomorphic style GUI was a massive success in its early products. The development of the anthropomorphic style has gone through many changes, from the original Aqua style to the brushed metal style to the new anthropomorphic style, whose ease of use, aesthetics, and other features have significantly impacted later interface designs. However, with the advancement of technology, the anthropomorphic style graphical user interface also gradually revealed its limitations; the interface style slowly appeared to need to be updated, unable to meet the user's higher requirements for visual effects and functionality. Apple began to abandon the anthropomorphic style in favour of a flatter and minimalist design style (Fig. 4).

Fig. 4. Pseudo physical style user interface

Flat Style. Flat style is based on simplifying and removing redundant design elements to make the interface look more balanced, cleaner, and intuitive. This design style emphasises simple, two-dimensional graphics and eschews excessive shadows, textures, and other decorative effects to provide a straightforward, intuitive, and easy-to-understand user experience. In 2013, Apple introduced flat design in iOS 7, which marked a massive shift in Apple's design style. The flat design eschews the decorations and textures of the anthropomorphic style in favour of clean graphics and sharp colour contrasts. Colour, shadow, and transparency create a sense of hierarchy and space. Richer animations are introduced to make the interface more vivid and fluid. Brighter and more vibrant colours make the interface livelier and more appealing. iOS 7's Messages icon has changed from a 3D bubble to a simple flat combination of green and white bubbles, a more modern design emphasising the direct presentation of content and functionality. Apple Watch interface has been flattened to fit its small screen size. Simple icons and text make the watch's interface easy to read and manipulate. MacOS Yosemite also uses a flat style but retains some anthropomorphic elements such as shadows and textures. While maintaining simplicity, this blend also preserves some of the user's habits. The flat style has been widely used in Apple products for a better user experience. Although flat design has many advantages, not all applications are suitable for flat design, and designers must choose the right design style according to the situation to achieve the best design effect. Apple will continue to evolve and refine its flat style to make it more user-friendly, personalised, and easy to use. Apple will continue exploring new design styles to give users a richer and more diverse experience (Fig. 5).

Fig. 5. Flat Style User Interface

Neuorphism Style. Neumorphism is a design trend and style that evolves and improves upon the traditional anthropomorphic style. It combines the simplicity and modernity of the flat style with the realism and emotional connection of the anthropomorphic style to create a more balanced and subtle approach to design. It uses soft shadows and lighting to contrast light and dark, producing a raised or recessed relief effect. Low saturation colours give the interface a smoother, more refined, and premium look— simple geometric shapes and icons to avoid excessive details and decorations and keep the interface simple. Uniform light source direction elements in the interface maintain a consistent light and shadow effect. Apple has updated all MacOS Big Sur application icons to be more uniform and coordinated while retaining their features and functionality. The application icons have a rounded rectangular shape and use soft shadows and light effects to contrast light and dark, producing a raised or recessed relief effect. The colours of the application icons are also more vivid and rich, using low-saturation colours to make the interface look softer, more refined, and more advanced. For example, the Finder icon uses rounded shapes and subtle shadows to give it a more three-dimensional look while maintaining an overall flat appearance. iOS 13's volume control icon uses a new mimetic style that mimics the shape and texture of a physical button through light and shadow effects, making it intuitive for users to understand and operate. Apple Watch dials are more realistic with neomorphic styles, such as the weather dial that simulates actual weather conditions. Neomimetic style is a design language that is still evolving and will be used in more Apple products and apps in the future. In the meantime, Apple will continue to explore and refine the biomimetic style to make it more mature and easier to use and to meet the psychological needs and changing aesthetic trends of today's users. The development of the neomorphic style will significantly impact future interface design (Fig. 6).

3.3 Spatial User Interface

Apple Vision Pro is a revolutionary spatial computing device powered by the visionOS operating system that provides an immersive, intuitive and efficient user experience. It marks the dawn of a new spatial computing era, bringing users an unprecedented hardware experience. The product features an advanced Spatial User Interface customised for Apple Vision Pro, a mixed-reality device. Unlike traditional 2D user interfaces, the Spatial User Interface utilises 3D space to present information and human-computer interaction. The Spatial UI incorporates natural input methods such as eye movements, gestures and voice and uses visual elements such as glass, 3D icons and dynamic fonts to create an immersive spatial computing experience. Its glass mimetic style is a new design language designed to provide a more immersive and natural mixed reality experience. The interface is made of a glass-like material that is translucent and lightweight and blends seamlessly with the natural environment. The material simulates light and shadow changes to enhance the interface's hierarchy and realism, automatically adjusting brightness and colour based on ambient light. Vibrancy technology indicates text and symbols and fills hierarchies through light and colour changes. Foreground content is brighter and more eye-catching; background content is softer and easier to read. This technology enhances the depth of the interface and creates a more immersive visual

Fig. 6. New pseudo physical style user interface

experience. On Apple Vision Pro, users can control apps with gestures, such as pinching to zoom in and out of an image or swiping to scroll a page. Users can also use eye tracking to control apps, such as by gazing at a button to activate it. Apps can utilise the spatial awareness capabilities of vision, such as adjusting the display based on the user's position and perspective. Apple Vision Pro will open up a new paradigm in interaction design, delivering immersive, intuitive, and interactive experiences that will continue to revolutionise and evolve the human-computer interaction paradigm.

The Spatial User Interface is a revolutionary design that allows users to interact with digital content in real space, providing an immersive experience. This innovation is realised through Virtual Reality (VR) and Augmented Reality (AR) technologies, which together build an interface that can be interacted with in three-dimensional space. Apple Vision Pro Spatial User Interface design not only represents the direction of the future development of user interfaces but also reveals unlimited potential and broad prospects for development. As the technology matures and the application scenarios become more affluent and prosperous, we can foresee that the spatial user interface will bring more advanced, personalised and humanised interactive experiences (Fig. 7).

All in all, Apple has enormously contributed to the history of user interface development. From pixel style to anthropomorphic style, from anthropomorphic style to flat style, and from flat style to neomorphic style. From the original command line user interface to the graphical user interface, from the user interface to the spatial user interface.

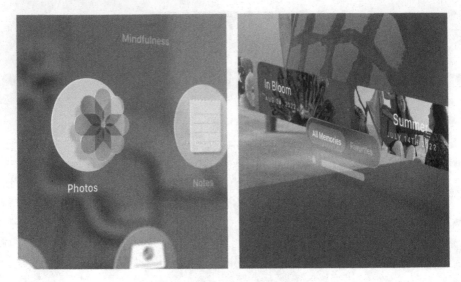

Fig. 7. visionOS User Interface.

User interfaces have evolved and innovated to provide users with a more intuitive, easy-to-use, and beautiful experience. Apple will continue exploring and innovating the user interface, incorporating technologies such as artificial intelligence, augmented reality, and virtual reality into interface design to give users a more intelligent, personalised, and immersive experience (Fig. 8).

Fig. 8. Spatial User Interface

4 Discussion

In the evolution of Apple's graphical user interface design, every style change is closely related to technological progress, user needs, and aesthetic trends. Analysing some content shows how Apple can solve specific problems, improve user experience, and lead the industry trend through interface design. The pixel-style graphical user interface provides intuitive visual symbols, greatly simplifying computer operation. However, with the development of technology and users' higher pursuit of beauty and functionality, the pure pixel art style can no longer meet the demand. Pseudo-pseudo-physical style followed. It created a friendly interactive environment for users by imitating objects in the real world. Still, it was also criticised for its excessive decoration, which promoted the rise of flat style. Flat design is loved by users for its simplicity and modernisation, but it also faces some challenges in functionality and usability. The new mimicry style tries to overcome these problems by balancing beauty and function through fine shadow and light effects. In addition, Apple's design of spatial interfaces marks a new era of user interface design. With the maturity of AR and VR technologies, future user interfaces may pay more attention to the sense of space and immersive experience. Designers will face new challenges, but they will also allow users to interact more naturally and efficiently. However, the progress of technology and design has also brought some things that could be improved. For example, the learning curve of the new design style may need to be clarified for some users, especially those who are used to the old interface version. In addition, the rapid changes in design may also cause some users to feel uncomfortable or dissatisfied. Therefore, while pursuing innovation, designers should consider the needs and receptivity of different user groups to ensure the universality of design.

5 Conclusion

The graphic user interface design of Apple products reflects technological innovation and the evolution of aesthetic concepts. Apple continues to explore and innovate in interface design, providing users with a richer and more intuitive interactive experience. From the command line interface to the graphical user interface and then to the spatial user interface, each change highlights Apple's unremitting efforts to pursue excellent user experience and design innovation. Apple's design evolution improves its products' ease of use and attractiveness, sets a benchmark for the entire technology and design industry, and continues to lead its development. In the future, with the continuous progress of technology, user interface design will continue to evolve, and more brand-new design concepts and interaction methods may appear. In the exploration process of user interface design, maintaining the usability, accessibility, and aesthetics of the user interface has become an essential task for designers. Ultimately, these efforts all point to a common goal - creating a more humanised and user-friendly interactive experience.

Funding. This Study Was Supported by the Shandong Social Science Planning Fund Program (23CLYJ04).

References

1. Apple human interface guidelines. https://developer.apple.com/design/human-interface-gui delines/
2. Norman, D.A.: The design of everyday things: revised and expanded edition New York: Basic Books (2013)
3. Tognazzini, B.: Tog on Interface Reading. Addison Wesley, Boston, MA (1992)
4. Johnson, J.: Designing with the mind in mind: a simple guide to understanding user interface design rules Morgan Kaufmann (2010)
5. Manovich, L.: The Language of New Media. MIT Press, Cambridge, MA (2001)
6. www.apple.com
7. Tiantian, D.: Research on Flat Design in the Context of Contemporary Thought. Mentor: Cui Tianjian Southeast University (2015)
8. Jing, H.: Research on Game APP Interface Design Based on Cognitive Psychology of Preschool Children. Mentor: Sun Yayun China University of Mining and Technology (2015)
9. Liling, Z.: Research on interface design of flat Internet products based on user experience. Mentor: Gao Ying Zhejiang University of Business and Technology (2014)
10. Jiali, Y.: Research on Visual Design of Children's Internet Product Interface Based on Emotional Design. Mentor: Zhang Dalu Suzhou University (2014)
11. Huan, Y.: Research on Interface Design of Smart Phone Mobile Internet Application. Mentor: Zhu Mingjian Wuhan University of Technology (2013)
12. Xinxin, S.: Research on Interaction Interface Design Based on User Unconscious Behavior. Mentor: Li Shiguo Jiangnan University (2013)
13. Songyan, M.: Design and implementation of fitness application based on iOS platform. Mentor: Que Xirong Beijing University of Posts and Telecommunications (2013)
14. Shanshan, M.: Research on icon design style of mobile phone graphics interface. Mentor: Zhai Ying Beijing Institute of Fashion (2012)
15. Yin, Q.: Research on user expectations in the design of smartphone application software for college students. Mentor: Li Shiguo; Li Binbin Jiangnan University (2011)
16. Min, F.: Research on graphic user interface design from the perspective of cultural communication. Mentor: Liao Jun Suzhou University (2009)
17. Xiangliang, Y., Junshun, Y., Yanlin, C.: Research on the application of UI design in shaping product image. Packaging Engineering (2007)
18. Furen, H.: Research on human-machine interface design. Mentor: Chen Hanqing Wuhan University of Technology (2003)
19. The History of the GUI. https://www.britannica.com/technology/graphical-user-interface
20. The Xerox Alto. https://en.wikipedia.org/wiki/Xerox_Alto
21. The Xerox Star. https://en.wikipedia.org/wiki/Xerox_Star
22. The Macintosh. https://en.wikipedia.org/wiki/Macintosh

Wings of Imagination: Strengthening Avian Embodiment and Flight Immersion in Virtual Reality Through Multisensory Haptic Feedback

Ziqi Wang[1], Mengyao Guo[2], Yikun Fang[3], Kexin Nie[4], Hanbing Wang[5], Xingzhi Shi[6], Yifan Li[7], and Ze Gao[8(✉)]

[1] Tsinghua University, Beijing, China
[2] Shenzhen International School of Design, Harbin Institute of Technology, Shenzhen, China
[3] Royal College of Art, London, UK
[4] University of Sydney, Sydney, Australia
[5] Goldsmiths, University of London, London, UK
[6] Pratt Institute, New York, USA
[7] Royal Melbourne Institute of Technology, Melbourne, Australia
4063821@student.rmit.edu.au
[8] Hong Kong Polytechnic University, Hong Kong SAR, China
zegao@polyu.edu.hk

Abstract. This research develops an integrated system using multimodal haptic feedback to enhance users' sense of body ownership when embodying avian avatars in virtual reality. The hardware components include retractable bands to guide limb movements and inflatable cushions to simulate environmental conditions during flight. The system aims to replicate key aspects of avian embodiment through synchronized virtual and physical stimuli. A user study evaluates the potential of this approach to strengthen feelings of ownership over non-human avatars. Results demonstrate moderately positive overall usability, with variable individual responses. Spatial haptics augmented realistic wing simulations for over half of the participants. However, limitations exist regarding personalized interactions and simulating comprehensive tactile sensations. This pioneering work contributes an innovative methodology for prototyping and assessing bodily transformations in virtual environments. It advances avatar embodiment knowledge and underscores the nuanced interplay of multisensory feedback. Further refinements may build empathy and connections with the natural world.

Keywords: Wearable Haptic Devices · Virtual reality · Body Ownership

1 Introduction

Throughout history, humanity has yearned for the ability to soar through the skies and has dedicated significant efforts toward advancing aerial technology.

© The Author(s), under exclusive license to Springer Nature Switzerland AG 2024
N. A. Streitz and S. Konomi (Eds.): HCII 2024, LNCS 14719, pp. 411–432, 2024.
https://doi.org/10.1007/978-3-031-60012-8_26

However, birds can achieve flight without needing mechanical energy; instead, they utilize their bodies to overcome the force of gravity and ascend into the sky. Humans have never experienced the physical sensation of birds defying the forces of gravity and air resistance. The inquiry into the disparities between avian and human anatomical encounters poses a challenge in enhancing the human embodiment of bird avatars, warranting further investigation. This study aims to improve the users' sense of immersion and ownership over virtual bodies by employing multimodal haptic feedback interactions. Specifically, we focus on enhancing body and space simulation, developing a design framework to expand the study of avatar diversity in virtual reality, and examining the individual and combined impacts of these two simulations on haptic feedback through quantitative and qualitative research.

The theoretical framework in the field helps this study. First, this study provides users with the body senses of a bird in flight, which belongs to beyond-real haptic feedback simulations, showing that humans and birds have different movement mechanisms and living environments. For instance, the avian's musculature and respiratory system have all evolved to accommodate flight and high altitude. Abtahi has proposed the concept of Beyond-Real transformations in virtual reality [2]. He explored how visual information input in the virtual world affects the sensory-motor loop, centring on the central nervous system when the Beyond-real transformation occurs. His proposed model links the user's physical body with the user's vision in the virtual world, which helped this study establish interaction design between wearable devices and VR headsets. Secondly, this study introduces the formula for haptic feedback fidelity proposed by Muender to conduct a quantitative analysis of haptic feedback data [5]. This formula quantifies the haptic feedback fidelity into specific values for comparison and exploration. The above theoretical framework provides a reference and basis for using haptic feedback in conjunction with VR to transcend the human body's limitations in daily life.

In this study, we researched the above body mechanisms and spatial transformation and designed wearable hardware for haptic feedback and software in a VR headset for vision. The body simulation hardware comprises a retractable strap system, and space simulation hardware consists of an inflatable airbag and a wind blower. Users wear wings and counterweights for controlled experiments to compare with the body simulation hardware. Furthermore, the space hardware will combine the other two sets separately for simulation. In all, we recruited a total of 15 participants for the experiment. To better evaluate the user experience, the System Usability Scale and haptic fidelity factors questionnaires were sent to the participants after the experiment. Based on the collected data, this study uses the formulas proposed by Muender to get the quantitative haptic feedback fidelity values and the formula of the System Usability Scale (SUS) to derive the participants' experience using this system. In addition to data collection, this study also conducted interviews with participants to collect personalized comments and suggestions. We also calculated the mean, median, mode, range, variance, standard deviation, and P-value in the Analysis of

Variance of the haptic fidelity scores for each group of devices, and we discussed device evaluation and future development.

This study concludes with four main contributions. Firstly, it develops a design methodology to enhance body ownership by simulating the movement mechanisms of non-human avatars through haptic feedback. Based on this, an interaction design framework is established for how the software interface in a virtual environment cooperates with haptic feedback hardware devices in the physical world. Additionally, this study evaluates the effects and issues of combining spatial and bodily haptic feedback devices and analyzes opportunities for future development. Furthermore, it enhances the field's understanding of how space simulations interact with body simulation through haptic feedback in beyond-real virtual reality environments. Finally, from an evaluation perspective, this study establishes a framework for assessing haptic feedback based on factors influencing users' sense of body ownership.

2   Related Works

The allure of avian flight taps into a profound existential yearning inherent to the human condition - our restless impulse to evolve and transcend the limitations of earthly existence. Soaring freely through the skies is akin to transcending the flesh, momentarily casting off our terrestrial bodily forms to glimpse an elevated state of being unhindered by physical laws, symbolizing our deepest aspirations for liberation from the constraints of material reality. Pioneers like Leonardo da Vinci dedicated their brilliance to designing exotic ornithopters and aircraft [20]. The dawn of the modern industrial age brought forth machines capable of achieving lifelong dreams of mastery over the skies. Early planes took to the air, swiftly followed by developments in aeronautical engineering that swiftly progressed from frail wood and fabric contraptions to reliable metal giants spanning the globe [21].

On a metaphysical level, flying symbolizes humanity's quest to reconcile our heightened consciousness and intelligence with our ephemeral mortal nature [25]. It speaks to our dual nature - the conflicting desires to embrace our animal roots yet flee the inevitability of earthly decay through transcendence into higher spheres of thought and being. Birds traversing the boundary between heaven and earth with ease remind us of possibilities beyond the narrow confines of our average worldly experience. At the same time, the dream of flight touches on humanity's search for meaning and purpose beyond our fleeting individual lives. Taking to the skies on wings like birds allows us to view life from a loftier, more celestial vantage point and contemplate our place in the grand universal order.

However, all of the above flying dreams are covered by tangible objects instead of human bodies. This highlights the limitations of current technology in achieving accurate human flight without external aids. The critical difference between bird flying and human arm waves is the specialized wing musculature that the birds possess is not found in humans, while both human arm swinging and bird wing flapping involve coordinated movement of antagonistic muscle pairs across the body in a rhythmic pattern to flex and extend the limbs, utilizing muscles like deltoids and supraspinatus to abduct and horizontally extend the arms or wings [26]. As birds use powerful pectoralis and supracoracoideus muscles to power the downstroke, they require more significant overall muscular effort against gravity given their more enormous wings, and their movement is more synchronized in a backward elliptical stroking motion versus human arms [22]. Birds do not have rotational elbow joints but have additional wing bones and joints to fold feathers tightly. Their wing feather proportions allow more efficient conversion of muscle work to propulsion than arms.

Consequently, our work aims to allow people to experience relaxation and effectiveness through extreme movement simulation that transcends human limitations. Physically, extreme sports push the body to its limits and induce a "runner's high" effect where the release of endorphins counters feelings of stress. Psychologically [23], engaging in virtual high-risk activities in a safe environment satiates our innate thirst for adventure while providing feelings of control over dangerous situations. It also allows people in increasingly sedentary lifestyles to fulfil basic human needs for the challenge, stimulation, and complex movement. By simulating experiences we cannot access in reality, this study aims to create an interactive system that could deliver positive mental health benefits of relaxation through immersion in intense sensations.

After thoroughly researching the relevant works, we have identified several key studies that inform our research on the sense of immersive realism, the materiality of virtual embodiment, and genuine haptic feedback mechanisms.

The projects investigating animal avatars in virtual reality, such as "Haptic Around," employ a hybrid system that provides various haptic sensations in VR using wind blowers, heat blowers, misters, and heat lamps [1]. Oyanagi's, on the other hand, focuses on the illusion of ownership in non-human avatars, specifically a bird in VR, building upon previous research on embodiment [19]. Krekhov investigates the utilization of animal avatars in virtual reality, employing body-tracking techniques to maneuver various creatures such as spiders and bats [13]. Other studies have highlighted valuable methodological advancements, such as Grabbe's semiotic analysis of "TreeSense," which investigates the physical nature of virtual embodiment. This study demonstrates the correlation between the physical characteristics of signals and how users perceive them, expanding semiotic theory to include dynamic, embodied virtual reality interactions [3]. The remaining efforts focus on user immersion in virtual reality. Freude's work explores how virtual body ownership and agency can be enhanced through virtual reality, suggesting that additional control devices can improve the sense of ownership [11]. Wee et al.'s study examines haptic interfaces for virtual reality and highlights essential challenges and future research directions in this field [17]. The study emphasizes ongoing issues such as adaptability, size reduction, integration of multimodal feedback integration, and the replication of bi-manual interactions. It suggests that overcoming these hurdles is crucial for advancing the realism and functionality of VR haptic systems.

The absence of genuine haptic feedback integration also greatly inspired us. Michael's research examines the constraints of kinesthetic feedback in consumer-grade VR technology, which does not incorporate authentic haptic feedback mechanisms [18]. Visual-based feedback, also known as pseudo-haptics, may undermine the authenticity of the kinesthetic experience, highlighting a need to assess the genuine effectiveness of haptic feedback. Richard's research centres on examining the influence of haptic feedback on the feeling of being fully present in virtual environments, particularly in the context of VR drawing tasks [12]. These findings emphasize the intricate connection between the ownership of one's body and the ability to exert control, as well as the significance of receiving feedback through multiple sensory channels. Upon reviewing the related works, several recurring limitations were identified that inform the focus of our research, centred around the narrow representation of avatars, incomplete evaluation of fidelity factors, lack of genuine haptics, and focus on individual modalities rather than holistic multisensory experiences. We introduce diverse avatar representations while thoroughly evaluating fidelity across modalities. Specialized hardware provides authentic haptics within complex flight simulations, such as the connecting muscles added to mimic the bird's wing. A user-centred mixed interview methods approach assesses synergistic multisensory effects beyond singular components. Through these enhancements, we seek to advance the authenticity and generalizability of embodied virtual experiences.

3 Study Overview

To address the current issue, this study examined the pertinent material. It determined that a sophisticated amalgamation of hardware, software, and interaction design is necessary to integrate human and animal movement experiences seamlessly. The Double Diamond design model is the basis of our methodical approach, comprising four distinct stages: Discover, Define, Develop, and Deliver Phases [24]. This model guarantees our project a meticulous and all-encompassing development process, from the initial concept to the final execution.

In the **Discovery Phase**, we analyzed the limitations of current VR technology and user requirements for immersive avian experiences through a literature review. Its multi-faceted understanding of our project context was enhanced through the amalgamation [16]. The reviewed literature focused on recent sources from 2019, ensuring updated data and information and a clearer comprehension of the latest haptic feedback advances in virtual reality. The **Definition Phase** involved synthesizing our findings to pinpoint critical areas for development. By studying bird flight movement mechanisms to inform our hardware design approach, where we carefully selected key components - a microcontroller, sensors, and operators - and prototyped a blower and inflatable airbag to simulate bird flight transformations through haptic sensations in space. During the **Development Phase**, we translated defined requirements into a tangible haptic interface through iterative prototyping to perfect feedback factors, and the software integrated sensory data to create a cohesive VR experience. Thus, we developed a series of wearable devices incorporating retractable straps and inflatable airbags, building on our research to enhance the feeling of acting like a bird. These devices simulate a bird's movements during takeoff and flight sensations like air resistance and temperature through our digitally mapped interaction model [14]. After the development, we implemented the complete system and conducted user'testing for validation to guarantee the further development of **Delivery Phase**. Experimental processes and data collection were designed based on the System Usability Scale (SUS), and adjustments were made based on feedback to ensure the interaction design facilitated convincing body ownership and met haptic immersion outcomes.

4   Hardware Design and Implementation

Our design strategy is to simulate the bird flight sensation from spatial and bodily perspectives with haptic feedback. The hardware design focuses on the bird's movement mechanism to give users haptic feedback on bird flight, and the software design in the VR headset provides a visual experience.

4.1   Birds Movement Mechanism Research

Birds overcome air resistance and gravity through evolved movement mechanisms, including their respiratory, structural, and force-exertion adaptations suited for flight. Birds have developed air sacs within their chest cavities to aid oxygen uptake under the low pressures experienced during lift-off in the perspective of respiratory physiology [9]. They possess well-developed pectoral muscles and feather-covered wings, allowing for continuous flapping to generate lift to counteract air resistance and support body weight in structural biomechanics [6]. Regarding force exertion dynamics, birds lower their centre of mass by bending their bodies downward during takeoff. We studied the avian flight mechanics through the lens of these above factors to inform the design of interactive hardware devices that mechanically transform these elements of the bird movement mechanism to enhance the sensory experience of embodied avian flight simulation.

4.2   Hardware Design Approach

The hardware design includes space simulations that imitate the environment transformations and body simulations that mimic the body movement. The space simulations mainly involve the air sacs in birds' respiratory systems and cold, strong wind in high altitudes. Birds' respiratory system bears more burden than humans in fighting against the lack of oxygen at high altitudes. Therefore, we placed an inflatable airbag on the user's chest, designed to simulate the air sacs of birds. The higher the user rises in VR, the more the airbag expands, bringing extra pressure to the user's chest, and a wind blower is equipped to simulate the strong wind in the air.

Bodily simulations targeted mimicking avian movement biomechanics. Primary avian flight muscles include the pectoral and scapular muscles evolved for power output [4]. Birds exploit drag and lift forces through the coordinated activity of back muscles and flapping wings to generate upward thrust and partially support weight [6]. Research indicates biceps and deltoid activity corresponds to locations of important avian flight musculature [7]. Accordingly, retractable elastic straps linked the user's upper body muscles, such that shortening one strap would drive surrounding straps to mobilize target areas. Besides, considering the flight movements of birds begin with a lowering gravity centre and a quick flap of the wings, the chest strap is shortened by the hardware when the user takes off, guiding them to bend over. Moreover, elastic bends tie the arm and the waist, making it difficult for users to flap fast, simulating the burden of real wings.

4.3   Retractable Straps System

Retractable Straps System is an integral component of the VR setup, including the straps and waist belt with arm cover.

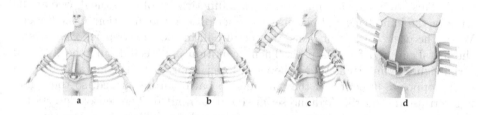

Fig. 1. The Hardware Design Model.

Straps. The straps offer direct force feedback by reducing the distance between the chest and waist, decreasing the wearers' centre of gravity. The user's upper chest is restrained by four inelastic nylon straps, which are fastened in a crisscross pattern in front of the chest (see Fig. 1a), and the same nylon straps are wrapped around the armpits on either side. This guarantees that the chest remains stationary during physical activity. The stretch straps were placed into each arm and the matching side of the waist (see Fig. 1b).

Waist Belt and Arm Cover. From the view of holding the whole weight of the device, considering that the servo motor is limited to be placed in front of the waist to complete the telescoping of chest straps, the supporting position stays the waist and arm, we develop waist belt and forearms covering. The waist brace consisted of a laser-cut galvanized steel base plate covered with 3D printed components inspired by avian bone structure (see Fig. 1c). The servo is secured in front of the waist for diverse body sizes, and the back side of the belt has adjustable elastic nylon straps that pass through the waist. Solid metal side strips fixed the elastic bands (see Fig. 1d). The basement of the arm cover is made of metal plates covered with hollowed-out 3d printed parts designed to reduce weight and provide support. The arm cover is attached to the waist near the inside of the body by elastic straps, simulating the tension received by a bird's wings in flight, aiming to mimic wing tension dynamics during avian flight. This brace configuration distributed device weight across the waist, arms and chest while retaining the range of motion.

4.4   Controlling System Design

The core of the controlling system is an Arduino microcontroller with an RDS5180 servo (80 kg-cm), an inflatable airbag with two air pumps, and an SW-520D vibration sensor. The Arduino is responsible for reading the data from the vibration sensor (0 or 1) and controlling the servo's motion accordingly.

Arduino with Vibration Sensor. The Arduino microcontroller acts as the system's brain and is responsible for processing the input signals and controlling the output. The sensor (SW-520D) detects vibration or motion in the environment. This study uses its tipping detection function by placing the device at the wrist or the hand back and placing its copper post in the direction of the fingers. When the users raise their arms, the metal ball inside the copper post slides to the metal pin and forms a path. Then, a motion is detected, and the Arduino serial signal is inputted. When the users lower their arms, the metal ball slides in the opposite direction of the pin, and no path can be formed, so the signal is interrupted, and the Arduino serial signal is input 0. The sensor detects the signal once every 1 s to prevent accidental touching. This time is the same or longer than most users' flapping once. The coding logic is to detect two flappings within 3 s as the official start. When the user's arm has been down for over 10 s, then Arduino serial signals are 0 at the official end.

Arduino with Servo Motor and Inflatable Airbag. The servo is set on the metal waist belt connecting with a non-elastic strap to the chest metal plate. The motor receives control signals from the Arduino and performs precise angle adjustments based on these signals. In our experiment, the servo motor range is 0 to 160 °C. When the servo is at 0 °C, the user can stand straight naturally, and when the servo is at 160 °C, the user needs to bend down.

The inflation system consists of two 40 L/min air pumps, two relays, a set of tubes, a tee device, and an airbag. The two air pumps are connected to a tee device through tubes; the pump inflates one tube, and the other is deflated. For safety reasons, the deflated air pump is used as a pressure relief valve for the inflated air pump to prevent the airbag from exploding due to overfilling. The third port of the teeing device is connected via a tube to the airbag, which is placed between the body and the metal plate on the chest. When the airbag is inflated, the non-stretchable nylon straps hold the metal plate and squeeze the airbag. Instead resulting in a feeling of compression by users.

5   Software Design and Implementation

For our user research and application development, we implemented VR games using the Meta Quest 2 virtual reality headset and the Unity game engine (version 2021.3.19f1c1). We utilised the XR Interaction Toolkit to develop user interactions within the VR games. We programmed two triggers for character control - one positioned above and one below the user's head position in VR space. When the Meta controller touched either the upper or lower trigger, it would prompt the character to move forward or upwards. By varying the relative distance between the triggers and the head position, we were able to test different avian flight postures. We also obtained terrain assets from the Unity Asset Store to construct virtual environments for testing. This setup allowed us to prototype our avian avatar simulations for evaluation with participants.

6   Interaction Design Approach

The interaction design approach relies on a harmonized interaction between software and hardware, crucial for creating immersive user experiences with minimal delay.

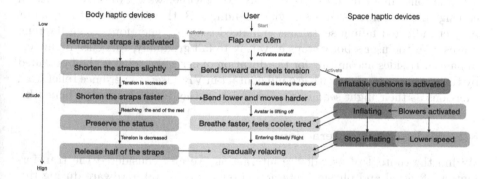

Fig. 2. The Flowchart of the Interaction between Haptic Feedback Devices and the User During the Taking-off Process.

6.1   Start and End Triggers

The delay and misunderstanding will decrease with the same command reacted to by visual and haptic feedback. Maintaining the synchronicity of software and hardware's start and end triggers is the key to immersive experiences. The hardware and software components ensured prompt triggering by accurately detecting the number of hand waves.

Hardware. The hardware setup utilizes key components to simulate flight motions in a logical sequence (see Fig. 2). This logical sequencing of hardware components and interaction settings aims to seamlessly translate natural avian motions into an immersive VR flight experience through realistic haptic feedback. At startup, the system initializes with the servo motor in the 0-degree position and the air pump switched off. In this system, we established two conditions to trigger the start and end of flights. The vibration sensor continually monitors for tilt cues from the user. When two flap motions are detected within a 3-second window, this is recognized as the official start signal.

Upon receiving the start signal, the servo motor transitions the apparatus from 0 to 160 °C. Simultaneously, the inflatable air pump activates the inflation of the wearable airbag. Throughout flight simulations, the sensor evaluates motion cues every 1 s. So long as the movement continues to register within each 10-second interval, the current operational state is maintained. However, if no motion signal arises for ten whole seconds, the system interprets this as the end of the flight. In response, the servo motor reverses course to return from 160 to 0 °C. Concurrently, the air pump switches modes to initiate the deflation of the inflated airbag.

Software. To enhance the immersion experience for users, the start and end triggers are synchronous with the hardware. The start signal was set consistently as two detected flaps within a 3-second window, aiming to translate natural motions smoothly into VR takeoffs. Meanwhile, we established a natural end signal that helped seamlessly guide landings. Rather than abrupt stops, our project indicated falling sensations enhanced realism. Therefore, when flapping ceases, and the user's body stops elevating to fall gradually, this cues flight termination. Besides accounting for the duration of descents, relief is then provided by the system in tandem with ground contact in VR. Users experience relief from exertions as their flight seamlessly concludes on the digital landscape beneath.

6.2 Multisensory Interaction

Within the context of user-device interaction, we also considered the transformation of visual and physical interaction on software and hardware during this project.

Hardware. For the hardware to translate avian motions, our project designed it to fit diverse body types. All joints and strap lengths are designed to be adjustable to accommodate varying human anatomies. When flight commences, haptic cues guide the user's posture and movements. Initially, tension is applied as the servo shortens straps connected at the waist, shoulders, and forearms. This gently pulls the user's posture downward, mobilizing back and arm muscles to simulate an avian stance against gravity. From this balanced position, further interactions cue realistic motions. Increased tension on the forearm straps with each flap simulates the muscular exertion of wings, coordinating with the user's physical actions. As the user responds instinctively through emulated flapping motions, corresponding haptic feedback loops recreate the experience of lift, thrust, and changing air pressures felt during avian flight. From initial posture cues through motion-guided feedback, our system aims to elicit natural movements that seamlessly translate the user's physical actions into an immersive virtual flight simulation. The user will receive commands not through words or verbal means but through haptic cues and react with motion.

Software. Users who interact with the software in a VR headset need clear visual feedback. In this project, we render a 3D forest environment scaled to a bird's perspective in flight (see Fig. 3). Plants appear comparatively larger than from a human viewpoint, filling more of the visual frame. Additionally, two square elements placed before the user represent their avian wings for easy position tracking. The user's altitude and location are readily discernible using these wings and the scaled forest scenery. Lower flights see tower plants encompassing most of the view. The software transitions the perspective upward as the user mobilizes their wings through physical flapping mirrored in VR. Trees gradually diminish in size as the view elevates through the forest canopy. Eventually, at high altitudes, the tops of tree silhouettes come into view, signalling the user has broken through to the open sky. This vertical visualization cues a natural sense of increasing elevation through bodily movement more intuitively than isolated readouts.

Fig. 3. The 3D Wild Forest in the VR.

7   Experiment and User Study

The study concluded with a user evaluation of this installation, which incorporated the experiential design, methodology, participant composition, and questionnaire.

7.1   Experiment Design

This experiment aims to help users experience the haptic feedback and score the hardware. The users will be experimenting with both space and body simulations, and this experiment design aims to explore the interaction between space and body simulation.

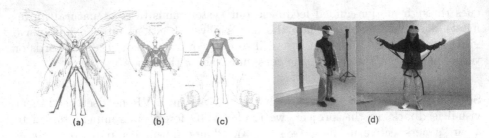

Fig. 4. The Single Simulation Groups and Records of Experiment.

Experimental Setup. As the equipment applied in this experiment consisted of software and hardware, we programmed and developed our scenario in Unity and imported it into the Meta Quest2 headset. The hardware includes three sections: realistic simulation, movement simulation, and space simulation. These first two sections are body simulations. The first, including the feather wings and the counterweight (see Fig. 4a). While having lower versatility than other designs due to storage and transport difficulties, this direct representation of wings allows more intuitively natural flapping motions. It compares with the second simulation to analyze the fidelity of haptic feedback. The second section is the criticaly hardware device developed in this research to study the flight mechanism of birds and change human movement and muscle force. The device uses the strap and servo motor to provide force feedback to guide the user's movements (see Fig. 4b). Lastly, the third section is the space simulation, which includes a wind blower and an airbag to simulate the drop in atmospheric pressure and high winds at high altitudes (see Fig. 4c) . The airbag was fixed beneath chest straps and inflated to generate pressure sensations in the experiments. Meanwhile, the external blower provided surrounding wind cues.

Group Classification. We separated the experiment participants into five groups. The first three groups are single simulation groups, testing the hardware of each section independently. Meanwhile, the latter two groups are combination groups, combining realistic and movement simulations with space simulations. Each participant has attempted five flights as a result.

Experiment Site. Due to the huge wings and considering the requirements of this experiment, the test should take place in an empty room, free of obstructions, able to provide adequate power connections, and able to accommodate other waiting participants.

7.2 Participants Information

For the experiment, fifteen volunteers between the ages of 19 and 40 were selected from the social community. The average age of the participants was roughly 25.7 years. The gender distribution was quite even, consisting of seven males and eight females, contributing to maintaining gender balance in the outcomes analysis. The participants in this study consisted mostly of university students and professionals from various sectors, such as interface design, finance, business management, computer science majors, programmers, professional photographers, and freelancers. The wide array of professional backgrounds brought forth a plethora of viewpoints and experiences for the study.

Significantly, 60% of the participants (nine persons) had previous familiarity with virtual reality haptic devices, whereas the remaining 40% (six individuals) did not. This broad composition is essential for examining the variances in responses and preferences across users with varying degrees of experience. Experienced participants can offer feedback that is grounded in their real-world usage. Conversely, viewpoints from novice people may provide more instinctive and sensory observations, which are crucial for understanding the usefulness and acceptance of a gadget.

7.3   Experiment Process

Upon arrival at the experimental site, participants are given the initial project overview with the organizer's help. The participants must read the project description, which contains the experimental purpose of this study, the experimental procedure, and the privacy protection and rights statement. The privacy statement includes the purpose and scope of the data collection, how the data is processed and stored, the rules for data use, the rights of the participants, and the privacy protection measures. All participants sign the document after indicating their approval of its content.

Following that, participants wear hardware equipment and VR headsets with our assistance. They individually wear the three pieces of hardware, corresponding to the contents of single simulation groups, as described in the group classification (see Fig. 4d). Subsequently, we initiate the activation of the combined sets of equipment to carry out the fourth and fifth flights successfully. Once all flights have concluded, participants proceed to dismantle the equipment and proceed to submit the questionnaire on the Qualtric platform, marking the completion of the experiment.

7.4   Questionnaire and Interview

We conducted two questionnaires and interviews with participants after they experienced the single and combined simulation groups.

The SUS Questionnaire and Calculating Methodology. This study used the SUS (System Usability Scale) questionnaire to investigate software and hardware user experience [8]. It evaluates a system's usability, complexity, and technical support. The SUS is generated with a ten-item questionnaire, which has standardized entries and is used to assess a system's or product's usability.

Participants rated their level of agreement with each statement on a 5-point Likert scale ranging from "Strongly Disagree" (1 score) to "Strongly Agree" (5 scores), where odd-numbered questions are positives, and even-numbered questions are negatives. To calculate the score for this study, the researchers followed the standard SUS procedure: subtracting 1 from odd items, subtracting scores from 5 for even items, summing the adjusted scores, and multiplying by 2.5 to scale the final result from 0 to 100. Higher SUS scores indicate better usability of the system.

Haptic Fidelity Questionnaire and Interview. We also refer to Muender's research on the evaluation framework for the fidelity of haptic feedback [5], in which Muender proposed 14 factors, among which there are six limiting factors and eight foundational factors, and a formula for calculating the haptic fidelity score based on these factors. This formula uses a 5-point Likert scale (0–4) to assess the factors, where the foundational factors are averaged, and the limiting factors are scored by inverting squaring and combining them with a specific exponential function to calculate a number between 0 and 1. Finally, this number is multiplied by the average of the foundational factors to arrive at a value between 0 and 4; 4 is perfect, and 0 is the lowest (see Fig. 5). Muender has proposed that the framework's validity and reliability are supported by its development process, which involves an iterative approach, a literature review on human haptic sensing, and feedback from experts in VR and haptic feedback.

Due to limited participants, this study focuses on five foundational factors: body location, hardware precision, sensory integrity, magnitude, and degrees of freedom. We also consider three limiting factors: side effects, constraints, and hardware latency. Every questionnaire item is designed to fit each factor, with 5 equipment groups in the scoring section. This allows for horizontal comparison of the same factors score among the equipment groups. After the questionnaires, the participants' scores are calculated using the formula. As the calculation of haptic fidelity here is not based on all 14 factors but on 8 of them, the result could not represent the total fidelity scores. The remaining six factors, software precision, software latency, dependency, distinguishability, stimuli, and body area, will be measured in the future with a larger capacity of participants and refined software.

In addition to the scoring items, the study also included open-ended interview questions in the questionnaires, for instance, suggestions they wanted to give the organizers, other species avatars they would like to play in VR, and their imaginings of bird body senses. The participants communicate with the researchers and discuss their experiences after the experience, and these feedbacks allow us to consider its updated version.

$$\text{Haptic Fidelity Score} = \left(\frac{\sum_{i=0}^{N_F} X_{F_i}}{N_F} \right) \times e^{-0.0027 \times \left(\sum_{j=0}^{N_L} X_{L_j}^2 \right)^2}$$

Fig. 5. The Haptic Fidelity Score Formula.

7.5 Data Analyzing Method

Finally, the SUS and haptic feedback fidelity scores were calculated using the mean, median, range, mode, variance, and standard deviation to summarize the data. The scores can also be calculated for the p-value of one-way ANOVA to analyze the significance between each group. Based on this study's design and common conventions in the field, we set the significance level at 0.05. If the p-value is less than or equal to 0.05, we consider the difference between at least two groups significant.

Those scores and figures are presented in tables or histograms, and the trend of specific groups of factor scores will be displayed in line graphs. In the graphs or tables, the users are listed according to age, from youngest to oldest. The higher the number, the older the age, so the relevance between age and data can be discerned.

8 Result Analysis

The quantitative and qualitative research results from the data collected through the SUS and haptic feedback questionnaire are shown below.

8.1 SUS Score Analysis

Based on the users' scores on the ten items shown in the SUS questionnaire, this study obtains a composite score for each user, and we compile a histogram after calculation (see Fig. 6).

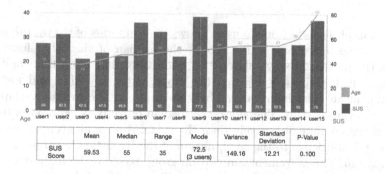

	Mean	Median	Range	Mode	Variance	Standard Deviation	P-Value
SUS Score	59.53	55	35	72.5 (3 users)	149.16	12.21	0.100

Fig. 6. The SUS Score with Age.

From the graph, the mode figure shows that 72.5 appeared three times in the ratings, which accounts for the mean being 4.53 higher than the median. At the same time, the variance in this data is 149.16, and the standard deviation is 12.21. These two values are relatively high, indicating high volatility in the data. Thus, in this case, the median, 55, is a more objective representative than the mean. It suggests that more than half of the users rated above average.

Realistic Simulation							Movement Simulation							Space Simulation						
User	1	2	3	4	5	6	7	1	2	3	4	5	6	7	1	2	3	4	5	6	7
Score	3.9	1.6	3.0	2.4	2.9	4	1.9	2.6	2	3.6	2.4	3.4	0.9	2.7	4	1.8	3.99	1.0	4	0.4	1.8
User	8	9	10	11	12	13	14	8	9	10	11	12	13	14	8	9	10	11	12	13	14
Score	1.6	3.2	4	2.4	2.6	0	0	0	3	4	2.9	2.6	0	0	0.5	3.2	3.6	0.6	3.6	0	0
User	15							15							15						
Score	4							4							4						

(a) Single Simulation Groups

Realistic Simulation+Space simulation							Movement Simulation + Space Simulation						
User	1	2	3	4	5	6	7	1	2	3	4	5	6	7
Score	3.8	3.2	3.8	0.4	3.8	3.4	3.4	2.873	4	3.8	0	3.8	0.19	4
User	8	9	10	11	12	13	14	8	9	10	11	12	13	14
Score	1.3	0.8	3.2	1	3.8	0	0	0.21	2.7	3.8	1.2	1.8	0	8
User	15							15						
Score	4							3.8						

(b) Combination Simulation Groups

Fig. 7. THe Fidelity Scores of Three Single Groups and Two Combination Groups.

8.2 Haptic Feedback Fidelity Analyzation

According to the framework proposed by Muender, below are the scores based on the eight factors of haptic feedback fidelity for the single simulation groups (see Fig. 7a) and combination simulation groups (see Fig. 7b). This study analyses data with these scores (see Fig. 8).

Haptic Feedback Fidelity Scores Analyzation of Five Groups

	Realistic Simulation	Movement Simulation	Space Simulation	Realistic+ Space	Movement+ Space
Mean	2.51	2.28	2.17	2.37	2.01
Median	2.60	2.70	1.80	3.20	2.70
Mode	4 (3 times)	0 (3 times)	4 (3 times)	3.8 (3 times)	0 (3 times)
Range	0-4	0-4	0-4	0-4	0-4
Variance	1.62	1.99	2.71	2.51	3.02
Standard Deviation	1.27	1.41	1.65	1.58	1.74
ANOVA P-Value	0.9382				

Fig. 8. The Data Analysis of Three Single Groups and Two Combination Groups.

Analysis of the data from 15 users shows that, in terms of the overall median, except for the Space Simulation group, the median of the other four groups exceeds the mean and stays above 2.60, indicating that more than half of the users gave high ratings. Regarding the mode, extremely high and low scores affect the mean. The high values show volatility in the overall variance and standard deviation data. Therefore, the median objectively represents the evaluation situation more objectively than the mean. Among all groups, the highest median of 3.20 belongs to the combination of the Realistic Group + Space Simulation group. The Movement Simulation group received the highest median of 2.70 among the three single-device groups. The P value of the one-way ANOVA analysis is 0.9382, higher than 0.05, so there is no significant difference in haptic fidelity scores between the five simulation groups, given the volatility in the data. The following result analysis and group comparison will be divided into **Realistic Simulations and Movement Simulations**, and the **Relationship between Space Simulations and Body Simulations**.

Realistic Simulations and Movement Simulations. According to the data analysis table (see Fig. 8), it could be found that the Realistic Simulation has the highest mean. However, its median is lower than that of Movement Simulation, and the mode is 4, occurring thrice, indicating that these high scores pull up the mean. On the other hand, the movement group's mode is 0 and occurs thrice as well, suggesting that the low scores pull down the mean. As a result, for Movement Simulation, more than half of the users' ratings are higher than or equal to 2.70, indicating that more than half of users evaluate it as high or medium, and a portion of users' ratings are low, even 0.

As for the formula of haptic feedback fidelity [5], the mean of the foundational factors scores and the sum of the limiting factors scores are the two variables (see Fig. 5). The fidelity score is positively correlated with the mean of the foundational factor scores (see Fig. 9a) and negatively correlated with the sum of the scores of the limiting factors (see Fig. 9b) so that this study will be further analyzed in depth based on these two data sets.

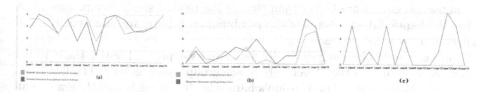

Fig. 9. The Foundational Factors Scores and Limiting Factors Scores of Realistic Simulation and Movement Simulation and Side Effect Factor Scores of Movement Simulation.

In the questionnaire results, the mean of the limiting factors sum in the Realistic Simulation group is 2. In contrast, the Movement Simulation group is 3.07, 1.5 times higher than the Realistic Simulation group. According to the line graph (see Fig. 9b), several extremely high limiting factors are in the Movement Simulation group, which lead to the corresponding haptic fidelity score of 0. On the other hand, the fidelity score positively correlates with the foundational factors scores, with a mean of 3.18 in the Realistic Simulation group and 3.05 in the Movement Simulation group. This indicates that the difference in foundational scores between these two groups is much smaller than in limiting scores. A user interview was conducted to explore this issue further.

Some users considered the physical exertion of the device to be a side effect, one of the limiting factors. Therefore, I scored high on that item in the interview. On the other hand, some users were amused by the physical exertion of flapping their arms and felt their immersion was enhanced. The polarized scores of the side effect factor can be seen in the figure (see Fig. 9c). For instance, user No.13 scored highly on foundational factors, indicating that she was optimistic about foundational factors. However, she noted that the soreness in her arms was very difficult, so she scored extremely high on the side effects factor. After calculating her perceived haptic fidelity, her score in all five groups was 0. This type of exception due to personality differences is additionally informative for this study.

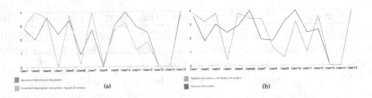

Fig. 10. The Haptic Feedback Fidelity Score of Single Group with Corresponding Combination Group.

Relationship between Space Simulations and Body Simulations. Based on the data in the table (see Fig. 8) and the line chart (see Fig. 10), it can be seen that the median of the combination groups is equal to or higher than that of the corresponding single group. The variance and standard deviation of the combination groups are higher than that of the related single group, suggesting that the haptic fidelity scores of the combination groups are more volatile and affected by very low scores.

Subsequently, the analysis is divided into two parts. Firstly, there is the Movement group and the Movement+Space group (see Fig. 10a). The line chart shows the Movement + Space group's haptic fidelity score is slightly lower than the Movement group's. The mean decreased from 2.28 to 2.01; however, the median value remained at 2.70, which indicates that the decrease in the mean is related to some shallow scores. Considering the interview in the previous section, the low scores are associated with the extra discomfort of the added airbag. However, the three high scores for the combination group in the graph and the median of 2.70 imply that the simulation of atmospheric pressure by the airbags did not make this physical sensation a negative experience for all portions of users.

The second part compares the Realistic Simulation and the Realistic + Space groups. Compared to the Realistic group median of 2.60, the Realistic + Space group median rises to 3.2, which indicates that more than half of the users rated high with the space device combined with feather wings (see Fig. 10b). At the same time, users with low scores remained, so the variance of this group increased further.

The haptic fidelity scores of the five groups have a median in the medium-high range, together with volatility, which is caused by participants' differences in ratings of the limiting factors.

9   Discussion, Limitation, and Future Work

The study provides a haptic feedback design framework centred on movement mechanisms by investigating space and body transformations in VR. It proposes a hardware design concept using an Arduino microcontroller, vibration sensors, and servo motor as the controlling system, which provides a reference for more haptic feedback hardware design in the future. In this project, immersive sharing of the physical sensations of birds can help humans better understand the stresses of the natural environment that birds may undergo in flight and the hardships of long-distance flight and build up empathy for birds that migrate long distances. It allows for body transformations and enhances the naturalness and intuitiveness of users' movements in VR. This research establishes the synchronization of sensations and perceptions between the physical and virtual bodies as the avatar of a bird. It is not limited to reducing the intensity of each part of the haptic feedback, coordinating the sequence in which the different haptic feedbacks occur, and adjusting the haptic magnitude to account for other users' acceptance levels.

From quantitative and qualitative research perspectives, the medium-high median of the haptic feedback fidelity scores shows that more than half of the participants validated the realism of the haptic feedback. In contrast, the high scores of variance and standard deviation and the polarized scores of side effect factors are related to personal preferences and body condition, consistent with the interviews. Some participants found the tiredness of arm flapping and the oppressive force in front of the chest unacceptable, while others found it amusing. This fact is also related to the limited number of participants, fifteen people-the small sample size limited diversity in identities, personalities, preferences, and body sizes. Therefore, the study will recruit more participants from different backgrounds, preferences, and body sizes in the future. This will enable the questionnaire to assess all fourteen factors more comprehensively while decreasing the impact of outlier data.

However, the current adjustment methods, especially the connecting muscles, are limited to calibrating variables like air pressure levels and motor ranges according to individual body sizes and weights. This diminishes the potential for optimal comfort across different user profiles. The software's bird takeoff functionality will be enhanced in the subsequent release due to the reduced accuracy with which the joystick and headset are recognized at low power levels. Meanwhile, the system is also confined by only promoting embodiment sensations from the waist up; the future versions must aim higher by pursuing whole-body ownership translations to exploit its immersive capabilities, such as placing the experiment in the vertical space of the loose ribbon to experience parallel flight. Even in the depth of the interview aspects, we consider our participants' feedback that when facing a sky view, they would like to scream out for relaxation, so the next version will incorporate speech controls to dynamize surroundings based on voice volume, cultivating a stronger sense of forward momentum, to achieve the flying speed control management.

We aim to widen content coverage to include additional globally significant heritage sites, artifacts, and architectural works that have the potential to broaden societal impacts. For example, extensions into virtual preservation initiatives and intangible cultural promotion could spurn valuable real-world applications. Still, they require the involvement of many participants, and the users can view them from a whole perspective. Moreover, the six factors not yet thoroughly examined within our evaluation framework, the Software Precision, Software Latency, Dependency, Distinguishability, Stimuli, and Body Area, will be assessed in forthcoming studies. These studies will feature an expanded participant pool and enhanced software capabilities to facilitate a more comprehensive evaluation to facilitate their classification and analysis in conjunction with scoring.

10   Conclusion

This research aimed to enhance users' sense of body ownership when embodying avian avatars in virtual reality. Our approach focused on developing an integrated system leveraging multimodal haptic feedback to mimic critical aspects of avian flight. The hardware components, including retractable bands and inflatable cushions, were designed to simulate avian movement mechanisms and environmental conditions during flight. The visualizations and interactions in VR software provided complementary virtual feedback synchronized with the haptics.

The user study results demonstrate the potential of this multisensory approach to strengthen feelings of body ownership for non-human avatars. The overall system usability ratings were moderately positive, with some variability based on individual preferences. The analysis of haptic fidelity factors indicates that refinements to limit side effects and constraints could further improve user experience. Interestingly, while the realistic wings simulation received higher fidelity scores, adding spatial haptics like air cushions and wind improved the ratings for over half the participants. This points to the value of coordinated multimodal feedback.

It contributes an innovative methodology for prototyping and evaluating bodily transformations in VR. The focus on replicating the motor experiences of avian flight advances avatar embodiment knowledge. The findings also underscore the nuanced interplay between multiple sensory stimuli in immersive environments. Potential social impacts include building empathy and connections with the natural world.

However, limitations remain regarding user sample diversity and the ability to simulate comprehensive tactile flight sensations within current technological constraints. Future work should explore more personalized and adaptive multisensory interactions based on user profiles. Investigating other non-human embodiments would also be valuable. This research pioneers new territory in reimagining and experiencing our embodiment potential.

Acknowledgments. The authors would like to express their sincere gratitude to IEEE VR for the opportunity to present our work in a poster session. This platform allowed us to showcase our research and provided us with invaluable feedback and insights from our peers in the field. We sincerely appreciate the support and the engaging discussions that have contributed to the refinement and improvement of our research.

References

1. Han, P.-H., et al.: Haptic around: multiple tactile sensations for immersive environment and interaction in virtual reality. In: Proceedings of the 24th ACM Symposium on Virtual Reality Software and Technology (VRST 2018), Article 35, pp. 1–10. Association for Computing Machinery, New York, NY, USA (2018). https://doi.org/10.1145/3281505.3281507
2. Abtahi, P., et al.: Beyond being real: a sensorimotor control perspective on interactions in virtual reality. In: CHI Conference on Human Factors in Computing Systems (2022). https://doi.org/10.1145/3491102.3517706
3. Grabbe, L.C.: The Image Becomes a Body: Avatarial Embodiment in the Context of a Body Ownership Illusion. Virtual Images: Trilogy of Synthetic Realities I **5**, 218 (2021)
4. Tobalske, B.W.: Biomechanics of bird flight. J. Exp. Biol. **210**(18), 3135–3146 (2007)
5. Muender, T., Bonfert, M., Reinschluessel, A.V., Malaka, R., Döring, T.: Haptic fidelity framework: defining the factors of realistic haptic feedback for virtual reality. In: CHI Conference on Human Factors in Computing Systems (2022). https://doi.org/10.1145/3491102.3501953
6. Chin, D.D., Lentink, D.: Birds repurpose the role of drag and lift to take off and land. Nat. Commun. **10**(1) (2019). https://doi.org/10.1038/s41467-019-13347-3
7. Bennett, A.I., Todd, A.I., Desai, S.D.: Pushing and pulling, technique and load effects: an electromyographical study. Work **38**(3), 291–299 (2011). https://doi.org/10.3233/wor-2011-1132
8. Bangor, A., Kortum, P., Miller, J.: Determining what individual SUS scores mean: adding an adjective rating scale. J. Usability Stud. **4**(3), 114–123 (2009)
9. Wang, Y., Claessens, L.P., Sullivan, C.: Deep reptilian evolutionary roots of a major avian respiratory adaptation. Commun. Biol. **6**(1) (2023). https://doi.org/10.1038/s42003-022-04301-z
10. Albayrak, A., Goossens, R.H.M., Snijders, C.J., de Ridder, H., Kazemier, G.: Impact of a chest support on lower back muscles activity during forward bending. Appl. Bionics Biomech. **7**(2), 131–142 (2010). https://doi.org/10.1080/11762320903541453
11. Freude, H., Reßing, C., Mueller, M., Niehaves, B., Knop, M.: Agency and body ownership in immersive virtual reality environments: a laboratory study (2020). https://doi.org/10.24251/HICSS.2020.188
12. Richard, G., Pietrzak, T., Argelaguet, F., Lécuyer, A., Casiez, G.: Studying the role of haptic feedback on virtual embodiment in a drawing task. Front. Virtual Reality. **1**, 573167 (2020). https://doi.org/10.3389/frvir.2020.573167
13. Krekhov, A., Cmentowski, S., Krüger, J.: The illusion of animal body ownership and its potential for virtual reality games. In: 2019 IEEE Conference on Games (CoG), London, UK, pp. 1–8 (2019). https://doi.org/10.1109/CIG.2019.8848005
14. Jacob, R.: Reality-based interaction. **201** (2008). https://doi.org/10.1145/1357054.1357089
15. Raposo, D., Neves, J., Silva, J. (eds.): Perspectives on Design II. SSDI, vol. 16. Springer, Cham (2022). https://doi.org/10.1007/978-3-030-79879-6
16. Crowe, S., Cresswell, K., Robertson, A., Huby, G., Avery, A., Sheikh, A.: The case study approach. BMC Med. Res. Methodol. **27**(11), 100 (2011). https://doi.org/10.1186/1471-2288-11-100. PMID: 21707982; PMCID: PMC3141799

17. Wee, C., Yap, K.M., Lim, W.N.: Haptic interfaces for virtual reality: challenges and research directions. IEEE Access **9**, 112145–112162 (2021). https://doi.org/10.1109/ACCESS.2021.3103598
18. Michael, R., Florian, G., Julian, F., Enrico, R.: Conveying the perception of kinesthetic feedback in virtual reality using state-of-the-art hardware. In: Proceedings of the 2018 CHI Conference on Human Factors in Computing Systems (CHI 2018). Association for Computing Machinery, New York, NY, USA, Paper 460, pp. 1–13 (2018). https://doi.org/10.1145/3173574.3174034
19. Oyanagi, A., Ohmura, R.: Conditions for inducing sense of body ownership to bird avatar in virtual environment. J. Comput. **13**(6), 5 (2018)
20. Hallion, R.: Taking Flight: Inventing the Aerial Age, from Antiquity Through the First World War. Oxford University Press (2003)
21. Wegener, P.P.: What Makes Airplanes Fly?: History, Science, and Applications of Aerodynamics. Springer Science & Business Media, New York (1997). https://doi.org/10.1007/978-1-4612-2254-5
22. Cao, T., Jin, J.P.: Evolution of flight muscle contractility and energetic efficiency. Front. Physiol. **11**, 1038 (2020)
23. Boecker, H., et al.: The runner's high: opioidergic mechanisms in the human brain. Cereb. Cortex **18**(11), 2523–2531 (2008)
24. Gustafsson, D.: Analysing the Double diamond design process through research & implementation (2019)
25. Wilson, E.O.: The Meaning of Human Existence. WW Norton & Company (2014)
26. Altshuler, D.L., et al.: The biophysics of bird flight: functional relationships integrate aerodynamics, morphology, kinematics, muscles, and sensors. Can. J. Zool. **93**(12), 961–975 (2015)

Exploring Key Issues Affecting Consumers' Intention to Use Chatbots in Cross-Border E-Commerce Activities

Shao Xixi and Xing Fei[✉]

Suzhou Institute of Trade and Commerce, Suzhou 215009, China
3371369379@qq.com

Abstract. Cross-border e-commerce enterprises are increasingly using conversational AI (chatbots) for customer service due to the perceived benefits and reduced operational costs of this emerging technology. However, despite the significant improvement in accuracy and effectiveness of chatbots, consumers are still in a passive state regarding its usage. This paper aims to investigate the key issues towards chatbots use across cross-border e-commerce activities. Fifteen in-depth semi-structured interviews were conducted that involved in cross-border e-commerce activities, and the interview data was then analyzed through a thematic analysis method. A concept map was developed in the final that represent the identified themes. The findings indicated that perceived ease of use, technology maturity, forced to use, perceived value and psychological needs have an impact on consumers' intention to adopt chatbots. Results of the study offered meaningful implications for cross-border marketer to optimize customer service capabilities and develop their marketing plan and strategy.

Keywords: Chatbots use · Key issues · Consumers Intention · Cross-border e-commerce

1 Introduction

Over the years, as ecommerce has become more popular, cross-border e-commerce has also seen a prominent growth. According to a survey by Statista, cross-border e-commerce was responsible for 15% of global ecommerce shipments in 2016, and it's been expected to reach 22% in 2022 [1]. Meanwhile, Zion Research indicates that cross-border B2C e-commerce in specific will reach USD 4856 billion by 2027, from USD 562 billion in 2018 [2]. Customer service is a bridge for communication and exchange between businesses and customers, and the quality of it is related to the image of businesses and customer experience. As the development of artificial intelligence, intelligent customer, so called as chatbots are changing the customer service industry. Chatbot is an automated chat agent program with a user interface that allows humans to talk in natural language [3]. It communicated in human language via text or audible communication with people or other chatbots through using NLP and sentiment analysis [4]. Compared to traditional manual customer service, chatbot can bring various advantages to enterprises, including

N. A. Streitz and S. Konomi (Eds.): HCII 2024, LNCS 14719, pp. 433–442, 2024.
https://doi.org/10.1007/978-3-031-60012-8_27

24-h online, simultaneous response to multiple consumer needs, rapid problem solving, and deep mining of data value. According to Rajaobelina & Ricard (2021), the market size of chatbots is predicted to yield from $3.7 billion in 2021 to $9.4 billion by 2024, and chatbots in customer service, in particular, is expected to be the fastest growing market segment between 2021 and 2026.

Chatbots have various applications in business, but the most common are in customer service sales. At present, chatbots are increasingly being employed in various cross-border e-commerce enterprises, because they provide round-the-clock customer service, increased revenue and engagement, automatic lead capture, lower operating costs, a competitive advantage, and significant time savings [5]. For example, Lego introduced Ralph – a Facebook Messenger chatbot which was designed to help customers quickly navigate through a large product portfolio and pick a perfect gift. Similarly, Amazon, the world's largest cross-border e-commerce platform, began to deploy chatbots in 2017 to promote new products and provide live support to customers [6].

However, despite the widespread availability of chatbots, they often fail to meet customer expectations due to a lack of understanding of input. Therefore, many consumers are unwilling to use chatbots in their shopping experience. According to Gartner, self-service solutions like chatbots only solve 9% of customer queries without needing to bring in an agent. At the same time, more than half of U.S. e-commerce shoppers say that interacting with a chatbot had a negative impact on their shopping experience, according to a Forrester study [7]. Further, current literature and studies have examined different types of chatbots and their effects on users' response as well as factors influencing user acceptance and adoption of chatbots [8, 9]. Yet, these studies mainly concentrate on chatbots from a technical perspective, there is little empirical research studying chatbots in consumers intention context. Indeed, the development of chatbots are highly dependent on the technology itself. However, its successful use still relies on the on the level of consumer acceptance. In other words, if consumers are unwilling to adopt chatbots, then no matter how smartness the chatbots are, they are meaningless. Based on the discussion above, there is a need to understand the key issues that affect consumers' intention to use chatbots in cross-border e-commerce activities. Therefore, the following research question (RQ) were developed to address the knowledge gap and pave the way for more substantial study.

- RQ: What key factors lead to consumers using chatbots in their cross-border e-commerce activities?

To answer the question, in-depth interviews were conducted with 15 participants who have more than five years' experience in cross-border e-commerce activities. Meanwhile, the entire interview will be recorded with the consent of the interviewees for better data analysis. In addition, the interview manuscript transcribed into text will also be handed over to the interviewees for verification to ensure the accuracy of the information. In the end, the outcomes of the qualitative data analysis resulted in establishing a framework that includes sixteen factors divided into five major categories.

The rest of the paper is structured as follows. First, a systematic review of literature on chatbots adoption and consumer use intention before we present the research methods used in the study. Subsequently, the findings derived from the interviews were presented and discussed. In the final, this study's overall conclusion is put forward.

2 Literature Review

2.1 Related Studies on Chatbots Adoption

Innovative technologies based on artificial intelligence (AI) have attracted increasing attention in recent years through both academic research and practice. The application fields of AI are very broad, from autonomous vehicles (such as Tesla) to intelligent customer service in daily life, all of which are applications behind technological development [10]. Chatbots are one of the rapidly growing industries that offers unrivalled commercial possibilities. Several services have found use for chatbots, including those aimed at facilitating student-teacher interactions, tourist-visitor interactions, and online shopper interactions [9].

Since the concept and application of chatbots was developed and implemented, there are multiple streams of existing research on chatbots, academic researchers and practical practitioners have investigated it. The studies can be further grouped into two categories. The first are conceptual studies which provide valuable research directions. For example, Jeon & Lee (2023) developed a conceptual framework of speech-recognition chatbots for language learning [11]. A conceptual modeling approach for the rapid development of chatbots for conversational data exploration was proposed by Tran et al. [6]. Moreover, many systematic review studies on the applications of chatbots in education, tourism, and on-line shopping, etc. have been conducted [9].

The second studies that focus on the technology and implications for consumers like chatbot designs and cues. To be specific, multiple studies have applied anthropomorphism theory to explore how humanlike versus non-humanlike chatbot design can trigger different perceptions and behaviors among users [12]. In order to avoid customer dissatisfaction, chatbots can be manipulated with service scripts, language, and tone. For instance, chatbots automatically capture valuable customer data during interaction, which can be used for data analysis and generating customer insights [13].

Despite the existing literature, there remains a need for further research on the issues of chatbots adoption and use by consumers. Indeed, the technical sophistication of chatbots particularly its algorithm has fundamentally affected the response speed during the interaction between consumers and chatbots. Some other socio-technical factors will also affect the quality of their interaction, for instance, attributes such as perceived usefulness and perceived ease of use both have a positive effect on chatbot adoption and use [14]. Hence, compared with numerous papers from a technical perspective, few studies concentrate on the socio-technical view to explore the key issues.

2.2 Related Studies on Consumer Use Intention

The research on consumer usage intention is one of the important directions in the field of information systems research. Researchers in the field of behavioral science mainly explore the motivations and obstacles for users to adopt and continue using chatbots from the perspective of technological diffusion [15]. For example, a questionnaire study was conducted involved more than 200 chatbots users who reported on episodes of chatbot use that they found particularly satisfactory or frustrating [16]. Verkijika & Neneh (2021) indicated that pragmatic attributes such as efficient assistance (positive) and problems with interpretation (negative) were two main important elements in the study.

Researchers from management and marketing field pay more attention to user attitudes and experiences towards consumer use particularly in intelligent customer service, such as satisfaction and loyalty, trust, and aversion [17, 18]. For instance, Brill et al. (2022) concluded that expectations and confirmation of expectations have a positive and significant relationship on customer satisfaction with digital assistants through the survey of 244 response [18]. As e-commerce companies integrate the intelligence customer service applications into their operations, they have to help consumers properly define what to expect from the e-commerce firm's interactive experience. In addition, information systems success model and theory of reasoned action were adopted by Roh et al. (2022), they indicated that three main dimensions affecting the attitudes toward intelligent services and consumers' intentions to use, namely the quality of system, information, and service [19]. Similarly, consumers' perceived security and privacy are positively related to consumers' trust in such services, which in turn encourages the use of the system [20].

2.3   Review Summary

Although these studies have provided a better understanding of the use of intelligent customer service or chatbots in customer service, they are still insufficient to explain the acceptance behavior of users towards them, especially the lack of avoidance of using chatbots. On one hand, refusal to use behavior is considered any attempt to downregulate an unpleasant experience through avoidance, avoidance, inhibition, distraction, or control [21]. According to the research conducted by Roh et al. (2022), communication and interaction both influence consumer purchasing decisions whether online or offline. When intelligent customer service reduces consumer service experience or deprives consumers of the right to seek assistance from human customer service, it will directly affect consumer purchasing intention.

On the other hand, existing literature mainly adopts quantitative methods for research, they lack depth and breadth of understanding of the causes of user avoidance behavior [22]. At present, there are few studies that use qualitative methods for exploratory attempts in chatbots study. Adopting qualitative research methods will be beneficial for gaining a deeper understanding of the interviewees' true thoughts and perspectives, and for better understanding their behavior. In this situation, the paper aims to empirically investigate the key issues that affect consumers' intention to use chatbots in cross-border e-commerce activities.

3   Research Methods

3.1 Data Collection

Given the qualitative nature of the research question, an inductive approach was followed. Considering the fact that the selected interviewees are those who have used chatbots in cross-border e-commerce, our selection of cases followed criteria of: 1) individuals have more than five years in cross-border activities, and 2) they are currently experiencing the use of chatbots. As a result, 15 users who meet the requirements of this interview were selected. We show the profiles of the 15 participants in Table 1.

Table 1. Profile of Interview Participants

ID	Jobs	E-commerce platform	Years of Experience
Participant-1	University Teacher	Amazon	7
Participant-2	Student	Amazon	6
Participant-3	Student	Amazon	6
Participant-4	Student	Shein	7
Participant-5	Chef	AliExpress	8
Participant-6	Doctor	Amazon	13
Participant-7	University Teacher	Shein	12
Participant-8	Student	AliExpress	7
Participant-9	Student	Shein	6
Participant-10	Student	AliExpress	6
Participant-11	Student	Shein	5
Participant-12	Administrative Staff	Amazon	8
Participant-13	Administrative Staff	Amazon	9
Participant-14	Administrative Staff	AliExpress	6
Participant-15	Administrative Staff	Shein	10

3.2 Data Analysis

The interview data was then analyzed through a thematic analysis approach, which typically contains five steps, as shown in Table 2. The interview data was transcribed into text so that researchers could become familiar with the data. Following these steps, we distributed all identified codes and regrouped into five major themes. All the codes and quotations for coherent pattern checking in the final stage are reviewed. A concept map was developed that represent the identified themes, as shown in Fig. 1.

Table 2. Five steps of Thematic Analysis

Step	Description of the process
1. Familiar with the data	Getting to know the data through transcription, reading
2. Coding the data	Developing a coding scheme: all codes emerged from data, coding textual data systematically
3. Connecting codes and identifying themes	Collating codes into potential themes
4. Reviewing themes	Checking if the themes work concerning the coded quotes and the entire data set
5. Developing concept maps and writing the report	Final analysis of selected quotes, relating back to the research question, producing the chapter of findings

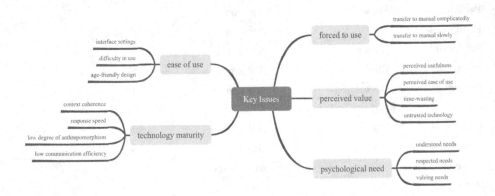

Fig. 1. Concept Map for the Data Analysis

4 Key Issues Affecting Consumers' Intention to Use Chatbots in Cross-Border E-Commerce Activities

4.1 Ease of Use

Ease of use is defined as the degree to which a person believes that using a particularly would be free from effort [23]. If the chatbots is easy to use, then the barrier is conquered. If it is not easy to use and the interface is complicated, no one has a positive attitude towards it. Therefore, majority of consumers considered ease of use a priority in the use of chatbots. Furthermore, according to the classic TAM model in information systems research, perceived ease of use directly affects users' adoption and sustained use of new information technologies [24]. For instance, smart city app is a service-oriented app, and its key purpose is to provide faster life service projects for the people. Zhang et al. (2022) considered that one of the biggest problems with smart city apps is their difficulty in use, especially for elderly users [25]. Therefore, developers of cross-border e-commerce platforms need to pay attention to the difficulty of operation when designing chatbots, particularly considering aging friendly designs.

4.2 Technology Maturity

A mature technology is a technology that has been in use for long enough that most of its initial faults and inherent problems have been removed or reduced by further development [26]. Ideal chatbots of cross-border e-commerce platform not only solve various problems encountered by consumers, but also reduces labor costs and improves service efficiency for enterprises. However, chatbots currently faces problems such as low response speed, low degree of anthropomorphism, and low communication efficiency. As confirmed by participant 3: *I have currently used several platforms, such as Amazon, Wish, eBay, etc. However, I have experienced that chatbots are not very intelligent, and many questions are a bit off topic. For example, one time before I bought clothes, I wanted him to recommend sizes to me. I reported my height and weight to him, but the result I got was not what I wanted. Later, I didn't place an order.*

4.3 Forced to Use

Consumers from cross-border e-commerce platform are forced to use chatbots during their shopping experience. Although the use of chatbots can effectively save labor costs, in reality, some e-commerce platforms overly rely on chatbots and even cancel manual customer service to save labor costs, which resulted in poor communication between consumers and businesses, continuous complaints, and seriously affecting the consumer experience [27]. As one of participants complained: *Nowadays, most online shopping platforms have automatic replies, but often the answers that are automatically replied to are not what I want. But when I want to switch to manual customer service at this time, it's very slow and I need to wait for a long time. Sometimes, I can't wait anymore and just quit.* Furthermore, in previous research on digital transformation of enterprises, it was found that if information technology is forcibly adopted, users will exhibit refusal to use it [28].

4.4 Perceived Value

Perceived value is the customers' evaluation of the merits of a product or service, and its ability to meet their needs and expectations, especially in comparison with its peers [29]. Perceived value is significant in marketing. Consumers who think the chatbots are worth it are willing to use. They probably will not use or use it rarely if they feel the product isn't worth it. As highlighted by one participant: *Intelligent customer service is the trend of the future. Apart from e-commerce platforms, many tourism products now use artificial intelligence customer service. However, as a consumer, may be due to unmature technology. Currently, I have not felt its true value, nor is it very convenient, and even many times I cannot understand what I mean.* As Zhang et al. (2021) confirmed, when users perceive that the benefits outweigh the losses, the perceived value of positive adoption intention will be stronger.

4.5 Psychological Need

Psychological need can be defined as a psychological condition in which something is required or wanted [30]. Consumers will go to e-commerce platforms to purchase items when their demand are generated. When consumers hesitate to choose a product, they will ask customer service personnel. Consumers hope that their needs can be respected, understood, and valued by customer service. However, as one of the participants stated: *the response from the intelligent customer service is slow each time, and I do not get the answer I want, which greatly affected my shopping experience. Considering the possible time difference with cross-border e-commerce merchants, many transactions cannot be communicated at the same time. However, we hope that intelligent customer service can do better in the future.* As discussed by Wang et al. (2023), in the area of motivation, researchers have described the three fundamental psychological needs that drive human behavior – Autonomy, competence and relatedness. Consequently, as new technology can effectively meet consumer needs, they will be willing to accept the new pattern.

5 Conclusions

As cross-border e-commerce retailers increase their use of chatbots as a form of customer service, there is an increasing need to gain more knowledge and insights about it. Particularly, it is important for cross-border e-commerce retailers and academic scholars to understand the key issues of affecting consumers' adoption and use in chatbots. This study investigated the factors that have led consumers to embrace the use of chatbots for cross-border e-commerce retail purchasing. The chatbots for planning purchases are user-friendly and can be used from any computer, tablet, or smartphone. The study revealed that perceived ease of use, technology maturity, forced to use, perceived value and psychological needs have an impact on consumers' intention to adopt chatbots. Meanwhile, a concept map was developed in the final that represent the identified themes. Furthermore, the popularity of chatbots largely depends on their usability. Anxiety over using technology can make people reluctant to do so. Customers are savvy when it comes to using various forms of e-commerce technology.

In addition, this study also has several limitations, the interviews were conducted with a relatively small group of participants, although the selected interviewees are highly experienced. Therefore, a questionnaire survey may validate the list of identified factors in the future.

References

1. Chen, W.H., Lin, Y.C., Bag, A., Chen, C.L.: Influence factors of small and medium-sized enterprises and micro-enterprises in the cross-border e-commerce platforms. J. Theor. Appl. Electron. Commer. Res. **18**(1), 416–440 (2023)
2. Ahi, A.A., Sinkovics, N., Sinkovics, R.R.: E-commerce policy and the global economy: a path to more inclusive development? Manag. Int. Rev. **63**(1), 27–56 (2023)
3. Pizzi, G., Scarpi, D., Pantano, E.: Artificial intelligence and the new forms of interaction: who has the control when interacting with a chatbot? J. Bus. Res. **129**, 878–890 (2021)

4. Lalwani, T., Bhalotia, S., Pal, A., Rathod, V., Bisen, S.: Implementation of a chatbot system using AI and NLP. Int. J. Innov. Res. Comput. Sci. Technol. (IJIRCST) **6**(3) (2018)
5. Rajaobelina, L., Ricard, L.: Classifying potential users of live chat services and chatbots. J. Financ. Serv. Mark. **26**, 81–94 (2021)
6. Tran, A.D., Pallant, J.I., Johnson, L.W.: Exploring the impact of chatbots on consumer sentiment and expectations in retail. J. Retail. Consum. Serv. **63**, 102718 (2021)
7. Rapp, A., Curti, L., Boldi, A.: The human side of human-chatbot interaction: a systematic literature review of ten years of research on text-based chatbots. Int. J. Hum Comput Stud. **151**, 102630 (2021)
8. Chaves, A.P., Gerosa, M.A.: How should my chatbot interact? A survey on social characteristics in human–chatbot interaction design. Int. J. Hum.-Comput. Interact. **37**(8), 729–758 (2021)
9. Huang, W., Hew, K.F., Fryer, L.K.: Chatbots for language learning—are they really useful? A systematic review of chatbot-supported language learning. J. Comput. Assist. Learn. **38**(1), 237–257 (2022)
10. Nicolescu, L., Tudorache, M.T.: Human-computer interaction in customer service: the experience with AI chatbots—a systematic literature review. Electronics **11**(10), 1579 (2022)
11. Jeon, J., Lee, S., Choe, H.: Beyond ChatGPT: a conceptual framework and systematic review of speech-recognition chatbots for language learning. Comput. Educ. 104898 (2023)
12. Luo, B., Lau, R.Y., Li, C., Si, Y.W.: A critical review of state-of-the-art chatbot designs and applications. Wiley Interdisc. Rev. Data Min. Knowl. Discov. **12**(1), e1434 (2022)
13. Haugeland, I.K.F., Følstad, A., Taylor, C., Bjørkli, C.A.: Understanding the user experience of customer service chatbots: an experimental study of chatbot interaction design. Int. J. Hum Comput Stud. **161**, 102788 (2022)
14. Kang, W., Shao, B., Du, S., Chen, H., Zhang, Y.: How to improve voice assistant evaluations: understanding the role of attachment with a socio-technical systems perspective. Technol. Forecast. Soc. Chang. **200**, 123171 (2024)
15. Dinh, C.M., Park, S.: How to increase consumer intention to use Chatbots? An empirical analysis of hedonic and utilitarian motivations on social presence and the moderating effects of fear across generations. Electron. Commer. Res. 1–41 (2023)
16. Følstad, A., Brandtzaeg, P.B.: Users' experiences with chatbots: findings from a questionnaire study. Qual. User Experience **5**(1), 3 (2020)
17. Verkijika, S.F., Neneh, B.N.: Standing up for or against: a text-mining study on the recommendation of mobile payment apps. J. Retail. Consum. Serv. **63**, 102743 (2021)
18. Brill, T. M., Munoz, L., Miller, R.J.: Siri, Alexa, and other digital assistants: a study of customer satisfaction with artificial intelligence applications. In: The Role of Smart Technologies in Decision Making, pp. 35–70. Routledge (2022)
19. Roh, T., Yang, Y. S., Xiao, S., Park, B.I.: What makes consumers trust and adopt fintech? An empirical investigation in China. Electron. Commer. Res. 1–33 (2022)
20. Kim, J., Giroux, M., Lee, J.C.: When do you trust AI? The effect of number presentation detail on consumer trust and acceptance of AI recommendations. Psychol. Mark. **38**(7), 1140–1155 (2021)
21. Chen, Y., Zhou, S.: Avoiding pre-roll ads: Predictors of online video consumption. Comput. Hum. Behav. **142**, 107652 (2023)
22. Ahmed, O., Siddiqua, S.J.N., Alam, N., Griffiths, M.D.: The mediating role of problematic social media use in the relationship between social avoidance/distress and self-esteem. Technol. Soc. **64**, 101485 (2021)
23. Peng, G., Clough, P.D., Madden, A., Xing, F., Zhang, B.: Investigating the usage of IoT-based smart parking services in the borough of Westminster. J. Global Inf. Manag. (JGIM) **29**(6), 1–19 (2021)

24. Bryan, J.D., Zuva, T.: A review on TAM and TOE framework progression and how these models integrate. Adv. Sci. Technol. Eng. Syst. J. **6**(3), 137–145 (2021)

25. Zhang, B., Peng, G., Xing, F., Liang, X., Gao, Q.: One-stop smart urban apps and determinants of their continuance usage: an empirical investigation based on CSCM. J. Global Inf. Manag. (JGIM) **29**(6), 1–21 (2021)

26. Gao, Z., Xing, F., Peng, G.: Research on the capability maturity model of data security in the era of digital transformation. In: Moallem, A. (ed.) HCII 2023. LNCS, vol. 14045, pp. 151–162. Springer, Cham (2023). https://doi.org/10.1007/978-3-031-35822-7_11

27. Alzoubi, H., Alshurideh, M., Kurdi, B., Akour, I., Aziz, R.: Does BLE technology contribute towards improving marketing strategies, customers' satisfaction and loyalty? The role of open innovation. Int. J. Data Network Sci. **6**(2), 449–460 (2022)

28. Xing, F., Peng, G., Wang, J., Li, D.: Critical obstacles affecting adoption of industrial big data solutions in smart factories: an empirical study in China. J. Global Inf. Manag. (JGIM) **30**(1), 1–21 (2022)

29. Li, Y., Shang, H.: Service quality, perceived value, and citizens' continuous-use intention regarding e-government: empirical evidence from China. Inf. Manag. **57**(3), 103197 (2020)

30. Wang, C., Li, Y., Fu, W., Jin, J.: Whether to trust chatbots: Applying the event-related approach to understand consumers' emotional experiences in interactions with chatbots in e-commerce. J. Retail. Consum. Serv. **73**, 103325 (2023)

Magnet Haptic: Using Magnets and Conductive Ink to Self-fabricate Interactive VR Devices

Cheng Yao[1]([✉]), Shuyue Feng[2], Shichao Huang[2], Mengru Xue[3], Yuqi Hu[4], Haowen Ren[5], Fangtian Ying[6], and Ran Wan[7]

[1] College of Computer Science and Technology, Zhejiang University, Hangzhou, China
yaoch@zju.edu.cn
[2] School of Software Technology, Zhejiang University, Ningbo, China
{shuyuefeng,huangshichao}@zju.edu.cn
[3] Ningbo Innovation Center, Zhejiang University, Ningbo, China
mengruxue@zju.edu.cn
[4] University of Nottingham Ningbo, Ningbo, China
yuqi.Hu@nottingham.edu.cn
[5] Jiangxi University of Finance and Economics, Nanchang, China
[6] MACAU University of Science and Technology, Macau, China
[7] Architecture and Design College, Nanchang University, Nanchang, China
wanran@ncu.edu.cn

Abstract. Magnet Haptic method presents an innovative approach for quickly creating tactile input devices tailored to enhance multisensory experiences in virtual reality (VR) environments. This technique utilizes a unique combination of magnets and conductive ink, allowing users to design and fabricate tactile feedback mechanisms easily. By exploiting the magnetism of the magnets to form various tactile structures and integrating the conductive properties of the ink for signal transmission, this method seamlessly bridges the tactile interaction with VR devices. A prototype was developed and evaluated with the participation of eight users, who engaged in both the creation and usage of the tactile devices. Their experiences, gathered through semi-structured interviews, provided insights into the usability and versatility of the method. Additionally, the durability and performance of the hardware were rigorously tested in multi-layer configurations and through repeated use, demonstrating its potential for diverse and complex VR applications. This research contributes significantly to the field by offering a fast, customizable solution for developing tactile interfaces in VR, marking a step forward in achieving comprehensive multisensory virtual experiences.

Keywords: Device Design · Manufacturing Methods · Haptic Interaction

---

C. Yao and S. Feng—Contributed equally to this work.

N. A. Streitz and S. Konomi (Eds.): HCII 2024, LNCS 14719, pp. 443–455, 2024.
https://doi.org/10.1007/978-3-031-60012-8_28

1 Introduction

1.1 A Subsection Sample

With the advancement of hardware devices like VR, the public can now purchase such devices to enjoy the fun of virtual reality. While these devices satisfy visual requirements, meeting the multisensory experiences of users in virtual reality environments, especially tactile experiences, remains a challenge. Although many researchers have developed various forms of tactile input hardware [1–3], more than a single device can meet the diverse needs in complex and variable virtual reality scenarios. Therefore, a method enabling users to quickly create simple tactile input devices is critical, allowing them to rapidly develop tactile input devices based on their actual needs.

Based on these issues, we propose 'Magnet Haptic,' a manufacturing method using magnets and conductive ink to help users quickly create tactile input devices. We created five basic structures using the magnetism of the magnets, which can help users make the desired tactile feedback forms. We also utilized the conductivity of the magnet's surface coating and conductive ink, combining the magnet structure and circuitry. This directly implements signal input based on the tactile feedback structure, achieving interaction with VR devices.

Using our method, we created a hardware prototype and invited eight users to experience its effects and personally make a similar device. We also conducted a performance evaluation of our hardware method to test its performance in multi-layer structures and repeated usage.

Our contributions are as follows:

1. Proposed a method for quickly creating tactile input prototypes, allowing users to rapidly build the needed tactile interaction hardware by themselves.
2. Invited eight users to participate in making and using tactile hardware, conducting semi-structured interviews with them.
3. Evaluated the durability of the hardware system and its applicability in complex situations.

2 Related Work

2.1 Hearing Substitute System

In the field of Human-Computer Interaction (HCI), tactile interaction has made significant progress, primarily driven by the demand for more immersive and intuitive user experiences. The essence of tactile interaction lies in its ability to simulate real-world sensations, providing a multi-sensory approach to digital interaction. Clement et al. proposed a tactile feedback device fabricated using a laser cutter on acrylic plates for precise force control [4]. This is particularly relevant in areas such as Virtual Reality (VR) and Augmented Reality (AR), where the tactile dimension adds a layer of realism to digital experiences.

The development of tactile technology plays a crucial role in tactile interaction. Notable among these are techniques using origami, shape memory alloys, magnets, and pneumatic structures. Origami technology enables the creation of structures with strength far exceeding the material itself from a single sheet of paper [5, 6]. Shape memory alloys can change shape in specific environments, triggering tactile feedback [7, 8]. Magnets can be used to quickly create simple tactile feedback structures due to their magnetic properties [9]. Pneumatic structures can change shape through inflation and deflation, providing force feedback [10, 11].

In summary, tactile interaction in HCI is rapidly evolving and positively impacting various fields. The ongoing improvements in tactile technology and the integration of artificial intelligence are paving the way for more nuanced and realistic tactile experiences in digital interfaces.

2.2 Accessible Communication Technology

In the realm of HCI, using magnets for haptic interaction [12–14] and as functional physical inputs [15, 16] is increasingly prevalent. GaussBricks [17] explores the potential of static magnet chains to create various elastic textures like clicking, bending, stretching, and squeezing, simplifying prototype fabrication for users with limited mechanical expertise. Additionally, magnetic fields have been employed for data input. For instance, Lamello [18] leverages a microphone to interpret inputs from audio signals produced by 3D-printed tines.

Beyond HCI, innovative materials combining conductive and magnetic properties have been developed. Magnetic Liquid Metal [19], created by infusing liquid metal with magnetic materials, and a flexible paper [20] composed of graphene and iron are examples of such advancements. These hybrid materials find extensive use in industries and consumer electronics [21]. However, their production often requires specialized knowledge and equipment, making them less accessible for individual makers.

In our research, we utilize commercially available neodymium magnets, which possess both magnetic and conductive properties. By merging movable structures with more complex mechanical movements and electronic circuits using neodymium magnets, users are empowered to customize and reliably produce interactive prototypes.

3 The Basic Principles of Magnet Haptic

3.1 Method

We suggest a collection of fundamental mechanical building blocks that serve as a source of inspiration for users to craft distinctive and increasingly intricate structures. These foundational mechanical-electronic functional units comprise an endless rotation structure, a straight-line motion structure, a compressive structure, a finite rotational structure, and a rotational-linear translation structure (see Fig. 1). Here is a brief overview of each structure:

1. Endless Rotation Structure: This design connects two elements using magnets that draw them together, enabling limitless rotation. This ensures that the circuit continues to conduct electricity as the structure spins.

2. Straight-Line Motion Structure: In this design, the top component glides along a groove in the bottom piece, facilitating linear movement. Equipped with a single magnet, the principal component attaches to the bottom one, which contains a linear arrangement of three magnets. These magnets allow the top piece to lock into place after moving a specific distance while keeping the circuit unblocked at each locked position.

3. Compressive Structure: This setup involves an upper component that sits atop the lower one, each embedded with repelling magnets. This mechanism functions like a button that can be pressed down and will automatically rebound. When the button is depressed, bringing the two magnets into contact, the circuit becomes active.

4. Finite Rotational Structure: This arrangement includes a central magnet and a ring of surrounding magnets in both components, enabling polar rotation. In this basic unit, the components lock every 36 degrees, conducting electricity at each position.

5. Rotational-Linear Translation Structure: This structure features a round component with a ring of magnets for rotation, while the linearly moving piece is embedded with a line of magnets. The rotation of the circular component can drive the linear one to move in a straight line and vice versa. In this fundamental setup, the circuit remains conductive.

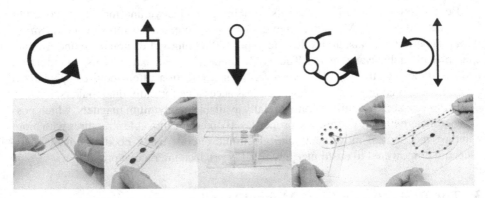

Fig. 1. Five different input structures were created using magnets.

3.2 Assembly Principle

In this innovative approach, we utilize acrylic plates as the foundational material for our construction method. Acrylic, known for its durability and clarity, provides an ideal base for incorporating magnetic components. To precisely assemble the magnets, we employ a technique involving laser cutting, a process that offers high precision and clean cuts, essential for the accuracy required in our design.

The process begins with carefully selecting acrylic plates, ensuring they are of optimal thickness and quality. The plates serve as a sturdy and transparent base, allowing for the visibility of the internal magnet arrangement, which is not only functional but also aesthetically pleasing.

Instead of using adhesive materials like glue, which can be messy and potentially weaken over time, we opt for a more robust and efficient method. By avoiding glue, we streamline the manufacturing process and ensure a more durable and reliable end product. The absence of glue also facilitates easy disassembly and reassembly, allowing for modifications and repairs without damaging the acrylic or magnets.

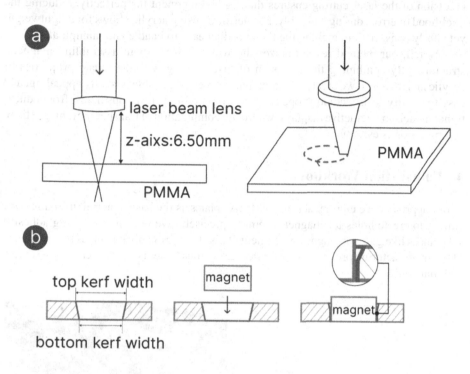

Fig. 2. Schematic diagram for making holes using laser cutting

The key to this method lies in the precision of laser cutting (see Fig. 2). We use a state-of-the-art laser cutter that can accurately cut the acrylic to our specified dimensions. When the laser beam, which is inherently conical in shape, passes through the focusing lens, it creates a hole that is not perfectly cylindrical. Instead, the hole has a tapered profile-wider at the top and narrower at the bottom – resembling a truncated cone.

This tapered hole design is critical for securing the magnets without adhesive. We carefully calculate the dimensions, ensuring that the diameter of the hole is slightly smaller than the diameter of the magnet at the bottom but slightly larger at the top. This size difference is meticulously calibrated – the diameter of the magnet (d) minus 0.22mm serves as the guideline for the laser-cut hole's diameter.

The magnets, selected for their strength and size compatibility with the acrylic plates, are inserted into these holes. The slightly smaller diameter at the bottom of the hole ensures a snug fit, preventing the magnet from falling out or moving. At the same time, the larger top diameter allows the magnet to be easily inserted into the hole. The elasticity of the acrylic plays a crucial role here. It exerts just enough pressure on the magnets to hold them securely in place, yet it's flexible enough to allow for easy insertion and removal if necessary.

This method has several advantages. Firstly, it provides a clean and efficient way to assemble magnetic structures without additional bonding materials. Secondly, the precision of the laser cutting ensures that each component fits perfectly, reducing the likelihood of errors during assembly. Furthermore, using acrylic allows for a lightweight yet sturdy construction, making the final product easy to handle and manipulate.

Overall, our method revolutionizes the way we think about assembling magnetic structures. By combining the precision of laser cutting with the innate properties of acrylic and magnets, we create a system that is efficient, reliable, visually appealing, and easy to modify. This technique opens up new possibilities in various fields, from educational models to interactive displays, where the combination of transparency, magnetism, and precision is essential.

4   Fabrication Workflow

In our approach, we employ acrylic (PMMA) plates as the base material, utilizing laser cutting to create holes for magnet assembly precisely. We refrain from using adhesive substances like glue for magnet attachment. This choice not only enhances the efficiency of the manufacturing process but also offers numerous benefits, such as ease of assembly and maintenance.

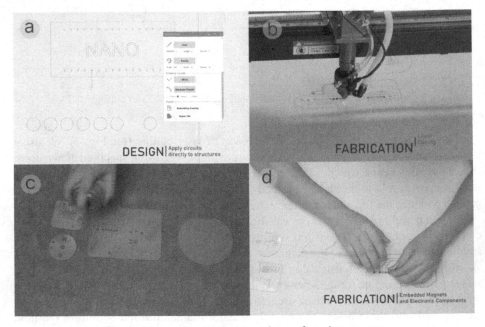

Fig. 3. Magnet Haptic design and manufacturing process

The process is initiated by importing pre-created files into our design software (see Fig. 3a). Users can then add slots for electronic components and magnets on the PMMA layers through the software interface. The software allows for easy positioning and moving of these components and joints. Once the positions are set, slots for the magnets and components are automatically generated, simplifying the process of aligning magnets and commonly used components. A critical aspect to note is the kerf created by the laser cutting process, which is inclined due to the lens converging the laser beam. Our software compensates for this sloped kerf, ensuring a secure fit for the magnets and components. The compensation involves reducing the generated magnet slot diameter by 0.22 mm, a parameter determined through iterative testing and shown to hold magnets without glue securely. This evaluation is further detailed in Sect. 5. Additionally, the software automatically generates a separate PMMA board for the Arduino, facilitating easier replacement.

After adding electronic components and mechanical joints, users can use the software to connect these slots and form specific circuits. Upon completion, the software enables the generation and exportation of a laser cutting file, where the paths for slots (corresponding to electronic components and mechanical structures) and the paths for electronic circuits are stored in separate layers. This separation allows for different laser cutting configurations to be applied (see Fig. 4): cutting through the PMMA layer for slots (black lines) and cutting through the paper membrane covering the PMMA for circuit paths (red lines).

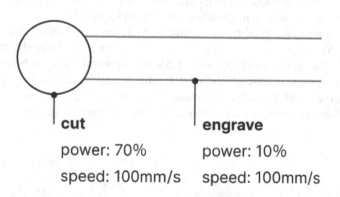

cut

power: 70%

speed: 100mm/s

engrave

power: 10%

speed: 100mm/s

Fig. 4. Different operating powers for laser cutting (Color figure online)

For laser cutting (see Fig. 3b), we use a commercial laser cutter (RS-1390 from HONG XIN LASER TECH) on PMMA plates covered with a paper membrane. Different configurations are used to cut slots and circuit paths to meet the requirements. The PMMA is cut through for slots, and the paper membrane is engraved for circuits.

After laser cutting, users must remove the PMMA in the slots and peel off the paper membrane from the circuit paths to reveal the components (see Fig. 3c). These are then sprayed with conductive silver ink, ensuring coverage of all slots and circuit paths. Slots for chip package electronic components are partially covered with sticky tape during spraying to prevent short circuits. The ink from a commercial source solidifies in about 15 min at room temperature or 2 min with a blow dryer at 50 °C. This solidification process, repeated thrice, ensures stable circuitry.

Finally, users embed electronic components and magnets into the PMMA board's slots (see Fig. 3d). For magnet orientation, magnets are aligned, similar to a pen, and embedded from bottom to top. Thicker than the PMMA board, Magnets protrude for direct contact between PMMA components, ensured by pressing them against a flat platform during embedding. After snapping, this method ensures a firm touch between scattered and row-aligned magnets to the PMMA boards.

5 Electrical Performance Evaluation

We conducted an evaluation of the success rate of our fabrication method and its durability in complex environments.

1. Assembly Success Rate Assessment (see Fig. 5a). We tested the connectivity of circuits with 100 magnets and surface-mounted resistors assembled into acrylic, as well as the connectivity of the pin legs of 10 Arduinos assembled into acrylic boards. We found that all 100 magnets were connected successfully, and all pin legs of the 10 Arduinos were connected. However, two of the surface-mounted resistors were not connected. Upon investigation, we discovered that these two resistors had connection issues due to acrylic board deformation caused by heat. This occurrence is very rare. Therefore, our fabrication method has a very high success rate.
2. Circuit Connectivity Quality in Complex Multi-layered Circuit Structures (see Fig. 5b). We assembled a component with a 10-layer multi-layered circuit. At the top of this structure was an LED, and a 1.5V battery was fitted at the bottom. We performed 20 repeated disassemblies and assemblies of this structure. We found that the LED lit up successfully each time, leading us to conclude that our method maintains good performance even when constructing complex circuit structures.

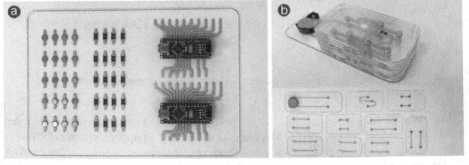

Fig. 5. Electrical performance evaluation: (a) assembly stability and success tests; (b) multilayer circuit connection stability tests.

6   User Study

We provided a completed prototype, a piano with tactile feedback (see Fig. 6a), and invited eight users to create and experience it from scratch using our method (see Fig. 6b). After completion, the users were asked to wear VR devices and interact with a music game (see Fig. 6c) using the hardware they had built. Following this, we conducted semi-structured interviews with the eight participants. Below are the results.

Feedback from Beginners. Our case studies showed that our basic mechanical structural units significantly aided users new to mechanical and electrical structures. These users viewed the units as templates, quickly incorporating them into their design drafts. This observation has motivated us to develop additional units to cater to a broader range of design needs in the future. One participant, unfamiliar with laser cutting (P6), found the software's feature for exporting files to the laser cutter particularly beneficial. He remarked, "I can concentrate on my structures and circuits." A beginner (P1) made a mistake while spraying conductive silver ink directly downward, leading to an excessive PMMA coating. However, this did not majorly affect the functionality of the end product. Beginners in electrical circuitry often viewed the conductive ink path as a significant aesthetic element of the product. P1 commented, "The look of the circuit matters to me since it's visible on the surface, forming part of my design." Nonetheless, those new to circuitry often faced challenges in establishing electrical connections. For instance, P7 frequently consulted with her partner to verify the circuit connections. It would be beneficial to incorporate features like automatic circuit generation and error detection in the software to assist those new to circuit design.

Efficiency in Design. Over half of the participants appreciated the software's automatic slot generation feature, efficiently creating magnet-involved circuits. P6 expressed, "The slots appear as soon as I place the electronic components, which is fantastic." Magnet Haptic simplified the integration of movable components and mechanical structures, which might otherwise require complex modeling and 3D printing. P6 noted, "There's no need to consider integrating mechanical structures into the prototype since they're inherently included." Our magnet-handling technique, like holding a pen, allowed participants to easily insert magnets into slots without confusion over their orientation. However, some participants (P1, P4, P5) mentioned needing to consider orientation when switching to a different PMMA board. Post-design, groups 2 and 4 compared their electronic circuits in the software with their sketches to ensure accuracy. P3 suggested developing a 3D view in the software for clearer circuit and structure design. P4 faced challenges in removing the paper membrane but noted that a blow dryer facilitated this process by reducing the membrane's stickiness. Generally, participants could successfully identify different magnetic poles by their attraction and repulsion. Marking magnetic poles in the software would be a helpful future enhancement.

Perception of the Fabrication Process. Students reported little difficulty in understanding and utilizing the pipeline. They could implement their design ideas effectively, finding the prototype fabrication process quick and straightforward. Most students found designing mechanisms and circuits in Magnet Haptic easier than traditional methods, particularly for creating mechanical structures with moving parts. P8 described the method as an "upgrade," more enjoyable than previous techniques, while P1 likened it to playing with block toys. The majority were keen on using this method for future prototypes. They also observed that this integrated fabrication approach allowed them to consider circuitry and structure concurrently during their design's immersion and ideation stages, inspiring them to create innovative and varied interactive devices.

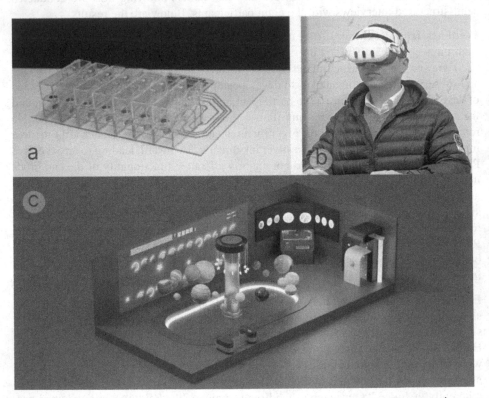

Fig. 6. (a) A haptic input device we designed; (b) A user is experiencing a VR game using our hardware; (c) A virtual environment we designed for a VR game in which the user interacts while playing music.

7 Discussion and Future Work

Magnet Haptic, which integrates electronic circuits, mechanical structures, and magnets into interactive laser-cut objects, has limitations and potential for future development. Key aspects are as follows:

1. Magnet Integration in Prototypes: Magnets in Magnet Haptic enable detachability and replaceability, like in the Rotatable-Switch-Controlled Lamp example, where the lamp part magnetically attaches to the base. However, excessive force can disassemble the magnetic connections. Using stronger magnets or electromagnets could enhance connection strength and add interactive capabilities.

2. Circuit Connectivity and Power Efficiency: Magnet Haptic uses magnets and conductive silver ink for circuit paths, simplifying traditional wiring methods. However, this raises issues with circuit stability and power efficiency. While the magnetic connections are secure, varying materials may require compensation adjustments. The silver ink circuit paths have higher resistance than copper wires, which is less efficient for high-power applications. Future improvements could include lower-resistance conductive ink or copper tape. Covering exposed circuits with extra PMMA can also prevent short circuits in higher-power setups.

3. Semi-Automatic Prototyping Process: The current process combines laser cutting with manual operations like spraying conductive paths. Future developments could see more automated methods for applying silver ink and assembling components, reducing manual labor. Magnetic connections facilitate easy assembly and part replacement, as our user study showed participants adjusted components like lamp bases for better stability.

8 Conclusion

This paper introduces Magnet Haptic, a method for rapidly fabricating tactile feedback devices for VR using magnets and conductive ink. We conducted a series of evaluations to determine the technical parameters and demonstrate the practical feasibility of our fabrication pipeline. Additionally, we organized a workshop with eight participants to confirm the creative uses of interactive prototypes. Magnet Haptic can enable users to quickly create tactile devices for interaction using simple materials like PMMA, magnets, and silver ink. Our pipeline also simplifies complex tasks such as wiring and soldering, making connections more convenient and replaceable. Furthermore, we envision Magnet Haptic utilizing standard laser cutting technology to provide product design iterations to a broad range of users.

Acknowledgments. This research was supported by the Fundamental Research Funds for the Central Universities, the Engineering Research Center of Computer-Aided Product Innovation Design Ministry of Education, National Natural Science Foundation of China (Grant No. 52075478), and National Social Science Foundation of China (Grant No. 21AZD056).

Disclosure of Interests. The authors have no competing interests to declare that are relevant to the content of this article.

References

1. Di Campli San Vito, P., Brown, E., Brewster, S., et al.: Haptic feedback for the transfer of control in autonomous vehicles. In: 12th International Conference on Automotive User Interfaces and Interactive Vehicular Applications, pp. 34–37 (2020)
2. McClelland, J.C, Teather, R.J., Girouard, A.: Haptic feedback with HaptoBend: utilizing shape-change to enhance virtual reality. In: Proceedings of the 5th Symposium on Spatial User Interaction, pp. 150–150 (2017)

3. Muender, T., Bonfert, M., Reinschluessel, A.V., et al.: Haptic fidelity framework: defining the factors of realistic haptic feedback for virtual reality. In: Proceedings of the 2022 CHI Conference on Human Factors in Computing Systems, pp. 1–17 (2022)
4. Zheng C, Yong Z Z, Lin H, et al. Shape-haptics: planar & passive force feedback mechanisms for physical interfaces. In: Proceedings of the 2022 CHI Conference on Human Factors in Computing Systems, pp. 1–15 (2022)
5. Zheng, C., Oh, H.J., Devendorf, L., et al.: Sensing kirigami. In: Proceedings of the 2019 on Designing interactive Systems Conference, pp. 921–934 (2019)
6. Chang, Z., Ta, T.D., Narumi, K., et al.: Kirigami haptic swatches: Design methods for cut-and-fold haptic feedback mechanisms. In: Proceedings of the 2020 CHI Conference on Human Factors in Computing Systems, pp. 1–12 (2020)
7. Muthukumarana, S., Messerschmidt, M.A., Matthies, D.J.C., et al.: Clothtiles: a prototyping platform to fabricate customized actuators on clothing using 3D printing and shape-memory alloys. In: Proceedings of the 2021 CHI Conference on Human Factors in Computing Systems, pp. 1–12 (2021)
8. Messerschmidt, M.A., Muthukumarana, S., Hamdan, N.A.H., et al.: Anisma: a prototyping toolkit to explore haptic skin deformation applications using shape-memory alloys. ACM Trans. Comput.-Hum. Interact. **29**(3), 1–34 (2022)
9. Zheng, C., Kim, J., Leithinger, D., et al.: Mechamagnets: designing and fabricating haptic and functional physical inputs with embedded magnets. In: Proceedings of the Thirteenth International Conference on Tangible, Embedded, and Embodied Interaction, pp. 325–334 (2019)
10. Yao, L., Niiyama, R., Ou, J., et al.: PneUI: pneumatically actuated soft composite materials for shape changing interfaces. In: Proceedings of the 26th Annual ACM Symposium on User Interface Software and Technology, pp. 13–22 (2013)
11. Ou, J., Skouras, M., Vlavianos, N., et al.: aeroMorph-heat-sealing inflatable shape-change materials for interaction design. In: Proceedings of the 29th Annual Symposium on User Interface Software and Technology, pp. 121–132 (2016)
12. Boldu, R., Jain, S., Forero Cortes, J.P., et al.: M-Hair: creating novel tactile feedback by augmenting the body hair to respond to magnetic field[C]//Proceedings of the 32nd Annual ACM Symposium on User Interface Software and Technology. 2019: 323–328
13. Wolf, K., Bennett, P.D.: Haptic cues: texture as a guide for non-visual tangible interaction. In: CHI'13 Extended Abstracts on Human Factors in Computing Systems, pp. 1599–1604 (2013)
14. Yasu, K.: MagneLayer: force field fabrication by layered magnetic sheets. In: Proceedings of the 2020 CHI Conference on Human Factors in Computing Systems, pp. 1–9 (2020)
15. Yasu, K.: Magnetact: magnetic-sheet-based haptic interfaces for touch devices. In: Proceedings of the 2019 CHI Conference on Human Factors in Computing Systems, pp. 1–8 (2019)
16. Strohmeier, P., McIntosh, J.: Novel input and output opportunities using an implanted magnet. In: Proceedings of the Augmented Humans International Conference, pp. 1–5 (2020)
17. Liang, R.H., Chan, L., Tseng, H.Y., et al.: GaussBricks: magnetic building blocks for constructive tangible interactions on portable displays. In: Proceedings of the SIGCHI Conference on Human Factors in Computing Systems, pp. 3153–3162 (2014)
18. Savage, V., Head, A., Hartmann, B., et al.: Lamello: passive acoustic sensing for tangible input components. In: Proceedings of the 33rd Annual ACM Conference on Human Factors in Computing Systems, pp. 1277–1280 (2015)
19. Guo, R., Sun, X., Yuan, B., et al.: Magnetic liquid metal (Fe-EGaIn) based multifunctional electronics for remote self-healing materials, degradable electronics, and thermal transfer printing. Adv. Sci. **6**(20), 1901478 (2019)

20. Liang, J., Xu, Y., Sui, D., et al.: Flexible, magnetic, and electrically conductive graphene/Fe3O4 paper and its application for magnetic-controlled switches. J. Phys. Chem. C **114**(41), 17465–17471 (2010)
21. Ding, L., Xuan, S., Feng, J., et al.: Magnetic/conductive composite fibre: a multifunctional strain sensor with magnetically driven property. Compos. A Appl. Sci. Manuf. **100**, 97–105 (2017)

Author Index

Printed in the United States
by Baker & Taylor Publisher Services